TRADEMARK ACKNOWLEDGMENTS

Que Corporation has made every attempt to supply trademark information about company names, products, and services mentioned in this book. Trademarks indicated below were derived from various sources. Que Corporation cannot attest to the accuracy of this information.

ANSI is a registered trademark of American National Standards Institute.

Apple and Macintosh are registered trademarks of Apple Computer, Inc.

AutoCAD is a registered trademark of Autodesk, Inc.

Batcom is a trademark of Wenhem Systems.

Bernoulli Box is a registered trademark of Iomega Corporation.

COMPAQ is a registered trademark of COMPAQ Computer Corporation.

CP/M is a registered trademark of Digital Research Inc.

DESQview is a trademark of Quarterdeck Office Systems.

FASTBACK PLUS is a registered trademark of Fifth Generation Systems.

IBM, IBM PC, IBM Personal Computer AT, and Quietwriter III are registered trademarks and Proprinter is a trademark of International Business Machines Corporation.

Intel is a registered trademark of Intel Corporation

Linotronic is a trademark of Allied Corporation.

Lotus Manuscript is a trademark and 1-2-3, Freelance Plus, Lotus, and Magellan are registered trademarks of Lotus Development Corporation.

Mace Utilities and Mace Vaccine are registered trademarks of Paul Mace Software, Inc.

Microsoft, MS-DOS, Microsoft Word, Microsoft Windows, OS/2, Smartdrive, and XENIX are registered trademarks of Microsoft Corporation.

PageMaker is a registered trademark of Aldus Corporation.

Paradox is a registered trademark of Borland/Ansa Software.

PC Tools is a trademark of Central Point Software.

RamQuest 50/60 is a trademark of Orchid Technology, Inc.

Seagate is a registered trademark of Seagate Technology.

SideKick Plus is a registered trademark of Borland International.

Super PC-Kwik Power Pak is a registered trademark of Multisoft Corporation.

The Norton Commander, The Norton Utilities, and The Norton Integrator are trademarks of Peter Norton Computing.

UNIX is a trademark of AT&T.

VOPT is a trademark of Golden Bow Systems.

WordPerfect is a registered trademark of WordPerfect Corporation.

WordStar is a registered trademark of MicroPro International Corporation.

XTreePro is trademark of Executive Systems, Inc.

Using Your Hard Disk

Robert D. Ainsbury

que ®
CORPORATION
LEADING COMPUTER KNOWLEDGE

Using Your Hard Disk

Library of Congress Catalog No. 90-61521

ISBN 583-1

93 92 91 90   8 7 6 5 4 3 2 1

Interpretation of the printing code: the rightmost double-digit number is the year of the book's printing; the rightmost single-digit number, the number of the book's printing. For example, a printing code of 90-4 shows that the fourth printing of the book occurred in 1990.

DEDICATION

To my Great Aunt Doris.

ABOUT THE AUTHOR

Bob Ainsbury is the Senior Developer at TechnoJock Software, Inc., a Houston-based software company specializing in Pascal software development tools. Bob has been active in the personal computer industry for eight years and regularly speaks at PC conventions and meetings of computer-user groups. He is also the author of the *Lotus Add-In Toolkit Guide*, published by Que Corporation. His favorite film is *Fletch*, and his favorite hobby is aerobics.

Publishing Director

David Paul Ewing

Product Development Director

David Solomon

Acquisitions Editor

Terrie Lynn Solomon

Acquisitions Editorial Assistant

Stacey Beheler

Developmental Editor

Lois Sherman

Editor

Tim Huddleston

Technical Editor

David Knispel

Jerry Ellis

Indexers

Hilary Adams

Sharon Hilgenberg

Book Design and Page Layout

Dan Armstrong

Lois Sherman

Tim Huddleston

Book Production

Sally Copenhaver

Mary Beth Wakefield

Don Clemens

Bruce Steed

Travia D. Davis

This book was written and typeset in Times Roman, Helvetica, and Courier, using Lotus Manuscript, Release 2.1 and Lotus Freelance Plus. Screen images were captured with the Lotus Manuscript Screen Capture program. Camera-ready copy was produced using a Linotype L300.

CONTENTS AT A GLANCE

Introduction 1

Part I. Hard Disk Basics

Chapter 1   Understanding Computers and Hard Disks 9
Chapter 2   Operating Systems and the Hard Disk 27
Chapter 3   Understanding How a Hard Disk Works 43

Part II. DOS Basics

Chapter 4   Understanding Basic File Operations....................... 77
Chapter 5   Managing Files and Directories........................... 105
Chapter 6   Understanding Batch Files 139

Part III. Hard Disk Organization and Management

Chapter 7   Configuring a Hard Disk 177
Chapter 8   Organizing the Hard Disk 205
Chapter 9   Using Batch Files to Manage a Hard Disk................. 231

Part IV. Getting the Most from Your Hard Disk

Chapter 10   Improving Hard Disk Performance 261
Chapter 11   Using File-Management Tools............................ 301
Chapter 12   Understanding Operating Environments 337

Part V. Maintaining Hard Disk Security

Chapter 13   Keeping Data Backups 387
Chapter 14   Avoiding Hard Disk Disasters 419
Chapter 15   Recovering from Disk Disasters 443
Chapter 16   Securing Your Data 473
Chapter 17   Safeguarding against Viruses............................ 497

Appendixes

A   Operating System Command Reference 515
B   Selecting a Hard Disk... 591
C   OS/2 and the Hard Disk... 597
D   Sources of Programs.. 603
E   Using the Programs Disk 607

Glossary of Hard Disk Terms... 615

TABLE OF CONTENTS

Introduction 1
  Who should Read This Book? 1
  The Details of This Book 2
  Conventions Used in This Book 4
  Other Que Titles 6

Part I   Hard Disk Basics

1 Understanding Computers and Hard Disks 9
  Personal Computer Hardware 10
    The Microprocessor 10
    The Computer Display 12
    The Computer Keyboard 13
    The Computer Disk Drives 14
  Computer Memory and Disk Storage 15
  Hard Disk Features 16
    Hard Disk Components 17
    Basic Hard Disk Operation 17
    Hard Disk Storage Capabilities 19
    Hard Disk Speed 19
  Operating Systems 20
  Hard Disk Utilities 21
    Performance Enhancers 21
    Batch File Enhancers 22
    File Managers 22
    Menu Systems 23
    File Backup Programs 23
    Data Security Tools 24
    Disaster Recovery Programs 24
  Summary 24

2 Operating Systems and the Hard Disk 27
  The Role of the Operating System 27
  Operating Systems Used On Personal Computers 29
    DOS 30
    OS/2 30
    UNIX 32
  Components of an Operating System 33
    The Basic Input/Output System 33
    The Command Interpreter 34

The Utilities 34
Understanding the Booting Process 34
  Performing a Cold Boot 35
  Performing a Warm Boot 36
Using Operating System Commands 37
Summary 41

3 Understanding How a Hard Disk Works 43
Understanding the Hard Disk Drive 44
  Hard Disk Components 44
  Disk Surface Organization 47
    Disk Tracks 48
    Disk Cylinders 49
    Disk Sectors 49
    Low-Level Formatting 51
    Interleaving 52
  Hard Disk Performance Factors 54
    Average Access Time 54
    Transfer Rate 55
  Data Storage and Retrieval 55
    The Formatting Process 55
    Clusters 56
    FAT 57
    Directories 58
    Putting it All Together 58
      File Reading 58
      File Saving 59
      File Deleting 60
  Understanding Partitions 60
  Disk Problems 62
    The Human Problem 62
    Drive Alignment 62
    CRC Errors 63
    Cluster Errors 64
    Drive Head Problems 65
    Mechanical Failures 65
  Understanding Disk Controllers 66
    Interface Standards 66
      ST506/ST412 66
      ESDI 67
      SCSI 67
    Data-Encoding Schemes 68
      MFM 68
      RLL 68

Other Storage Devices 69
    Cache Controllers 69
    Hard Cards 70
    The Bernoulli Box 70
    High-Capacity Floppies 71
    CD-ROM 71
Summary 72

Part II DOS Basics

4 Understanding Basic File Operations 77
Understanding File Concepts 78
  File Characteristics 78
    File Names and Extensions 79
    File Size 79
    File Date/Time Stamp 80
Naming Files 80
  Rules for Naming Files 81
  Avoiding Reserved Names 82
  Establishing Naming Conventions 83
Listing, Displaying, and Printing Files 84
  Understanding Directories 84
  Listing Files with DIR 85
    Using the Basic DIR Command 85
    Listing Too Many Files 86
    Printing a Directory Listing 88
    Using Wild-Card Characters with DIR 89
  Displaying File Contents 93
    Using the TYPE Command 93
    Understanding the TYPE Command 95
  Printing Files 96
Finding Text in Files 98
  Issuing the FIND Filter 98
  Using FIND as a Word-Search Utility 101
  Using FIND as a COMMAND Filter 101
Summary 102

5 Managing Files and Directories 105
Directory Concepts 106
  Understanding the Root Directory 106
Using Hierarchical Directories 108
  Understanding the Concept of Paths 109
  Understanding the Current Directory
  and Relative Paths 110

Making Directories 111
   The Operation of the MD Command 112
   The Directory Entries . and 113
Changing the Current Directory 113
   The Operation of CHDIR 114
Using the PROMPT Command 115
Revisiting the DIR Command 116
Viewing the Directory Hierarchy
with the TREE Command 117
Deleting or Removing Directories 118
   The Operation of the RD Command 119
Using Shortcut Path Commands 120
Using the COPY Command 120
   Copying Files 121
     Copying Files from One Disk to Another 122
     Copying Files from Directory to Directory 122
     The Operation of the COPY Command 123
     Respecting the COPY command 124
   Concatenating Files 125
   Using Devices with COPY 126
Setting the Path 128
Understanding the Environment 131
Redirecting File Input/Output
with Pretender Commands 132
   Using ASSIGN 132
     The Operation of the ASSIGN Command 133
   Using JOIN 134
     The General Rules of the JOIN Command 135
   Using SUBST 135
Summary 137

6 Understanding Batch Files 139
Editing Text Files 140
   Using EDLIN 140
   Using a Word Processor 142
   Using a Text Editor 143
Understanding Batch File Concepts 144
Building a Simple Batch File 145
   Rules for Creating Batch Files 145
   Executing Batch Files 146
   A Simple Batch File 146
   Hiding the Action with ECHO OFF 148
   Annotating with REM 150
   Displaying Messages 151
     Echoing Messages 151

Using PAUSE 153
Suppressing Extraneous Messages 154
Calling Other Batch Files 155
   The Batch File Subcommand CALL 155
   Calling a Batch File with COMMAND /C 156
Batch File Programming 157
   Passing Parameters to a Batch File 158
      Passing Multiple Parameters to a Batch File 160
      Using Shift To Adjust Parameters 162
   Branching With GOTO 163
   Understanding the IF statement 164
      Comparing Parameters and Strings 165
      Testing for Missing Parameters 166
      Checking for Files with IF EXIST 167
      Checking Program Error Levels 169
      Using NOT with IF 169
   Understanding the FOR..IN..DO Statement 170
Summary 172

Part III   Hard Disk Organization and Management

7 **Configuring a Hard Disk** 177
Low-Level Formatting 178
Understanding Partitions 180
Partitioning a Hard Disk 182
   Using the FDISK Command 183
      Using FDISK with DOS V3.2 and Earlier 184
      Using FDISK with DOS V3.3 and V4 185
         Creating a Primary DOS Partition 187
         Creating an Extended DOS Partition 188
         Creating Logical Drives in the Extended Partition 189
         Setting the Active Partition 189
   Changing Hard Disk Partition Settings 190
Using Third-Party Hard Disk Configuration
Utilities 192
Using Disk Manager 193
Using SpeedStor 195
High-Level Formatting 197
Installing the Operating System 199
Installing a Second Hard Disk 201
Summary 202

8 Organizing the Hard Disk 205
  Organizing the Directory Structure 206
    Using a Hard Disk Template 207
      Keeping the Root Directory Clean 209
      Installing New Software 210
        Understanding Install Programs 210
        Loading Programs Manually 210
      Isolating Program Files 211
      Using a KEEP Directory 212
      Using a TEMP Directory 212
  Building the CONFIG.SYS File 213
    Using the BREAK Directive 215
    Setting BUFFERS 217
    Using BUFFERS with DOS V4 and Later Versions 219
    Installing Device Drivers with DEVICE 220
    Setting FILES 222
    Using LASTDRIVE 223
    Using the SHELL Directive 224
    Setting up a CONFIG.SYS File 225
  Building the AUTOEXEC.BAT File 226
    The AUTOEXEC.BAT File's Rules 227
    The AUTOEXEC.BAT File's Contents 227
  Summary 229

9 Using Batch Files To Manage a Hard Disk 231
  Building a Batch File Menu System 231
    Overall Structure of a Menu 232
    Developing the Menu Screen 232
    Using Batch Files to Call Programs 235
    Adding Color with ANSI.SYS 236
    Rules for Displaying Color Screens 237
      Using Batch Files To Set Colors 239
  Batch File Utilities 240
    Displaying Program Files 240
    Maintaining Multiple Boot Configurations 242
    Swapping and Extending the Search Path 245
  Using Batch File Enhancers 246
    Using WHAT 247
      Getting User Input with WHAT 248
      Temporarily Changing the Directory 249
      Checking the Printer 250
    Using the Norton Utilities 250
      Getting User Input with ASK 251
      Screen Drawing 252
      Sounding the Speaker 253

Using the Batcom Batch File Compiler 254
Summary 257

Part IV   Getting the Most from Your Hard Disk

10 Improving Hard Disk Performance 261
　Using Disk Caches 263
　　Disk Cache Theory 264
　　　Mirroring 264
　　　Track Buffering 265
　　　Write Buffering 265
　　　Redundancy Checking 266
　　Disk Cache Considerations 266
　　Disk Cache Problems 267
　　"Free" Disk Caches 268
　　　IBMCACHE 268
　　　COMPAQ CACHE 269
　　　SmartDrive 272
　　Commercial Disk Caches 272
　　　Super PC-Kwik 273
　　　Mcache from Mace Utilities 276
　　　PC-CACHE from PC Tools 277
　Using RAM Disks 278
　　Comparing RAM Disks to Disk Caches 279
　　Good RAM-Disk Applications 279
　　　Temporary Files 280
　　　Program Overlay Files 280
　　　Spell Checkers 281
　　　Copying Files between Floppy Disks 281
　　　Laptop Computers 282
　　　Linked Worksheets 282
　　Using Operating System RAM Disks 282
　　PC-Kwik Power Pak RAM Disk 283
　　RAM.SYS 284
　Defragmenting a Hard Disk 285
　　Understanding Fragmentation 286
　　How Defragmenters Work 287
　　Benefits of Defragmenting 288
　　Commercial Defragmentation Programs 289
　　　Multisoft's Power Disk 289
　　　VOPT 291
　　　Utility Programs 292
　　　　PC Tools' COMPRESS 292
　　　　Mace Utilities' UNFRAG Program 294

The Norton Utilities' Speed Disk 295
Economical Optimization with DOS 296
   Directory Organization 296
   Optimizing the PATH and APPEND Commands 297
   Optimizing BUFFERS 298
   Using FASTOPEN 298
   The Impact of VERIFY 299
   Defragmentation on a Budget 299
  Summary 300

11 Using File-Management Tools 301
  Using Menus 302
   Menu Features 303
   Using PowerMenu 306
   Using Automenu 309
   Using Direct Access 311
  Using File Managers 314
   File Manager Features 315
   File-Management Software 317
    Managing Files with Lotus Magellan 318
    Managing Files with Norton Commander 319
    Managing Files with XtreePro Gold 321
    Managing Files with PC Tools 323
    Using QFILER 324
  Using Small File Utilities 325
   FGREP—a Text Searcher 326
   FINDIT—a File Finder 327
   LIST—a File Browser 328
   MOVE—a File Mover 330
   PCOPY—a File Copier 331
   PKZIP—a File-Compression Utility 332
   VTREE—a Directory-Tree Builder 334
  Summary 335

12 Understanding Operating Environments 337
  Environments Supplied with the Operating System 339
   The DOS Shell 339
    An Overview of the DOS Shell 339
    Creating DOS Shell Menus 342
    Creating a New Group 343
    Adding Programs to a Group 345
    Using the DOS Shell's File Manager 348
    Using the File Menu 350
     Opening a File 350
     Printing a File 351

Associating a File 351
Moving a File 352
Copying, Deleting, and Renaming Files 352
Changing File Attributes 353
Viewing Files 353
Creating a Directory 353
Selecting and Deselecting Files 353
Using the Options Menu 353
Display Options 353
File Options 354
Show Information 354
Using the Arrange Menu 355
Understanding DOSSHELL.BAT 356
OS/2 Presentation Manager 359
Managing Groups 361
Swapping Tasks 362
Using the File System 363
Using Presentation Manager Utilities 366
Independent Operating Environments 367
Using Microsoft Windows 3.0 368
Windows Fundamentals 369
Common Window Characteristics 370
Window Icons 373
Using the Program Manager 373
Using the File Manager 376
Using DESQview 379
Managing DESQview Applications 379
Using the DOS Services 382
Summary 384

Part V   Maintaining Hard Disk Security

13 Keeping Data Backups 387
Understanding Data Backup Needs 388
Backup Programs 388
Backup Frequency 388
Incremental Backups 389
Multiple Backups 391
Storing Backups 391
Restoring Backups 392
Using DOS Commands for Backups 392
Using BACKUP 392
The Operation of the BACKUP Command 395
Making A Full Backup 396

Making an Incremental Backup 397
Making a Partial Backup 398
Using RESTORE 398
The Operation of the RESTORE Command 401
Performing a Complete Restore 401
Performing a Selective Restore 403
Using XCOPY 404
Understanding XCOPY's Switches 405
Using XCOPY for Backups 406
The Operation of XCOPY 407
Using Commercial Backup Programs 408
Using FASTBACK PLUS 409
Features of FASTBACK PLUS 409
Installing FASTBACK PLUS 410
Making a Backup with FASTBACK 411
Restoring FASTBACK PLUS Files 414
PC Tools' Backup Utility 415
Using Tape Backup Devices 416
Summary 417

14 Avoiding Hard Disk Disasters 419
Preventing Hardware Failures 419
Parking Drive Heads 422
Protecting Important Files with ATTRIB 423
Avoiding a Hard Disk Format 426
Using a FORMAT Batch File 427
Using Commercial Formatting Programs 428
Using CHKDSK 430
Using Commercial Disk Analyzers 435
Using The Norton Utilities To Analyze the Hard Disk 435
Checking the Disk with Mace Utilities 436
Verifying Disk Integrity with PC Tools 438
Using SpinRite II for a Low-Level Format 439
Using SpeedStor's Disk Diagnostics 440
Viruses 442
Summary 442

15 Recovering from Disk Disasters 443
Using Data Recovery Snapshots 444
Making Snapshots with The Norton Utilities 444
Storing Disk Information with Mace Utilities 446
Tracking Disk Information with PC Tools 446
Undeleting a File 447
Understanding How Files Are Undeleted 448
Unerasing Files with The Norton Utilities 450

      Undeleting Files with Mace Utilities 452
      Undeleting Files with PC Tools 454
   Repairing Damaged Files 457
      Repairing 1-2-3 Spreadsheets 457
      Repairing dBase Files 460
   Undoing a Disk Format 462
      Using The Norton Utilities' Format Recover Program 463
      Using Mace Utilities' UNFORMAT Program 464
      Using PC Tools' REBUILD 464
   Recovering From a "Dead" Disk 465
      Using Norton Disk Doctor 465
      Using Emergency Room 467
      Using PC Tools' DISKFIX 469
   Editing a Disk Directly 470
   Summary 471

16 Securing Your Data 473
   Understanding the Need for Security 473
   Bogus Security Techniques 474
      Password-Protecting the AUTOEXEC.BAT File 474
      Excluding Programs from the Path and Menu 474
      Hiding Files 475
      Creating Hidden Directories 475
   Password-Protecting the System 475
   Software/Hardware Computer Locks 477
   Physical File Security 478
   "Shredding" Hard Disk Data 479
      Using the Norton Utilities To Erase Data 479
      Using the Mace Utilities' DESTROY 482
   Encrypting Confidential Data Files 483
      Using SuperKey 485
      Using PC SECURE 486
      Password-Protecting Data Files 490
      Password-Protecting 1-2-3 Worksheets 491
      WordPerfect File Protection 492
      Paradox Security Facilities 493
   Summary 494

17 Safeguarding against Viruses 497
   Worms 497
   Trojan Horses and Viruses 498
   How Viruses Propagate 500
   The Damage Caused by Viruses 501
   How To Identify Viruses 502
      Logging Program Files 502

Scanning Files for Patterns 503
Maintaining File Check Values 503
Intercepting Suspicious Disk Writes 504
Eradicating a Virus 504
Using Virus-Protection and Eradication Utilities 505
Using Mace Vaccine 506
Virus Detection with Lotus Magellan 509
Using McAfee Associates Virus Products 510
Summary 514

Appendixes

A   Operating System Command Reference................................... 515

B   Selecting a Hard Disk... 591

C   OS/2 and the Hard Disk 597

D   Sources of Programs... 603

E   Using the Programs Disk 607

Glossary of Hard Disk Terms 615

Index 635

ACKNOWLEDGMENTS

Thanks, Erica, for all your support, encouragement, and help. Special thanks to my talented editors, Lois Sherman and Tim Huddleston, for all the guidance and late nights. To everyone at Que who has contributed to the book, especially Terrie Solomon, Stacey Beheler, David Solomon, Tim Stanley, and Jerry Ellis.

—RDA

Introduction

The introduction of hard disks helped transform the personal computer from yet-another-office-machine to the indispensable productivity tool it is today. There are tens of millions of personal computers being used in America and throughout the world, and the vast majority include a hard disk storage device.

Using Your Hard Disk offers you all the information you need to get the most from your hard disk. It covers the operating system commands related to hard disks and discusses some of the myriad programs that help you leverage your hard disk investment.

Who Should Read This Book?

Using Your Hard Disk is written for a wide range of computer users. It is a valuable reference for both new and experienced hard disk users.

If you are new to hard disks, all areas of the book will be relevant, but the first two parts of the book will be especially useful. The book begins with an introduction to computer hardware and explores the relationship between the hard disk and the operating system. The concept of files is explained, as well as how files should be organized.

Experienced hard disk users will be particularly interested in the later chapters, which explain how to get optimum performance from a hard disk and how to avoid and recover from hard disk disasters.

Whether you are a new or experienced hard disk user, you will find this book packed with practical insights into how to manage your hard disk.

The Details of This Book

The book is organized into the following five major parts:

Part I: Hard Disk Basics
Part II: DOS Basics
Part III: Hard Disk Organization and Management
Part IV: Getting the Most from Your Hard Disk
Part V: Maintaining Hard Disk Security

The first three chapters are designed for new hard disk users. Experienced users will find these chapters of interest, but they can be more selective in their reading. Each part of the book builds on concepts and material addressed in earlier chapters. The book also includes a set of useful appendixes. The diskette that accompanies the book includes evaluation copies of some of the most popular public-domain and user-supported hard disk utility programs.

Part I introduces hard disks and describes how they fit into the framework of personal computers and operating systems. Chapter 1 describes the components of a personal computer, focusing on the hard disk, and presents the main categories of hard disk utilities. In Chapter 2, the close relationship between the operating system and the hard disk is explored, and computer booting operations are explained. In Chapter 3, you look "under the hood" to see how a hard disk physically works. Each major component of the hard disk is reviewed, and logical organization of the hard disk surface is explained. Understanding the surface organization is especially useful when you need to use any of the disaster recovery programs discussed in Part V.

Part II discusses the operating system commands that help you to control and manage the data on your hard disk. Chapter 4 introduces the concepts of files and file-naming conventions. This chapter shows you how to view and print files, as well as how to search a set of files for a specific word or phrase. Chapter 5 shows you how to organize your files into a manageable directory structure. The directory-related operating system commands, such as MD, RD, and CD are explained in detail, together with file-manipulation commands, such as COPY, DELETE, and RENAME. In Chapter 6, you learn how to create batch files to automate command sequences and make the computer easier and simpler to use.

The chapters in Part III show you how to configure a hard disk and how to organize the hard disk for your particular needs. Chapter 7 describes the various stages of hard disk preparation, including low-level formatting, partitioning, and drive formatting. The use of third-party utilities for configuring non-standard drives is also discussed. In Chapter 8, you learn the importance of the start-up files CONFIG.SYS and AUTOEXEC.BAT. A hard disk directory template gives you some guidelines on how to create an effective hard disk directory structure that is tailored to your software. Chapter 9 builds on the knowledge of batch files gained in Chapter 6 and explains how to use batch files to get the most from your hard disk. You are guided through the steps needed to build a menu system driven by batch files, and special batch file enhancement software is reviewed.

Part IV explains how to get the most performance from your hard disk and how operating systems and file-management software can simplify your file-management tasks. Chapter 10 concentrates on techniques for squeezing optimum performance from your hard disk by using operating system device drivers and third-party software. Chapter 11 shows you how specialist third-party software tools can help you manage the files and data on your hard disk. In Chapter 12, some of the most popular operating environments are reviewed, including the DOS V4 Shell and Microsoft Windows 3.

Part V explains how you can secure your data to safeguard it against unintentional—or deliberate—destruction. In Chapter 13, you learn the importance of maintaining complete and frequent data backups. Operating system commands are covered in detail, together with some of the most popular third-party backup programs. Chapter 14 explains many varied techniques that will help you to avoid accidental data loss, including protecting against unintended file deletion and drive formatting. Third-party disk analyzers, which check the integrity of the disk surface media, also are reviewed. In the event that data loss does occur, Chapter 15 discusses ways to recover and rebuild damaged data. "Undeleting" files and "unformatting" disks are discussed, along with specialist programs designed to recover damaged binary files, such as spreadsheets. Chapter 16 concentrates on ways of securing your disk-based data to ensure that an intruder cannot gain access to confidential or private data files. In Chapter 17, the subject is computer viruses. This chapter explains what a computer virus is, how it propagates, and how you can identify and eradicate a virus if your computer becomes infected.

Using Your Hard Disk includes five appendixes and a glossary of computer terms related to hard disks. Appendix A provides a comprehensive command reference for all the DOS commands related to hard disk management. In Appendix B, the major criteria for selecting a hard disk are reviewed. Appendix C provides an overview of the OS/2 operating system and explains the high-performance file system introduced with OS/2 V 1.2. Many third-party programs are reviewed in this book, and Appendix D provides a list of the developers, with addresses and telephone numbers. Appendix E explains how to install onto your hard disk the programs included on the companion disk.

At the back of the book is a disk that contains several very popular public-domain and user-supported programs that can help you manage your hard disk. These programs include a text file editor, a file-management program, a file browser, a text search program, an advanced file-copying utility, a file-compression program, and more. Some of these programs are included for evaluation only. If you decide to use the product, you should register your copy with the author.

Conventions Used in This Book

Uppercase letters are used to distinguish file names and operating system commands. When you need to press a special key combination, the two keys are hyphenated. For example, Ctrl-Break means hold down the Ctrl key and press the Break key, and Alt-X means hold down the Alt key and press X.

Words or phrases described for the first time appear in *italic* characters. Words or phrases that you type appear in **boldface** characters.

Uppercase letters are usually used in the examples to indicate what you type, but you can type commands in either upper- or lowercase letters. For a few commands, the case of the letters makes a difference. When the case is significant, the difference is specifically mentioned in the discussion of the command.

In many cases, a command is explained by describing the full syntax of the command. For example, the syntax of the FIND command is shown as follows:

　　　*d:path***FIND** *switches* **"string" filename** ...

Two typefaces are used to distinguish between optional and mandatory parts of the command. Items in **boldface** are mandatory; you must always specify this part of a command. In this case you must issue the command FIND.

For many mandatory items, you must substitute the appropriate information. In the case of FIND, **"string"** should be replaced by the character, word, or phrase to search for, and **filename** should be replaced by the name of a file. An ellipsis (...) indicates that more than one of the preceding items can be specified. In this case, multiple file names can be used.

Items in *italic* are optional; you supply these items only when needed. For example, *switches* represents optional switches that further control how the FIND operation will function. In some cases, the switches will be specifically identified, for example */C /N /V*.

Throughout the book, you will find the following icons used to identify important text:

NOTE — Provides extra information which, while not crucial to the topic being discussed, extends your knowledge of a subject.

DISK — Indicates that the program being discussed is included on the accompanying companion disk.

OS/2 — Identifies text that describes differences between OS/2 and DOS for the command being discussed.

WARNING — Warns that the command being discussed is powerful and should be used with caution.

UTILITY — Indicates text that describes a program providing a specific file- or disk-management function.

Other Que Titles

As you will see as you read this book, the topic of hard disk management cannot be separated easily from other computer-related topics. For that reason, you will see references in the text to books that provide specialized information on subjects that don't fit into a book on hard disks.

One example is the topic of operating systems, which is closely connected to the topic of hard disks. Que's *Using DOS* and *Using OS/2* provide a wealth of information to help you get the most from your computer's operating system. If you want a more visual approach to operating systems, you may be interested in *MS-DOS QuickStart*.

If reading this book inspires you to open the computer case and tinker, you will find *Upgrading and Repairing PCs* an excellent companion volume. Mark Brownstein of *InfoWorld* calls this book "one of the best books about the workings of personal computers I've ever seen. . ."

Many general-purpose and speciality programs are described throughout this book. Que publishes a full line of microcomputer books, including books on some of these programs. The following titles may be of particular interest to you: *PC Tools™ Quick Reference*, *Using Microsoft Windows 3*, *Using Lotus Magellan*, *Norton Utilities Quick Reference*, and *Using Paradox 3*.

All these books can be found in better bookstores worldwide. In the United States, you can call Que at 1-800-428-5331 to order books or obtain further information.

Using Your Hard Disk follows the Que tradition of providing quality text that is targeted appropriately for users at various levels of skill. Because of the dedication to this goal, Que ultimately has only one way of getting better—by hearing from you. Let Que know how you feel about this book or any other Que title. Que wants to keep improving its books, and you are the best source of information.

Part I

Hard Disk Basics

Understanding Computers and Hard Disks

Operating Systems and the Hard Disk

Understanding How a Hard Disk Works

1

Understanding Computers and Hard Disks

In 1983, IBM introduced the IBM PC XT. This new computer was just like its predecessor, the IBM PC, except that it sported a *hard disk*—a permanent storage device that could hold 10 megabytes (10M) of data. These new machines were expensive, but everybody seemed to want one.

Since those modest beginnings, computer users have watched the storage capacity of hard disks increase by 5,000 percent. Similarly, operating speed has improved by a factor of 10. Meanwhile, the relative cost of hard disks continues to fall. Although many "diskless" PCs are still in operation, the vast majority of personal computers have hard disks.

The way you organize and use a hard disk has a significant impact on your computer's performance. This chapter offers a quick overview of PC hardware, and explains the principal benefits of using a hard disk. The following chapters offer detailed discussions of hard disk components and operations.

Personal Computer Hardware

Today's market is virtually flooded with different brands of PCs, including
IBM, Compaq, AST, Epson, and many others. Fortunately, despite all the
marketing hype you may hear, these systems are quite similar in their
design and operation. Even a PC that fits in a briefcase has the same major
components as a desktop PC. These components include a display, a
keyboard, a microprocessor with supporting circuitry, one or more floppy
disk drives, and a hard disk. The computer's physical components are
collectively referred to as *hardware*.

Hardware falls into two main categories: *system hardware* and *peripheral
hardware*. System hardware is directly associated with processing or
computing activity. The microprocessor is the main system hardware
component, because it is central to the computer's operation. Because of its
central role, the microprocessor is often called the *central processing unit*,
or CPU.

A *peripheral* is any device used by the computer for input or output of data.
Displays, printers, modems, keyboards, and disk drives are all peripheral
hardware. Peripheral hardware supports the system hardware's computing
activity.

The Microprocessor

The *microprocessor* is a computer chip that performs the computer's
primary computing tasks. In short, the microprocessor is the computer's
brain. The microprocessor coordinates the many complex tasks that are
required to execute a program and control peripheral devices, such as the
display or a printer. The microprocessor is supported by a variety of chips
and circuits, which help perform specific operations and communicate with
the peripheral hardware. The microprocessor and the supporting circuitry
usually are located on a single circuit board, called the *motherboard*.

Original PC microprocessors were manufactured by Intel Corporation.
Although other companies now make microprocessor chips and circuits,
microprocessors are still classified according to Intel's product numbering
scheme. The original PCs used the 8088 and 8086 microprocessor. The last
few years, however, have brought great advances in the computational
power of microprocessors. Today's most powerful PCs use the 80486 chip.
A general guide to a microprocessor's power is processing speed, which is
measured in megahertz (MHz). Most microprocessors can operate at a
variety of speeds. Table 1.1 lists microprocessors commonly found in PCs
today.

Table 1.1
PC Microprocessors

Microprocessor	Use
8086, 8088	Used in IBM PCs and XTs. In the early PCs, these chips operated at a speed of 4.77 MHz. The operating speed of these chips has since been boosted to 10 MHz and greater.
80286	Used in IBM Personal Computer ATs. The 80286 chip originally ran at 6 MHz, but now operates at speeds of 8, 12, 16, and 20 MHz.
80386	Used in "386-based" computers, such as the Compaq Deskpro 386, and the IBM PS/2 model 70. These chips initially ran at 16 MHz, and now operate at speeds as high as 33 MHz.
80386SX	Used in "SX" computers. This special chip combines the design principles of the 80386 microprocessor with the capability of interacting with other circuity in the same manner as an 80286 chip. The 80386SX chip operates at 16 MHz and 20 MHz.
80486	Used in "486-based" computers, such as the Compaq System Pro. Although these chips currently operate at 25 MHz, their overall performance is superior to other PC microprocessors.

The microprocessor can manipulate only small amounts of data at any one time. The microprocessor relies on the computer's *random access memory*, or RAM, to store programs and data while the computer is turned on. Data is pushed from RAM to the microprocessor, and the results of the microprocessor's computations are sent back to RAM. System *read-only memory*, or ROM, contains permanently stored programs. These programs control some of the most fundamental PC operations, such as checking the circuitry when the computer is turned on. The microprocessor can retrieve information from ROM, but cannot store any new information there. Because ROM contains programs, or *software*, but is actually part of the hardware, it is often *called firmware*—half software, half hardware.

The microprocessor steps through a program in order to execute it. To coordinate the complex interactions between the microprocessor and other electronic parts, such as RAM and ROM, the microprocessor relies on a consistently timed set of electronic pulses. These pulses are produced by a clock-timing generating circuit.

Only one instruction is performed for every *tick*, or cycle, of the clock. The faster the clock speed, the faster the computer. Every action of the computer requires at least one clock cycle; most actions require multiple cycles. An 8086 chip, for example, requires 4 cycles to transfer data from the microprocessor to RAM. The clock's timing is rated in MHz; therefore, a 16 MHz microprocessor can process twice as many tasks as an 8 MHz microprocessor, in the same amount of time.

With some computers, the microprocessor can manipulate data faster than the data can be transferred to and from RAM. Such systems must be configured with a one-tick delay period—called a *wait state*—during which the processor waits to receive more data from RAM. If RAM can keep pace with the microprocessor, the computer is said to have *zero wait states*.

The Computer Display

The computer *display*—also called the monitor, VDU, CRT, or simply the screen—produces the computer's visual output. A variety of technologies go into the construction of computer displays. The most common type of display is similar to a television, and uses a *cathode ray tube* (CRT) to produce images.

With the introduction of portable, laptop, and briefcase-size computers, however, manufacturers had to develop alternative display technologies that required less power and space. The two main alternative technologies are *gas plasma displays* and *liquid crystal displays*. Gas plasma displays produce orange characters, which appear light against the screen's dark background. Liquid crystal displays (LCDs) work on the same principle as digital watch displays. Most LCDs produce dark characters, which appear against a lighter background. Some LCDs employ a backlight to increase display contrast. Color LCDs are emerging as the new standard for portable computers.

Regardless of the display type, all displays have one function in common. They take electrical signals and translate them into patterns of tiny picture elements, called *pixels*, that you can recognize as characters or figures. Not all displays produce the same number of pixels. Generally, the more pixels a monitor produces, the sharper and clearer that monitor's image will be. The image's sharpness is referred to as *resolution*; image resolution is a function of the display and the display adapter.

The *display adapter* is a collection of circuits that serve as an interface between the display and the system hardware. The display adapter controls the computer display. The display circuitry can be part of the motherboard, or can be located on a separate board that fits into a slot on the motherboard. The display adapter can be a monochrome display adapter (MDA), color graphics adapter (CGA), enhanced graphics adapter (EGA), video graphics array adapter (VGA), or some less common type of special display adapter.

The display and the display adapter must be compatible. For example, a VGA monitor will not function with a computer that has an EGA display adapter. Some monitors are designed to work with several types of adapters; others function with only one specific adapter.

All PC display systems can display text. Some also can display graphics, such as charts, drawings, digitized pictures, and animated game characters.

The Computer Keyboard

Like displays, keyboards can differ from one PC to the next. Apart from variations in quality, keyboards can vary in the number and arrangement of keys they use. Special keys may have different locations on keyboards of different brands. All PC keyboards, however, share some common characteristics.

Like most typewriter keyboards, a PC's keyboard utilizes the traditional QWERTY layout for the alphabet keys. But a computer keyboard differs from a typewriter keyboard in several important ways. The primary difference is that a computer keyboard has a number of special keys. These special keys include 10 or 12 *function* keys (labeled F1 to F12), one or two Alt keys, one or two Ctrl keys, and several special cursor-movement keys.

The special keys may have many different purposes, and this is important to remember when you use any computer program. Although some de facto standards are observed, the special keys' functions are controlled by the software. In most programs, for example, a press of the F1 key brings helpful or explanatory text to the screen (this is called a *help screen*), but such is not always the case. One notable exception is WordPerfect, in which the F1 key activates the program's cancel or "undelete" function. Many software packages include a keyboard template, which is a plastic strip or card that can be placed on the keyboard. The template reminds the user of the special keys' functions for that particular program.

The Computer Disk Drives

The *disk drive* is perhaps one of the most important pieces of peripheral hardware on any computer. Disk drives enable you to store data permanently in magnetic form. If this were not possible, computers would not be nearly as useful as they are today. Imagine the drudgery of typing your data into the computer each time you wanted to work with it! Without the help of disks and disk drives, such would be the computer user's life.

You must use disks for long-term data storage, because data that is stored in RAM is volatile. That is, RAM's contents are erased when the machine is turned off. You must store data on a disk, if you want to maintain the data permanently. The process of transferring information between RAM and a disk is called *reading* and *writing*. The computer can read data from a disk into memory, and the computer can write data onto a disk from memory.

When the computer writes data to a disk, the data is stored as a named collection of information called a *file*. A disk's primary job is to act as a storage medium for files.

Most computers can utilize two types of disks (and their drives); both types are available in a variety of sizes and storage capacities. Disks are either *floppy* or *hard*. Floppy disks, also called *diskettes*, can be removed from the computer, but have a lower storage capacity than hard disks. Hard disks, also called *fixed disks*, are nonremovable, high-capacity disks that store data on rigid platters.

A computer can have a number of attached disk drives. Your computer, for example, may have two floppy disk drives and a hard disk. Whenever a program needs to access files on a disk, it must determine which disk drive to use. Each disk drive, therefore, is assigned an identifying letter. For example, the top (or leftmost) floppy disk drive usually is identified as *drive A*. The other floppy drive is referred to as *drive B*. If the computer has only one floppy disk drive, it can be referred to as either drive A or drive B. The primary hard disk normally is identified as *drive C*. If a computer program asks you for a file's name, you normally can prefix the file name with the appropriate drive letter and a colon—for example, **c:filename**. This command instructs the program to access the file from a specific drive (in this case, drive C).

Computer Memory and Disk Storage

Nearly all data manipulation takes place in memory, not on disk. When you start a program, the operating system loads the program from disk and transfers it into RAM. Typically, you then load into RAM a copy of a *data file* that you saved to disk during a previous session. Otherwise, you create a new file (such as a new letter or worksheet) in memory, where it temporarily resides with the program.

It is important to understand that when you make changes to a data file, those changes occur in memory. Again, RAM is temporary, and all data stored in RAM is lost when the machine is switched off or when the program ends. Therefore, data in memory must be saved to disk if you want to re-use the data later. Most applications programs have options that enable you to save data to disk while you are working in the program. Lotus 1-2-3's /**F**ile **S**ave command is a good example of such an option. When you select such a file-saving command, the data in memory is transferred to disk. When you save a file while using an applications program, the disk drive light usually flickers, indicating disk access.

You should think of memory as temporary working storage where data can be viewed and modified. The hard disk, on the other hand, is a permanent storage area that holds data for later use. Conceptually, the hard disk is like a filing cabinet and memory is like a desk. To work on a file, you must take it out of the cabinet and put it on the desk. However, the file must be put back in the storage cabinet if the changes are to be stored permanently.

Most computer users know what it's like to work on a project for thirty minutes or more without saving the data onto a disk, only to experience power or program failure. When this happens, the computer loses all the new and revised data that has not been saved to a disk. When you must work on a project for any length of time, you should save the data to disk frequently. A good general rule of thumb is to save your data every 5 minutes.

NOTE

In some applications, such as databases, files are often too large to fit into memory. In such cases, the program usually loads part of the file into memory so that it can be modified, and then automatically saves this data back to disk before loading a different part of the file. In such applications, the program automatically saves the data to disk for you. Newer versions of some programs (such as word processors) can be set to save data to disk automatically, at specified intervals. Such features enable the user to continue working without remembering to save data every few minutes.

Hard Disk Features

As noted previously, a hard disk is a nonremovable disk drive assembly with a built-in data storage disk. Today, every computer should have a hard disk (unless the computer is connected to a remote disk via a network). A hard disk is a high-capacity storage device that can be accessed quickly by the computer's operating system. With a hard disk, the computer user no longer has to keep inserting and removing floppy disks in order to run a program. More and more software vendors are marketing their products with hard disk users in mind; in fact, some programs run only on a PC fitted with a hard disk. Other software packages operate without a hard disk, but these programs can exhaust the user because they require constant diskette swapping. Once installed on a hard disk, a program is ready to run almost instantly.

A hard disk's storage capacity is many times greater than that of a floppy disk. In fact, a beginning user might even be lulled into thinking that a hard disk has almost limitless storage space. A hard disk enables you to store programs and data together on one device. Further, a hard disk drive can read and write data much more quickly than a floppy disk drive. Because most PC operations involve the transfer of data to and from a disk, the hard disk's speed is a significant factor in computer performance.

Hard disks are available in a variety of capacities. A small hard disk can hold the equivalent of 30 floppy disks; some of the largest hard disks currently in use can store as much data as 2,000 floppy disks.

The hard disk usually is installed in one of the storage bays at the front of the computer; the number of available bays depends on the computer model. Hard disks are available in *full-height* and *half-height* dimensions, and in a variety of widths to fit desktop and portable computers. Most bays are 6 inches wide, and can accept one full-height device (about 3 1/2 inches deep) or two half-height devices. See Appendix B for more information on selecting and installing hard disks.

NOTE

As manufacturers develop new forms of disk storage, it becomes increasingly difficult to define what a hard disk is (and for that matter, what a PC is). A number of vendors now sell removable hard disks. These transportable disks have all the properties of a standard hard disk, along with connectors that permit the disk to be pulled out of the drive (like a two-inch-thick floppy disk). Iomega Corporation markets a unique storage device, called a Bernoulli drive, that can store huge amounts of data on a high performance 1/4-inch-thick removable cartridge. Refer to Chapter 3 for more information about Bernoulli drives.

The following sections introduce various hard disk components and operations; Chapter 3 discusses these topics in detail.

Hard Disk Components

Figure 1.1 shows a cutaway view of a typical hard disk drive. Data is stored on the magnetized surfaces of circular aluminum platters that are positioned in a vertical stack. Data is transferred to and from the disk through disk drive *heads*. Each side of every platter has its own drive head on an armature, which operates like a tonearm on a record player. When the drive leaves the factory, the internal components are not exposed; the drive is sealed shut. The seal keeps dust, hair, dirt, smoke, pizza(!), and other contaminants out of the delicate mechanical parts within the drive. The head glides just thousandths of an inch above the platter's magnetized surface. You can imagine the problems that can be caused by dirt on the platter.

Unlike a floppy drive, a hard disk drive's platters constantly rotate while the computer is turned on. This constant rotation enables the head to move rapidly to the appropriate area of the disk, without waiting for the platter to start rotating.

Basic Hard Disk Operation

The hard disk drive is controlled and operated by a *hard disk controller*. The controller usually is a separate add-in computer board that is plugged into the motherboard and connected to the hard disk by one or more ribbon wires. Some of the newest disks feature built-in controller circuitry; these disks usually are installed in portable computers, where space is at a premium.

A hard disk stores data in a structured manner, to provide fast and efficient access to any file on the disk. Each platter surface is organized logically, into a series of concentric rings of data. These rings, or *tracks*, are divided into sections, called *sectors*. Each sector can store up to 512 bytes (or characters) of data. By specifying the appropriate platter, track, and sector, the computer can access a specific part of the disk. The computer maintains a detailed inventory of all the information stored on the disk, including the disk areas that are not currently in use. The computer also internally logs the specific address of each sector that contains all or part of a file.

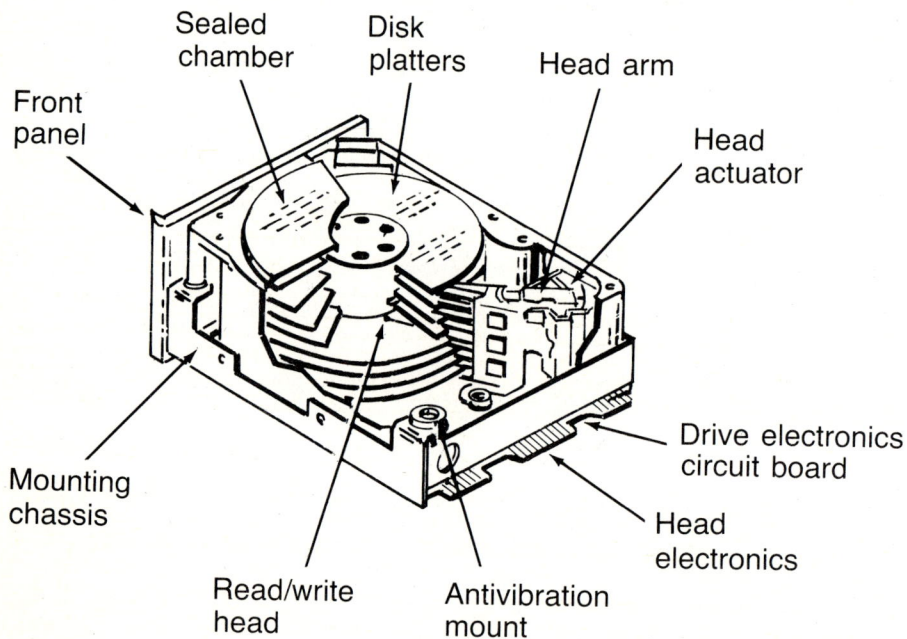

Fig. 1.1 An internal view of a hard disk's main components.

The disk controller instructs the disk to move the drive heads over a specific track and sector of a platter. The heads then can read data from or write data to the disk. To save a file on disk, data is passed from RAM to the controller and then to a specific location on the disk. The operation works in reverse when data is read from the disk.

Hard Disk Storage Capabilities

The smallest hard disk in popular use today can store 10 megabytes (10M) of data; larger disks can store 500M or more. A *byte* is the standard unit of storage on a computer, and represents the amount of space required to store a single character. A *megabyte* is approximately the space required to store one million characters. The average printed page holds about 2,500 characters, so a 500M disk can store the equivalent of 200,000 pages of text. You may be familiar with the old saying about closets: "If you've got the space, you'll fill it." The same is true of hard disks. Even if you use a large hard disk, you inevitably run out of space.

A number of factors ultimately determine how much data a hard disk can hold. The data itself is stored as magnetic charges on the disk platter's surface. The more platters (and, as a result, platter surfaces) a disk contains, the greater the disk's storage capacity. By using special data compression techniques, and by engineering the drive head to pass extremely close to the platter's surface, disk designers have increased the amount of information that can be stored on a square inch of platter surface. Data storage capabilities have improved dramatically over the last few years, and the trend certainly will continue.

Most computer users purchase 20M hard disks, and recent sales indicate that most new hard disks purchased have a storage capacity in the range of 20M to 110M. If you buy a hard disk that is too small, you may not be able to load all your programs onto the disk, and you will have to swap floppy disks for your least-used programs. When shopping for a hard disk, however, economics should be your primary consideration. That is, use the same principle you would use when buying a house: the bigger the better, as long as you can afford it.

Hard Disk Speed

Hard disk speed significantly affects your computer system's performance, especially if you regularly use disk-intensive programs, such as databases. Several types of measurements can be used to define a disk's speed, including seek time, average access time, and transfer rate.

The most commonly used measurement of disk speed is *average access time*, which is the amount of time required for the head to move from one random location on the disk to another. Access time usually is measured in milliseconds (ms). Some of the fastest hard disks sport average access times of 10 ms to 20 ms; the slowest disks operate in the range of 60 ms to 100 ms. The average access time of most new hard disk drives is between 20 ms and 30 ms.

Disk performance also depends on factors such as the disk controller interface and sector interleave. See Chapter 3 for more information on disk performance.

Operating Systems

An operating system is a set of programs that operate and control the computer's memory and peripheral devices. The operating system performs all the detailed tasks that control the computer's low-level operation. For example, the operating system recognizes key presses, or that a floppy disk has been loaded in the disk drive. The operating system is accessed by both the user and the applications program. Whenever you type an instruction, the operating system inspects the input and determines which action to take (that is, load a program, copy a file, change the system time, and so on).

Because the operating system must have full control of the computer hardware, each operating system is designed to work with a specific type of computer. Most computers can use more than one operating system, but one operating system—the Disk Operating System (DOS)—generally dominates the market.

Microsoft Corporation originated the MS-DOS (Microsoft Disk Operating System) operating system, and subsequently licensed DOS to other hardware vendors, so that those vendors could distribute DOS with their computers. Each licensee modified the product name: IBM distributed DOS as PC DOS, Compaq sold Compaq DOS, an so on. Today, DOS is still the most widely used operating system for PCs. Although many variations of DOS exist, they all utilize the same commands and provide the same services.

DOS has been upgraded and enhanced several times since the original version (V1.0) was released. DOS now features an extensive set of commands that helps the user manage disks and files. To manage large numbers of files, for example, DOS enables you to organize files into groups (called *directories*) by using special commands that create and remove directories.

The latest operating system for the PC computer market is Operating System/2 (OS/2), which works on PCs fitted with an 80286 (or later) processor. OS/2 provides all the features and services of DOS, but also gives the user access to larger amounts of memory. Further, OS/2 is a *multitasking* operating system, in that it enables the computer to perform more than one task at a time.

Hard Disk Utilities

As hard disk storage capacity has increased during the past few years, file-management tasks have become commensurately more difficult. Since the introduction of hard disks in PCs, however, many companies have developed programs to help users get the most benefit from their hard disks. Having gone to the expense of buying a hard disk, you should consider the advantages of owning one or more hard disk *utility programs*. Such programs can simplify file management, increase the disk's effective speed, and make programs easier to access and run.

You should, however, avoid becoming a utility junkie. Most of us know at least one computer "guru" who has so many utilities on the hard disk, there is hardly any room left for data files! Every hard disk user should try to gain a good understanding of the operating system commands before becoming dependent on third-party utilities. Armed with an understanding of the operating system and a few good utilities, managing your hard disk will be a breeze.

Performance Enhancers

As you already have seen, a hard disk drive accesses data much more quickly than a floppy disk drive. As you grow accustomed to the hard disk's speed, however, don't be surprised if you begin craving even better performance.

Hard disk performance can be improved in several ways. Arguably, you can realize the most dramatic improvements by using a *disk cache*. A disk cache is an area of memory that is reserved to quicken data transfer rates. A disk cache operates on the following basic principle: When a program requests a block of data from the disk, the disk drive reads the requested data, as well as the next block of data. Both blocks are stored in the cache area of memory. If the program then requests the second block of data, the memory cache can pass the data to the program instantly, so that the program does not have to access the disk. Disk performance can improve by more than 40 percent when a disk cache is used.

When the operating system saves a file to disk, the disk drive uses the first available space on the disk. If this space is not large enough to store the entire file, the next available space is located and the next part of the file is stored there. The operating system repeats this process until the whole file has been saved to disk. If pieces of files are scattered all over the disk's platters, the disk has become *fragmented*. A fragmented disk performs inefficiently because the disk takes longer to locate and load each part of the desired file. (For more information on fragmented disks, see Chapter 3.) Some types of utilities can reorganize a disk so that the various parts of files are grouped together. This process is referred to as *defragmenting*, or *optimizing*.

Chapter 10 describes several methods and utilities you can use to improve your hard disk's performance.

Batch File Enhancers

The operating system includes a set of commands for creating and running *batch files*, which you can use to store a series of commands. When you execute a batch file (by entering the batch file's name), the operating system executes the commands stored in the batch file. With the help of batch files, you can combine a series of potentially complex commands into one simple command.

As explained in Chapter 6, batch files are useful and can significantly simplify the operation of the hard disk. As good as they are, however, batch files have a number of weaknesses. For example, a batch file does not provide a way of prompting the user to enter data, and large batch files are slow. Batch file enhancers provide more batch file commands, enable you to draw custom displays, and often improve operating speed.

File Managers

Most hard disks can store thousands of files, but managing these files can be a demanding chore. You can spend a long time looking for a file, if you cannot remember which directory contains the file. This search is like trying to find a needle in a haystack. As the disk begins to fill, you will want to erase old files, but which ones? A relatively straightforward task—such as changing a disk's directory structure—can be a long and tedious process.

File management programs ease the burden of controlling and administering your files. Such programs typically can search one or more disks for a specific file or set of files, and enable you to view a file's contents. File management programs also simplify the tasks of deleting, copying, and moving groups of files.

Using a hard disk without a file manager is like going on a touring vacation without a map. If you have a large hard disk, a file manager can be a real productivity booster. See Chapter 11 for more information about file managers.

Menu Systems

A menu program enables you to execute other programs with ease. If you want to run a program by issuing basic operating system commands, for example, you may have to do the following: (1) change to the drive where the program is stored; (2) change to the specific program directory; and (3) enter the program's execution command, followed by any other information required by the program.

A menu system frees you from such drudgery, by entering all the program execution commands for you. A menu program presents a list of all the programs on your hard disk, and you specify the program you want to run. The process is like ordering a meal from a restaurant menu. When you choose a menu option, the menu program issues all the commands required to start the program. Some menu programs include file management tools, and provide additional utilities, such as maintaining a log of program usage, or executing a program at a specific time of day. For example, a menu program might automatically execute a communications program to download your electronic mail at 10 p.m., while you are at home watching TV.

File Backup Programs

The primary disadvantage of using a hard disk is that you are storing all data and programs together on a single device. If the unit suffers a mechanical failure, or if an errant program corrupts the data on the disk, you may have a problem.

This drawback, however, is no reason to avoid using a hard disk. Rather, you should take precautions to protect your data. For example, every hard disk should be *backed up* frequently. When you back up a hard disk, you copy the data from the disk onto another file storage medium, such as floppy disks or a tape drive. You then stash this copy in a safe place. If a problem arises with your hard disk, you can have the problem fixed and then restore the data from the backup copies.

The operating system provides the commands BACKUP and RESTORE specifically for making data backups. While these commands do offer backup capabilities, they often are criticized for being cumbersome and slow. Many third-party backup programs can run several times faster than these operating system commands. Third-party programs bypass the operating system's normal disk drive services and simultaneously read the hard disk while writing to the output device. Generally, such programs also are more flexible than BACKUP and RESTORE, offering file compression, directory selection, script files to record backup settings, and other options.

Frequent data backup is an essential duty for a hard disk user. Chapter 13 explores the data backup tools provided with the operating system, as well as commercial backup programs.

Data Security Tools

If you store classified, private, or confidential data on your computer, you should take measures to secure the data. A number of products can help you prevent intruders from gaining access to such data. One way of securing data is to keep files on a removable medium, such as a floppy disk or a Bernoulli cartridge, rather than storing the files on the system's internal hard disk. The removable storage device can be locked away in a safe when it is not being used.

Special software programs enable you to encode confidential files, by using government-approved encryption techniques. The file is compressed, scrambled, and assigned a user-supplied password. After encryption, the file is unreadable until it is decrypted. The file can be decrypted only when the correct password is given to the program.

Certain hardware/software combinations permit the computer to start up only when a password is entered. This type of protection ensures that only authorized users can access the PC after it has been turned off. For a detailed discussion of data security, turn to Chapter 16.

Disaster Recovery Programs

Whether caused by computer malfunction or operator error, things do go wrong. An important file may be accidentally deleted, or perhaps a disk will not operate properly when the computer is turned on. Some specialized programs help you "turn back the clock" and recover from such problems.

Disaster recovery programs can diagnose disk errors, resurrect deleted files, and even restore a disk after it has been erased with a FORMAT command. The best form of insurance is a frequent data backup; if you do not have a good backup, a good disaster recovery program can be worth a fortune. (Disaster prevention and recovery are discussed in Chapters 14 and 15.)

Summary

This chapter introduced you to PC hardware, and summarized a hard disk's main features. In this chapter you learned the following key points:

- System hardware performs the computer's "computing."

- Peripheral hardware provides the PC with input and output.

- PCs use a variety of displays that can display text in different resolutions. Some displays can show graphic images.

- The keyboard offers standard typewriter keys, as well as special keys (such as the function keys). Software determines the use of special keys.

- Most PCs use either a hard disk drive, one or more floppy disk drives, or a combination of the two types of drives.

- A hard disk provides large data storage capacity and fast access speeds.

- Utility programs can help you get the most from your hard disk.

The next chapter shows you how the operating system manages data stored on the hard disk.

Operating Systems and the Hard Disk

When you use a hard disk, you are using a collection of programs called an operating system. This chapter explains the relationship between the operating system and the hard disk in your computer.

The Role of the Operating System

An *operating system* is a collection of computer programs that provides recurring services to other programs or to the user of a computer. These services consist of disk and file management, memory management, and device management. Computers need software to provide these services. If the computer's operating system did not provide these services, the user or the user's applications program would have to deal directly with the details of the PC's hardware, file system, and memory utilization.

The hard disk is the main data storage reservoir in the computer. All the programs you run, including the operating system itself, and all the data files, such as spreadsheets, letters, and mailing lists, are stored on the hard disk. It is the responsibility of the operating system to ensure that the data is stored on the disk in such a way that it can be easily and efficiently retrieved. As far as the hard disk is concerned, the operating system provides three very important tasks: it allows the computer to automatically install the operating system when the computer is turned on, it organizes the hard disk to facilitate the storage and retrieval of data, and it provides a set of file management commands for creating, manipulating, and deleting files.

The operating system must *format* the hard disk before it can be used for file management. When a disk is formatted, the operating system creates a special area on the outer edge of the first disk platter to store information about the rest of the disk. This reserved area contains a detailed index of information about all the files on the disk. To maintain the file index, the operating system logically divides the surface of the hard disk into a series of small units known as clusters. The index contains a record of every cluster on the disk—which ones are occupied, which ones are free for new files, and which are bad and should not be used. Every time data is accessed on the hard disk, the operating system looks at the index to decide which cluster(s) to go to.

If the hard disk is the disk you will start the system from, the format operation also writes a special block of information to the beginning of the disk. This information contains data used to start the operating system when the computer is first turned on.

The operating system includes a set of commands designed specifically to help you manage the files on your hard disk. The commands are used to copy files from one disk to another, delete unwanted files, rename files, and update files with new information. To manage the files, all you have to do is use the appropriate operating system command. The operating system interprets your instructions, or the instructions issued by a program you are running, and translates them into the very detailed commands required to operate the computer's components.

For example, if you want to copy a file from a diskette to the hard disk, you enter a simple copy command. The operating system reads the command and then proceeds to guide and control the floppy disk drive, RAM, and the hard disk through the copy operation. The operating system makes sure that the diskette is loaded in the drive and that the drive door is closed. It then reads a special area of the diskette to find the physical location of the file on the diskette. The diskette is rotated so that the appropriate area of the disk is beneath the read-write head, and the data is transferred into a free area of RAM. The operating system then continues with the detailed process of storing the file information in a new file on the hard disk. As you can see, the operating system has to manage a lot of tasks just to perform a "simple" file copy operation.

Without a disk operating system, every computer program would have to contain instructions listing each step the hardware should take to do a job, such as storing a file on disk. Early computers did not have operating systems; every program had to control the computer hardware directly. The first modern-day computer, in the 1940s, was called ENIAC. ENIAC was as large as a house and performed computations that now can be performed on a pocket calculator. Even the computers of the 1950s, such as the UNIVAC 1103A, didn't have an operating system. To enter data into the system, you had to convert the numbers into octal format (as opposed to decimal), punch the information in a special format onto paper tape, and feed the tape into the computer. The computer would then follow the precise instructions on the paper tape and compute a result. Because there was no operating system or output device, the answer could only be accessed by instructing the computer to dump its core memory. This core dump was than translated, by hand, back into decimal format.

Not only were programs for such computers very time-consuming to write, they would run on only one specific set of hardware. If the computer were modified in any way, the chances were that the program would no longer function.

An operating system provides a layer between the computer hardware and the applications program, and this layer makes the application software independent from the hardware. For example, when 3 1/2-inch disk drives were introduced in PCs, the operating system was upgraded to operate this new type of drive. None of the existing applications programs (for example, Lotus 1-2-3) needed to be modified; the operating system accepted the same commands from programs and provided the same data back. The program was not affected by whether the data was being read from a 5 1/4-inch or a 3 1/2-inch drive. Without the operating system "layer," all the applications programs would have to be modified with every introduction of a new peripheral device.

Operating Systems Used On Personal Computers

When personal computers were introduced in the early eighties, a number of vendors tried to establish their operating system as the standard for all

PCs. The two main contenders were CP/M-86 from Digital Research and 86-DOS from Seattle Computer Products. Microsoft Corporation bought the 86-DOS operating system and renamed it MS-DOS. In 1981, when IBM was aggressively developing a personal computer, IBM selected Microsoft's operating system, and distributed the software under license as PC DOS. When IBM introduced the IBM PC, MS-DOS quickly became the operating system of choice for PCs.

Today, two main operating systems designed exclusively for the IBM-compatible personal computer market are available: DOS and OS/2. Another operating system, UNIX, is available on a wider variety of hardware and is gaining popularity as a PC operating system.

DOS

Because the operating system has a very close relationship with the hardware, most major hardware vendors have tailored the basic operating system to work efficiently with their hardware. Microsoft Corporation is the leading developer of DOS, and manufacturers such as IBM, Compaq, and Toshiba have produced their own variations under license from Microsoft. The manufacturers may put their own names on the disks and include different manuals with the operating system, but all the DOS variations are very similar when they operate on a PC.

Since its initial release in 1981, DOS has undergone considerable improvement and change. Two major releases have been largely related to hard disk management. In 1983, DOS V2.0 (for *version* 2.0) was introduced, and with it came the capability to support hard disks with up to 32 megabytes (32M) of storage space. DOS V4.0 was released in 1988, and was able to accommodate disks much larger than 32M. Table 2.1 details the evolution of the DOS operating system from 1981 to 1990.

DOS is the predominant operating system in use on PCs today, and will continue to be enhanced and improved in the future. For instance, DOS will continue to be upgraded to support new devices, such as new formats of diskette drives or maybe 132-column monitors. With the introduction of DOS V4, a file manager called the DOS Shell was shipped as part of the operating system. Future releases of DOS may have further additions in the area, and may even adopt a fully graphical interface.

OS/2

OS/2, or *Operating System/2*, is the latest operating system from Microsoft Corporation. The new operating system's primary purpose is to replace

DOS and provide a wealth of additional features, the most notable of which is multitasking—the capability of running several programs at the same time on a single computer.

Table 2.1
Quick Reference to Versions of DOS

DOS Version	Significant Change
1.0	Original version of DOS
1.25	Accommodates double-sided disks
2.0	Includes multiple-directory capability, needed to organize hard disks
3.0	Uses high-capacity floppy disks, RAM disks, volume names, and the ATTRIB command
3.1	Includes provisions for networking
3.2	Accommodates 3 1/2-inch floppy disk drives
3.3	Accommodates high-capacity 3 1/2-inch drives; includes new commands
4.0	Introduces the DOS Shell and the MEM command; accommodates larger files and disk capacities

The reception of OS/2 within the PC community has been much cooler than Microsoft expected. Although OS/2 is clearly a more powerful and flexible operating system, it demands more resources of the computer—it uses much more disk space and memory than DOS, and it really needs an 80386 microprocessor to perform acceptably. These resource demands, together with a shortage of software applications that can take advantage of OS/2, have contributed to lackluster OS/2 reception. As OS/2 matures, and as more software applications, such as Lotus 1-2-3/G, are written to take advantage of OS/2, it will probably gain in popularity and significantly increase its market share.

Microsoft designed OS/2 to be the natural successor to DOS. Most of the commands introduced in DOS are also available, in virtually identical form, in OS/2. In fact, one of the multiple sessions running under OS/2 can be a standard DOS session that uses the DOS operating system and runs DOS applications programs.

> In the discussions of operating system commands, this text focuses primarily on DOS commands and DOS-compatible software. Note that many DOS commands are included in OS/2. A special sidebar marked OS/2 will indicate if the OS/2 version differs from the DOS command. Appendix C provides further information about OS/2 V1.2

UNIX

The UNIX operating system was around long before the advent of PCs. The first version of UNIX was developed in 1969 at AT&T Bell Laboratories, for a Digital Equipment Corporation DEC PDP-7 computer. When AT&T originally licensed UNIX, the company offered the source code for a modest fee. Many programmers purchased licenses for the source code and modified it for their own use. In fact, UNIX was designed by programmers primarily to make programming easier. As a result, several variations of UNIX have evolved from the original form.

UNIX has been growing and evolving for 20 years and, arguably, the main reason UNIX has not stormed the PC market is a lack of standards, with too many variations of UNIX. In an attempt to resolve the problem, AT&T has tried to establish a standard specification for the UNIX operating system, referred to as *System V Interface Definition*. A number of significantly different UNIX systems still exist, but UNIX vendors and the standards commissions are close to establishing a single UNIX standard.

Standards notwithstanding, UNIX is a very capable and mature operating system that offers a number of features attractive to the PC user:

- UNIX was designed for a shared computing environment. It supports multitasking and enables multiple users to utilize the same computer (networking).

- UNIX is available on PCs, mini computers, and mainframes, and UNIX users have no difficulty switching computer platforms.

- UNIX uses a flexible memory-management system that allows the program to use varied forms of memory, without the need for special drivers or memory emulators.

- UNIX includes a rich set of operating system commands, together with text editors and a powerful "better-than-batch-files" programming facility.

- UNIX includes built-in communications software that permits remote systems to transfer files and data via phone lines or network cables. For example, UNIX includes a MAIL command for sending electronic mail to other users.

Many respected PC authorities believe that UNIX is superior to OS/2, and think it will be the PC operating system of the 1990s.

Components of an Operating System

All PC operating systems share the same basic structure. That is, each includes an operating system *kernel*, which controls memory management and manages the transfer of data to and from the peripheral devices. Every operating system features an *interpreter*, which intercepts all the input commands and decides which service to invoke. Finally, operating systems include *utilities*, such as file editors, backup programs, and others.

In the case of DOS, these components are known as the basic input/output system, the command interpreter, and the utilities.

The Basic Input/Output System

The so-called "hidden" or *system* files are another part of the operating system. These two or three special files (the number depends on your computer) define the hardware to the software. When you start up a computer, these system files are loaded into memory. Combined, the files provide a unified set of routines for controlling and directing the computer's operations. These files comprise the input/output system.

The hidden files interact with special read-only memory (ROM) on the motherboard. The special ROM is called the *ROM Basic Input/Output System*, or ROM BIOS for short. Responding to a program's request for service, the system files translate the request and pass it to the ROM BIOS. The BIOS provides a further translation of the request that links the request to the hardware.

The Command Interpreter

The command interpreter is the part of the operating system that you directly access and use. The DOS command interpreter is the program COMMAND.COM, which interacts with you through the keyboard and the display when you operate your computer.

When you enter a command, you are communicating with the program COMMAND.COM, which then interprets what you type and processes your input so that the operating system can take appropriate action. COMMAND.COM manages such tasks as displaying a list of the contents of a disk, copying files, and starting applications programs. Commands processed solely by COMMAND.COM are referred to as *internal* commands. COMMAND.COM doesn't carry out most of the commands itself, however. It tells other parts of the operating system that the task needs to be performed. Commands that cannot be handled directly by COMMAND.COM are referred to as *external* commands.

The Utilities

The operating system utilities carry out a variety of useful housekeeping tasks, such as preparing disks, comparing files, finding the free space on a disk, and printing. The utility programs are files that reside on disk and are loaded into memory by the command interpreter (COMMAND.COM) when you type their command names.

The more recent versions of some operating systems (for example, DOS 4.0 and OS/2 V1.1) provide powerful utilities that are more like applications programs than utilities. For example, DOS V4 includes the DOSSHELL program, which provides sophisticated file-management facilities (see fig. 2.1). OS/2 V1.1 also includes a file-management system, together with a powerful program manager, known as the Presentation Manager.

Throughout this book you will learn how the operating system utilities help you to get the most from your hard disk.

Understanding the Booting Process

The operators of early computers started their computers by entering a short binary program and then instructing the computer to run the program. This binary program was called the "bootstrap loader" because the computer, through the bootstrap program, figuratively pulled itself up by the bootstraps to perform the task. The early computer operators shortened the name of the start-up process to *booting*, and the term stuck. Today, *booting the computer* still refers to the start-up procedure. Fortunately, the process of booting is now relatively automatic.

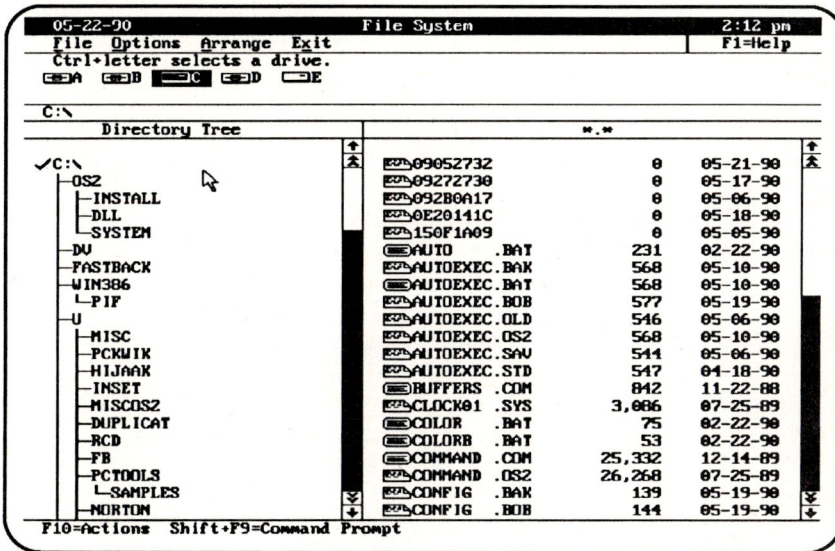

```
┌──────────────────────────────────────────────────────────────────┐
│ 05-22-90                        File System              2:12 pm   │
│ File  Options  Arrange  Exit                             F1=Help   │
│ Ctrl+letter selects a drive.                                       │
│ ═A  ═B  ═C  ═D  ═E                                                 │
│ ─────────────────────────────────────────────────────────────────│
│ C:\                                                                │
│      Directory Tree                          *.*                   │
│ ✓C:\                          09052732            0    05-21-90    │
│   ├─OS2             ▷        09272730            0    05-17-90    │
│   │ ├─INSTALL                092B0A17            0    05-06-90    │
│   │ ├─DLL                    0E20141C            0    05-18-90    │
│   │ └─SYSTEM                 150F1A09            0    05-05-90    │
│   ├─DV                       AUTO    .BAT      231    02-22-90    │
│   ├─FASTBACK                 AUTOEXEC.BAK      568    05-10-90    │
│   ├─WIN386                   AUTOEXEC.BAT      568    05-10-90    │
│   │ └─PIF                    AUTOEXEC.BOB      577    05-19-90    │
│   ├─U                        AUTOEXEC.OLD      546    05-06-90    │
│   │ ├─MISC                   AUTOEXEC.OS2      568    05-10-90    │
│   │ ├─PCKWIK                 AUTOEXEC.SAV      544    05-06-90    │
│   │ ├─HIJAAK                 AUTOEXEC.STD      547    04-18-90    │
│   │ ├─INSET                  BUFFERS .COM      842    11-22-88    │
│   │ ├─MISCOS2                CLOCK01 .SYS    3,086    07-25-89    │
│   │ ├─DUPLICAT               COLOR   .BAT       75    02-22-90    │
│   │ ├─RCD                    COLORB  .BAT       53    02-22-90    │
│   │ ├─FB                     COMMAND .COM   25,332    12-14-89    │
│   │ ├─PCTOOLS                COMMAND .OS2   26,268    07-25-89    │
│   │ │ └─SAMPLES              CONFIG  .BAK      139    05-19-90    │
│   │ ├─NORTON                 CONFIG  .BOB      144    05-19-90    │
│ F10=Actions  Shift+F9=Command Prompt                               │
└──────────────────────────────────────────────────────────────────┘
```

Fig. 2.1. *The file manager DOS Shell is included with DOS V4.*

A *cold boot* occurs when the computer power is first switched on. If you reboot the computer by pressing the reset button (on some computers), or by pressing the key combination Ctrl-Alt-Del, the computer performs what is known as a *warm boot*.

Performing a Cold Boot

As soon as the power supply switch is turned on, the computer performs a *power-on reset* (POR). The random-access memory, microprocessor, and other circuits are cleared (or zeroed out), and the system begins a *power-on self test* (POST). The POST ensures that the computer is fully functional and operating normally. For example, the memory chips are tested to see whether they are responding normally. During this test you may notice the computer displaying a memory count in the upper left corner of the display.

When the POST is completed, you hear one beep and drive A starts activity. The bootstrap loader checks to see if there is a disk in drive A, and if there is, it will try to load the operating system from that disk. *Booting from a floppy* refers to booting the system with an operating system disk in drive A. On systems equipped with a hard disk, you should leave drive A empty, and the system will switch to the hard disk to load the operating system files.

You can create two files that control booting tasks: CONFIG.SYS and AUTOEXEC.BAT. CONFIG.SYS instructs the operating system to load specific *device drivers*. A device driver is a file that enables the operating system to communicate with a device, such as a mouse or a tape backup unit. Then AUTOEXEC.BAT file executes some operating system commands as soon as the PC is booted. For example, you may instruct the operating system where to look for program files, using the PATH command, or what to display in the command interpreter prompt, using the PROMPT command. This files saves you from having to type these commands every time you boot the system. You learn more about these special start-up files in Chapters 3 and 4.

> ✓
>
> OS/2
>
> The file AUTOEXEC.BAT is not used in the OS/2 booting process. Most of the user-definable boot information is located in the CONFIG.SYS file. OS/2 introduced a new file, STARTUP.CMD, which can start one or more programs automatically when the system is booted.

Performing a Warm Boot

The warm boot differs very little from the cold boot. The primary difference is that the POST is not performed; that is, the system does not check that computer components such as memory chips are functioning normally. You may need to warm boot your PC for several reasons. If you change your system's start-up files, CONFIG.SYS or AUTOEXEC.BAT, you have to reboot the system to activate the changes. If your system becomes "hung" or unresponsive because of a program error, you might perform a warm boot. You can even start a different version of DOS from a floppy disk by performing a warm boot.

Whether you have cold booted through a power-up or warm booted through a Ctrl-Alt-Del key combination, your PC is reset, refreshed, and ready for a new computing session.

Using Operating System Commands

To communicate your need for service to the operating system, you enter commands at the operating system prompt. Commands are made up of groups of characters, separated or *delimited* by certain other characters. The operating system responds to more than 75 different commands, but you have to type the commands in the correct format or *syntax*.

One of the simplest operating system commands is VER. The VER command tells you the *version* number of the operating system you are using. You can determine the version number of your operating system by typing the following command:

VER

and pressing the Enter key. The operating system will display the operating system version number, probably with a company name or copyright notice.

Unlike many operating system commands, VER has no options and can only be entered in this one form. Other commands accept a variety of different options. You identify these additional options by adding extra characters to the command before you press Enter. These extra elements of the command are known as *parameters* or *switches*. Sometimes the parameters are mandatory; other times they are optional. These options are used to change the way the command is executed. For example, the command **DIR** displays a list of files, but if the extra parameter /W is added to the command line (that is, **DIR /W**), the file list is displayed in wide format. You learn more about the DIR command in Chapter 3.

The parameters and switches are usually separated by one or more spaces or by a slash (/). Because many commands have various parameters, switches, and defaults, various forms of these commands may be correct.

Table 2.2 summarizes all internal and external operating system commands available with DOS V4.

Table 2.2
A Summary of the DOS V4 Commands

Command	Description
APPEND	Sets a search path for data files
ASSIGN	Assigns a drive letter to a different drive
ATTRIB	Sets or displays file attributes
BACKUP	Backs up files from one disk to another
BREAK	Sets the status of the Ctrl-C check
CHCP	Displays or sets the current code page
CHDIR (CD)	Displays or sets the default directory
CHKDSK	Scans a disk for errors
CLS	Clears the screen
COMMAND	Starts the command processor
COMP	Compares two sets of files for exact likeness
COPY	Copies files
CTTY	Changes the input device
DATE	Displays or sets the date
DEL (ERASE)	Deletes files
DIR	Lists the files in a directory
DISKCOMP	Compares two disks for exact likeness
DISKCOPY	Copies contents of one floppy disk to another
ECHO	Batch file command for displaying messages
EXE2BIN	Converts EXE files to binary format
EXIT	Terminates a secondary copy of COMMAND.COM
FASTOPEN	Caches directories

Command	Description
FC	Compares two files or sets of files
FDISK	Partitions a hard disk
FIND	Searches for a specific phrase or string
FOR	Batch file command for controlling program flow
FORMAT	Formats a disk
GOTO	Batch file command for program branching
GRAFTABL	Enables extended character set on a CGA system
GRAPHICS	Enables printing of graphics screens
IF	Batch file command for controlling program flow
JOIN	Joins a disk drive to a specific path
KEYB	Loads a keyboard program
LABEL	Displays or sets a disk volume label
MEM	Displays memory status
MKDIR (MD)	Makes a new directory
MODE	Sets operating characteristics of peripheral devices
MORE	Displays output one screen at a time
NLSFUNC	Loads country-specific information
PATH	Sets the directories to be searched for program files
PAUSE	Batch file command to suspend processing
PRINT	Prints text file(s)
PROMPT	Changes the operating system command prompt
RECOVER	Tries to recover data from corrupted files
REM	Batch file command to denote a comment or remark

Command	Description
REN (RENAME)	Changes the name of a file
REPLACE	Updates old versions of files
RESTORE	Restores files from backup
RMDIR (RD)	Removes or deletes an empty directory
SELECT	Creates AUTOEXEC.BAT and CONFIG.SYS files
SET	Displays or sets data in the environment
SHARE	Controls file sharing and locking
SHIFT	Batch file command to adjust passed parameters
SORT	Sorts data output from another command
SUBST	Substitutes a string for a path
SYS	Transfers operating system files to a drive
TIME	Sets the PC's internal time clock
TREE	Displays the directory hierarchy for a disk
TYPE	Displays the contents of a text file
VER	Displays the DOS version number
VERIFY	Displays or sets the file copy verification status
VOL	Displays the disk volume label and serial number
XCOPY	Copies files and directories

The following chapters focus on those operating system commands that can help you to manage your hard disk. Appendix A provides a complete reference for the commands that are directly related to hard disk management.

Summary

A major responsibility of the operating system is to organize and manage the data stored on a hard disk. In this chapter you learned the following key points:

- The operating system provides a layer between the computer hardware and the computer user or the applications program.

- The most common personal computer operating systems are DOS, OS/2, and UNIX.

- Operating systems include a command interpreter, basic input/output services, and utilities.

- Recent versions of operating systems include powerful disk management utilities, such as the DOS Shell and the OS/2 Presentation Manager.

- Booting is the process of initially loading the computer's operating system. A cold boot occurs when the system power is turned on, and a warm boot occurs when the computer is reset (usually by pressing Ctrl-Alt-Del).

- There are a variety of operating system commands, and many commands can be used with switches to precisely define the actions of the command.

Chapter 3 discusses the detailed workings of the hard disk.

3

Understanding How a Hard Disk Works

So far, this text has shown you how to use and manage information stored on a hard disk. This chapter explains, in plain English, the disk drive's physical operation. Just as a good driver needs an appreciation of a car engine's inner workings, a computer user should have an understanding of the mechanics behind that flashing disk light.

A hard disk unit has two main components: the disk drive itself, and the disk drive controller. In this chapter you will learn about the disk drive hardware, problems that commonly afflict hard drives, and some modern data-storage alternatives to the hard disk. If you know how a hard disk works, you will have a clearer understanding of the file- and disk-related commands discussed in this text. This increased understanding also should help you prevent problems with your disk drive and recover from problems that do occur.

Understanding the Hard Disk Drive

Hard disks have evolved considerably since the first 10M disks were introduced with the IBM PC XT. Hard disk units are now available in a variety of sizes, storage capacities, performance categories, and prices. Yet, just as all modern-day car engines are broadly similar, all hard disks follow the same basic principles of operation.

A hard disk's workings fall into three general categories: the disk drive's physical characteristics, the organization of the disk's data storage surfaces, and the logical methods used by the operating system to store and retrieve data.

Hard Disk Components

Chapter 1 briefly explained the structure of a hard disk. Remember that the hard disk's primary component is a stack of aluminum platters (see fig. 3.1). The platters are coated with a magnetic oxide material that can store a positive or negative charge. To maximize the disk's storage capacity, both sides (that is, the top and bottom) of the platter are used to store data.

Hard disks rarely have more than 16 platters, and typically have fewer than 8 platters. The top side of the top platter is sometimes referred to as side 0; the underside of the top platter is called side 1. Unlike a floppy disk, a hard disk's platters continually rotate at a speed of 3,600 r.p.m.—that's 60 full rotations every second—while the computer is turned on.

Data is transferred to and from the platter's surface through a *disk drive head*. The drive head is attached to an armature that moves the head across the platter's surface. The head assembly is similar to the tonearm on a record player.

Disk drive heads come in various shapes and sizes. Figure 3.2 shows two of the more common types. The head glides just above the platter's surface, senses the magnetic polarity of a tiny region of the disk, and converts this magnetic signal into an electrical charge. The head itself is held in position by a flexible metal head-holder assembly. A set of wires, which carries electrical signals to and from the head, connects to the head and passes through the head-holder assembly. The wires then connect to a flexible ribbon cable. The ribbon cable absorbs wire movements when the head assembly moves.

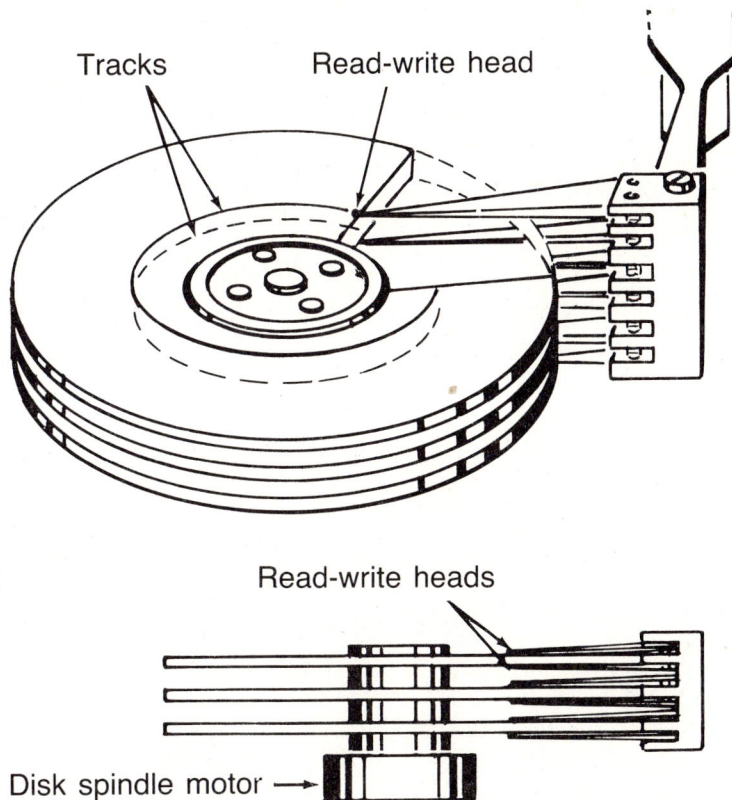

Fig. 3.1. *A typical hard disk.*

The head assembly's light weight provides greater start-stop control when a head is in position over a specific area of the disk. If the disk drive used only one head, the armature would have to move not only across one platter's surface, but also from one platter to another, to read and write data on other surfaces. A single-head hard disk drive, therefore, would be slow and difficult to engineer. To optimize performance and simplify the unit's mechanics, a hard disk usually has one drive head for every platter surface. If a drive has 7 platters, for example, it has 14 drive heads and armatures.

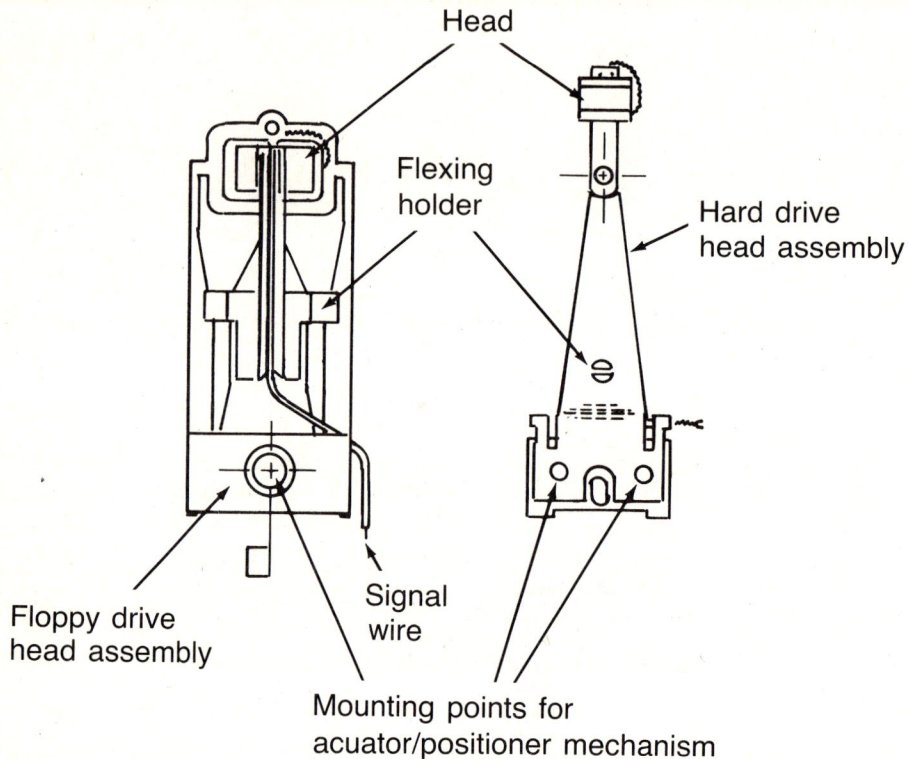

Fig. 3.2. *Typical disk drive head assemblies.*

Some of the newest hard disks use two (or more) heads for each surface to improve performance and reduce the time required to move a head to the correct part of the disk. They can even write data to two parts of the platter's surface simultaneously. These disks are complex to engineer and expensive to manufacture and are, therefore, not commonplace in PCs.

The hard disk assembly is a tremendous feat of engineering, especially when you consider how accurate and reliable hard disks are. Users always want more powerful computers that take up less space, and these demands certainly extend to hard disks. To increase hard-disk capacity, engineers have designed platter surfaces that store magnetic charges closer together. In order to read these magnetic charges, the drive head must be extremely close to the disk's surface, but can never actually touch the surface. In fact, a typical drive head glides just one ten-thousandth of an inch above the platter's surface—that's much less than the thickness of a hair—as the disk rotates 3,600 times a minute. In some units, the tolerance is even closer. These tolerances have been compared to the accuracy required to fly a jet at 500 miles per hour an inch above the surface of a runway. Now that's engineering.

If the disk drive head is too close to the platter's surface, friction builds up, and the system becomes vulnerable to problems caused by minute particles of dust. If a disk drive head actually touches the platter's surface (such an occurrence is called a *head crash*), the data on that part of the disk is destroyed. If the head glides too far above the surface, the head cannot read the magnetic charge accurately. The solution, therefore, is to make the drive head extremely light, and use the natural air current generated by the disk's rotation to *float* the drive head over the surface. You can compare the head's behavior with that of a large Hovercraft floating just above the surface of the water.

You can easily imagine the havoc created by dust and dirt in this environment. The hard disk chassis is sealed to keep foreign material away from the disk's surface. Most hard disk assemblies feature an air inlet, which is covered with a fine gauze filter to keep dirt out.

Disk Surface Organization

The disk drive must be able to store and retrieve data quickly. The disk surfaces, therefore, are organized into a *coordinate* system. This system is used to position the correct drive head over the area containing the desired data. The coordinate system divides each platter into tracks, cylinders, and sectors.

Each of the disk's sectors must be given an identifying number. This numbering is accomplished through an addressing scheme called *disk interleave*. Interleave has a significant impact on the drive's overall performance. Other factors affecting the disk's performance are more directly related to hardware components.

Disk Tracks

When a disk drive head is positioned over the rotating platter, the head can access an area of the disk's surface that describes a circle. After the platter completes a revolution, the head repositions itself over another part of the platter. If the head moves inward toward the disk's center, or outward toward the edge, it can read another "circle" of data on the disk. A full ring of information on the disk is referred to as a *track*.

The track of magnetically recorded data is like a ring on an archery target, except that the track is not visible to the eye. Figure 3.3 illustrates the organization of tracks on a disk platter. The tracks form perfect concentric circles. The number of tracks available on one disk's surface is determined by the head positioner's mechanical tolerances. The smaller the stepping distance, the narrower the track width and the tighter the track pattern. The more tracks on a platter, the greater the disk's storage capacity.

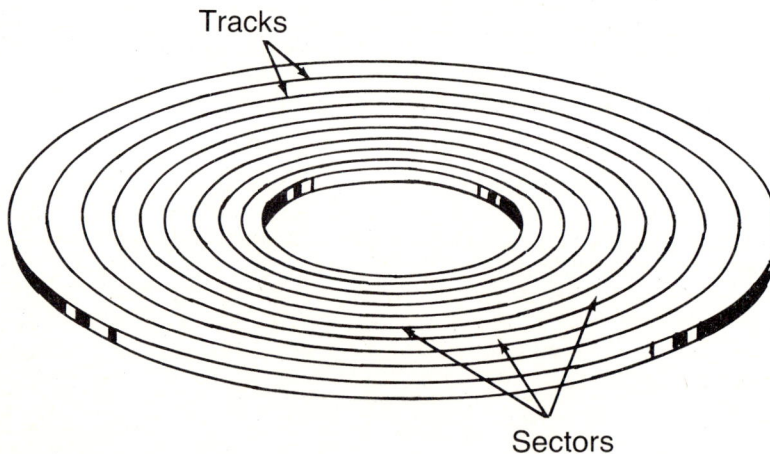

Fig. 3.3. Concentric tracks on a disk's surface.

There are typically between 500 and 750 tracks per inch across the diameter of a platter. The outermost track on the disk is referred to as track 0; the next track in is track 1, and so on. Both sides of a platter have an identical number of tracks.

Disk Cylinders

All the disk drive heads are mounted on a single mechanism, which moves the heads together in a vertical column. When the head on the platter's top side is over track 5, therefore, the head on the platter's underside also is over (or strictly speaking, beneath) track 5. In fact, all the heads are in position over track 5 on all platter sides.

The primary time delay in accessing data on a hard disk is the time required to move the head into position over a specific track. To optimize reading and writing speed, data often is accessed from the same track (for example, track 5) on both sides of each platter, rather than from multiple tracks on one platter. This means that multiple tracks can be read without moving the drive heads. Ten heads are better than one! A vertical column of aligned tracks is called a *cylinder*.

A cylinder is like a three-dimensional track; the terms "cylinder" and "track" are often used interchangeably. If a disk's platters each have 2,000 tracks, then the tracks line up vertically to form 2,000 cylinders. Cylinders use the same numbering scheme as tracks, with the outermost cylinder being cylinder 0, the next being cylinder 1, and so on.

Disk Sectors

The volume of data that can be stored on a single track depends on the data-encoding scheme used by the disk. (You will learn more about data encoding in the discussion of hard disk controllers.) Typically, one hard disk track can store about 10K. To use this available storage space more efficiently, however, the minimum data storage unit must be less than one track. Tracks, therefore, are further divided into *sectors*. A sector is one segment of a track (see fig. 3.4). The number of sectors in a track depends on the type of hard disk and controller. Usually, a track contains 17 or 26 sectors, and a sector contains 512 bytes.

> ✓
> NOTE
>
> Both DOS and OS/2 expect the disk's sector size to be 512 bytes, and they make no provision to alter this setting. Some disk utility programs, however, use a special technique to increase the sector size to 1,024 or 2,048 bytes. This technique enables the disk to store more information, and further enables DOS to reference drives larger than 32M—the storage limit until the appearance of DOS V4.

Sector

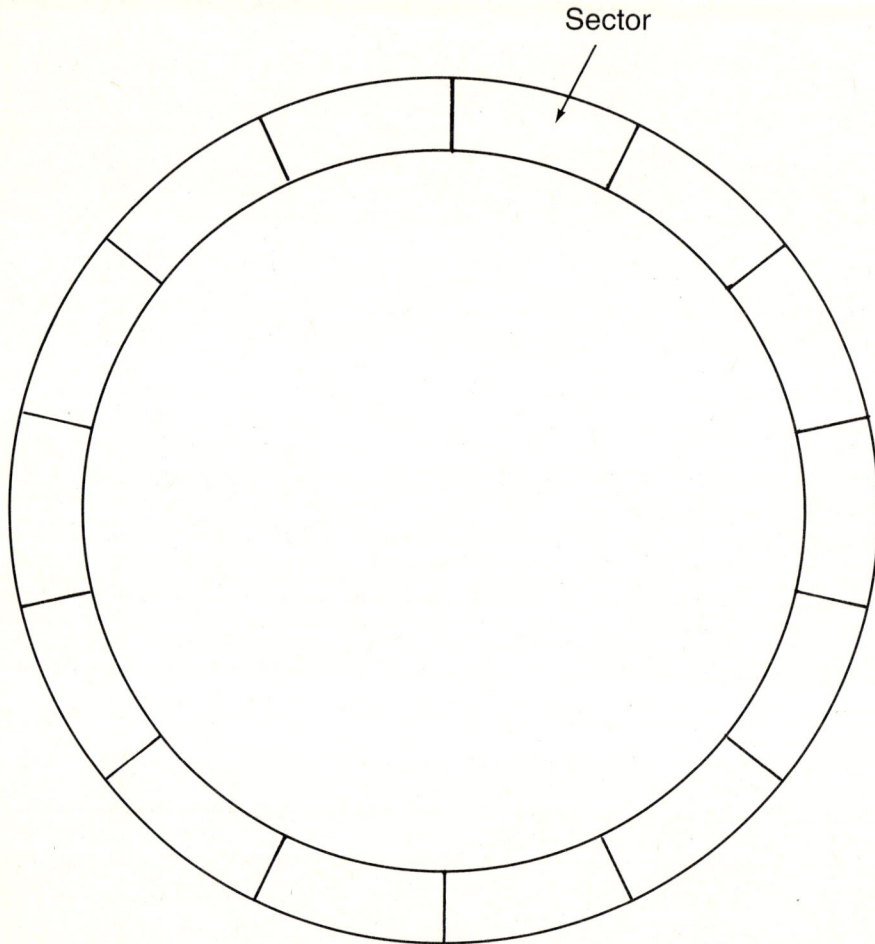

Fig. 3.4. A track is subdivided into 512-byte sectors.

Although the disk's outer tracks have a greater surface area, they store the same amount of data as the innermost tracks. By maintaining the same sector-addressing scheme and track width, the operating system does waste some storage capacity, but it also simplifies disk operation and improves performance. In fact, even the disk's innermost tracks have a gap between the sectors to improve performance.

To find a specific data element, the disk must know which platter, track, and sector to search for the data. Each platter, track, and sector is identified by a unique number. Later in this chapter, you will learn how the operating system uses this addressing scheme to access data on the disk.

Low-Level Formatting

Before it is ready for daily use, the hard disk must undergo *low-level formatting*. The low-level format organizes the disk's magnetic surfaces into tracks and sectors. During low-level formatting, the disk surface is checked and any bad or unusable sectors are marked so that the operating system cannot use them.

For performance reasons, a track's sectors do not necessarily line up in sequential order. For example, sector 1 may be followed by sector 7. (The following section explains the reasons behind this arrangement.) The first few bytes of each sector contain the sector's identifying number. These initial bytes—called the *sector header*—eliminate the need for an index that keeps track of each sector's location (see fig. 3.5). To find a specific sector, the drive head moves along the appropriate track and reads each sector header until the right sector is found. This coding scheme is referred to as *soft sectoring*.

The header information is written into each sector during low-level formatting. The sector address contains the track number, the head number, and the sector number. The track number is included in case the drive head is mistakenly positioned over the wrong track. If this happens, the head recognizes the error after reading the current address, and orders the armature to move. Following the sector address, additional bytes indicate that sector data follows. The sector address is written only once, during low-level formatting; it is never written again.

The hard disk's distributor normally performs low-level formatting when the unit is new. If not, the disk should include a program that enables you to perform low-level formatting.

The second stage of hard disk preparation includes *high-level formatting* (also called *logical formatting*), which prepares the disk for use with an operating system. High-level formatting is discussed later in this text.

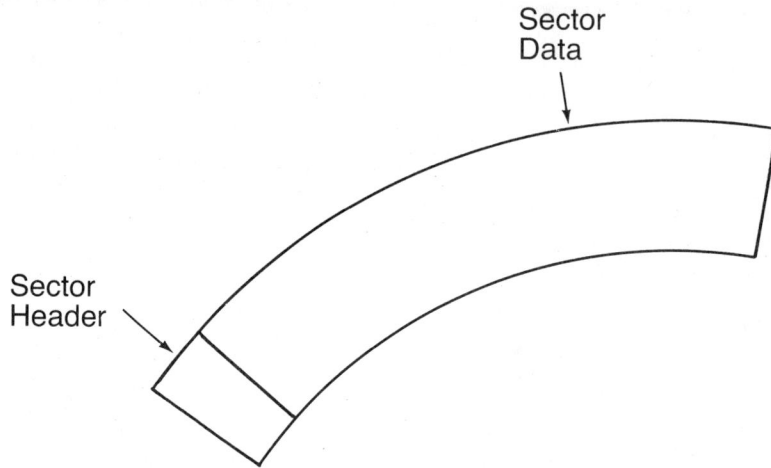

Fig. 3.5. *The sector header contains the sector's identifying number.*

Interleaving

When you save a file on the hard disk, your computer's operating system writes the file to one or more sectors. Suppose that a file is to be stored in three sectors, and that all the sectors in a track are free. The drive head moves to the appropriate track, and when the head is in position over sector 1, it writes the first part of the file to that sector. The disk controller then ships the next part of the file to the drive head. Because a small but measurable amount of time is required to send the next block of data to the drive head, the head already may be positioned halfway over sector 2 by the time the data reaches the head. (Remember that the disk rotates at 3,600 revolutions per minute.) The disk must make nearly another full revolution before the beginning of sector 2 is again below the drive head. Then the head can write the second part of the file into sector 2. By the time the controller has sent the final part of the file, the drive head may be halfway along sector 3, and so the disk has to rotate another revolution before the third part of the file can be saved. In the worst case, the disk may have to complete 17 revolutions before a full track of data can be saved (a track is usually divided into 17 sectors).

If your computer, drive controller, and hard disk operate at high levels of performance, they may be fast enough to ship data to the drive head before the head passes the beginning of the next sector. Many systems, however, simply are not so fast. With slower machines, therefore, sectors should not be ordered consecutively. Rather than numbering sectors adjacent to each other, the operating system can *interleave* the sectors so that sector 2 is located two or more sectors after sector 1. When interleaving is used, the controller has more time to pass data to the drive head.

To achieve the best possible configuration, the drive head is positioned over the target sector header just when the data is ready to be written. This arrangement is called *optimum interleave*. Figure 3.6 shows three different interleave ratios. A drive has a 1:1 interleave ratio when adjacent sectors are numbered consecutively (1, 2, 3, 4, and so on). A drive has 2:1 interleave when its sectors are numbered alternately (1, 10, 2, 11, 3, 12, and so on). Typical interleave ratios range from 1:1 to 8:1.

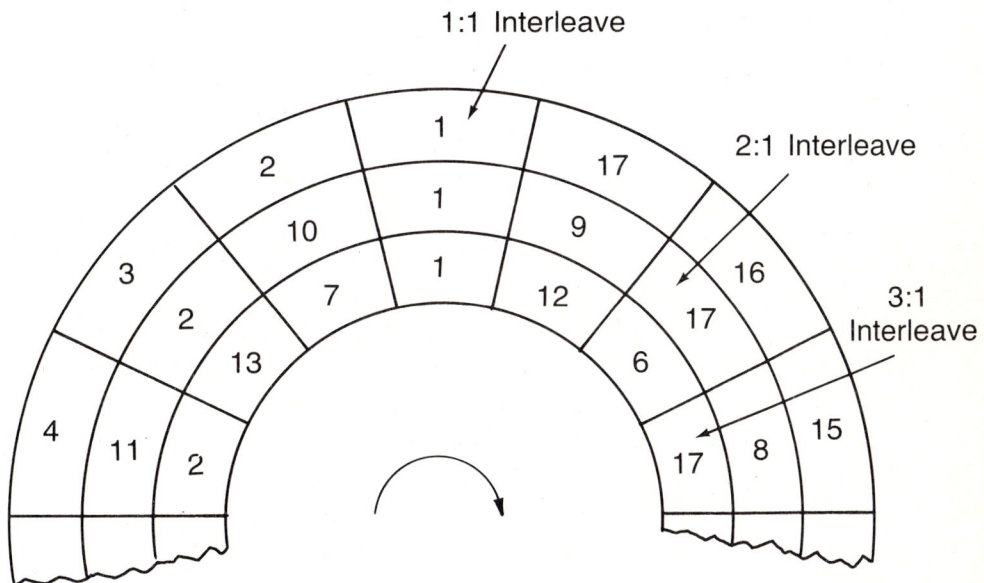

Fig. 3.6. *Possible interleave ratios on a track that contains 17 sectors.*

Interleave ratio has a profound effect on a hard disk's performance. If the ratio is too small, the controller cannot ship data to the drive head quickly enough, forcing the disk to make almost one revolution before the target sector is positioned below the drive head. If the interleave ratio is too high, the head is ready to write the data before the target sector is in position, causing unnecessary idle time.

UTILITY   SpinRite II (Gibson Research Corporation) tests and calibrates hard disks. This utility program checks drive alignment and determines the disk's optimum interleave ratio. For more information on this product, see Chapter 14.

Hard Disk Performance Factors

Aside from microprocessing speed, the hard disk has the most significant impact on a computer's overall performance. A number of statistics can be used to evaluate a disk's capabilities. If you ask car enthusiasts which is the most informative statistic about a car engine, you might get many different responses: top speed, acceleration, horsepower, number of valves, engine capacity, and so on. You can expect a similar range of replies if you ask computer buffs about hard disks.

Realistically, no single statistic accurately describes a hard disk's overall performance. You can rely on two primary performance attributes, however, to describe a hard disk's speed. These attributes are the disk's *average access time* and *transfer rate*.

Average Access Time

When the computer requests data from the hard disk, the drive head must move from its current position to the track where the requested data is stored. The time required to move the head to its new position is called *seek time* or *access time*.

Access time depends on the distance from the head's current position to the target track, and can vary with every data transfer request. To quantify the performance accurately, engineers perform multiple tests to find the average amount of time the head needs to access a random track. The target track may be close to or remote from the head's current position. The random tests normally compute the time required for the head to seek across one-third of the tracks on a platter. *Average access time* is the average duration of these random seek tests. Average access time is the most commonly used measurement of overall disk performance.

Average access time is measured in milliseconds (ms); that is, thousandths of a second. The first IBM PC XT hard disks had an average access time of between 80 ms and 110 ms. Many hard disks now in use have average access times of about 65 ms. Newer hard disks, however, sport average access times between 15 ms and 30 ms. If you plan to buy a new hard disk soon, look for one with an average access time of 28 ms or less.

Once the disk head is in position over the desired track, the computer must wait for the appropriate sector to move into place beneath the drive head. This waiting period is called drive *latency*. Statistically, the average wait will be the time taken for the disk to rotate half a revolution; this measurement is called *average latency*. Because all hard disks rotate at 3,600 r.p.m., they all have the same average latency of 8 ms. Average latency, therefore, is not a useful statistic for comparing the performance of PC hard disks.

Transfer Rate

The rate at which data can be transferred to and from the hard disk is called *transfer rate*. Transfer rate is measured in megabits per second (mps).

Because all personal computer hard disks rotate at the same speed, the only factor that influences transfer rate is the amount of information that can be stored in each sector or track. This storage capacity is the disk's *density*. Density is largely determined by the type of controller interface and data-encoding method used. (These factors are discussed later.) Transfer rates of 5 mps are common, but disk and controller manufacturers are closer to making cost-effective systems that transfer more than 20 mps.

Data Storage and Retrieval

While tracks and sectors are the foundation of a data storage system, they do not, alone, provide sufficient control of an efficient *file* storage and retrieval system. You can use the operating system command FORMAT to add another "layer" of addressing schemes, which manage data that has been organized into files.

The Formatting Process

When a disk undergoes low-level (or physical) formatting, the disk's physical space is organized into tracks and sectors. The available platters, sides, tracks, sectors per track, and bytes per sector are the physical elements that allow the division and addressing of the disk's storage space.

Your computer's operating system uses a logical scheme for managing files. This scheme not only improves speed, but enables you and your programs to access the disk without using the physical addressing scheme. The FORMAT program further organizes the hard disk and establishes this logical drive format. (FORMAT works with floppy disks, as well.) See Appendix A for more information about the FORMAT command.

FORMAT adds special information to the first few tracks on a disk, starting at sector 1, track 0, side 0. The operating system uses this information as the basis for managing all other areas of the disk. The information includes the *boot record*, the *file allocation table* (FAT), and the *root directory*. Subdirectories are created from the root directory, so the FORMAT command only needs to create the root directory; you can use the MKDIR (Make Directory) command to create all other descendant directories.

The FORMAT command erases all the data stored on a disk. Do not invoke this command until you fully understand its use and potential consequences.

When you boot your computer, it automatically accesses the boot record. Generally speaking, the boot record gives the computer just enough information to start operating. Specifically, the boot record instructs the computer as to the hard disk's physical characteristics (the number of sides, heads, tracks, sectors, and so on), and then helps the computer locate the operating system files. The computer then accesses the operating system files, and the booting process completes.

Clusters

The smallest unit of storage on the disk is a 512-byte sector. The operating system has to know which sectors are in use—that is, which sectors currently contain data—and which sectors are available for storing new data. Further, the operating system must keep track of all the sectors that each file is stored in.

A 100M hard disk holds nearly 200,000 sectors. The operating system would be overburdened if it had to manage each individual sector. Certainly, a computer could manage a list of 200,000 items, but file access would be unacceptably slow. To make the disk more manageable, the operating system uses a referencing scheme that considers a group of sectors together as a single unit. Such a group of sectors is called a *cluster*.

The number of sectors in a cluster is determined by the operating system's version number and the hard disk's storage capacity. On hard disks with a capacity of 16M or more, the default cluster size is 4 sectors (2K). Smaller drives may use 8 (4K) or 16 (8K) sectors per cluster. For small drives using DOS V4, the default cluster size is 8 sectors.

When the computer stores data on the disk, the operating system maintains a record of the disk clusters used to store the data. (This record is maintained in the file allocation table, which is discussed in the following section.) By maintaining clusters rather than sectors, the operating system reduces its management burden by a factor of 4 or more.

This scheme has a down side as well, however, because one cluster is the smallest space that can be allocated to a file. Even a 50-byte batch file must be allocated an entire cluster. Similarly, if a file has to be saved in multiple clusters (because it is too large to fit in one), the last part of the file is allocated a full cluster whether the entire cluster is needed or not. Depending on the system's cluster size, this wasted storage space can range from 2K to 8K per file.

FAT

The file allocation table (FAT) is the primary file "bookkeeping" area, which maintains a record of all the clusters on the disk. When writing a file to the disk, the operating system searches the FAT to determine the location of the next available free cluster. The FAT also tells the operating system which clusters are being used by a file, and identifies reserved or unusable clusters.

Every cluster in the disk's data area (that is, the area not reserved for the boot record and FAT) receives a unique reference number. This number is different from track and sector numbers, which are relative to a specific side or track of the disk. The FAT maintains one entry (or record) for every cluster on the disk, and the cluster number is used as the primary index.

Each entry in the FAT maintains two bytes of information that indicate the cluster's current status. Each cluster falls into one of the following five status categories:

- The cluster is available.

- The cluster is being used by a file. The record actually indicates the next cluster that is used by the same file.

- The cluster is being used by a file and is the last cluster containing data for that file.

- The cluster is reserved.

- The cluster occupies a bad spot on the disk and should not be used.

Directories

The operating system uses another "bookkeeping" area, called a *directory*, to record information about each file. The disk's root directory is automatically created when the disk is formatted. A directory contains one entry (or record) for every file in the directory; each record includes the information shown in table 3.1.

Each directory entry takes up 32 bytes; an extra 10 bytes are reserved for potential future use. Notice that the information includes the starting cluster number, which provides a link to the FAT.

The root directory's size is fixed during formatting. All disks, therefore, have a maximum number of files that can be stored in the root directory. Typically, this maximum is 512 files.

A directory is actually a special file that stores information about other files. Any file in the root directory can itself be a directory, storing information about yet more files. The root directory can therefore store data files and directories of other files. Each of *these* directories also can keep records of additional data files and additional directories. Although the number of files in the root directory is limited, you can create many directories spawning from the root to provide a directory hierarchy, limited only by the total storage space available.

Putting it All Together

When the operating system is instructed by a program (such as EDLIN or Lotus 1-2-3) to read, save, or delete a file, the operating system uses the directory and the FAT to find all the information needed to process the file. Each one of these processes is managed in a different way.

File Reading

To load a file, the operating system must find the cluster(s) in which the file is stored. The operating system uses the file's directory entry to determine the number of the file's first cluster, and then references the FAT to determine whether other clusters are used to store the entire file. If the cluster is marked in the FAT as being the last cluster in the file, the operating system knows that the file is stored in just one cluster. If the FAT entry points to another cluster, however, the operating system must read the current sector and then move to the next cluster. The operating system then checks the FAT to determine whether the second cluster is the last cluster containing data for the current file. The operating system repeats the process until all the file's clusters are read.

Table 3.1.
File Information Contained in Directories

File Information	Description
File name	The file's eight-character root name
Extension	The file name's three-character extension
Attributes	An indicator of certain aspects of the file's status, such as read/write, hidden, system, archive, or volume label
Time	The time the file was last saved to disk
Date	The date the file was last saved to disk
Cluster	The number of the cluster in which the first part of the file is stored
Size	The file's size in bytes

File Saving

If a new file is being saved to disk, the operating system checks the FAT to locate the first available cluster on the disk, and then writes the data into that cluster. If all the data can be saved in one cluster, that cluster receives a "last cluster" entry in the FAT. If another cluster is needed, the operating system checks the FAT to find the next available cluster; this cluster number is recorded in the first cluster's FAT entry, creating a *cluster chain*. The process is repeated until all the data has been saved. After filling the file's last cluster with data, the operating system places a "last cluster" entry in the FAT for that cluster. The file's directory entry is then updated with the necessary details about the file, including the starting cluster number.

If the file already has been saved on the disk, the operating system finds the file's existing directory entry. The operating system searches the directory and the FAT to locate the clusters that store the existing version of the file. Once the clusters are found, the operating system overwrites the old data with the new. If the new file is smaller than the original, the unused clusters are marked as free in the FAT. If the new version of the file is larger than the old version, the operating system searches the FAT to find the next free cluster, and extends the cluster chain.

Over time, the hard disk performs thousands of file creations and deletions. As a result, empty clusters may be randomly scattered all over the disk. When new files are saved to the disk, they may be saved in many different tracks, depending on the available clusters' locations. When parts of files are located all over the disk in this manner, the disk is said to be *fragmented*. A fragmented disk's performance is slow because the drive heads have to make many seeks to access data.

> UTILITY
>
> You can use a number of programs to defragment a disk. Such utility programs can improve your hard disk's performance significantly. See Chapter 10 for more information.

File Deleting

When the operating system deletes a file, it does not physically erase the file from the disk. Rather, the operating system finds the file's directory entry, and replaces the file name's first character with a special character (ASCII code 229). This special character signifies that the file has been deleted. The operating system then searches the FAT, and marks as free the clusters used by the deleted file.

The deleted file's clusters continue to store the file's data until they are overwritten by a new file. This data-deletion method enables you to *unerase* a deleted file if you have limited your file-saving activity since the file was deleted.

> UTILITY
>
> Operating systems do not provide an unerase command, but many third-party programs do provide this facility. These utilities are discussed in detail in Chapter 15.

Understanding Partitions

You can configure a single physical hard disk so that it works like multiple disks. You can accomplish this through a process called *partitioning*, which tricks the operating system into treating one disk as multiple disks. Each partition functions like an independent disk. Disks usually are partitioned for one of the two following reasons:

- To allow different parts of one disk to be used and structured by different operating systems. The operating system determines the disk's logical organization. DOS and OS/2 structure the disk with a boot record, a FAT, and a root directory. One of your hard disk partitions could be used for DOS, and another for UNIX. Because of the separation, each operating systems is "tricked" into recognizing its partition as an entire disk.

- To divide a large disk into smaller logical disks that are each 32M or less in size. Before the introduction of DOS V4 (or Compaq DOS V3.31), DOS could access only 32M of disk space—the FAT was too small to manage any more clusters. Disk storage capacities, however, have grown considerably beyond 32M. You can imagine how frustrating it would be to have a 100M hard disk and an operating system that could access only 32M!

You can use your operating system's FDISK program to partition a disk, but FDISK must be run before the FORMAT command is used. FDISK creates a *partition table* that stores all the information about the hard disk partitions. The partition table precedes the boot record at the beginning of the disk, on side 0, track 0. The partition table actually includes a dummy boot record that is referenced when the computer is booted.

The partition table details the total number of partitions on the disk and the dimensions of each partition, and, with a special flag, indicates which partition is the *primary partition*. The primary partition refers to the partition that contains the operating system files needed to boot the computer. When first booted, the computer reads the dummy boot record in the partition table, then the partition table, and then the real boot record in the primary partition. Chapter 7 discusses disk partitioning in detail.

The operating system assumes that each formatted partition is a separate drive. To change from one DOS (or OS/2) drive to another, you enter the partition's logical drive name, such as D:.

See Chapter 7 for more information on FDISK.

Disk Problems

As you can now appreciate, the hard disk is an engineering wonder, and the operating system must perform sophisticated tasks to access the data on the disk. In an environment of such close tolerances, problems inevitably arise.

The Human Problem

Arguably, the most common cause of disk problems is the user (you and me excepted, of course). The user might delete the wrong file or accidentally erase a file by copying another file over it. A much more significant problem occurs if the user accidentally erases all the files in a directory, or—worse yet—formats the disk and erases *all* the files.

No matter what precautions you take, however, the unexpected can always happen. To reduce the effect of accidental data loss, back up your data as often as possible. Data backup techniques are covered in Part V.

Drive Alignment

You may recall that the low-level format organizes the disk into tracks and sectors, and that the sector number is recorded at the beginning of each sector. This sector number is never rewritten.

The accurate alignment of the drive head over each track is critical to the drive's operation. The drive head is attached to an armature, which is mechanically moved into position by a stepping motor. When mechanical operations are involved, mechanical wear is always a danger. In the case of a hard disk, the drive-alignment mechanism can suffer wear and fail to position the drive head exactly over the target track. Although new data will be written along this new path, the original sector addresses remain in the same physical location where they were originally written. Figure 3.7 shows a magnified view of a sector suffering a drive alignment problem. The sector numbers are stored in the drive head's old location (before the alignment failure), and data is stored in the drive head's new location (after failure).

If the alignment error is too large, the drive head cannot read the sector number, and the operating system generates a `Sector not found` message.

If the drive mechanism is still healthy, the disk can be reused after undergoing a new low-level format. The low-level formatting positions the sector numbers along the drive head's new path.

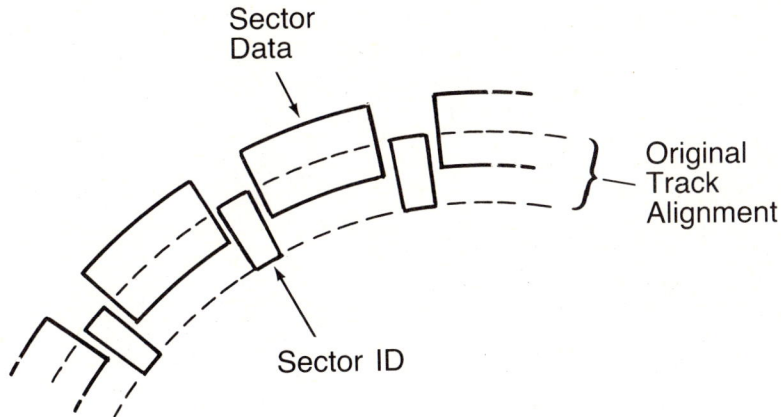

Fig. 3.7. *A worn stepping mechanism can cause drive heads to go out of alignment.*

Most low-level formatting programs erase all the data on the disk. The SpinRite program (discussed in Chapter 14) performs low-level formatting without disrupting the data. Using such a program is a good option when you are trying to recover from a drive-alignment problem.

CRC Errors

When the operating system writes data to a specific sector, it performs a quick computation based on the data written, and writes the resulting value at the end of the sector. The value is like a subtotal. When the disk reads the data from a sector, the same computation is performed, and the computed value is compared to the value stored at the end of the sector. This procedure is called a *cyclic redundancy check*, or CRC. If the values are different, a problem has occurred during the writing or reading of the data. When such an error is discovered, the operating system generates a message such as **CRC ERROR READING DRIVE C**. The operating system then searches the FAT and marks as unusable the cluster containing the faulty sector.

When VERIFY is active, or when the /V option is used with the COPY and DISKCOPY commands, the CRC value is checked after each sector is written. That is, each sector is read as soon as it is written, and the computed CRC value is compared to the stored CRC value. These file commands do not actually compare the source and target data.

If the operating system encounters a CRC error when the data is written to the disk, the cluster is marked as bad, the data is automatically written elsewhere, and a new CRC check is performed. In other words, the operating system corrects the problem and no data is lost. Rarely does an unrecoverable CRC error occur while the operating system is reading information from the disk. Usually, the controller instructs the drive to reread the sector, and the problem is resolved. If the data cannot be successfully read, the file may be unusable. In such cases, you may be able to resurrect the unusable file with help from a disaster recovery program (as discussed in Chapter 15).

Cluster Errors

The FAT and the directories maintain a detailed record of all the clusters on the hard disk. Cluster errors occur when these records contain contradictory information. Errors usually occur when the computer is turned off during a file-writing operation or when a program crashes (stops unexpectedly) during a file-writing operation.

If a cluster is in use (that is, if it is being used to store data for a file), an entry in the FAT points to it, or it is referenced as a file's starting cluster in the directory cluster. A *lost cluster* occurs when the FAT indicates that a specific cluster is in use, but other records in the FAT and the disk's directories indicate that the cluster is not referenced by any file in the system.

A similar problem occurs when two files point to the same cluster; that is, the cluster is claimed by two or more files. Files that share a cluster are called *cross-linked* files.

A third problem occurs when one cluster points to a second cluster as part of a cluster chain, but the second cluster is classified (in the FAT) as free. The first cluster is said to contain an *invalid next-cluster-in-chain value*.

You can use the external CHKDSK command to identify and correct cluster errors. CHKDSK is discussed in Chapter 14, but for a thorough explanation of CHKDSK, see *Using DOS* (published by Que Corporation) or your operating system manual.

Drive Head Problems

A *head crash* occurs when the drive head actually strikes the disk platter's oxidized surface, and destroys the data on that part of the disk. Head crashes can be caused by a malfunctioning drive or by a sudden jolt to the computer (and, therefore, the drive). Such movements can occur whether the system is turned on or off.

A less dramatic problem may occur when you turn on your computer. Like many electronic systems, a computer suffers a small power surge when the electrical current is first turned on. If this impulse occurs while the drive head is located above the disk surface, the charge on the surface may be weakened.

Modern disk drives move the head away from the disk's surface when the system is shut down, but older disk drives do not. If you are not sure whether your system has this capability, you should always *park* the disk drive before turning off your computer. Parking is the action of moving the drive head mechanism to the side of the platter, well away from the disk surface. The diagnostics disk supplied with your computer may include a head-parking program. Some third-party utilities also can park the heads. Refer to Chapter 14 for more details.

Mechanical Failures

Hard disks can suffer from serious mechanical failure that render them inoperative, with data loss a frequent result. If the drive simply stops functioning, a program can do little to fix the problem. However, most computer repair shops can repair a disk and get it functioning. Some companies will, for a price, recover all the data on a damaged disk by duplicating the data on a working drive. If you have lost valuable data because of a mechanical failure, take the drive to a reputable dealer; they may be able to fix the drive or recover the data. Do not try to open the disk drive and repair it yourself.

You may be able to recover "lost" data caused by certain disk problems. Chapter 14 explains how you can avoid data loss, and Chapter 15 shows how you might be able to recover from a disaster, if one should occur.

Even if the disk suffers a major mechanical failure, there is a reasonable chance that some data can be recovered. OnTrack Data Recovery, Inc. (see Appendix E) and other companies specialize in the recovery of data from "trashed" disks. If your data is very important, and you do not have a backup, custom data recovery may be the ideal solution.

Understanding Disk Controllers

In most computers, the *disk drive controller* is a separate piece of circuitry that controls the disk drive's physical operation. Most controllers take the form of a plug-in card that is inserted in one of the computer's motherboard slots. In some of the most modern computer systems (particularly laptops and briefcase-size systems), the controller circuitry is built into the motherboard or the disk drive.

The controller instructs the disk drive to position the drive head, and sends and receives the data that is accessed on the disk. Usually, two ribbon-type cables extend from the controller to the disk drive; one cable transfers data, and the other transmits the mechanical instructions.

Like hard disks, floppy disk drives cannot operate without the aid of a controller. In the first PCs fitted with hard disks, one controller operated the floppy disk drive and another controller managed the hard disk. Now, one controller usually controls both the floppy and hard disk drives.

Ever since hard disks were introduced, computer users have demanded greater storage capacity and speed, at a smaller size and price. Hardware manufacturers have met these demands by improving the interface between the controller and the drive, and by changing the data-encoding method used to store the data on the disk. The hard disk and the controller must use compatible interface and data-encoding methods.

Interface Standards

The *interface* is the connection between the controller and the disk drive. The interface specifies how the controller is wired to the drive, what protocol is used to transmit instructions, and how multiple drives are connected to the controller. The three main interfaces currently employed on hard disks are ST506/ST412, ESDI, and SCSI.

ST506/ST412

The ST506/ST412 interface was first developed by Seagate and was the original interface used on PC hard disks. Unlike other interfaces, the ST506/ST412 operates at a fixed data-transfer rate of 5 megabits per second. An overwhelming majority of computers use this interface standard. Western Digital's WD-1003-WA2 controller, the IBM PC XT, and the IBM Personal Computer AT all use the ST506/ST412 interface.

By today's standards, the ST506/ST412 interface is conservative in its operating design. The interface's primary goal, however, was reliability and economy of production.

ESDI

The *enhanced small device interface* (ESDI) is an extension of the original ST506/ST412 interface. The interface between the controller and the drive looks the same as the ST506/ST412, but is slightly different—sufficiently different that a ST506/ST412-type drive cannot be driven by an ESDI controller.

The ESDI interface employs a superior interface protocol, which makes an ESDI system twice as fast as an ST506/ST412 system. The ESDI controller also can handle larger and faster drives. Compaq Deskpro 386 computers use the ESDI interface.

SCSI

The third primary interface standard is the *small computer system interface* (SCSI). The SCSI interface design is quite different from its predecessors. The SCSI interface enables the computer manufacturer to chain multiple devices (in parallel) to a single controller. For example, one SCSI interface might control two hard disks, a tape drive, and a CD-ROM drive. As many as eight independent devices can be daisy-chained to the controller.

The performance of the early systems that used the SCSI interface was disappointing. But recent refinements in data-transfer protocols have significantly improved the interface's performance, making the SCSI the interface of choice for many hard disk aficionados. The SCSI is potentially more than twice as fast as the ESDI interface, and many experts believe that SCSI will become the predominant interface in the 1990s.

You do not need to buy a very high-performance (and expensive) drive interface if your computer cannot transfer data to the controller at a rate equivalent to that of the interface. In such a mismatched configuration, the drive must continually wait for the computer to "catch up." The ESDI and SCSI interfaces are best suited to high-performance 80286 systems (which operate at speeds of 12 MHz and above) and 80386 systems.

Data-Encoding Schemes

Another major influence on the hard disk's overall performance is the disk controller's data-encoding scheme. *Data encoding* is the process of converting bits of data into magnetic charges on the disk's surface. The two predominant data-encoding standards are MFM and RLL.

MFM

Most disk drive systems use the *modified frequency modulation* (MFM) data-encoding scheme. This coding scheme is generally used with the ST506/ST412 controllers.

An MFM system transfers a single bit of data to a single location on the disk's surface. A system that uses the MFM coding scheme with an ST506/ST412 interface has a maximum data transfer rate of 5 mps.

RLL

The other major encoding method is the *run-length limited* (RLL) scheme. The RLL scheme packs more information onto the disk. An RLL system effectively uses a compression algorithm or coding scheme to convert a stream of bits into a compacted code of variable length. This encoding scheme can place up to three times as much data on a disk as the MFM scheme. A disk that uses the RLL scheme usually has 26 sectors per track, compared with 17 sectors per track for MFM.

RLL encoding not only increases drive capacity, but also improves overall data throughput. In an RLL system using an ST506/ST412 interface, average throughput is 7.5 mps. Throughput jumps to 10 mps with an ESDI interface.

Theoretically, any hard drive can use the RLL encoding method, but the disk is subjected to significantly greater strain because it must do much more work. Only RLL-certified drives should be used with controllers that employ RLL encoding.

The *advanced run-length limited* (ARLL) scheme is a refinement of the RLL standard. By using a more advanced encoding scheme, ARLL increases disk density by more than 25 percent over RLL. Similarly, the ARLL throughput rate climbs to 9 mps, when used with an ST506/ST412 interface. The ARLL scheme also operates on a wider range of drives than the RLL scheme.

Other Storage Devices

A number of innovative storage devices provide good alternatives to the traditional hard disk. Some of these devices offer the potential for incredible storage capacities with excellent access times; others offer an economical alternative to the 3 1/2- and 5 1/4-inch hard drives. The following sections describe some of the currently available alternative data storage technologies.

Cache Controllers

A new breed of disk controller may significantly improve hard disk performance. These controllers include their own memory for caching data, and are known as *cache controllers*. The amount of memory on the board varies from product to product, but cache controllers often contain 4M or more.

In principle, a cache controller operates in much the same manner as a software cache. Both take advantage of the fact that the operating system can access RAM much more rapidly than it can access data on a disk. When a program requests data, the controller reads the requested data and more. While the drive head is positioned over the disk surface, the overhead of loading the extra data is negligible. The additional data is read into a memory buffer on the cache controller. If the program then requests data that has been read into the cache memory, the data can be transferred to the program directly from the cache memory, eliminating the need to access the disk again.

Similarly, data can be transferred to the cache buffer before it is saved on disk. By buffering the data in this fashion, the cache controller releases the computer to proceed with the next task.

Highly complex caching algorithms determine which data must be loaded into the cache, and which data should be discarded from the cache when new data is accessed. Different manufacturers employ different techniques.

The user gains two advantages by using a cache controller rather than a software cache. First, the cache controller frees valuable system RAM for other uses. Second, cache controllers generally use an optimized caching algorithm that works with the specific drive configuration. Software caches, however, are much cheaper than cache controllers. If you are looking for fast performance from a hard drive, a cache controller is a good solution. Cache controllers are available for MFM- and RLL-encoded ESDI drives.

Hard Cards

A *hard card* is a disk drive and a controller on a single card. The entire mechanism fits into one slot on the motherboard. Early hard cards had a capacity of 10M and slow access times. Today's hard cards can store 80M or more and feature access times of 28 ms or less.

Hard cards are easily installed and do not require a drive bay; all you need is a spare slot on the motherboard. Although hard cards utilize only one expansion slot, some of the bulkier cards effectively take up two slots because they do not leave enough room to put another device in the adjacent slot. Hard cards provide a very convenient way of upgrading early-model PCs—those PCs have no space for a hard disk (unless you remove a floppy disk drive) and have only a small power supply, which would not be capable of driving a traditional hard disk drive.

The Bernoulli Box

Iomega Corporation has developed a unique storage system that takes advantage of Bernoulli technology. The first Bernoulli products were introduced in 1983, and could store 10M of data on an 8-inch removable cartridge. In 1989, the 44M 5 1/4-inch Bernoulli cartridge was introduced. This cartridge fits in a special drive, which can be installed in a standard half-height bay. In effect, a Bernoulli cartridge is a 5 1/4-inch (by 1/4-inch thick) 44M removable disk.

The Bernoulli system uses the same basic magnetic storage method as a floppy or hard disk. The big difference is that the drive head on a Bernoulli system travels extremely close to the disk surface. To be accurate, it is the surface of the disk that moves, not the drive head. The data is stored on a very thin, flexible disk that floats toward the drive head when the drive is rotated. The air flow generated by the rotating disk curves the disk around the drive head. The aerodynamic principles were first postulated by Daniel Bernoulli, an eighteenth-century mathematician—hence the product's name.

The drive head's close proximity to the disk enables the system to pack data very densely onto the disk's oxidized surface. The drive uses an SCSI interface that transfers data at a rate of 12 megabits per second. With a software cache, the Bernoulli system has an average access time of nearly 22 ms.

In simple terms, a Bernoulli cartridge is like an extremely fast, high-capacity floppy disk. The cartridge works like a hard disk (except that when the disk fills, you can just put another cartridge in), or it can be used for external storage, such as backups and data transfers between machines.

> *A **note from the author** ...* I have been using Bernoulli drives for a number of years, and I would be lost without them. I use them for data security, data backup, and to store programs and data that I use infrequently.

High-Capacity Floppies

Many hardware companies are aggressively developing new high-capacity 3 1/2-inch floppy disk drives. Normally, 3 1/2-inch drives store 720K or 1.44M of data on a single floppy disk. Some new drives can store 2.8M and, if production costs can be reduced, you can expect floppy disk drives with storage capacities of 5M and more in the near future.

CD-ROM

One of the hottest technologies of the late 1980s was CD-ROM. A CD-ROM disk is a compact disk (like the ones used for music and, to a lesser extent, video) that stores computer data. The promise of CD-ROM is outstanding; a single CD-ROM disk can store more than 650M of data.

CD-ROM, however, has not exploded onto the computer scene as originally expected. One of the most significant drawbacks to this technology is that engineers have been unable to produce a viable drive that can write data to a CD-ROM disk. A hard disk uses magnetic flux to store data, but CD-ROM uses tiny bumps on the disk's surface. For this reason, CD-ROM data can only be read on a PC; new data cannot be saved back to the drive. Undoubtedly, read-write CD-ROM drives will be introduced in the future.

Another problem with CD-ROM technology is that drive-access time is relatively slow, ranging from 300 ms to 800 ms. When you can access vast volumes of data, however, a wait of a second or two is not too inconvenient.

CD-ROM, therefore, provides a means of accessing large volumes of data in a read (not write) environment. Today, the majority of information stored on CD-ROM is not volatile—that is, it does not change frequently. The earliest CD-ROM applications were dictionaries, thesauruses, and the like. A growing number of vendors provide CD-ROM-based data on a variety of technical subjects. Examples of CD-ROM titles are the *Original Oxford*

English Dictionary, *The CIA World Factbook*, *The New Grolier Encyclopedia*, and (my favorite) *The Guinness Disk of Records*. Other, more specialized titles include the *Medical Year Book on Disc*, *U.S. Patent Database*, and *Spectrum Clip Art*. Some CR-ROMs are updated regularly (usually monthly or quarterly), and are distributed to registered users.

CD-ROM drives are now being installed in stacks on networks to provide users with as much as six gigabytes of on-line data. You don't need much imagination to see the potential of CD-ROM!

Summary

A hard disk is a storage device that provides fast access to large volumes of data. Although many data storage alternatives exist, the hard disk remains the primary mass storage device currently in use in PCs. In this chapter you learned the following key points about hard disks:

- A hard disk contains aluminum platters stacked in a vertical column, with one drive head for each platter surface.

- A low-level format organizes the disk into tracks and sectors; a column of aligned tracks is called a cylinder.

- Disk interleave determines the numbering of individual sectors on a disk. Optimum interleave varies from system to system.

- The FDISK utility can partition a single drive into multiple logical drives.

- The FORMAT command prepares the disk for everyday use, and adds a boot record, a FAT, and a root directory.

- A cluster is a group of sectors, and the FAT keeps track of the status of each sector on the disk.

- The directory records information about every file, including the starting cluster number.

- Data is transferred from RAM to the hard disk via the disk controller.

- The disk controller interface and data-encoding method have a significant influence on the hard disk's capacity and performance.

This chapter concludes Part I of this text. Part II explains how the operating system interacts with the hard disk to provide an efficient file storage system.

Part II

DOS Basics

Understanding Basic File Operations

Managing Files and Directories

Understanding Batch Files

Understanding Basic File Operations

A hard disk's primary purpose is to store large volumes of data, so that the computer can quickly access and manipulate the data. The computer's operating system organizes the stored data into discrete blocks of related information, which are called *files*. If you use a word processing program to write a letter, for example, the document's text and formatting information are stored in a single file. To get the most from your hard disk, you need a good understanding of how to organize and utilize such data files.

Every file has a set of characteristics that describes its properties. For example, each file has a name; when you create a new file, you must assign the file a name. Because the operating system places certain restrictions on file names, however, you should adopt good file-naming conventions, so that you can create names that will help you remember the contents and purpose of each file. Further, you can use a variety of operating system commands to help you determine a file's purpose. Such commands can display and print a file's contents, for example, or search files for a specific word or phrase.

By learning to understand basic file characteristics and to use the operating system's file management commands, you are taking an important first step toward effective hard disk management. This chapter introduces essential file concepts, and explains the following primary file commands:

- DIR
- TYPE
- MORE
- PRINT
- FIND

Understanding File Concepts

A file is a collection of related information that is grouped together as a single unit. A file's size (or *length*) varies according to the amount of information in the file. This information may be data (such as your daily schedule or a to-do list), or it can be part of a program (such as the software you use to display your calendar and print a to-do list). In some instances, files can store a combination of data and programs.

If you use more than one software program on your computer (and you should!), then your hard disk probably contains hundreds of different files. Certain files are required by the operating system, and each applications program needs its own program files in order to operate. Further, you create data files when you use a program. If you use Lotus 1-2-3 to create worksheets, for example, the program stores each worksheet in a file on the hard disk. Similarly, when you use a word processor to create a letter or report, the document is stored in a file on the hard disk.

File Characteristics

Aside from the data it contains, a file has characteristics that describe its own unique properties. The most obvious characteristic is the file name. Others include the file's size, date/time stamp, and attribute flags.

The operating system maintains an index of the characteristics of every file on the disk. Such an index is called a *directory*. Figure 4.1 shows how one file's characteristics might appear in a typical directory listing. (Directories are discussed in detail later in this chapter, and in Chapter 5.)

```
CONFIG   SYS    106   6-03-90  10:53a
```

CONFIG is the file's root name. The root name can contain up to eight characters.

SYS is the file name extension.

106 is the file size in bytes.

This file was created or last modified on June 3, 1990.

The file was created or last modifed at 10:53 a.m.

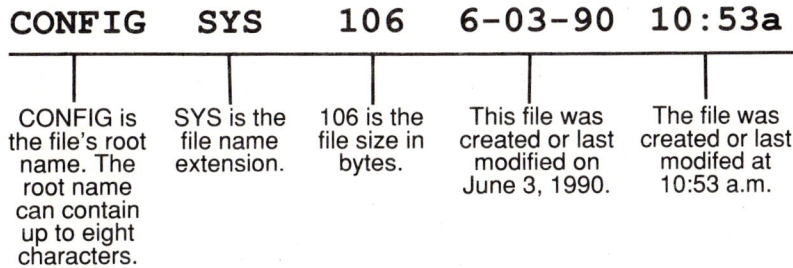

Fig. 4.1. *A typical directory listing.*

File Names and Extensions

A file name has two parts: the *root name* and the *extension*. The root name can contain as many as eight characters; the extension can include up to three characters. A period separates the root name from the extension. Examples of acceptable file names are BUDGET.WK1, LETTER.DOC, and MENU.BAT.

Figure 4.1 shows that, in a directory listing, the file's root name and extension are separated by one or more spaces rather than a period. This format simply makes the directory listing more readable. When you specify a file name in a command, or enter a file name in an application (such as WordPerfect), you must use the normal *name-period-extension* convention.

An upcoming section discusses file-naming rules in detail, and explains how you can simplify file management by following good naming conventions.

File Size

Size is another file property. A byte is the basic unit of size for a file. An empty file, for example, is zero bytes in length; that is, the file has a name but contains no data. Files can grow to be millions of bytes long. A character (such as the letter *e*) is one byte in size; therefore, the terms "character" and "byte" often are used interchangeably. Imagine that one of this book's pages contained 3,000 characters of text. If you stored that page in a data file, the file would be approximately 3,000 bytes in size.

NOTE

A *bit* is the primary (or smallest) storage unit in a PC. A group of 8 bits is called a byte. When memory capacity and disk storage capacity are discussed, the byte unit is often too small to be of much meaning. A *kilobyte* is 1,024 bytes, and the word "kilobyte" is often abbreviated as K, as in a 360K floppy disk. A *megabyte* is 1,024 kilobytes or 1,048,576 bytes, and is abbreviated as M. You may wonder why a kilobyte does not contain exactly 1,000 bytes, or why a megabyte does not contain exactly 1,000,000 bytes. The short explanation is that the computer uses a binary numbering system rather than the decimal system most people use. All the numbers discussed here are derived by raising 2 to a power. For example, 2 to the power 10 is 1,024, and 2 to the power 20 is 1,048,576. Another common value in computer discussion is 64K, which is actually 65,536 bytes, or 2 to the power 16. Don't worry, however. You do not need to be a scholar of binary mathematics to use your hard disk! You'll be safe if you follow the normal assumption that 1K is a thousand bytes and 1M is a million bytes.

In figure 4.1, the file's size is listed in bytes in the third column.

File Date/Time Stamp

Another useful file characteristic is the file *date/time stamp*. This marker indicates the date and time that the file was last saved to disk. The computer's internal clock determines the date and time, so make sure that the date and time attributes are set correctly on your computer by using the operating system commands DATE and TIME. The time stamp can help you determine which version of a file is the most recent.

In figure 4.1, the directory listing's last two columns show the date and time when the file was created or most recently modified and saved to disk.

As your computing expertise grows, you will use these file characteristics to help you manage your data. For example, you might list all the files according to size, so that the biggest files are listed first, or you might look at all files that have been updated in the last week.

Naming Files

Most of your work at the computer will involve the updating of data in files. To gain access to any file, you must supply the file's name. You use file names when entering operating system commands, and when you load and save files in applications programs. As mentioned earlier, the operating system restricts the file name's length and characters. Therefore, file management is easier if you follow certain conventions when naming your files.

You will create many different files over time, and you may not always be able to remember all their names. If a file name in some way describes the file's contents, you can more easily remember the file's purpose. A file called BUD90, for example, might contain information about your 1990 budget.

Rules for Naming Files

Each file name in a directory must be unique, but this is not always easily guaranteed, because you must adhere to a number of rules when you name a file. As mentioned earlier, the operating system actually considers a file name as having two parts: the root name and the extension. The root name can be up to eight characters long and the extension can be up to three characters long. These two parts are separated by a period (.); when used in this manner, the period is called a *delimiter* or a *separator*.

NOTE The 8-character root name and 3-character extension have always been considered a significant restriction for PC users. Many users have difficulty thinking of a truly descriptive 11-character file name. DOS adopted the file-naming rules from the CP/M operating system, which was popular in the early days of PCs. At that time, DOS and CP/M were competing to become the operating system of choice for PC users. The DOS developers thought users would more readily migrate from CP/M to DOS if the file-naming concepts were alike. In fact, many of the file-related concepts in DOS were adapted from the CP/M operating system. Although OS/2 V1.2 enables you to use much longer file names, applications programs probably won't be modified to use this extended facility for some time. For more information on OS/2 V1.2, see Appendix D.

A valid file name can contain any letter of the alphabet (either upper- or lowercase), the numerals 0 to 9, and any of the following special characters:

~ ' ! @ # $ ^ & ( ) - _ { }

The operating system does *not allow* any escape or control characters (such as Esc and Del) or blank spaces in a file name. Novice users commonly try to insert one or more blank spaces in file names, but the operating system does not accept this. Instead, use the underscore character (_) as an alternative to a space. Further, the following special characters cannot be used in a file name:

+ = / [ ] " : ; , ? * \ < > |

The operating system disallows certain characters because those characters (either singly or in combination) have a special meaning for the operating system. When you press the Esc key, for example, the operating system uses the resulting character to cancel a command. Control characters, which you produce by pressing the Ctrl key in combination with another key, also have special meanings. The Ctrl-G combination, for instance, tells the operating system to sound a beep from the PC's internal speaker. You can imagine how confused the operating system would become if it encountered these special characters in a file name.

Table 4.1 lists some invalid file names, and explains why the file names are not acceptable.

Table 4.1
Invalid File Names

File Name	Cause of Problem
file A.txt	Blank spaces are not accepted in file names.
september.dat	The root name is longer than eight characters.
may.data	The extension is longer than three characters.
Tome=one.txt	The equal sign character (=) is not allowed.
sales:doc	The delimiter must be a period (.).

Avoiding Reserved Names

The operating system reserves certain names as *device names*. You can refer to various parts of the computer by using one of these special names. If a printer is attached to your computer, for example, you can refer to the printer by using the device name PRN. Whenever you enter a file name, the operating system determines whether one of the special device names has been specified. If so, the data is transferred directly to the specified device.

You should never assign a reserved device name to a data file. Table 4.2 defines the operating system device names.

Table 4.2
Operating System Device Names

Name	Device
AUX	Communications port
COM*x*	A specific serial communications port. In this generic sample format, the *x* represents a port number, such as COM2.
CON	The console, which is either the display or the keyboard
LPT*x*	A specific parallel port. The *x* represents the port number, such as LPT1.
NUL	A "do-nothing" device name that is often used to suppress operating system messages
PRN	The printer

All the device names have a root name and no file extension. Technically, you can use these reserved device names for a file name if you add an extension. The file name PRN.ABC, for example, is different from the device name PRN, and is therefore acceptable. To save confusion, however, avoid using a device name as any part of a file name.

Establishing Naming Conventions

Traditionally, the root name describes a file's contents, and the extension describes the file's format. If you want to create a file that contains a letter of resignation, for example, you might name the file I_QUIT.DOC. Always try to use a file name that will help you (or another user) remember what is in the file. You will be amazed at how quickly you can forget file names!

Many applications programs actually control the extensions of data file names. Lotus 1-2-3 Release 3 automatically appends the extension WK3 (for **W**orksheet Release **3**) to its data files' names, and Microsoft Word appends the extension DOC (for **doc**ument). On the other hand, many popular programs (such as WordPerfect and WordStar) do not set restrictions on extensions.

Some extensions tell the operating system that a file has a special purpose. The extensions EXE and COM are reserved for executable programs, for example, while BAT (DOS) and CMD (OS/2) indicate batch files. The SYS extension identifies special system files that can be loaded into memory when the system is booted.

In many cases, you do not have to use an extension with a file name. The operating system and most applications programs will accept a file without an extension. In such cases, however, you should add an extension, because it provides a further means of identifying and determining the purpose of a file. You might name all your legal contracts with a CTR extension, for example, or your planning files with a PLN extension.

For a detailed list of extensions commonly used by popular programs, see *Using DOS* or *MS-DOS User's Guide*, Special Edition, published by Que Corporation.

Listing, Displaying, and Printing Files

Like an attic, a hard disk can become cluttered. Eventually, your disk will begin to fill up with unused files, even if you are a good housekeeper. A number of operating system commands, however, enables you to list, view, and print any of the files on your hard disk. You should use these housekeeping commands routinely, to "clean out" unneeded files.

The following sections review some of the most useful operating system commands. If possible, read the text near a PC, and practice executing the commands.

Understanding Directories

If the hundreds of files on your hard disk were stored in one large pool, file management would be a nightmare. Your computer's operating system, however, enables you to divide the hard disk into discrete sections, with each section devoted to a group of related files. These sections are called *directories*. The computer's concept of directories is similar to placing paper files in separate filing cabinets. Further, any directory can be divided into *subdirectories*, just like the drawers in a filing cabinet.

By separating groups of files into different directories, you can organize your files logically, in the same way you might arrange a filing system in an office. A good directory structure helps you manage and locate files. In fact, most commands and programs that accept a file name also accept a directory name, or *path*, which specifies the directory in which the file is stored.

Organizing a good directory structure is as important as establishing a good file-naming covention. Chapter 5 focuses on the broader issues of directory management.

Listing Files with DIR

The operating system command DIR displays a list of the files stored in a specific directory or subdirectory. The command quickly produces a list of the file names, showing each file's size, as well as the date and time each file was last saved.

Using the Basic DIR Command

At the DOS prompt, you can produce a listing of a directory's files by typing **DIR** and then pressing Enter. DIR tells the operating system to display a list of files. You can issue the DIR command in different ways by specifying certain kinds of information along with the command. To create a listing of the files on the floppy disk in drive A, for example, enter the following command:

DIR A:

In this form of the command, the **A:** is called a *parameter*, and it instructs the DIR command to read the files on the disk in drive A. Try this form of the command only if you have loaded a floppy disk in drive A. If there is no disk in the drive, the operating system displays an error message, along with a prompt asking if you want the program to abort, retry, or fail. You can either abort the command, or insert a disk in drive A and press R to try the command again. Figure 4.2 illustrates a typical directory display generated by the DIR command.

```
A:\>dir

 Volume in drive A has no label
 Directory of  A:\

AUTOEXEC BAT      440    3-29-90    4:42p
12       DOC    27929    3-26-90    5:31p
T2       EXE    42064    3-26-90    9:55a
CRYPT    WK3      459    3-21-90    8:54p
FASTTTT5 PAS    11858    2-28-90    7:21a
ABC      WK3      433    2-19-90    2:03p
HELPME!  DOC    11031   10-09-89    2:00a
GREP     COM     7029   10-09-89    2:00a
NOTEPAD  HLP    22834   11-15-88    1:00a
MORTGAGE TXT     2467   11-15-88    1:00a
DOSKEY   COM     1644    6-01-88   12:00p
MAPMEM   COM    16706    3-05-87   10:55a
FINDIT   COM    16244    3-19-86   12:13p
KEY-FAKE COM      536    1-29-86    9:46a
VTREE    COM      512    1-23-86    8:11a
        15 File(s)    192512 bytes free

A:\>
```

Fig. 4.2. A sample directory generated by the DIR command.

Listing Too Many Files

If the directory contains so many files that they cannot all fit on-screen at the same time, the list scrolls up and off the top of the screen before you can read the file names. You can use two command options (or parameters) to avoid this problem.

The first alternative is to add the parameter /P to the command line, so that the command appears as follows:

DIR /P

The /P is the *pause* parameter, which tells the operating system to pause after displaying a full screen of file names, and to wait for the user to press a key before displaying the next full screen. Figure 4.3 shows a typical display after the DIR /P command has been issued.

You can use the /W parameter rather than the /P parameter when you must view a long directory listing. When issued with the /W parameter, the DIR command appears as follows:

DIR /W

The /W is the *wide* parameter, and it instructs the operating system to condense the directory listing by displaying four file names per line on-screen, instead of devoting a full line to each file name. Figure 4.4 shows a typical display after the DIR /W command has been issued.

```
.              <DIR>      1-17-90    8:29a
..             <DIR>      1-17-90    8:29a
PCSETUP  EXE   135981     3-24-90    6:00p
PCSETUP  CFG     5610     3-24-90    6:00p
README   TXT    16683     3-27-90    6:00p
PC-CACHE COM    63373     3-24-90    6:00p
PCSECURE EXE   114963     3-24-90    6:00p
PCSECURE HLP     7807     3-24-90    6:00p
DISKFIX  EXE   174625     3-24-90    6:00p
MIRROR   COM    15897     3-24-90    6:00p
REBUILD  COM    17504     3-24-90    6:00p
UNDELETE EXE    15925     3-24-90    6:00p
PCFORMAT COM    16960     3-24-90    6:00p
COMPRESS EXE    70683     3-24-90    6:00p
COMPRESS HLP     6337     3-24-90    6:00p
MI       COM     4256     3-24-90    6:00p
SAMPLES        <DIR>      3-28-90    9:32p
OLDSHELL CFG      269     3-29-90    4:41p
KILL     EXE     1586     3-24-90    6:00p
BINARY   VWR    10923     3-27-90    6:00p
LLS      EXE    57216     3-27-90    6:00p
PCSHELL  EXE   141974     3-27-90    6:00p
TEXT     VWR     9780     3-27-90    6:00p
Strike a key when ready . . .
```

Fig. 4.3. The display produced by the DIR /P command.

Notice, however, that the DIR /W command displays only the names of the files in the current directory. This version of the command does not display the size, date, and time information for any of the files.

If you prefer the wide format, and if the current directory contains too many files to fit on-screen, you can combine the /W and /P parameters as follows:

DIR /W /P

This version of the command tells the operating system to display the list of file names in wide format, and to pause after displaying a full screen of names. After viewing the first part of the listing, the user then can press any key, and the next screenful of file names appears.

```
C:\U\NORTON>dir/w

    Volume in drive C is TECHNOJOCK
    Directory of  C:\U\NORTON

    .                     ..              READ    ME      FR      EXE     NDD      EXE
NU        EXE    NU        HLP    DS      EXE     DT      EXE     FF       EXE
NCC       EXE    NCD       EXE    NI      EXE     QU      EXE     SD       EXE
SF        EXE    VL        EXE    BE      EXE     DI      EXE     FA       EXE
FD        EXE    FI        EXE    FS      EXE     LD      EXE     LP       EXE
TM        EXE    SI        EXE    TS      EXE     UD      EXE     WIPEDISK EXE
WIPEFILE  EXE    FILEINFO  FI     MARY            BEDEMO  BAT     BEDEMO   DAT
MENU      DAT    MAKE-TUT  BIN    MAKE-TUT BAT    TUT-READ ME
         39 File(s)    6369280 bytes free

C:\U\NORTON>
```

Fig. 4.4. The display produced by the DIR /W command.

Printing a Directory Listing

Sometimes when you are reviewing all the file names in a directory listing, you may need a hard copy of the listing. You can, of course, press Shift-PrtSc (print screen) to print an exact image of the monitor display. To create a printout of a directory listing, you can include the pause (/P) parameter in the DIR command, and then press Shift-PrtSc each time the listing pauses on-screen. This method works, but you can use a simpler approach.

Remember that the operating system reserves some names for use as device names. The device name PRN represents the printer. By using the *redirector* symbol (>) and the PRN device name as parameters, you can instruct the operating system to print the directory listing rather than displaying it on-screen. Simply add these two parameters to the end of the command line, as follows:

DIR /W > PRN

If your printer is not connected and ready, the operating system tries to activate the printer. If the printer does not respond within about 40 seconds, the operating system displays an error message and prompts you to abort, retry, ignore, or fail the attempt. If you do not have a printer, press A to abort. If you do have a printer, make sure that it is hooked up and operational, and then press R to try again.

> **NOTE** The redirector symbol (>) instructs the operating system to redirect output. That is, the output normally produced by the command on the symbol's left side is transferred to the device or file specified on the right side. Printing output is a common use for the redirector. You also can use this symbol to redirect command output to the NUL device (for example, *command* > NUL). This has the effect of suppressing the output from the command.

Using Wild-Card Characters with DIR

Many operating system commands can operate on one or multiple files. When you issue the DIR command, for example, you can tell the operating system to perform the command on one or several files. With the help of special characters, called *wild cards*, you can type only one file name to specify a group of files. The operating system recognizes the asterisk (*) and the question mark (?) as wild-card characters.

Each wild-card character has its own meaning. The **?** represents any character in a specific character position. In a root name or extension, the ***** matches all characters in that part of the full file name.

Earlier, you learned that the DIR command can be used with a drive indicator, as in the syntax **DIR A:**. You also can include a file name with the command, to indicate which file (or files) you want to be listed. In its generic format, the long form of the DIR command looks like this:

   DIR *d:filename.ext*

You should replace the *d:* with the appropriate drive indicator (such as A:, B:, or C:). Omit the drive indicator if you want to list the files on the current drive. In place of the *filename.ext*, use a specific file name, such as BUDGET.WK3. Suppose that you want to make sure that the file named BUDGET.WK3 resides in the current directory on the current disk. Type the following command:

   DIR BUDGET.WK3

This command instructs the operating system to list all files that *match* the file name BUDGET.WK3. Because no two files can have the same name and reside in the same directory, however, only one file can have the name BUDGET.WK3. When the preceding command is issued, the operating system lists only this file. You can use the command in this manner to ensure that a specific file resides in a directory, without listing all the files in the directory. (Remember: if you don't specify a file name, DIR lists all the files.)

By using wild-card characters, you can instruct DIR to list a group of files. If you want to see a listing of all files whose extension is WK3, for example, you can replace the root name with the asterisk (*) wild-card character. The following command produces a list of all files (in the current directory) that have a WK3 extension:

DIR *.WK3

This command tells the operating system to list every file with the WK3 extension, regardless of its root name. When one or more wild cards are used, the file name is referred to as a *file mask*.

You also can precede the asterisk (*) with one or more characters, as the following sample command shows:

DIR BU*.WK3

This command tells the operating system to list every file whose file name begins with the characters BU and has a WK3 extension.

You will not get similar results, however, by placing an alphabetical character after a wild card in a root name or an extension. If you use the asterisk (*) wild-card character at the beginning of a file's root name or extension, the operating system ignores any characters that follow the asterisk in the same part of the name. The command DIR *ET.WK3 command, for example, lists *all* files that have an extension of .WK3, not just the ones with the root name ending in ET.

X
WARNING

The file mask ***.*** tells the operating system to match *every* file, because a matching file has any root name and any extension. Use ***.*** with caution, because the command operates on *all* files in the directory. For example, you can use the DEL command to delete files; therefore, the command **DEL *.*** deletes all the files in the directory!

Use the question mark (**?**) wild-card character when you want to select files more precisely. Suppose, for example, that the current directory contains the following files:

```
QTR191.WK1
QTR191.WK3
QTR291.WK2
QTR391.WK3
QTR491.WK3
QTR91.WK3
QTR91A.WK3
QTRAB91.WK3
QTRT91.WK3
```

Now, suppose that you issue the following command:

DIR QTR?91.WK3

This command tells the operating system to list all files that have the characters QTR in the first 3 positions, *any* character in position 4, the characters 91 in positions 5 and 6, and an extension of WK3. The following files match the specified file mask:

```
QTR191.WK3
QTR291.WK3
QTR391.WK3
QTR491.WK3
QTRT91.WK3
```

The file name QTR191.WK1 does not match, because its extension is different from the one specified in the DIR command. The file name QTR191A.WK3 does not match, because the file mask does not include a character in the seventh position (the A). The file name QTR91.WK3 does not match, because the characters 91 are not in positions 5 and 6, as specified in the command. The same is true for the file name QTRAB91.WK3, where the characters 91 are in the sixth and seventh positions.

If you need to make exact file selections, and still want to select several files at the same time, you can use the asterisk (*****) and the question mark (**?**) together. Consider, for example, the following command:

DIR QTR?91.*

This sample command lists all files that have the characters QTR in the first 3 positions, any character in position 4, the characters 91 in positions 5 and 6, and *any* extension.

Table 4.3 offers a few sample file masks, and shows what kinds of files the operating system will match with each file mask:

Table 4.3
Sample File Masks

File Mask	Matching Files
*.WK3	All files with a WK3 extension
MON*.DAT	Every file that begins with MON and has a DAT extension
PLANS.*	All files that have a root name of PLANS and any or no extension
EARN?23.XLS	Every file that begins with EARN, has any character in position 5 followed by the characters 23, and has an XLS extension
.	All files
????.*	Any file with a four-character root name
*.	All files with *no* extension

You will reap dividends if you use foresight in naming your files. If you develop and adhere to naming conventions, you usually will be able to manipulate all related files in one block. If all the files associated with Project X have file names beginning with PX, for example, then you can use the file mask PX*.* to manipulate all these related files as a group.

If you use one of the powerful operating system commands, such as ERASE or COPY (these commands are discussed later), and you are not sure of the precise file mask, test the file mask on the DIR command first and see if the expected files are listed. If not, try DIR with a different file mask. When you are confident you are using the correct file mask, execute the real command using the same file mask.

> ✓
> OS/2
>
> If you use OS/2, the DIR command enables you to specify more than one file name or file mask on the command line.

Displaying File Contents

Before you remove an unwanted file from the disk, or when you are trying to determine a file's purpose, you should view the file's contents. You can use the TYPE command to display a file's contents on-screen.

The information stored in a file is classified as either ASCII or binary. ASCII is an acronym for American Standard Code for Information Interchange, and ASCII files often are referred to as *text files*. An ASCII file contains only text characters (such as letters, numbers, and punctuation) and hidden characters that indicate the end of each line and the end of the file. The standard ASCII alphabet contains 128 characters; the extended ASCII alphabet contains another 128 characters, making 256 characters in all. Extended characters include mathematical symbols, foreign letters, and box- or line-drawing characters. You can use DOS to read or print an ASCII or text file; you do not need to use an applications program.

A binary file contains raw data that is not formatted to be read as text. A 1-2-3 worksheet file, for example, contains detailed information about the worksheet in encoded form. An ASCII file stores the number 35730 as the characters "35,730." In a binary file, however, the number might be stored as "8B92." Binary files are designed for efficient, compact storage of information, and are not concerned with the data's appearance. If you use an operating system command in order to view a binary file, garbage scrolls across the screen, and the system may beep a number of times. The beeping occurs when the operating system tries to display the Ctrl-G character, which is an instruction that tells the operating system to beep.

Use the TYPE command to view only text or ASCII files. If you try to use the command to view binary files, garbage (unreadable characters) appears on-screen. Normally, you can read a binary data file's contents by executing the program that generated the file, and then loading the file. If the file is itself a program (with an EXE or COM extension), you should check your software documentation to see which software the program belongs to.

Using the TYPE Command

In its most basic form, the TYPE command takes the following syntax:

TYPE *filename*

In this command, *filename* is an individual file name. If you want to view the contents of your AUTOEXEC.BAT file, enter **TYPE AUTOEXEC.BAT**. If necessary, you can include a drive identifier and path with the file name (these syntax elements are discussed later).

Figure 4.5 illustrates the display generated when the TYPE command is used to list the contents of a typical AUTOEXEC.BAT file. Your computer's AUTOEXEC.BAT file probably is different from the one shown here.

```
E:\>type autoexec.bat
@echo off
path c:\win386;c:\;c:\dos;c:\batfiles;c:\p\brief;C:\U\PCTOOLS;
set btmp=e:\
prompt $p$g
doskey
typemat
ver


E:\>
```

Fig. 4.5. Display produced by the command TYPE AUTOEXEC.BAT.

If you want to view a file that is too large to be read in a single screen display, the file scrolls off the screen before you have time to read it. You may recall that the DIR command presents a similar problem. You can solve this problem in a couple of ways.

If you are nimble fingered, you can press either Ctrl-Num Lock, Ctrl-S, or Pause (on newer keyboards) to *freeze* the computer. The faster the computer, the faster your reactions have to be! Any one of these commands causes the computer to stop scrolling, and freezes the display. The computer resumes scrolling after you press another key.

A better approach, however, is to instruct the operating system to pause after displaying a full screen of information. You can accomplish this by adding the characters | **MORE** to the end of the TYPE command. The vertical bar (|) is a special operating system character, called the *pipe character*. A pipe character instructs the operating system to send a command's output to the *filter* that follows the pipe character. By piping the output to the MORE filter, you cause the output data to be interrupted when the screen is full. The system then pauses until you hit a key, and the next full screen is displayed. The following command, for example, displays the contents of the file README.TXT, and pauses between each screenful of information:

> **TYPE README.TXT | MORE**

A note from the author... You might have expected the TYPE command to have a pause parameter (/P). This would make TYPE consistent with the DIR command, after all, but things are not always so easy! The TYPE command does not support /P. Later, you will learn that other operating system commands also use MORE to pause the display. So some consistency can be found in all this. If you use OS/2, you also can use MORE with the DIR command.

Understanding the TYPE Command

You must supply a literal file name when you issue the TYPE command. TYPE does not accept wild-card characters in the file name, and therefore is limited to use with only one file at a time.

The operating system's TYPE program does not recognize the difference between text files and binary files. If you issue the TYPE command to view a binary file—such as a COM or an EXE file—TYPE's output includes graphical characters, control characters, sequences, beeps, and other "garbage" that you cannot read. When used with a binary file, the TYPE program may even cause your computer to lock up. A locked computer does not respond to keyboard input, and must be rebooted.

You can terminate the output of TYPE by pressing Ctrl-C or Ctrl-Break.

☑

OS/2

In OS/2, the TYPE command supports the display of multiple text files. To see more than one file, you simply specify more than one file name on the command line. You also can specify wild cards in the file name to view multiple files.

> *A note from the author* ... As you read more of this text, you will realize that the PC enables you to perform many tasks in many different ways. You can use one of several excellent utility programs, for instance, that can help you manage your PC effectively. In fact, these programs often are superior to the operating system commands. Before you become dependent on such a program, however, you should master some of the primary operating system commands. This is similar, in principle, to learning some basic math before relying on a calculator. Rest assured that you will not be forced to read about and learn obscure commands that are of little use to the average user. At several points in this book, therefore, you will find special text marked with an icon (such as the following), introducing utilities that can help you perform difficult or tedious tasks. Later chapters offer detailed discussions of many kinds of utilities.

UTILITY

The utility program LIST is a good replacement for the TYPE command. LIST enables you to view multiple files at once, search for text in a file, print a file's contents, scroll forward and backward through the text, and much more. Refer to Chapter 12 for more information about LIST.

Printing Files

You often may find yourself in need of a printout of a text file. As with most operations, of course, the computer gives you more than one way to print a file's contents. One technique is to issue the TYPE command with the redirector symbol (>), to redirect the output to the printer. You learned a similar technique for printing a directory listing by redirecting the DIR command's output to the printer. To print a file named README.DOC, for example, you can execute the following command:

TYPE README.DOC > PRN

This command, however, does not separate the text into pages. The file's contents, therefore, are printed continuously, even over the perforations on continuous paper.

Such quick and dirty printing chores are more easily accomplished when you use the operating system's PRINT command. The PRINT command prints the contents of one or more *text* files (PRINT cannot print binary files). The unique feature of the PRINT command is that you can do other computing chores while the files are printing. You can issue the command to print some files, for example, and then execute and use Lotus 1-2-3 while the files are being printed. This facility is referred to as *background printing*. If the computer is performing an active task while the PRINT program is running, the active task is called the *foreground task*.

The PRINT command supports a variety of switches and options. Because the command can become fairly convoluted, most people shy away from it. You can use PRINT to good effect, however, with just a few simple options.

In its basic form, the PRINT command takes the following syntax:

PRINT *filname1 filename2 ...*

The PRINT command is followed by one or more file names. If you want to print multiple files, you can specify them separately. If the files have similar names, you can specify the appropriate file mask. Files that are waiting to be printed are said to be in the *print queue*. Usually, the print queue can hold up to 32 files.

For example, to print the files README.DOC and AUTOEXEC.BAT, you would enter the following command:

PRINT README.DOC AUTOEXEC.BAT

PRINT does not check the printer's status before starting the print operation. If the program determines that the printer is not ready, it waits in the background until the printer is readied. Make sure that the printer is operational before issuing the PRINT command.

You can use a number of switches with the PRINT command, to control print operation. The most popular switch is the /T (terminate) switch, which stops all printing. Once the operating system encounters the /T switch, it cancels all the files waiting in the print queue, as well as the file currently being printed. To stop the print operation, enter the following command:

PRINT /T

Refer to the Appendix A for information about the other PRINT command switches.

Finding Text in Files

Sometimes you want to search one or more files to see if a file contains a specific word or phrase. You might need to find the file that contains Helen's address, for example, but you can't remember the file's name. The operating system command FIND is handy in such situations.

You can use FIND to search text files for a string; that is, a specific character, word, phrase, or sentence. This search facility saves you the trouble of using the TYPE command on several files, and reading each one yourself. You also can use FIND to search the output from another command. FIND can intercept the output from the DIR command, for example, and search for a string. When used in this manner, FIND acts as a command *filter*, because it filters out any output which does not include the specified string.

Issuing the FIND Filter

To search text files, FIND takes the following syntax:

FIND */C* */N* */V* *"string" d:filename ...*

The /C switch instructs FIND to count the number of lines containing the search string.

The /N switch instructs FIND to display the line number of each line of text displayed.

The /V switch reverses the search's meaning, so that the command displays any lines that do not match the specified search string.

In the preceding generic syntax, *"string"* is the character, word, or phrase to be searched for. When you enter the FIND command, you must enclose the search string in quotation marks.

You can instruct FIND to search one or more files, indicated by *filename...* in the generic syntax.

To illustrate the FIND command's use, suppose that the file RECIPE.BOB contains the following text:

```
Wash and dry the zucchini and trim off both
ends. Grate the zucchini into a bowl and toss
them with a dash of salt. Leave for 10 minutes.
Using a large frying pan, saute the onion and
garlic in the oil, stirring until they are
softened but not allowing them to change color.
Squeeze the liquid from the zucchini by handfuls
and then add the zucchini to the pan. Discard
the liquid. Stir the zucchini over a medium heat
for a few minutes, season and then set aside.

Take a sip of wine; you've earned it. Eat the
zucchini.
```

If you want to search the file for every occurrence of the word *zucchini*, enter the following command:

FIND "zucchini" RECIPE.BOB

Alternatively, you can display the corresponding line numbers by adding the /N switch, as follows:

FIND /N "zucchini" RECIPE.BOB

Figure 4.6 illustrates the output from these two commands.

If you use the /V switch, FIND displays the lines that do not contain the search string (see fig. 4.7).

FIND generally is used to search larger files or multiple files. Keep the following principles in mind whenever you use the FIND command:

- The *"string"* parameter is case-sensitive. You must enter upper- and lowercase letters correctly when you specify the search string.

- You must always enclose the search string in quotation marks when you specify the string in the FIND command. If the string already contains quotation marks, you must further enclose that material with an extra set of quotation marks. Suppose that you want to search for the string *The girl said "Hello" to me*. To specify this sentence as the search string, you must type **"The girl said ""Hello"" to me."**

- You cannot use wild-card characters when you specify a file name to the FIND command.

```
F:\MS\DISK>FIND "zucchini" RECIPE.BOB

---------- RECIPE.BOB
Preheat the oven. Wash and dry the zucchini
and trim off both ends. Grate the zucchini into
Squeeze the liquid from the zucchini by handfuls
and then add the zucchini to the pan. Discard the
liquid. Stir the zucchini over a medium heat for
zucchini.

F:\MS\DISK>FIND /n "zucchini" RECIPE.BOB

---------- RECIPE.BOB
[1]Preheat the oven. Wash and dry the zucchini
[2]and trim off both ends. Grate the zucchini into
[7]Squeeze the liquid from the zucchini by handfuls
[8]and then add the zucchini to the pan. Discard the
[9]liquid. Stir the zucchini over a medium heat for
[13]zucchini.

F:\MS\DISK>
```

Fig. 4.6. FIND displays the lines that contain the search string.

```
F:\MS\DISK>FIND /V "zucchini" RECIPE.BOB

---------- RECIPE.BOB
a bowl and toss them with a dash of salt. Leave for
10 minutes. Using a large frying pan, saute the onion
and garlic in the oil, stirring until they are
softened but not allowing them to change color.
a few minutes, season and the set aside.

Take a sip of wine, you've earned it. Eat the

F:\MS\DISK>
```

Fig. 4.7. FIND also can display lines that do not contain the search string.

Using FIND as a Word-Search Utility

The FIND filter is a handy word-search utility. Suppose, for example, that you have forgotten the name of a memo you recently sent to your boss. You know that it is either MEMO1, MEMO2, or MEMO3, and that you always use your boss' title, *Supervisor*, in memos. You can use *Supervisor* as a search string by typing the following command:

FIND "Supervisor" MEMO1 MEMO2 MEMO3

The FIND program searches each of the specified files to locate occurrences of the word *Supervisor*, and displays each line that contains the string. The listing appears in the following form:

```
---------- MEMO1
---------- MEMO2
Supervisor of Communications
---------- MEMO3
```

The desired file is MEMO2. FIND displays the line that contains the word *Supervisor*. No lines are listed under MEMO1 or MEMO3.

> You can use a number of text-searching utilities that are faster and more flexible than the FIND command. See Chapter 12 for a discussion of one such utility, called FGREP.
>
> UTILITY

Using FIND as a COMMAND Filter

As mentioned previously, you can use the FIND command for more than simple text searches. You also can use FIND as a filter to search the output from another command.

For instance, the DIR and FIND commands can be combined to provide a useful file management utility. Remember that DIR lists all the files in a directory, and that DIR also can display files whose names match a specified name. To list all the files that have a DOC extension, for example, enter the following command:

DIR *.DOC

You also can use FIND with the DIR command. If you want to search the current directory for all files that *do not* have a DOC extension, for example, type the following command:

DIR|FIND /V ".DOC"

The pipe character (|) instructs the operating system to pass the output from the DIR command to the FIND command rather than to the monitor. Because the DIR command has been issued without any parameters, it sends a list of all the file names to FIND. Further, because the /V switch has been specified with FIND, FIND displays all the lines that do not include the string *.DOC*. In this example, therefore, the FIND command lists all the files that do not have a DOC extension.

Remember that the FIND command is case-sensitive, and all operating system output is in uppercase. Always specify the FIND search string in uppercase letters when filtering the operating system commands.

Summary

A hard disk is like a warehouse for your files. You would have a great deal of trouble finding files in this vast storage space, however, if not for the help of operating system commands.

In this chapter you learned the following key points about file management:

- The operating system stores information in files.

- A file name can contain as many as eight characters for the root name and three characters for the extension. Certain characters are not allowed in a file name. Certain names are reserved by the operating system, and should not be used in data file names.

- By convention, certain file names refer to specific types of files. You can ignore file-naming conventions, but file management is easier when you observe them.

- The operating system records information about files in a directory. This information includes the file's name and size, as well as the date and time the file was last saved to the disk.

- You can use the DIR command to list all the files in a directory.

- You can use the TYPE command to display a text (or ASCII) file's contents on-screen.

- You can use the PRINT command to print text files.

- By placing the redirector > and filter | characters in certain commands, you can manipulate the commands' output.

- You can use the FIND filter to search text files or command output for a character, word, or phrase.

Chapter 5 explains how files can be organized into hierarchical directories, and teaches you how to copy, delete, and rename files.

5

Managing Files and Directories

A single hard disk is capable of storing tens of thousands of files. If all those files were stored together, they would be almost impossible to manage, because the operating system sets restrictions on the way you name files. Just how many meaningful eleven-character names are there? Finding a file would be like finding a needle in a haystack.

In this chapter, you learn how to organize and use in a logical and efficient way the files on a hard disk, and to use the following commands:

- ASSIGN
- CHDIR or CD
- COPY
- DIR
- ERASE or DEL
- JOIN
- MKDIR or MD
- PATH
- PROMPT
- RENAME or REN
- RMDIR or RD
- SET
- SUBST
- TREE

Directory Concepts

The organizational objectives that guide storing computer files on a hard disk are very similar to the objectives of using a paper filing system in an office. The filing system must be *well structured* so that a file can be quickly located. It must be *flexible* so that new files can be easily added to the system. And the system must also be *logical* so that you can easily determine where to store a particular file.

In an office filing system, files are organized into various general subject groups, such as Sales, Purchasing, Personnel, and so on. Each general group is further subdivided into more specific categories. For example, the Sales section might be subdivided into North America, International, and General. Depending on the number of files to be stored in each category, there might be further subcategories—for example, East Coast, Central, and West Coast could be subcategories of the North America group. After three to five levels, all the files are stored in chronological or alphabetical order.

This kind of filing system is known as a *hierarchical* filing system because the file categories are organized into a logical hierarchy, with detailed categories being grouped within more general categories. Such a system meets the filing goals: files can be located quickly, new categories and sections can be easily added within the overall structure, and you can readily determine where a new file should be stored.

The hierarchical filing system has been around since the ancient Greeks stored parchment scrolls, and has certainly stood the test of time. It should come as no surprise that the early PC developers decided to use a similar hierarchical system for storing files on a hard disk.

Logically, a PC's hard disk can be organized into major categories called *directories*. These directories can be further subdivided into *subdirectories*, and subdirectories themselves may be further subdivided into additional subdirectories. Files can be stored in any directory or subdirectory.

Understanding the Root Directory

When a disk is formatted, the operating system creates a single directory, which is called the *root directory*. This directory can store information about a fixed number of files—the absolute number varies with the operating system and the disk format, but is typically 512 files.

I know what you must be thinking—if a disk is formatted to hold a fixed number of files in the root directory, how can the disk be used to store thousands of files? The answer is that some of the "files" in the root directory may themselves be directories. The operating system uses a special type of file to store directory information.

Every file has a set of *attributes* that describes some of the technical properties of the file. One of these attributes indicates whether the file is actually a directory. If you use the DIR command to display a directory listing (see fig. 5.1), the directory entries are displayed differently from the normal data files. The directory's files, or *directory entries*, are marked with a **<DIR>** symbol rather than the file size.

The information in a directory listing includes every data file's *starting cluster*—the location where the first part of the file is physically stored on the hard disk—although this information is not displayed in the directory listing. The starting cluster is used by the operating system in conjunction with the file allocation table to access the file contents.

```
E:\>dir

 Volume in drive E is QUEDISK
 Directory of  E:\

123R3        <DIR>      4-07-90   10:04a
WORD5        <DIR>      4-07-90   10:04a
HELP     CRC   19892    3-26-90    9:30a
AUTOEXEC BAT     440    3-29-90    4:42p
CONFIG   SYS     233    2-07-90    1:17p
COMMAND  COM   25332   12-14-89    9:57p
MOUSE    SYS   14394    8-01-88   12:00a
DOS          <DIR>      4-07-90   10:15a
TREEINFO NCD     187    4-07-90   10:15a
PCFDB        <DIR>      4-07-90   10:20a
BATFILES     <DIR>      6-07-90   10:21a
UTILS        <DIR>      6-07-90   10:21a
        12 File(s)   2002432 bytes free

E:\>
```

Fig. 5.1. A directory listing showing directories and data files.

The operating system also stores the disk's volume label as a special file. The file is marked with a volume-label attribute. The operating system uses the combined file name and extension to form an eleven-character name. For example, the volume label "TECHNOJOCKS" is actually a special file with the name TECHNOJO.CKS. The file name is not displayed in the directory listing; the label is displayed in the heading above the file names.

Using Hierarchical Directories

The root directory can spawn many directories, and each of these directories can store data files and still more directories. That is how a disk with a limited root directory can store thousands of files. Since all the files and directories are either in the root directory, or are descendants of the root directory, the directory network forms a hierarchy stemming from the root.

In an office filing system, the main file categories are used to group a large number of files that have some common theme, such as Sales, Purchasing, or Personal. On a hard disk, the main file categories might correspond to a specific software product. For example, the root directory can include one directory for Lotus 1-2-3 Release 3, another directory for Microsoft Word, another directory for the DOS operating system files, and so on. The Lotus 1-2-3 Release 3 directory may contain all the program files, together with a number of subdirectories for storing worksheets. For example, there may be one directory for storing the department's operating budget worksheets, and another for storing personnel worksheets. In a similar way, each of the other directories that hold an applications program can include directories for storing files. Fig. 5.2 shows the directory hierarchy of a hard disk that has been organized in this fashion.

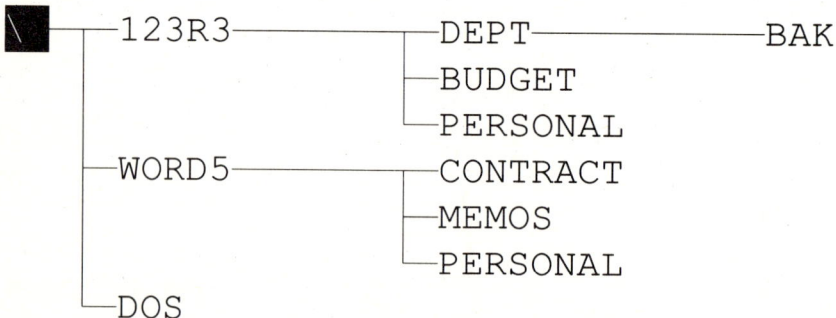

```
\ ──┬─123R3──────────┬─DEPT────────────BAK
    │                ├─BUDGET
    │                └─PERSONAL
    ├─WORD5──────────┬─CONTRACT
    │                ├─MEMOS
    │                └─PERSONAL
    └─DOS
```

Fig. 5.2. A sample hard disk directory hierarchy.

To develop and use a good directory structure, you need to understand the concept of paths—explicit descriptions of a file's location within the overall directory hierarchy. You also need to understand how to create, navigate, and delete directories.

Understanding the Concept of Paths

Every file in a directory must have a unique name. However, there can be more than one file on a disk with the same name, provided the files are located in different directories. To distinguish between the files, the file name can be referenced in commands by preceding the file name with the path. A file name preceded by the drive specifier and the path is referred to as a *fully qualified file name*.

The *path* is a chain of directory names that tells the operating system how to find a file you want. Each directory name is separated from the others by the backslash (\) character. A file's full path (including the drive specifier) is the name that indicates absolutely where the file is located. Using symbolic notation, the path for a file is as follows:

d:\dir1\dir2\dir3...\filename.ext

d: is the name of the disk drive. The first \ represents the root directory. *dir1\dir2\dir3...* indicates a chain of directories leading from the root directory down the hierarchy to the directory that contains the file. The ellipses (...) indicates that more (or fewer) directory names are allowed. All the characters between the first \ and the last \ comprise the directory path. *filename.ext* is the name of the file that is in the final directory.

The specification of the file path is very similar in function to the filing number that is written on the docket of an office file. For example, the file number 2-16-12-1 indicates that the file should be located in major section 2, subsection 16, and within subsection 16 it should be filed in category 12, subcategory 1. By specifying the full filing number, you identify exactly where the file should be stored. The path is just like a full filing number, except that each filing category is usually a name, and the delimiter must be a backslash.

Look again at the hard disk directory hierarchy shown in figure 5.2. Imagine that the hard disk contains a budget worksheet file called TENYEAR.WK3. Assuming that the hard disk is drive C, the full file name including the path would be

C:\123R3\BUDGET\TENYEAR.WK3

This file name indicates that the file TENYEAR.WK3 is stored on drive C and is located in the directory BUDGET, which is located in the directory 123R3, which in turn is located in the root directory.

Similarly, a letter (to Dad asking for money) written in Microsoft Word might have the following full file name:

C:\WORD5\PERSONAL\SENDCASH.DOC

Understanding the Current Directory and Relative Paths

The *current directory* is the path used when no path is specified in an operating system command; it also is referred to as the *default directory*. Behind the scenes, the operating system stores the current directory in an internal location. For example, when you execute the DIR command without specifying any parameters or switches, the operating system lists all the files in the current directory. The operating system also stores the name of the *current drive*. This is the drive accessed unless the command includes a different drive name.

In the following sections, you learn how to use several operating system commands that manipulate directories and files: DIR, COPY, MD, CD, DEL, and REN. All these commands accept paths as parameters. When the path begins with the backslash (\), the operating system knows that the path is being specified from the root directory; that is, the path is fully qualified. If the leading backslash is omitted, the operating system assumes that the path is relative to the current path, and that the path extends from the current, or default, directory.

For example, if your current directory is \WORD5, and you specify the directory DOCS without a leading backslash, the operating system knows you are specifying a path relative to the current directory, and actually interprets the path by combining the current directory with the specified directory—\WORD\MEMOS.

All the commands that accept a path specifier support both the explicit path specified from the root and a path relative to the current directory. Both techniques will be illustrated as we investigate each of the commands.

A hierarchical directory is similar to a family tree, with one family spawning many descendent families. Quite often, the term *parent directory* is used to refer to the directory from which the current directory stems. For example, if the current directory is \WORD5\DOCS, then the parent directory is \WORD5. Sometimes the term *subdirectory* is used to refer to directories that descend from (or are children of) another directory. For example, the DOCS directory would be a subdirectory of the WORD5 directory.

You can use the following three guidelines for specifying a path:

- If the path specifier begins with the backslash character (\), the operating system interprets the path as being from the root directory.

- If the path specifier does not begin with a backslash, the operating system interprets the path as stemming from the current directory.

- If the path specifier is omitted, the operating system assumes that the path is the path of the current directory.

Making Directories

When a hard disk is initially formatted, the disk is created with a root directory and no other directories stemming from it. The operating system command MKDIR or MD is used to make a directory.

When you issue the MD command, you are instructing the operating system to add a new subdirectory to some part of the hierarchical directory structure. The syntax of the MD command is

MD *d:path***directoryname**

where *d:* optionally specifies where the new directory is to be added. If *d:* is omitted, the current drive is used. *path* is the optional path to which the new directory will be added. **directoryname** is the name for the new directory.

The length of the full path (drive, path, and new directory name) must not exceed 63 characters, including delimiters. The full path is the measure for length. If you are creating a directory relative to your current directory, you must count your current directory's full path length from the implied root \ character as being part of the 63-character limit.

The directory name must follow the same rules as those for standard file names (see Chapter 4). Although the directory name can have a file name extension, normal practice is not to use one.

When you try to create a new directory, the operating system checks that the directory name is unique, that is, that the parent directory does not include another directory or file with the same name. If the operating system cannot create the directory, it displays the message **Unable to create directory**. If this occurs, check that you have used a legal file name and that the parent directory does not include another directory or file with the same name.

To create a new directory called MISC from the root directory, you enter the following command:

MD \MISC

The \ indicates that the directory is to be created from the root directory. If the current directory is the root, the command **MD MISC** has the same effect, because the relative path implies that the directory is to be created from the current directory—the root.

To create a directory called MENU branching from the MISC directory, enter the following command:

MD \MISC\MENU

The MD command can be used to create only one directory at a time. In the preceding examples, the directories \MISC and \MISC\MENU were created. They could *not* have been created with the single command MD\MISC\MENU because you would be asking the operating system to create more than one directory in a single statement. The parent directory must be created first.

The Operation of the MD Command

- MD and MKDIR are different names for the same command. Both names produce identical results.

- The rules for a directory name are the same as the rules for a file name, but it is normal practice to not use an extension in a directory name.

- A directory name cannot duplicate a file name in the intended parent directory.

- Only one directory can be created with one command.

- MD does not change the current directory to the new directory. To change to the new directory, use CD.

The Directory Entries . and ..

When the operating system creates a directory, it adds two special entries to the new directory. The first directory entry's name is **.** (pronounced "dot"). The dot name is used internally by the operating system to identify the full directory entry itself. The dot directory entry has the same name as the directory in which it is stored. You will learn later how to take advantage of the dot directory entry to abbreviate certain commands that accept a directory path specification.

The second directory entry is named **..** ("dot-dot"). The operating system uses the dot-dot entry to find a directory's parent directory, regardless of what that parent directory is named. Later in this chapter you will learn how the dot-dot directory entry can be used as a shortcut way of specifying a path.

Both the dot and dot-dot entries are displayed when you list all the directory entries using the DIR command. You cannot delete or modify these specific directory entries.

Changing the Current Directory

When you boot the computer, the operating system sets the current drive to the hard disk (assuming that the PC wasn't booted from a floppy disk) and the current directory to the root. If you enter the DIR command after booting the system, you get a listing of all the files in the root directory. To change the current directory, you use the operating system command CHDIR. The command can be abbreviated CD, which most people prefer to CHDIR. Whichever name you use, the same command is invoked. It is the command you use to position yourself in different directories.

The syntax of the change directory command is

CD *d:path*

where *d:* is the optional drive name for the current drive, and *path* is the directory you want to make current. For example, to change to the directory 123R3, enter the following command:

CD \123R3

If you do not begin the path with a backslash, the operating system assumes that you want to move to the path relative to the current path. For example, suppose that the current directory is \123R3, and you enter the following command:

CD BUDGET

The operating system changes the current directory to the BUDGET directory that stems from the 123R3 directory. In other words, the new current directory will be \123R3\BUDGET.

A common mistake hard disk users make is to precede a relative directory with a backslash. For example, if you enter the command **CD\BUDGET**, the operating system tries to change to a BUDGET directory situated off the root directory. The initial backslash indicates to the system that you are specifying a directory from the root. Omit the backslash if you are specifying a path relative to (or down from) the current directory.

To change to the root directory of the current drive, you enter the command as follows:

**CD **

If you use the CD command with no path specifier, the operating system displays the name of the current directory. Every disk drive in the system has a current directory. To change the current drive, you must enter the drive letter followed by a colon (:). For example, to change to drive A, you enter the following command (assuming that there is a disk in drive A):

A:

When you change drives, you are automatically located in the current directory for that drive.

If a specified path (either fully qualified or relative) does not exist, the operating system issues the message **Invalid directory** and does not change the current directory.

The Operation of CHDIR

- CH and CHDIR are different names for the same command. Both names produce identical results.

- If the path specifier begins with a backslash, the CD command assumes that the directory path is from the root directory.

- If the path specifier does not begin with a backslash, the CD command assumes that the path is relative to (or below) the current directory.

- When the CD command is specified with no parameters, the current directory is displayed. If the CD command is used with only a drive specifier—for example **CD A:**, the current directory of the specified drive is displayed.

- The drive and path specifiers in the command must be valid.

Using the PROMPT Command

When you are moving around a directory using the CD command, it is always useful to know what the current directory is. To give you visual confirmation of your current logged drive and the current directory, the operating system provides the internal command PROMPT.

Every time the operating system is ready for you to enter a command, it displays a prompt: >. You can use the PROMPT command to make this display much more informative. For example, the following command instructs the operating system to display the current drive and directory:

PROMPT pg

If the current directory is \123R3 on drive C, the following prompt is displayed:

```
C:\123R3>
```

The **$p** specifier in the PROMPT command tells the operating system to display the full directory path as part of the prompt. The **$g** tells the operating system to display the > character at the end of the prompt. When your prompt is established in this manner, you have a visual reminder of where you are working in the hierarchical directory system.

The PROMPT command supports a number of other parameters that can be used to further customize the prompt. For example, **$d** displays the date. See Appendix A, "Operating System Command Reference," for more information about the PROMPT command.

You can change the prompt by entering the command at the system prompt, but as soon as you reboot the computer, the prompt returns to its former

appearance. If you want the expanded prompt to be permanent, add the PROMPT command to your AUTOEXEC.BAT file. See Chapter 8 for more details on creating an AUTOEXEC.BAT file.

Revisiting the DIR Command

Now that you have learned about paths, reviewing the DIR command is worthwhile.

In Chapter 4 you learned that the DIR command displays all the files in a directory. You may recall that the command accepts a file name, which can include wild-card characters, and the optional switches /P and /W, which pauses the listing after each full screen and displays the listing in a wide display format, respectively. The full syntax of the DIR command is as follows:

DIR *d:path\filename /P /W*

When used without any optional parameters, the DIR command lists all the files in the current directory. If you specify a path without a file name, the operating system lists all the files in the specified path. For example, if the current directory is the root, you can list all the files in the \WORD5 directory by entering the following command:

DIR \WORD5

To list only the files in that directory that have a DOC extension, enter the following command:

DIR \WORD5*.DOC

If the current directory is not the root, and you want to see all the files in the root directory, enter the following command:

**DIR **

To see all the files with a TXT extension in the INFO directory on the disk in drive A, enter the command **DIR A:\INFO*.TXT**.

> ✓ NOTE
> The command **DIR *.** displays a list of all the subdirectories that extend from the current directory. This form of the command instructs the operating system to list all the files in

the current directory that have no extension. Since most file names normally have an extension, and directory names generally don't, you will often get a listing of all the subdirectories.

Viewing the Directory Hierarchy with the TREE Command

With any filing system, having a summary of the filing system structure is useful, and a hard disk is no exception. As you learn to segregate different programs into different directories and create subdirectories to organize the data used by these programs, you will develop a very structured hard disk. As the number of directories and files grows, your ability to remember the directory names and the directory structure will diminish.

The operating system provides an external command TREE to inform you of the directory structure of a disk.

The TREE command has been significantly improved in recent releases of DOS and OS/2. The most noticeable improvement is with DOS V4, where the hierarchy is displayed in an easy-to-view graphical format (see fig 5.3). The earlier versions used a listing to display the directories. If you are using an earlier version of the TREE command, see the utility sidebar at the end of this section.

The syntax of the TREE command is

TREE *d:path\ /F /A*

In this generic syntax, *d:* is the optional name of the disk drive that holds the directories you want to list. If you omit the *d:*, TREE lists all the directories on the current drive. The TREE command in MS-DOS V3.3 and PC DOS V4.0 accepts the optional *path* specifier. The path specifier names the directory where TREE starts processing the listing. If the path is omitted, TREE displays all directories.

The TREE command in DOS V3.3 and earlier versions accepts only the single switch */F*, which directs the TREE to list all the *files* in the directories. Use this switch if you are trying to locate a file. If you do not use this switch, TREE displays only the disk's directories—not the disk's files.

Using V4 of DOS, the /A switch can instruct TREE to avoid the use of special line-drawing characters when the visual tree structure is displayed.

```
E:\>TREE
Directory PATH listing for Volume QUEDISK
E:.
├───123R3
│   ├───DEPT
│   │   └───BAK
│   ├───BUDGET
│   └───PERSONAL
├───WORD5
│   ├───CONTRACT
│   ├───MEMOS
│   └───PERSONAL
├───DOS
├───PCFDB
│   ├───TTT
│   └───MAILLIST
├───BATFILES
└───UTILS
    ├───NORTON
    ├───MAG2
    ├───PCTOOLS
    └───FASTBACK

E:\>
```

Fig. 5.3. *The graphical directory display from the TREE command.*

With a large or very structured hard disk, the output from TREE may be too large to display on the screen. You can use the MORE filter to instruct the operating system to pause after each full screen, as with the TYPE command: **TYPE | MORE**, for example. Alternatively, you can use the redirection symbol > to redirect the output to the printer: **TREE > PRN**, for example.

> ✓ **UTILITY**
> If you are using a version of the operating system that does not support the graphical display of the directory hierarchy, the public domain program VTREE provides a similar function. See Chapter 11 for more information about VTREE.

Deleting or Removing Directories

The operating system includes the command RMDIR or RD, which is used to remove directories. As with other directory commands, the operating system provides two names to execute the same command. Most users prefer the short command, RD.

The syntax of the RD command is

RD *d:path***directoryname**

In this generic syntax, *d:* is the optional disk drive name where the RD command will search for the directory to remove. If *d:* is omitted, the operating system assumes that the directory is on the current drive.

path is the path to the **directoryname**. If the path specifier is omitted, the operating system assumes that **directoryname** is a subdirectory of the current directory of *d:*. If path begins with a backslash, the path is assumed to be fully qualified. If the path does not begin with a backslash, the operating system assumes that the path to the **directoryname** is relative from the current directory *d:*.

directoryname is the name of the directory to be removed. The directory name must be specified; that is, it is not optional.

If the operating system cannot remove a directory, it displays the message `Invalid path, not directory, or directory not empty`. The operating system can remove a directory only if the directory is empty. In other words, the directory must not contain any files or any subdirectories. If you want to delete a directory and all its subdirectories, you must go to the lowest level in the directory structure and delete all the files and subdirectories. Note that you cannot remove a directory if it is the current directory. You must change to another directory and then enter the RD command.

If the current directory is \WORD5, and you want to remove the subdirectory \WORD5\TEMP, enter the following command:

RD TEMP

The TEMP directory also could be removed from any other directory or drive by specifying the drive and the full path:

RD C:\WORD5\TEMP

The Operation of the RD Command

- RD removes only empty directories.

- A directory affected by the SUBST command cannot be removed.

- You should not remove directories from a drive that is affected by a JOIN or ASSIGN command.

- You cannot remove the root directory.

The SUBST, JOIN and ATTRIB commands are discussed later in this chapter.

> ☑ **NOTE** The operating system does not provide a way of renaming a directory (although there are utilities that do). To give a directory a new name, you must create a new directory and copy the files from the old directory to the new directory. Then you should remove the old directory.

Using Shortcut Path Commands

Every directory (other than the root directory) includes a **..** directory entry. This directory is a link between the current directory and the parent directory. You can use the dot-dot entry in commands when you want to identify the parent directory in a path. For instance, assume that the current directory is \MISC\MAIL\HOME, and you want to change the current directory to the parent of the HOME directory, \MISC\MAIL. One way would be to use the CD command as follows:

CD \MISC\MAIL

However, you can use the shortcut dot-dot path name as follows:

CD ..

Similarly, if you want to change from the directory \MISC\MAIL\HOME to the directory \MISC\MAIL\BUSINESS, you can use the dot-dot shortcut, as follows:

CD ..\BUSINESS

The **..** instructs the CD command to substitute the full name of the parent directory: \MISC\MAIL.

The dot-dot shortcut can be used with all operating system commands that accept a path. For example, you can display the files in the parent directory by entering the following command:

DIR ..

Using the COPY Command

The COPY command is arguably the most frequently used operating system command. The primary purpose of the COPY command is to copy one or more files from one drive or directory to another. However, the COPY command is very versatile and can be used to combine two or more files into one, to create new files, to print files, and much more.

Copying Files

In its basic form, COPY is easy to use and understand. The syntax of the basic copy command is

> **COPY** *d:path1***filename1.ext1** *d:path2***filename2.ext2** */V*

d:path1 and *d:path2* are the optional source and destination disk drive and directory path. If you omit a source drive or directory path, the default is assumed.

filename1.ext1 is the name of the file to be copied. It may include wild-card characters to copy all files matching a pattern. If **filename1.ext1** is not specified, but the file path is, all the files in the specified directory are copied.

The COPY operation can copy a file and give it a new name. **filename2.ext2** is the name to be given to the new file. The file name may include wild-card characters. If the **filename2.ext2** is omitted, but a path is specified, the COPY command will give the new file the same name as the source file.

The optional */V* switch instructs the command to verify that the file is successfully copied. If specified, the COPY command performs read-after-write verification of the output sectors of the destination file; that is, the system checks to see if it can read the data it has just written to the disk. The destination file is not compared to the source file. This option simply insures the integrity of the new file.

Unlike the RENAME command, COPY actually duplicates the data in a file. Data is read from the source file into a temporary RAM buffer. When this buffer is full, the COPY command writes the data to the new target file. COPY then reads more data from the source; the cycle repeats until all the data is copied from the source to the destination file.

✓ The operating system command VERIFY is used to set the
NOTE   computer to verify newly written files automatically after a
       copy operation. See Appendix A, "Operating System
       Command Reference," for more information about the
       VERIFY command.

Copying Files from One Disk to Another

You can copy one or many files to another disk for safe keeping, to move
data to another computer, or for any other purpose. To do so, simply use the
COPY command with a file name or a wild-card that matches the file(s)
you want to copy to the disk. For instance, to copy all the files with the
extension WK3 from the current directory to the root directory of a diskette
in drive A, enter the following command:

COPY *.WK3 A:

The file name *.WK3 does not include a drive or path in the name, so the
COPY command assumes that the files to be copied are in the current
directory of the current drive. The second parameter, A:\, identifies the
destination drive and directory, but does not specify a new file name. The
COPY command therefore creates files on drive A with the same file names
as the source files. The command **COPY *.WK3 A:*.WK3** would have
the same effect.

Similarly, if you want to copy all the files from the root directory of a
diskette in drive A to the root directory of a diskette in drive B, you can
enter the following command:

COPY A:*.* B:

In the preceding example, the drive and path of the source files are
explicitly identified. Notice that the file mask *.* represents the files with
any name and any extension, that is, *all* files.

Copying Files from Directory to Directory

As a hard disk user, you will often want to copy files from one directory to
another. For example, you can copy the file AUTOEXEC.BAT from the
root directory to the \TEMP directory by entering the following command:

COPY \AUTOEXEC.BAT \TEMP

The first parameter is the name of the file to be copied, including the path (in this case the root \), and the second parameter is the destination directory. Because a new file name is not specified, the COPY command creates a file with the same name—AUTOEXEC.BAT. If you do not want the copied file to have the same name, you can explicitly specify the new name for the destination file:

COPY \AUTOEXEC.BAT \TEMP\AUTO.TMP

The file AUTOEXEC.BAT is copied from the root directory to the \TEMP directory and given the new name AUTO.TMP.

Provided that the destination file name is different from the source file name, you can copy files that are in the same directory. To copy all the files in the current directory with an extension DOC and give them the extension BAK, enter the following command:

COPY *.DOC *.BAK

> ✓
> **NOTE**
> In a copy operation, the dot directory name can be used as a terse alternative to the *.* file mask. For example, the command **COPY . \TEMP** copies all files from the current directory to the \TEMP directory. The dot directory name also may be used in the RENAME and DELETE commands.

The Operation of the COPY Command

- The source parameter must contain at least one of the following: a drive specifier, a path specifier, or a file specifier.

- If the source drive or path specifier is omitted, the default drive and directory are used.

- If the source-file specifier is omitted, all files in the specified directory on the specified (or default) drive are copied. This situation is equivalent to supplying *.* as the source-file specifier.

- The destination parameter consists of a combination of drive, path, and file-name specifiers. An omitted drive or path specifier assumes the value of the current drive or directory. An omitted file-name specifier assumes the value of the source-name specifier.

- If COPY detects an attempt to copy a single source file onto itself (same drive, directory, file name, and extension), the copy operation is aborted.

- The /V parameter instructs the COPY command to verify the data as it is written to the destination file.

- If the source-file parameter matches multiple files, and if the destination file is a literal file name, the destination file is the concatenation of all the source files.

Respecting the COPY command

The COPY command is very powerful and useful, but if used carelessly, you can destroy data without warning. Don't be too alarmed, however. With a good understanding of the COPY command and awareness of the potential problems, you can use it very effectively.

The primary thing to remember is that the COPY command *overwrites* any existing file with the same name as the destination file (unless the existing file has been made read-only). Suppose, for example, that you enter the following command:

COPY BUDGET.WK3 \FILES

If the file BUDGET.WK3 already exists in the directory \FILES, it is overwritten without warning. That is, the original file is replaced by the new file, and the old file no longer exists. Always be sure that a destination file does not already exist, unless you intend to overwrite it.

If you use wild cards in the source file name, there is the potential for overwriting many files in one quick command. Use wild-cards with caution. If you don't want files to be overwritten, be sure that no files exist with the same name in the destination path. If you confuse the source and destination when you copy a file, you can easily copy an old file over a current one. You might not even notice the error until you need today's work. Not all mistakes with COPY, however, overwrite current data. Some mistakes just create file-management messes.

For example, relying on default drive and directory values when using COPY is convenient. Yet, if your current drive or directory isn't what you think it is, you can copy many files to the wrong disk or directory with one COPY command. Cleaning the misplaced files from the erroneous directory or disk and getting the files into the correct location can be a tedious process.

This mistake can happen to you when you install new software. If you make a new directory for the program files, but forget to change to the new directory with CHDIR, your next COPY command can make a mess. You will need to copy these errant files one by one to their correct directory home.

To avoid sending files to the wrong directory, check the name of the logged disk or directory. Don't forget to check the name of the current directory on other drives of your system as well. Use the DIR command with drive and path parameters for the source and destination of your next COPY command. Viewing the directories takes a bit longer, but not as long as copying misplaced files one by one. For complete control of COPY, give the command the drive name, path, and file-name specifiers for both source and destination files.

A less well-known problem occurs when you use a wild card in the source file name, but a specific file name for the destination. All the files that match the source file mask are combined (or concatenated) into a single large file that has the destination file name. For example, the command

> **COPY *.* TEST.FIL**

combines all the files in the current directory into a single destination file called TEST.FIL.

Concatenating Files

The COPY command can be used to combine two or more files into a single file. The process of combining or merging files is referred to as *file concatenation*. Nowadays, this form of the COPY command is rarely used, but it is worthwhile to be aware of the facility.

The syntax of the COPY command when it is used for concatenation is

> **COPY**   *d:path1***filename1.ext1** */A/B +*
> *d:path2***filename2.ext2** */A/B + ...*
> *d:pathD***filenameD.extD** */A/B/V*

The command normally is entered on a single line, but here for clarity, the syntax is split onto three lines.

The first two file-name specifiers followed by the ... indicate that there are multiple source files. Each source file can have an optional drive and path specifier to indicate the source drive and directory.

The /A and /B switches are used to indicate whether the file is ASCII or binary. Use one switch or the other with each file, not both.

Using the /A parameter with the source files instructs the operating system to copy all data up to, but not including, the end-of-file character (^Z). When the /A switch is used with the destination file, an end-of-file character is embedded at the end of the destination file.

Using the /B parameter with the source files instructs the operating system to copy all the characters from the source file. Using the /B switch with the destination file prevents the COPY command from adding an end-of-file character to the end of the file.

The + sign is used to separate each of the source files and is the trigger that advises the COPY command to concatenate the files.

For example, to combine the files DICK.TXT and JANE.TXT into a new file called STORY.TXT, enter the following command:

COPY DICK.TXT /A + JANE.TXT /A STORY.TXT /A

> ✓
> **NOTE**
> Every ASCII file ends with a ^Z end-of-file character. When you combine ASCII files, you want only one ^Z character at the end of the file—to mark the end of the combined file. Binary files do not end with a ^Z character.

Using Devices with COPY

In Chapter 4 you learned that the operating system reserves certain names to indicate devices. The reserved device named CON (short for *con*sole) can be used with the COPY command to create a file. *Console*, in this case, refers to the keyboard. In effect, you are instructing the operating system to copy into a file data typed at the keyboard.

If you use the CON device as the source "file" in a COPY command, the operating system copies from the console to a file. That is, the command copies input from the keyboard to a file. You can type characters on the keyboard, and they are placed in the destination file.

Using the COPY command with the CON device name as a source parameter is so popular that many users refer to the "COPY CON" command when talking about the operation. By way of an illustration of this facility, you can create a batch file that will automatically start 1-2-3. (You will learn more about batch files in Chapter 6.)

The goal of the following command is to create a file in the root directory that automates the steps of changing to the \123R3 directory and executing the program LOTUS.EXE. The following command creates a file called RUN123.BAT:

COPY CON RUN123.BAT

When you press Enter, the cursor will shift to the next line, but the operating system prompt will not be displayed. The system is waiting for you to type characters into the new file. You can now start typing the file. Type the following line and press Enter:

C:

The cursor drops to the next line, indicating that you have created the first line of the file. Type the following line and press Enter:

CD\123R3

The cursor drops to the next line. Type the following command and press Enter:

LOTUS

At this stage, you have created a three-line file, and the system is waiting for the next line. You must press Ctrl-Z (or F6) to indicate that there are no more lines. The Ctrl-Z is known as the end-of-file marker. Then press Enter one last time. The operating system responds with the following:

`1 File(s) copied`

To confirm that the new file is correct, you can use the TYPE command to review the contents of the file.

In Chapter 4, you learned that a file could be printed by redirecting the output of the TYPE command, using > PRN. You also can use the COPY command to print a file by copying the file to the PRN device. For example, to print the file RUN123.BAT, you could enter the following command:

COPY C:\RUN123.BAT PRN

More recent versions of the operating system include two powerful new file-copy commands: REPLACE and XCOPY. See Appendix A for more information about these commands.

☑

UTILITY

The COPY CON facility provides a quick way of creating a small file, but its capabilities are very limited. For example, you cannot go back to a previous line to correct an error. The operating system also includes the program EDLIN, which provides more editing capabilities, but not much more. There are many different text-editor utilities that provide a quick and easy word processor-like facility for editing files (see Chapter 6).

Setting the Path

Every well-structured hard disk is organized into a variety of directories used to store programs and data. While this structure helps to keep the files segregated, it can pose problems for the operating system when you instruct it to execute a program.

With so many directories to choose from, the operating system may not know where to find a program file. Furthermore, two separate programs with the same name may exist in different directories. The operating system has to know which program to execute. The PATH command can be used to overcome these problems.

The operating system recognizes three types of files as programs that it can execute. These file names have the extensions COM, EXE, or BAT. (Batch files in OS/2 have an extension CMD, not BAT.) To execute (or run) a program, you type the program file name without the extension, and press Enter.

When you enter the command, the operating system first checks to see if the command is internal (such as the DIR command). If not, it searches the current directory for a file that has the same name and extension: COM, EXE, or BAT.

If you want to run a program located on a drive and/or directory other than the current, you can supply the drive and path information the operating system needs along with the command's name on the command line. For example, to
execute the external operating system command TREE stored in the \DOS directory of drive C, enter the following command:

C:\DOS\TREE

This form of the command explicitly instructs the operating system to access the file from the C:\DOS path. An alternative would be to use the CD command to make C:\DOS the current directory, before issuing the TREE command.

To run programs in this manner, you need to remember where every program is stored and change current directories or enter the full path of a command. Fortunately, the operating system provides a convenient way to overcome this problem. A directory search path can be established through the PATH command. The PATH command enables you to inform the operating system of the directories most likely to contain external commands, batch files, and programs.

The syntax of the PATH command is

PATH=*d1 :path1\;d2 :path2\;...*

The equal sign (=) is optional; you can simply use a space.

d1 :path1 is the first drive and path combination. The semicolon (;) following *path1* indicates that the end of the first path has been reached in the command.

d2 :path2 is a second drive and path combination to search, if the operating system does not find the program in the first path.

The ellipses (...) indicate that you can add more drive/path alternatives.

You do not have to give the drive specifiers with the path specifiers, but it is sensible that you always do. You don't want the operating system to search for a directory on the current drive that is really on another drive.

Nearly all hard disk users take advantage of the PATH command. It is normal practice to add the PATH command to the AUTOEXEC.BAT batch file so that the PATH is automatically set every time the computer is booted. See Chapter 6 for more information about AUTOEXEC.BAT.

All the PATH command does is tell the operating system to look for a program file if it can't find the file in the current directory. The directories specified in the command are referred to as the *search path*, because this is where the operating system is to search for programs.

For an example of setting a search path with the PATH command, suppose that you have a hard disk drive named C:. The DOS external program files are located in a directory named \DOS, as they would be if you used the DOS V4 installation program. To include the external commands in your search path, issue the following command:

PATH=C:\DOS

The operating system searches C:\DOS for a program that is not located in the current directory. If you have other program packages, you might add their directories to the path. For example, if you have the program dBASE IV stored in the directory C:\DBASE, you might use the following path command:

PATH=C:\DOS;C:\DBASE

Notice that the semicolon separates the two alternatives. If the file is not found in the current directory, DOS searches the C:\DOS directory for a program. Failing to find the program there, DOS searches the C:\DBASE directory where (one hopes) it will find the program file.

You can add as many directory paths as necessary to the PATH command, but usually there are no more than six or seven entries. You learn more about the PATH command in Chapter 8 when the subject of organizing a hard disk is addressed.

NOTE A command similar to the PATH command is APPEND, available in DOS V3.3 and V4.0 and in OS/2. APPEND can search for data files when a file name is specified in an operating system command. See Appendix A for more information on the APPEND command.

OS/2 OS/2 uses a technique for loading and running programs that is different from that used by DOS. OS/2 programs may be contained in several files—EXE files as well as DLL (dynamic link library) files. The command LIBPATH is used in the CONFIG.SYS file to instruct OS/2 where to find the program library files. There is also a DPATH command to instruct applications where to search for data files.

Understanding the Environment

The operating system uses a special part of RAM to record some information for controlling how the operating system functions. This area of memory is referred to as the *environment*.

In the environment, the operating system records information that it and other programs can reference. For example, when you specify a search path with the PATH command, the search path is stored in the environment. Every time you enter a command at the operating system prompt, the current directory is searched for the program. If the program file is not found, the operating system checks the environment to see which other directories are to be searched.

The default prompt, set with the PROMPT command, also is stored in the environment, as is the location of the command processor COMMAND.COM.

To display the complete environment, use the SET command. If you enter the command SET, you will see a display similar to the following:

```
COMSPEC=C:\COMMAND.COM
PATH=C:\WIN386;C:\;C:\DOS;C:\U\BAT
PROMPT=$p$g
```

The SET command also can be used to add entries to the environment. The syntax of the active SET command is

SET *name=value*

In this generic syntax, *name* is an identifier that is referenced by a program, and *value* is a string or expression that is assigned to the *name*.

If the *name* already exists, it is replaced with the new *value*. If no value is specified, the *name* entry is deleted from the environment.

Some applications programs check the environment to determine how to perform a particular function. For example, Aldus PageMaker checks the environment for the name TEMP, and the value is a directory where temporary files are to be stored. To instruct Aldus Pagemaker to use the C:\TRASH directory for temporary files, you enter the following command:

SET TEMP=C:\TRASH

The environment then includes a new entry for TEMP:

```
COMSPEC=C:\COMMAND.COM
PATH=C:\WIN386;C:\;C:\DOS;C:\U\BAT
PROMPT=$p$g
TEMP=C:\TRASH
```

Any changes to the environment are temporary and are erased when the operating system is rebooted.

> ✓ **NOTE**   The default size of the environment is 127 bytes. If you try to add too much information to the environment, you may get the message **Out of Environment Space**. The environment can be increased by using the /e switch with the SHELL command in the file CONFIG.SYS. See Chapter 6 for details.

Redirecting File Input/Output with Pretender Commands

Because the operating system manages disks in a logical rather than a strictly physical way, the operating system can "pretend" that a disk's identity differs from the disk's real name. Three commands can pretend that a disk's identity has changed. ASSIGN redirects disk operations from one disk to another. JOIN attaches an entire disk as a subdirectory to the directory structure of another disk. SUBST makes a directory of a disk appear to commands as a separate disk. When you issue commands that contain drive parameters, these pretender commands can alter the identity of the underlying drives. These three commands are discussed in the following sections.

Using ASSIGN

The external command ASSIGN redirects all disk activity from one drive to another. The syntax of the assign command is

> **ASSIGN** *d1=d2 ...*

In this generic syntax, **d1** is the drive letter for the original disk drive, and **d2** is the drive letter for the reassignment.

The ellipses (...) indicate that more than one drive can be reassigned on a single command line.

When you issue the ASSIGN command, the operating system redirects all I/O requests for d1 to d2. If you assign drive A to drive C, all commands referring to drive A actually are sent to drive C. The ASSIGN command should be used sparingly. If it is not required for a particular purpose, do not use it.

An example of where ASSIGN is useful is when you execute an installation program that transfers data from a floppy disk to the hard disk. Suppose that the software is on a 3 1/2-inch disk, and your 3 1/2 drive is drive B. The installation program starts to run and the drive A light illuminates, showing that the installation program is looking for the files in drive A. If the installation is unable to access drive B, you can use the following assign command to trick the installation program:

ASSIGN A=B

After you have reassigned drive A, the installation program is automatically redirected to read drive B.

To undo the drive reassignments, enter the command ASSIGN with no parameters:

ASSIGN

The Operation of the ASSIGN Command

- Both **d1** and **d2** must physically exist.

- You can use an optional colon after the drive letter only with DOS V4.

- Remove any ASSIGN settings before running FDISK, PRINT, FORMAT, BACKUP, or RESTORE.

- Do not use ASSIGN if either JOIN or SUBST are being used.

- Do not use ASSIGN prior to using the APPEND command.

- Beware of using CHDIR, MKDIR, RMDIR, LABEL, APPEND, and PATH with any reassigned drives.

- DISKCOPY and DISKCOMP do not recognize any drive reassignments.

Using JOIN

Whereas the ASSIGN command is used to make one disk drive appear to be a different drive, the JOIN command is used to make a drive appear to be one or more directories on another disk.

The external command JOIN enables you to have a floppy disk that appears to be part of a hard disk. The directory structure on the floppy disk is added to the directory structure of the hard disk. You also can use the JOIN command if you have two hard disks: drive C and drive D. You can use JOIN to attach drive D to a subdirectory on drive C.

To connect disk drives, use the following form:

JOIN d1: *d2:***directoryname**

To disconnect disk drives, use this form of the command:

JOIN d1: /D

To show currently connected drives, use the following form:

JOIN

d1: is the disk drive to be connected. This drive is often referred to as the *guest drive.*

d2: is the disk drive to which **d1:** is to be connected and is referred to as the *host drive.*

\directoryname is a subdirectory in the root directory of *d2:*, the host drive.

The /D switch *disconnects* the specified guest disk drive from its host.

For example, to JOIN drive B to drive C as a subdirectory called \DRIVEB, type the following:

JOIN B: C:\DRIVEB

Typing JOIN with no parameters or switches displays any drive reassignments. In this example, the following message appears:

```
B: => C:\DRIVEB
```

To remove this joined drive, type the following:

> **JOIN B: /D**

The primary use of the JOIN command is to overcome the 32M limitation on partition size in some versions of DOS.

The General Rules of the JOIN Command

- the directory **\directoryname** must either be empty or not exist.

- You cannot join a directory to the current directory.

- You cannot join a directory to the root directory of a drive.

- When a drive is joined to another drive, you cannot change to the drive using standard drive syntax. For example, if drive B is joined to drive C, you cannot switch to drive B with the command **B:**.

- The entire drive is joined with the JOIN command.

- You cannot specify a networked drive as either **d1:** or *d2:*.

- Do not use the JOIN command with ASSIGN or SUBST.

- Remove any JOIN settings before running DISKCOPY, DISKCOMP, FDISK, PRINT, FORMAT, BACKUP, or RESTORE.

- Beware of using CHDIR, MKDIR, RMDIR, LABEL, APPEND, and PATH with any reassigned drives.

Using SUBST

The external command SUBST is the opposite of the JOIN command. Rather than grafting a disk onto the tree structure of another disk, the SUBST command splits a disk's directory structure in two. In effect, the SUBST command creates an alias disk drive name for a subdirectory.

The syntax for the SUBST command has several different forms.

To establish an alias, use the following form:

> **SUBST d1:** *d2:***pathname**

To delete an alias, use this form:

> **SUBST d1: /D**

To see the current aliases, use this form:

> **SUBST**

d1: is a valid disk drive name that becomes the alias or nickname. d1: may be a nonexistent disk drive.

*d2:***pathname** is the valid disk drive name and directory path that will be nicknamed **d1:**

The **/D** switch deletes the alias.

The SUBST command replaces a path name for a subdirectory with a drive letter. Once a SUBST command is in effect, the operating system re-routes all access to a drive back to a specific directory.

> ✓ You can use the LASTDRIVE directory in the CONFIG.SYS
> file to allocate logical drives that may be referenced in a
> NOTE SUBST command.

For example, the following command assigns the alieas drive name E to the path C:\P\TURBO55\TEDDY:

> **SUBST E: C:\P\TURBO55\TEDDY**

You now can use drive E to prefix file names when you want to access the specific directory. To confirm that the substitution is active, enter the following command:

> **SUBST**

The following message should appear:

> `E: => C:\P\TURBO55\TEDDY`

To disconnect the substitution of drive E for the subdirectory C:\P\TURBO55\TEDDY, type the following:

> **SUBST E: /D**

The most common use for the SUBST command is to provide abbreviations for long path names. The SUBST command also can prove useful when a (poor and outdated) software program does not recognize directories, but does allow drive specifications.

Summary

This chapter showed you that the best way to organize files on a hard disk is to build a directory hierarchy. In this chapter you learned the following key points:

- All disks have a root directory, which is represented by the backslash (\).

- The MKDIR (MD) command creates (makes) new directories.

- The CHDIR (CD) command changes default (current) directories.

- The RMDIR (RD) command removes empty directories.

- The TREE command displays the directory hierarchy of a disk, and the PROMPT command can be used to remind you of the current directory.

- The COPY, REN, and DEL commands are used to copy, rename, and delete files.

- The PATH command is used to inform the operating system where to search for program files.

- The PROMPT command is used to identify the current directory every time the operating system is waiting for input.

- The environment is a special location in memory that is referenced by the operating system and by some applications programs.

- The SET command is used to view and modify the environment.

- You can modify drive and directory identities using the "pretend" commands ASSIGN, JOIN and SUBST.

In Chapter 6, you will learn how to create and use batch files.

A note from the author ... There are many excellent commercial utilities that make directory and file management much easier. You should consider using at least one disk-management utility program. These programs are reviewed in Chapter 11.

Understanding
Batch Files

You probably have found that you enter some command sequences over and over again. For example, to execute your spreadsheet program, you may change to a specific directory and then execute the program, or at the end of every day, you may copy all the files with a DOC extension from a directory to a diskette for safekeeping.

Fortunately, the operating system provides a simple and convenient way to carry out such routine tasks. It allows you to store operating system commands in a special text file called a *batch file*.

You place the desired commands in a batch file, and when you execute the batch file, all the commands in the file are invoked. Batch files therefore provide a way to combine a series of commands.

In this chapter you learn how to create and edit text files and how to make batch files that automate repetitive and complex tasks.

The following commands are discussed in this chapter:

- EDLIN   - COMMAND /C
- COMP   - GOTO
- REM   - IF
- ECHO   - FOR
- PAUSE   - PROMPT
- CALL

Editing Text Files

Batch files are ASCII or text files with the reserved file name extension BAT (or CMD in OS/2). In order to build and modify batch files, you need to learn how to edit text files in general.

In Chapter 5 you learned that the COPY CON command can be used to create a text file. This technique allows you to enter characters directly into a file, but it does not provide any editing capabilities. Its use, therefore, is limited to very short, simple files. COPY CON is not really suitable for developing batch files.

Most operating systems include a program that can be used to build text files. The DOS program is EDLIN. OS/2 has the program "E," and UNIX includes "ED." Alternatively, you can use a word processor that has an option to save plain text (or ASCII) files, or a text editor.

Using EDLIN

EDLIN is provided on the DOS disks and is normally located in the same directory as the operating system's external commands—C:\DOS, for example. If you cannot locate the file EDLIN.COM in your DOS directory, copy it from the original operating system diskettes to your operating system directory.

To run EDLIN, simply type **EDLIN** at the operating system prompt, followed by the name of the file you want to create or edit. EDLIN must be located in the current directory or in one of the directories listed in the operating system PATH.

Table 6.1 summarizes the EDLIN commands.

**Table 6.1
EDLIN Commands**

Command	*Function*
n	Edit line **n**
n1,n2D	Delete lines **n1** through **n2**
nD	Delete line **n** only
nI	Insert lines, starting at **n**
n1,n2L	List lines **n1** through **n2**
L	List from the current line to 23 lines down
A	Read more of the file from disk
n1,n2,n3C	Copy lines **n1** through **n2** to **n3**
E	Save file and exit
n1,n2,n3M	Move lines **n1** through **n2** to **n3**
n1,n2,P	List lines **n1** through **n2**; change current line (repeated **P** commands will move through the file)
Q	Exit without saving
n1,n2[?]Rs1^Zs2	Replace **s1** with **s2** in lines **n1** through **n2** (the **?** optionally requests confirmation with each change)
n1,n2[?]Ss1	Search lines **n1** through **n2** for string **s1**
nTfilename	Merge text from file **filename** to line **n**
nW	Write **n** lines to disk

In table 6.1, **n**, **n1**, and **n2** refer to line numbers, **s1** and **s2** refer to strings, and **^Z** is the Ctrl-Z end-of-file character.

You can use EDLIN's editing commands to edit or move an individual line, or to delete one or more lines. EDLIN places a temporary line number before each line of text in a file. The line numbers, however, are not part of the saved file.

For a detailed explanation of using EDLIN, see *Using DOS*, published by Que Corporation.

> ***A note from the author...*** There have been many heated discussions between experienced PC users about the value of EDLIN. Some say it is very poor, and others say it is excellent. I sit somewhere between the two extremes. The best thing about EDLIN is the price—it comes *free* with the operating system. Even if you use a more flexible text editor, you still should learn how to use EDLIN. Someday you may want to edit a file on a PC that is not equipped with a text editor, and EDLIN usually will be there.
>
> If you are an OS/2 user, you are in luck. OS/2 includes a very good text editor, tersely called E, a replacement for EDLIN. EDLIN is still provided for running in DOS mode.

Using a Word Processor

If you own a word processing program, you may prefer it to EDLIN for creating and editing text files. The main drawback is that most modern word processors do not save the file in plain ASCII or text form. The files usually include hidden formatting characters that record such things as the print margins, text font and style, and so on. Most good word processors do, however, have a special option that saves the file in text form. This option may be categorized as an *export* facility, or a *print-to-file* option.

You may find that the ASCII file created by your word processing program has a number of spaces or blanks at the beginning of each line. You should eliminate these spaces by altering the page or print margins in the word processor's settings.

Some word processors make it very easy to create plain ASCII files, and others don't. If you have difficulty using your word processor for this purpose, consider using EDLIN or a text editor.

Using a Text Editor

Text editors are like simple word processors that create and edit ASCII text files. They usually are smaller and simpler to use than word processors, and offer a friendly full-screen editing facility.

DISK

A simple, free text editor called TEDDY, which you can use to create and edit batch files is included on the disk that accompanies this book. TEDDY (see fig. 6.1) is designed for creating batch files and includes a help facility that explains each of the major batch file commands.

```
F1-Help               ♦♦♦ TECHNOJOCK's TEXT EDITOR II ♦♦♦
      Line 1    Col 2    Insert           C:AUTOEXEC.BAT
@echo off
path C:\WINDOWS;c:\;c:\dos;c:\u\bat;c:\u\misc;c:\123r3\tools;c:\p\brief;C:\U\PC
set bpath=;c:\p\brief\macros
set bhelp=c:\p\brief\help
set bfile=c:\p\brief\state.rst
set bbackup=c:\p\brief\backup
set bcasm="!\p\tasm\tasm %%s.asm"
set bcpas="\p\turbo\tpc /L /M %%s.pas"
set bpackages=doc,txt-txt:wp;asm:r;pas:r
set bflags=-bc1,2,3,2i120Mrt -mRDA -mrestore -D101key
set btmp=e:\
prompt $p$g
doskey
typemat
\u\norton\be ask "Do you want the disk cache loaded? ===> " YN
if errorlevel 2 goto skip
\pckwik\superpck
:skip
ver

set TEMP=C:\WINDOWS\TEMP

F2-Save F3-Load F4-DelLine F5-Copy F6-Move F7-Beg F8-End F9-Abort F10-Quit&Save
```

Fig. 6.1. TEDDY is a full-screen text editor.

TEDDY is a full-screen editor, which allows you to scroll text and move the cursor to any character or line. The program is like a simple word processor for plain text files. Although it is ideal for batch files, you also can use TEDDY to create and edit any text file.

Understanding Batch File Concepts

As mentioned previously, a batch file is a text file that contains a series of operating system commands. Most of the commands you use in batch files are the same as the commands you would enter at the operating system prompt. Other commands, however, are unique to batch files. These commands, referred to as *batch subcommands*, make batch files more powerful. The operating system executes the commands in a batch file one line at a time, treating them as though you had entered each one individually.

You can easily recognize a batch file in a DOS directory listing. Batch files have the file name extension BAT. When you type a batch file's root name (that is, the name without the extension) at the operating system prompt, COMMAND.COM looks in the current directory for that file name with a BAT extension, reads the file, and executes the commands contained in the file. The whole process is automatic. If the file is not found, the operating system looks through all directories in the search path (as described in Chapter 3). You just enter the batch file's name—the operating system does the work.

✓	All the DOS batch file commands discussed in this section also are supported in OS/2. The one major difference is that OS/2 batch files have the extension CMD, whereas DOS uses BAT. In the following sections, the text refers to BAT files. If you use OS/2, just substitute the extension CMD.
OS/2	

Batch files are useful for automatically issuing commands that are hard to remember or that are easy to mistype at the command line. One of the most common uses of a batch file is to simplify the running of a program. Such a batch file includes commands to change drives and directories and then run a program, including all the necessary switches and parameters. All you have to do is enter the name of the batch file.

Batch files can *echo* or display text you have entered into them. This text-display capability is useful for presenting instructions or reminders on the screen. You can compose messages that help you execute a command or that contain syntax examples and reminders. A batch file is not limited to displaying text contained within it, however. If a batch file includes the DOS TYPE command, it can display text from another file.

Building a Simple Batch File

The best way to learn about batch files is to create some. So that you can practice applying the principles of batch files, the following sections show you how to create a batch file that copies 1-2-3 worksheets to a diskette. You then learn how to improve and refine a batch file. Later sections discuss the constraints on batch file names, the rules for creating batch files, and techniques for modifying batch files.

First, consider the batch file's name. A batch file is an ASCII or text file that has the extension BAT. Avoid giving a batch file the same name as a DOS internal command or a program with a COM or EXE extension. The reason is that when a command is entered at the prompt, the operating system checks to see whether the command is an internal command (that is, part of COMMAND.COM). If not, the operating system then determines whether the command is a file with a COM or EXE extension. If the operating system still hasn't found the file, it checks to see if the file has a BAT extension. If you use a name that has already been used internally or with a COM or EXE file, the batch file will never be executed, because the other program file will always be executed first.

Rules for Creating Batch Files

Although batch files are easy to create and use, you still need to remember the following rules:

- Batch files must be ASCII text files.

- The batch file's name must be from one to eight characters in length, have a batch file extension, and conform to the operating system's naming conventions.

- The file's root name should not be the same as that of an internal command, or of any program with a COM or EXE extension.

- The batch file can contain any command that is valid at the operating system prompt. It may also contain subcommands meant expressly for use in batch files.

- You can include in the batch file any program name that you would usually type at the operating system prompt.

- Use only one command or program name per line in the batch file.

Executing Batch Files

DOS uses the same rules to execute a batch file as it does for COM and EXE files. If you do not specify the disk drive name before the batch file name, the operating system uses the current drive. If you do not give a path, the operating system searches through the current directory for the file. If the operating system cannot find the file in the current directory, and you did not precede the batch file name with a path, the operating system searches the directories specified in the PATH.

If there is an error in a batch file command line, the operating system displays an error message, skips the errant command, and continues with the next line in the batch file. You can stop a batch command by pressing Ctrl-C or Ctrl-Break. When you do, the operating system prompts you to confirm that you want to terminate the batch file. If you answer No, the operating system skips the current line of the batch file and resumes execution with the next command in the batch file.

If you execute a program from a batch file, the program is executed as though you had entered its name at the prompt. When the program is terminated, control is passed back to the batch file and the next line in the batch file is executed.

A Simple Batch File

This section examines a situation where a batch file might simplify hard disk management, and then shows you how to create a simple two-line batch file.

Imagine, for example, that you have stored some important 1-2-3 worksheets in the directory C:\123R3\PLANS. Your objective is to create a batch file that automatically copies the files to a diskette. The batch file is to be run every afternoon.

The batch file should include the following primary command:

    COPY C:\123R3\PLANS*.WK3 A:\

This command instructs the operating system to copy all the files with a WK3 extension to the root directory of drive A.

As a safety precaution, you should use the COMP command to verify that the files have been successfully copied. COMP compares files in two directories and ensures that they are identical. The batch file, therefore, should include a second command, as follows:

COMP C:\123R3\PLANS*.WK3 A:\

See Appendix A for more information about the COMP command.

As with all programs, when you enter the program name, the file must be located in the current directory or in one of the directories in the search path. To ensure that you will be able to run the batch file from any directory, create a new directory especially for storing batch files—named BATFILES, for example—which you add to the search path, by using the PATH command.

Remember that you execute a batch file by typing its name at the operating system prompt. Therefore, you should always give the batch file a sensible name. In this example, name the file BACK_WK3.BAT.

BACK_WK3.BAT, therefore, is to be created in the \BATFILES directory, and should contain the following two lines:

```
COPY C:\123R3\PLANS\*.WK3 A:\
COMP C:\123R3\PLANS\*.WK3 A:\
```

Notice that each command is typed on a separate line. Since COMP is an external command, the batch file assumes that the COMP program file is located in one of the directories identified in the search path.

That's all there is to creating a batch file. The batch file contains the commands that you would have typed at the operating system prompt.

To run the batch file, insert a formatted floppy into drive A, type **BACK_WK3**, and press Enter (see fig. 6.2).

In this example, only two files (ABC.WK3 & SALES.WK3) have the WK3 extension. Notice that the COMP command displays the message `EOF mark not found`. This is not an error. The message simply indicates that the files are binary, not ASCII. Having compared all the files, the COMP command automatically prompts to see if any more files are to be compared. Enter **N** to indicate that no more file comparisons are required.

```
C:\>COPY C:\123R3\PLANS\*.WK3 A:\
C:\123R3\PLANS\ABC.WK3
C:\123R3\PLANS\SALES.WK3
        2 File(s) copied

C:\>COMP C:\123R3\PLANS\*.WK3 A:\


C:\123R3\PLANS\ABC.WK3 and A:\ABC.WK3

Eof mark not found

Files compare ok


C:\123R3\PLANS\SALES.WK3 and A:\SALES.WK3

Eof mark not found

Files compare ok

Compare more files (Y/N)? n

C:\>
C:\>
```

Fig. 6.2. The display generated when BACK_WK3.BAT is executed.

Hiding the Action with ECHO OFF

As figure 6.2 illustrates, the operating system displays each line of the batch
file before it executes the line, and then the output generated by each
command is also displayed. These messages are reassuring when you are
testing a batch file, but they usually are not necessary when you know the
batch file is working correctly.

The re-displaying of every command in the batch file is referred to as
echoing (because the batch file echoes each command). The batch file
command ECHO OFF can be used to suppress the display of batch file lines
before they execute. ECHO OFF makes the display less "busy." The output
from each command executed is not suppressed (see fig. 6.3). The ECHO
OFF command usually is added to the first line of a batch file, as follows:

```
ECHO OFF
COPY C:\123R3\PLANS\*.WK3 A:\
COMP C:\123R3\PLANS\*.WK3 A:\
```

```
C:\>back_wk3

C:\>ECHO OFF
C:\123R3\PLANS\ABC.WK3
C:\123R3\PLANS\SALES.WK3
        2 File(s) copied


C:\123R3\PLANS\ABC.WK3 and A:\ABC.WK3

Eof mark not found

Files compare ok


C:\123R3\PLANS\SALES.WK3 and A:\SALES.WK3

Eof mark not found

Files compare ok

Compare more files (Y/N)? n
C:\>
```

Fig. 6.3. Using ECHO OFF to suppress command echoing.

Notice that the first command in the file, ECHO OFF, is itself echoed. This is because the command to suppress the echo has not yet been activated when the first line of the batch file is read. Beginning with DOS V3.3, you can use the @ character to prevent the ECHO OFF command from appearing on-screen. Any line that begins with @ is not displayed. If you have DOS V3.3 or later, add the @ character to the beginning of the first line, as follows:

```
@ECHO OFF
COPY C:\123R3\PLANS\*.WK3 A:\
COMP C:\123R3\PLANS\*.WK3 A:\
```

As figure 6.4 illustrates, even the ECHO OFF statement is now suppressed.

In figure 6.4 notice that the names of the files being copied are still displayed, even though ECHO OFF has been specified. ECHO OFF only suppresses the display of the batch file line being executed. If the executed command produces its own output (as COPY does), the output is not suppressed. Later in this chapter, you learn how even this output can be suppressed. In this example, however, the display of the file names is desirable.

```
C:\>back_wk3
C:\123R3\PLANS\ABC.WK3
C:\123R3\PLANS\SALES.WK3
        2 File(s) copied


C:\123R3\PLANS\ABC.WK3 and A:\ABC.WK3

Eof mark not found

Files compare ok


C:\123R3\PLANS\SALES.WK3 and A:\SALES.WK3

Eof mark not found

Files compare ok

Compare more files (Y/N)? n
C:\>
```

Fig 6.4. *@ECHO OFF suppresses all echoing.*

The ECHO OFF state is normally in effect for the whole batch file. However, the command ECHO ON can be used to reinstate echoing later in the file. You might use this command when you want to show that a specific command is being executed.

Annotating with REM

The batch file command REM is used to embed comments (or *rem*arks) and notes into a batch file. It is a good practice to enter at least one remark in a batch file to indicate what the batch file is used for. The batch file BACK_WK3.BAT, for example, might contain the following remarks:

```
@ECHO OFF
REM Copies 1-2-3 worksheets to drive A.
REM This file should be run every afternoon
REM after the daily worksheet updates.
COPY C:\123R3\PLANS\*.WK3 A:\
COMP C:\123R3\PLANS\*.WK3 A:\
```

The ECHO setting affects REM. If ECHO OFF is set, the REM messages are not displayed. If ECHO ON is set, REM messages are displayed. In this example, you do not want the remarks to be displayed; Hence, they are located after the ECHO OFF command. Since there are only two commands in the file, it is easy to interpret what the batch file is used for, and the remarks may seem unnecessary. However, with more complex batch files the purpose of the file is often less obvious and a few REM statements serve as valuable reminders.

Displaying Messages

Sometimes, you will want to display a message from a batch file to indicate progress or to remind you (or anyone else running the batch file) to perform a task—such as making sure that the printer is connected and on-line. You use the ECHO command to suppress or enable the echoing of batch file commands, but it also can display messages. To give the user time to read messages, use the batch command PAUSE to suspend the batch file's execution.

Echoing Messages

When used to display messages, ECHO takes the following syntax:

ECHO *anytext*

In this generic syntax, *anytext* can be any string of text containing up to 122 alphanumeric characters. Note that ECHO's ON and OFF parameters are reserved to indicate the echo state.

Any message following the ECHO command is displayed on-screen, even if ECHO OFF is active. The file BACK_WK3.BAT could advise the user of the tasks being performed, as follows:

```
@ECHO OFF
REM Copies 1-2-3 worksheets to drive A.
REM This file should be run every afternoon,
REM at the end of the day's worksheet updates.
ECHO Copying files ...
COPY C:\123R3\PLANS\*.WK3 A:\
ECHO Verifying copy ...
COMP C:\123R3\PLANS\*.WK3 A:\
```

Notice that two ECHO commands have been added to the file. Figure 6.5 illustrates the display when this modified batch file is run.

```
C:\>back_wk3
Copying files ...
C:\123R3\PLANS\ABC.WK3
C:\123R3\PLANS\SALES.WK3
        2 File(s) copied
Verifying copy ...


C:\123R3\PLANS\ABC.WK3 and A:\ABC.WK3

Eof mark not found

Files compare ok


C:\123R3\PLANS\SALES.WK3 and A:\SALES.WK3

Eof mark not found

Files compare ok


Compare more files (Y/N)? n
C:\>
```

Fig. 6.5. *Using ECHO to display messages.*

NOTE

If you want to get the user's attention, you can use the ECHO command to sound the computer's speaker. The special key combination Ctrl-G is interpreted by the operating system as an instruction to beep. To add a beep to a batch file, simply add the line **ECHO ^G**. Don't actually type the two characters; instead, hold down the control key and press G. The editor automatically inserts the **^G** symbol in the text. (If your editor does not support this key combination, or it is assigned another purpose, use EDLIN.) The Ctrl-G does not need its own line in the batch file, and can be embedded in a message, such as **ECHO The speaker^G beeps!**. The **^G** characters are not actually displayed in the echoed message.

You may want to separate parts of a long message with a blank line. However, if you add an ECHO statement with no text after it (or with spaces), the operating system thinks you are checking ECHO's status, and displays the message **ECHO ON** or **ECHO OFF**. To make ECHO display a blank line, use an invisible character as the ECHO message. The character whose ASCII value is 255 is non-displaying, or NUL. Therefore, to add a blank message line to a batch file, add the normal command ECHO, and then enter the special 255 character. To enter this character, hold down the Alt key, press the numbers **2 5 5** on the numeric keypad, and release the Alt key.

Using PAUSE

The BACK_WK3.BAT batch file copies files from the hard disk to a floppy disk. If the batch file is executed when there is no disk in drive A, the operating system presents the following uninformative message:

```
Not ready error reading drive A
Abort, Retry, Fail?
```

To avoid this problem, you can have the batch file remind the user to insert a disk into drive A. The PAUSE command can be used to suspend execution of the batch file to wait for such an action. When the operating system executes the PAUSE command, the message **Strike any key when ready . . .** is automatically displayed, and batch file execution is suspended until the user presses a key. The user can press Ctrl-C or Ctrl-Break to terminate the batch file. PAUSE gives the user the opportunity to read any messages and, if appropriate, terminate the program.

The operating system command CLS can be used at any time to clear the display and move the prompt to the top of the screen. The command is often added to the top of a batch file to focus the user's attention on the messages being written to the display.

By adding a CLS command, some informational messages using ECHO, and a PAUSE command, the BACK_WK3.BAT file is significantly improved:

```
@ECHO OFF
REM Copies 1-2-3 worksheets to drive A.
REM This file should be run every afternoon,
REM at the end of the day's worksheet updates.
CLS
ECHO ***     WK3 Backup Program      ***^G
ECHO Insert a formatted disk in drive A and
ECHO press any key, or press Ctrl-C to terminate.
PAUSE
ECHO Copying files ...
COPY C:\123R3\PLANS\*.WK3 A:\
ECHO Verifying copy ...
COMP C:\123R3\PLANS\*.WK3 A:\
```

When this modified batch file executes, the user is presented a clear display, the computer beeps, and the message is displayed (see fig. 6.6).

```
***     WK3 Backup Program     ***
Insert a formatted disk in drive A and
press any key, or press Ctrl-C to terminate.
Strike a key when ready . . .
```

Fig. 6.6. The modified batch file features more helpful messages.

It is unlikely that you have the exact directory or copy requirements that this batch file illustrates, but you can use the batch file as a template for your own batch file.

Suppressing Extraneous Messages

As you just learned, the ECHO OFF command suppresses the display of each line of the batch file before it is executed. This command does not, however, affect the output and messages generated by the actual commands called from the batch file. For example, the COPY command in the batch file BACK_WK3.BAT generates messages about the files being copied (see fig. 6.5). In this example, the messages are not a problem, but sometimes it helps to suppress messages to keep the screen from getting too "busy."

The redirector symbol > (which was introduced in Chapter 4) can be used to direct the output away from the screen to another device.

Typically, the NUL device is used to reduce the on-screen display of messages generated by a batch file. Redirecting the output to the NUL device simply suppresses the output. For example, to suppress the file-copying messages, the copy line in the BACK_WK3.BAT file could be adjusted as follows:

```
COPY C:\123R3\PLANS\*.WK3 A:\ > NUL
```

> ✓
> **NOTE**
> The use of the redirector is not restricted to batch files; you can use it directly whenever you enter a command at the operating system prompt.

Calling Other Batch Files

A batch file often is used to simplify the commands you need to enter in order to execute another program. When a line in a batch file contains a command that executes another program (or another batch file), the line is described as a program *call*.

When a batch file calls a program (a file with a COM or EXE extension), the program is executed, and when it terminates, the operating system returns to the batch file and executes the next line in the file. This is a very useful facility, because a single batch file can control the consecutive execution of multiple programs. For example, a batch file might call a program that performs a backup and, after that, call a program that defragments and optimizes the hard disk.

The situation is different when one batch file calls another batch file. If one batch file calls another batch file, control is not automatically returned to the first batch file when the second batch file finishes processing. You can, however, call the second batch file in a special way that ensures that control will return to the first batch file. If you are using DOS V3.3, V4, or a later version, you can use the CALL subcommand. With any version of DOS you can also use COMMAND.COM to achieve the same result.

The Batch File Subcommand CALL

The CALL command is used to call one batch file from another and return control to the calling batch file. CALL takes the following syntax:

CALL *d:path\filename parameters*

In this generic syntax, *d:path* is the optional disk drive and path name of the second batch file you want to execute. *filename* is the root name of the second batch file, that is, the file name without the BAT extension. *parameters* are the optional items that normally would be entered on the command line. Batch file parameters are discussed in detail in Chapter 9.

The CALL command is very easy to use. All you do is precede the command that calls the second batch file with the word CALL. The operating system then realizes that you want to return to the first batch file when the second one is finished. For example, the following line in a batch file executes the batch file BATCH2.BAT. Control does not return to the calling file, however, when BATCH2.BAT finishes executing:

```
BATCH2
```

IF the line is modified as follows, control does return to the calling batch file:

```
CALL BATCH2
```

The operating system uses 96 bytes of RAM to record the information required to return control to the original batch file. When the called batch file is completed, the 96 bytes are released.

The second batch file may *call* a third batch, and the third batch file may call a fourth, and so on. The technique of calling batch files from other batch files is referred to as *nesting*. Again, 96 bytes of RAM are temporarily used for each nested CALL command.

Calling a Batch File with COMMAND /C

The CALL command was first introduced in DOS V3.3. If you use an earlier version of DOS, you can use the command interpreter, COMMAND.COM, to call other batch files. The COMMAND subcommand takes the following syntax:

COMMAND /C *d:path\filename parameters*

In this generic syntax, *d:path* is the optional disk drive and path name of the second batch file you want to execute. *filename* is the root name of the second batch file, that is, the file name without the BAT extension. *parameters* are the optional items that normally would be entered on the command line.

The command's syntax is the same as that of the CALL statement, except that COMMAND /C is used rather than CALL.

When you use COMMAND /C, the operating system invokes a second copy of COMMAND.COM. The primary copy of COMMAND.COM (the one that interprets all the commands you enter at the operating system prompt) manages the calling batch file, and the second copy manages the execution of the called batch file. When the second batch file finishes executing, the second copy of COMMAND.COM shuts down, and the original copy regains control.

The batch file BATCH2.BAT could be called from another batch file as follows:

```
COMMAND /C BATCH2
```

COMMAND /C is almost identical to CALL. Each copy of COMMAND.COM, however, uses approximately 4,000 bytes of RAM. There is one other significant difference: because COMMAND loads a new version of COMMAND.COM, any changes you make to the environment (with the SET, PATH, or PROMPT commands) are lost when you return to the batch file that invoked COMMAND. If you use CALL, the environment changes are "permanent," since the environment accessed by the primary copy of COMMAND.COM is modified.

Batch File Programming

You can use batch files to do more than execute standard operating system commands and programs. Batch files also can include a collection of programming subcommands that enhance their capabilities beyond simple program execution. Don't be concerned if you are not a programmer; these subcommands are easy to learn and add power and flexibility to batch files.

Batch files usually execute one line at a time, starting at the first line in the file and proceeding until every line has been read. In some instances, you will want to test for a certain condition and execute commands selectively. For example, you may want to determine whether a specific file exists, or whether the batch file was executed with additional information (parameters) on the command line.

Batch files can access additional information that was typed on the command line when the batch file was executed, and batch files can access data stored in the operating system environment. Table 6.2 describes the three major batch file programming subcommands.

Table 6.2
Major Batch File Programming Subcommands

Subcommand	Purpose
GOTO	GOTO instructs the command processor to go to a specific line in the batch file to continue execution.
IF	IF can be used to verify a file's existence, the program completion code (or ERRORLEVEL) of a program just executed, and whether two strings are identical.
FOR	FOR repeats a command several times.

The following sections explore these batch file facilities, and show how they can be used to assist in hard disk management.

Passing Parameters to a Batch File

A *parameter* is any data typed after the program name on the command line. Each parameter on the command line is separated by one or more *delimiters*—usually spaces or forward slashes (/). Consider, for example, the following command:

    C:\> BATCH1 AB Hello 26

This command contains the batch file name BATCH1, followed by three parameters—AB, Hello, and 26. Using a special notation, the batch file can check the value of these parameters and use them within the batch file. Conceptually, the parameters can be directly substituted into the statements in the batch file. This facility allows you to make generic batch files that can be used in different ways, depending on the batch file parameters.

The best way to understand the usefulness of this facility is by example. In Chapter 4 you learned that the TYPE command is used to display the contents of a text file, and that the MORE pipe (|) can be used to pause the display after each full screen. The following sections show you how to create a generic batch file that displays text files on-screen. To view the file SHOPPING.LST, for example, you would enter the following command:

    TYPE SHOPPING.LST | MORE

This command could be put into a one-line batch file. However, you want the batch file to be able to list any text file, not just SHOPPING.LST. The trick is to create a batch file that is passed a single parameter—the name of the file to be displayed.

Each parameter passed to a batch file can be referenced by a special code inside the batch file. The code is a percent character (%) followed by the parameter number. For example, the first parameter can be accessed by using the code %1. Whenever the command processor sees the code %1 in the batch file, it substitutes the first parameter directly in its place.

Remember that all batch files should be located in a special directory, such as C:\BATFILES, which is included in the search path. This setup enables you to type the batch file command from any directory. Create the following one-line batch file, and call it TM.BAT—short for *type more*:

```
TYPE %1 | MORE
```

The command processor automatically substitutes for the %1 code the first parameter on the command line. For example, to display the contents of the file SHOPPING.LST, enter the following command:

TM SHOPPING.LST

This command instructs the operating system to execute the batch file TM.BAT and passes it a single parameter, SHOPPING.LST. When the command processor reads the first batch file line, it substitutes the parameter SHOPPING.LST in place of the %1 code. In other words, the command processor executes the following line:

```
TYPE SHOPPING.LST | MORE
```

As a result, the file's contents are displayed. Not only is typing reduced, but the batch file also can be used to list any file. All you have to do is change the file name you type on the command line; that is, change the *passed parameter*. For example, enter the following command to display the contents of the AUTOEXEC.BAT file:

TM C:\AUTOEXEC.BAT

Next, execute the batch file without any parameters, as follows:

TM

The command processor substitutes %1 with nothing and executes the following command:

```
TYPE | MORE
```

Because the file name is missing, the operating system responds with the following message:

```
Invalid number of parameters
```

Passing Multiple Parameters to a Batch File

Up to nine parameters can be directly accessed using %1, %2, and so on, up to %9. The SHIFT command, which is discussed in the next section, can also be used to provide access to more than nine parameters.

To illustrate the use of multiple parameters, suppose that you want to create another batch file. For example, you use several computers daily, but one of the hard disk systems is your primary "workhorse" where you store the files you want from all the computers you use. You use diskettes to move information between computers. You usually delete the file from the diskette after the file has been copied to a hard disk. Deleting the file "cleans" the file out of the process, so that the file won't be copied accidentally to the hard disk. You use the following steps to transfer data from a floppy disk to a hard disk:

1. Copy file from the diskette to the hard disk.

2. Erase the file from the diskette.

To simplify this process, you can create a batch file (named C&E.BAT, for copy and erase). Type the following commands into the file:

COPY A:%1 C:%2 /V
DEL A:%1

To use the C&E.BAT file, use the following command syntax at the operating system prompt:

C&E *oldfilename newfilename*

The first parameter, *oldfilename*, represents the name of the file you want to copy from the floppy disk to the hard disk; *newfilename* is the new name for the copied file (if you want to change the copied file's name).

Suppose that you put a diskette containing the file NOTES.TXT into drive A, and that you want to copy the file to the hard disk. Type the following at the operating system prompt:

C&E NOTES.TXT

The parameter NOTES.TXT replaces %1 in the batch file commands, and because there is no second parameter, %2 is replaced with "nothing." The command processor therefore executes the following two commands:

```
COPY A:NOTES.TXT C: /V
DEL A:NOTES.TXT
```

The operating system copies NOTES.TXT from drive A to drive C and then deletes the file on the diskette in drive A. The %2 parameter is dropped, and the file does not get a new name when it is copied.

One of the benefits of constructing a batch file that copies a file using parameters is that you can use a path as the second parameter. By specifying a path, you can copy the file from the floppy disk to a different directory on the hard disk. To copy NOTES.TXT to the directory called WORDS, for example, type the following:

C&E NOTES.TXT \WORDS

When the command processor executes the batch file, it substitutes the two parameters for the %1 and %2 entries in the commands. After the substitution, the following two commands are executed:

```
COPY A:NOTES.TXT C:\WORDS /V
DEL A:NOTES.TXT
```

Because \WORDS is a directory name, the operating system knows to copy the file NOTES.TXT into the directory \WORDS and not to give the new file the name WORDS. The operating system is doing nothing unusual here. It is simply following the rules of syntax for the COPY command. The batch file takes advantage of these syntax rules.

NOTE   The code %0 also can be referenced in the batch file. Whenever %0 is encountered in the batch file, the command processor substitutes the name of the batch file that is being executed. For example, in the preceding examples, %0 would refer to the name C&E.

Later in this section you will see how the IF and FOR commands can be used in conjunction with passed parameters to greatly increase the power and flexibility of a batch file.

Using Shift To Adjust Parameters

The batch file subcommand SHIFT can be used to reassign the parameters the command processor substitutes in the batch file commands. You already know that the first parameter is represented by %1, the second parameter is represented by %2, and so on up to the ninth parameter, which is represented by %9. When the command processor encounters the command SHIFT in a batch file, it moves the parameters in the command one to the left. After a SHIFT command, %1 refers to the second parameter. %2 refers to the third parameter, and so on, all the way to %9, which refers to the tenth parameter.

The following batch file, SHIFTIT.BAT, is a simple (and otherwise useless!) illustration of how the SHIFT command operates:

```
@ECHO OFF
ECHO %0 %1 %2 %3 %4 %5 %6 %7 %8 %9
SHIFT
ECHO %0 %1 %2 %3 %4 %5 %6 %7 %8 %9
SHIFT
ECHO %0 %1 %2 %3 %4 %5 %6 %7 %8 %9
SHIFT
```

This batch file simply echoes the parameters %0 through %9 three times. Between each message, however, the SHIFT subcommand shifts the parameters to the left.

Suppose that you execute the batch file with the following command:

SHIFTIT A B C D E F G H I J K L M N O P

The following output results:

```
SHIFTIT A B C D E F G H I
A B C D E F G H I J
B C D E F G H I J K
```

Each line of the output displays the parameters %0 through %9. The first line of the output displays SHIFTIT as the %0 parameter, and the letters A through I as the parameters %1 through %9. The second line shows the new parameter substitutions after the SHIFT subcommand has been executed. Now the %0 parameter is A, all the other parameters have been shifted once to the left, and the tenth parameter on the command line, J, has been shifted to %9. The third line shows the display after one further SHIFT. Now the eleventh parameter on the command line, K, has been assigned to %9.

There are two main uses for the SHIFT command. First, the SHIFT command provides a way to access more than nine parameters on the command line. Second, the SHIFT statement can be included in a program loop to simplify the processing of multiple parameters.

Branching With GOTO

Normally, the command processor executes a batch file one line at a time, starting with the first line and ending with the last line. With the subcommand GOTO, however, you can jump to another part of the batch file. The GOTO command uses a label to specify the destination. A *label* is a batch file line that starts with a colon (:), followed by a one- to eight-character name. The label name can be longer than eight characters, but only the first eight characters are significant as a label. The GOTO subcommand takes the following syntax:

GOTO *labelname*

In this generic syntax, *labelname* is the name of a label somewhere in the file, that is, a line whose contents is *:labelname*.

When the command processor encounters a GOTO command in the batch file, it searches from the beginning of the batch file until it finds a label matching the one specified by GOTO. Control then jumps to the line following the line with the label.

As an example, the batch file GOTOIT.BAT is listed here. This batch file has no practical use, but it does show how the GOTO command operates.

```
@ECHO OFF
:START
ECHO Hello, %1
PAUSE
GOTO START
```

Suppose that you invoke the batch file by typing **GOTOIT ERICA**. The screen shows the following:

```
Hello, ERICA
Strike a key when ready . . .
```

The batch file begins by echoing the message that includes the name
ERICA. The file then pauses so that you can press a key before it continues:

```
Hello, ERICA
Strike a key when ready . . .
```

After you press a key (for example, the space bar), the command processor
executes the GOTO START command. That is, it jumps to the line
following the :START label and continues. The GOTO statement passes
control back to the beginning of the batch file and forms a never-ending
loop:

```
Hello, ERICA
Strike a key when ready . . .
```

On the third time through the loop in the example, press Ctrl-C to stop the
batch file. (How many times do you want to see the message **Hello,
ERICA**?) The operating system asks whether you want to stop the batch file.
In this example, the response is yes, so that the processing of the batch file
stops and the system prompt returns:

```
Terminate batch job (Y/N)? Y
C:\>
```

Normally, the GOTO statement is used in conjunction with the IF statement
to provide very useful control of batch file execution.

Understanding the IF statement

The IF subcommand is a "test-and-do" command. When a condition is true,
IF executes the command on the line. When the condition is false, IF
ignores the line. The IF subcommand takes the following syntax:

IF *expression command*

In this generic syntax, *expression* is any logical test that has either a true or
false result, and *command* is any valid batch file command to be executed if
expression equates to true.

The IF subcommand can be used to determine whether parameters have
been passed to the batch file, to compare two strings, to ensure that a file
exists, and to determine whether a program was successfully executed.

Comparing Parameters and Strings

The IF subcommand can be used to determine whether string 1 equals string 2. When used to compare strings, IF takes the following syntax:

IF *string1* == *string2 command*

In this generic syntax, *string1* and *string2* are the strings to be compared, and *command* is the command that will be executed if the two strings are the same.

The term *string* simply means a collection of one or more characters. The following are examples of strings:

Goodnight mommy
bye
q
The time is 12:15

One of the strings in an IF command statement is often a batch file parameter. An example of a batch file that uses IF to check the value of a parameter is called GUESS.BAT. Create GUESS.BAT with the following contents:

```
@ECHO OFF
IF %1 == QUE ECHO CORRECT
```

All this batch file does is check to see if the first passed parameter is QUE. Type **GUESS QUE** at the operating system prompt, and you see the following response:

```
CORRECT
```

If you type something other than **QUE** (even **que**), nothing appears on-screen.

If you do not provide enough parameters with the IF command, the command processor replaces the % parameter markers with nothing. The command processor cannot compare empty, or *null*, parameters, so it displays the message **Syntax error** and aborts the batch file.

Testing for Missing Parameters

If a parameter has been specified, you can tell whether the parameter is null by using the following expression in a batch file:

```
"%1"==""
```

Earlier in the chapter, you created the file TM.BAT, which was used to display a file using the TYPE command with the | MORE pipe. This one-line file contains the following instruction:

```
TYPE %1 | MORE
```

If you recall, when the batch file was executed without parameters, the operating system displayed the message **Invalid number of parameters**. By combining an IF statement with a GOTO statement, that operating system error can be avoided. Modify the file TM.BAT as follows:

```
@ECHO OFF
IF "%1"=="" GOTO :MISSING
TYPE %1 | MORE
GOTO END
:MISSING
ECHO You must specify a file name
:END
```

If you execute the batch file by entering TM with no parameters, the following message is displayed:

```
You must specify a file name
```

Now examine how the batch file works. The first line simply turns off echoing. The second line checks the expression `"%1"==""`. If the result is true—that is, if no parameter was passed—the command `GOTO :MISSING` is executed and control jumps to the line following the label `:MISSING`. However, if the expression `"%1"==""` is false—that is, if a parameter was passed—control immediately passes to the next line, and the statement `TYPE %1 | MORE` is executed. Having displayed the file, the batch file then processes the statement `GOTO END` jumping to the label `:END`, thereby skipping the ECHO statement.

The IF and GOTO subcommands often are used in batch files in this way. The IF statement checks the passed parameters, and the GOTO statement branches to a specific part of the program.

Checking for Files with IF EXIST

The IF subcommand can be used to determine whether a file exists. When used in this manner, the IF subcommand takes the following syntax:

IF EXIST *filename.ext command*

In this generic syntax, *filename.ext* is any valid file name, including optional drive and path specifiers, and *command* is the command to be executed if the file is found.

Wild-card characters are allowed in the file name. When wild cards are used, the expression is true if any file matching the file mask is found.

Create the file FOUND.BAT as follows:

```
@ECHO OFF
IF EXIST %1 ECHO File %1 found!
```

To test the batch file, enter the following:

FOUND TM.BAT

If the file is found, the following message is displayed:

```
File TM.BAT found!
```

If the file is not found, no message is displayed.

Now use the IF EXIST command to build a more useful batch file. In Chapter 3 you learned about the RENAME command, which is used to give a file a new name. If the RENAME command fails, you are presented with the following all-encompassing message:

```
Duplicate file name or file not found
```

The following batch file, called RN (for ReName), is an improvement over the operating system command:

```
@ECHO OFF
IF "%1" == "" GOTO HELP
IF "%2" == "" GOTO HELP
IF EXIST %1 GOTO STAGE2
ECHO Rename failed. The file %1 doesn't exist.
GOTO END
:STAGE2
IF EXIST %2 GOTO NOTNEW
REN %1 %2
ECHO File %1 has been renamed %2.
GOTO END
:NOTNEW
ECHO Rename failed. The file %2 already exists.
GOTO END
:HELP
ECHO Execution error. The correct syntax is: %0
oldname newname
:END
```

The batch file provides the user with the command RN to rename a file. The main advantage of RN over the operating system command RENAME is that RN provides much better error messages. For example, if an error occurs, one of the following messages is displayed:

> **Execution error. The correct syntax is RN** *oldname*
> *newname*.
> **Rename failed. The file** *oldname* **doesn't exist.**
> **Rename failed. The file** *newname* **already exists.**

Also, if the file is renamed, the following reassuring message is displayed:

> **File** *oldname* **has been renamed** *newname*.

No more wondering if the command actually worked!

At first glance, this batch file looks very complicated, but it is actually very simple. Lines 2 and 3 ensure that two parameters have been passed, and if not, the **Execution error** message is displayed. Line 4 determines whether the source file exists. If it does, the command processor jumps to the line after the label **Stage2**. If the source file is not found, the second error message is displayed. In **Stage2**, a check is made to ensure that a file already exists that has the new name. If so, the third error message is displayed; otherwise the operating system command REN is called, and the success message is displayed.

Checking Program Error Levels

The IF statement also can be used to check the ERRORLEVEL of the last program executed. Before discussing how to use the IF statement in this context, it is worth reviewing the principles of error levels.

A better name for this condition would be "exit level." ERRORLEVEL is a code some programs leave for the operating system when they finish executing. In DOS V3.3 and later versions, only the BACKUP, GRAFTABL, KEYB, REPLACE, RESTORE, and XCOPY commands leave an exit code. Many third-party programs use exit codes.

An exit code of zero (0) usually means that everything is okay. Any number greater than 0 usually indicates that something went wrong when the program terminated. For example, no files were found, the program encountered an error, or the user aborted the program. Including an IF command in a batch file enables you to test ERRORLEVEL to see whether a program worked properly.

When used to check ERRORLEVEL, the IF subcommand takes the following syntax:

> **IF ERRORLEVEL** *value command*

In this generic syntax, *value* is a whole number you want to test for, and *command* is the command to execute if the expression is true.

The command processor actually determines whether the ERRORLEVEL returned by the program is equal to or greater than *value*. For example, if ERRORLEVEL is actually 5, the expression IF ERRORLEVEL 3 is true, and *command* is executed. If you want to go to a different label in the batch file based on a program ERRORLEVEL, then you must test for the values in *highest-first* order. The following extract from a batch file illustrates this technique:

```
IF ERRORLEVEL 5 GOTO BRANCHE
IF ERRORLEVEL 4 GOTO BRANCHD
IF ERRORLEVEL 3 GOTO BRANCHC
IF ERRORLEVEL 2 GOTO BRANCHB
IF ERRORLEVEL 1 GOTO BRANCHA
```

Using NOT with IF

You can reverse the meaning of any IF statement by using the NOT clause. That is, you can test whether an expression is false by adding the word

NOT after IF—remember that the standard IF command checks to see whether an expression is true. For example, you can use the following statement to determine whether a file does not exist on the disk:

IF NOT EXIST *filename*

If the result of the statement is true (the file does not exist), the command following the IF statement is executed.

You also can test for NOT *string1* == *string2* or NOT ERRORLEVEL. In any event, the command at the end of the IF test activates only if the condition is false—that is, if the condition does NOT occur.

Understanding the FOR..IN..DO Statement

FOR..IN..DO is an unusual and extremely powerful batch subcommand, which takes the following syntax:

FOR *%%variable* **IN** (*set*) **DO** *command*

In this generic syntax, *variable* is a one-letter name that takes on the value of each item in *set*. The double percent sign (%%) in front of the variable is important. If you use a single percent sign, the operating system confuses the symbol with the parameter marker and does not work properly.

set is the list of items, commands, or disk files of which you want *variable* to assume the value. You can use wild-card file names with this parameter. You also can use drive names and paths with any file names you specify. If you have more than one file, or other items in the set, use a space or comma between the names.

command is any valid command you want to perform on each item in the set. The command usually has a reference to the *%%variable* as one of the command parameters.

The best way to gain an understanding of the FOR..IN..DO subcommand is by example. The main purpose of the subcommand is to repeat a command again and again, using different command parameters. You can use the TYPE command to illustrate the subcommand.

Create a batch file called TM2.BAT (for Type More 2), as follows:

```
@ECHO OFF
FOR %%A IN (*.TXT) DO TYPE %%A | MORE
```

Because there are no passed parameters, you execute the command by entering the batch file name **TM2**.

This command finds every file that matches the file mask *.TXT and assigns the specific file name to the variable %%A. Each time a file is found, the TYPE command is executed, and the %%A in the command is replaced with the actual file name. When there are no more matching files found, the FOR statement ends, and the batch file terminates.

You can make the batch file more flexible by changing the set in the FOR subcommand to a passed parameter, as follows:

```
@ECHO OFF
FOR %%A IN (%1) DO TYPE %%A | MORE
```

You then can view all the files with a BAT extension, for example, by entering the command **TM2 *.BAT**. In this form, however, the batch file is not practical because the file contents scroll off the screen if there are too many files. To improve the batch file, you could call another batch file that contains the TYPE command and a PAUSE command.

UTILITY

Batch files provide a convenient, easy, and economical way of customizing a PC. After a short time, however, you will realize that batch files have a number of limitations. For example, there is no way in a batch file to prompt the user for input or to check the default directory. A number of excellent public domain utilities enhance batch file capabilities and overcome these weaknesses. There also are batch file compilers that make batch files faster and more powerful by converting them into EXE and COM programs. You learn more about these programs in Chapter 9.

OS/2

OS/2 supports all of the commands that have been covered in this chapter. Additionally, OS/2 includes the following three new batch file commands:

EXTPROC specifies a different command processor to OS/2's standard CMD.EXE for a particular batch file. This facility has been added in anticipation of third-party developers' writing powerful extensions to the batch file processor.

SETLOCAL allows the setting of a local environment that can be used temporarily by the commands in the batch file.

ENDLOCAL marks the end of the local environment, and switches the subsequent batch files to read the master environment.

Remember, an OS/2 batch file must have an extension of CMD, not BAT.

Summary

This chapter showed you how to use batch files to automate tasks and reduce a complex set of operating system commands to a single easy-to-use command. In this chapter you learned the following key points:

- You must give batch files the extension BAT (or CMD for OS/2).

- You invoke a batch file by typing the root name of the batch file and pressing Enter. You can specify an optional disk drive name and path name in front of the batch file name.

- You can use the ECHO subcommand to turn on or off the display of the command statements and to display messages.

- The @ character suppresses the display of a single line in a batch file (in DOS V3.3 and later).

- The PAUSE subcommand causes the batch file to suspend execution and displays a message on-screen.

- You can press Ctrl-C or Ctrl-Break to terminate a batch file while it is executing.

- The REM subcommand is used to annotate the batch file, to describe its purpose.

- The CLS command is used to clear the display and move the prompt to the top of the screen.

- COMMAND /C and CALL can be used to invoke a second batch file and return control of the computer to the first batch file.

- Each word (or set of characters) in a command, separated by a delimiter, is a parameter. When you use a batch file, the operating system substitutes the appropriate parameters for the variable markers (%0 to %9) in the file.

■ SHIFT shifts command parameters one to the left.

■ The GOTO subcommand can be used to branch to another location in a batch file.

■ The IF subcommand tests for a condition, and if the condition is true, the command on the line with the IF statement is executed.

■ The IF NOT clause is similar to IF, except that it tests whether a condition is NOT true.

■ The FOR..IN..DO subcommand can repeat a batch file command for one or more files or commands.

This chapter concludes Part II, DOS Basics. Part III shows you how to configure and organize your hard disk, and how batch files can be used to help you manage your hard disk.

Part III

Hard Disk Organization and Management

Configuring a Hard Disk

Organizing the Hard Disk

Using Batch Files To Manage a Hard Disk

7

Configuring a Hard Disk

If you have just purchased a new computer with a hard disk, or have just installed a new hard disk in your computer, you must *configure*—that is, prepare—the disk for everyday use. To be completely configured, a disk must undergo low-level formatting, partitioning, and high-level formatting. Finally, the operating system files must be copied onto the newly prepared hard disk. This chapter shows you how to configure a hard disk, and how to change the disk's partition structure, if necessary.

Over the last year or so, more and more computer distributors have been preparing hard disks before shipping, thus relieving the end user of the burden of setting up the disk. If a new computer can boot without a DOS operating disk in the diskette drive, then the hard disk already has been prepared. You can either accept the system as shipped, or you can modify the setup to suit your specific needs.

More and more hardware vendors are making it easier for the end user to prepare a hard disk. For example, Compaq Computer Corporation now provides a utility called FASTART. This easy-to-use program guides the user through all the required disk preparation tasks. Before rushing to set up the disk yourself, read the installation documentation to determine whether an all-in-one installation utility has been provided with your disk or operating system.

Low-Level Formatting

Low-level formatting is the first stage of hard disk configuration. Chapter 3 introduced the concept of the low-level format; the following sections explain the low-level formatting process in greater detail. Three primary tasks are performed during low-level formatting: surface structuring, interleave selection, and defect mapping.

When you buy a new computer or a new hard disk, the disk probably already has undergone low-level formatting. The low-level formatting usually is performed at the factory where the disk is constructed; otherwise, the disk's distributor performs the low-level formatting. You should not have to execute another low-level formatting program when you set up the system. Refer to the disk documentation, or check with the distributor to determine whether the drive already has undergone low-level formatting.

You may, however, need to perform a low-level format again if you have drive alignment problems, or if your disk controller expects the disk to have a different interleave ratio. (Chapter 3 discusses drive alignment and interleave ratios in detail.) Further, if your computer does not recognize the type of drive you are trying to install (that is, if the disk drive and computer are outwardly incompatible), you may need to use special disk management software to perform a new low-level format on the drive.

Low-level formatting programs usually come from one of three sources. In the early (and wacky) days of hard disks, the program was stored in a ROM chip on the disk drive controller. The user invoked the program by entering some cryptic codes into the operating system's DEBUG program. The disk controller then performed low-level formatting on the attached disk. Now, some hardware manufacturers provide disk-based low-level format programs with the hardware, such as the IBM Advanced Diagnostics disk. Otherwise, you can purchase a third-party utility program. Although the precise options and menus vary from program to program, all low-level formatting programs follow the same principles and perform the same basic task. This section focuses on the principles of low-level formatting; later sections introduce you to two specific products that can help you perform low-level formatting on your disk.

In the first phase of low-level formatting, a formatting program organizes the surface of each disk platter into tracks and sectors. This step is called *surface structuring*. You may recall that a track is a narrow "ring" of disk surface, which is accessed by the drive's read-write head as the disk rotates. Normally, the disk's surface contains between 500 and 750 tracks per inch. Each track is further subdivided into sections of equal size. These arc-shaped sections are called sectors; a typical disk has either 17 or 26 sectors per full track. During low-level formatting, each sector receives a unique identification number. During everyday operation, the hard disk controller uses these numbers to find specific sectors on the disk. This track-and-sector organization is the primary *disk-mapping* scheme (or *coordinate* scheme) used by the operating system when accessing data.

Organizing a disk into tracks and sectors is like drawing rule lines on a blank sheet of paper; the process provides a logical structure so that information can be easily written and read.

Because sector ID numbering depends on the disk's interleave ratio, the low-level formatting program always establishes disk interleave. Disk interleave dictates the number of times the disk platter must revolve for an entire track to be read. If a drive is set to an interleave ratio of 3:1 ("3 to 1"), that drive's disk must complete three revolutions in order for the disk head to read the data stored in one full track. A disk with a 1:1 interleave needs to rotate only once for an entire track to be read; such drives usually have the highest throughput. The optimal interleave setting depends on the disk drive, the drive controller, and the data-encoding method used. The important point to emphasize is that every drive-controller combination has an optimum interleave, and an incorrect interleave setting can dramatically reduce the disk's data transfer rate. Most low-level format programs automatically determine the system's optimum interleave.

When the disk drive originally undergoes low-level formatting at the factory, special hardware rigorously tests the disk's surface to ensure that every part of the disk is reliable. The process of checking the disk surface for defects is referred to as *defect mapping*. As defects are identified, they are noted on a label that is placed on the drive's side. If you ever need to perform another low-level format, your low-level formatting software should allow you to enter this list of defective tracks manually. Even though each low-level formatting program tests the disk for defects, you should mark the factory-identified faulty tracks rather then relying on your program to find the same problems. By entering the defective tracks manually, you ensure that data is never stored in these tracks.

As it organizes the disk into tracks and sectors, the low-level formatting program tests the integrity of the disk's surface. During these tests, the program writes data to the disk, and then reads the data back to ensure that the data was properly recorded. This test is similar to recording your voice on an audio tape, and then playing the tape to make sure that everything was recorded correctly. The disk test, however, is extremely rigorous; complex combinations of data may be written and tested as many as 32 times on each sector to make absolutely sure that the sector is reliable.

WARNING

Many low-level formatting programs will permanently destroy any data that is stored on a hard drive. If you want to perform a low-level format on a hard disk that contains data, you should consider using a special third-party program that does not destroy data. Regardless of the type of program you use, however, be sure to make a full backup of all the data on the disk before running the program.

Understanding Partitions

Prior to DOS V4, the operating system could only reference up to 32M of data from a hard disk. When hard disk capabilities were added to DOS, 32M seemed like a huge amount of data, but PC users quickly began to demand more storage capacity. The hardware manufacturers obliged by providing hard disks with much larger capacities. Still, however, a large hard disk is of no value if the operating system cannot access all of it! The operating system had to be modified, as well, so that it could access drives larger than 32M. Accommodating such system modifications turned out to be a monumental task, and engineers had to make significant changes to the operating system kernel.

NOTE

Prior to DOS V4, the FAT used a 16-bit number to store sector information. The largest number that can be specified in 16 bits is 65,535, and so earlier versions of DOS could only reference 65,535 sectors. Because each sector could hold 512 bytes, the maximum amount of data that could be referenced with a 16-bit FAT was 32M (that is, 512 bytes times 65,535 sectors).

Some third-party programs broke the 32M barrier by increasing the sector size from 512 bytes to 1,024, 2,048 or more. With a sector size of 2,048 bytes, the total storage capacity of a 16-bit FAT increased to 128M. This file allocation technique had a serious drawback, however, because it permitted small files to consume huge amounts of disk space. A 30-byte batch file occupying a single cluster, for example, might consume 8,000 bytes or more.

PC DOS V4 introduced a 32-bit FAT capable of addressing two million megabytes (a *terrabyte*). This storage scheme should keep users satisfied for a long time...maybe.

The personal computer already had the capability to subdivide a hard disk into different sections, so that different operating systems like DOS and UNIX each could "own" a section of the hard disk. This capability meant that one personal computer could be used to run multiple operating systems (though not simultaneously). Each of these sections on the hard disk is called a *logical drive*. Even though the computer may have only one physical disk drive, the system treats it like multiple smaller drives. The procedure for dividing a single disk into multiple logical drives is called *partitioning*.

Few computer users ever take advantage of this multi-system capability. Disk partitioning, however, provides a way to overcome the disk drive's inherent 32M data storage limit. Prior to DOS V4, the DOS program FDISK could create multiple DOS partitions, with each partition having a capacity of 32M or less. For example, you can divide a 70M hard disk into two 20M partitions and one 30M partition. After a disk is partitioned, the operating system regards each disk partition as a separate drive. In this example, the first 20M partition would be drive C, the second 20M partition would be drive D, and the 30M partition would be drive E. The partitioning process logically structures a disk so that the operating system(s) can access the disk as though it were actually several smaller disks. As a result, the operating system can access more than 32M of data on the hard disk. Remember, however, that each logical drive must be 32M or less.

With the introduction of MS-DOS V4 (and earlier versions of certain brand-specific DOS packages, such as COMPAQ DOS V3.31), the 32M limit was removed. The use of partitions solely to access large disks, therefore, became unnecessary. At first glance, you would expect any user to configure his system with a single large partition. After all, the obvious advantage of having a single large disk is that it can store all its files together in a single directory hierarchy. If you use a large-capacity hard disk with only one partition, however, you may experience one or more of the following problems:

- Some software packages were developed under the assumption that a single drive would never exceed 32M. Early versions of some programs that operate directly on the hard disk (such as data-recovery programs and back-up programs) will not function on partitions larger than 32M. Many of these programs, however, have now been updated to work with the new partition sizes.

- Because large partitions can store thousands of files, they often use complex directory structures. Many disk management programs operate at a significantly lower speed on a large partition, because more time is required to search these complicated structures.

- Larger disks tend to have a larger cluster size. (A cluster is the smallest unit of space referenced by the operating system; see Chapter 3 for more information on clusters.) This arrangement tends to increase data transfer speeds, but wastes space because every file, no matter how small, consumes at least one cluster. Note that 16M partitions and smaller also maintain large cluster sizes.

By setting up a number of smaller partitions, you can establish an effective means of structuring and organizing your data. For example, you might keep all your desktop publishing and word processing files on drive C, and your customer database on drive D. The separate logical drives enable you to manage the data separately; that is, you might backup drive C every day, and drive D once a week. You can often organize a single drive to achieve a similar degree of information segregation, but the directory structure tends to become more complex.

If you use DOS V4, you must decide whether to go with a single large partition or multiple smaller partitions. Assuming that your software will run on large disk partitions, there is no right or wrong answer. The choice is simply a matter of personal preference. If you do decide to segment a large drive into smaller partitions, avoid using partitions of 16M or less, because the disk's cluster size will jump from 2,048 bytes to 8,192 bytes.

Partitioning a Hard Disk

When the computer boots, the operating system reads the *partition table* from the first sector of the first track. The partition table contains a boot record (which provides essential data for booting the computer), data that shows how the disk is partitioned into logical drives, and a flag that designates the bootable drive (that is, the drive containing the operating system that should be loaded when the computer first boots). The partition that contains the boot copy of the operating system is called the *active partition*.

In DOS and OS/2, the external command FDISK manages the partition table. You can use FDISK to partition a new drive or to modify an existing drive's partitions. Third-party utilities also provide added flexibility for special situations. For example, you may use a third-party partitioning program to break the 32M limitation on a machine that uses a release of DOS prior to V4.

> **WARNING**
>
> You can use the FDISK command to delete an existing partition from the disk partition table. Be cautious when you use FDISK. If you delete an existing partition, all the files within that partition will be lost. Be sure that you have backed up or copied any data from the partition before you delete the partition from the disk. Do not experiment with FDISK unless your hard disk contains no data.

Using the FDISK Command

FDISK enables you to divide a hard disk into separate, isolated sections. DOS can use one partition while another operating system, such as XENIX, uses another partition. Non-DOS operating systems have their own versions of the FDISK command to manage their partitions.

The vast majority of hard disk users have only DOS partitions. With recent improvements to the operating system, many computers utilize only one partition, so that the entire disk is dedicated to DOS (or OS/2).

Even if you want your system to have only one DOS partition (so that the disk will operate as one large drive), you still must use FDISK to record this information in the partition table. Every hard disk must have a valid partition table. As with low-level formatting, however, the disk may already be partitioned when you receive it. If the computer boots straight out of the box, then the drive already has been partitioned, and you do not need to run FDISK.

> **NOTE**
>
> On some computers, such as the IBM Personal Computer AT, you must run the SETUP program before running the FDISK program. See Appendix B for more information on SETUP.

FDISK was overhauled with DOS V3.3; earlier versions of the command
operate in a slightly different fashion. Whichever version of DOS you use,
you first must boot the system from a floppy disk, and then execute the
FDISK command with no parameters, as follows:

FDISK

The FDISK program displays a series of menus that help you perform the
following disk-configuration operations:

- Create partitions

- Change the active partition

- Delete partitions

- Display current partition settings

- Review or modify the configuration of another physical drive in the
computer

Using FDISK with DOS V3.2 and Earlier

In versions of DOS predating V3.3, the FDISK command's primary
purpose is to enable you to install multiple operating systems on a single
drive, with a different operating system installed in each partition. If you
use an older version of FDISK to install a single DOS partition, then you
don't have much to do.

Figure 7.1 shows the FDISK command's main menu for DOS V3.2 and
earlier.

Select option 1 from the menu to install a new partition. If your disk already
has been configured with a DOS partition, FDISK displays the following
message:

```
DOS partition already exists
```

If this message appears, press Esc to return to the main menu. If the disk
has not already been configured with a DOS partition, the following
message appears:

```
Create DOS partition
Current Fixed Disk Drive: 1
Do you wish to use the entire fixed
disk for DOS (Y/N) ...........? [Y]
```

Simply press Enter to accept the default response of Y (for Yes). The system then updates the partition table. Reboot the system when FDISK is finished.

```
COMPAQ Personal Computer
Fixed Disk Management, Version 3.10
 (C)Copyright COMPAQ Computer Corporation 1983,84,85

* FDISK Menu *

Current  Fixed  Disk  Drive:  1
Available Fixed Disk Drives:  1

Choose one of these options:

     1.  Install MS-DOS Partition
     2.  Modify Active Partition
     3.  Remove MS-DOS Partition
     4.  List Partition Information


Enter your choice: [1]




Press ESC to return to MS-DOS
```

Fig. 7.1. The FDISK main menu for DOS V3.2 and earlier.

Using FDISK with DOS V3.3 and V4

In DOS V3.3 and later versions, FDISK is more sophisticated and permits the setup of multiple DOS partitions. That is, after defining a *primary* DOS partition, you can use these later versions of FDISK to define a single *extended* DOS partition, which you then can divide into one or more logical drives. Figure 7.2 illustrates the main FDISK menu that appears when you execute the program in DOS V3.3 and later versions.

```
                        MS-DOS Version 4.01
                      Fixed Disk Setup Program
                   (C)Copyright Microsoft Corp. 1983, 1988

                             FDISK Options

      Current fixed disk drive: 1

      Choose one of the following:

      1. Create DOS Partition or Logical DOS Drive
      2. Set active partition
      3. Delete DOS Partition or Logical DOS Drive
      4. Display partition information



      Enter choice: [1]




      Press Esc to exit FDISK
```

Fig. 7.2. The FDISK main menu for DOS V3.3 and V4.

If you are running FDISK on a system that has more than one physical drive, the menu offers a fifth option, as follows:

5. Select next fixed disk drive

Note that your system's menu options may be worded differently than those shown here, depending on the version of FDISK you are using.

If you select option 1, FDISK presents a prompt asking which type of DOS partition you want to create, as shown in figure 7.3.

If the disk already has an extended partition, this prompt provides a third option, as follows:

3. Create Logical DOS Drive(s) in the Extended DOS partition

You first must create a primary DOS partition, by selecting the first option from the menu shown in figure 7.3. If you want to subdivide your disk into a number of logical drives, you can create an extended partition and then assign logical drives in the extended partition.

```
Create DOS Partition

Current Fixed Disk Drive: 1



     1. Create Primary DOS partition
     2. Create Extended DOS partition




Enter choice: [1]




Press ESC to return to FDISK Options
```

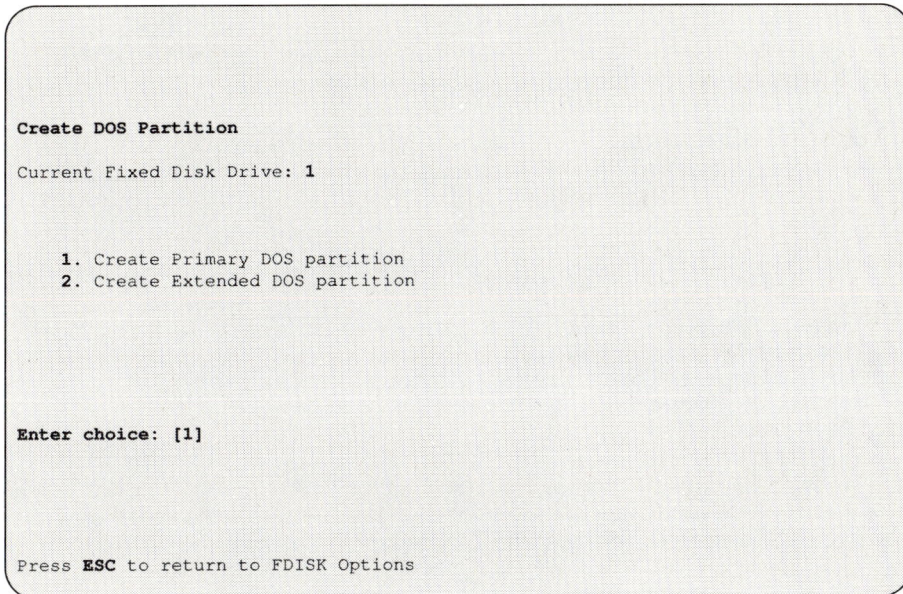

Fig. 7.3. *Creating a new DOS partition.*

NOTE   In the following examples, FDISK refers to disk capacity in megabytes. Some versions of FDISK use cylinders rather than megabytes. (Refer to Chapter 3 for more information on cylinders.) You can compute the relative sizes of the partitions by noting the total number of cylinders available on the disk. If an 80M hard disk has 1,024 cylinders, for example, a partition of 512 cylinders will be 40M.

Creating a Primary DOS Partition

To create a primary DOS partition, select option 1 from the Create menu (see fig. 7.3). FDISK then prompts you as follows:

```
Do you wish to use the maximum size
for a DOS partition and make the DOS
partition active (Y/N).........?  [Y]
```

If you want to use the entire hard disk for DOS in a single large drive, press Enter to accept the default Y response. (Note, however, that MS-DOS V3.3 will not permit you to create a primary partition that is larger than 32M.) FDISK updates the partition table, and the process is complete.

If you use DOS V3.3 on a drive that is larger than 32M, or if you want to create several partitions on a large drive, you should respond N to the preceding prompt. FDISK then presents a prompt similar to the following:

```
Total disk space is 300 Mbytes
(1 Mbyte = 1048576 bytes).

Maximum space available for partition
is 300 Mbytes (100%).
Enter partition size in Mbytes or percent
of disk space (%) to create a Primary
DOS partition........... [300]
```

The prompt displays the actual amount of space available on your hard disk. The partition's default size is the maximum available storage space on your hard disk. You need to advise FDISK how large you want the primary partition to be; specify the size in megabytes or as a percentage of available disk space. To set up a 30M primary partition, therefore, you can enter either 30 or 10% (in this example). The remaining space can then be used as an extended partition for adding further logical drives.

Creating an Extended DOS Partition

If you create a primary DOS partition that is less than the total disk capacity, you should then create an extended DOS partition. Select option 2 from the Create menu (see fig. 7.3), to create an extended partition. FDISK displays a prompt similar to the following:

```
Partition Status Type    Size in      Percentage
                         MBytes       of disk used
   C:1          PRI DOS               10
                           30

Total disk space is 300 Mbytes (1 Mbyte = 1048576
bytes).
Maximum space available for partition
is 270 Mbytes (90%).
Enter partition size in Mbytes or percent of disk
space
to create an Extended DOS partition....... [270]
```

The prompt displays the actual amount of space available for the extended partition on your hard disk. FDISK uses this amount as the default size for the partition. Unless you want to reserve some of the disk for a non-DOS partition, press Enter to select the total remaining space.

Creating Logical Drives in the Extended Partition

If you create an extended partition, you can divide it into logical drives by selecting option 3 from the menu. (Remember that this option appears on the menu only after an extended partition has been created.) Even if you want to use the entire extended partition as a single logical drive, you must select this option. When you select option 3, FDISK displays a prompt similar to the following:

```
Total partition space is 270 Mbytes
(1 Mbyte = 1048576 bytes).
Maximum space available for logical
drive is 270 Mbytes (100%).

Enter logical drive size............ [270]
```

If you want to assign all available space to a single drive, press Enter. Otherwise, you can further subdivide the extended partition by entering a smaller size (100, for example). FDISK continues prompting for information until all the extended partition space has been assigned to logical drives. In this example, if you respond to the prompt with 150 and then 120, FDISK creates a 150M drive named drive D, and a 120M drive named drive E, in addition to the 30M primary partition, drive C.

To review the partition settings, select option 4 from the main menu (see fig. 7.2).

Setting the Active Partition

You can establish an active partition only on a hard disk that is already partitioned with two or more operating systems. If you have created two partitions (with one partition containing DOS, and the other containing XENIX, for example), this option enables you to specify one of the partitions as active.

To designate an active partition, select the second option from the main
FDISK menu (see fig. 7.2). DOS responds with a prompt similar to the
following:

```
Partition Status Type    Size in     Percentage
                         MBytes      of disk used
    C:1      A    PRI DOS                  50
      2           non DOS    150           50
                             150

Total disk space is 300 megabytes.

Enter the number of the partition you
want to make active............... :[ 1]
```

In the **Status** column, an **A** indicates the currently active partition. To
make another partition the active partition, type the partition's number and
press Enter.

If DOS is the only operating system on your hard disk, you do not need to
select this option. In such a setup, only the primary DOS partition (that is,
the partition containing the DOS operating system files) can be the active
partition. If you attempt to activate an extended partition, the FDISK
program responds with the following message:

```
Partition selected (2) is not startable,
active partition not changed.
```

Changing Hard Disk Partition Settings

FDISK does not permit you to change the size of a partition once it has
been created. If you need to change the size of a partition, you must first
delete the partition(s) and then create a new partition of the appropriate size.

You can use the FDISK program to delete a primary partition, an extended
partition, or a logical drive from the extended partition. If you select the
Delete option from the FDISK main menu, the Delete DOS Partition
menu appears (see fig 7.4).

Select the menu's first option if you want to delete the primary DOS
partition. The system displays the current partition settings, and warns you
that data may be lost if you continue with the delete operation. If you press
Y (telling FDISK to proceed with the operation), FDISK deletes the
partition. If you press any other key, the program aborts the operation, and
returns to the Delete DOS Partitions menu.

```
Delete DOS Partition

Current Fixed Disk Drive: 1

Choose one of the following:

    1.   Delete Primary DOS partition
    2.   Delete Extended DOS partition
    3.   Delete logical DOS drive(s) in
         the Extended DOS Partition




Enter choice: [ ]




Press ESC to return to FDISK Options
```

Fig. 7.4. *The Delete DOS Partition menu.*

If you want to delete the extended partition, you first must delete the logical drives associated with it. To delete a logical drive from the hard disk, select the third option from the Delete DOS Partitions menu. The system displays a list of all currently configured logical drives. Select a logical drive from the list, and press Enter. As an added precaution (remember that you delete all the partition's files when you delete the partition itself), FDISK prompts you for the logical drive's volume label. You can delete the partition only if you supply the drive label. If you can't remember the label, quit the FDISK menu, and use the LABEL command to see the drive's label.

Having deleted the previously established partitions, you can create new partitions with new settings, following the steps outlined in the previous sections. You then can restore the files from your backup floppy disks, and start using the newly partitioned disk. The new logical drive sizes will be different from the old ones, and the backed-up files may not all fit on the new drives. If so, you will need to perform incremental file restores to the new target drives, reorganizing the directory structure in the process. See Chapter 13 for more information on data backups.

✓ OS/2

The OS/2 FDISK command operates in much the same way as the DOS FDISK command, with one other major feature. If you execute the OS/2 version of FDISK with the /MBR parameter, the operating system replaces the disk's *master boot record*. The master boot record contains the boot record and the partition table.

Some other operating systems (such as an auto-boot version of UNIX) may overwrite the master boot code with their own program. This program may not permit OS/2 to boot the system, even if the partitions are valid OS/2 partitions. To correct this condition, FDISK replaces only the master boot code (when it is run with the /MBR parameter).

Using Third-Party Hard Disk Configuration Utilities

Prior to the release of DOS V4, computer users were pretty much on their own when it came to "breaking down" the 32M barrier. Rather than using the FDISK program, many users turned to separate utility programs for help in partitioning their hard disks.

You also may need to use a third-party disk utility if you buy a hard disk separate from your computer. These programs enable you to install a nonstandard drive in a computer that normally does not support such a drive. Whenever you install a new hard disk in a computer, you must run the program SETUP to record the type of the hard disk in CMOS RAM. Because SETUP is provided by the computer's manufacturer, however, the program may not include the appropriate disk type in its menu of drive types. For example, the Compaq Deskpro 286 does not support a drive with 7 heads and 1,169 cylinders. The solution is to select a drive type with the same number of heads but fewer cylinders, and then use a special utility program to install a device drive. The program "tricks" the system into recognizing the additional drive cylinders. The utility software performs the trick by modifying CMOS RAM so that the computer recognizes the type of hard disk being installed. This step is similar to specifying the drive type in SETUP; unlike SETUP, however, the utility supports all types of drives.

✓ NOTE

The CMOS chip is a special RAM chip that is used to record the computer's SETUP information. This chip is powered by a small internal battery that has a life of between one and two years. When the battery expires, you will need to install a new one, or run SETUP every time you boot the system!

The introduction of DOS V4 has reduced the need for such third-party programs, but if you have a drive that is not recognized by SETUP, these utilities provide a good (and perhaps the only) solution. If your goal is to have a drive larger than 32M, you probably can satisfy your needs simply by upgrading to DOS V4.

Two popular third-party utility programs are Disk Manager (Ontrack Computer Systems, Inc.) and SpeedStor (Storage Dimensions, Inc.).

Using Disk Manager

Disk Manager is a hard disk utility program that often is "bundled" with Seagate and Miniscribe disk drives.

Disk Manager's primary program, called DM, can perform low-level formatting on the drive, and update the partition table. If you execute the program with no switches, DM works in automatic mode, guiding you through each stage of disk preparation. You also can run the program in manual mode, so that you can select the required operations from menus.

If you use Disk Manager to configure a hard disk, you first must modify the CMOS RAM configuration, so that the computer will recognize the type of hard disk being installed. This step is similar to specifying the drive type in SETUP; Disk Manager, however, supports all possible drive types.

Once you have updated CMOS, the drive is ready for low-level formatting. DM automatically checks the disk's surface, and identifies bad tracks (see fig. 7.5). You also can manually enter the numbers of any bad tracks that were identified during the manufacturer's disk test. You then select a drive interleave, and proceed with low-level formatting.

After low-level formatting, DM can build a partition table in much the same way as the DOS V4 FDISK program. Disk Manager supports as many as 16 partitions and 4 different operating systems (see fig. 7.6).

```
  HARD DISK MANAGEMENT PROGRAM  V4.02 - Drive 1, 1169 Cyls,  7 Hds, 17 Secs.

Cyl--Hd   Cyl--Hd   Cyl--Hd   Cyl--Hd   Cyl--Hd   Cyl--Hd   Cyl--Hd   Cyl--Hd
  57- 0   1012- 0   1069- 0    312- 1    738- 1    905- 1     21- 2    971- 2
1129- 4    965- 6




                       ─────── CURRENT DEFECT LIST ───────
INITIALIZATION MENU:              HELP AVAILABLE BY PRESSING F1.
(I)nitialize or (V)erify surface
(D)efect-list management, (R)eturn to main menu
Select an option (R): i
Is the above DEFECT-LIST accurate for this disk? (y/n):
```

Fig. 7.5. Disk Manager produces a list of defective tracks.

```
  HARD DISK MANAGEMENT PROGRAM  V4.02 - Drive 1, 1169 Cyls,  7 Hds, 17 Secs.

## START  END TYPE       BOOT NAME-VER   ## START  END TYPE      BOOT NAME-VER
 1     0  380 DOS          Y  IBM  3.3     9
 2   381  402 WRITE/READ   N  NOSYSTEM    10
 3   403  785 WRITE/READ   N  NOSYSTEM    11
 4   786 1168 WRITE/READ   N  NOSYSTEM    12
 5                                        13
 6                                        14
 7                                        15
 8                                        16
                     ─────── CURRENT PARTITION TABLE ───────
                          HELP AVAILABLE BY PRESSING F1.


Does the above PARTITION TABLE require modification? (y/n):
```

Fig. 7.6. Disk Manager can divide a hard disk into 16 partitions.

Using SpeedStor

SpeedStor is a multifunction disk utility that performs hard disk preparation and setup, disk diagnostics, and head parking.

SpeedStor's hard disk preparation capabilities include low-level formatting and disk partitioning, and you can instruct the program to perform these tasks in automatic or manual mode. In automatic mode, SpeedStor's INSTALL program executes whatever operations are required to configure the disk, and guides you through each step of disk preparation. You also can execute the utility's primary program, SSTOR, to prepare the disk manually.

The first stage of drive preparation is to identify the drive's manufacturer and model (see fig. 7.7). SSTOR includes an extensive list of manufacturers and models.

```
        SpeedStor(TM)  Disk Integration Software, version 6.0.3
        Copyright(C) 1985-1989 Storage Dimensions, Inc.  All rights reserved


         Use cursor keys to highlight the desired drive Model,
         and press <Enter> to accept the new drive type.
         IF you do not want to change the type, press ESC.

Drive      Manufacturer/Model     Cyls  Heads  Secs  Precomp  Lzone  TotalBytes
   1        <Standard Type 11>     925    7     17     128     924   56,357,888
                      M i n i S c r i b e   D r i v e   M o d e l s
        ModelName  Cylinders  Heads  Sectors  PreComp  LandingZone  TotalBytes

          3425        615        4      17       128        656     21,411,840
          3438        615        4      26       128        656     32,747,520
          3650        809        6      17       300        852     42,249,216
          3675        809        6      26       300        852     64,616,448
          3053       1024        5      17       512       1023     44,564,480
          3085       1170        7      17       512       1169     71,285,760
          3130E      1250        5      35      none       1249    112,000,000
          3180E      1250        7      35      none       1249    156,800,000
          6032       1024        3      17       512       1023     26,738,688
          6053       1024        5      17       512       1023     44,564,480
                      Home   PgDn  ↑  ↓  PgUp   End
```

Fig. 7.7. *Selecting a drive model in SSTOR.*

After selecting the appropriate drive type, you can proceed with low-level formatting. During this step, you should enter the manufacturer's defect map. You then can partition the drive, by following the menu shown in figure 7.8; SpeedStor supports up to 24 partitions (drives C through Z). The SpeedStor partition options can be used in place of the operating system commands FDISK and FORMAT. In addition to creating, deleting, and formatting DOS partitions, SpeedStor can manage partitions larger than 32M, and partitions spanning different physical drives.

```
          SpeedStor(TM)  Disk Integration Software, version 6.0.3
          Copyright(C) 1985-1989 Storage Dimensions, Inc.  All rights reserved
          ──────────────────────────────────────────────────────────────────
                           P A R T I T I O N    M A N A G E R
            NextDrive  AutoPart  Create  Status  Owner  Delete  Format  Quit

          Automatically create and format partition(s)

              Drive  Manufacturer/Model    Cyls Heads Sectors  TotalBytes   FreeBytes
                1     <Standard Type 11>    924    7     17     56,297,472   8,347,136
                                                        Cylinder
              No. Owner DOS Compatibility     Status    Start  End  Sectors     Bytes

               1   DOS  3.0 and later     BOOT (ACTIVE)    0   380   45,322   23,204,864
               2  ( 81) none              usable         786   144        0            0
               3  ( 81) none              usable         381   402    2,618    1,340,416
               4  ( 81) none              usable         403   785   45,577   23,335,424

                                          Free Block (1)  787  923   16,303    8,347,136
```

Fig. 7.8. SSTOR supports up to 24 partitions.

You can use SpeedStor's diagnostic options to locate system faults, to isolate problems with the hard disk or its controller, to find undetected surface defects, and to test the hard disk. During the hard disk testing, SpeedStor performs seek tests, read and write tests, as well as surface analysis.

Like Disk Manager, SpeedStor enables you to install nonstandard drives in any computer.

High-Level Formatting

After the hard disk has undergone low-level formatting and the partition table has been created, the drive is ready for final formatting. This stage is sometimes referred to as *high-level* or *logical* formatting, to distinguish it from low-level formatting. During high-level formatting, the disk's surface is readied to receive data. Whereas low-level formatting and partitioning are performed by a program devoted to such tasks, high-level formatting can be performed by the computer's operating system.

Each operating system has a unique method of addressing storage areas on the disk. DOS and OS/2, for example, logically organize the disk into a series of clusters, and then establish an addressing scheme that uses directories and a FAT. When the disk undergoes high-level formatting, the disk-filing scheme is established by creating a boot record, the FAT, and a root directory.

If you use DOS or OS/2, you can perform high-level formatting by invoking the operating system's FORMAT command. (See Chapter 3 for more details on the formatting process.)

⚠️ **WARNING** FORMAT is a powerful command that erases all files and data on a disk. Use FORMAT only if you fully understand its operation. FORMAT issues warning messages and prompts for verification before formatting a hard disk. Pay attention to the prompts and make sure that you intend to format the drive before permitting the operating system to continue with the FORMAT program. The FORMAT command is easy to use, but you first must be sure that you are formatting the correct disk. Use FORMAT with caution.

To initiate high-level formatting on the hard disk, boot the system with a bootable DOS disk in drive A. At the **A>** prompt, enter the following command:

FORMAT C:/S/V

The C: specifies the drive to be formatted, which in this case is drive C (the hard drive normally is named drive C). The /S switch indicates that you want to transfer the *system* files to the newly formatted drive. The /V switch tells the FORMAT program to prompt you for a *volume* label after the drive has been formatted. (A volume label is a name tag for the drive, and is not required. If you do not want to assign a volume label to the drive, omit the

/V switch.) The FORMAT command supports a number of other switches that are used primarily when formatting floppy disks; see Appendix A for a full description of the FORMAT command.

The system files, which are transferred to the hard disk when the /S switch is specified, include only COMMAND.COM and some special hidden files that are used internally by the operating system. These are the basic files needed to boot the computer. None of the other external operating system commands (such as XCOPY, TREE, and PRINT) are transferred during the FORMAT procedure. If you want to copy these files to the disk, you must do so after the disk has been formatted.

Remember that the FORMAT command is potentially destructive. For this reason, the program asks if you really want to format the hard disk (see fig. 7.9).

```
A>FORMAT C:/S/V
Enter current volume label for drive C: TECHNOJOCK

WARNING, ALL DATA ON NON-REMOVABLE DISK
DRIVE C: WILL BE LOST!
Proceed with Format (Y/N)?
```

Fig. 7.9. A FORMAT prompt verifies that you want to format a hard drive.

If you press Y in response to the verification prompt, the FORMAT program performs high-level formatting on the hard drive. The formatting process can take between 5 and 30 minutes, depending on the drive's speed and size.

If you include the /V switch in the FORMAT command, the operating system prompts you for a volume label after the drive has been formatted. Type a name up to 11 characters long, and press Enter. The label will appear in directory lists. If necessary, you can use the LABEL command to change the drive's volume label. Note that FORMAT prompts for the current volume label only if the drive already is formatted.

If you have created more than one logical drive (such as a drive D:, drive E:, and so on), you must format each drive separately. You do not need to transfer the system files to each of these drives; therefore, you can use the following command when formatting logical drives:

FORMAT D:/V

Again, you can omit the /V switch if you do not want to assign a volume label to the drive.

After you have formatted each drive, reboot the system without a diskette in drive A; the system should boot from the newly prepared hard disk. The hard disk is now ready to store and retrieve files.

Installing the Operating System

To complete the configuration process, you must transfer the operating system files to the hard disk.

If you use DOS V4 or OS/2, you can install the operating system manually, if you like. These two operating systems can install themselves automatically, however, as described at the end of this section. If you use an earlier version of DOS, you must install the operating system files manually. To do this, simply create a directory on the hard disk and copy the operating system files into the directory. For example, the following commands create a directory named DOS, and copy the files from drive A to the new directory:

```
C:
MD\DOS
COPY A:*.* C:\DOS
```

The operating system is supplied on more than one diskette. Insert each of the operating system diskettes in drive A and repeat the COPY command. The operating system files are now transferred to the hard disk, and you are ready to use the system. (The next chapter shows you how to create special start-up files that customize the computer to your preferences.)

DOS V4 and OS/2 automatically install themselves on the hard disk. All you have to do is boot the computer with the operating system Install disk in drive A. DOS V4 and OS/2 present a series of menus that enable you to customize the installation to suit your computer's configuration (see fig. 7.10).

```
                          Welcome

        Welcome to DOS 4.0 and the SELECT program.  SELECT
        will install DOS 4.0 on your fixed disk or diskette.
        If you install DOS 4.0 on a diskette, the number of
        blank diskettes you need depends on the type and
        capacity of your diskette drive:

            Drive Type (Capacity)       Number of Diskettes

            5.25-Inch Drive (360KB)     five  5.25 (360KB)
            5.25-Inch Drive (1.2MB)     five  5.25 (360KB)
            3.5-Inch Drive (720KB)      three 3.5  (720KB)
            3.5-Inch Drive (1.44MB)     three 3.5  (720KB)

        If you install DOS 4.0 onto a fixed disk, you need
        one blank diskette:

            5.25-Inch Drive             one   5.25 (360KB)
            3.5-Inch Drive              one   3.5  (1 or 2MB)

        Press Enter (◄┘) to continue or Esc to Cancel

  Enter    Esc=Cancel
```

Fig. 7.10. The opening screen of the DOS V4 automated installation program, SELECT.

UNIX distribution floppy disks usually have files saved in archived format. These are extracted during installation and loaded to the appropriate directories on the hard disk.

UNIX-based systems usually have a system administrator who sets up the hardware. Unless you are using a stand-alone UNIX system, you won't have too many installation issues to worry about. Unlike DOS, UNIX is so large that you must run it from the hard disk. A typical UNIX partition is at least 40M and, not uncommonly, 200M or more.

Installing a Second Hard Disk

If you install a second hard disk drive in your computer, you need to perform the same basic steps of low-level formatting, partitioning, and high-level formatting. To learn how to install a second hard drive, see *Upgrading and Repairing PCs*, published by Que Corporation.

When you run FDISK to partition a second hard disk, the program recognizes that your system has two hard drives installed, and permits you to partition both drives. Remember that the second drive's main impact is on the computer's drive *lettering* scheme. On a single-hard-disk system, the primary DOS partition is named drive C, the first drive in the extended partition is drive D, the second drive in the extended partition is drive E, and so forth. On a system with two hard drives, drive C is the primary partition of the first hard disk, drive D is the primary partition of the second hard disk, and additional drive letters then are assigned to the extended partition of the first drive, and finally to the extended partition of the second drive.

Suppose, for example, that your computer has two hard drives. The first disk is divided into three drives, and the second disk is divided into three drives. In this case, the operating system assigns drive letters as follows:

Drive C: Primary partition of disk 1

Drive D: Primary partition of disk 2

Drive E: First logical drive in the extended partition of disk 1

Drive F: Second logical drive in the extended partition of disk 1

Drive G: First logical drive in the extended partition of disk 2

Drive H: Second logical drive in the extended partition of disk 2

Summary

Before you can use your hard disk, it must undergo low-level formatting, receive a partition table, undergo high-level formatting, and receive the operating system files. These are the basic steps of hard disk configuration. One or more of these tasks may be performed by the disk's manufacturer or distributor.

In this chapter you learned the following key points about hard disk configuration:

- Low-level formatting tests the integrity of the hard disk's surface, and organizes the disk into tracks and sectors.

- Normally, the manufacturer or distributor performs low-level formatting on a new hard drive. If so, the user should not have to perform low-level formatting again, unless the disk must be reconfigured or a problem arises.

- The numbering scheme used on the sectors is known as disk interleave. Every system has an optimum interleave based on the speed of the hard disk, the disk controller, and the speed of the computer.

- A disk can be subdivided into partitions; each partition is treated like a separate drive.

- In DOS and OS/2, the FDISK program can be used to create and modify the hard disk's partition table.

- Before the introduction of DOS V4, hard drives were limited to a storage capacity of 32M. Special programs, however, can overcome this limit on disks used with earlier DOS versions.

- You can use special programs to configure and partition a new hard disk. These programs can even "trick" the computer into recognizing an incompatible hard drive.

- Once created, a disk partition's dimensions cannot be modified. To change a partition's dimensions, you must first delete the partition from the disk, and then create a new partition of different dimensions.

- The FORMAT command performs high-level formatting on the hard disk. The program also creates a boot record, a file allocation table, and a root directory.

■ All the commands for low-level formatting, partitioning, and high-level formatting are extremely powerful. Any of these commands can destroy files quickly. Use these commands with extreme caution on drives that already contain data.

Chapter 8 shows you how to create a practical directory hierarchy, and how to set up the AUTOEXEC.BAT and CONFIG.SYS files.

8

Organizing the Hard Disk

Once you have formatted and prepared your hard disk, you are ready to install programs and transfer files. In other words, you finally can use the hard disk in your day-to-day work. When the disk has just been initially prepared, it is largely empty or "clean." That is, the newly configured disk probably will contain only a root directory and perhaps a DOS directory for the operating system files.

Before you start creating other directories and loading files, you should think about the manner in which you will organize the hard disk. The disk's initial organization directly affects the computer's "friendliness." If you crowd too many subdirectories onto the disk, you may not be able to remember where all your programs and data files are located. On the other hand, if the disk is too loosely organized (with many unrelated files stored in too few directories), you run the risk of accidentally overwriting and deleting files. Further, files are just as difficult to find on an unstructured disk as they are on an overly structured disk.

Although a personal computer is highly adept at performing calculations, it is not intelligent; hard disk organization is your responsibility. Every hard disk user's needs are different, however, and there are no hard and fast formulas or rules that "lead" you to optimal organization. But by following a few generally accepted guidelines, you can build a soundly organized directory hierarchy. The first part of this chapter discusses these principles, and explains why a well-organized hard disk will help you in all aspects of computer use.

The latter part of this chapter discusses two special files, CONFIG.SYS and AUTOEXEC.BAT. These files enable you to customize the computer to meet your specific needs and requirements. By entering commands and instructions into these files, you can customize the system's configuration and arrange for certain commands to be invoked automatically when the computer boots. When these two files are properly configured, hard disk use becomes easier and more efficient.

Organizing the Directory Structure

The concepts used in hard disk organization are similar to the concepts used when organizing a library. Think of the disk as a library, and of each file as a book. Imagine a library where the books were randomly stacked in rows of shelves, and were not grouped by subject. You would have a real problem trying to find a specific book. The more books, the bigger the problem. Similarly, if all the hard disk's files were stored in the root directory, you would have chaos. This problem is even more dramatic when you consider that, unlike books, a file's name is restricted to a total of eleven characters, and there is a high probability that two files would have the same name.

A well-organized library usually is arranged by subject, with principal sections devoted to history, science fiction, geography, and so on. Each of the major subjects is divided into categories, which further classify books according to specific topics and subtopics. The geography section, for example, might feature separate categories of books devoted to each of the world's continents. As more books are devoted to a subject, the subject is further organized into subcategories; the section on Asian geography might be divided into categories on the Georgian plains, the Southeastern marsh lands, the Northern tundra, and many others. The library's organization, therefore, is determined by the subject matter of its books. As a result, the specific categories in an engineering library differ greatly from those in a children's library. The same principles, however, are adopted when organizing any library.

The same principles apply to a hard disk. The disk's organization should be a product of the number and types of files stored on the disk. The disk's directories and subdirectories are like the subjects and categories in a library.

On the flip side, your hard disk can be too organized. Some hard disk users go overboard creating complex directory structures. They spend as much time hunting for files as those users who keep all their files in one giant directory. Clearly, most of us do not need to develop a library management system for our meager collection of books at home. It is equally inappropriate to overstructure a hard disk. If you are organizing the hard disk of a network file server used by hundreds of people, you may need hundreds of directories. Most PC users, however, should strive for a simple and logical hard disk directory hierarchy.

If you fail to organize a hard disk well, many computer operations can be adversely affected. You may have difficulty finding files and programs, and you increase the risk of unintentionally overwriting valuable files. A poorly organized disk can cause the computer to function slowly. Finally, when your disk fills up (and it will), you may not be able to identify the files that should be removed.

On the other hand, you will enjoy the following benefits from a good hard disk directory structure:

- Data files and programs are easy to find.
- Less space is wasted on duplicate files.
- The chances are minimal of accidentally using the wrong file.
- Incremental data backups are simple.
- Disk housekeeping is easy.
- Other people can understand and use the system.

Because no two systems (or users) are the same, no hard and fast rules exist regarding directory organization. This does not mean, however, that you are completely on your own in designing a directory hierarchy; a few general guidelines can help you organize your hard disk efficiently. The following sections show you how to keep the root directory uncluttered, use different software installation methods, segregate program and data files, and use temporary directories.

Using a Hard Disk Template

To understand some of the principles of good hard disk management, consider the directory structure shown in figure 8.1. The sample directory "tree" includes the primary PC application software categories: a spreadsheet, a word processor, and a database. The disk also contains separate directories for the DOS operating system files, batch files, utilities, an operating environment, accessory programs, and miscellaneous data files. You can use this directory format as a template for your own hard disk's directory structure.

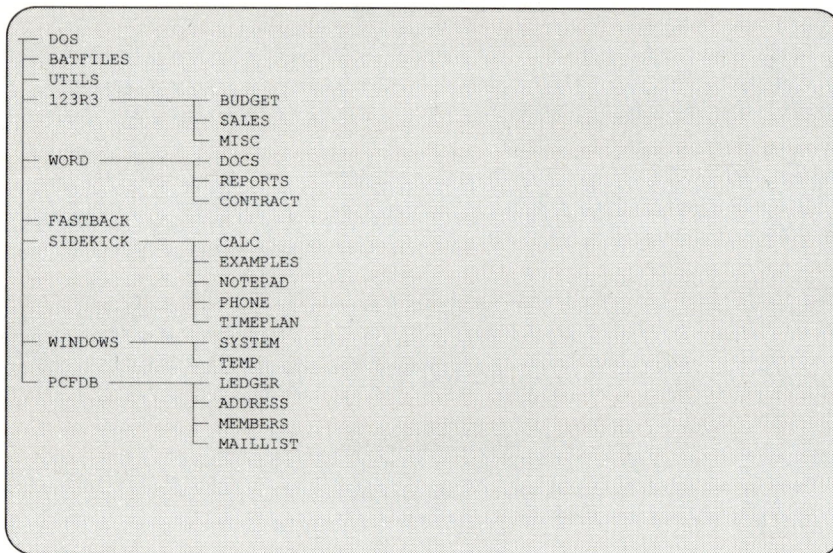

```
┬ DOS
├ BATFILES
├ UTILS
├ 123R3 ─────────┬ BUDGET
│                ├ SALES
│                └ MISC
├ WORD ──────────┬ DOCS
│                ├ REPORTS
│                └ CONTRACT
├ FASTBACK
├ SIDEKICK ──────┬ CALC
│                ├ EXAMPLES
│                ├ NOTEPAD
│                ├ PHONE
│                └ TIMEPLAN
├ WINDOWS ───────┬ SYSTEM
│                └ TEMP
└ PCFDB ─────────┬ LEDGER
                 ├ ADDRESS
                 ├ MEMBERS
                 └ MAILLIST
```

Fig. 8.1. A sample hard disk directory structure.

Chapter 5 introduced the concept of hierarchical directories and explained how you can use directories to segregate and categorize files on the hard disk. You may recall that the root directory is the parent of all other directories on the hard disk and is created when the disk is formatted. You can store files in the root directory, and create other directories within the root directory. Each of these directories can in turn spawn other subordinate directories. A directory that branches from another directory is often called a *subdirectory*; the directory from which it extends is referred to as the *parent directory*. On a hard disk, you have the potential to "nest" subdirectories several levels deep. *Level 1 directories* extend from the root directory, *level 2 directories* extend from level 1 directories, and so on. The directories in the template (see fig. 8.1) only extend to level 2.

As a rule of thumb, you should set up one major directory for each large software program on your system. Suppose, for example, that you are developing a computer system for engineering applications. You may set up a directory for a spreadsheet program, another for a CAD program, a third for a word processing program, and so on.

As the template illustrates, each of the major applications directories should include a series of subdirectories for storing data files. As well as separate directories for the major applications, most hard disks should be organized with one directory for the operating system, and another one for small utility programs (such as the programs described in Chapter 11).

The following sections discuss the principles that were used to develop the directory template. You can use this template together with the discussions that follow to help you plan your own hard disk directory structure.

Keeping the Root Directory Clean

The root directory includes system files (COMMAND.COM and some hidden files) that are used whenever the computer is booted, as well as the CONFIG.SYS and AUTOEXEC.BAT files. A well-organized hard disk has only these special files in the root directory. The root directory's primary purpose is to serve as a starting point from which new directories and subdirectories can be created.

Unfortunately, many computer users treat the root directory like the "General" or "Misc." drawer in a filing cabinet. That is, they store in the root directory all the miscellaneous files that really should be categorized and placed elsewhere in the system. Don't let yourself develop such a habit. Eventually, you may forget the purpose of such files, and won't know which ones are essential or can be deleted. The root directory should contain only the files that the operating system expects to find there.

Inexperienced users commonly load all the DOS files into the root directory, but this is a mistake. Place the external commands, device drivers, and other files that are provided on the DOS disks into a special directory, named DOS.

Although the following sections advise you to create various directories and subdirectories for specific purposes, you should be careful not to take this practice to extremes. Some novice hard disk users get "directory fever," and create dozens of directories and subdirectories, almost at random. Try to avoid having too many directories branching from the root directory (some experienced users set the limit at 15 to 20). Similarly, you should not nest directories more than 3 or 4 levels deep.

Installing New Software

Whenever you buy new software, you probably will want to load it onto the hard disk. To facilitate this process, most new programs include an installation or setup program that automatically transfers the files from the original floppy disks to the hard disk.

Before you copy any software program onto the hard disk, read the documentation and refer to the installation instructions. Many programs will not operate if they are simply copied to the hard disk. The installation program might perform configuration tasks, in addition to copying the software files.

Understanding Install Programs

Many popular software packages include a program that automatically installs the software on a hard disk. These install programs usually perform one or more of the following tasks:

- Create one or more directories on the hard disk and copy program files into these directories.

- Configure the software to work with your computer.

- Modify the operating system's AUTOEXEC.BAT and CONFIG.SYS files to add commands required by the new software.

- Provide you with new information that is not included in the product's documentation.

- Provide a brief overview of the software's use.

Always follow the install program's instructions carefully. As the program runs, it probably will prompt you for information about your computer and peripherals. If you are not sure how to answer any of the questions, accept the default answer provided by the program. Configuration options usually can be adjusted after the software has been installed.

Loading Programs Manually

Some software packages do not feature such automatic installation programs. If you need to load a software package that does not have an install program, carefully read the installation instructions in the product's documentation.

Normally, you must complete two tasks when manually loading new software:

- Create a new directory for the program.

- Copy the software from the original floppy disks to the newly created directory on the hard disk.

Just copy the program files from the floppy disk to the hard disk, as you would copy files from any diskette. The documentation may include instructions to help you modify your system's CONFIG.SYS and AUTOEXEC.BAT files. (These files are explained in detail later in this chapter.) If so, edit the files as instructed, and reboot the system.

After installing the software, you may want to perform two more chores. First, you might create one or more data directories beneath the main program directory. These subdirectories can store data files used with the program. Second, if you use a menu system for calling up your applications programs, you probably will want to add the new program to the menu.

Isolating Program Files

When you load a large software program onto the hard disk—either manually or via an install program—you should make sure that the program resides in its own unique directory. That is, the directory should be devoted to storing that program's files only.

Remember that many different programs use files with similar names. Therefore, by storing each program in its own directory, you avoid the risk of overwriting a file from one program with a file of the same name that belongs to a different program. Further, if you keep each application in its own directory, you can more easily remove the program from the disk when you need to free up disk space.

You should not, however, create a new directory for every small utility and accessory program that you load onto the hard disk. Keep a separate directory, named UTILS, especially for these utilities. If a program consists of only a few files, it is a good candidate for the UTILS directory.

Remember: Before you copy any program into the UTILS directory, make sure that the directory does not already contain any files with the same name as the new program's files.

Just as you should isolate large programs from each other on the disk, you also should avoid placing program files and data files in the same directory.

By keeping data and programs in separate directories, you simplify the process of finding and making backup copies of data files. A good practice is to store a particular application's data files in subdirectories beneath the main program directory.

In the sample directory structure (see fig. 8.1), the level 2 directories BUDGET, SALES, and MISC have been created to store 1-2-3 worksheet files. Similarly, the level 2 directories DOCS, REPORTS, and CONTRACT are used to store Microsoft Word documents.

Using a KEEP Directory

Nearly every data file eventually outlives its usefulness, but you may not always be sure that you want to delete such a file from the disk. You can create a directory named KEEP (or something similar) to store these files. If a file is of questionable future use, but you do not want to decide its fate right away, copy the file to the KEEP directory and delete the original file from the current data directory.

Be careful, however, or this catch-all directory will quickly grow out of control. When disk space is short, or when KEEP grows beyond 360K, you should review the directory's contents and decide which files can be deleted. If you need to make room on the hard disk, but still are not sure that you want to delete the files permanently, simply copy the files from KEEP to a floppy disk. Then you can safely erase the files from the hard disk. It's just like putting old clothes in the attic!

Using a TEMP Directory

A temporary directory can hold files that you are readying for final disposition. After reading this chapter, for example, you might decide to reorganize your hard disk directory structure. You can use a TEMP directory to store files while you are splitting up groups of files for assignment to new directories. In other words, a TEMP directory can serve as a file clearinghouse.

If your computer has only one floppy disk drive, you have experienced the inconvenience of trying to use the machine to copy one floppy disk's contents to another floppy disk. Even if you use the DISKCOPY command, you must frequently swap the source and target disks to transfer a great deal of data through RAM. The process is especially frustrating if you must make multiple copies of an original floppy disk. You can make such copies quickly and easily, however, with the help of a TEMP directory. Simply copy the source diskette's files to the *empty* TEMP directory. You then can copy the files from the TEMP directory to one or more destination diskettes. This process reduces disk swapping, and you can make copies faster thanks to the hard disk's extra speed. When the duplication is done, you can erase the files from TEMP.

(If you must make multiple copies of a floppy disk, you can simplify the process even further by using a RAM disk. See Chapter 10 for more information on RAM disks.)

Building the CONFIG.SYS File

Because your computer's hardware and operating system are flexible, you can customize many of the computer's characteristics to meet your specific needs. In the early days of personal computers, users could modify a system's settings only by opening up the unit, and changing jumpers and switches on the computer circuitry. Fortunately, many operating characteristics are now software-controlled and can be modified through configuration commands, rather than hardware adjustments.

Many of these configuration commands—called *directives*—must be stored in the special configuration file CONFIG.SYS. When you boot the computer, the operating system searches the root directory of the start-up drive (usually drive C) for the CONFIG.SYS file. The operating system then reads this file and configures the computer according to the instructions in the file. The CONFIG.SYS file, for example, tells the system whether memory above 640K should be configured as expanded or extended memory.

Most of the configuration file's commands control the computer's characteristics for the entire session. In other words, you cannot change the settings midway through a session. If you want to change the system's configuration, you must modify the commands in the CONFIG.SYS file and reboot the computer. The operating system then completely resets, and adopts the commands in the revised CONFIG.SYS file.

The CONFIG.SYS file is especially important to hard disk users. Many of the file's commands directly affect hard disk performance and file management.

Certain CONFIG.SYS commands are provided with the operating system files. The FILES command, for example, controls the number of files that can be open at one time, whereas the BUFFERS command determines the amount of memory that can be dedicated to improving the speed of file reading. The LASTDRIVE command dictates the highest drive letter that the computer recognizes. Later in this section, these configuration commands are discussed in detail.

You also can use CONFIG.SYS to install commercial *device drivers*, which are special programs that enable the operating system to operate a nonstandard device. Many of these devices directly affect the computer's speed and file storage capabilities. Such device drivers can control Bernoulli and tape drives, for example, and "software" devices such as disk caches and RAM disks. You can install these device drivers by placing a DEVICE command in the CONFIG.SYS file. Chapter 10 introduces several such devices.

Your system may not currently have a CONFIG.SYS file. To find out, enter the following command at the DOS prompt:

TYPE \CONFIG.SYS

The CONFIG.SYS file contains directives that alter some of the operating system's functions. If the TYPE command does display the contents of a CONFIG.SYS file, two settings may appear as part of the file:

```
FILES   = 20
BUFFERS = 15
```

The CONFIG.SYS file is a plain text (or ASCII) file. If you do not have one in the start-up drive's root directory, you can create a CONFIG.SYS file by using EDLIN or any other text editor. Table 8.1 lists the directives you can use in your CONFIG.SYS file and describes the operating system function affected by each directive.

Some of the directives (such as COUNTRY) are not related to hard disk management. The following sections examine commands that directly affect hard disk operations, including BREAK, BUFFERS, DEVICE, FILES, LASTDRIVE, and SHELL. For more information on all CONFIG.SYS directives, see *Using DOS*, published by Que Corporation.

Table 8.1
CONFIG.SYS Directives

Directive	Action
BREAK	Determines when the operating system recognizes the Ctrl-Break sequence
BUFFERS	Sets the number of file buffers used by the operating system when accessing files
COUNTRY	Sets country-dependent information
DEVICE	Permits different devices to be used with the system
FCBS	Controls DOS's reactions to a program's use of DOS V1 file handling
FILES	Sets the number of files that can be active at one time
INSTALL	Installs specific memory-resident programs (DOS V4 and later versions only)
LASTDRIVE	Specifies the highest allowable disk drive letter
REM	Enables the user to insert remarks in the CONFIG.SYS file, which DOS ignores when the computer is booted (DOS V4 and later versions only)
SHELL	Tells the operating system which command processor to use and where that processor is located
STACKS	Sets the number of stacks used by the operating system
SWITCHES	Disables extended keyboard functions (DOS V4 and later versions only)

Using the BREAK Directive

When you enter a command by mistake, you usually want to interrupt the command and stop it from executing. Suppose, for example, that you issue a DEL command in the wrong directory. You doubtlessly should try to stop the command before too much damage is done. The best safeguard, of course, is to be cautious with potentially destructive commands, and make sure that the command is accurate before you press the Enter key. But for those times when you do make a mistake, the operating system offers a means of interrupting or *breaking out* of a command. The special key combinations Ctrl-Break and Ctrl-C (both key sequences have identical purpose) can be used to stop a command from continuing. They are helpful (but not foolproof) "panic buttons" that you can use to stop commands in mid-execution. The operating system does not respond instantaneously to Ctrl-Break or Ctrl-C, because the operating system only looks for these commands at intervals. If the system were always checking for Ctrl-Break, the computer's operation would be considerably slower. The CONFIG.SYS directive BREAK tells the operating system when to check for the Ctrl-Break key sequence. Note that the BREAK directive does not enable or disable your ability to use Ctrl-Break to abort an operation. Rather, the directive merely influences how often the keys are checked.

You can use either of the following settings for BREAK in the CONFIG.SYS file:

BREAK = ON
BREAK = OFF

The default setting is **BREAK = OFF**.

If you set BREAK on, the operating system checks to see whether you have pressed Ctrl-Break whenever a program asks the operating system to perform an operation. If BREAK is off, the operating system checks for the Ctrl-Break sequence only when working with video display, keyboard, printer, or communications ports.

If you use a program that accesses the disk a great deal, but uses the keyboard or screen only minimally, you may want to set BREAK on. This setting increases your chances of terminating an unwanted or destructive operation in a timely fashion.

Some programs can disable the Ctrl-Break function, preventing you from typing this sequence to exit the program. Such programs do not permit you to use Ctrl-Break, no matter how the BREAK directive is configured in your CONFIG.SYS file.

As well as including the BREAK directive in the CONFIG.SYS file, you can execute a BREAK command at any time during a session. In other words, you have two different ways of controlling the intervals at which the operating system checks for the Ctrl-Break sequence. Both techniques yield precisely the same result. If you enter the BREAK command without any parameters at the operating system prompt, the system displays the ACTIVE break setting on-screen. Alternatively, you can pass a parameter to control the BREAK setting, by typing either BREAK ON or BREAK OFF. Note that the equal sign (=), which is required in the CONFIG.SYS file, is not required when the command is typed at the operating system prompt. If you set BREAK in the CONFIG.SYS file, you can overwrite the setting during the session by using the BREAK command. You can choose the method you prefer to set the BREAK status. Most users place the command in the CONFIG.SYS file.

Setting BUFFERS

The BUFFERS directive affects your hard disk's operating speed, by telling the operating system how many disk buffers to use. A disk buffer is an area of RAM in which the operating system can store data temporarily. When the operating system reads a required block of data from the disk, the system also can read "extra" data into the buffer portion of RAM. Then, if the operating system needs data that already is loaded into a buffer, the system can use the "buffered" data rather than going back to the disk. Because the operating system can access RAM much more quickly than it can access a disk, a large disk buffer can significantly improve the system's operating speed.

(If you use DOS V4 or a later version, you should note that your system's BUFFERS directive has been significantly enhanced. These changes are discussed later in this chapter.)

A single buffer contains about 512 bytes (plus 16 bytes for overhead). The BUFFERS directive dictates the number of disk buffers your computer can use. The BUFFERS directive takes the following basic syntax:

    BUFFERS = *value*

In this generic syntax, *value* represents the number of buffers to be specified to the operating system. Therefore, if you want to tell the operating system to set aside 20 disk buffers in RAM, type the following directive into the CONFIG.SYS file:

    BUFFERS = 20

If you use a version of DOS prior to V4, you can specify any number of buffers, from 1 to 99. If your system's CONFIG.SYS file does not contain a BUFFERS directive, DOS uses a default number of buffers. The default BUFFERS value depends on the type of disk you have, the amount of memory the computer has, and the operating system version you use. Table 8.2 lists the default configurations for the BUFFERS directive.

Table 8.2
Default Number of Disk Buffers

DOS Version	Number of Buffers	Hardware
DOS V3.3 and earlier	2	No hard disk
	3	Hard disk
DOS V3.3 and later	2	360K floppy disk drive
	3	Other floppy or hard drives
	5	More than 128K of RAM
	10	More than 256K of RAM
	15	More than 512K of RAM

As a rule of thumb, the more buffers the system can access, the better the disk's performance. Remember, however, that buffers eat up valuable RAM. Two buffers, for example, use approximately 1K of memory.

You should specify a BUFFERS value according to the programs you use and the amount of memory the computer has. If you do not use the computer for accounting or database work, 10 to 20 buffers should be plenty. If the computer must perform a great deal of accounting or database work, you probably need to specify from 20 to 40 buffers. Your system's performance may suffer, however, if you specify more than 40 (unless you use DOS V4), because the operating system must spend too much time managing the buffers.

NOTE Disk caches have pushed aside the BUFFERS directive as a way to increase disk performance. A disk cache is like a large and intelligent disk buffer designed specifically to reduce direct disk access. Chapter 10 discusses disk caches in detail. You can purchase a disk cache program from the manufacturer of your hardware or operating system, or from a third-party vendor. To conserve memory, most disk cache manufacturers advise that three to five buffers be specified when a disk cache is being used.

If you do not have a disk cache, then you can use the BUFFERS directive to improve performance.

Using BUFFERS with DOS V4 and Later Versions

With the introduction of DOS V4, important new options were added to the BUFFERS directive. If you use DOS V4 or a later version, and if your computer system utilizes expanded memory, you can set as many as 10,000 buffers. Users of DOS V4 or later also can take advantage of a special buffer, which increases disk efficiency even further.

DOS V4 introduced support for expanded memory, and the BUFFERS directive plays an important role in this support. If you add the /X switch to the BUFFERS directive in your CONFIG.SYS file, the operating system stores buffered data in expanded memory. You must, of course, have an expanded memory driver to use this facility.

The operating system uses *look-ahead* buffers to store data read from the sectors that are directly ahead of the sector requested by the operating system during a disk read. A single look-ahead buffer uses 512 bytes of memory; you can specify as many as 8 look-ahead in the BUFFERS directive. Suppose, for example, that you specify 5 look-ahead buffers. Afterward, every time DOS reads a sector from the disk, it also reads the five following sectors, storing the additional data in the look-ahead buffers. This disk access method is fast and efficient because the disk's read/write head is positioned directly on the first look-ahead sector. This improves performance because, the next item required from the disk often already is loaded in the look-ahead buffers.

The DOS V4 BUFFERS directive, with parameters for expanded memory and look-ahead buffers, takes the following syntax:

BUFFERS = *buffers, look-ahead_buffers* /X

Suppose, therefore, that you specify the following BUFFERS directive in your system's CONFIG.SYS file:

BUFFERS = 100, 8 /X

This directive tells the operating system to set aside 100 standard buffers and 8 look-ahead buffers, using expanded memory. The default is one look-ahead buffer; to gain a real performance improvement, however, you should initially specify at least eight look-ahead buffers.

If the system does not have enough expanded memory to accommodate this, the entire BUFFERS directive is ignored and the operating system uses the default settings in conventional memory. You can use the MEM command to ascertain your computer's memory configuration.

Because DOS V4 and later versions support buffers in expanded memory, you might be thinking of setting hundreds of buffers to gain full advantage of this memory. Realistically, however, the amount of improvement diminishes as the number of expanded memory buffers grows beyond 100. A better way to enhance the disk's operating speed is by using a disk cache. If you do use a disk cache, you should reduce the BUFFERS setting to 10 or less; large BUFFERS settings are inefficient when you use a cache. Disk caches are discussed in Chapter 10.

Installing Device Drivers with DEVICE

Device drivers are special software additions and extensions to the operating system's basic input/output system. The operating system includes a wealth of device drivers that can help you make better use of your computer hardware. Some add-on hardware components (such as a mouse or a tape drive) come with device-driver files that enable the hardware to function with your system. To inform the operating system which device drivers you want to use, include one or more DEVICE directives in the CONFIG.SYS file. The DEVICE directive takes the following syntax:

DEVICE = *d:path\filename.ext* /*switches*

In this generic syntax, *d:path* is an optional drive and directory that contains the device driver file. You must replace *filename.ext* with the driver file's name (device driver files normally use the extension SYS). Replace the /*switches* parameter with any special parameters required by the device driver.

You can load as many device drivers as you need, but you must use a separate line in the CONFIG.SYS file for each device directive. As each device driver is loaded, the operating system extends its control to that device. Table 8.3 lists the device drivers that are included with the operating system.

Table 8.3
Operating System Device Drivers

File Name	Purpose
ANSI.SYS	Customizes keyboard and screen operation
DISPLAY.SYS	Supports code-page switching
DRIVER.SYS	Supports external floppy drives
PRINTER.SYS	Provides code-page support for the printer ports
RAMDRIVE.SYS	Creates a RAM disk drive
SMARTDRV.SYS	Provides disk caching capabilities

NOTE

The actual device drivers vary from one operating system version to another. Further, the hardware manufacturer may provide device drivers that enable you to use a particular component with your system (such drivers may be named VDISK.SYS, IBMCACHE.SYS, CEMM.EXE, and so on).

The following listing is an extract from a CONFIG.SYS file that includes six DRIVER directives:

```
DEVICE=C:\U\RCD\RCD.SYS /F
DEVICE=C:\DOS\MSMOUSE.SYS
DEVICE=C:\DOS\CACHE.EXE 2048 ON /EXT
DEVICE=C:\DOS\VDISK.SYS 2048 256 512 /E
DEVICE=C:\DOS\CEMM.EXE 4096 ON
DEVICE=C:\DOS\ANSI.SYS
```

The number of DEVICE directives you use depends on the equipment you have installed. Chapter 10 discusses device drivers that enhance computer performance.

WARNING

Some device drivers are not installable. That is, they are used by the operating system, and should not be added to the CONFIG.SYS file with a DEVICE directive. The drivers COUNTRY.SYS and KEYBOARD.SYS are noninstallable device drivers; you must use other commands (such as COUNTRY) to instruct the operating system to use these drivers. If you accidentally add a noninstallable device driver to the CONFIG.SYS file, the system will not boot. To correct this problem, you must boot the computer from a floppy disk and remove the offending driver from the CONFIG.SYS file.

Setting FILES

Many programs must access more than one file at a time. A spreadsheet program may open a configuration file, two worksheet files, and a printer file. To gain access to a file, the applications program tells the operating system that it needs a file. The operating system responds by assigning a *file handle* (a two-byte identifier) to the file. Thereafter, the program uses the file handle to refer to the physical file.

The operating system can accommodate a specified number of file handles at any one time. You can modify this number by using the FILES directive in CONFIG.SYS. The FILES directive takes the following syntax:

>   **FILES** = *value*

value represents the maximum number of file handles that can be open at one time. The minimum (and default) value is 8 files; the maximum value is 255. If you specify a value less than 8, or if you omit the directive, the operating system automatically uses the default value of 8 files. Each additional file handle increases memory usage by 39 bytes.

The name FILES is somewhat misleading, because both files and devices use file handles. Standard devices, such as the display, keyboard, or printer, for example, automatically consume one file handle each. In fact, the operating system allows 5 handles for standard devices, leaving only 3 handles for your program, if you use the default value of 8. As a rule of thumb, you should specify at least 10 files in the FILES directive; increase the value to 20 or more for file-intensive applications. Programs that require a large number of file handles usually state their requirements in the installation instructions. The following directive should allow sufficient file handles for most popular programs:

FILES = 20

Using LASTDRIVE

The LASTDRIVE directive tells the operating system how many disk drives your system is using. The LASTDRIVE command takes the following syntax:

LASTDRIVE = x

In this generic syntax, x represents an alphabetical character signifying the last drive on the system. For this value, you can use any of the letters A through Z, in either uppercase or lowercase. If you want to specify the letter G as the last drive letter on your system, for example, type the following directive into the CONFIG.SYS file:

LASTDRIVE = G

If you do not use a LASTDRIVE directive in the CONFIG.SYS file, the operating system uses a default setting. The minimum default value is drive E. If you have one or more partitioned hard disks, the operating system automatically sets the LASTDRIVE default to the last logical drive. If your computer has a single hard disk divided into 4 partitions, for example, the LASTDRIVE default is drive F (because the partitions are assigned the drive letters C, D, E, and F). If you specify a letter that is less than the number of actual drives (including partitions) installed on your system, the operating system ignores the specification, and uses the default.

You should use the LASTDRIVE directive if you want to create multiple RAM disks. Suppose that you have a system with two floppy drives (drives A and B) and a hard drive (drive C). By default, you only have the capacity for two RAM disks, named drives D and E. The operating system will not recognize any references to drives F or later. To create a third RAM drive, issue the following directive:

LASTDRIVE = F

You might also use LASTDRIVE to reserve some drives before connecting to a network.

Using the SHELL Directive

The SHELL directive's original purpose was to enable programmers to replace the command processor, COMMAND.COM, with other command processors. The directive has since evolved, however, and now serves two other purposes. You can use this directive to place the command processor file in any directory, not just the root. You also can use SHELL to expand the size of the environment. See Chapter 5 for a discussion of the operating system environment.

> ⊠
> **WARNING**
>
> Improper use of the SHELL directive can lock the system. Make sure that you understand its use before you add a SHELL directive to the CONFIG.SYS file. If you can't boot the system after entering a bad SHELL command, boot the computer from a floppy disk, and correct the problem.

The SHELL directive takes the following syntax:

> **SHELL** = *d:path***filename.***ext d:\\path* **/P** /E:*size*

In this generic syntax, *d:path* is the name of the disk drive and directory where the command processor currently is located.

Next, **filename.***ext* is the name of the command processor. This file name is nearly always COMMAND.COM; if no extension is specified, the operating system automatically appends the extension COM to the specified root name.

> ✓
> **NOTE**
>
> DOS V4 enables you to specify an optional /MSG switch, which instructs the operation system to load all the operating system messages into RAM. This switch improves performance to a degree, while requiring only about 1K of RAM.

The second *d:\path* parameter is the disk drive and path name to the command processor. The operating system uses this to place the COMSPEC entry in the environment. This path should correspond with the *d:path* that was specified in the first parameter. Technically this second path specification is optional, but you should always include it in the command.

The **/P** (*permanent*) switch instructs the operating system to load and keep resident a copy of the command processor. Without the /P switch, the system loads the command processor, executes the AUTOEXEC.BAT file and then stops. Unless you are performing some very specialized operation, you should always specify the /P switch.

The */E:size* switch is optional. This switch sets the amount of memory used by the environment. The */E:size* switch is available only with DOS V3.1 and later.

The SHELL command is most commonly used to increase the environment space. If the operating system ever displays the `Out of environment space` message, use the SHELL directive with the */E:size* option to expand the environment, and then reboot the system. Normally, the *size* option is specified in bytes. If you specify a size that is not evenly divisible by 16, the operating system adjusts to the next higher multiple of 16. The default environment size is 160 bytes, but the size can be increased up to 32,767 bytes. You normally should not need to increase the environment's size to more than 800 bytes.

A typical SHELL directive might appear as follows:

SHELL = C:\COMMAND.COM C:\ /P /E:800

✓
NOTE

If you use DOS V3.1, you must specify environment size in 16-byte *paragraphs*, or blocks. In DOS V3.1, the environment size starts at 128 bytes. You can use the SHELL directive to change the environment's size from 11 (that is, 11 times 16, or 176 bytes) to 62 (62 times 16, or 992 bytes). If you use a number less than 11 or greater than 62, the operating system displays an error message and ignores the /E switch.

Setting up a CONFIG.SYS File

You can use a text editor to create or modify your CONFIG.SYS file. Remember that you must reboot the computer, so that the changes to the file become operative.

A typical CONFIG.SYS file's contents might look like the following:

```
BUFFERS = 10
FILES = 20
DEVICE=C:\DOS\MSMOUSE.SYS
DEVICE=C:\DOS\ANSI.SYS
SHELL = C:\COMMAND.COM C:\ /P /E:800
```

NOTE

If you use DOS V4, you can place three additional commands in your CONFIG.SYS file. The REM directive enables you to place notes within the file, in the same way you can use REM in batch files. You can use the SWITCHES = /K directive to turn off Enhanced Keyboard functions. This may resolve problems caused by the inability of some programs to access enhanced keyboards. Use the INSTALL directive to install certain programs that remain in memory. In versions of DOS before V4, you had to load these programs from the DOS prompt or in a batch file. The INSTALL command can save thousands of kilobytes of memory, compared with the old installation process. You can use FASTOPEN.EXE, KEYB.COM, NLSFUNC.EXE and SHARE.EXE with the INSTALL directive. For example, you can load SHARE.EXE by typing **INSTALL = C:\DOS\SHARE.EXE**. You also may be able to install other third-party memory-resident programs with the INSTALL directive.

OS/2

OS/2 is a far more complex and flexible operating system than DOS. As a result, you can use many more options with CONFIG.SYS. A typical CONFIG.SYS file in OS/2 is between 40 and 50 lines long. For that reason, this book cannot address all OS/2 CONFIG.SYS options. For more information on using the CONFIG.SYS file in OS/2, see *Using OS/2*, published by Que Corporation.

Building the AUTOEXEC.BAT File

Chapter 6 showed you how to create simple batch files, and discussed the importance of batch files to the operating system. One particular batch file—named AUTOEXEC.BAT—is especially significant to the operating system. AUTOEXEC.BAT is the *auto-execution* batch file. As the computer boots, the operating system looks for the AUTOEXEC.BAT file in the root directory. If the file resides in the root directory, the operating system executes commands stored in the file during booting.

A well-designed AUTOEXEC.BAT is an ideal partner for a hard disk. Before the introduction of personal computer hard disks, the AUTOEXEC.BAT file was utilized only little. You can use the AUTOEXEC.BAT file just like any other batch file. In other words, the file can include operating system commands, as well as commands that invoke other programs stored on the hard disk. The advantage of the AUTOEXEC.BAT file is that just by turning the computer on, you can ensure that a sequence of commands and programs are always executed.

Although you do not have to set up an AUTOEXEC.BAT file in your system's root directory, you should take advantage of this enormously helpful batch file, just the same. The AUTOEXEC.BAT file enables you to make sure that certain commands are automatically executed whenever the computer boots, including customized initialization commands such as PROMPT and PATH. Without an AUTOEXEC.BAT file, you must manually type in these commands every time you turn on or reboot the system. Why bother with all that typing, when the system can do it for you?

Normally, AUTOEXEC.BAT files are not distributed with the operating system files, because different users need different commands. Each AUTOEXEC.BAT file's contents reflect the individual user's start-up needs.

> **NOTE** During the installation process, DOS V4.0 creates a file called AUTOEXEC.400, which includes commands that you might want. You can use the RENAME command to change this file's name to AUTOEXEC.BAT.

The AUTOEXEC.BAT File's Rules

Except for the fact that the AUTOEXEC.BAT file is automatically executed when the system boots, this file is like any other batch file. You can include any commands you want in the AUTOEXEC.BAT file, provided you follow certain rules:

- The full file name must be AUTOEXEC.BAT, and the file must reside in the root directory of the boot disk.

- The AUTOEXEC.BAT file's contents must conform to the rules for all batch files. See Chapter 6 for a general discussion of batch files and an explanation of the rules applying to batch files.

- The operating system does not prompt for the date and time when executing ATUOEXEC.BAT, unless you have included the DATE and TIME commands in the file. Normally, you do not use DATE and TIME if the system has an automatic clock.

The AUTOEXEC.BAT File's Contents

The AUTOEXEC.BAT file should include commands for programs you want to have in effect for the full session. Normally, the file at least includes a PATH command and a PROMPT command. The PATH command usually is located at the beginning of the AUTOEXEC.BAT file, so that the file's remaining program execution commands can take advantage of the path.

You also should consider the following types of programs for loading with your AUTOEXEC.BAT file:

- Utility programs that speed up the keyboard's repeat rate

- Memory-resident programs that you can "pop up" during the session (such as SideKick Plus or PC Tools)

- Disk-caching programs

- Screen-blanking programs that suppress the display after a specified period of inactivity

- SET commands that place information in the environment

- Virus-detection programs

The AUTOEXEC.BAT file's contents depend on the way you use your system and the software you have installed. If you execute the same commands every time you boot the computer, you should consider adding these commands to the AUTOEXEC.BAT file.

The batch file's final line often calls a menu program, which displays a list of options (see Chapter 9 for more details on these menu programs). The menu spares the user from facing a dormant C> prompt!

A typical AUTOEXEC.BAT file might contain the following commands:

```
@ECHO OFF
PATH C:\WIN386;C:\;C:\DOS;C:\BATFILES;C:\U\MISC
PROMPT $P$G
```

The @ECHO OFF command can be used to suppress the display of the batch file's contents as each line is executed. The command eliminates the "garbage" that is displayed when the computer boots.

Summary

A well-organized hard disk significantly improves system performance and makes the computer easier to use. In this chapter you learned the following key points:

- A well-organized directory structure helps simplify file management and promotes data integrity.

- The CONFIG.SYS file is used to alter the system settings.

- The CONFIG.SYS file must be in the root directory of the boot disk.

- Device drivers are special software additions and extensions to the operating system's basic input/output system. You can assign new drivers by using the DEVICE directive in the CONFIG.SYS file.

- Disk buffers improve disk performance, and are assigned with the BUFFERS directive.

- The FILES directive sets the maximum number of file handles that can be open at one time.

- The LASTDRIVE directive specifies the letter of the last disk drive installed in your system.

- You can use the SHELL directive to replace the command processor program file and increase the size of the operating environment.

- When you alter CONFIG.SYS or AUTOEXEC.BAT, the changes do not take effect until the system is rebooted.

- Every time the system boots, the operating system searches for, and executes, a special batch file called AUTOEXEC.BAT.

- The AUTOEXEC.BAT file stores commands and programs that are executed as soon as the session starts.

Chapter 9 shows you how to build batch files that help can you manage the hard disk. You also will learn batch file enhancement techniques.

Using Batch Files To Manage a Hard Disk

The batch file commands you learned to use in Chapter 6 provide a way of combining a set of potentially complex commands into one easy-to-execute command. In this chapter you learn how to use batch files to simplify using your hard disk. A potpourri of sample batch files is reviewed, along with techniques for building a batch file menu system. You also learn how batch file enhancement programs can be used to make batch files more flexible and powerful.

Building a Batch File Menu System

In the PC world, a *menu* refers to a list of items that identify the programs available on the computer. To run a program, the user chooses an item from the menu, and the program is executed. When the user terminates the program, the menu reappears. The use of a menu makes the programs very easy to access, and the user is spared from having to remember all the directories and program execution names. Batch files enable you to create customized menus that simplify hard disk management.

NOTE   If you want a menu to appear as soon as the computer is booted, you need to add to the end of the C:\AUTOEXEC.BAT file the menu-display batch file command.

Overall Structure of a Menu

Menu systems driven by batch files have two elements. First, there must be a batch file that displays all the options (or choices) on the menu; and second, there is at least one batch file for each program on the menu. Both elements should be located in a single directory, and this directory should be included in the search path. A good location for the files is C:\BATFILES.

Before you build a menu system for your computer, you need to know the operating system commands used to execute each program you intend to include on the menu. Specifically, you need to know the drive and directory where each program is located and the command you ordinarily enter to start the program. Armed with this information and a text editor, you can create a custom menu system in just a few minutes.

Developing the Menu Screen

The first task in developing a menu is to create a text file that presents a list of all the options on the menu. As well as listing the options, you can use special ASCII characters to give the menu a distinctive and professional look. For example, you might draw a box or fancy border around the options. The ASCII character set includes a number of geometric characters that can be used to construct lines and boxes. In this section, some of the most popular ASCII graphics characters are shown, together with the special techniques needed to enter them into text files (see fig 9.1).

Every ASCII character has a three-digit code, ranging from 000 to 255. The characters that do not have their own keys on the keyboard can be entered into a file by using the character's three-digit ASCII code. To enter a code, hold down the Alt key and press the three numbers of the code on the numeric keypad, located on the right of the keyboard and then release the Alt key. These keystrokes automatically enter the special character into the file. Note that you must use the keys on the numeric keypad to enter the numbers—not the keys located above alphabet keys.

NOTE: Some word processors and text editors do not allow you to enter the special characters in the manner described. If the expected character does not appear when you type Alt and the ASCII code, consult the documentation. If you are still having problems, use EDLIN to create the file.

Single-Line Box

218 196 194   191
* *   *   *   **

179 *

195 *   *   * 180
*   197*

*   *   *   **
* 192   193   217*

Double-Line Box

201 205 203   187
* *   *   *   **

186 *

204 *   *   * 185
*   206*

* *   *   **
* 200   202   188*

Enter Key

*   ^Q***
* 017 + 196 + 217*

Block Characters

* 176 **
* 177 **
* 178 **
* 219 **

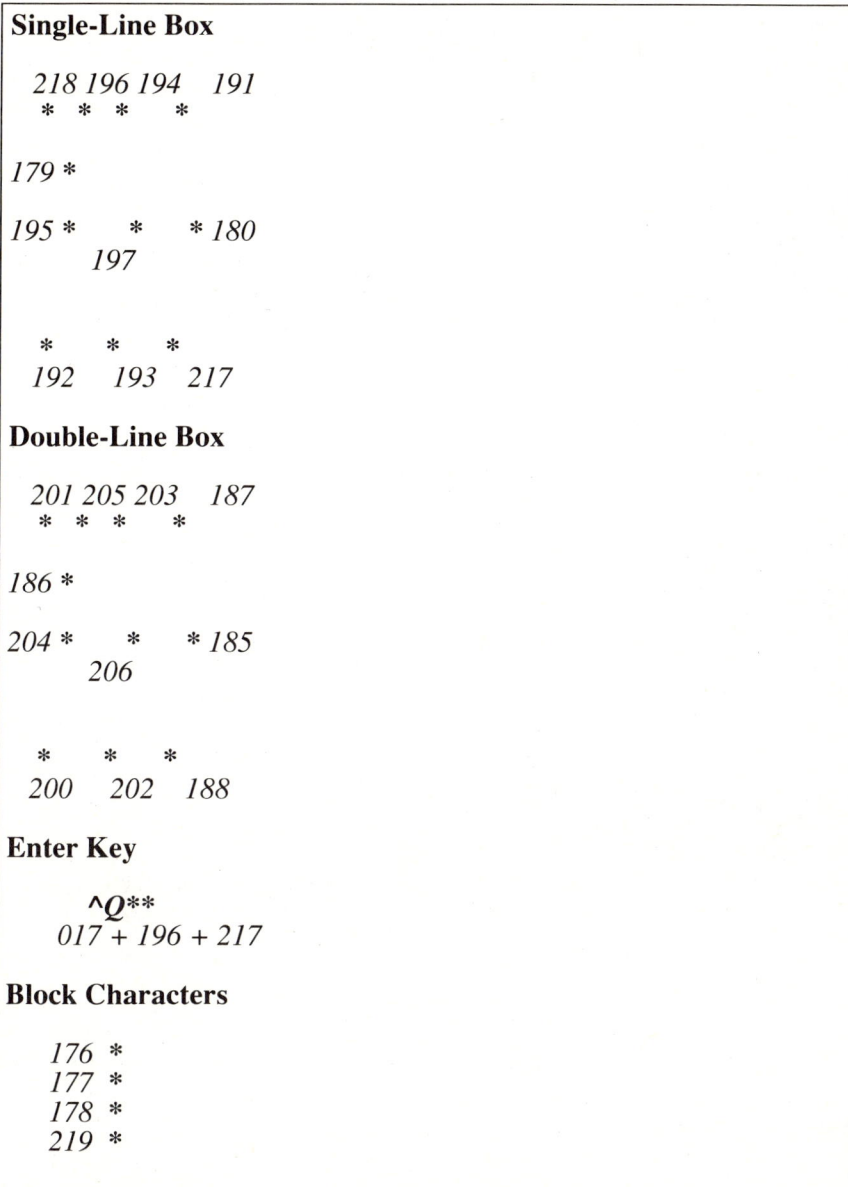

Fig. 9.1. *The ASCII codes for some box-formatting characters.*

To work through the menu system example, create a file and call it MAINMENU.TXT. This file will present the main menu to the user. In this file, you should create a menu box that includes a title, a list of all the programs as menu options, and some instructions to the user on how to execute a program.

The top line of the file will probably be the top of the box, and so to get started you press Alt-2-1-8 to embed the top-left corner character. Press Alt-1-9-6 to create the first character of the horizontal line. Keep adding line characters (or use a copy command if your editor has one—EDLIN doesn't) and then add the top-right corner character by pressing Alt-1-9-1. Continue in this manner to create an ASCII file similar to the following one:

```
* * * * * * * * * * * * * * * * * * * * * * * * * * * * * * * * * * * * * * * * *
*            ******* ERICA's MAIN MENU *******           *
*                                                         *
*                                                         *
*        1        Lotus 1-2-3 Release 3                   *
*                                                         *
*        2        Lotus Manuscript                        *
*                                                         *
*        3        PC File                                 *
*                                                         *
*        4        Aldus PageMaker                         *
*                                                         *
*        5        File Management Program                 *
*                                                         *
*        6        Daily File Backup                       *
*                                                         *
*                                                         *
*                                                         *
* Type the option number and press Enter (^Q**)  *
* * * * * * * * * * * * * * * * * * * * * * * * * * * * * * * * * * * * * * * * *
```

To create a space below the menu, add two or three blank lines to the end of the file. The actual text in the menu will vary, depending on the software you have installed on your system. The actual format of this file is purely cosmetic, and you can modify it to suit your taste. (I know you engineers won't use fancy boxes!)

The next task is to create a small batch file that displays this menu on the screen. The operating system command CLS can be used to clear the screen, and the TYPE command can be used to display the file. Create the file MENU.BAT as follows:

> **@ECHO OFF**
> **CLS**
> **TYPE C:\BATFILES\MAINMENU.TXT**

You might want to execute this batch file from any drive or directory, so the first task is to change drive and directory to C:\BATFILES. The user can enter MENU at any time to display this menu (see fig. 9.2).

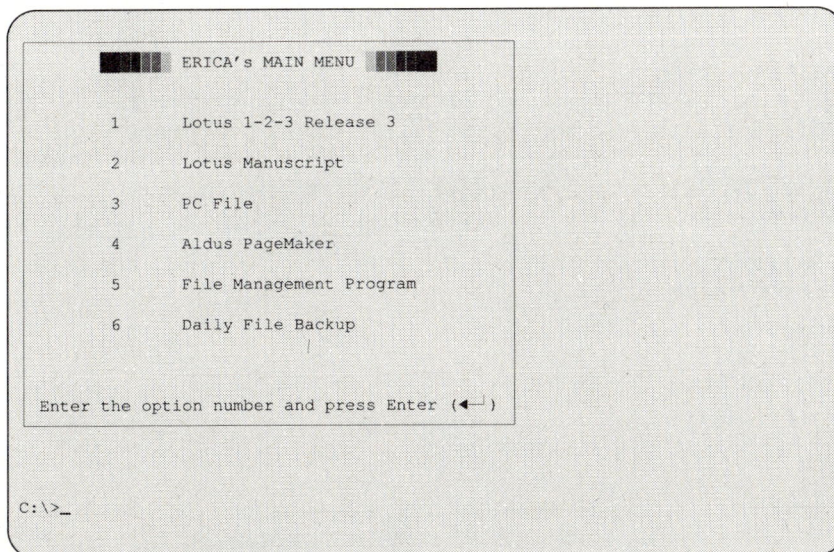

```
          ████ ██  ERICA's MAIN MENU  ██ ████


      1       Lotus 1-2-3 Release 3

      2       Lotus Manuscript

      3       PC File

      4       Aldus PageMaker

      5       File Management Program

      6       Daily File Backup


  Enter the option number and press Enter (◄─┘)




C:\>_
```

Fig. 9.2. The display created by MENU.BAT

Using Batch Files to Call Programs

In the menu screen you just created, each topic on the menu is preceded by a number. The instructions to the user indicate that he/she should type the menu option number and press Enter. All the user is really doing is entering the name of—and thereby executing—a batch file, 1.BAT, for example.

The final step in creating the menu is to build one batch file for each program on the menu. The batch file to execute the first program should be called 1.BAT, the batch file to load the second program should be 2.BAT, and so on.

In the example, the first option is Lotus 1-2-3, and the 1.BAT file might be as follows:

```
@ECHO OFF
CLS
ECHO LOADING 1-2-3 Release 3.0
CD\123R3
LOTUS
MENU
```

This batch file turns off the echoing, immediately clears the screen, and displays a message, so that the user knows something is happening. The next commands in the batch file are the commands required to load the program. In the example, this simply involves changing the directory to C:\123R3 and executing the command LOTUS. The last command in the file is MENU, which is a call to the original batch file to display the menu again. When the user exits the program LOTUS, the main menu is displayed once more, and the user can make another selection.

For the second program in this example system, the 2.BAT file contains the following commands:

```
@ECHO OFF
CLS
ECHO LOADING Lotus Manuscript
CD\MS
MS
MENU
```

If the user enters a command other than the batch file menu commands, the operating system will try to execute the command as usual. At any time, the user can enter the MENU command to redisplay the menu.

Adding Color with ANSI.SYS

Even on expensive color systems, DOS usually uses plain old white on black for the screen "colors." If you have been thinking there must be a way to display colorful menus, you are right. You can use the PROMPT command to instruct DOS to display characters in color (on color systems, of course). But to do so, you must use a special device driver called ANSI.SYS. The ANSI.SYS device driver comes with DOS and has a number of potential uses. It can be used to move the cursor, to redefine the meaning of keys on the keyboard, and—most commonly—to add color to the operating system prompt on computers fitted with a color-display system, such as CGA, EGA, and VGA.

If you want to use ANSI.SYS to have colorful operating system screens, you must add the line **DEVICE=ANSI.SYS** to the file CONFIG.SYS in the root directory of the hard disk. (If this file does not exist, you can create it with COPY CON, EDLIN, or a text editor. The CONFIG.SYS file is discussed in Chapter 6.) You also should copy the file ANSI.SYS from the DOS disk to the root directory of the hard disk. Remember that any time you make a change to CONFIG.SYS, you must reboot the system for the changes to take effect.

With the ANSI.SYS device driver installed, you use the PROMPT command with special character sequences to instruct DOS to use color. In this context, the syntax of the PROMPT command is

PROMPT $e[#;..#m

where **$e** is the special character sequence for Esc when used with the PROMPT command. (**$e** is referred to as a PROMPT metacommand. See Appendix A for a list of other metacommands supported by PROMPT.) [is a delimiter that always follows **$e**. #;..# represents a series of numerical values that define which display colors to use. One or more values may be specified. If more than one value is specified, each value must be separated by a semicolon. **m** is a special character that signifies the end of the command.

Rules for Displaying Color Screens

- You must have the device driver ANSI.SYS installed in the CONFIG.SYS file.

- The PROMPT command is used with the $e metacommand to adjust the display colors.

- A batch file must be in an ECHO ON state for the PROMPT command to be effective.

- The default operating system prompt will be switched off by the color statements and must be reset, with the command **PROMPT pg** for example.

- The screen must be cleared in a batch file (using CLS) to set the full screen to the new colors.

Table 9.1 lists the values that can be used with the PROMPT command.

Table 9.1
Color Values Used by ANSI.SYS

Value	Description
0	All attributes set to default (usually light gray on black)
1	Bold on (high intensity)
2*	Low intensity on
3*	Italic on
4	Underscore on (monochrome adapters only)
5	Blink on
6*	Rapid blinking on
7	Reverse video on
8	Cancel on (invisible characters black on black)
30	Black foreground
31	Red foreground
32	Green foreground
33	Yellow foreground
34	Blue foreground
35	Magenta foreground
36	Cyan foreground
37	White foreground
40	Black background
41	Red background
42	Green background
43	Yellow background
44	Blue background
45	Magenta background
46	Cyan background
47	White background
48*	Subscript
49*	Superscript

Older versions of ANSI.SYS may not support all the values.
* indicates that the feature is not supported on VGA monitors.

Using Batch Files To Set Colors

Normally, these special PROMPT commands are created in a batch file. For example, the following batch commands set the background to blue and the foreground to light cyan:

```
PROMPT $e[44m
PROMPT $e[36m
PROMPT $e[1m
@ECHO OFF
PROMPT $p$g
CLS
```

The first line sets the background to blue. The second line sets the foreground to cyan. The third line sets the foreground intensity on, that is, light cyan. The batch file must be in an ECHO ON state (default) for these commands to be operative. After the special PROMPT commands execute, the batch file can be switched to the ECHO OFF state. The PROMPT command is normally used to display the default drive and directory (see Chapter 3), but the special use of the PROMPT command disables the normal prompt. The fifth line resets the operating system prompt to display the default drive and directory. The last line is the command CLS to clear the screen. This batch file makes the full display use a blue background with light cyan lettering.

If you run this batch file and the colors do not change, check that you have the statement **DEVICE=ANSI.SYS** in the CONFIG.SYS file and that the file ANSI.SYS is in the root directory. If they are, you probably forgot to reboot the system after you changed the CONFIG.SYS file. Reboot and try again.

You can combine the three color settings in the preceding batch file into a single statement as follows:

```
PROMPT $e[44;36;1m
ECHO OFF
PROMPT $p$g
CLS
```

The following batch file can be used to reset the colors to the default of light gray on black:

```
PROMPT $e[0m
ECHO OFF
PROMPT $p$g
CLS
```

Earlier, you learned that the Ctrl-G character can be used to beep the speaker to get the user's attention before a PAUSE statement. The following batch file illustrates how to set the colors so that the message **Strike any key when ready . . .** flashes or blinks to call attention to itself:

```
PROMPT $e[5m
CLS
@ECHO OFF
REM
REM Your message would go below here
REM
PAUSE
ECHO ON
PROMPT $e[0;44;36;1m
ECHO OFF
PROMPT $p$g
CLS
REM
REM    Your commands would go below here
REM
```

You can use this batch file as a template for your own applications. The first line sets the blink attribute on. Then the screen is cleared. You add "ECHO *text*" statements before the PAUSE command to present the user with a warning message. After the PAUSE statement, the colors are set back to light cyan on blue. That is, blinking is turned off, and the normal operating system prompt is reset. You can append other batch file commands to the end of the file to perform the appropriate tasks.

Batch File Utilities

A few simple batch files can make the chore of managing a hard disk much more straightforward. In this section a variety of utility batch files are presented.

Displaying Program Files

Sometimes you may want to list all the executable files in a directory—all the files with a *COM, *EXE, or *BAT extension. One approach would be to create a batch file (called DIRPROGS.BAT here) that contains three DIR commands as follows:

```
@ECHO OFF
IF EXIST *.COM DIR *.COM /W/P
IF EXIST *.EXE DIR *.EXE /W/P
IF EXIST *.BAT DIR *.BAT /W/P
```

Each of the three main lines is similar. The IF command checks whether any matching files are found, and if so, the DIR command displays them. The /W switch provides the wide format of the directory display, thereby showing as many files on the screen as possible, and /P pauses the output if any of the individual listings extends beyond one screen. Fig. 9.3 shows an example of the output from DIRPROGS.BAT.

```
C:\MAG2>DIRPROGS

 Volume in drive C is TECHNOJOCK
 Directory of  C:\MAG2

INSTALL COM    MG        COM    MERGE    COM    MG94       COM
       4 File(s)   7585792 bytes free

 Volume in drive C is TECHNOJOCK
 Directory of  C:\MAG2

MGUNZIP EXE    README    EXE    MGZIP     EXE    MAGINDEX EXE
       4 File(s)   7585792 bytes free

 Volume in drive C is TECHNOJOCK
 Directory of  C:\MAG2

MGFAST   BAT
       1 File(s)   7585792 bytes free
C:\MAG2>_
```

Fig. 9.3. The display created by DIRPROGS.BAT.

An alternative technique for displaying all the program files would be to use the batch file programming subcommand FOR as follows:

```
@ECHO OFF
FOR %%A in (*.COM,*.EXE,*.BAT) DO ECHO %%A
```

When executed, this batch file lists all the files with a COM extension, all the files with an EXE extension, and all the files with a BAT extension (see fig. 9.4).

```
C:\MAG2>PROGS
INSTALL.COM
MG.COM
MERGE.COM
MG94.COM
MGUNZIP.EXE
README.EXE
MGZIP.EXE
MAGINDEX.EXE
MGFAST.BAT
C:\MAG2>_
```

Fig. 9.4. Using the FOR subcommand to display program files.

Maintaining Multiple Boot Configurations

The special files CONFIG.SYS and AUTOEXEC.BAT define how your system should be configured and which commands execute when the computer is booted. If you have a diverse set of programs installed on your computer, you may want to use various configurations during certain sessions.

For example, some of the programs on your computer may require expanded memory, whereas other programs will use only extended memory. The dilemma is that the instructions to set the computer's memory to expanded or extended have to be placed in the file CONFIG.SYS. You therefore have to change the parameters for the memory device driver in CONFIG.SYS (and reboot the system) each time you want to switch from a program that uses expanded memory to a program that uses extended memory.

The situation is further complicated if you also have to make modifications to the AUTOEXEC.BAT file to run different programs. For example, you may want to use different search paths or avoid the automatic loading of memory-resident programs for certain memory-hungry applications.

The solution to these dilemmas is to create multiple sets of CONFIG.SYS and AUTOEXEC.BAT files and to use a batch file to activate the appropriate set. In the \BATFILES directory, you might create the following four files:

```
CONFIG.1
AUTOEXEC.1
CONFIG.2
AUTOEXEC.2
```

CONFIG.1 and AUTOEXEC.1 are copies of the CONFIG.SYS file and AUTOEXEC.BAT files used for one of your setups, and CONFIG.2 and AUTOEXEC.2 are an alternative set. The following batch file, SETSTART.BAT is used to install the appropriate files:

```
@ECHO OFF
IF "%1"=="1" GOTO PROCEED
IF "%1"=="2" GOTO PROCEED
ECHO ERROR! You must specify the files you want to
copy.
ECHO The valid values are 1 and 2, e.g. SETSTART 1
GOTO END
:PROCEED
C:
CD\BATFILES
COPY CONFIG.%1 \CONFIG.SYS
COPY AUTOEXEC.%1 \AUTOEXEC.BAT
ECHO System now set to use configuration %1.
ECHO Press Ctrl-Alt-Del to reboot the system.
PAUSE
:END
```

To execute the batch file, you pass the parameter 1 or 2 to indicate which set of files you want to use, and the batch file copies the appropriate files into the root directory. However, the system must be rebooted before the changes are effected. Fig. 9.5 illustrates the display generated by the SETSTART batch file.

```
C:\BATFILES>setstart 1
        1 File(s) copied
        1 File(s) copied
System now set to use configuration 1.
Press Ctrl-Alt-Del to reboot the system.
Strike a key when ready . . . _
```

Fig. 9.5. Using the SETSTART batch file to maintain multiple boot files.

If you establish a system like this, you must remember to avoid making changes directly to the CONFIG.SYS and AUTOEXEC.BAT files. If you, or a program, make changes to the files, be sure to copy those changes to the appropriate copy of the file in the \BATFILES directory. Otherwise, the changes will be overwritten the next time you run SETSTART. The following batch file, GETSTART, can be used to automate this reverse-copy procedure:

```
@ECHO OFF
IF "%1"=="1" GOTO PROCEED
IF "%1"=="2" GOTO PROCEED
ECHO ERROR! You must specify the files you want to
update.
ECHO The valid values are 1 and 2, e.g. GETSTART 1
GOTO END
:PROCEED
C:
CD\BATFILES
COPY \CONFIG.SYS CONFIG.%1
COPY \AUTOEXEC.BAT CONFIG.%1
ECHO Set %1 configuration files updated
:END
```

Swapping and Extending the Search Path

In Chapter 4, you learned that the environment is an area of memory reserved to provide the operating system and other programs with information. The SET command can be entered with no parameters to view the information in the environment. If parameters are added in the following format, the environment is updated with the new information:

SET *name=value*

An example of the information in the environment is

```
COMSPEC=C:\COMMAND.COM
PATH=C:\WIN386;C:\;C:\DOS;C:\U\BAT
PROMPT=$p$g
TEMP=C:\TRASH
```

You can access the data stored in the environment from batch files. This access allows you to build variables that check the environment to determine which part of the batch file to execute. To access the data in the environment, the environment name must be written inside two % signs as follows:

%name%

The command processor will substitute the actual environment value for the specified name in the place of this marker. For example, if the contents of the environment were as listed above, the entry %TEMP% in a batch file would be interpreted as:

```
C:\TRASH
```

A useful application of this facility is to build a batch file that adds a directory path to the environment. To do this, create the following ADDPATH.BAT file:

```
@ECHO OFF
PATH=%PATH%;%1
```

This simple batch file is very useful if you want to temporarily add a directory to the path. To add a path, you would execute the batch file and pass a single parameter that is the additional search path directory. For example, the following command adds the C:\TEST directory to the search path:

```
ADDPATH C:\TEST
```

The command processor substitutes the %PATH% entry in the batch file for the current PATH. A semicolon and the new path (%1) are then added to form the new PATH. For example, after the substitutions the batch file would execute the following command:

```
PATH=C:\WIN386;C:\;C:\DOS;C:\U\BAT;C:\TEST
```

Two simple batch files can be created that allow you to temporarily change the path and then subsequently restore the old path. The following batch file, NEWPATH, sets the new path:

```
@ECHO OFF
SET OLDPATH=%PATH%
PATH=%1
```

The second line in this batch file saves the current path setting in the environment, using the SET command. The PATH command is then called and the path is set to the first passed parameter. Here is an example of calling this batch file:

```
NEWPATH C:\TEST;D:\BATFILES
```

The following batch file, OLDPATH.BAT, is used to restore the PATH to its original setting:

```
@ECHO OFF
PATH=%OLDPATH%
SET OLDPATH=
```

The second line of the batch file restores the old path by accessing the environment entry OLDPATH. The OLDPATH entry is then removed from the environment by assigning nul (or nothing) to OLDPATH.

Using Batch File Enhancers

This section discusses three products that illustrate the value of batch file enhancers: WHAT, a public domain utility included on the disk that accompanies this book; BE, the batch-enhancement program included in the Norton Utilities; and Batcom, a commercial product that extends the programmability of batch files and compiles BAT files into EXE and COM files. These three products include most of the features available for batch file enhancement.

Batch files have a number of weaknesses, and batch file enhancement programs are designed to overcome these weaknesses and give batch files greater flexibility and ease of use. For example, when you use the standard batch file subcommands (or any other operating system command for that matter), there is no way to prompt the user for input. Without an enhancement, the only way to get batch file input is to pass parameters on the command line.

Batch file enhancement programs range from simple programs that communicate to the batch file via the environment to programs that extend batch file programming facilities and actually create EXE or COM programs from plain batch files.

Using WHAT

DISK

WHAT.EXE is a small public-domain (free) program that provides a variety of useful extensions to the standard batch file subcommands.

This easy-to-use utility has the following capabilities:

- Waits until the user inputs one of a set of characters
- Prompts the user to enter some text
- Determines the amount of free disk space
- Determines the size of all files matching a file specification
- Determines how much free memory exists
- Determines if a printer is attached and onlline
- Determines the video mode being used
- Determines if a math coprocessor is installed
- Determines if ANSISYS is installed
- Saves the current directory

All these features are packed into a program that is only 3,200 bytes in size.

WHAT is designed to be executed from a batch file, and is passed one or more parameters to indicate the information you are trying to retrieve. WHAT gets the information and places it in the environment, assigned to the environment variable WHAT. You can then access this data in a batch file using the %WHAT% statement.

The basic format for using WHAT is

WHAT id *switches*

In the syntax, **id** is a letter or number to indicate the information you want, and *switches* is additional parameters required with some **id** options.

The WHAT has many useful applications. Three of them—getting user input, temporarily changing directories, and checking the printer—are discussed in the following sections.

Getting User Input with WHAT

WHAT can be used in a batch file to wait until one or a set of characters is pressed. The command is:

WHAT C *"prompt" allowchars*

C is the switch to indicate single-character input, *"prompt"* is an optional prompt that will be displayed, and *allowchars* is the set of allowable characters.

This command line displays the specified prompt and waits for the user to press one of the specified characters. If the user presses an invalid character, WHAT ignores it. The actual character (converted to uppercase if appropriate) is stored in the WHAT environment variable.

The following batch file extract waits for the user to press 1, 2, or Q, and then branches to another part of the batch file:

```
WHAT C "Press (1) Lotus (2) Word or (Q) to Quit "
12Q
IF %WHAT%==1 GOTO LOTUS
IF %WHAT%==2 GOTO WORD
IF %WHAT%==Q GOTO END
```

The first line instructs WHAT to prompt the user for input and to wait until the user presses 1,2, or Q. WHAT then saves the value of the pressed key in the environment variable WHAT. The remaining three lines check the environment variable for each of the three possible values and then branch to another part of the batch file where the label LOTUS, WORD, or END is situated.

The file MENU.BAT, discussed earlier in the chapter, could be enhanced as follows:

```
@ECHO OFF
C:
CD\BATFILES
CLS
TYPE MAINMENU.TXT
WHAT C "Press 1, 2, 3, 4, 5, 6 or Q " 123456Q
```

```
IF  %WHAT%==1  1
IF  %WHAT%==2  2
IF  %WHAT%==3  3
IF  %WHAT%==4  4
IF  %WHAT%==5  5
IF  %WHAT%==6  6
```

The advantage of using WHAT for user input is that the user is restricted to entering one of the menu options, rather than any command whatsoever. With traditional batch file techniques, the user's input cannot be resticted. Any value could be entered, not just the ones listed in the menu. If an invalid value were entered, for example, one for which there is no corresponding batch file, the operating system would respond with the message **Bad command or filename**. Because WHAT continues to prompt until the user enters an acceptable value, only valid batch file commands will be executed.

WHAT also can be used to get text from the user, by specifying the S (for string) switch. The syntax for using WHAT for string input is

WHAT S *"prompt"*

S is the switch to indicate string input, and *"prompt"* is an optional prompt that will be displayed.

WHAT will wait for the user to type characters and press Enter. The input data (converted to upper case) is assigned to the environment variable WHAT.

For example, to request a user's name, you could create the following batch file:

```
WHAT S "Enter your name ===> "
IF "%WHAT"=="LOIS" FULLMENU
IF "%WHAT"=="TIM" PARTMENU
SLIMMENU
```

If the user enters LOIS, lois, or some other variation, the batch file FULLMENU will be called. If the user enters TIM, the batch file PARTMENU will be called; otherwise the batch file SLIMMENU is called.

Temporarily Changing the Directory

The Y switch is used to save the current directory in the WHAT environment variable. The following batch file, TEMPCD.BAT, can be used to temporarily change to another directory:

```
@ECHO OFF
WHAT Y
SET OLDDIR=%WHAT%
CD %1
```

The second line of the batch file instructs WHAT to save the current directory in the WHAT variable. The next line saves the value of the WHAT environment variable in the OLDDIR environment variable. This command ensures that the directory will not be overwritten if WHAT is subsequently used for some other purpose. The following batch file, CDBACK.BAT, can be used to change back to the original directory:

```
@ECHO OFF
CD %OLDDIR%
```

Checking the Printer

Before you run a PRINT command, you might want to confirm that the printer is connected and on-line. WHAT will check the printer status (on LPT1 only) when the P parameter is specified. If the printer is active, the WHAT environment variable is updated with a 1; otherwise it is set to 0.

The following batch file, PRNT.BAT, checks the printer status before issuing the operating system PRINT command:

```
@ECHO OFF
WHAT P
IF %WHAT%==0 GOTO OFFLINE
PRINT %1 %2 %3 %4 %5 %6 %7 %8 %9
GOTO END
:OFFLINE
ECHO Error! The printer is not active.
:END
```

Line 1 turns off the echoing. Then the WHAT command is used with the parameter P to check the status of the printer. WHAT updates the environment variable WHAT with a 0 if the printer is inactive, and a 1 if the printer is active. The third line of the batch file checks whether the WHAT environment variable is set to 0; if so, the batch file branches to the label OFFLINE and displays an error message. If the printer is online, the fourth line of the batch file calls the PRINT command and passes to it all the parameters that were specified when PRNT was executed.

Using the Norton Utilities

The Norton Utilities contains a large group of utilites to help you with your hard disk management. One of the programs in the Norton utilities package is BE.EXE (short for Batch Enhancer), which is packed with features to improve the capabilities of batch files. Like the WHAT enhancement program, BE is a multipurpose batch file enhancer that is passed a switch, together with optional parameters that indicate how you want to use the switch.

The general syntax of the BE command is:

> **BE subcommand** *switches*

> or

> **BE filename**

subcommand is one of the following subcommands: ASK, BEEP, BOX, CLS, DELAY, PRINTCHAR, ROWCOL, SA, or WINDOWS. *switches* are the parameters required with some of the subcommands.

filename is a file that includes only BE subcommands, or remark lines starting with REM. BE reads the file and activates the commands as though they were embedded in the batch file.

BE includes a rich set of commands for prompting for user input, drawing colorful screens, and sounding the speaker.

Getting User Input with ASK

The ASK subcommand is used to display a prompt and get input from the user. ASK can be used to get only a single character, and the pressed character is determined by checking the ERRORLEVEL set by BE.

The syntax of the ASK subcommand is

> **BE ASK "prompt"** *keys DEFAULT=char TIMEOUT=n ADJUST=n color*

where **"prompt"** is a word or phrase that will be displayed on the screen.

keys is an optional list of allowable keys.

TIMEOUT=n is the maximum time, in seconds, that ASK will wait for input (optional).

DEFAULT=char is the character returned if no key has been pressed within the timeout period (optional).

ADJUST=n is an optional factor to adjust the returned error level. This parameter allows one batch file to handle multiple inputs.

color is the foreground and background display colors (optional).

When the user chooses one of the valid keys, ASK terminates and sets the
DOS ERRORLEVEL. The batch file can then check the ERRORLEVEL to
determine which key the user pressed. The following batch file waits for the
user to press the key 1,2,3 or Q:

```
BE ASK "Select a menu option ===> "123q
IF ERRORLEVEL 4 GOTO QUIT
IF ERRORLEVEL 3 GOTO OPTION3
IF ERRORLEVEL 2 GOTO OPTION2
IF ERRORLEVEL 1 GOTO OPTION1
```

Note that the ERRORLEVEL codes must be checked in reverse order (see
Chapter 6). If the user presses the fourth key—Q or q,—the batch file
branches to the label QUIT. If the third key is pressed, 3, the batch file
branches to the label OPTION3, and so on.

Screen Drawing

The real power of BE is in its screen-display capabilities. BE includes the
subcommands BOX, PRINTCHAR, ROWCOL, and WINDOW that can
create menus and other custom screens.

The BOX subcommand is used to draw a single- or double-line rectangle
anywhere on the screen. The WINDOW subcommand draws a rectangle,
but it also clears the area inside the rectangle, and can optionally produce a
drop-shadow effect. You can even have the window zoom onto the display,
that is, grow dynamically onto the screen. The ROWCOL subcommand is
used to write text in a specific location on the screen, and PRINTCHAR can
be used to print a character repeated many times. The coordinates used with
these commands are 0 to 24 for the row and 0 to 79 for the column.

The following batch file illustrates how easy it is to create a display that
looks professional, using the BE command:

```
@ECHO OFF
CLS
BE WINDOW 0,0,23,79 BRIGHT WHITE ON BLUE EXPLODE
BE WINDOW 4,11,20,68 BLACK ON CYAN EXPLODE SHADOW
BE ROWCOL 8,33  " Erica's menu" BLACK
BE ROWCOL 10,25 "1     Lotus 1-2-3 Release 3" BRIGHT
    WHITE
BE ROWCOL 11 25 "2     Lotus Manuscript      " BRIGHT
    WHITE
BE ROWCOL 12,25 "3     PC Tools              " BRIGHT
    WHITE
BE ROWCOL 13,25 "4     File backup           " BRIGHT
    WHITE
```

```
BE  ROWCOL 14,25 "Q      Quit                      " BRIGHT
    WHITE
BE  ROWCOL 18,20
BE  ASK "Select a program number or press Q ===>
    "Q1234
IF  ERRORLEVEL 5 4
IF  ERRORLEVEL 4 3
IF  ERRORLEVEL 3 2
IF  ERRORLEVEL 2 1
BE  ROWCOL 24,0
```

When the batch file is executed, a large box explodes onto the screen and a smaller shadowed box explodes inside the first box (see fig. 9.6).

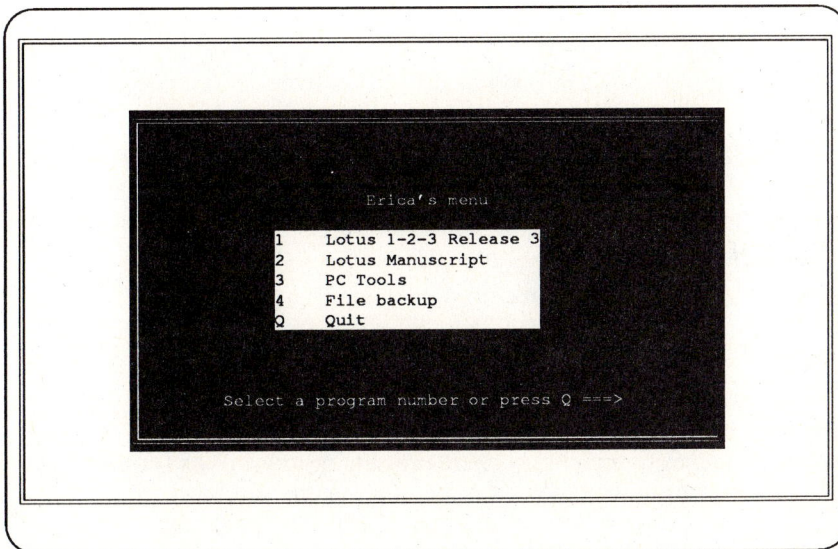

Fig. 9.6. *BE can draw colorful, exploding boxes and text.*

Another BE subcommand, SA, can be used to set the screen attributes used at the operating system prompt. Behind the scenes, SA uses ANSI.SYS to set the display colors, and so ANSI.SYS must be installed in the CONFIG.SYS file for SA to be effective.

Sounding the Speaker

The BEEP subcommand is a simple utility for sounding the computer speaker. The PC speaker is very crude, so don't expect to be able to create a symphony or rock concert! BEEP is designed to be used in a batch file to signal certain events. For example, you could use BEEP to grab the user's attention just before prompting for input.

The syntax of the BEEP command is

BE BEEP */Dn /Fn /Rn /Wn*

or

BE BEEP *filename /E*

where */Dn* is the duration of the tone, and n is the number of eighteenths of a second. For example, /D9 sounds the tone for half a second.

/Fn is the frequency of the tone in Hertz.

/Rn repeats the tone *n* times.

/Wn is the wait (in eighteenths of a second) between repetitions.

BEEP also can read the settings from a separate file if a *filename* is specified. The */E* option instructs BEEP to echo each line to the screen as it is played.

The following command sounds the speaker four times in a high-pitched beep (2000 hertz) for one eighteenth of a second.

```
BE BEEP /F2000 /D1 /R4
```

Using the Batcom Batch File Compiler

When you create a batch file, you are actually programming. The batch file subcommands provide an elementary programming language that can greatly simplify repetitive tasks, such as running a program or finding a file. The main programming weaknesses of batch files are that batch files are slow to execute and have a very limited set of programming commands.

Batcom, from Wenhem Systems, is a batch file compiler designed to overcome these weaknesses. A compiler is a program that creates executable programs with a COM or EXE extension. Batcom can read a batch file and create an EXE file that runs faster than a batch file and that cannot be tampered with. Batcom also adds a wealth of extra features that extend the programmability of batch files.

If you create only small batch files for your own use, then you may not need a batch file compiler, but if you want to create more sophisticated batch files that you can distribute to others, Batcom is an excellent tool.

In Chapter 6, you created a batch file, RN.BAT, which was an enhancement to the DOS command RENAME. Batcom can be used to compile this file with the following command:

```
BATCOM RN.BAT
```

Batcom reads the statements in the batch file and automatically creates a compiled file RN.EXE. The program RN.EXE performs exactly the same tasks as RN.BAT.

In this particular example, there are very few advantages to compiling the file. The original batch file runs quickly, so the speed advantages of running the EXE program are minimal. The only real advantage is that users are prevented from editing the file (since it is binary), and so tampering is unlikely.

Some batch file compilers create EXE files that are much larger than the source BAT file, but Batcom is very efficient. The size of the RN.EXE file is only 2892 bytes, compared to the original RN.BAT file size of 447 bytes. The smaller the file, the less space is consumed on the hard disk to store it. Batcom goes to great lengths to keep the files as small as possible.

As well as compiling standard batch files, Batcom provides a rich set of *language extensions*, which give you more programming capabilities and allow you to build sophisticated programs. Without a batch file compiler, like Batcom, you would have to learn a programming language to create programs. The Batcom extensions include: local variables, support of mathematical operations such as plus, minus, times, and divide, the ability to ascertain the amount of free memory and disk space, user input, and much more.

We don't have the space to fully explore the features of Batcom, but listed below is a program, called CHKFILE, which uses a number of Batcom's language features to report how much space is used by a set of files and how much free disk space and memory are available. CHKFILE is somewhat similar to CHKDSK.

```
(1)    REM Displays disk space used and free memory
(2)    LET %!F = %1
(3)    IF "%!F" = "" LET %!F = *.*
(4)    LET %!S = %!F
(5)    FILESIZE %!F
(6)    FREEDISK %!D
(7)    FREEMEM %!M
(8)    echo The total size of the file(s) %!S is %!F.
(9)    echo The total free disk space is %!D.
(10)   echo You have %!M bytes of memory available.
```

The first line describes the purpose of the file, and the second line assigns the value of the first passed parameter %1 (the same as in standard batch files) to the variable %!F. The value of %!F is then checked to see whether it is null, that is, whether no parameters were specified. If so, the value *.* is assigned. The third line stores the value of %!F in another variable, %!S. Line four calls the special Batcom command FILESIZE and passes the variable %!F, which identifies the name of the file or files (wild-card characters are supported) whose size is to be checked. FILESIZE then updates the variable %!F with the total size of all the files. The sixth line calls the Batcom command FREEDISK to report the total available space on the disk, and the value is assigned to the variable %D. Line seven uses another command, FREEMEM, to update the variable %!M with the total free memory. The last three lines of the batch file echo the results by embedding the variable names within the message text—in just the same way as the parameters %1..%9 can be used in ordinary batch files.

The preceding explanation is intended to give you an awareness of how batch file compilers can extend the power of batch files. The resultant program is 2878 bytes in size. Fig. 9.7 illustrates the output generated when CHKFILE was run three different ways: with no paremeters, with *.DOC, and with *.SCR.

```
C:\MS\DISK2>chkfile
The total size of the file(s) *.* is 1674360.
The total free disk space is 2125824.
You have 458048 bytes of memory available.

C:\MS\DISK2>chkfile *.doc
The total size of the file(s) *.doc is 776347.
The total free disk space is 2125824.
You have 458048 bytes of memory available.

C:\MS\DISK2>chkfile *.scr
The total size of the file(s) *.scr is 0.
The total free disk space is 2125824.
You have 458048 bytes of memory available.

C:\MS\DISK2>_
```

Fig. 9.7. The output generated by CHKFILE.

Summary

In this chapter, you learned how to use batch files to make hard disk management more straightforward. You learned how to develop a few small batch files that create a very useful menu system and how to use ANSI.SYS to give your display some color. Batch file enhancers can further extend the value of batch files by adding more power and flexibility to the batch file subcommands.

In Part IV you learn how to improve the performance of your hard disk and how special programs can make file management much easier.

Part IV

Getting the Most
from Your Hard Disk

Improving Hard Disk Performance

Using File-Management Tools

Understanding Operating Environments

10

Improving
Hard Disk
Performance

All PC users wish that their machines were faster. Since the operating speed of a hard disk has a significant impact on the overall speed of the machine, the best way of improving your PC's overall speed—short of buying a faster microprocessor—is to squeeze the most performance out of your hard disk.

You can "fine-tune" your system in many ways to reduce the amount of time wasted while data is read from or written to the hard disk:

- The most dramatic performance improvements are realized by reducing the amount of disk access. Memory access is much faster than disk access, and *disk caches* and *RAM disks* improve performance by storing data in memory, rather than on disk.

- Significant performance gains can be realized by *defragmenting* the files on the hard disk. Over time, different parts of each file tend to be stored in different locations on the disk surface. To access a file, the disk read-write head has to move all over the disk, and this movement wastes time. When a file is defragmented, all the parts of the file are gathered up and stored in one contiguous area of the disk.

- The organization of your directory hierarchy and the setting of the search path have an impact on disk performance.

- DOS and OS/2 include a number of utilities expressly designed to improve hard disk performance—for example, the BUFFERS and FASTOPEN commands.

Some performance gains can be realized just by optimizing your DOS *settings*. However, the most noticeable gains are realized when you use commercial disk utilities. If you have paid for a hard disk, you ought to consider leveraging your investment by purchasing some disk-optimization software.

A note from the author ... Many different specialty products can enhance one aspect or another of disk management. There are programs dedicated to disk caching, data recovery, defragmenting, file management, and so on. If you purchase all the specialty products, you will certainly have an arsenal of high-powered disk-management software. But you also will have spent hundreds of dollars.

Alternatively, there are a number of products designed to provide a broader base of disk-management tools in a single package. Three of the most popular and acclaimed all-purpose disk-management programs are

PC Tools from Central Point Software
Mace Utilities from Fifth generation Systems
The Norton Utilities from Peter Norton Computing

Throughout Parts IV and V of this text, we look at one or more specialty products and then discuss the related utilities available in each of these three all-purpose utility programs.

Optimizing a hard disk does not always improve the speed of your application. Optimizing can improve tasks only if they normally involve disk access. For example, improving disk performance does not reduce the time required to "recalculate" the values in a spreadsheet, since recalculation (usually) does not involve disk access. A math coprocessor is the solution to that problem. Nevertheless, the time required to load and save a worksheet is reduced. The most dramatic speed improvements are realized with disk-intensive applications, such as a database. You also realize significant performance benefits with memory-hungry programs (such as desktop publishing packages) that create temporary disk files to store data when they run out of RAM.

Failing to optimize your hard disk is like driving a car without keeping the engine tuned. In this chapter, you learn many different ways to improve the performance of your hard disk.

Using Disk Caches

Of all the measures you can take to improve hard disk performance, a disk cache has the most impact. A disk cache increases overall performance by temporarily storing copies of disk data in RAM to reduce disk activity. By reducing the amount of disk access, a disk cache can dramatically reduce the number of physical disk operations; as a result, applications run significantly faster.

In the early days of PC hard disks, nobody every dreamed of using a disk cache because every last drop of memory was usually required by the applications software. Besides, memory was one of the most expensive commodities used in the PC; it made more sense to develop faster hardware than to use expensive memory. Since those days, however, the price of memory has been reduced, and advances in memory-management technology have made disk caches viable.

Nowadays it is cheaper to get more memory and install a disk cache than it is to buy a faster disk drive. In fact, the faster the processor and memory chips, the greater the advantage of a disk cache. It is a common misconception that an 80386-based computer with a fast hard disk does not need a disk cache. No matter how fast the system is, performance can still be improved with a disk cache.

Disk caches are ideally suited to laptop machines, where disk activity is a major drain of battery power. When outfitted with a cache, the laptop can run faster and last longer between charges.

The great thing about a disk cache is that it doesn't interfere with the way you use the computer. Once a disk cache program has been activated, you use the computer as usual. You are aware of the disk cache only because your system operates faster—sometimes a lot faster. The performance improvement can range from 10 percent to 60 percent on disk-intensive operations. If you don't already have a disk cache on your computer, you should get one!

Disk Cache Theory

A disk cache reserves a portion of memory for storing disk-related data. The best disk-cache programs allow the cache to be located in conventional, extended, or expanded memory, and usually some combination thereof. A disk cache uses this memory in four main ways to improve performance: mirroring, track buffering, write buffering and redundancy checking.

Mirroring

The most common form of caching is referred to as *mirroring*. The first time a file is read, the disk cache keeps a copy of the file in memory, that is, a mirror image. If, some time later, the application program tries to read the same file, the cache can provide the file directly from memory, avoiding the need to read the file from disk again. The first time the file is read, there is no performance advantage. In fact, the file might even be slightly slower to load because the cache intercepts data as it is read from disk. However, any subsequent attempt to read the file will be orders of magnitude faster because there is no need to load the file again from the hard disk.

You might think that very little data is read multiple times from the disk, but that is not the case. For example, if you use a spell checker (and my editor wishes I did!), the dictionary is usually stored on disk and has to be searched every time you check the spelling in a document. Also, many large programs keep some of the program code on disk in an overlay file. When you select certain commands, the program has to access the overlay file. If you have ever run a large program from a diskette, you can appreciate how many times overlay files are accessed while a program is being used.

The data in the cache usually is managed by sectors. Every time a sector is read from disk, a copy is retained in memory. Once the cache fills all its available memory, the cache must decide which data to remove from the cache to make way for new data. Good cache programs use a special algorithm that removes the *least recently used* data. To do this, the cache must retain information about which data is accessed from the cache and how frequently. When a new sector is read from disk, the cache finds the least recently used sector in the cache and overwrites it with the new sector. If the discarded sector is requested by the applications program, it must be read from disk again.

Track Buffering

Whenever a sector is read from the hard disk, there is a good chance that the data from the next sector also will be required. Having just read one sector, the read-write head is already positioned over the next sector on the track. A cache that employs track-buffering goes ahead and reads additional sectors, whether they are requested or not. If any more data is requested from that track, it can be transferred directly from the cache. There will be occasions when an applications program will not need the other data on the track, and the extra data will have been read unnecessarily.

Unlike mirroring, track buffering reduces the time required to read a file the first time it is read. Overall, the performance gains are most apparent on disks that are not fragmented, that is, on disks where files are physically located on contiguous sectors. (File fragmentation is discussed later in this chapter.) If data is randomly scattered all over the disk, you may find that the cache slows down the operation—this occurs because the cache is continually reading and discarding data that is not needed.

Write Buffering

Most disk caches reduce the disk access time required when a file is *read* from the disk, but the more advanced disk cache programs also can speed up the time taken to *save* a file to the disk.

With write buffering, the file to be saved is first transferred to the cache. The application can then proceed with other operations while the cache takes care of writing the file in the background. Write buffers are similar, in principle, to print buffers because the main application program is not held up waiting for the task to be completed.

As well as freeing the user to perform other tasks, write-buffering techniques also can increase the amount of data written to the disk in each rotation and can reduce the amount of disk read-write head movement.

Most disk caches immediately transfer data from the cache to the disk and do not wait for an extended period of user inactivity. This reduces the chances of data loss if the computer unexpectedly crashes.

Because a write cache saves the data in the background, a delay may occur before the data is saved to disk if the computer is busy with a foreground task. If the computer is rebooted or turned off before the cache has a chance to save the data, data loss can occur. The problem is not a major one, however, because even in the background the cache saves data within a matter of seconds.

Most disk cache programs provide a way to disable background write-buffering so that the data is saved as quickly as possible in the fore-ground. But even with background writing disabled, the disk cache still reduces the overall time taken for the data to be written to the disk.

Redundancy Checking

A few disk cache programs compare each sector to be saved to the sector on disk. If they are identical, the cache doesn't bother to save the data again. This technique is referred to as *redundancy checking*, but it usually does not save much time, because the time taken to check the data is almost as long as the time taken to save the data.

Not every disk cache program includes all the caching technologies described here, but the majority of good ones do. Upcoming sections review the capabilities of a variety of popular disk cache programs. Most good disk caches allow you to choose which features you want enabled, as well as the amount and type of memory to dedicate to the cache.

Disk Cache Considerations

Disk caches work by reserving a portion of memory to store data. As a general rule, the greater the amount of memory allocated to the disk cache, the greater the performance improvement. If you are using a machine with only 640K of memory, however, you may not be able to spare much room for a disk cache.

If a disk cache is less than 64K, it is usually insufficient to be an effective cache. In conventional memory, a 128K cache provides a very noticeable increase in performance. Good disk caches also support extended and expanded memory, with a small portion of the cache (less than 20K) residing in conventional memory.

If you have an 80286 (or later) computer, you may have the option of selecting extended or expanded memory for the cache. Which should you choose? As a general rule, extended memory is faster than expanded memory; therefore, you might expect an extended memory cache to be faster than an expanded memory cache. This, however, usually is not true.

For example, PC-Kwik from Multisoft Corporation requires less conventional memory and runs slightly faster if it is installed in expanded memory. Check your documentation to determine which option is faster.

If you have a lot of memory installed, you should consider increasing the disk cache to 1M or even 2M. If your software application does not use all your RAM, you might as well dedicate it to a disk cache. With some disk cache programs, you can even change the memory settings without rebooting. You might have a large 2M cache for a database program, but reduce the cache to 500K when running a spreadsheet program.

Each cache program has its own rules about how you specify the amount of memory to dedicate to the cache, as well as the memory type. You will learn about some popular cache programs shortly.

Disk Cache Problems

In some situations, a disk cache does not work, at best, and at worst, crashes the system. These problems usually arise when a cache is installed and another program uses a nonstandard technique for accessing data. That is, the program bypasses the operating system's disk read-write functions. Generally, caches are very stable and robust, but you may experience problems in the following areas:

- A disk cache may not work with backup programs that use the DMA chip for optimum backup speed. Everything may appear to be working correctly, but the files may not be successfully backed up. Be sure to test your backup to see if the files really are being saved when you use a disk cache. See Chapter 13 for more information about data backups.

- The cache may not work with certain RLL disk controllers, disks that use a nonstandard sector size, or disk device drivers such as Disk Manager.

- Programs that use special "DOS extender" technology may conflict with the cache. For example, some caches are incompatible with Lotus 1-2-3 Release 3.

- Some "clone" machines do not send a signal to the operating system when a diskette is swapped in a drive. As a result, a cache sometimes transfers data from memory to an applications program, not knowing that a switched diskette with different data has been inserted into the drive.

- Usually, disk caches do not function on network drives. This is not likely to cause a problem, but no performance improvements are realized on network drives.

- Using two different disk caches at the same time does not double the performance! In fact, doing so may cause your computer to hang.

These problems are no reason to avoid using a disk cache. If you discover a conflict, disable the cache while that particular program is running and enable it again afterwards.

"Free" Disk Caches

You may be surprised to find that you already have a disk cache program. Some hardware vendors, such as IBM and COMPAQ, now ship disk caches with their computer systems. Also, DOS V4 includes a disk cache program.

These "free" disk caches do improve overall system performance, but they are not generally as flexible, and their performance is not as good as that of commercial third-party disk cache programs. However, if you decide not to buy a commercial program, and your system includes a cache utility, then you should use it. The price is right, and you will obtain a noticeable increase in disk performance.

> **NOTE** These disk caches are not really free—they are bundled with some other product you have purchased. The programs are subject to software copyright law and may not be copied freely for others.

IBMCACHE

IBMCACHE.SYS is a device driver file that accompanies any IBM PS/2 system that uses extended memory (excluding Models 25 and 30). IBMCACHE is specifically made for PS/2 computers and is shipped on the Reference Disk included with the system.

To install the cache on your computer, insert the Reference Disk into drive A and enter the following command:

A:IBMCACHE

You are then presented with a variety of menu selections that copy the device driver IBMCACHE.SYS to your hard disk, add a line to your CONFIG.SYS file, and set the parameters to meet your requirements. Thereafter, you can modify the cache settings either by running the IBMCACHE.COM program or by directly editing the entry in the CONFIG.SYS file.

The options with IBMCACHE are limited. You can specify the size of the cache and whether it should be installed in conventional memory (also referred to as "low" memory) or extended memory. You also can specify the number of sectors that are loaded in each disk read, that is, the number of track buffers. The syntax of the IBMCACHE.SYS entry in the CONFIG.SYS file is

DEVICE = *d:path***IBMCACHE.SYS** *size /Psectors /E or /NE*

d:path is the optional disk drive and directory path to the file named IBMCACHE.SYS.

size is the size of the cache in kilobytes, limited only by the total amount of memory available.

/Psectors identifies the number of sectors that are read every time the disk is accessed. The acceptable settings are 2, 4, or 8.

The */E* and */NE* switches designate where the cache is to be placed. /E designates extended memory, and /NE designates conventional memory. You can use either switch, but not both.

After you change the cache settings, you must reboot the system for the settings to take effect.

COMPAQ CACHE

Every COMPAQ computer now ships with the program CACHE.EXE on the User Programs disk. CACHE.EXE is commonly regarded as the best "free" cache available. CACHE is a versatile program that supports mirroring and track buffering for read operations, as well as write buffering and redundancy checking (if the program is writing a single sector at a time) for write operations.

Like IBMCACHE, CACHE must be installed as a device driver in the CONFIG.SYS file. If it has been installed, you execute the CACHE.EXE program from the command line to change some of the setting and review the effect of the cache. The syntax for using CACHE as a device driver is

DEVICE = *d:path***CACHE.EXE** *ON or OFF size /BAS or /EXT or /EXP /Q*

d:path is the optional disk drive and directory path to the CACHE.EXE file.

The switch *ON* or *OFF* is used initially to enable or disable the cache. Use the OFF parameter if you want to install the cache, but have it initially disabled. The cache can be activated later with the CACHE ON command. (The default is ON.)

size is the size of the cache in kilobytes. The size can range from 128K to 15,232K.

The switch */BAS* or */EXT* or */EXP* is used to install the cache in conventional (referred to as *base*), extended, or expanded memory, respectively. (The default is /EXP.)

The */Q* switch is used to enable the use of write buffering (referred to as *queued* writes). Write buffering is not supported on 8086- and 8088-class machines.

The following statement in the CONFIG.SYS file creates a 2,048K cache in extended memory, with the main cache enabled and with no write buffering:

```
DEVICE=C:\DOS\CACHE.EXE 2048 ON /EXT
```

After the device driver has been installed, you can execute the CACHE program to set the status of the cache device driver, to enable or disable queued writes, to reset or display the disk cache statistics, or to display a brief help screen. The syntax of the CACHE command is

CACHE *ON or OFF QUEUE or NO QUEUE CLEAR HELP*

The *ON* switch is used to enable the cache and *OFF* disables the cache. When the cache is disabled, the memory used by the cache is free to be used by other applications.

The *QUEUE* and *NOQUEUE* switches are only applicable if the device driver was installed with /Q in effect. NOQUEUE disables write buffering, and QUEUE enables it again.

CLEAR resets the performance statistics, which are maintained by CACHE for information purposes.

HELP instructs CACHE to display a help screen explaining the switches.

One of the major strengths of the CACHE program is that the cache memory can be temporarily released for use by a program without needing to reboot the system.

If CACHE is executed with no parameters, a list of the CACHE statistics for the current session is displayed (see fig. 10.1).

```
C:\>cache

COMPAQ Disk Cache  Version 1.43
(C) Copyright Compaq Computer Corporation 1986, 1989


    Type of Cache Memory . . . . . .   EXTENDED
    Size of Cache Memory . . . . . .   2048 KB
    Disk Cache (ON/OFF)  . . . . . .   ON
    QUEUED Writes  . . . . . . . . .   NOT AVAILABLE
    Total Number of Reads  . . . . .   1303
    Number of Reads from Cache . . .   1098
    Number of Reads from Disk  . . .    205

C:\>
```

Fig. 10.1. COMPAQ's CACHE program displays performance statistics.

SmartDrive

Microsoft Corporation distributes the SmartDrive disk cache with MS-DOS V4 and with Microsoft Windows. Like IBMCACHE and COMPAQ's CACHE, SmartDrive is installed as a device driver in the CONFIG.SYS file. The name of the program is SMARTDRV.SYS.

SmartDrive is a "no-frills" disk cache that can be installed in expanded or extended memory. SmartDrive's main advantage is that it automatically frees memory if that memory is required by Microsoft Windows. That is, Smardrive is designed especially to work with Windows. The cache cannot, however, be disabled (without rebooting) if a non-Windows program needs additional memory.

The syntax of SMARTDRV.SYS is

DEVICE = *d:path***SMARTDRV.SYS** *size* /A

d:path\ is the optional disk drive and directory where the file SMARTDRV.SYS is stored.

size is the size of the cache in kilobytes. (The default is 256K.)

The /A switch forces the cache to use expanded memory.

If you use Microsoft Windows to run most of your applications, then SmartDrive with its Windows awareness may be the most appropriate disk cache to use.

Commercial Disk Caches

You can choose from several very good and economical disk cache programs. These programs generally offer improved performance gains and greater flexibility than the products discussed so far.

Before you buy a disk cache, you may want to consider how important the following are to you:

   Memory usage. If you have extended or expanded memory, you will want to keep conventional memory consumption to a minimum. The amount of conventional memory required varies from product to product.

Flexibility. Unless you enjoy keeping multiple CONFIG.SYS files, you should look for a cache program that can be reconfigured without rebooting the system.

Compatibility. Check with the vendor to see if the program is compatible with your hard disk and controller, as well as with your major applications programs.

Write buffering. Not all caches support write buffering, and this deficiency reduces performance gains if you frequently save files.

Floppy disk support. If you frequently access data on floppy disks, look for a cache that supports floppy disk drives.

Device support. If you use an external storage device, such as a Bernoulli drive, look for a cache that supports the device.

Performance. The main reason you want to use a disk cache is to improve hard disk performance. However, the performance of the cache itself is not usually a major factor. All the commercial disk caching programs offer great performance improvements, and benchmark tests indicate there are only marginal differences between them.

The following discussion covers three popular disk cache programs: Super PC-Kwik, Mcache from Mace Utilities, and PC Tools.

Super PC-Kwik

Super PC-Kwik is a critically acclaimed disk cache from Multisoft Corporation. The program is fast, easy to install, rich in features, and flexible.

The main Super PC-Kwik program is SUPERPCK.COM. It includes an automatic installation facility that checks the computer's memory as well as the disk and controller, and chooses the most appropriate settings (see fig. 10.2). The cache is not loaded as a device driver in CONFIG.SYS. To install Super PC-Kwik, execute the following command:

SUPERPCK

If you do not want to use the automatic settings, the program includes a variety of switches that strictly control how the cache functions. The following switches can be specified when you first install SUPERPCK:

Switch	Function
/A+	Use expanded memory.
/C+	Use conventional memory.
/E+	Use extended memory.
/EM	Minimize the amount of conventional memory used when the /E+ parameter is in effect.
/R:size	Reserve an amount of the available memory (determined by *size* in kilobytes) to be used by other programs and use the rest for the cache.
/S:size	Allocate *size* kilobytes for the cache.
/?	Display a help screen.

```
Super PC-Kwik(TM) Disk Accelerator, Version 3.53, S/N 317827
Copyright 1986, 1989 Multisoft Corporation, All Rights Reserved.
Program licensed exclusively for use on a single computer.
Subset of program (SUPERPCK.SB6) loaded.
Following is a list of the parameters in effect:
 /D+ Advanced support of diskette transfers.
 /H+ Advanced support of hard disk transfers.
 /B+ Perform batch copies to/from cache.
 /O- Standard algorithm for advanced support.
 /Q- Return DOS prompt normally.
 /T+ Track buffering using a 33-sector buffer.
 /V+ Use volume change hardware.
 /W+ Check write requests for redundancy.
 /-D Drive D cannot be cached -- physical unit unknown.
 /A+ 4048K Expanded memory cache has been set up as follows:
                      Conventional      Expanded
         DOS/Resident      122K            384K
         PC-Kwik            24K           4096K
         Available         494K              0K
         Total             639K           4480K
Super PC-Kwik program successfully installed.   Type "SUPERPCK /?" for help.

C:\PCKWIK>
```

Fig. 10.2. *SUPERPCK automatically selects the most appropriate cache settings.*

Once the disk cache has been installed, the following switches can be used to review and modify the settings:

Switch	Function
/D	Disable the cache, but keep the cache's memory reserved.
/E	Enable the cache, if it has been disabled with the /D parameter.
/F	Flush all data from the cache.
/M	Display the cache statistics for the current session (see fig 10.3).
/P	Display all the current settings.
/U	Uninstall the cache and release the memory.
/?	Display a help screen.

```
Super PC-Kwik(TM) Disk Accelerator, Version 3.53, S/N 317827
Copyright 1986, 1989 Multisoft Corporation, All Rights Reserved.
Program licensed exclusively for use on a single computer.
Super PC-Kwik program was previously installed and caching is enabled.
Measurements are as follows:
    4,301  logical transfers.
      963  physical transfers.
    3,338  transfers saved.
       77  percent saved.

C:\PCKWIK>
```

Fig. 10.3. *Super PC-Kwik's /M parameter displays the cache statistics.*

In addition to supporting most of the available hard disk drives and
controllers, PC-Kwik also supports floppy disk drives and Bernoulli drives.

> ✓
> **NOTE**
> Super PC-Kwik can be purchased as a single product or with a
> bevy of other programs in the PC-Kwik Power Pak. The
> Power Pak includes a RAM disk, a print spooler, a screen
> utility, and a keyboard enhancer. The unique feature of the
> Power Pak is that the disk cache, RAM disk, and print spooler
> can all share the same memory—the disk cache automatically
> frees cache memory if it is required by the print spooler or the
> RAM disk. When the memory is no longer required, the disk
> cache reclaims it.

Mcache from Mace Utilities

The Mace Utilities package includes a utilitarian disk cache, called Mcache.
There are actually three different cache programs, any one of which can be
loaded in the CONFIG.SYS file as a device driver. There is one driver for a
conventional memory cache, another for an extended memory cache, and a
third for an expanded memory cache. The syntax for each device driver is

DEVICE =*d:path***driver** */size* */d*

d:path\\ is the optional disk drive and directory path to the device driver file.

driver is one of the Mcache device drivers. Use MCACHE.SYS for
conventional memory, MCACH-EM.SYS for expanded memory, or
MCACH-AT.SYS for extended memory.

/size is the size of the cache in kilobytes.

/d is an optional parameter to restrict caching to a single physical hard disk.
Use /1 for the first hard disk, /2 for the second, and so forth.

Mace Utilities also includes a program called CACHCTRL.EXE, which
reports and adjusts the cache settings during a session. CACHCTRL can be
used with the switches ON, OFF, and TEST to enable or disable the cache
or to perform a benchmark test that indicates the effectiveness of the cache.

Although Mcache is a reasonable performer, it has a number of
shortcomings: when the cache is disabled, the memory is not released;
parameters cannot be modified without modifying CONFIG.SYS and
rebooting; and all partitions on a drive must be cached.

PC-CACHE from PC Tools

PC Tools includes the disk cache program PC-CACHE. Prior to version 6 of PC Tools, the disk cache was actually a slimmed-down version of the PC-Kwik disk cache. Starting with PC Tools version 6, however, Central Point Software implemented its own disk-cache technology; PC-CACHE is no longer a hybrid of PC-Kwik.

PC-CACHE is an executable program (not a device driver), which can provide a cache in conventional, expanded, or extended memory. The PC-CACHE.EXE command takes the following syntax:

PC-CACHE */SIZE=nnn or /SIZEEXP=nnn or /SIZEEXT=nnn switches*

/SIZE, /SIZEEXP, or */SIZEEXT* is specified for conventional, expanded, or extended memory respectively. *nnn* is the size of the cache in kilobytes.

switches are a variety of optional switches that can further control the characteristics of the cache. If the /? switch is used, the program displays a help screen detailing all the switches (see fig. 10.4).

```
C:\U\PCTOOLS>pc-cache /?
                  PC-CACHE, Version 6
    Copyright 1990, Central Point Software Inc., All Rights Reserved.
                  Summary of Parameters

    /EXTSTART=xxxxK  Don't use extended memory below xxxxK.
    /FLUSH           Flush cache -- set the cache to empty.
    /Ix              Do not cache drive x.
    /INFO            Display drive information.
    /MAX=xx          Cache no more than xx sectors at a time.
    /MEASURES        Display measurements.
    /NOBATCH         Don't batch copy to/from the cache.
    /PARAM           Display parameters in effect.
    /PAUSE           Pause before installing.
    /QUIET           Don't display status messages.
    /SIZE=xxxK       Set up xxxK cache in conventional memory.
    /SIZEXP=xxxxK    Set up xxxxK cache in expanded memory.
    /SIZEXT=xxxxK    Set up xxxxK cache in extended memory.
    /UNLOAD          Un-install the cache.
    /WRITE=xx        Set disk write optimization period to xx.
    /?               Display this information.

C:\U\PCTOOLS>
```

Fig. 10.4. *The /? parameter displays a list of optional switches.*

If PC-CACHE is executed without any parameters, the default cache settings are used: 256K of extended or expanded memory, if available; otherwise 64K of conventional memory; 4 sectors track buffered; and no delay on write buffering.

The cache supports up to four drives, but it automatically caches all partitions for a drive. The cache does not support floppy drives or Bernoulli drives (unlike earlier versions). The cache can be removed from memory without rebooting the system.

Using RAM Disks

A RAM disk is a portion of memory that is disguised as a disk drive. The operating system and programs treat a RAM disk like any other drive in the system—it is assigned a letter name (E:, for example), files can be copied to the drive and executed, and so on. RAM disk files are "stored" in a reserved portion of memory and can be accessed almost instantly. The main difference between a normal disk and a RAM disk is that the RAM disk is blazingly fast, because all the files are in memory, not on a physical disk; there are, therefore, no read-write heads or actuator arms to slow things down.

RAM disks usually are created by adding a device driver to the CONFIG.SYS file. Most versions of DOS later than V3 and of OS/2 include a RAM disk device driver. The RAM disk normally can be situated in conventional, expanded, or extended memory, and the size of the disk is definable. The larger the RAM disk, the more files can be stored.

When RAM disks are named, drive letters are first assigned to all physical drives and partitions. Then the next available letter is assigned to the RAM disk. For example, if you have one hard disk in your system, it is drive C, and the RAM disk becomes drive D.

⊠
WARNING
When the computer is turned off (or rebooted), all the files and data in a RAM disk are lost. When you save a file to a RAM disk, you are not permanently saving the file to a disk. Make sure that you copy any modified files from the RAM disk to the hard disk before turning off or rebooting the computer.

Comparing RAM Disks to Disk Caches

RAM disks are often confused with disk caches. They both use a reserved portion of memory to reduce disk activity and improve the effective operating speed of the computer, but they are used very differently.

When a disk cache is installed, it monitors all disk activity and automatically improves disk performance. A RAM disk, on the other hand, has no "intelligence" and can only speed access to files that you or a program have placed on the RAM disk drive. Unlike a disk cache, a RAM disk does not improve performance when you access the hard disk. You must explicitly access the files on the RAM disk to gain a performance advantage.

A cache automatically discards any sectors of data not required to make way for more frequently used data. When you use a RAM disk, you must decide which files are to be copied to or deleted. A disk cache can speed access to a file that does not completely fit in the allotted memory, but a RAM disk must have room for the entire file.

When a file is saved, a disk cache ensures that the file is promptly and permanently saved on the physical disk. A RAM disk does not transfer files back to the disk. You must manually copy the files from the RAM disk to the hard disk.

Generally, a disk cache is much easier to use than a RAM disk and provides better overall performance, but there are some good applications for a RAM disk.

Good RAM-Disk Applications

When a RAM disk is first created, it is empty; it contains no files. The primary purpose of a RAM disk is to temporarily store files that can then be accessed very quickly by the operating system or by an applications program. RAM disks normally should be used for files that do not change, are short-lived, or are frequently used.

There is little point in copying files to a RAM disk if the files are used infrequently. For example, if you use 1-2-3, all the program files are loaded into memory when the program is first executed, and they are not accessed on the disk again. There is little point in transferring 1-2-3 program files to a RAM disk. In fact, a RAM disk used this way wastes valuable memory and restricts the space available for spreadsheet data.

The following sections describe a number of situations where a RAM disk can be put to good use.

Temporary Files

Behind the scenes, many programs create temporary (or scratch) files to store data during program execution. Most programming-language compilers and many Windows applications, such as Aldus PageMaker, create temporary files. Normally these temporary files are created on the hard disk, and this fact can result in a significant degradation of operating speed. The program has to create a temporary file, transfer data from memory to the file, perform the operation that needs the extra memory, and then reload the data from the temporary file.

The majority of these types of programs can be instructed where to store temporary files, either by specifying a switch when the program is executed or by adding a variable to the environment. (See Chapter 5 for more information on the environment.) For example, Aldus PageMaker checks the environment to see if a directory is assigned to the environment variable TEMP. If so, all temporary files are created in the specified directory.

If your RAM disk has been assigned to drive D, you can instruct a program like PageMaker to use the RAM disk for temporary files by entering the following command at the operating system prompt:

    SET TEMP=D:

With a RAM disk, you will normally experience a very significant performance improvement in those program operations that need to create a temporary file. If you find that the program operates more slowly after you have assigned a RAM disk, try making the RAM disk larger.

Program Overlay Files

Some large programs keep a part of the program in separate files called overlay files. The main program file usually has a COM or EXE extension, and the overlay files usually have an OVR or OVL extension or something similar. Whenever the main program performs a task that needs code from an overlay, the overlay file is read from disk into memory, and the code is executed. A popular program that uses this technique is AutoCAD.

The time taken to load the program overlay is significant, and you may notice that the program seems slow during certain operations. If you notice activity on your hard disk, it is likely that the program is loading an overlay file.

A RAM disk provides a very convenient way of speeding up this whole operation. The basic approach is to copy the main program and all the overlay files onto the RAM disk and then execute the program from the RAM disk. Whenever the program needs an overlay file, it is instantly available from the RAM disk. If you find no significant improvement in program speed, the chances are that the program automatically loads the overlays into expanded or extended memory and doesn't look for them on the disk anyway.

For safety's sake, double-check to make sure that you are saving your data files to the hard disk, and not to the RAM disk.

Spell Checkers

Most popular word processors include a spell checker and a thesaurus as writing aids. Usually, the spell checker's dictionary and the thesaurus are stored in very large, external files. Every time one of these utility files is needed, the main program opens the file and searches through it for data. Copying these files to a RAM disk can produce a significant improvement in the operating speed of the program.

Some word processing programs allow you to specify the drive where the utility files are to be stored. If not, you have to copy all the word processor program files onto the RAM disk and execute the entire program from the RAM disk.

Copying Files between Floppy Disks

If you have a single floppy disk drive in your system, a RAM disk can provide a very convenient way of copying files from one floppy disk to another. You insert the source disk in the floppy disk drive and copy all the files to the RAM disk. If the diskette includes subdirectories, you can use the XCOPY command to copy all the files in all directories. Assuming that the RAM disk is drive E, use the following command to copy all the files to the RAM disk:

XCOPY A:*.* E: /S/E

Then insert the formatted target diskette into drive A and copy the files to it by entering the following command:

XCOPY E:*.* A: /S/E

Copying in this manner is faster than copying files to a temporary directory on the hard disk, and is usually faster than the DISKCOPY command, especially on computers with a single drive, or when you are trying to make multiple copies of a disk.

Laptop Computers

The main drain of power for a laptop computer is running the disk drives. An excellent way of conserving energy is to create as large a RAM disk as you can afford and copy all the programs you will be using onto the RAM disk. The less frequently you use the hard disk, the longer your battery will last. If you use a laptop with no hard disk, a RAM drive can really speed up program operation.

Linked Worksheets

Some spreadsheet programs allow you to link cells in the active worksheet (the worksheet loaded in memory) to cells and ranges in other worksheets that are disk-based. When you first load the worksheet into memory, and whenever you perform a full recalculation, the worksheet files on disk must be opened to obtain the values for the specified cells and ranges. Although disk-linked worksheets are a convenience, they tend to slow down the application. You will realize a real performance improvement if you copy the worksheets to a RAM disk and link to them there. The linked cells are recalculated almost as quickly as the cells in the active worksheet.

Using Operating System RAM Disks

Versions of DOS after V3 include with the operating system a device driver for a RAM disk. To set up a RAM disk using DOS 3.x and later, all you need to do is add a device driver to the CONFIG.SYS file. Depending on which version of DOS you have, the RAM disk may be called either RAMDRIVE.SYS or VDISK.SYS. The following text refers to RAMDRIVE.SYS, but the information is equally applicable to the VDISK.SYS driver.

The syntax for the RAMDRIVE.SYS device driver is

DEVICE = *d:path***RAMDRIVE.SYS** *disksize sectorsize entries /E or /A*

d:path is the optional disk drive and directory path to the device driver file.

disksize is the size of the RAM disk in kilobytes. (The default is 64K.)

sectorsize is the sector size in bytes. The allowable sizes are 128, 256, 512, and 1,024 bytes. (The default is 512.)

entries specifies the maximum number of root directory entries. The minimum is 4, and the maximum is 1,024. (The default is 64.)

If */A* is specified, the RAM disk is placed in expanded memory; if /E is specified, the disk is placed in extended memory. Otherwise the disk is placed in conventional memory.

The following entry in the CONFIG.SYS file creates a 360K RAM disk in extended memory, with a 512-byte sector and 64-file limit in the root directory:

```
DEVICE=RAMDRIVE.SYS 360 512 64 /E
```

PC-Kwik Power Pak RAM Disk

Few of the disk utility programs include RAM disk software, because the one provided with the operating system is perfectly adequate. One notable exception is the RAM disk provided in the PC-Kwik Power Pak from Multisoft Corporation.

The PC-Kwik RAM disk is a simple RAM disk that shares memory with the PC-Kwik disk cache (discussed earlier in this chapter). When the RAM disk has no files, all of the memory is available to the disk cache. When you copy files to the RAM disk, the memory is taken from the pool of memory shared by the disk cache and the RAM disk. When files are deleted, the RAM disk memory is released and is once again used by the disk cache. This intelligent utilization of memory makes using a RAM disk much more attractive, because the memory is not wasted when the RAM disk is not being used.

The PC-Kwik RAM disk is a device driver called PCKRAMD.SYS. It is installed in the CONFIG.SYS using the following syntax:

DEVICE = *d:path***RAMDISK.SYS** */S:nnn /D:nnn*

d:path is the optional disk drive and directory path to the device driver file.

/S:nnn is the maximum size of the RAM disk in kilobytes. (The default is 128K.)

/D:nnn is the maximum number of root directory entries. (The default is 64.)

If you want to have multiple RAM disks (and if you have sufficient memory), add additional RAMDISK.SYS entries in CONFIG.SYS.

RAM.SYS

On the disk that accompanies this book is an excellent public-domain RAM disk utility. The RAM.SYS and SETRAM.EXE files provide a flexible RAM disk. Install the RAM disk by including the following statement in the CONFIG.SYS file:

DEVICE=RAM.SYS

If the RAM.SYS device driver is not in the root directory, precede the file name with the drive name and the path to the file.

DISK   RAM.SYS is a public-domain disk utility that provides a conventional-memory RAM disk, which can be adjusted in size without rebooting the computer.

After you enter the command, reboot the computer, and an empty RAM disk is created. The program SETRAM.EXE is used to set the amount of memory used by the RAM disk. The syntax of the SETRAM command is

SETRAM drive size

drive is the drive letter for the RAM disk, and **size** is the size of the RAM disk in kilobytes.

The following command sets the RAM disk to 360K:

SETRAM D 360

The main drawback of RAM.SYS is that the RAM disk must reside in conventional memory. A handy aspect of this utility is that you can modify the amount of memory allocated to the RAM disk without rebooting the computer. All you have to do is empty the RAM disk with the command **SETRAM** *d*, where *d* is the name of the drive, and reallocate a different size using the full syntax.

To modify the RAM disk to a 100K in size, for example, enter the following two commands:

SETRAM D
SETRAM D 100

Further documentation for RAM.SYS is included on the disk that accompanies this book, in the text file RAM.DOC.

Defragmenting a Hard Disk

Over time, you may notice that file operations (saving a large worksheet, for example) seem to take longer and longer. This may be just because the file size has increased, but it also could be because the hard disk has become *fragmented*. That is, the files are not stored efficiently on your disk. If you are unaware of file fragmentation and have taken no steps to rectify it, your disk is probably operating significantly below its optimum speed.

Every active hard disk should be regularly defragmented. Various utility programs can reorganize the files so that they are stored efficiently. The fastest way to defragment a disk is with a commercial defragmentation program, although you also can use a combination of operating system commands (discussed in the section "Defragmentation on a Budget").

Defragmentation takes time, and the more sophisticated programs allow you to select how thoroughly you want to defragment the disk. In the fastest mode, the files are not completely defragmented—they may be organized into two or three different fragments, but that is much better than a dozen! In an intermediate mode, the files are completely defragmented, but the free space on the disk may be split into several areas of the disk. In the most thorough mode, all the file-optimization operations are performed.

If you frequently defragment your disk, you might include a quick defragmenter in your AUTOEXEC.BAT file and run a thorough defragment once a week.

Understanding Fragmentation

Chapter 5 described the way files are physically saved on the disk. You may recall that the operating system maintains a list of all the clusters on the disk. The clusters are categorized as empty, in use, or unusable. When a new file is saved to the hard disk, the operating system checks in the file allocation table to see where the first empty cluster is on the disk. The file is saved in this cluster. If the file is too large to fit in one cluster, the operating system checks the FAT again and looks for the next free cluster. The process repeats until all the file has been saved. The operating system then records in the file's directory entry the cluster where the first part of the file is saved. In the FAT, the first cluster points to the second cluster, the second to the third, and so on, to form a *cluster chain*. By referencing the directory entry and the FAT, the operating system can determine all the clusters where a file is stored.

When a disk is first formatted and used, all the clusters are empty, and so the files are stored in adjacent clusters. The next free cluster is always adjacent to the cluster to which the file was just partially written. Files stored in this manner are very quick to read because movement of the disk read-write head is minimal. Moving the read-write head to another track is one of the slowest operations in the whole file-reading process.

When a file is deleted, the clusters that were allocated to the file are marked as free and can be used when new data is saved to the disk. After just a few weeks (or even days) of disk usage, a typical drive has free clusters scattered all over the disk. Now when a file is saved to such a disk, the chances are slim that it is saved in a neat block of contiguous clusters. The first free cluster may be on one track, and the next free cluster may be on a remote track. Files stored in different remote clusters are said to be *fragmented*.

File fragmentation also occurs when you save a new version of a file to the disk. If the file is larger than the old version stored on disk, the last part of the file must be located in the next available cluster(s). The free cluster may not be situated near the first part of the file.

Defragmenting a disk can significantly increase the overall speed of reading and writing hard disk data. For a badly fragmented disk, the improvement can be as much as 200-400 percent. That's a performance improvement worth having!

How Defragmenters Work

A commercial defragmentation program reorganizes hard disk data so that every file is stored in adjacent clusters. To do this, the utility must move data from one cluster and place it in a different cluster. In a badly fragmented disk, you may find that the data on every cluster is moved to another location. That hard disk really gets a workout during the defragmentation process!

Each file is processed in turn. The directory and FAT are accessed to find the location of each cluster used by a file. The program then moves these clusters to an area of the disk where they can be stored together (see fig. 10.5). The process is complicated by the fact that there may not be enough space available to store the newly organized file. In this situation, the program has to move some other clusters to make room for the file.

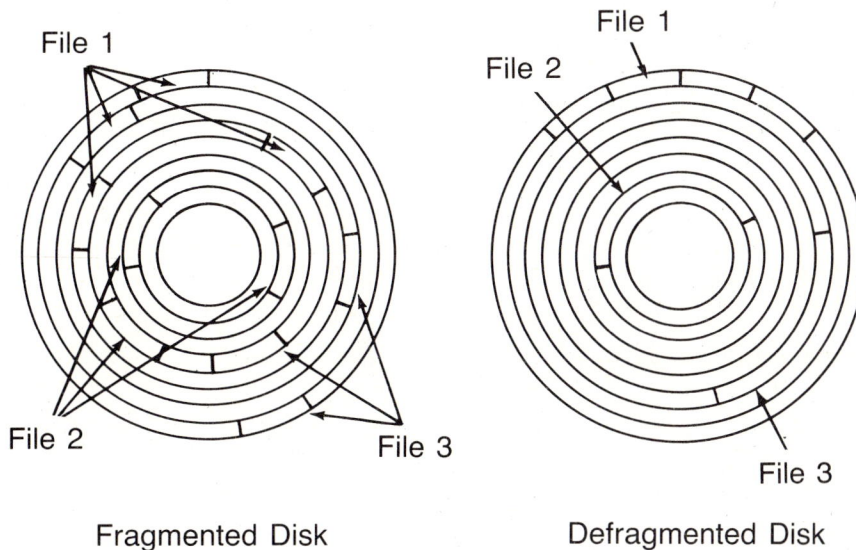

File 1

File 2

File 1

File 2

File 3

File 3

Fragmented Disk

Defragmented Disk

Fig. 10.5. A hard disk before and after defragmentation.

Defragmentation programs use remote parts of the disk (where no data is currently stored) as a temporary holding place for clusters. Clusters are also temporarily held in RAM while other clusters on the disk are reorganized. Most defragmentation programs display a graphical map of the disk, which shows the clusters being moved around during the defragmentation process.

Most defragmenters do not move hidden files. The main reason is that the hidden files may form part of a copy-protection scheme that requires the files to be stored in a specific sector. If the hidden file is moved, the protected program may not function, because it suspects that there has been a copy violation.

The time required to reorganize a hard disk depends on the size of the disk, the degree of fragmentation, the speed of the computer, and the speed of the defragmentation program. The time can range from 5 to 45 minutes. If you regularly defragment your disk, the defragmenter will have less work to do, and the time can be reduced to a few minutes. The frequency with which you should defragment your disk is influenced largely by how often you use your hard disk, but it is usually somewhere between once a week and once a month.

☒ **WARNING**	During the defragmentation process, the data on the hard disk is constantly being moved around and reorganized. If you turn off the computer or interrupt the program while the disk is being processed, you may trash the FAT and lose data.

Some of the most advanced defragmentation programs have a safety valve that prevents any data loss if the program is interrupted. Unless you are confident you are using one of these programs, however, do not interrupt.

Benefits of Defragmenting

The most obvious benefit of keeping a disk defragmented is that disk access is much faster, because the read-write heads move less to read all the file's clusters. There also are a number of less obvious benefits:

- Whenever a file is accessed on the disk, the operating system checks the directory entry and the FAT before reading the file data. On a defragmented disk, the directory files can be moved to the outermost tracks, adjacent to the FAT, to reduce read-write head movement while the file bookkeeping details are accessed.

● Defragmenters move all the files to the outside area of the disk, as near as possible to the file allocation table. This rearrangement reduces the distance the read-write head has to move.

● Defragmentation programs can verify the integrity of the disk surface and provide an early-warning system if there is a marked increase in bad sectors.

● It is much easier to automatically recover a deleted file if the file's data is stored in contiguous clusters. Avoiding hard disk fragmentation enhances your chances of data recovery. See Chapter 15 for more information about data recovery.

Commercial Defragmentation Programs

Many commercial disk defragmentation programs are available, and their flexibility and speed vary considerably.

The speed with which a defragmenter performs a task is not necessarily an indication of the thoroughness of the program. The most advanced defragmentation programs use very complex algorithms and sophisticated data movement tricks to reduce the time taken to process the disk. Slower is not always better!

The following sections discuss two of the most popular commercial defragmentation programs, as well as the defragmentation programs bundled with the multipurpose disk-utility programs PC Tools, Mace Utilities, and The Norton Utilities.

Multisoft's Power Disk

Power Disk was developed by the creators of the PC-Kwik disk utilities, Multisoft Corporation. Power Disk is a fast program, which offers a variety of options and modes that allow you to strictly control the defragmentation process.

Power disk includes the following four modes of operation:

Directories in order. The most thorough option, which defragments all files, fills all space, and organizes the files in the same order as the directories. By using a special control file, you can place any file toward the front or end of a disk's data area.

Speedy reorganization. All files are defragmented and all empty space is filled, but the files are not reorganized in directory order. This option is faster to execute than *directories in order*.

Fragmented files last. Places currently fragmented files at the end of the disk, with all nonfragmented files at the front. This operation is quick to run, but doesn't provide total defragmentation.

Partial defragment only. This strategy defragments as many files as possible into empty space without closing up all the empty spaces. This is usually the fastest option to execute, but it promotes future fragmentation.

Power Disk can be run from the command line, by passing switches, or it can be executed as a menu-driven program, with no switches. One of the excellent safety features of Power Disk is the capability of interrupting the program without corrupting data. You can even switch the computer off without damaging the file data. Power Disk also prevents you from popping-up any terminate-and-stay resident (TSR) programs, since they may inadvertently cause data loss.

An interesting feature of Power Disk is the Disk Explorer (see fig. 10.6). The Disk Explorer allows you to graphically view (and explore) any part of the disk. You can pinpoint a specific file's location and zoom in on any part of the disk to see how every single cluster is being deployed.

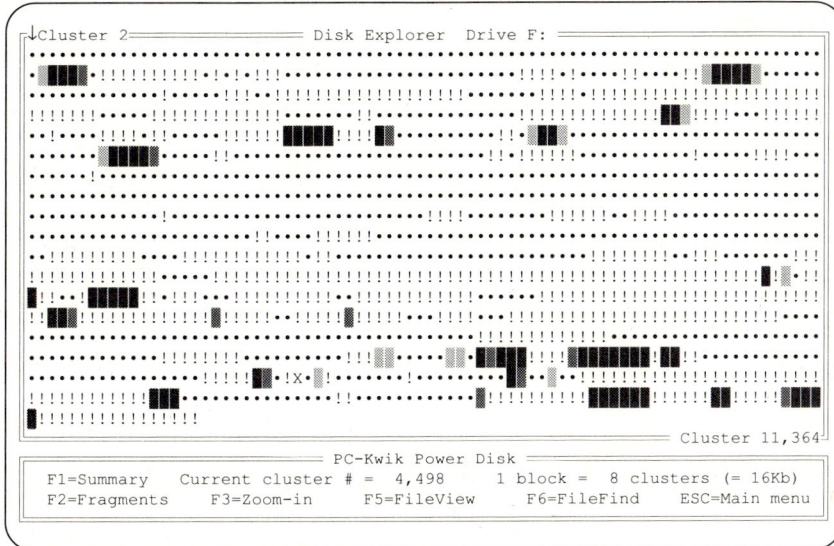

Fig. 10.6. Power Disk includes the Disk Explorer.

VOPT

VOPT, from Golden Bow Systems, is acknowledged as one of the fastest disk defragmenters in the market place. VOPT is a "no frills" program with few options and switches. VOPT is greatly optimized for speed and is fast enough that you can include it in your AUTOEXEC.BAT file.

The VOPT package contains a simulation program, SHOWVOPT, that emulates all the operations performed by VOPT, but does not actually write any changes to the disk. This is a useful utility if you want to perform a "dry run" to see what will happen when you try to defragment a disk.

When VOPT is executed, a depiction of the disk's organization is shown, and you can watch the activity while VOPT defragments the disk (see fig. 10.7). Nearly all disk defragmentation programs have a similar graphical display.

```
Vopt version 2.2                        ┌──── Cluster Map of C: ────┐
Copyright (C) Golden Bow Systems 1987   │ Lo Cluster=101  Scale: ■=15 Clus.
                                        │  •-Empty ■-Used ▓-Fragm ?-Bad
Volume TECHNOJOCK
   45196 sectors total disk space
     108 sectors in 3 hidden files
     176 sectors in 36 directories
   41360 sectors in 887 user files
      60 sectors marked bad
    3492 sectors available on disk

      17 empty files
     290 erased files
    3940 clusters in 93 fragmented files
   11299 is the highest used cluster
     844 is the lowest empty cluster
     872 free clusters in the used space

Files Moved     1
```

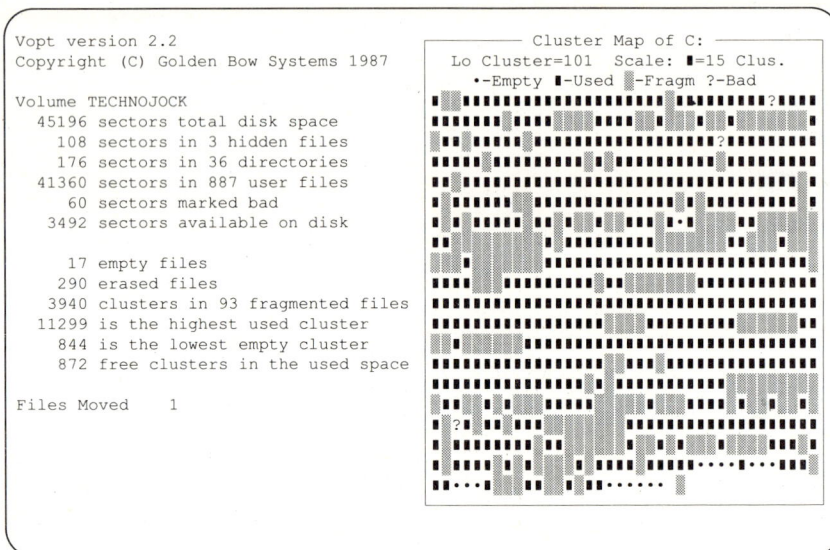

Fig. 10.7. VOPT graphically displays the defragmentation progress.

The VOPT package also includes various utility programs, including a better- than-DOS CHKDSK, and VMARKBAD, which finds and marks bad clusters.

Utility Programs

PC Tools, Mace Utilities, and The Norton Utilities each include a disk-defragmentation program. These programs do not defragment the drive as quickly as the Power Disk or VOPT, but they are all solid programs that perform adequately. If you own one of the utility programs, there is little reason to buy a specialty defragmentation program.

PC Tools' COMPRESS

The PC Tools defragmentation program is (somewhat misleadingly) called COMPRESS. COMPRESS can analyze a disk and report the degree of disk fragmentation. You can select which defragmentation technique you want the program to use.

COMPRESS also allows you to specify the order in which you want the files to be physically placed on the disk (see fig. 10.8). The standard order

places all subdirectories first, but you can instruct COMPRESS to situate
COM and EXE files at the beginning of the disk and specify that the files
and directories be grouped in ascending order.

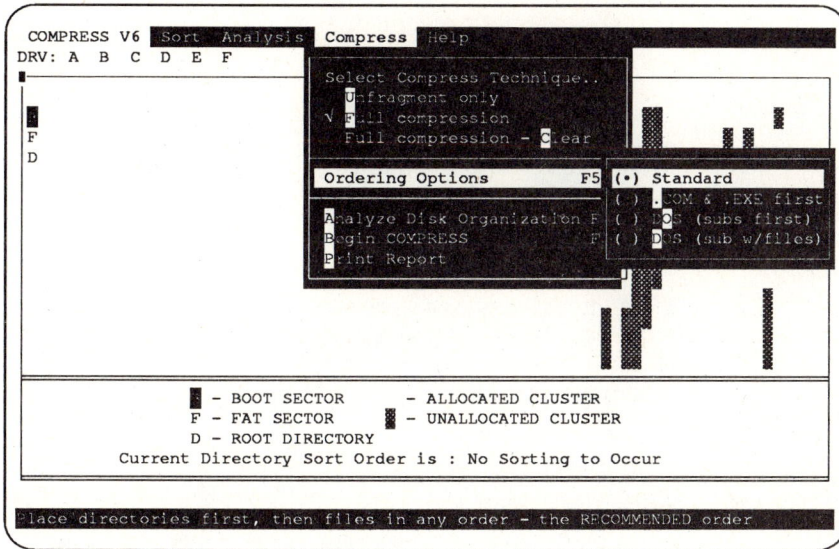

```
COMPRESS V6  Sort  Analysis   Compress  Help
DRV: A B C D E F
■                        Select Compress Technique..
■                          Unfragment only
F                        √ Full compression
D                          Full compression - Clear

                         Ordering Options          F5    (•) Standard
                                                         ( ) .COM & .EXE first
                         Analyze Disk Organization F     ( ) DOS (subs first)
                         Begin COMPRESS            F     ( ) DOS (sub w/files)
                         Print Report


              ■ - BOOT SECTOR       - ALLOCATED CLUSTER
              F - FAT SECTOR      ■ - UNALLOCATED CLUSTER
              D - ROOT DIRECTORY
        Current Directory Sort Order is : No Sorting to Occur

Place directories first, then files in any order - the RECOMMENDED order
```

Fig. 10.8. COMPRESS can sort the files in one of four orders.

COMPRESS offers three disk defragmentation options:

Unfragment only. All files are defragmented, but the free space is not reorganized. This is the quickest option to run, but new files tend to fragment quickly.

Full compression. All files are defragmented, and all free space is moved to the back (or inside) of the disk.

Full compression with clear. This option performs all the same operations as full compression and additionally erases all the data in unused sectors. This can improve your chances of data recovery if, later on, a file is accidentally deleted or destroyed.

Mace Utilities' UNFRAG Program

The Mace Utilities package includes the program UNFRAG. When UNFRAG is executed, the program first analyzes the disk and displays a list of all the fragmented files (see fig. 10.9). The program then defragments the disk according to the command-line switches specified.

```
v1990          M A C E   F R A G M E N T A T I O N   C H E C K        12-15-89

     FILE                                                 FRAGMENTS
   E:\BBS502\WINTTT5.PAS                                      3
   E:\BBS502\WINTTT5.QPU                                      2
   E:\BBS502\NESTTTT5.TPU                                     2
   E:\BBS502\DIRDEM2.EXE                                      2
   E:\TEMP\WINTTT5.PAS                                        2
   E:\BRIEF\READ.ME                                          2

   Press a key...
   E:\BRIEF\MACROS                                            2
   E:\BRIEF\MACROS\STARTUP.CM                                 2
   E:\BRIEF\MACROS\AUTOSAVE.CB                                2
   E:\BRIEF\MACROS\KEYBOARD.H                                 3
   E:\BRIEF\MACROS\PROCS.CM                                   2

   Total number of fragmented files: 53
   Total number of fragments: 125

   Done; press a key...
```

Fig. 10.9. *UNFRAG lists all the fragmented files.*

UNFRAG options can be set with the following switches:

Switch	Function
/R	Reorganizes the files to match the directory structure. All the files are placed on the disk in the same order as the directory structure.
/P	Packs the disk, moving all the files to the front of the disk and all empty clusters to the back.
/1	Instructs UNFRAG to execute another MACE program, REMEDY (discussed in Chapter 14), to test the disk surface.

The Norton Utilities' Speed Disk

Speed Disk (SD.EXE) is the Norton Utilities disk defragmentation program. Speed Disk can be run from the command line by specifying switches, or in full-screen menu mode (see fig. 10.10).

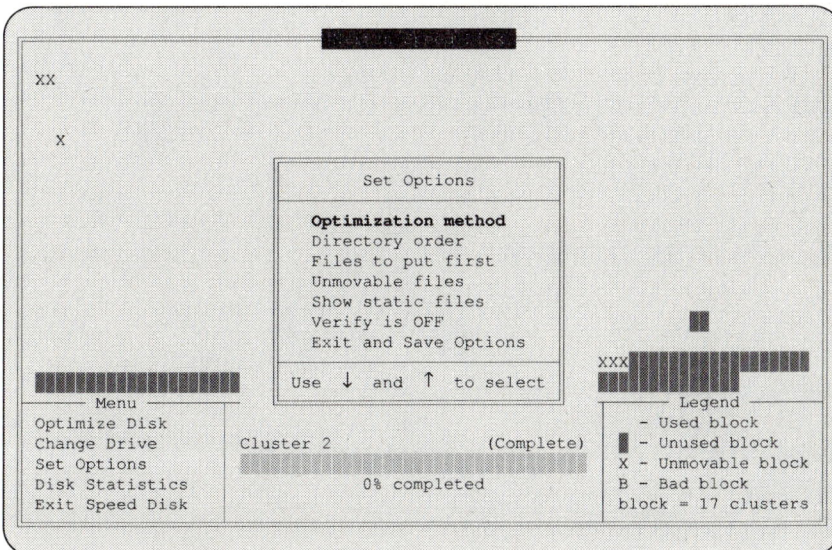

Fig. 10.10. *SD has a variety of defragmentation options.*

Speed Disk allows you to specify which files you want moved to the front of the disk and even which files you do not want moved. Speed Disk provides the following four optimization techniques:

Complete optimization. As the name suggests, this optimization is the most thorough. Once all files are unfragmented, the appropriate files and directories are moved to the front of the disk, and all free space is moved to the inside of the disk.

File unfragment. This option is less thorough (but faster) than the complete optimization, with the potential for some large files to remain fragmented and some empty clusters to remain in the data storage area.

Directories only. This is a very fast option that defragments directory files only.

Quick compress. Files are not defragmented, but all empty space is moved to the inside of the disk. This is a fast method that reduces the incidence of fragmentation in new files.

Economical Optimization with DOS

If you do not want to purchase a specialty disk optimization program, such as a disk cache or a defragmenter, there are still some measures you can take to improve your hard disk speed, just by using operating system commands. These methods involve changing the settings of various operating system commands and taking disk optimization into consideration when you use certain other commands.

Directory Organization

A significant amount of your disk activity is probably time spent searching for files. If you try to access a file from a nested subdirectory, the operating system has to find the parent directory entry in the root, jump to another part of the disk where the next level subdirectory file is stored, and so on, until the specific nested subdirectory is found, and the specific file's location is established. This kind of directory search happens when you load or access any file.

When you build your hard disk directories, you should avoid building a highly nested structure that extends many subdirectories deep. Chapter 8 provides some further guidelines on how you should organize the directories on a hard disk.

Avoid having huge directories that contain hundreds of files. Every time you enter a command in one of these directories, the operating system has to search through all the files, looking for the appropriate program file. Furthermore, large directories will not fit in a single cluster, and the operating system will have to look in two or more clusters just to find the file entry in the directory.

Following these guidelines for hard disk structure will not only speed your disk read-write operations, but also will make the disk easier to manage in general.

Optimizing the PATH and APPEND Commands

In Chapter 5 you learned that the PATH command is used to instruct the operating system where to search for programs. If you enter a command at the operating system prompt, the operating system looks in the current directory for a file with a COM, EXE, or BAT extension. If the file is not found, the operating system accesses the PATH specified in the environment and continues searching in each of the directories specified in the PATH. The number of entries and the order of the entries on the PATH command line can have a significant impact on the speed with which programs are found and executed.

Avoid having too many entries in the PATH. If you enter an invalid command (for example, DRI instead of DIR), the operating system will have to search through every directory on the path, only to respond with **Bad command or filename**.

The operating system searches the directories in the order specified in the PATH. Thus, you should put the most-used directories toward the front of the PATH statement: C:\DOS;C:\BATFILES;C:\UTILS. Avoid having deeply nested directories specified in the path. Otherwise, the operating system will have to jump all over the disk to locate files. If the files are used frequently, place them in a directory off the root directory.

Like the PATH command, APPEND instructs the operating system where to search for data files. If you use the APPEND command, follow the same principles as for the PATH command to optimize performance.

Optimizing BUFFERS

In Chapter 8 you learned how to use the BUFFERS command in the CONFIG.SYS file. The BUFFERS command is similar in principle to a disk cache, and it has a significant impact on disk read operations.

> ☑ **NOTE** Most disk cache programs provide their own read buffering. If you use a commercial disk cache program, check to see whether the documentation recommends an optimum setting for the DOS buffers. Having too many DOS buffers wastes memory without improving performance.

The BUFFERS command specifies how much RAM to reserve for track buffering. When data is read from the disk, some extra data is read into the buffers. When more data is requested, the operating system checks to see if the data is already loaded in the buffer. If it is, the data is quickly transferred from RAM and the disk is not accessed.

The exact number of buffers you need depends on your computer, disk drive, and disk activity. Usually, a BUFFERS value in the range of 10 to 20 is optimal for a 640K system. See Chapter 8 for additional information on buffers.

Using FASTOPEN

The operating system command FASTOPEN was introduced with DOS V3.3 and improves the performance of computers with hard disks. Because the file allocation table is so frequently accessed, it is usually stored in the disk buffers. The directory entries, however, are not. The FASTOPEN command reserves memory to cache the directory entries. Whenever the operating system searches for files, the directory details can be quickly read from the cache, rather than from the disk.

Every time a file or directory is opened, FASTOPEN records its name and location. With DOS V4, FASTOPEN also keeps a map of the file's physical location on the drive. If a file or directory already recorded by FASTOPEN is reopened, the access time is greatly reduced.

If you don't have a commercial disk cache and you are using DOS V3.3 or later, you should use the FASTOPEN command. See Appendix A for further details about FASTOPEN.

The Impact of VERIFY

The DOS VERIFY command controls the data checking performed when a file is written to the disk. If the verify indicator is on, the data written to the disk is verified. If the verify indicator is off, the data written to the disk is not verified.

Verifying data during disk writes is inherently slower than not verifying data. In most disk-intensive activities, a program will be 20% to 40% slower during disk read-write operations if verification is on. If you are looking for optimum speed, turn off disk verification, and if you are looking for maximum data integrity, turn on verification.

It is normally not necessary to have verification permanently on. By default, verification is off, but you should then turn it on for sensitive or important tasks.

You can determine your current setting for the VERIFY command by entering **VERIFY** with no switches. The operating system will report the current state of verification, for example, `VERIFY is on`. You can control the verification state by using the switches ON and OFF; that is, enter **VERIFY ON** or **VERIFY OFF** to set the verify state.

Defragmentation on a Budget

DOS does not provide a defragmentation program, but with a little patience, you can defragment a disk by using standard DOS commands.

The basic approach is to back up the entire disk, by using the BACKUP command (or a third-party backup program). You then can format the disk by using the FORMAT command. This step erases all the files on the disk. Finally, you RESTORE the files from the backup. When the files are restored to the disk, they will not be fragmented.

> ⊠
> **WARNING**
> Before formatting your disk, make *absolutely* sure that you have successfully backed up the data. Try to restore some of the files to make sure they were really backed up, and browse the file backup log to see that every directory was included. See Chapter 13 for further information on data backups.

Backing up and restoring an entire disk is a slow process, especially if you do not have a commercial backup program. But your disk has the potential to run a lot faster after the defragmentation. Further, the process provides a full backup of your data!

DISK

In Chapter 3 you learned that the hard disk cannot perform optimally unless the disk's optimum interleave ratio is set. Included on this book's companion disk are the programs SPINTEST.COM and SPINTIME.COM. You can use these programs to determine your hard drive's interleave ratio and the precise speed at which the disk revolves. Refer to Appendix E for details on these helpful programs.

Summary

The primary speed characteristics of the drive are hardware-dependent, but significant performance gains can be realized by keeping the disk fully optimized. The following optimization techniques were discussed in this chapter:

- Disk caches reduce the amount of disk activity by mirroring, track buffering, write buffering, and redundancy checking. Caches can have a profound impact on the overall performance of your system.

- Recent versions of DOS and OS/2 include disk cache software, but commercial cache programs usually offer superior performance gains and greater flexibility.

- RAM disks are like disk drives in memory, and they can be used to improve performance by temporarily storing frequently accessed files.

- Disk fragmentation significantly impairs disk performance. All hard disks should be regularly defragmented.

- The most significant optimization is achieved with commercial software, but performance gains also can be realized by fine tuning operating system settings, such as PATH, APPEND, BUFFERS, FASTOPEN, and VERIFY.

In Chapter 11, you will learn how to use various file-management tools to improve hard disk performance.

11

Using File-Management Tools

This chapter reviews some of the most popular hard disk management programs, including utility programs that help you manage the information on your hard disk. The discussion focuses on three programs that provide menu-creating capabilities, on five useful file-management programs, and on seven handy file utilities included on the disk that accompanies this book.

In Chapter 9 you learned how to develop a menu system from a set of batch files. As alternatives, literally dozens of specialized menu programs exist that simplify the process of finding and executing programs. The first part of this chapter describes the features and capabilities of three popular menu programs.

One of the most valuable programs you can add to your set of hard disk tools is a file manager. File managers help you to manipulate the files on your hard disk, and they provide much more power and flexibility than the standard operating system commands. For example, you can move files, reorganize the directory structure, manipulate files in groups, search for a specific phrase, and much more. We review some of the best disk-management tools in the second part of the chapter.

DISK

Most hard disk users also have a collection of utilities that provide a quick and easy way of performing specific file-management tasks, such as listing the contents of a file or finding a file. In the last section of this chapter, we review some of the most popular disk-utility programs (all of which are included on the disk that accompanies this book).

A note from the author ... It used to be that if your computer had a hard disk, you needed a menu program and a file manager. But more and more disk-utility programs are providing a broad range of features that address more than one area of hard disk management. Some file managers include menu capabilities, and some menu programs include file-management capabilities. It is becoming increasingly difficult to categorize utility programs. If you do not own a file manager or a menu program, you might want to consider buying one program that meets both requirements.

Using Menus

The primary purpose of a menu is to provide quick and easy access to programs. The instructions on how to execute each program are stored in one or more menu files, and when you select a topic from the menu, the program executes the appropriate instructions. For example, the menu program might change the default directory and execute a program with some predetermined parameters—and *voilà*, you have activated the chosen program. A menu provides a controlled environment to access all the applications programs on your hard disk. You no longer have to remember the operating system commands needed to start the programs. When you quit the applications program, you are returned to the menu.

To execute operating system commands, you can quit the menu program and return to the system prompt. Some programs provide a gateway that executes operating system commands, but does not free you to enter any command you want.

A major consideration when choosing a menu program is the amount of RAM required to run the menu. Some menu programs stay in memory and execute the applications program as a "child process." If the menu program consumes too much memory, there may not be enough memory to run the applications program. For example, Paradox and Aldus PageMaker are two programs that each require nearly 640K of memory and cannot be run from memory-hungry menu programs unless you have memory beyond 640K.

Some menu programs consume no memory whatsoever. This feat usually is achieved through the clever technique of building temporary batch files. When you select an option from the menu, the menu program terminates, the temporary batch file is executed to start the applications program, and when the program finishes, the temporary batch file calls the menu program again. The menu, therefore, is not in memory when the program executes.

If a goal of your menu system is to restrict a user's access to the system—for example, to prevent use of such DOS commands as FORMAT and DELETE—you will want to avoid menu systems that use this temporary batch file trick. During the brief time period when the temporary batch file is running, the user can press Ctrl-Break to halt the batch file and exit to DOS.

Menu Features

Most good menu programs do more that just execute a program; they provide a variety of additional features. The following list shows some of the extra capabilities you might find in a good menu program.

Automatic menu creation. Whey you install some menu programs, they automatically scour the hard disk, looking for well-known applications programs. These programs are then automatically added to an appropriate menu. With this feature, you are relieved of the task of manually adding each of your programs to the menu, that is, adding a new menu topic that identifies the program and identifying the drive/directory where the program is stored and the command used to execute the program. If a menu-installation program doesn't load some of your programs (because they are less well known), you can always manually add them after installing the menu program.

Parameter prompting. Some programs require a number of parameters or switches to be specified when the program is executed, and you may want to specify certain switches every time you select the program. For example, with a text-editing program, such as EDLIN or TEDDY, you need to specify the name of the file you want to edit. Good menu programs provide a facility to prompt you for data before executing the program, thereby allowing you to specify different parameters each time the program is run.

Password protection. If your PC is going to be used by more than one person, you may want to password-protect certain programs—your name and address book, for example. If you select a protect option from the menu, the menu program prompts you to enter a password. Only if you enter the password correctly will the program be executed. *Note: securing a program by adding a password to the menu provides only modest protection. Most knowledgeable intruders would be able to circumvent this form of security. See Chapter 16 for more information on data security.*

Activity logging. If your PC is used in a multiuser environment and you want to monitor the system usage, or if you are trying to keep track of how much time you spend using each application (for billing purposes, for example), then you should use a menu that has an activity-logging feature. The menu automatically notes in a file the time each application is started and finished. You can browse this file to review the computer's activity. Menu activity logging is useful only up to a point because many users tend to leave a PC idle in an application—1-2-3 in 1-2-3 READY mode, for example. The log will imply that the system was being used for 1-2-3 work when it may have been idle. However, if users consistently terminate applications and return to the menu, the activity log can be very informative.

Mouse support. Menus make it easy to access applications software, and menu programs that provide mouse support are usually the easiest of all to use. All you have to do is drag the mouse and click the button. More and more menu systems are incorporating mouse support.

Screen blanking. When the computer is idle, the main menu probably is displayed. Over time, the image can "burn-in" to the phosphor of the monitor tube and leave a permanent shadow of the menu imprinted on the monitor. This problem is particularly evident in monochrome displays. One remedy is a menu system that has an automatic "dimmer," which blanks the screen after a specified period of inactivity. The screen is automatically refreshed when you press a key.

Restricted operating system access. If you are creating a menu for an inexperienced computer user, you may not want him to leave the menu system and use operating system commands. Some menu programs enable you to password-protect or otherwise prevent the user from gaining direct access to the operating system.

Virus Detection. Computer virus programs propagate by modifying program code when the program is executed. Some contemporary menu systems provide in-built virus-detection software that can help identify and prevent the propagation of computer viruses. For more information on computer viruses, see Chapter 17.

Network Support. Not all menu programs work in a network environment. Some menu programs create one or more temporary files that are accessed when the applications program is terminated, that is, when the user is trying to return to the menu. In a multiuser environment, the menu program needs to create a separate temporary file for each active user; otherwise one user's temporary file will be overwritten by someone else's.

Built-in file manager. Some menu programs include a file manager to help you manage the data on your hard disk. These utilities are not directly related to menu creation, and are provided as a value-added tool to increase the usefulness of the overall product.

Table 11.1 summarizes the features available in the three menu programs discussed in this chapter.

Table 11.1
Summary of Menu Program Features

Feature	PowerMenu	Automenu	Direct Access
Activity Logging	✔	✖	✔
Automatic Menu Creation	✔	✖	✔
File Manager	✔	✖	✖
Memory Consumption	4K	0/27K	0K
Mouse Support	✖	✔	✔
Network Support	✖	✔	✖
Parameter Prompting	✔	✔	✔
Password Protection	✔	✔	✔
Restricted DOS Access	✔	✔	✔
Screen Blanking	✔	✔	✔
Virus Protection	✖	✖	✔

Before buying a menu program, decide which features you want and choose a program that offers those features. Remember that there are dozens of reliable menu programs available, and you do not need to restrict your selection to the ones discussed in this section.

Using PowerMenu

PowerMenu from Brown Bag Software, Inc. ($89.95 retail) is an easy-to-use menu system. It combines standard menu facilities with a file manager, called Disk Manager, and various system utilities, such as a file finder.

When you install PowerMenu, you can instruct it to search for programs on your hard disk. The installation program searches for a limited number of programs, however, and the list is somewhat out-of-date. For example, the program did not find Lotus 1-2-3 Release 3 or Microsoft Word for Windows on my hard disk. Further, PowerMenu automatically adds certain topics to the menu, whether they are found on the disk or not. Presumably, this is to "pad out" the menu to give you examples of different program calls. If you select one of the phantom programs, PowerMenu responds with the message `Invalid Directory`.

PowerMenu's installation program is weak, but adding your own menu topics manually is very easy, provided that you know the program directory and the name of the main program file (including the extension). PowerMenu allows you to list up to 10 topics in each menu panel, and any of these topics can load another menu panel or execute a program. You can nest menus up to four levels deep, for 10,000 separate menu topics. If you choose a topic that calls another menu panel, the second menu displays on top of the parent menu (see fig. 11.1).

To execute a program from PowerMenu, you can either move the highlight bar to the appropriate topic or type the number of the topic. When a program executes, PowerMenu unloads most of its program from memory, leaving a 4K program *stub* in memory. The stub is used to reload the main menu program code after the applications program terminates. PowerMenu does not use temporary batch files to execute the called program.

To add or change a menu topic in PowerMenu, all you have to do is highlight the topic and press Ins. An input panel pops up and allows you to change the topic details. The panel includes entries for the menu description, the directory where the program is stored, and the name of the program (see fig. 11.2). If you want to pass parameters to one of your programs, you can either set the parameters on the Parameters line or set a flag to indicate that PowerMenu should prompt for parameters before the program executes.

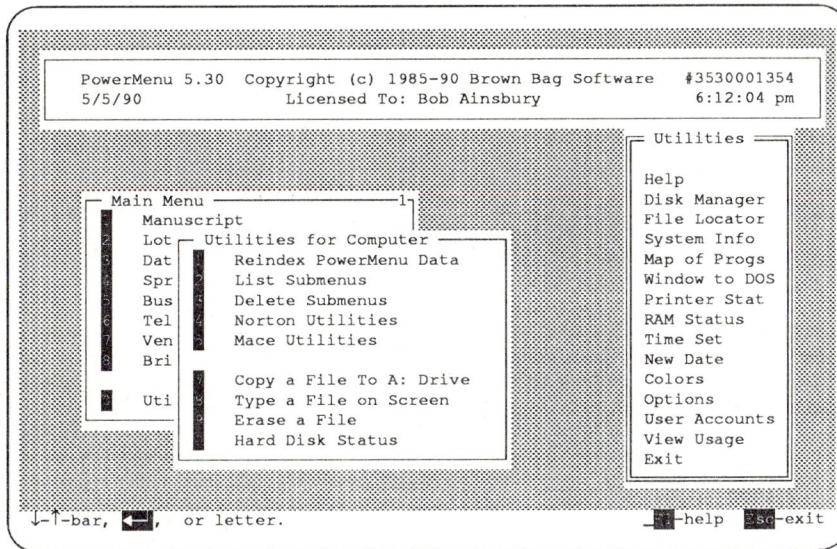

```
PowerMenu 5.30   Copyright (c) 1985-90 Brown Bag Software    #3530001354
5/5/90                   Licensed To: Bob Ainsbury              6:12:04 pm
                                                    ┌─ Utilities ══╗
                                                    │ Help
                                                    │ Disk Manager
   ┌─ Main Menu ──────────────1┐                    │ File Locator
   │  Manuscript               │                    │ System Info
   │  Lot ┌─ Utilities for Computer ─────┐           │ Map of Progs
   │  Dat │   Reindex PowerMenu Data     │           │ Window to DOS
   │  Spr │   List Submenus              │           │ Printer Stat
   │  Bus │   Delete Submenus            │           │ RAM Status
   │  Tel │   Norton Utilities           │           │ Time Set
   │  Ven │   Mace Utilities             │           │ New Date
   │  Bri │                              │           │ Colors
   │      │   Copy a File To A: Drive    │           │ Options
   │  Uti │   Type a File on Screen      │           │ User Accounts
   │      │   Erase a File               │           │ View Usage
   │      │   Hard Disk Status           │           │ Exit
   └──────└──────────────────────────────┘           └──────────────┘
↓-↑-bar, ←┘, or letter.                              ■-help  ■■-exit
```

Fig. 11.1. PowerMenu displays overlapping, nested menus.

You also can set an option to indicate that the system should wait for a key to be pressed before returning to the menu. This feature is useful when you want to see the final output from a program before returning to the menu. For example, if the menu executes the DIR command, you might want to pause before returning to the menu and read the directory listing.

If you want to password-protect a topic, you also enter a password in the input panel. This password must then be entered when you execute the program and when you press INS to edit the topic details.

PowerMenu provides commands to move and delete topics once they have been created.

Figure 11.1 also shows a list of the utility programs included with PowerMenu. In addition to the collection of miscellaneous utilities, the Disk Manager program provides a variety of file-management tasks, including copying, moving, erasing, sorting, finding, and browsing. Disk Manager displays the entire contents of the hard disk in a graphical tree (see fig. 11.3), which makes it easy to navigate the directory hierarchy quickly.

```
PowerMenu 5.30   Copyright (c) 1985-90 Brown Bag Software   #3530001354
5/5/90                  Licensed To: Bob Ainsbury            6:12:58 pm
```

```
┌─ Main Menu ──────────────────────────────────────┐
│ ┌─ Main Menu  -  Edit Window ═══════════════════┐ │
│ │ ┌──────────────────────────────────────────┐  │ │
│ │ │ Manuscript                               │  │ │
│ │ Directory: \MS                            │  │ │
│ │ Cmnd Name: MS.EXE                         │  │ │
│ │ Parametrs:                                │  │ │
│ │ Password : SODOFF                         │  │ │
│ │ Pause?   : N        Prompt for Parametrs? N │ │
│ │                                          │  │ │
└─ ↓-↑-move bar.  Enter title, directory, cmnd name, etc.    F1-help  ESC-exit
```

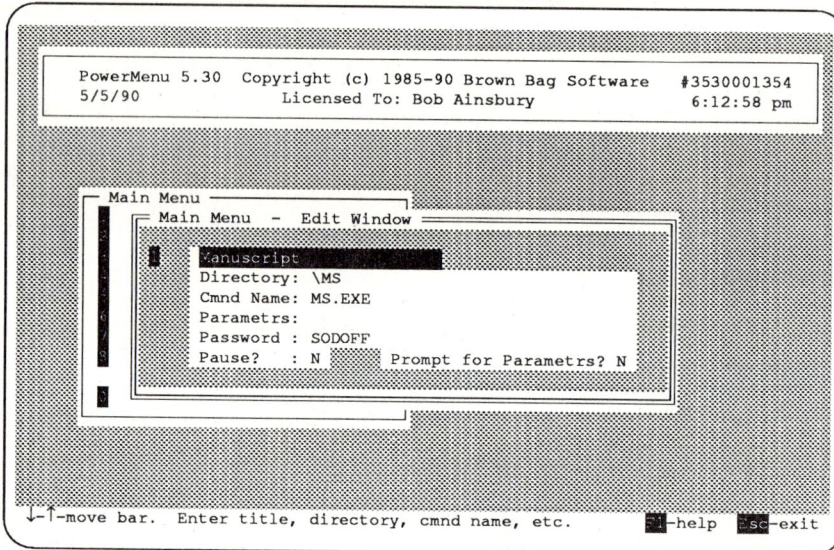

Fig. 11.2. *Editing a PowerMenu topic.*

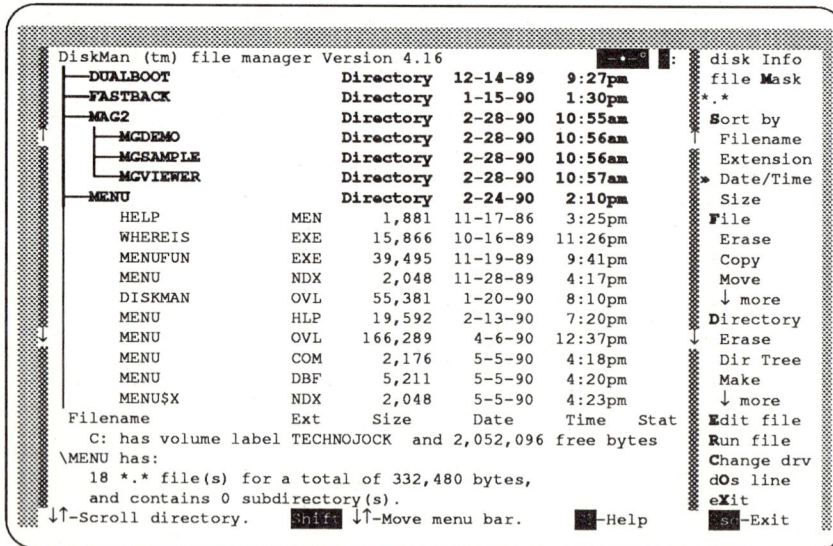

```
DiskMan (tm) file manager Version 4.16        ·:  disk Info
├─DUALBOOT              Directory  12-14-89   9:27pm    file Mask
├─FASTBACK              Directory   1-15-90   1:30pm    *.*
├─MAG2                  Directory   2-28-90  10:55am    Sort by
│  ├─MGDEMO             Directory   2-28-90  10:56am     Filename
│  ├─MGSAMPLE           Directory   2-28-90  10:56am     Extension
│  └─MGVIEWER           Directory   2-28-90  10:57am   ▸ Date/Time
├─MENU                  Directory   2-24-90   2:10pm     Size
   HELP        MEN         1,881  11-17-86   3:25pm    File
   WHEREIS     EXE        15,866  10-16-89  11:26pm    Erase
   MENUFUN     EXE        39,495  11-19-89   9:41pm    Copy
   MENU        NDX         2,048  11-28-89   4:17pm    Move
   DISKMAN     OVL        55,381   1-20-90   8:10pm    ↓ more
   MENU        HLP        19,592   2-13-90   7:20pm    Directory
   MENU        OVL       166,289   4-6-90   12:37pm    Erase
   MENU        COM         2,176   5-5-90    4:18pm    Dir Tree
   MENU        DBF         5,211   5-5-90    4:20pm    Make
   MENU$X      NDX         2,048   5-5-90    4:23pm    ↓ more
Filename       Ext       Size      Date      Time  Stat  Edit file
  C: has volume label TECHNOJOCK  and 2,052,096 free bytes  Run file
\MENU has:                                                Change drv
  18 *.* file(s) for a total of 332,480 bytes,            dOs line
  and contains 0 subdirectory(s).                         eXit
↓↑-Scroll directory.    Shift ↓↑-Move menu bar.    F1-Help  ESC-Exit
```

Fig. 11.3. *PowerMenu includes Disk Manager, a file-management program for hard disks.*

Version 5 of PowerMenu introduced an activity-logging feature as well as multiuser support. With these two features, you or the menu administrator can specify a list of valid users and their passwords, as well as a list of projects to which any of the users can assign their time. Every time the menu is started, or when the menu is put into *login* mode, the user must enter a valid name, password, and project. All subsequent activity is then logged to the specific user and project. PowerMenu includes an activity-log viewing and printing option, and the log can be filtered to display data for a specific subset of users, projects, and time periods.

Using Automenu

Automenu is the very popular shareware menu program from Magee Enterprises, Inc. (Automenu's licensing fee is $69.95.) The heart of Automenu is AUTOMENU.COM, an executable file that displays menus on-screen (see fig. 11.4) and lets you execute menu selections. The program can list up to eight menu topics per page, and up to eight pages of topics in each menu. You use the PgUp and PgDn keys to move through each page in the menu.

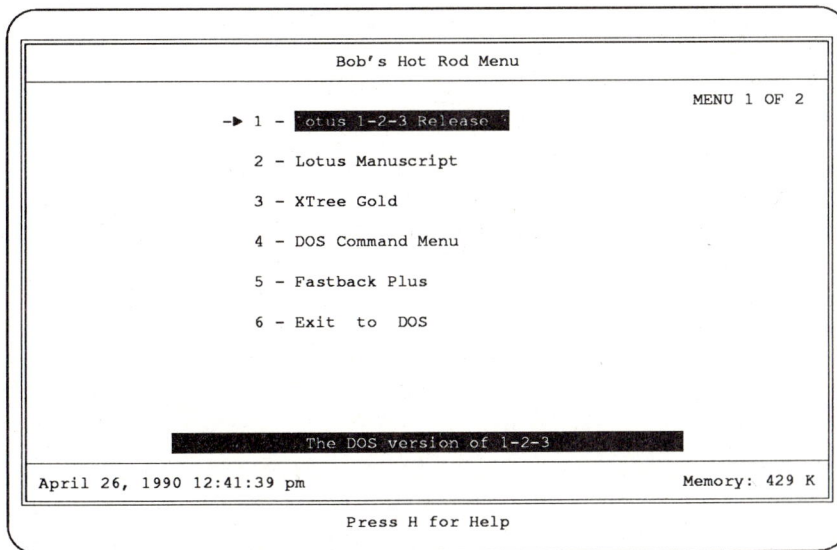

```
                        Bob's Hot Rod Menu

                                                   MENU 1 OF 2

              -▶ 1 - Lotus 1-2-3 Release

                 2 - Lotus Manuscript

                 3 - XTree Gold

                 4 - DOS Command Menu

                 5 - Fastback Plus

                 6 - Exit  to  DOS




                      The DOS version of 1-2-3

  April 26, 1990 12:41:39 pm                        Memory: 429 K

                        Press H for Help
```

Fig. 11.4. *A sample Automenu display.*

The Automenu install program does not have a program-search facility to build a customized menu for your hard disk. However, the program includes a sample menu, which you can easily modify to suit your needs.

Menu contents are stored in *menu definition files*, which have an MDF extension. A separate program, AUTOMAKE.EXE, is used to build and modify the menu definition files. The MDFs are plain ASCII files that contain all the instructions required to display menus and execute programs.

AUTOMAKE is a special text editor, which provides a number of aids to help you build the MDFs (see fig. 11.5). It includes an on-line help system and the capability of encrypting files so that unauthorized users cannot view or modify MDFs. Figure 11.5 shows the commands used to execute Lotus 1-2-3 Release 3.

Automenu interprets the commands in the MDF and creates a temporary batch file when a menu option is selected. This batch file is then executed to call the applications program.

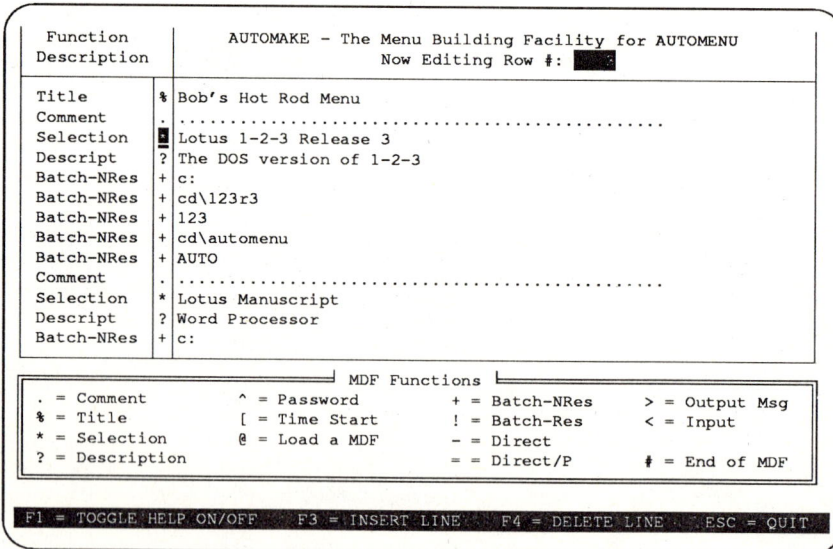

```
┌─────────────────────────────────────────────────────────────────────┐
│  Function          AUTOMAKE - The Menu Building Facility for AUTOMENU │
│  Description               Now Editing Row #: ▓▓▓▓                    │
│ ┌───────────────┬───────────────────────────────────────────────────┐│
│ │ Title        %│ Bob's Hot Rod Menu                                 ││
│ │ Comment      .│ ...................................................  ││
│ │ Selection    ▪│ Lotus 1-2-3 Release 3                              ││
│ │ Descript     ?│ The DOS version of 1-2-3                           ││
│ │ Batch-NRes   +│ c:                                                 ││
│ │ Batch-NRes   +│ cd\123r3                                           ││
│ │ Batch-NRes   +│ 123                                                ││
│ │ Batch-NRes   +│ cd\automenu                                        ││
│ │ Batch-NRes   +│ AUTO                                               ││
│ │ Comment      .│ ...................................................  ││
│ │ Selection    *│ Lotus Manuscript                                   ││
│ │ Descript     ?│ Word Processor                                     ││
│ │ Batch-NRes   +│ c:                                                 ││
│ └───────────────┴───────────────────────────────────────────────────┘│
│ ┌═══════════════════════ MDF Functions ═══════════════════════════════┐│
│ │  . = Comment      ^ = Password     + = Batch-NRes   > = Output Msg  ││
│ │  % = Title        [ = Time Start   ! = Batch-Res    < = Input       ││
│ │  * = Selection    @ = Load a MDF   - = Direct                      ││
│ │  ? = Description                   = = Direct/P     # = End of MDF  ││
│ └─────────────────────────────────────────────────────────────────────┘│
│ ┌─────────────────────────────────────────────────────────────────────┐│
│ │ F1 = TOGGLE HELP ON/OFF   F3 = INSERT LINE   F4 = DELETE LINE  ESC = QUIT││
│ └─────────────────────────────────────────────────────────────────────┘│
└─────────────────────────────────────────────────────────────────────┘
```

Fig. 11.5. *AUTOMAKE is used to edit MDF files.*

When you select a topic from the menu, Automenu can stay resident in memory and execute the temporary batch file as a child process (thereby avoiding the Ctrl-Break problem discussed in the introduction to this section). Or Automenu can be terminated and reloaded afterwards. Automenu also includes a facility to execute a program option at a specific time of day. For example, you can set up a program so that a disk defragmenter runs at noon every day. Note that for this feature to operate, the system must be idle and Automenu must be using the MDF that includes the timed execution topic. Otherwise the program will not be run.

Using Direct Access

Direct Access ($89.95 retail) is a feature-packed menu program from Delta Technology International, Inc. Direct Access includes a usage-tracking system and virus-detection software.

When Direct Access is installed, the program searches the hard disk for well-known programs (see fig. 11.6) and creates an initial set of menus that provides you with immediate access to these programs. The installation programs can recognize a remarkable variety of programs and even can identify individual Microsoft Windows applications.

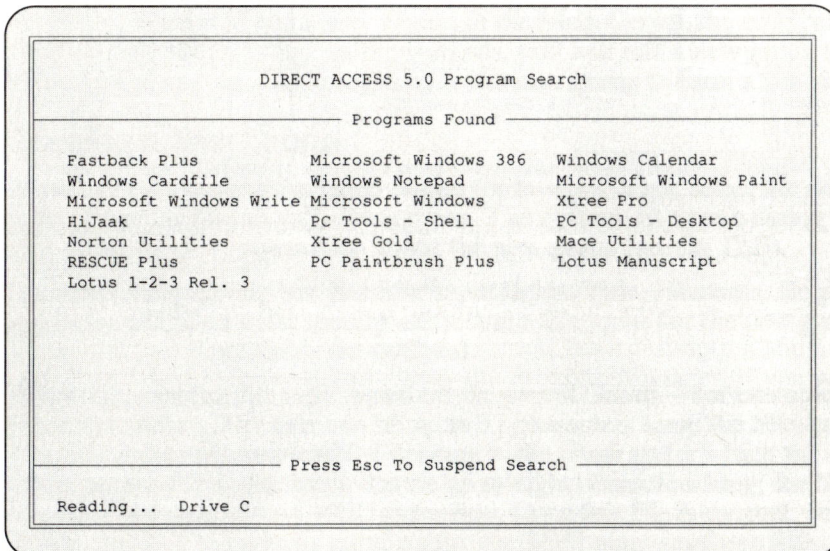

```
                  DIRECT ACCESS 5.0 Program Search
                  ───────── Programs Found ─────────

  Fastback Plus          Microsoft Windows 386    Windows Calendar
  Windows Cardfile       Windows Notepad          Microsoft Windows Paint
  Microsoft Windows Write Microsoft Windows       Xtree Pro
  HiJaak                 PC Tools - Shell         PC Tools - Desktop
  Norton Utilities       Xtree Gold               Mace Utilities
  RESCUE Plus            PC Paintbrush Plus       Lotus Manuscript
  Lotus 1-2-3 Rel. 3




                  ───── Press Esc To Suspend Search ─────

  Reading...  Drive C
```

Fig. 11.6. The Direct Access installation program searches the hard disk for program files.

The Direct Access main menu can include up to 26 topics (see fig. 11.7), and any of these topics can call a submenu. Each submenu can hold 26 topics, and any topic in a submenu can call another submenu, thereby providing an almost limitless menu capacity.

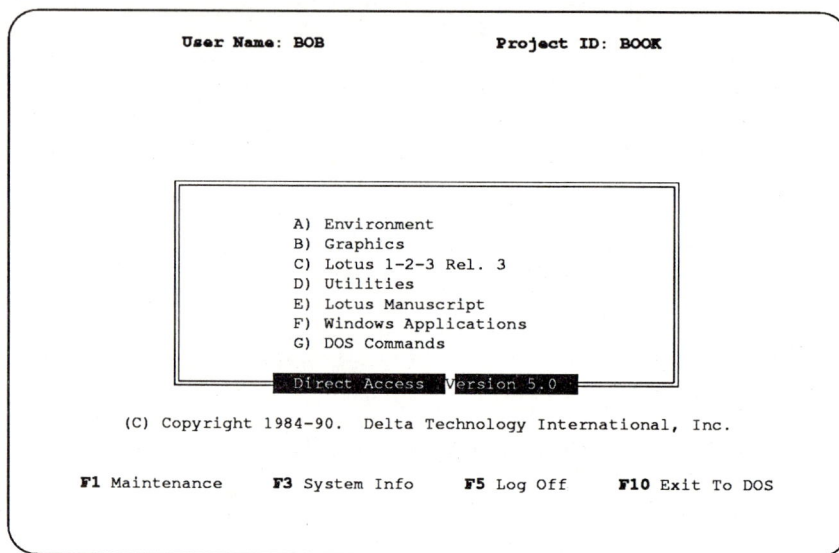

```
        User Name: BOB                    Project ID: BOOK




                    A)  Environment
                    B)  Graphics
                    C)  Lotus 1-2-3 Rel. 3
                    D)  Utilities
                    E)  Lotus Manuscript
                    F)  Windows Applications
                    G)  DOS Commands

                    Direct Access Version 5.0

      (C) Copyright 1984-90.  Delta Technology International, Inc.


    F1 Maintenance    F3 System Info    F5 Log Off    F10 Exit To DOS
```

Fig. 11.7. An example of a Direct Access main menu.

The main-menu display program includes a variety of built-in menu maintenance options, which you can invoke by pressing F1. The maintenance option can be suppressed and/or password-protected if you want to stop a user from modifying the menu configuration. The menu maintenance subprogram allows you to make changes to the main and submenus, modify the menu configuration options, and change the usage-tracking options.

Each topic on the menu must have the following basic information defined: the menu description, the drive and directory where the program is located, and the name of the program. You can optionally password-protect any option, disable Ctrl-Break to stop the user from exiting to DOS, pause after an application has terminated, or exit to DOS after the application finishes.

To help you enter a topic, file name, and directory, Direct Access displays a directory tree from which you can select any program file. You can even ask Direct Access to search the hard disk for a specific file. These extra utilities make Direct Access one of the easiest menu systems to maintain.

Like Automenu, Direct Access allows you to define a series of commands to be executed when a topic is selected from the menu. These commands can be DOS or batch file commands, program file names, or special Direct Access prompting commands. Prompting commands display a message in a pop-up box, requesting that the user input data. Input can be limited to alphanumeric characters or to special prompts, such as Yes/No/Cancel and OK/Esc.

Other menu-maintenance options allow you to change global settings, such as the main menu heading, whether the date and time are displayed, and whether all programs should be checked for viruses before they are executed.

Like PowerMenu, Direct Access includes a usage-tracking facility, which makes it an ideal choice for computers used by more than one person, or for individuals who want to record the time spent in an applications program. You can define a list of users and a list of projects that each user may work on. Whenever the menu program is started, the menu system can be configured so that every user must input a name, an optional password, and a project name. Any subsequent activity on the computer is recorded in the usage log. When one user has finished using the computer, the login screen can be invoked, and the next user must enter a name and project ID before proceeding. In addition, a menu topic can be configured so that the user is automatically logged out of the menu system when the application program has finished.

The menu-maintenance facility includes a section for managing the usage log. The log can be browsed (see fig. 11.8) or printed in a variety of formats. The log also can be cleared.

Direct Access is not network-compatible. However, Delta Technology sells a network version of the program, called Direct Net.

```
PROJECT                                         TIME     TIME     TOTAL
ID            USER NAME  APPLICATION NAME   DATE     IN       OUT      TIME

DAY STARTING: 04-26-90

BOOK          BOB        Log On to Direct Access 04-26-90   9:00a   9:00a    0:00
              BOB        Lotus 1-2-3 Rel. 3      04-26-90   9:00a  10:23a    1:23
              BOB        Lotus Manuscript        04-26-90  10:23a   1:12p    2:49
              BOB        Log Off Direct Access   04-26-90   1:12p   N/A      N/A
              BOB        Maintenance             04-26-90   1:12p   1:12p    0:00

              SUBTOTAL          TIMES USED: 5   TOTAL TIME: 4 Hr 12 Min

MISC          LOIS       PC Tools - Desktop      04-26-90   1:12p   1:12p    0:00
              LOIS       Log On to Direct Access 04-26-90   1:12p   N/A      N/A
              LOIS       Xtree Pro               04-26-90   1:12p   1:44p    0:32
              LOIS       Lotus Manuscript        04-26-90   1:44p   3:55p    2:11
              LOIS       Maintenance             04-26-90   3:55p   N/A      N/A

              SUBTOTAL          TIMES USED: 5   TOTAL TIME: 2 Hr 43 Min


D A Y    T O T A L        TIMES USED: 10   TOTAL TIME: 6 Hr 55 Min

   More Output Follows, Press Any Key To Continue, [ESC] to cancel report
```

Fig. 11.8. A Direct Access usage log.

Using File Managers

Hard disks have grown larger and larger in the last few years, and file manager programs have, not surprisingly, become much more popular. The more files you have to manage, the more useful a file manager becomes.

For even the most skilled users, DOS provides a limited set of commands for large-scale manipulation of files. For example, DOS has no move command—a file must be copied from one directory to another, and then the original file must be deleted. Simply finding a file in one of the subdirectories can be a challenge.

Note: The DOS Shell, introduced with DOS V4.0, extends the capabilities of the operating system commands and includes a file-move option (see Chapter 12.)

Nowadays, fortunately, there are dozens of top-quality programs designed to simplify the management of the files on your hard disk—and they work! Arguably, every hard disk user should have a file manager. This section looks at some of the distinguishing features of the most popular file managers.

File Manager Features

The primary goal of every file-management program is to make it easy for you to locate and manipulate files on your hard disk. Most file managers offer many of the features described in the following list.

Graphical disk map. One of the easiest ways to quickly see the directory hierarchy of a hard disk is by looking at a display of the directory in a tree diagram. Most file managers provide a tree-like view of the disk.

File finding. Good file managers help you to find any file on the disk. The program searches the entire disk and displays the location of the file(s).

Text search. Sometimes you know you have a file that contains specific text, but you cannot remember the name of the file. For example, you may have written a letter to Lois Sherman, and you know the file contains the text *Lois Sherman*, but the file's name is a mystery. Some file managers search all the files in a directory, or even the entire hard disk, looking for the specified text. Without a file manager, you have to keep loading files into your word processor until you find the letter.

File tagging. You will frequently want to manipulate a group of files that do not share a common file specification; that is, they do not match a specific wild-card name. File managers provide a way of tagging or selecting files. These files then can be manipulated *en masse*— copied, deleted, and so on. The file manager usually displays statistics about the tagged files, for example, the number of tagged files or the total size of the tagged files. These statistics are useful when you are tagging files to be copied to a diskette, because you can see how many of the files fit on the diskette.

Copying, erasing, and moving. A basic task of a file manager is to provide easy ways of copying, erasing, and moving groups of files. Some programs even include directory *prune and graft* tools to help you reorganize your directory structure, using a few simple commands.

File viewing. More and more file managers now offer file-viewing capabilities. The first file managers on the scene allowed you to browse plain ASCII files, but they were unable to show binary files in any readable form. Some recently released file managers let you browse spreadsheets, word processor files, graphics files, databases, and the like. This capability enables you to navigate the hard disk quickly and look at the contents of binary files without executing the applications program. For example, you can view a Lotus 1-2-3 spreadsheet (for example, a file with a WK1 extension) without running Lotus 1-2-3.

File editing. Certain file managers include built-in editors that enable you to edit ASCII files, such as batch files and the CONFIG.SYS file. Other file managers do not include an editor, but they provide a way of *hooking* your own editor into the program. When you instruct the file manager that you want to edit a file, it loads your editor for you.

Program launching. Managing files on your hard disk is only one of the tasks you perform on the computer. Most of the time (hopefully) you are running applications software. Some file managers are able to recognize the applications program used to create and modify a particular file. For example, a file with a WK3 extension is created by Lotus 1-2-3 Release 3. At the press of a key, some file managers can look at a selected file, determine the appropriate applications program, automatically execute the program, and load the file. This technique is called *program launching*.

Menu building. Many file managers provide some modest menu capabilities, so that you can create your own menus.

Laptop connectivity. If you are fortunate enough to own a laptop computer and a desktop computer, you are only too aware of the problems of keeping the latest data files on both computers. Some file managers provide software that can greatly simplify the process of transferring files between the computers. If you connect two computers with a cable between serial ports, the file manager can transfer files between them. No more floppy disk transfers!

Communications and miscellaneous features. In a continuing attempt to stand out from the crowd, a number of file managers bundle extra utilities that are not directly related to file management. For example, The Norton Commander now has a link to the MCI mail service via a modem, and PC Tools includes an array of utility programs ranging from file backup to an appointment scheduler. These additional features are far from gimmicks, and they may provide just that feature which makes one file manager more appealing to you than the rest. That is precisely why these extra features are added.

File-Management Software

In this section we review some of the capabilities and features of the most popular file-management programs. Table 11.2 provides a quick summary of the features and facilities available in the commercial products reviewed in this chapter.

Table 11.2
File-Management Software—Summary of Features

Feature	Lotus Magellan	Norton Com-mander	XTree-Pro Gold	PC Tools
Basic File Management	✔	✔	✔	✔
Communications	✖	✔	✖	✔
Custom Menus	✔	✔	✔	✔
File Archiver	✔	✖	✖	✔
File Editor	✔	✔	✔	✔
File Transfer	✖	✔	✖	✔
File Viewers	✔	✔	✔	✔
Memory Overhead	10K	13K	7K	10K
Mouse Support	✔	✔	✔	✔
Pop-Up TSR Mode	✖	✖	✖	✔
Program Launch	✔	✔	✔	✔
Text Search	✔	✔	✔	✔

The look and feel of a file-management program has a very significant influence on whether you use it, and although this is true of most computer software, it is especially so with file managers.

Managing Files with Lotus Magellan

Named after the famous Portuguese explorer, Magellan from Lotus Development Corporation is a hard disk "explorer," which has set a new standard for file-management utilities. Magellan enables you to view files, execute programs, and search the hard disk for files matching some specific criterion.

Although it includes the standard file-manipulation facilities, such as file copying, renaming, and deleting, Magellan's real strength is in its file exploring, viewing, and launching facilities.

Unlike its competitors, Magellan uses an advanced indexing technique, which maintains a special index of all the files on your hard disk. When the program is installed (or later if you prefer), Magellan inspects every file on the hard disk and builds the special index file. This file contains a compact summary of all the data stored in the files. The primary advantage of the index file is speed. For example, if you ask Magellan to display all files that contain the characters "green", Magellan can very quickly search the information in the index and display a list of all files that include the word (see fig. 11.9). Magellan refers to the process of selecting a specific subset of the files on your disk as *exploring*.

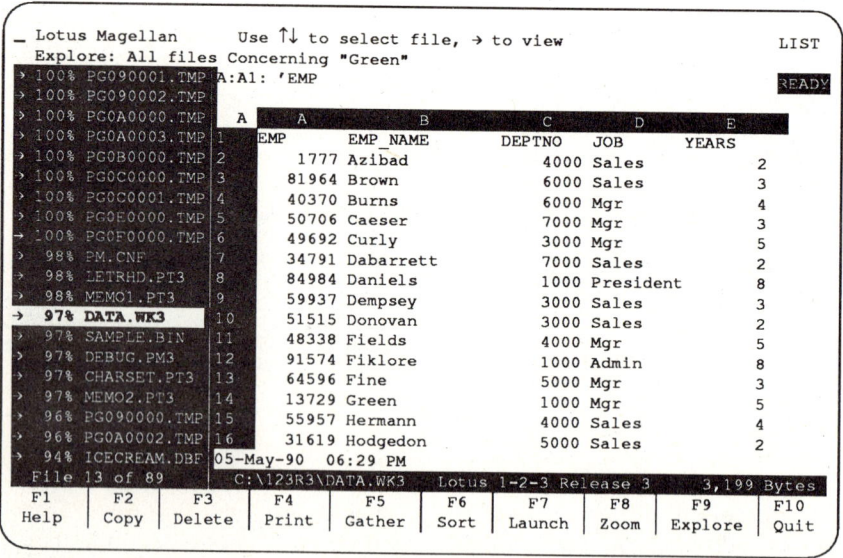

Fig. 11.9. *Magellan can search and display files that contain a specific word or phrase.*

If multiple files contain the search text, Magellan lists them in priority order, with the files containing the most occurrences of the string listed first. Magellan also supports complex search criteria. For example, it can search for all files modified since June 1, 1990, which contain the phrase "nutritious food", but not the word "ice cream".

Whether you use the browse facility to select a file, or are simply scrolling through a list of files in a directory, Magellan can display a view of the file's contents. In figure 11.9, the highlighted file is DATA.WK3, a Lotus 1-2-3 Release 3 worksheet, and the contents of the file are displayed in the main viewing window, formatted just as in a real 1-2-3 worksheet. Not only can you view the start of the file, you can press the TAB key to scroll around the file and view any part of the worksheet.

Magellan allows you to view most of the popular file formats, including all the files created by products from Lotus Development Corporation, text files, dBASE DBF files, WordPerfect files, and Paradox tables. Magellan can even display PCX, CGM, and GIF graphics files.

If you have special binary files that Magellan does not recognize (an RBase file, for example), you still can view the text in the file, in an unformatted but readable layout.

If you decide you want to edit the files you are viewing in Magellan, all you have to do is press the launch key (F7). Magellan automatically loads the appropriate program and the file you were viewing, ready for you to edit. If the highlighted file is an ASCII file, Magellan loads a text editor of your choice, or you can use Magellan's built-in editor. During the installation process, Magellan searches your disk and automatically identifies the programs you have installed and their directories. The Launch facility turns Magellan into a very flexible menu program.

In addition to its primary browsing, viewing, and launching facilities, Magellan can compress (or zip) a group of files to save disk space. You still can view and search the compressed files, recover or unerase deleted files, grab text from a file and export it to another file, print a file's contents or details, and compare the contents of two files or directories.

Managing Files with Norton Commander

The Norton Commander, from Peter Norton Computing, Inc., is a popular file-management program that offers full access to DOS and to a comprehensive set of file viewers.

Many hard disk users do not like to use a file manager or DOS shell program because they lose the ability to execute familiar DOS commands quickly and easily. The Norton Commander combines the benefits of a file manager with the familiarity of the DOS prompt. Norton Commander allows you to have two active windows, which can point to any drive or directory. Either window can be set to display a directory tree or a file list. Or either window can be turned off. In figure 11.10, the left window shows the directory hierarchy of the disk in a tree diagram, and the right window shows the files in the default directory.

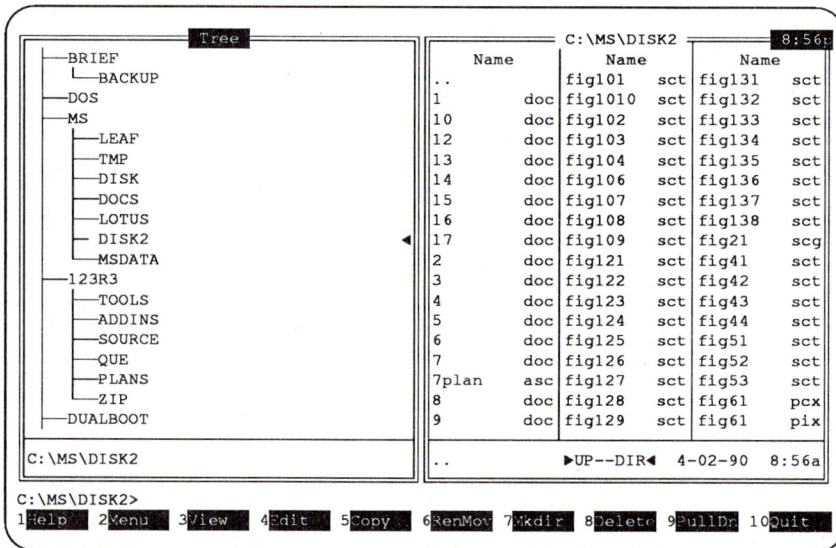

```
                Tree                          C:\MS\DISK2            8:56:
  ─BRIEF                           Name          Name           Name
    └─BACKUP                   ..          fig101    sct  fig131    sct
  ─DOS                         1      doc  fig1010   sct  fig132    sct
  ─MS                          10     doc  fig102    sct  fig133    sct
    ├─LEAF                     12     doc  fig103    sct  fig134    sct
    ├─TMP                      13     doc  fig104    sct  fig135    sct
    ├─DISK                     14     doc  fig106    sct  fig136    sct
    ├─DOCS                     15     doc  fig107    sct  fig137    sct
    ├─LOTUS                    16     doc  fig108    sct  fig138    sct
    ├─ DISK2              ◄    17     doc  fig109    sct  fig21     scg
    └─MSDATA                   2      doc  fig121    sct  fig41     sct
  ─123R3                       3      doc  fig122    sct  fig42     sct
    ├─TOOLS                    4      doc  fig123    sct  fig43     sct
    ├─ADDINS                   5      doc  fig124    sct  fig44     sct
    ├─SOURCE                   6      doc  fig125    sct  fig51     sct
    ├─QUE                      7      doc  fig126    sct  fig52     sct
    ├─PLANS                    7plan  asc  fig127    sct  fig53     sct
    └─ZIP                      8      doc  fig128    sct  fig61     pcx
  ─DUALBOOT                    9      doc  fig129    sct  fig61     pix

C:\MS\DISK2                    ..          ▶UP--DIR◄  4-02-90   8:56a

C:\MS\DISK2>
1Help  2Menu  3View  4Edit  5Copy  6RenMov  7Mkdir  8Delete  9PullDn  10Quit
```

Fig. 11.10. Norton Commander offers two file windows, a set of a file-management features, and direct access to DOS.

Immediately below the left window is the DOS prompt. With Norton Commander, you can use one of the special keys or the mouse to invoke a Norton Commander utility, or you can enter a standard DOS command, just as you would at the DOS prompt. Further, the last ten DOS commands you issue are recorded. To reissue a command, press Alt-F8 and select the command from the pop-up window.

The last line of the display summarizes the purpose Norton Commander assigns to each special function key. Press F9 (or click the mouse at the top of the screen) to display the pull-down menus for controlling file-selection and window-display criteria. You can customize the F2 function key to display a pop-up menu that gives you direct access to your main programs.

Norton Commander has all the usual file-copying, deleting, and renaming facilities. Files can be manipulated individually, one directory at a time, or as a group of tagged files. Norton Commander provides a simple text editor and, in addition, includes a rich set of file viewers that enables you to browse binary files in their applications format. Although Norton Commander does not support Lotus Development Corporation products or graphics files as well as Magellan, it does provide support for other vendors' file formats, including the RBase and Reflex database files.

Norton Commander includes the program Commander Link for transferring files between two PCs connected by a serial cable. The Commander package also includes a special program, Commander Mail, which provides an easy and convenient way of accessing the MCI Mail system via a modem.

Managing Files with XtreePro Gold

XtreePro Gold, from XTREE Company, includes file-viewing and menu capabilities, but its main strength is file manipulation. The original Xtree program was one of the first file managers available for hard disk users. It was good then, and it is even better now.

When the program is executed, it searches the disk drive and builds a list of all the files on the drive. This procedure takes a few seconds, and then provides instant access to any of the files on the drive. You can instruct XtreePro Gold to *log* additional drives—as many as 26 drives logged at any one time. To switch the display to show another logged drive, you press the plus sign (+), or you can split the display to show two drives (see fig. 11.11).

XtreePro Gold enables you to tag files and manipulate them as a group and, unlike many competitors, it even allows you to tag files across drives. XtreePro Gold streamlines file-manipulation tasks. You tag the appropriate files, and then you can copy, rename, delete, or move the files as a block. You can even move a subdirectory hierarchy from one branch of the directory tree to another—a process referred to as *pruning and grafting*.

```
  C:\OS2\INSTALL                      D:\CORELDRW\MY_ART
  ┌<disk: *.*>─────────              ┌<disk: *.*>─────────
  ├──MENU                            ├──COLORIX
  ├──MENUS                           │   └──RIXHELP
  ├──MS                              ├──CORELDRW
  │   ├──DISK                        │   ├──CLIP1
  │   ├──DISK2                       │   ├──CLIP2
  │   ├──DOCS                        │   ├──CLIP3
  │   ├──LEAF                        │   ├──CLIP4
  │   ├──LOTUS                       │   ├──CLIP5
  │   ├──MSDATA                      │   ├──CLIP6
  │   └──TMP                         │   ├──MY_ART        ←
  ├──OAD                             │   └──TASK1
  ├──OS2                             ├──QPRO
  │   ├──DLL                         │   └──FONTS
  │   └──INSTALL                     └──TP

  INSTALL .LOG     5,067  ....  12-14-89    ALL      .CDR   84,970 .a..  4-11-90
  SYSLEVEL.OS2       169  r...   7-25-89    KID1     .CDR   22,298 .a..  4-11-90
  SYSIUTIL.EXE     3,912  ....   7-25-89    UPRIGHT1.CDR   21,814 .a..  4-11-90
  SYSINST .LIB   101,376  ....   7-25-89    GIRL1    .CDR   14,063 .a..  4-11-90

  DIR        Available  Delete  Filespec  Global  Invert   Log disk  Makedir
  COMMANDS   Print  Rename  Showall  Tag  Untag  Volume  eXecute  Quit
  ↵  file  F7 autoview  F8 unsplit  F9 menu  F10 commands    F1 help  +/- select
```

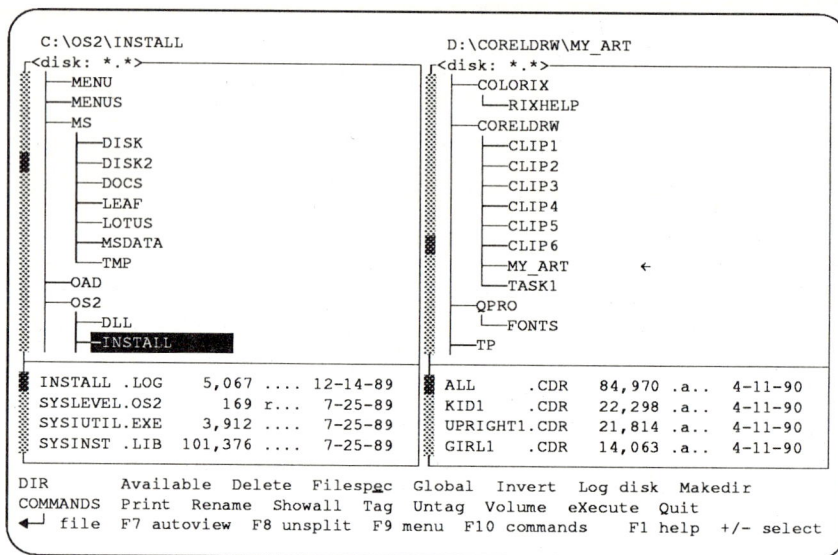

Fig. 11.11. *XtreePro Gold shows the contents of two drives on a split screen.*

To execute a program, you can either add a topic to a user-definable menu, or you can highlight the program file and press X to execute the program directly. You also can use the X function to execute any standard DOS command. If you copy, delete, or rename any files from the DOS prompt, however, the changes are not reflected in the XtreePro Gold display until you relog the disk.

XtreePro Gold includes a set of file viewers that can be used to view the contents of files in their native format. A variety of word processing viewers are supported, but the only spreadsheet viewer is for Lotus 1-2-3. The only database viewer is for dBASE. XtreePro Gold also includes a feature-packed editor to help you edit ASCII files.

All the XTreePro Gold commands are invoked by pressing a single key or by pressing the same key in conjunction with the Ctrl or Alt keys. It is this cleverly designed, intuitive interface that helps XtreePro Gold to excel on the file-management scene. The program also provides full mouse support.

Managing Files with PC Tools

Describing PC Tools as a file manager is like calling a Swiss Army knife a screwdriver. PC Tools is packed with hard disk utilities. Throughout this book you read about many of PC Tools' diverse features. This section is restricted to the file-management capabilities of PC Tools.

The file-management element of PC Tools is in the program PCSHELL, which is the main program from which all other PC Tools options can be called. Like Norton Commander, PC Tools displays the DOS prompt at the next-to-last line of the display. You can either enter DOS commands or use a function key or special key combination to invoke one of the PCSHELL options. If you enter a DOS command, PCSHELL automatically clears the display and waits for you to press a key before filling the screen with its windows. This delay gives you a chance to look at the output from a DOS command before it is obscured by the PCSHELL display. Both the DOS prompt and the pause-on-command options can be configured to be ON or OFF.

The PC Tools file-display windows are very flexible. Using a mouse or special key combinations, you can stretch and zoom the display windows to meet your preferences. In figure 11.12, three main windows are displayed: a tree view of the directory hierarchy, a file list for the highlighted directory, and a viewer window showing the contents of the highlighted file. PCSHELL includes more than 30 viewers for displaying a wide range of binary files in their application format. Figure 11.12 shows the Lotus 1-2-3 WK1 file viewer, as well as a pop-up window that describes the properties of the file being viewed.

If you press the Launch key (Ctrl-Enter or a nominated function key), PCSHELL automatically loads the parent program and installs the file being viewed, making it ready for you to edit. One of the pull-down menus is the Applications menu, which is really a 15-topic menu. When you install PC Tools, the drives are automatically scanned for applications programs, and these programs are added to the Applications menu. At any time, you can change, add, or delete options on the menu. To run a program from the menu, you pull down the Applications menu and select the desired program.

PCSHELL includes a rich set of file-selection and manipulation tools for file-deletion, copying, renaming and moving, directory pruning and grafting, text searching, file comparing, and so on. Some of the other file-management tools include a built-in editor for editing ASCII and binary files, a file undelete option, a file-transfer facility via serial cable (Laplink), and a modem-communications program.

```
PC Shell V6  File  Disk  Options  Applications  Special  Help           3:05pm
Drive A  B  C  D                                           Advanced Mode
┌──ID = TECHNOJOCK──┐      ┌═══════ Lotus 123 Viewer ═══════┐
│  └─MSDATA          ^║    A1: 'Office Expenses              ^
├─123R3              ║                 A   °       B        C
│  ├─TOOLS           ║     1  Office Expenses
│  ├─ADDINS          ║     2
│  ├─SOURCE          ║     3                    01-Jan   01-Feb
│  └─QUE             v║    4                   ─────────────────
│                    ║     5  Depreciation
│  10,125,312 Bytes F┌───── File Information ──────┐
│                    │ File name    EXPENSES.WK1   │
├─────C:\123R3\*.*───│ Last Updated  06/19/89      │
│  DBT14S   WK3   SALE│ Rows   10   Columns    5   │
│  MAC17S   WK3   ACCT└─────────────────────────────┘
│  EMPFILE  DBF   MFG      WK3 ║11           ─────────────────
│  SAMPMACS WK3   SHOES    WK3 ║12
│ 1 EXPENSES WK1  DATA     WK3 ║13
│  CONSOL   WK3   TABLES   WK3 ║14
│  SUMMARY  WK3   123      CNF v║15
│                              ║16
│  1 Selected =     2,315 bytes║17                               v
│                              ║                                 =▪
C:\123R3>                      └─────────────────────────────────┘
1Help   2Info   3Exit   4Launch 5Goto  6    7Search 8Zoom  9NextF 10Menu
```

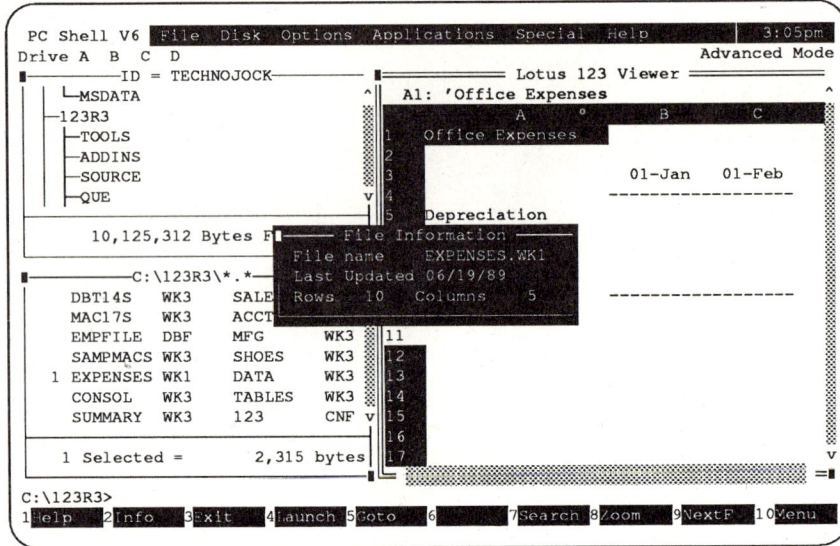

Fig. 11.12. PC Tools supports multiple file windows, including a file list and file viewer.

Using QFILER

DISK

QFILER (short for "quick filer") is a shareware file-management program from Jamestown Software. An evaluation copy of the program is included on the disk for you to try. Also included on the disk is an ASCII copy of the documentation that describes QFILER features in detail. See Appendix E for instructions on installing this evaluation copy of the software.

QFILER is not a full-featured desktop accessory like some of the products discussed so far. For example, it does not include binary file viewers, editors, communications links, and the like. It is simply a good file-management program designed to help you copy, rename, delete, and move files.

QFILER uses two windows to display file listings or directory trees. The lower part of the screen is reserved for the menu and status lines (see fig. 11.13). The windows can be used to display different directory listings in each window.

```
                      TECHNOJOCK            name              C:\U\QFILER
                  C:\U\QFILER                           ┌─MACE
  <PARENT>        <DIR>    050590 17:23               ─┤─MISC
  665                 45  022889 14:31a               ─┤─MISCOS2
  ARCE     COM      7128  020688  3:13a               ─┤─NC
  ARCE     DOC     13098  020688  8:59a               ─┤─NORTON
  COPYRITE          383  022889 14:31a               ─┤─PBRUSH
  QF101KEY TXT     7831  012488 10:16a                 │  └─BOOK
  QFILER   DOC    56847  022289 14:32a               ─┤─PCKWIK
  QFILER   EXE   115520  022089 15:18a               ─┤─PCTOOLS
  QFINST   EXE    31456  112988 20:39a                 │  └─SAMPLES
  QFKB5151 TXT     7990  020388 23:47a              ► ─┤─QFILER            ◄
  QFKBF12  TXT     7728  022089 11:22a               ─┤─QUE
  QFKEYS   TXT     4604  121387  4:00a                 ├──4DOS
  QFUPDATE DOC    33430  022089  2:11a                 ├──DISK
  WFU      ARC    70224  122788 11:48a                 ├──EBL
                                                       ├─FGREP
                                                       ├─LHARC
                                                       ├─P
                                                       ├─PCUTIL
                                                       ├─PERFECT
                                                       └─SECURE
  dir:  356K  tag:    0K  left:10104K    └1 └2 └3 └4 └5 └6 └7 └8    (Level)
  Use cursor keys to select directory.   <ESC> Abort.   <P> Print.   <C> Clear.
    Press ◄─ to move tree to left side, ◄┘ to display selected dir on left.   _
```

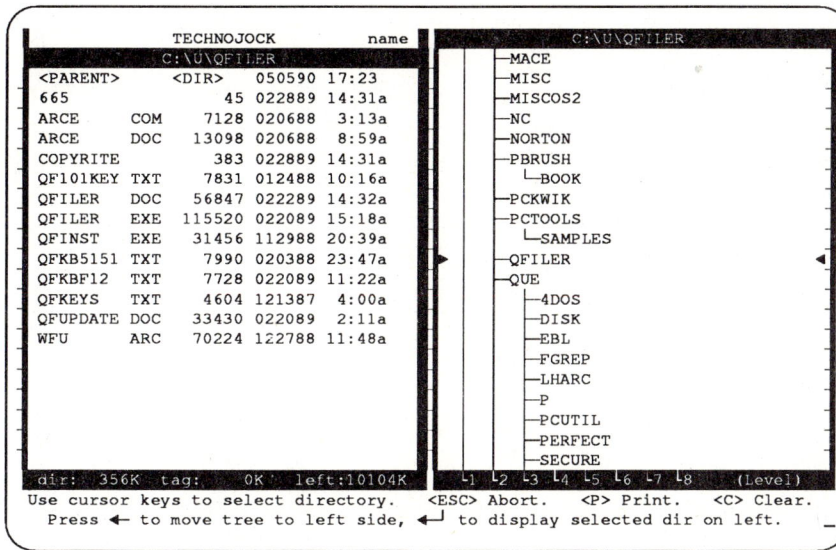

Fig. 11.13. QFILER uses two windows to display file details.

Virtually all the QFILER commands can be invoked by pressing a special key combination. Once you have learned the special keys, you can manipulate groups of files very quickly and efficiently. QFILER also provides full mouse support with pull-down menus. QFILER does not include an editor or a file viewer, but you can configure the program to load your favorite utility—both an editor (T2) and a file browser (List) are included on the disk that accompanies this book.

If you want to run a program, you highlight the program file and press the E key (for execute). QFILER prompts you for any passed parameters or switches. You then press Enter to start the program. *Note that QFILER is a shareware program and that the copy is included for your evaluation. If you decide to continue using the program, you should register the copy. Further details are included in the on-disk documentation.*

Using Small File Utilities

Some hard disk users like the features offered in a file manager, but do not want to be forced to execute a large file-manager program every time they want to perform a small task. For those users, there are a multitude of small, easy-to-use utility programs that provide a very specific hard disk management function: listing a file, moving a file, searching for a file containing specific text, and so on. If you don't want the expense and confinement of a full file-management program, but you do want some file-management capabilities, a few hard disk utilities will serve you well.

This section looks at some of the most popular special-purpose hard disk management utilities. All the programs reviewed in this section are included on the accompanying disk. Further, the disk includes the author's documentation, which provides more information about each program.

FGREP—a Text Searcher

FGREP, written by Chris Dunford, is an excellent utility for searching files for a word or phrase. It is blazingly fast and leaves the DOS FIND utility in the dust for both performance and flexibility.

FGREP searches text or binary files for a sequence of characters, using the following basic syntax:

FGREP *-switches* **"search string" filename**

In this generic syntax, *-switches* represents a variety of switches that control search criteria and the output format. For example, the *-c* switch indicates that the search should be case-sensitive.

"search string" is the character, word, or phrase to be looked for. If the string includes spaces, the string must be delimited with a character other than a space. You can use any character to delimit the string, providing that character does not appear in the string itself. For example, you could use the percent character to delimit a string that includes spaces and quotation marks—%"No," he screamed%.

filename is the name of the file (wild-card characters are supported) to be searched. You can optionally specify multiple files and directories, and FGREP searches all of them.

See the file FGREP.DOC on the accompanying disk for additional information.

Figure 11.14 illustrates a search in the directory \MS\DISK2 for all files with a DOC extension that include the word *sector*. The *f* switch instructs FGREP to display file names of files where the text is found. The *0* switch instructs FGREP not to display the line in the file where the text is located.

The *0* switch is particularly useful when you are searching binary files in which the "line" may be hundreds of characters long. Displaying such a line may consume five lines or more and, if multiple files are found, the all-important file name may scroll off the display before you get a chance to read it.

```
C:\>FGREP -f0 "SECTOR" \MS\DISK2\*.DOC
fgrep 1.71 (c) Copyright 1985-1989 by Chris Dunford
**File \MS\DISK2\15.DOC
**File \MS\DISK2\16.DOC
**File \MS\DISK2\14.DOC
**File \MS\DISK2\3.DOC
**File \MS\DISK2\1.DOC
**File \MS\DISK2\4.DOC
**File \MS\DISK2\8.DOC
**File \MS\DISK2\5.DOC
**File \MS\DISK2\7.DOC
**File \MS\DISK2\10.DOC

C:\>
```

Fig. 11.14. FGREP displays the file names where the search string is found.

FINDIT—a File Finder

FINDIT is a small public-domain utility, written by Larry McMains, which searches any drive for a file that matches a file specification.

You may know, for example, that you have a file called RECIPE.DOC, but you can't remember which directory it is in. If you enter the following command, FINDIT searches the drive and tells you the file's location:

FINDIT RECIPE.DOC

As well as specifying individual file names, you can use wild-card characters, and FINDIT displays all files on the drive that match the file specification. Figure 11.15 illustrates a search for all files with an INI extension.

```
C:\>findit *.ini

 Filename      Size     Date      Time    Drive:Path
------------ ------- -------- -------- ----------------------
SD      .INI    2497 04/21/90 17:54:16 C:\
OS2     .INI   16150 03/10/90 09:28:22 C:\OS2
WIN     .INI    6772 03/28/90 21:56:58 C:\WIN386
NC      .INI     476 05/05/90 21:12:24 C:\U\NC
MCI     .INI     287 05/05/90 20:52:24 C:\U\NC
Search Complete, 5 files found.

C:\>
```

Fig. 11.15. FINDIT searches any directory, looking for matching files.

LIST—a File Browser

> DISK

List is Vernon Buerg's classic file browser. It is a direct substitute for the DOS TYPE command, but has dozens more features.

List can be used to browse any text or binary file, and the standard cursor-movement keys can be used to scroll through the file. List includes a print facility, a search facility, and much more. Once you use List, you may wonder how you survived without it.

The accompanying disk includes three copies of the List program: LISTR.COM is the regular list program, LISTS.COM is a smaller version with fewer features than the regular version, and LISTP.COM is the plus version that includes all the bells and whistles. The programs on the enclosed disk are for evaluation purposes, and if you want to continue to use the program, Vernon encourages you to send a donation. The LIST command takes the following syntax:

LIST /*switches filename...*

where /*switches* are a variety of command-line switches. For example, /*M* enables mouse support.

filename... is a list of one or more file names to be browsed (wild-card characters are supported).

See the file LIST.DOC on the accompanying disk for further information.

Figure 11.16 shows the LISTP program being used to list the file LIST.DOC.

```
LIST     452            05-06-90 18:56 ◆ LIST.DOC

Command line switches

            /S          indicates viewing a piped or redirected file

            /J          sets Junk filter on
            /7          sets 7-bit display
            /8          sets 8-bit display
            /*          sets star filter on

            /W          sets Wrap on
            /H          sets Hex dump mode
            /L          sets pre-Loading on
            /M          allows use of a mouse for moving the cursor

            /Ftext      tells LIST to Scan for 'text' immediately

    The command line switch character is normally a slash, "/", but LIST
    will use whatever  character that is  defined to DOS  as the command
    line switch character, e.g. a  dash, "-".  Depending on your  needs,
    you could load LIST using  any of these command line  switches, such
    as:

Command▶ _                            Keys: ↑↓← PgUp PgDn F10=exit F1=Help
```

Fig. 11.16. LIST can be used to browse both text and binary files.

MOVE—a File Mover

DISK

The program MV.EXE by Bryan Higgins is an efficient file mover, which significantly simplifies file-moving operations.

One of the "missing" commands from DOS is a file-moving program. Using DOS, the only way to move a file is to copy the file to the new directory and then delete the original file (unless you use the DOS Shell available with DOS V4 and later). This is both awkward and slow.

MOVE solves both problems. If a file is being moved to a different directory on the same drive, the file is not physically moved by MOVE. Rather, the disk directory entries are simply updated to place the logical location of the file in the new directory. This provides a very significant speed advantage over copying the file to the new location. Figure 11.17 illustrates a command to move all COM and EXE files to the \UTILS directory.

MV takes the following syntax:

MV -*switches* **filename**... *target*

In this generic syntax, -*switches* are a variety of switches that control the move operation. For example, the -*n* parameter instructs MV to warn you before it overwrites any files already present in the target directory.

filename is the name of the file(s) to be moved. Wild-card characters are supported, and multiple file names are allowed.

target is the name of the target drive or path; that is, the location the files will be moved to. If only one *filename* is specified, and *target* is omitted, then the target is assumed to be the default directory.

```
C:\U\QUE\THEDISK>MV *.COM *.EXE \UTILS
Moving LISTS.COM --> \UTILS\LISTS.COM ... Done
Moving LISTR.COM --> \UTILS\LISTR.COM ... Done
Moving LISTP.COM --> \UTILS\LISTP.COM ... Done
Moving FGREP.COM --> \UTILS\FGREP.COM ... Done
Moving FINDIT.COM --> \UTILS\FINDIT.COM ... Done
Moving T2.EXE --> \UTILS\T2.EXE ... Done
Moving PCOPY.EXE --> \UTILS\PCOPY.EXE ... Done
Moving MV!.EXE --> \UTILS\MV!.EXE ... Done
Moving MV.EXE --> \UTILS\MV.EXE ... Done
Moving CIPHER.EXE --> \UTILS\CIPHER.EXE ... Done
Moving WHAT.EXE --> \UTILS\WHAT.EXE ... Done

C:\U\QUE\THEDISK>
```

Fig. 11.17. MV can move multiple files with a single command.

PCOPY—a File Copier

DISK

PCOPY, a shareware program from the prolific programmer Norm Partreqin, is packed full of file-selection and copying options.

Since DOS provides the COPY and XCOPY commands, you might be surprised to see a copy program in a list of useful utilities. But once you use PCOPY, you begin to realize how many copy options are missing from its DOS counterparts.

PCOPY takes the following syntax:

PCOPY filename *target* /*switches*

In this generic syntax, **filename** is the name of the file(s) to be copied. Wild-card characters are supported.

target is the target drive or directory to which the files are to be copied. If no directory is specified, the default is assumed.

/*switches* are optional switches that control the copy operation. For example, /*U* copies only files that do not exist on the target directory or that have an earlier file date and time stamp than the source file.

PCOPY can be used to copy files based on date, time, file attributes, whether the file exists on the target, and so on. Although PCOPY has many switches, it can be used without any switches as a replacement for the DOS COPY command. Even in its basic form, PCOPY is superior to DOS COPY because it creates the target directory if no directory exists and warns you if a file already exists in the target directory.

PCOPY provides a full-screen display of the copy operation. Figure 11.18 illustrates the output from the command PCOPY *.EXE \SAVE.

PCOPY can even be used as a simple backup program, since it can copy source files to multiple diskettes on a target drive. For further information about this very flexible and useful utility, see the file PCOPY.DOC on the accompanying disk.

Note that PCOPY is a shareware program and that the copy is included for your evaluation. If you decide to continue using the program, you should register the copy. Further details are included in the on-disk documentation.

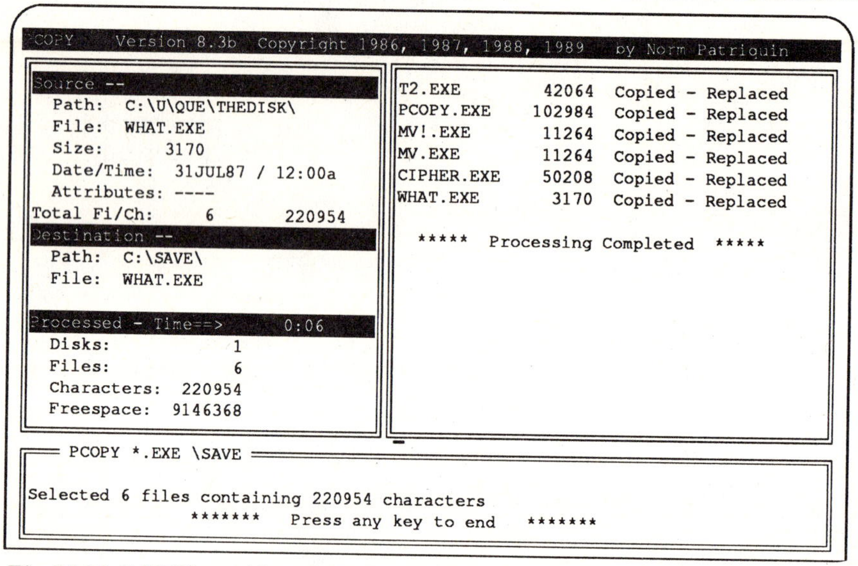

```
PCOPY    Version 8.3b  Copyright 1986, 1987, 1988, 1989   by Norm Patriquin

Source --                              T2.EXE          42064  Copied - Replaced
  Path:  C:\U\QUE\THEDISK\             PCOPY.EXE      102984  Copied - Replaced
  File:  WHAT.EXE                      MV!.EXE         11264  Copied - Replaced
  Size:      3170                      MV.EXE          11264  Copied - Replaced
  Date/Time:  31JUL87 / 12:00a         CIPHER.EXE      50208  Copied - Replaced
  Attributes: ----                     WHAT.EXE         3170  Copied - Replaced
Total Fi/Ch:    6       220954
Destination --                           *****   Processing Completed   *****
  Path:  C:\SAVE\
  File:  WHAT.EXE

Processed - Time==>        0:06
  Disks:          1
  Files:          6
  Characters:  220954
  Freespace:  9146368

 = PCOPY *.EXE \SAVE =

Selected 6 files containing 220954 characters
           *******   Press any key to end   *******
```

Fig. 11.18. PCOPY provides a full-screen display of its progress during a copy operation.

PKZIP—a File-Compression Utility

DISK

PKZIP, from PKWARE, Inc., is Phil Katz's well-known set of shareware utilities for compressing and combining files into a single, very compact file.

The primary reason for *zipping* files is to save space. If you are short of disk space, you might combine all the files in one directory into a compacted ZIP file, that is, a file with a ZIP extension. You can save as much as sixty percent of your disk space by zipping the files. And by keeping your least-used files zipped, you can free up space for other files.

The files contained in the ZIP file cannot be directly accessed. You must unzip them first. Zipping and unzipping are similar in principle to stacking a set of books on the side of the desk. You can't read any of the books while they are in the stack, but stacking does make room on your desk for other books!

The PKZIP routines are used throughout the PC community. The ZIP technology is even bundled with Lotus Magellan. And one of the PC Tools viewers enables you to browse the contents of a ZIP file.

The ZIP routines are especially popular on electronic bulletin boards because the file transfer times via modem are directly proportional to the size of the file. If you zip a file, uploading and downloading from a bulletin board is quicker and cheaper.

The two main programs are PKZIP, for compressing files, and PKUNZIP, for decompressing files—splitting a ZIP file back into its component files. The PKZIP command takes the following syntax:

PKZIP *-options* **zipname** *filename...*

In this generic syntax, *-options* are one or more switches to indicate the operation to be performed. For example, *-a* indicates that the files are to be added to the ZIP file, *-v* instructs PKZIP to list all the files in the specified ZIP file, and *-es* indicates that a fast-compression technique should be used.

zipname is the name of the ZIP file to be created or referenced. If an extension is not used, a default of ZIP is assumed.

filename... is the name of the file(s) to be processed; wild-card characters are supported.

The PKUNZIP command takes the following syntax:

PKUNZIP *-options* **zipfile** *d:path\filename*

In this generic syntax, *-options* are optional extraction switches. For example *-n* instructs PKUNZIP to extract only newer files or files that don't exist on the target directory. For example, the *-n* switch instructs PKUNZIP to extract files that do not exist in the target directory or files in the target directory whose date and time are older than those of the copy being unzipped.

zipfile is the name of the zip file from which the files will be extracted.

d:path is the optional directory where the unzipped files are to be stored, and *filename* is the optional name of the file to be unzipped. If no filename is specified, all files will be unzipped.

Figure 11.19 illustrates a PKZIP operation to compress all the files (*.*) in a directory into the file DOCS.ZIP.

```
C:\ZIPPED>PKZIP -A DOCS.ZIP *.*

PKZIP (tm)   FAST!   Create/Update Utility   Version 1.02   10-01-89
Copyright 1989 PKWARE Inc.   All Rights Reserved.   PKZIP/h for help

Creating ZIP: DOCS.ZIP
   Adding: 6.DOC         imploding (68%), done.
   Adding: 5.DOC         imploding (69%), done.
   Adding: 2.DOC         imploding (63%), done.
   Adding: 1.DOC         imploding (62%), done.
   Adding: 4.DOC         imploding (67%), done.
   Adding: 12.DOC        imploding (66%), done.

C:\ZIPPED>
```

Fig. 11.19. PKZIP displays the compression method and percentage of reduction as each file is zipped.

PKZIP is a shareware program. The copy on the accompanying disk is included for your evaluation. If you decide to continue using the program, you should register the copy. Further details are included in the on-disk documentation.

VTREE—a Directory-Tree Builder

VTREE is a simple, public-domain program that displays the directory hierarchy of a disk.

VTREE creates a display similar to the one generated by the DOS V4 TREE command. VTREE works on any system using DOS V2 or later. It provides a quick way of seeing how a hard disk is organized.

Figure 11.20 illustrates a sample display generated by VTREE.

```
 — 123R3 ————————— TOOLS
                  — ADDINS
                  — SOURCE
                  — QUE
                  — PLANS
                  — ZIP

 — DUALBOOT
 — SPOOL
 — TEMP
 — AUTOMENU
 — ZIP
 — BATFILES
 — MENU
 — MAG2 ————————— MGSAMPLE
                 — MGDEMO
                 — MGVIEWER

 — OAD
 — DOS401
 — PCKWIK
 — BATCOM ——————— BATDEMO
 — SAVE
 — DA5
 — ZIPPED

C:\MS>
```

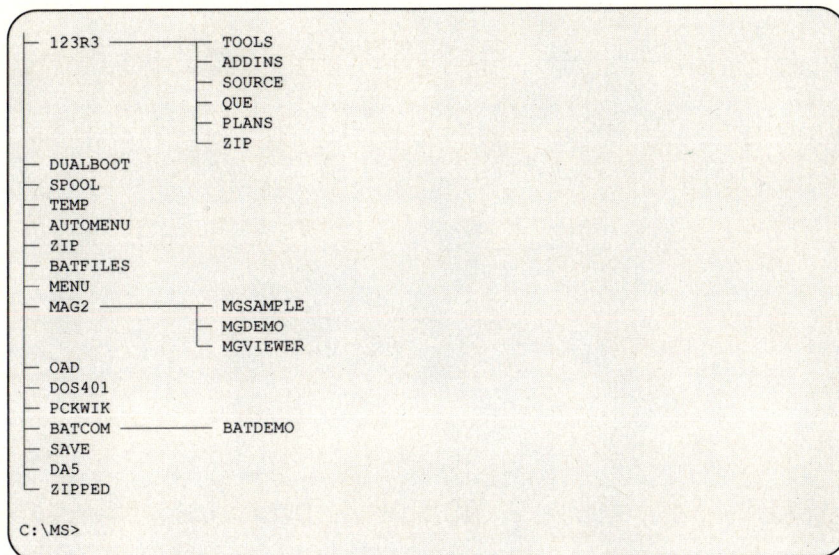

Fig. 11.20. VTREE displays a visual tree diagram of the directory hierarchy.

Summary

In this chapter, you learned about the capabilities of specialty hard disk programs and saw how they can help you to manage the information on your hard disk. Included in the discussion were the benefits of using menu programs, powerful file managers, and small utilities that focus on specific file-management tasks.

In Chapter 12, you learn about operating environments. These are programs that combine sophisticated program-execution facilities with file-management capabilities to provide you with a user-friendly interface to your programs and hard disk files.

12

Understanding Operating Environments

For a number of years, DOS has been criticized for being unfriendly and difficult to use. This situation is in marked contrast to other computer platforms, such as the Apple Macintosh, whose interface has been praised as being intuitive and satisfying for novice and experienced users alike. As a result, a few companies in the PC world are developing their own "friendly" programs, which provide many DOS services while freeing the user from the detailed syntax of DOS commands. These programs provide a layer between the user and DOS, and are known collectively as *operating environments*.

An operating environment's primary goals are to make the PC easy to use, and to extend the power of the operating system by permitting multiple programs to run simultaneously. The more powerful operating environments also enable the user to transfer data between diverse programs. You might use the operating environment's capabilities to cut a graph from a graphing program, for example, and paste it into a word processing program.

From a software developer's viewpoint, operating systems also provide a layer between the applications program and the hardware. The operating environment may provide printer drivers, for example, to save each program-development team from writing separate print routines to support all the printer makes and models. They can just use the ones included in the operating environment kernel.

With the release of DOS V4, Microsoft Corporation began shipping a program with the operating system called the DOS Shell. The DOS Shell is meant to be a useful and intuitive user interface, which simplifies file management and program execution. The DOS Shell is not a full operating environment, however, because it does not enable you to run multiple programs simultaneously. Nevertheless, the DOS Shell does make DOS easier to use and it is provided as part of the operating system; therefore, the program qualifies as a budget operating environment.

Similarly, the first implementation of the Extended Edition of OS/2 included an operating environment called Presentation Manager. Presentation Manager provides a graphical user interface from which you can start programs, switch between active applications, and manage files.

Long before the DOS Shell and Presentation Manager were developed, Microsoft (the developers of the DOS and OS/2 operating systems) introduced Microsoft Windows, a true operating environment that is in many ways similar to the acclaimed Macintosh interface. Microsoft Windows runs in graphics mode (as opposed to text mode), makes extensive use of graphical images and icons, and provides full mouse support. Although Windows receive a lackluster response at first, the product has since undergone major enhancements, and Microsoft Windows V3.0 (introduced in May, 1990) is recognized as the premier graphical operating environment for the PC.

Since Microsoft developed all three programs, you won't be surprised to hear that the DOS Shell, Presentation Manager, and Windows are quite similar. Although different technologies were used to develop these programs, they share a common look and feel, and use similar terminology (all three products refer to a menu as a "group," for example). If you can use any one of the three products, you can quickly master the others.

DESQview (Quarterdeck Office Systems) is another popular operating environment. This menu-driven program's main strength is its capability to manage and execute multiple programs at one time. DESQview works with almost any program that runs under DOS, and each program can be run in its own window on the display. You can display a graphics program in one window, and a text-based program in another. The program windows can be shrunk, zoomed, resized, and closed. Few operating environments offer such flexibility.

This chapter discusses the DOS Shell and Presentation Manager operating environments, which now are bundled with their parent operating systems. You also will learn about the two most popular third-party operating environments, Windows and DESQview.

Environments Supplied with the Operating System

Soon after the introduction of hard disks in personal computers, commercial software developers began to write third-party "shell" programs. These programs simplified many of the file-management tasks that previously could be performed only by using operating system commands, such as COPY and DELETE.

Now, the operating system software itself includes file-management and program-execution software. Since the introduction of DOS V4 and OS/2 Extended Edition, these operating systems have included their own operating environment software, the DOS Shell and the OS/2 Presentation Manager.

The DOS Shell

The DOS Shell is a menu system and file manager combined in a single program. As you install the operating system on your computer, the DOS Shell programs are copied onto the hard disk. The DOS Shell program already is configured with a number of menu options; to get the most from the Shell, however, you should customize it to meet your specific needs. For example, you can add menu options that automatically run your applications programs, and you can configure the graphics display and colors to your preference.

The following sections examine the DOS Shell's overall capabilities. If you already use the Shell, these sections show you how to create menus to access your programs, and how to get the most from the DOS Shell's file system.

An Overview of the DOS Shell

When you install DOS on your computer's hard disk, the DOS Shell is placed in the same directory as the operating system. To run the DOS Shell, switch to the directory containing the operating system, and enter the command **DOSSHELL**. Figure 12.1 shows a typical DOS Shell start-up screen. (To quit the DOS Shell, you can press F3 or select Exit.)

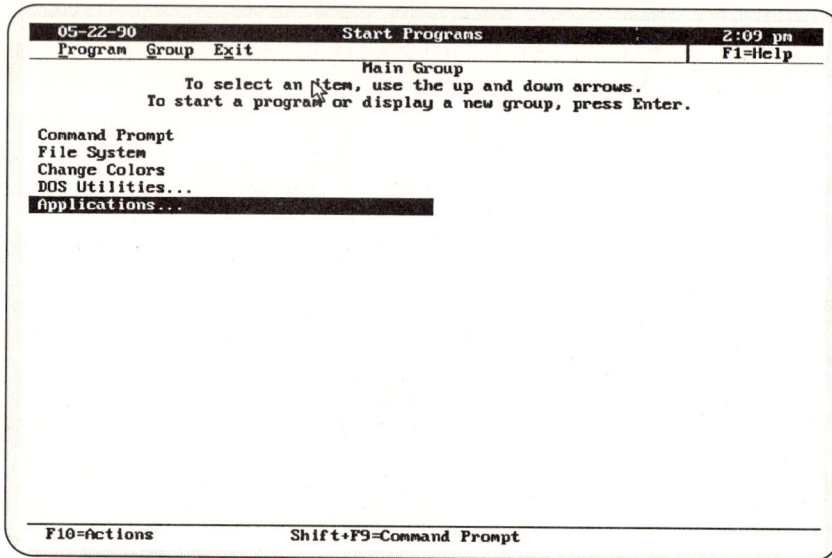

```
┌─────────────────────────────────────────────────────────────┐
│ 05-22-90                  Start Programs            2:09 pm   │
│ Program  Group  Exit                               F1=Help   │
│                         Main Group                           │
│           To select an item, use the up and down arrows.     │
│        To start a program or display a new group, press Enter.│
│                                                              │
│ Command Prompt                                               │
│ File System                                                  │
│ Change Colors                                                │
│ DOS Utilities...                                             │
│ █Applications...████████████████████████████████████         │
│                                                              │
│                                                              │
│                                                              │
│                                                              │
│                                                              │
│                                                              │
│                                                              │
│                                                              │
│                                                              │
│ F10=Actions              Shift+F9=Command Prompt             │
└─────────────────────────────────────────────────────────────┘
```

Fig. 12.1. The DOS Shell's opening screen.

You can set the Shell to display to one of four modes. Figure 12.1 shows the Shell in 25-line color graphics mode, which is the mode preferred by most users with an EGA or VGA display. The Shell also operates in text mode, which works best with monochrome and CGA systems. If you use a VGA system, you also can set the Shell to display in 30-line color or 30-line black-and-white modes. Throughout this section, DOS Shell screens are shown in 25-line graphics mode. You will learn how to configure the Shell to your system later in this chapter.

The Shell's information panel appears at the top of the display; the panel's second line shows the headings for the program's *pull-down menus*. To select options from the pull-down menu, you can either press the F10 key. If you use a mouse, move the pointer to the desired menu heading and click the left mouse button once. Figure 12.2 shows the display with the Group pull-down menu activated.

```
05-22-90                    Start Programs                2:09 pm
Program┃Group┃Exit                                        F1=Help
        ┌─────────────┐     Main Group
        │Add...       │ n item, use the up and down arrows.
        │Change...    │ ram or display a new group, press Enter.
        │Delete...    │
Command │Reorder...   │
File Sys└─────────────┘
Change Colors
DOS Utilities...
Applications...




F10=Actions              Shift+F9=Command Prompt
```

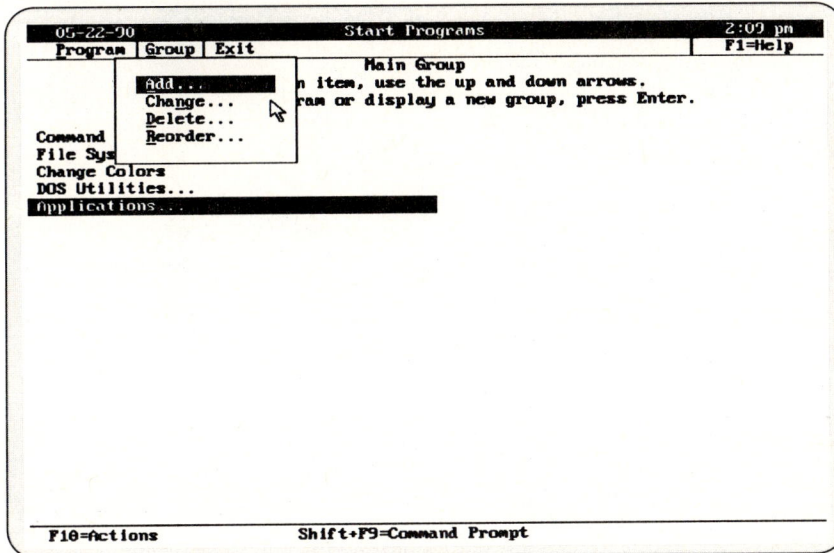

Fig. 12.2. The Group pull-down menu.

Normally, you use the Main Group menu's options to select programs, and the pull-down menus only for system maintenance and administration. You use the Group menu, for example, to modify the menu settings. (Again, in the DOS Shell's terminology, you can think of a "group" as a "menu.")

As shown in figure 12.1, the majority of the display is devoted to the Main Group's options. To select an item from the menu, use the cursor keys to highlight the desired item, and press Enter; if you have a mouse, place the pointer over the desired item, and click the left mouse button once. The following section shows you how to customize the Main Group menu.

If you select the DOS Utilities option from the Main Group, a pull-down menu appears, and offers quick access to a number of operating system commands. Figure 12.3 shows the display when the Set Date and Time Option has been selected from DOS Utilities menu. A *pop-up dialog box* appears, and prompts for user input—in this case, a new date. The DOS Shell enables you to build your own custom dialog boxes, which prompt for data after the user selects a menu option. Each dialog box includes a number of *action buttons*, which you can activate by clicking the mouse directly on the button, or by pressing the specified key.

```
┌─────────────────────────────────────────────────────────────────┐
│ 05-22-90                    Start Programs              2:09 pm   │
│ Program  Group  Exit                                   F1=Help   │
│                          DOS Utilities...                        │
│              To select an item, use the up and down arrows.      │
│           To start a program or display a new group, press Enter.│
│                                                                  │
│  ████████████████████                                            │
│  Set Date and Time                                               │
│  Disk Copy                                                       │
│  Disk Compare                                                    │
│  Backup Fixed Disk                                               │
│  Restore Fixed Disk                                              │
│  Format                                                          │
│                    ┌─────────────────────────────┐              │
│                    │   Set Date and Time Utility  │              │
│                    │                              │              │
│                    │                              │              │
│                    │   Enter new date ??-??-??    │              │
│                    │                              │              │
│                    │   Parameters . . [        ]  │              │
│                    │                           ▷  │              │
│                    │  (←┘=Enter)(Esc=Cancel)(F1=Help)│            │
│                    └─────────────────────────────┘              │
│                                                                  │
│  F10=Actions  Esc=Cancel  Shift+F9=Command Prompt               │
└─────────────────────────────────────────────────────────────────┘
```

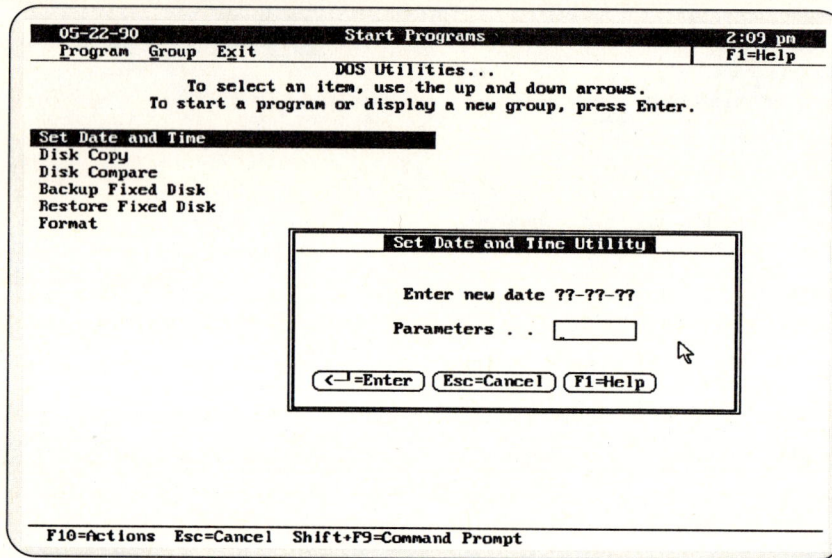

Fig. 12.3. *Pop-up dialog boxes prompt for data.*

The Shell does not only enable you to execute DOS commands quickly and easily. The program also features a useful file manager, which is accessed through the File System option in the Main Group (see fig. 12.4). You can use the file manager to review files on the disk, as well as to copy, rename, and delete groups of files. Like most of the Shell's options, the file manager enables you to perform basic tasks with a few clicks of the mouse or a few simple keystrokes—without remembering or entering convoluted DOS commands.

The Shell also features an extensive help system. If you are not sure how to use a command, press Help (F1) to invoke the help system.

Creating DOS Shell Menus

You can easily add new groups (or menus) to the DOS Shell, and you can just as easily add programs to the new groups. The Main Group screen can contain as many as 16 entries, and each entry can be either a single program or the name of a group of programs. If the entry is a group name, it is followed by three periods (such as DOS Utilities...), indicating that a menu of choices will appear when that entry is selected.

```
┌─────────────────────────────────────────────────────────────────┐
│ 05-22-90                    File System                   2:12 pm │
│  File  Options  Arrange  Exit                          │ F1=Help  │
│ Ctrl+letter selects a drive.                                      │
│ ▭A  ▭B  ▣C  ▭D  ▭E                                                │
│─────────────────────────────────────────────────────────────────│
│ C:\                                                               │
│     Directory Tree                            *.*                 │
│─────────────────────────────────────────────────────────────────│
│ ✓C:\                          ▲  📁09052732         0   05-21-90 ▲│
│  ├OS2                         ▲  📁09272730         0   05-17-90 ▲│
│  │ ├INSTALL        ⇖             📁092B0A17         0   05-06-90  │
│  │ ├DLL                          📁0E20141C         0   05-18-90  │
│  │ └SYSTEM                       📁150F1A09         0   05-05-90  │
│  ├DV                             📄AUTO    .BAT   231   02-22-90  │
│  ├FASTBACK                       📁AUTOEXEC.BAK   568   05-10-90  │
│  ├WIN386                         📄AUTOEXEC.BAT   568   05-10-90  │
│  │ └PIF                          📁AUTOEXEC.BOB   577   05-19-90  │
│  ├U                              📁AUTOEXEC.OLD   546   05-06-90  │
│  │ ├MISC                         📁AUTOEXEC.OS2   568   05-10-90  │
│  │ ├PCKWIK                       📁AUTOEXEC.SAV   514   05-06-90  │
│  │ ├HIJAAK                       📁AUTOEXEC.STD   547   04-18-90  │
│  │ ├INSET                        📄BUFFERS .COM   842   11-22-88  │
│  │ ├MISCOS2                      📁CLOCK01 .SYS 3,086   07-25-89  │
│  │ ├DUPLICAT                     📄COLOR   .BAT    75   02-22-90  │
│  │ ├RCD                          📄COLORB  .BAT    53   02-22-90  │
│  │ ├FB                           📄COMMAND .COM 25,332  12-14-89  │
│  │ ├PCTOOLS                      📁COMMAND .OS2 26,268  07-25-89  │
│  │ │ └SAMPLES                 ▼  📁CONFIG  .BAK   139   05-19-90 ▼│
│  │ ├NORTON                    ▼  📁CONFIG  .BOB   144   05-19-90 ▼│
│─────────────────────────────────────────────────────────────────│
│ F10=Actions   Shift+F9=Command Prompt                            │
└─────────────────────────────────────────────────────────────────┘
```

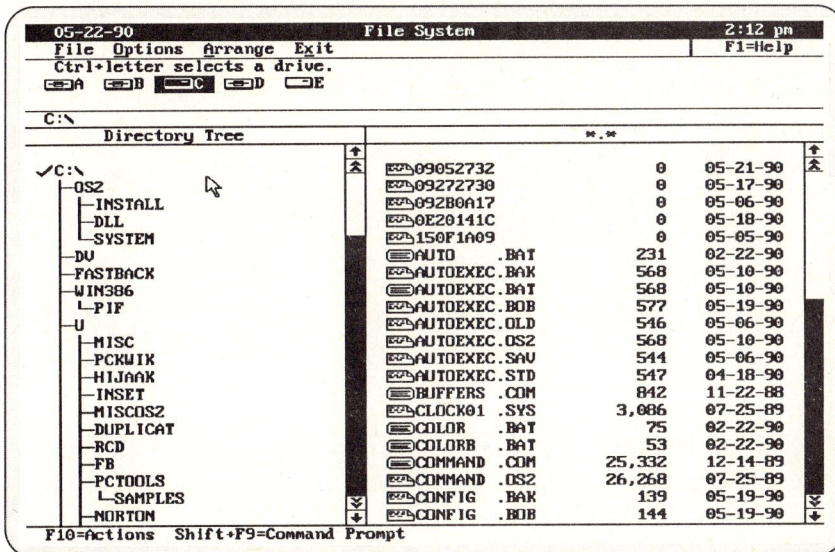

Fig. 12.4. *The DOS Shell's file-management menu.*

Normally, when you add a new option to the Main Group, the entry will be the name of another group. In other words, you will add a new group to the Main Group, and then add programs to the new group to form a sub-menu.

Creating a New Group

To add a new group to the Main Group (or to any group), select the Add option from the Group pull-down menu. The system displays a dialog box, which prompts for information about the new group (see fig 12.5).

The Add Group dialog box has four input fields: Title, Filename, Help Text, and Password. You must specify a title and a file name for the new group; the second two input fields are optional.

Title is the name of the topic listed on the parent Group—for example, Word Processing. The title can be up to 37 characters long; the Shell adds the trailing dots automatically. Filename is the name under which the new menu is stored. The file name can be up to eight characters long; the Shell automatically appends an MEU extension. Once this file is created, you should not need to enter its name again; the Shell manages these files behind the scenes. Still, you should assign a meaningful file name to the new menu. Choose a file name that best describes the group's purpose. If you are adding a group of word processing programs, for example, you might assign the root name WORDP to the file.

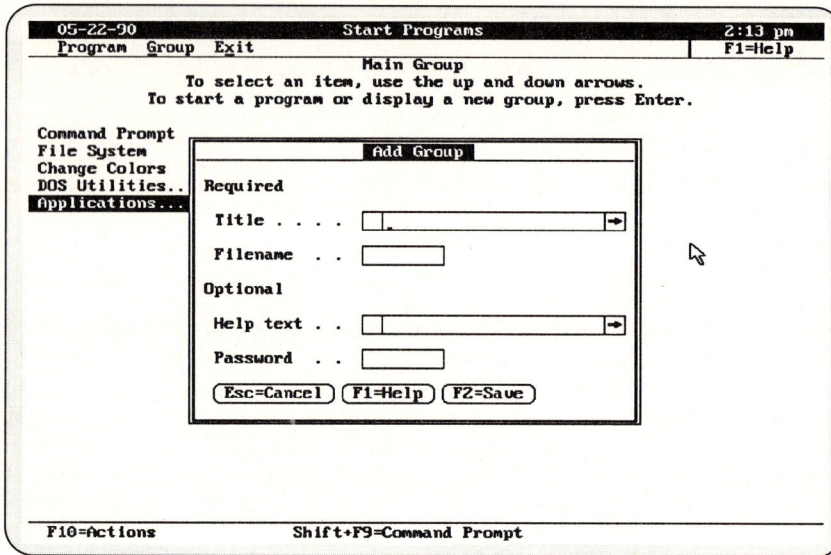

Fig. 12.5. *Adding a new group to the Main Group.*

In the Help Text field, you can enter descriptive text that is automatically displayed when the user calls the help routine for the new group. The help text can contain up to 478 characters, which appear just as you type them, with upper- and lowercase letters and blank spaces. The text is automatically adjusted to fit in the help text box, but you can force text to a new line by preceding it with an ampersand (&).

If you want to password-protect your new group, enter the password in the Password field.

After you enter the requested data, press F2 (or click on the Save button) to save the new group. The newly added group now appears on the Main Group menu. If you select the new group, the Shell displays a new screen and the message `The Group Is Empty`. The message appears because you have not yet added any programs to the group. You will learn how to do this shortly.

After you have added a new group to the main menu, you can modify the group's details by selecting Change from the Group pull-down menu. You also can delete a group by selecting the menu's Delete option. The Reorder option enables you to change the order in which the topics appear in the group.

Adding Programs to a Group

Suppose that you have just created a new group called Word Processing, and you want to add some programs to this group. The first step is to display the new group by selecting the Word Processing... option from the Main Group. Next, select the Add option from the Programs pull-down menu; an Add Program dialog box appears (see fig. 12.6).

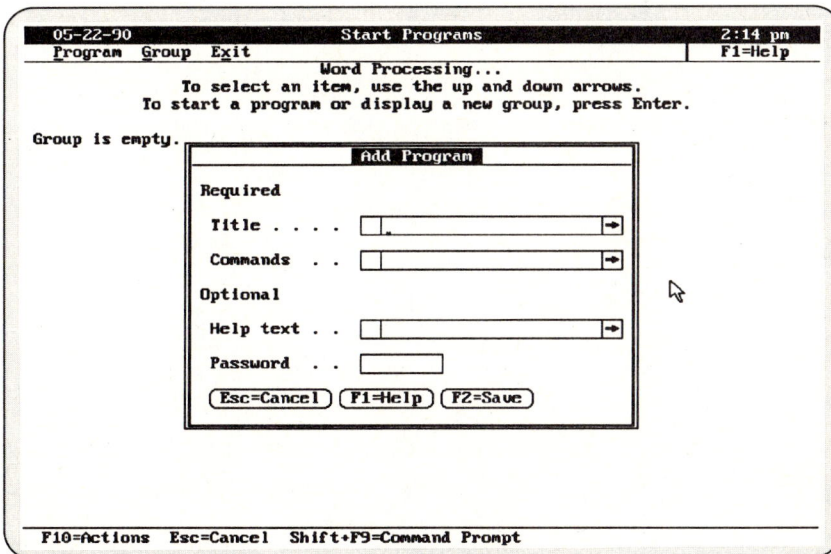

Fig. 12.6. *Adding a program to the Word Processing Group.*

The Add Program box is similar to the Add Group box, in that you must provide information for the first two fields, while responses to the second two fields are optional. First, you must specify the program's title. This title will be displayed in the group list, and can be up to 40 characters long.

The second required parameter is the set of commands that the Shell must execute to load the program. You can provide the commands in one of two ways. First, you can type all the commands needed to load the program, using up to 500 characters, in the Commands field. Alternatively, you can type all the commands in a batch file, and type CALL and the batch file's name in the Commands field. If you want to enter all the commands directly into the field, press F4 to indicate the end of each command or line. If you want to load Lotus Manuscript (a word processing program), for example, enter the following commands:

C:<F4>CD\MS<F4>MS

Remember to press the function key F4 at the end of each command or line; do not actually type the characters "<F4>."

When you press F4, a double vertical bar appears, indicating the next command's location. The preceding sample line is equivalent to the following three commands in a batch file:

```
C:
CD\MS
MS
```

Once you have defined the command, you can optionally enter some help text and a password. To save the program details, press F2. The Shell then returns to the Group display, which now should include the new program entry.

You also can use the Command field to develop sophisticated custom dialog boxes that request further information from the user when the program is selected. You create these custom dialog boxes by embedding commands between the special characters [and] in the Command field. When you create the custom dialog box, use the /T parameter to specify the box's title and the /P parameter to specify the prompt text. /I specifies instructional text at the bottom of the dialog box. Figure 12.7 shows the dialog box created by the following series of commands:

```
cd\123r2<F4>123 ["/T"Worksheet AutoLoad",
/I"Enter a spreadsheet to be loaded",
/P"Filename"]
```

Table 12.1 summarizes the options you can use when building a customized dialog box. For more information on custom dialog boxes, see *Using DOS*, published by Que Corporation.

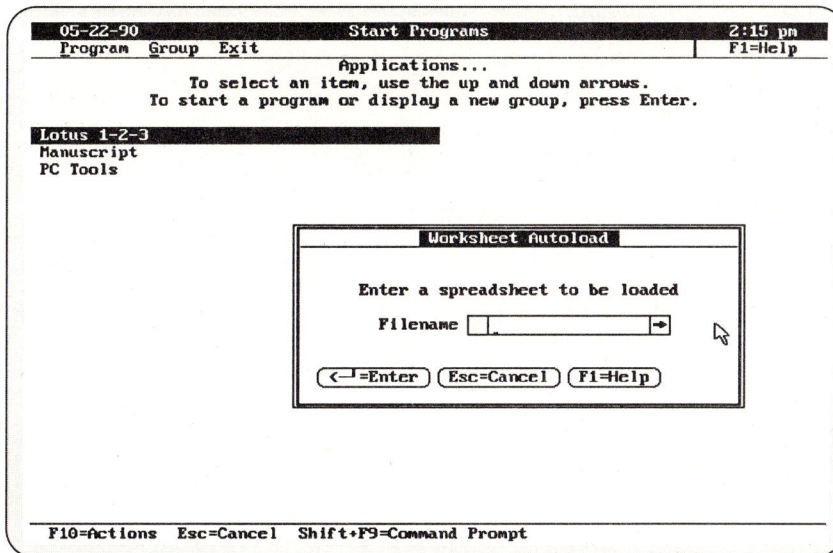

Fig. 12.7. The DOS Shell can create custom dialog boxes.

Table 12.1
Custom Dialog Box Parameters

Parameter	Description
[ ]	Special characters used to denote the beginning and end of the parameters. The Shell ignores the brackets, and displays a standard dialog box if no characters are entered between the brackets.
/T	Specifies the *title* that will be displayed at the top of the dialog box.
/I	Specifies the *instructions* (up to 40 characters) to be displayed above the input dialog box.
/P	Specifies the *prompt* text (up to 20 characters) to be displayed to the left of the input field.
%n	The %n variable is similar to variable markers used in batch files. It assigns the information entered by the user to a variable with the name *n*—for example, %1. Up to 10 variables can be assigned in one dialog box.

Parameter	Description
/D	Specifies the *default* field value; that is, the value that is displayed when the field is first entered.
/D"%n"	Indicates that the value assigned to variable *n* should be used as the default.
/R	Specifies that the default value will be erased when a user presses a key.
/L"Max"	Limits the number of characters the user can enter. *Max* can range from 1 to 128.
/M"E"	Instructs the Shell to accept only *existing* file names in the dialog box.
/C"%n%	Instructs the Shell to save the variable information assigned to variable *n*, so that the same value appears the next time the program is selected.

Once you have added a program, you can change it, delete it, or reorder all the programs in a Group, by selecting the other options from the Program pull-down menu.

Using the DOS Shell's File Manager

The DOS Shell File System group enables you to perform many file-management operations, without using complicated DOS commands. To access the program, select File System from the Main Group menu. DOS reads directory information and displays the introductory screen (see fig. 12.8).

Like the Main Group screen, the second line of the File System's display lists the available pull-down menu categories. The File System has four pull down menus: File, Options, Arrange, and Exit. The following sections examine each menu's function. Below the menu line appear letters or icons (depending on whether your Shell is in graphics or text mode), which indicate the disk drives available on your system. The current disk drive is highlighted.

The lower portion of the screen is split, to display two types of information. The left side contains a directory tree that shows how the directories are arranged on your disk. The active directory is highlighted. The right side of the screen displays a list of the active directory's files. If you use graphics mode, you should see an icon or character next to each file name, indicating the file's type (program, data, and so on). The file's size and last modification date also are displayed.

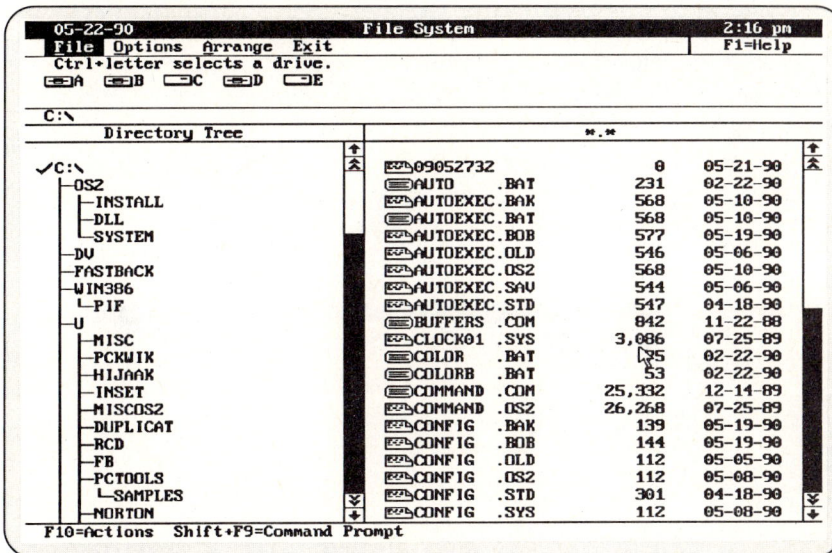

Fig. 12.8. *The main File System display.*

If the screen cannot display all the files at one time, you can scroll back and forth through the directory listing. If you have a mouse, move the pointer to the *scroll bar* to the right of the listing, and click on the up or down directional arrow. If you are using the keyboard, use the Tab key to jump to the file window, and then use the up- and down-arrow keys to scroll through the file listing.

If you want to change to a different drive or directory, click the mouse on the appropriate disk icon at the top of the screen, or on the desired directory on the tree display. If you are using the keyboard, press the Tab key to move into the appropriate window, and then use the cursor keys to change selections.

By using special keys or pull-down menus, you can manipulate files, sort directories and launch programs.

Using the File Menu

When you select the File option from the File System group, the File pull-down menu appears. As shown in figure 12.9, this menu lists 12 operations that you can perform on files that you have selected from the active directory. If you have selected more than one file, the File operation will be performed on all of the selected files. If some of the menu options do not appear on the pull-down menu, those options are not currently selectable. Many of the file options are available only if one or more files are marked as selected in the directory listing.

You can select a file from the active directory listing by clicking the mouse (once) on the desired file's name, or by pressing the keyboard's space bar when the file is highlighted. You can "deselect" a file in the same way.

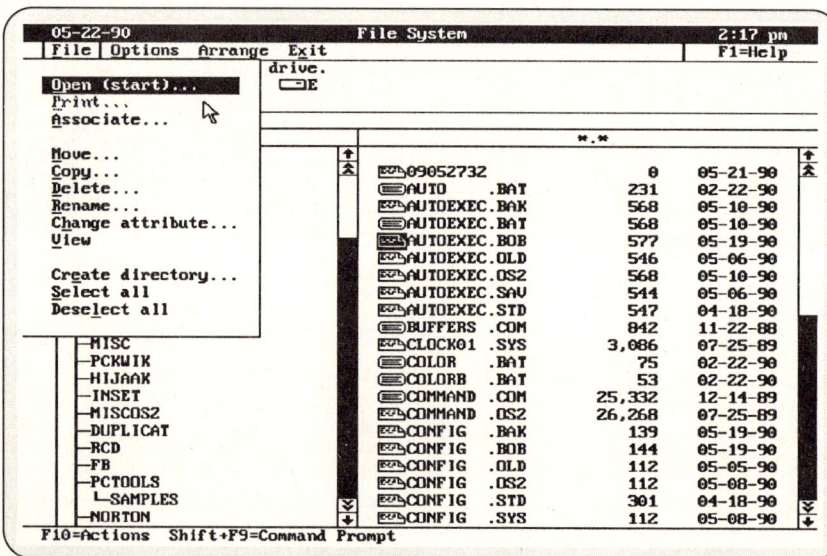

```
 05-22-90                        File System                      2:17 pm
 File  Options   Arrange   Exit                                  F1=Help
                           drive.
 Open (start)...           ▭E
 Print...
 Associate...      ▷

 Move...                              *.*
 Copy...                     09052732            0      05-21-90
 Delete...                   AUTO     .BAT     231      02-22-90
 Rename...                   AUTOEXEC .BAK     568      05-18-90
 Change attribute...         AUTOEXEC .BAT     568      05-18-90
 View                        AUTOEXEC .BOB     577      05-19-90
                             AUTOEXEC .OLD     546      05-06-90
 Create directory...         AUTOEXEC .OS2     568      05-18-90
 Select all                  AUTOEXEC .SAV     544      05-06-90
 Deselect all                AUTOEXEC .STD     547      04-18-90
                             BUFFERS  .COM     842      11-22-88
       MISC                  CLOCK01  .SYS   3,086      07-25-89
       PCKWIK                COLOR    .BAT      75      02-22-90
       HIJAAK                COLORB   .BAT      53      02-22-90
       INSET                 COMMAND  .COM  25,332      12-14-89
       MISCOS2               COMMAND  .OS2  26,268      07-25-89
       DUPLICAT              CONFIG   .BAK     139      05-19-90
       RCD                   CONFIG   .BOB     144      05-19-90
       FB                    CONFIG   .OLD     112      05-05-90
       PCTOOLS               CONFIG   .OS2     112      05-08-90
        SAMPLES              CONFIG   .STD     301      04-18-90
       NORTON                CONFIG   .SYS     112      05-08-90
 F10=Actions   Shift+F9=Command Prompt
```

Fig. 12.9. The File pull-down menu.

Opening a File

To start an applications program, double-click the mouse pointer on a file entry in the directory listing window. If you don't have a mouse, use the arrow keys to highlight the desired entry and press Enter. The Shell can execute valid COM, EXE, or BAT files. If you have used the Associate option (this option is discussed later) to link a file extension to an application, you can start a program by clicking on an associated data file's name.

In addition to double-clicking on a program file name, you can execute a program by selecting the Open option from the File menu when the program file name is highlighted in the directory listing. When selected, the Open File dialog box is displayed. This box allows you to specify parameters or switches that should be executed along with the program. For example, if you select a word processing program, you might specify the name of the document file to be loaded.

Printing a File

The Shell's Print option is similar to the one available at the DOS prompt. When you use the Shell's Print option, however, you cannot specify all the print switches that are available at the DOS prompt.

You must load the PRINT command prior to running the DOS shell if you want to use this option. Refer to Chapter 4 for more information on the PRINT command.

Associating a File

The Associate option enables you to associate certain program applications with various file extensions. For example, you might associate the extension WK3 with the program 123.EXE. After you associate an applications program with a particular file extension, you can start the application by selecting a data file that has the correct extension.

To create an association, highlight the program file (such as 123.EXE) and select the Associate option from the File menu. Then, enter all the extensions associated with this program (see fig. 12.10). The Shell asks whether the program should pause for input before loading.

The advantage of creating an association is that you are saved from having to select a program from a directory. Unfortunately, the Shell only loads the program; it does not automatically load the data file for you.

```
 05-22-90                      File System                    2:10 pm
 File  Options  Arrange  Exit                               F1=Help
 Ctrl+letter selects a drive.
 ⊡A  ⊡B  ⊡C  ⊡D  ⊡E
 C:\123R3
     Directory Tree                                     *.*             ↑
    ┌─────────────────┤ Associate File ├─────────────────┐           ▲
    ├─BRIEF    │                                          │  03-26-90 │
    │ └─BACKUP │                                          │  12-14-89 │
    ├─DOS      │  Filename . .: 123.EXE        1 of    1  │  06-19-89 │
    ├─MS       │                                          │  06-19-89 │
    │ ├─LEAF   │  Extensions. . │WK1 WK3              │→│ │  06-19-89 │
    │ ├─DISK   │                                          │  06-19-89 │
    │ ├─DOCS   │                                          │  06-19-89 │
    │ ├─LOTUS  │                                 ▷        │  06-19-89 │
    │ ├─DISK2  │                                          │  06-19-89 │
    │ ├─MSDATA │                                          │  06-19-89 │
    │ ├─TMP    │                                          │  06-19-89 │
    │ └─FIG12  │ ┌─────────┐ ┌──────────┐ ┌─────────┐    │  06-19-89 │
  ✓ ├─123R3    │ │ ←┘=Enter│ │ Esc=Cancel│ │ F1=Help │   │  04-09-90 │
    │ ├─TOOLS  └────────────────────────────────────────┘  06-19-89
    │ ├─ADDINS            ▨AI050LAA.LRF        36,738       06-19-89
    │ ├─SOURCE            ▨AI100LAA.LRF        84,332       06-19-89
    │ ├─QUE               ▨AJ033LAA.LRF        20,700       06-19-89
    │ ├─PLANS             ▨AJ066LAA.LRF        54,898       06-19-89
    │ ├─ZIP               ▨BC008LBA.LRF         6,418       06-19-89
    │ └─FINISHED    ⊻      ▨BC010LBA.LRF         6,783       06-19-89  ⊻
    └─DUALBOOT     ↓      ▨BC018LBA.LRF         9,527       06-19-89  ↓
 F10=Actions   Shift+F9=Command Prompt
```

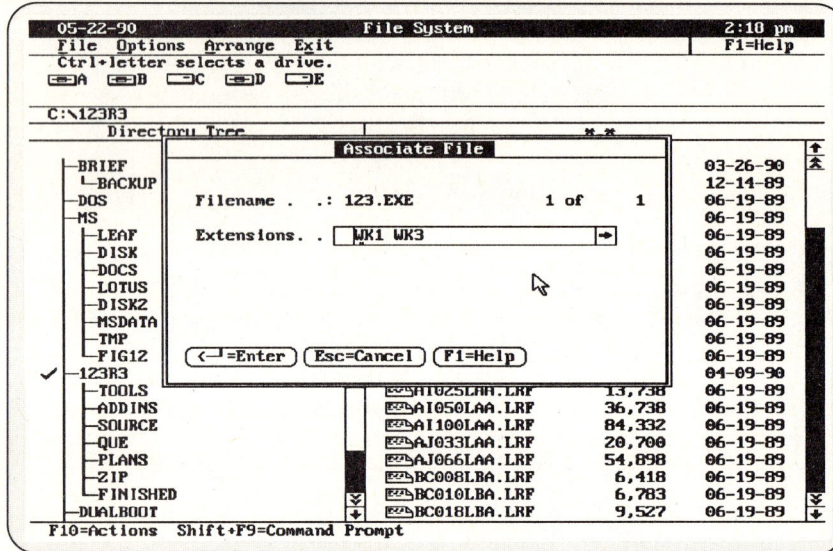

Fig. 12.10. Program files can be associated with file extensions.

Moving a File

Select the Move option from the File menu if you need to move one or more files from one directory to another. The move operation affects all the marked files in the directory list. The marked files' names are displayed in the MOVE dialog box. If you have activated the *Confirm or Delete* option in the File System Options menu, the shell prompts for confirmation before deleting the file from the old location. The Shell moves a file by copying it from the old location to the new location, and deleting the original file from its original location.

Copying, Deleting, and Renaming Files

The File menu's Copy option is used to copy one or more files to a new name or directory. The Delete option is used to delete files, and the Rename option is used to rename files. The advantage of using the Shell's Copy, Rename, and Delete options is that you can mark files that don't share a common file mask and manipulate them together.

For example, the files RESIGN.DOC, SALES.TXT, and STUFF.NOT do not share a common file mask (like *.DOC) and if they are stored in a directory with other files, they cannot all be copied together with a single

COPY command. However, using the Shell, the three files can be highlighted and then copied together by selecting the COPY option from the File menu.

Changing File Attributes

You can use the File menu's Change Attributes option to modify the hidden and read-only file attributes. The menu enables you to change all the marked files at once, or change each file individually.

Viewing Files

The View option enables you to browse the contents of ASCII files by pressing the PgUp and PgDn keys, or by clicking on the icons. Press Esc to return to the directory display.

Creating a Directory

To create a new directory from within the Shell, select the Create Directory option from the File menu. An input panel appears, in which you type the name of the directory to be created.

Selecting and Deselecting Files

The File menu's final two options enable you to select or deselect all files in one quick command, which saves a lot of mouse clicking and spacebar pressing!

Using the Options Menu

The second item on the File System's pull down is the Option menu, which has three entries: Display Options, File Options, and Show Information. These menus are used to configure the Shell to your specific needs, as well as to display summary information about the drive. You can control which files are displayed and the order in which they are displayed. You also can control whether the Shell prompts for confirmation before overwriting or deleting files. The following sections describe these entries in detail.

Display Options

The Display Options selection controls the order in which files are displayed in the file window. You can tell the Shell to sort displayed files by name, extension, date, size, or disk (unsorted) order. The display order does not affect the order in which the files are stored on disk.

File Options

You can use the File Options menu to toggle the following settings ON or OFF:

Confirm on delete. Set to ON if you want the Shell to prompt for confirmation before deleting a file.

Confirm on replace. If set to ON, the Shell prompts you for confirmation before copying a file over another file with the same name.

Select across directories. Ordinarily, any selected files are automatically deselected when you change directories or drives. When this option is turned on, you can select files even if they are stored in different directories; that is, the selections are not cleared when you change directories.

Show Information

When this option is selected, the Shell displays information about the selected file, directory, and disk drive (see fig. 12.11).

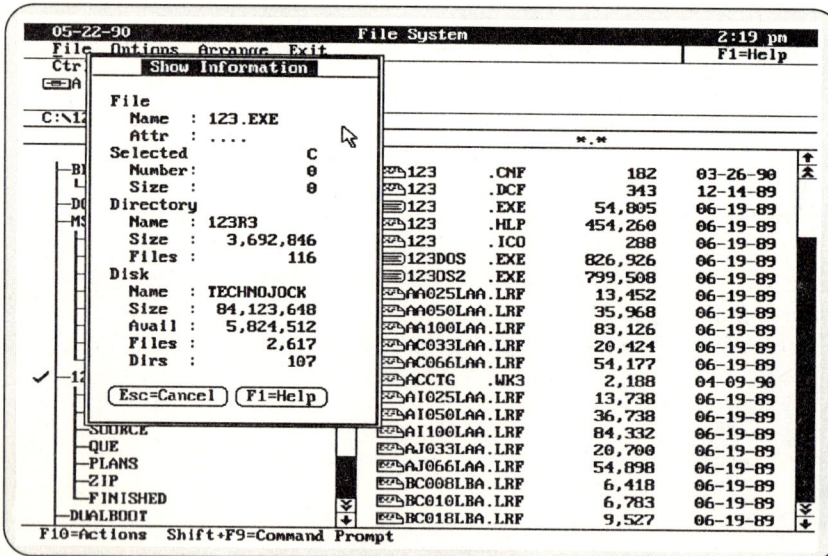

Fig. 12.11. The Shell shows information about the selected file, directory, and drive.

The Show Information panel's File section displays the file's name (including the extension) and attributes. Each attribute set is indicated on the Attr line by a character: *r* for read-only, *h* for hidden, *s* for system, and *a* for archive bit. Any of these characters, none of them, or all four may appear on the line, depending on the file.

To the right of the Selected heading in the panel appear the names of the drives currently stored in the Shell's buffer. If more than one drive is "memorized," this entry and the Number and Size entries have two columns, one for each of the drives. The Number entry indicates how many files have been marked in the directory listing for that drive. The Size entry shows the total number of bytes taken up by the selected files in that drive.

The panel's Directory section displays the name of the currently selected directory, the total size of all the files in that directory, and the total number of files in that directory.

The Disk section covers information about the disk drive itself. The Name entry is the label applied during formatting or with the LABEL command. The Size entry represents the total disk space, and the Avail entry signifies the free space available for new files. The Files entry shows the number of files stored on the disk. The last entry, Dirs, shows the number of subdirectories on the disk.

Using the Arrange Menu

You can use the Arrange menu to control the File System's overall look. Files can be displayed in a single listing (the default option), in a double display that enables you to view two drives or directories (see fig 12.12), or in a full listing that sorts files by name, extension, and so on.

When you select the Arrange menu, the three options Single File List, Multiple File List, and System File List are displayed, but only two will be selectable. The non-selectable option indicates the setting currently in effect.

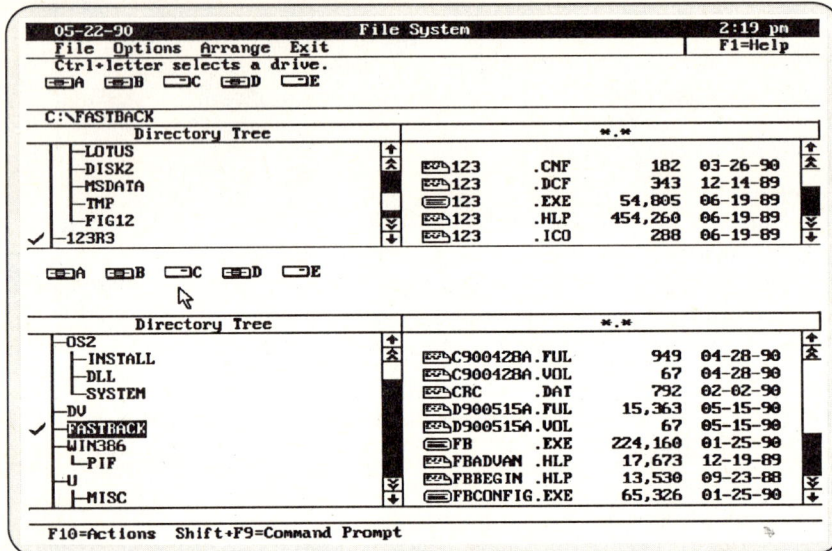

Fig. 12.12. The File System menu can display the contents of two drives and directories at the same time.

Understanding DOSSHELL.BAT

When you install DOS V4, the SELECT utility creates a batch file similar to the DOSSHELL.BAT file described in this section. Your file may differ slightly from the one shown here, depending on the options you select and the changes you make to this file.

```
(1)  @ECHO OFF
(2)  C:
(3)  CD \DOS
(4)  SHELLB DOSSHELL
(5)  IF ERRORLEVEL 255 GOTO END
(6)  :COMMON
(7)  @SHELLC/MOS:PCIBMDRV.MOS/TRAN/COLOR/DOS/MENU
     /MUL/SND/MEU:SHELL.MEU/CLR:SHELL.CLR/PROMPT
     /MAINT/EXIT/SWAP/DATE
(8)  :END
(9)  CD\
```

Each line in this sample batch file is numbered for easy reference. The line numbers are not part of the batch file, however, and should not be included if you copy this file or create one of your own from scratch. Each line performs the following functions:

Line 1 turns off the echoing of commands so that they are not displayed on-screen as DOS carries them out. Line 2 changes the current drive to drive C, in case you are using another drive when you call DOSSHELL.BAT. Line 3 changes the current directory to \DOS, which stores the programs you need to run the Shell. Line 4 summons a program called SHELLB.COM, which loads several key functions into memory. These functions take up less than 4K of DOS memory. SHELLB.COM checks for any errors that might prevent the Shell from running properly. If any errors are found, a value of 255 is loaded into the special DOS memory register, which stores the current ERRORLEVEL setting. SHELLB.COM then notes the name of the batch file you want to use to call up the DOS Shell. The default name is DOSSHELL. In network environments, customized batch files can be used for each node using the Shell on the same server.

Line 5 checks the value in ERRORLEVEL to see whether SHELLB.COM found any errors. If an error is found, control passes to line 8 (:END), and the batch file terminates. If this happens, you may have to run the SELECT program again, making sure you correctly define your system. Line 6 marks the portion of the batch file that calls the SHELLC.COM program. When you run a program from the DOS Shell, or leave the Shell to access the DOS prompt, DOS returns to this line in the batch file to reload the Shell. You must be careful to specify to SHELLB.COM the name of the file you want to use; you also must use only the :COMMON label to mark this point in the batch file. If you don't specify the name of the file, DOS does not know where to look. If you use some label other than :COMMON, DOS cannot find the correct starting place. Line 7 does most of the work in setting up the DOS Shell. Each key word following a slash (/) controls the Shell's settings and attributes. Line 8 marks the end of the section of the batch file that calls SHELLC.COM. Line 9 changes the current subdirectory to the root directory.

The seventh line of the sample file calls the SHELLC.COM program and specifies a list of options that customize the Shell. As you specify options in the DOSSHELL.BAT file, remember that no spaces can precede the slashes for the options in the SHELLC line.

Table 12.2 summarizes all the valid Shell customization options.

Table 12.2
DOS Shell Customization Options

Option	Purpose
/ASC:file	Specifies the name of the special-association file that records all the program-data file associations. By default, all file associations are stored in the file SHELL.ASC. Use this option to specify a different file.
/B:n	Limits the amount of memory used by the Shell for buffers.
/CLR:file	Specifies the color configuration file.
/CO1 /CO2 /CO3	Specifies the Shell display mode.
/COLOR	Enables the color-changing facility.
/COM2	Instructs the Shell to use COM2 for the mouse.
/DATE	Turns on the date and time display.
/DOS	Enables the File System option.
/EXIT	Enables the user to quit the Shell.
/LF	Swaps the purpose of the mouse buttons.
/MAINT	Enables the Shell maintenance menu options.
/MENU	Activates the Start programs menu.
/MEU:file	Specifies the menu file to use for the main menu.
/MOS	Specifies the mouse driver.
/MUL	Instructs the File System to monitor multiple drives.
/PROMPT	Enables the drop-to-DOS feature.
/SND	Turns on the Shells beep capability.
/SWAP	Instructs the Shell to maintain file details in a swap file.
/TEXT	Instructs the Shell to use text mode on CGA and monochrome systems.
/TRAN	Sets *transient* mode to reduce the amount of memory used by the Shell.

> ☑️ **NOTE** Several Shell customization options regulate the user's interaction with the Shell. In particular, the /PROMPT, /EXIT, and /MAINT options prevent the user from leaving or modifying the Shell.

To learn more about customizing the DOS Shell, see *Using DOS*, published by Que Corporation.

OS/2 Presentation Manager

OS/2 is a multitasking operating system; that is, it allows you to run multiple programs concurrently. To help you to execute and manage these programs, OS/2 includes the Presentation Manager, a graphical user interface for managing multiple OS/2 sessions. There are two main elements to the Presentation Manager: the menus and a file manager.

When you install OS/2, the system is configured to display the Start Programs menu at boot-up. Each menu set is referred to as a group (see fig. 12.13).

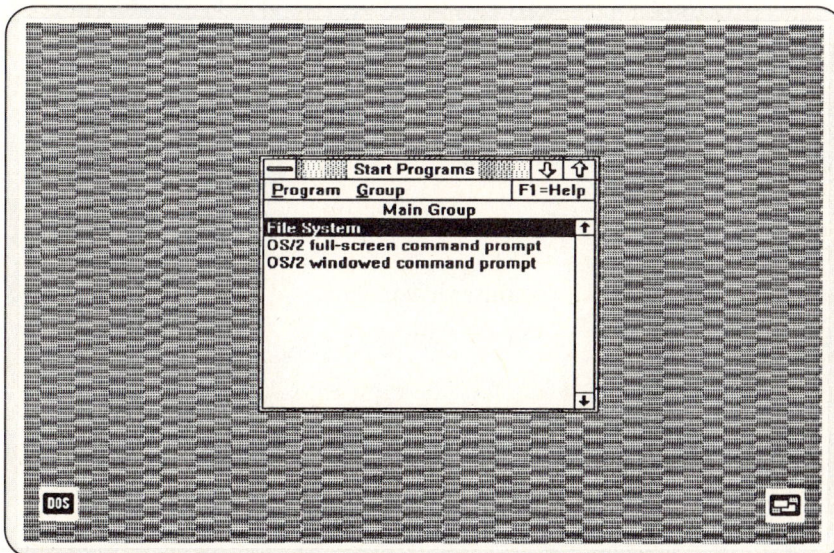

Fig. 12.13. The Start Programs menu in Presentation manager.

At the bottom of the screen are task icons. These icons represent active
programs or tasks, and in this case there are just two: a DOS session and a
Presentation Manager tool called the Task Manager. The Task Manager
provides a menu of all the active tasks and allows you to activate or
terminate any of them.

To start a program, you double-click the mouse on that program's menu
topic. (The Presentation Manager can be run from the keyboard, but it is
much easier to use with a mouse.) The Start Programs menu is displayed in
a window, and all Presentation Manager windows share some common
features. For example, the top line of the window has a title bar and
minimize and maximize arrows. These arrows can be used to change the
window to an icon or zoom the window so that it fills the entire display. By
holding down the left mouse button somewhere along the title bar and
moving the mouse, a window can be dragged to another position on the
display. Windows also can be stretched into a different shape (although the
shape will still be rectangular) by holding the mouse button down on the
window border and moving the mouse. Figure 12.14 illustrates the Start
Programs menu after it has been stretched and moved.

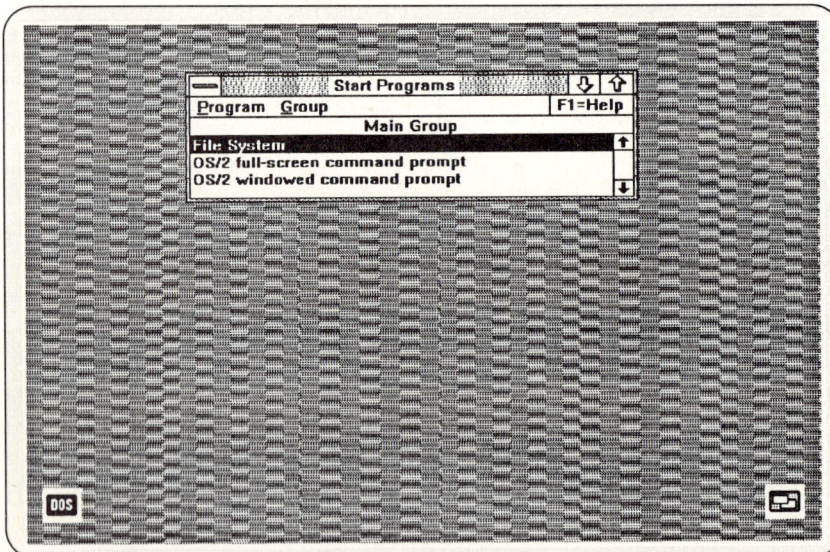

Fig. 12.14. Windows can be stretched and moved easily.

Most of the windows-management features in Presentation Manager are identical in Windows 3.0. See the section on Microsoft Windows for more information regarding window manipulation.

The Start Programs windows can be used to invoke programs, which are organized into groups. Once you have activated multiple programs, you can jump from one active program to another by using the Task Manager.

Managing Groups

The Start Programs menu provides two pull down menus: Program and Group. Like the DOS Shell, these menus are used to add, change and delete a group or programs within a group. To change to a different group of programs, pull down the group menu and select the desired group. The name of the active group will change, and the Start Programs menu will display all the programs in the newly selected group. In figure 12.15, the Lotus 1-2-3 Menu group is displayed.

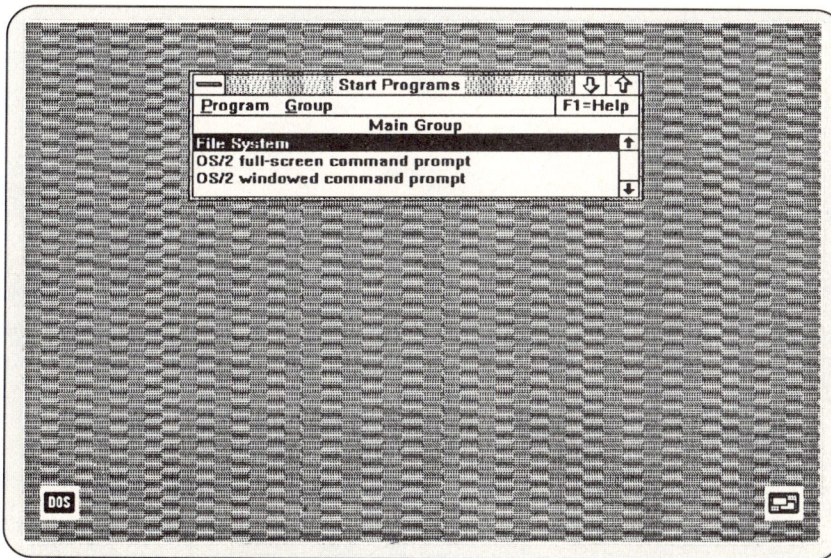

Fig. 12.15. *The Lotus 1-2-3 Group.*

When you select a program from the menu, the program is executed, and you are switched into the newly activated program. For example, if you select the Lotus 1-2-3 Release 3 program, the screen will be cleared, 1-2-3 will be started, and you will be positioned at the READY prompt in 1-2-3. At any time, you can press the key combination Ctrl-Esc to return to the Presentation Manager display. You can then execute another program or swap to an already active task.

Swapping Tasks

Every time you select a program from the Start Programs menu, an additional icon will be displayed. Figure 12.16 shows a busy OS/2 session where there are seven programs active, each one represented by an icon. In this example, the active programs are a DOS session (running Lotus Manuscript), Lotus 1-2-3, Aldus PageMaker, the OS/2 File Editor, the Presentation Control panel (used to change PM settings), the File System, and—over on the right—the Task Manager icon.

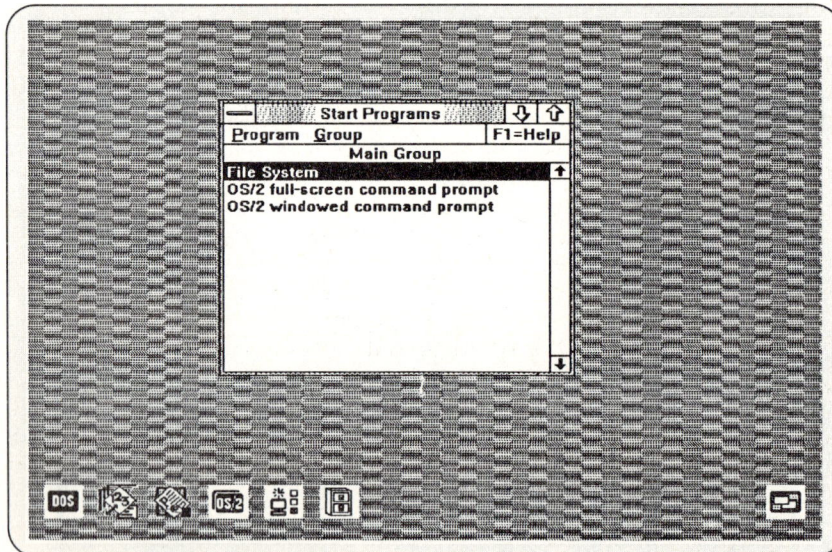

Fig. 12.16. Each active program task is represented by an icon.

To "jump into" an active task, you double-click the mouse on the icon. In addition to displaying icons for each active program or task, the Presentation Manager also keeps a list of all the active programs in a special menu, appropriately referred to as the Task Manager. The Task Manager menu can be activated by clicking on the Task Manager icon. Every time you press Ctrl-Esc to jump back to the Presentation Manager from an application, the Task Manager menu is automatically displayed (see fig. 12.17).

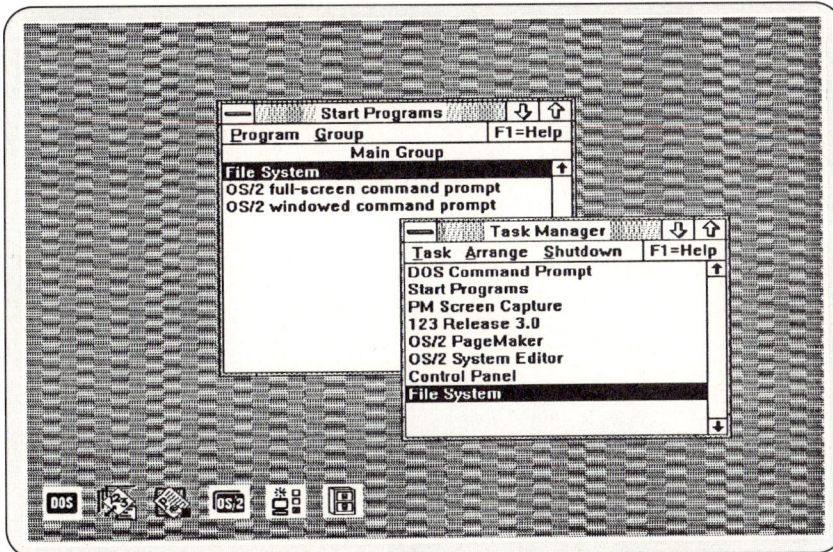

Fig. 12.17. *Every active program task is listed in the Task Manager menu.*

To select a task from the Task Manager, you double-click on the task's name. You also can press Alt-Esc repeatedly to cycle through each active application. To close a program, you can use the Task Manager by selecting the program name and then choosing Close from the Task pull-down menu.

If you close an application, that is, you quit the program, the corresponding icon will be removed, and the item will be removed from the Task manager menu.

Using the File System

If applications programs are written specifically to be controlled by the Presentation Manager, they can operate in a display window on the screen (that is, they don't have to take full control of the screen, like Lotus 1-2-3 Release 3). And they can take advantage of the Presentation Manager's built-in device support for devices such as print drivers. (An example of a commercial program written specifically to run in Presentation Manager is Aldus PageMaker for OS/2.) The Presentation Manager also ships with another PM-specific program called the File System. This is a windows-based file-management program to help you manage your hard disk.

The File System is similar in overall design to the file manager bundled with the DOS Shell. The program allows you to look easily at the files on your disk, and it provides ways to copy, rename, move and delete files, either individually or as a group. When you access the File System, a directory tree of the hard disk is displayed (see fig. 12.18).

The File System window provides the following series of pull down menus:

File. Includes options to manipulate files and directories, such as copy, delete, and open. Also includes the associate option to identify data files with programs.

Options. Controls the type of files to be included in the file list and the amount of data to display about each file.

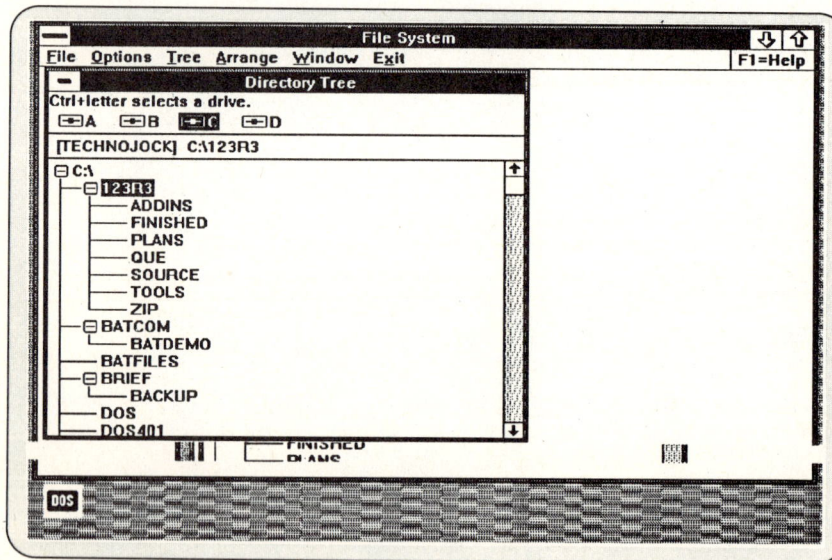

Fig. 12.18. The Presentation Manager File System.

Tree. Controls the level of detail to display in the disk directory tree. The File System allows parts of the tree to be expanded and contracted to control how many directory levels are displayed.

Arrange. Provides a quick way to rearrange the file-system windows after you have stretched and moved them.

Window. Used to instruct the file system to refresh all the windows; also includes options to delete windows that are no longer required.

Exit. Closes the File System.

To manipulate one or more files, you must select a directory from the directory tree. When you double-click on a directory name, the File System opens a directory window that lists all the files contained in the directory (see fig. 12.18).

Adjacent to each file in the directory window is an icon. Each icon provides an indication of the file's purpose. For example, there are icons to represent subdirectories (beside ZIP in the figure), data files (beside 123.CNF), and

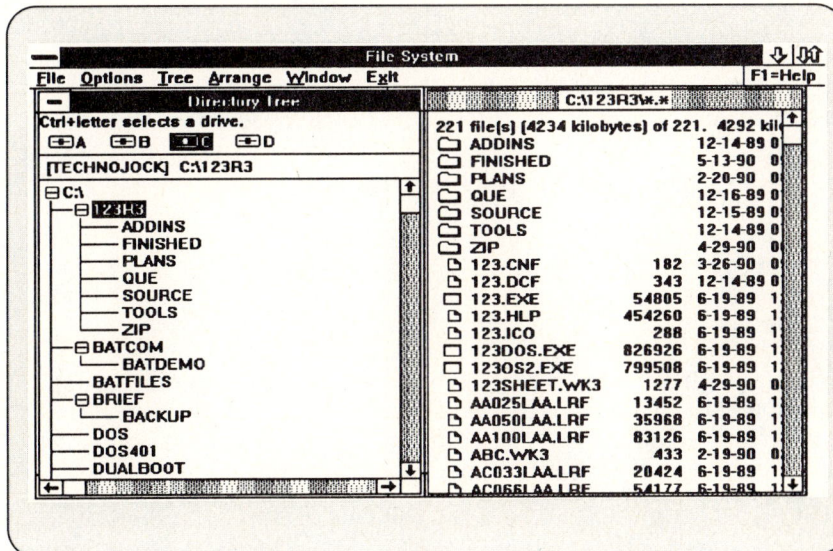

Fig. 12.19. *The directory window for C:\123R3.*

programs (beside 123.EXE). From the Options menu, you control which of these file types you want displayed. By default, the directory list will include all files.

You can use the File menu to copy and move files and so on, but you also can use the file-name icon. This is a good illustration of how graphical user interfaces can greatly simplify the computer interface. If you have two or more directory windows open, you can copy files from one directory to another just by depressing the mouse button on the file-name icon and dragging the icon to the window that is displaying the target directory. As soon as you release the mouse button, the file is copied.

The same operation can be used to move a file, the only difference being that you hold down the Alt key when you first select the file-name icon.

You can manipulate multiple files at one time. To select a single file, you click on the file name. To select more than one file, you hold down the Ctrl key while you select each file. In this manner, you can select a few files from different positions in the directory. If you want to select a contiguous range of files, click on the first file. Then move the mouse to the last file in the list, hold down the shift key, and click once. All the files between these two will then be selected.

In the section on the DOS Shell, you learned how to execute a program by selecting an item from one of the groups in the Start Programs menu. You also can execute a program by double-clicking the mouse on the program's file name. As in the DOS Shell, you also can execute a program by clicking on a data file, provided that file's extension has been associated with a specific program (using the Assoc menu).

Using Presentation Manager Utilities

In addition to the File System, the Presentation Manager includes some smaller utility programs that can help you manage and configure your system. These programs can be accessed from the Utility Programs group, which is automatically added to the Start Programs menu when you install OS/2. This group includes a text file editor, the CHKDSK program to check your hard disk, and a very useful utility called CONFIG.

The CONFIG program is used to edit the contents of the CONFIG.SYS file. OS/2 has a far greater number of commands in the CONFIG.SYS file than DOS, and this program makes updating the configuration file easy. The program is not an editor—all changes are made to the CONFIG.SYS file behind the scenes. By selecting options from menus and dialog boxes, you inform CONFIG of the desired settings. There are options to modify the settings for the country, keyboard, DOS session, OS/2 session, memory management, mouse, and virtual disk (see fig. 12.20).

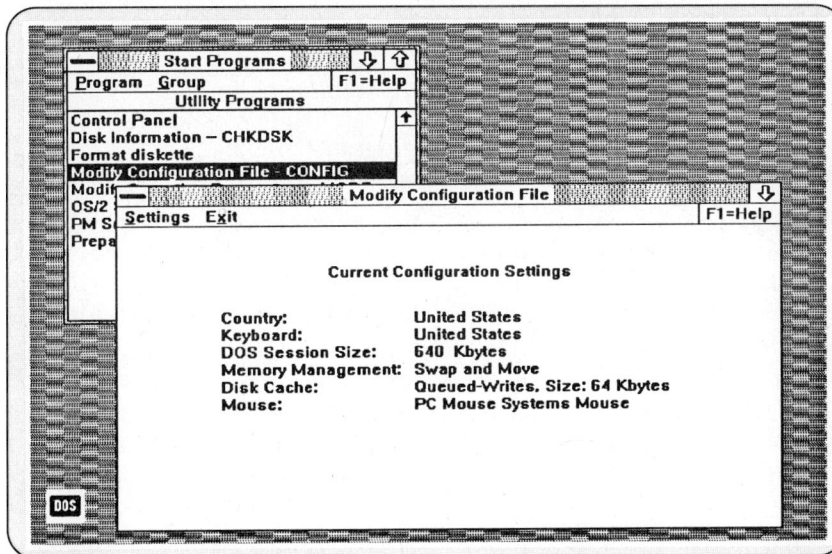

Fig. 12.20. Changing the system configuration with CONFIG.

See Appendix C for a discussion of OS/2 features that relate to hard disk mangement.

Independent Operating Environments

Since the mid-eighties, operating environments have been available from third-party developers. These programs can be bought off-the-shelf, and are often bundled with other software and hardware products. For example, if you buy a certain mouse, you may be given a copy of Microsoft Windows; or if you buy a memory-expansion card, you may receive a complimentary copy of DESQview.

Although other operating environments have come and gone, Microsoft Windows and DESQview are established as two of the most popular operating environments. Both these products have leveraged the power of the 80286 and 80386 microprocessors and allow you to run multiple applications at the same time. In the remainder of this chapter, you learn about the capabilities of these two products, with the primary focus on those features that help you to get the most from your hard disk.

Using Microsoft Windows 3.0

Microsoft Windows 3.0 (Windows) incorporates many of the features of the DOS Shell and the OS/2 Presentation Manager and provides an excellent graphics-based operating environment. Windows offers a complete work environment from which you can execute programs, manage data on your hard disk, and transfer data between applications.

Windows used to be sold in two different packages: *Windows 286* for 80286-based machines, and *Windows 386* for 80386-based machines. With the release of Windows version 3.0, the products were combined. Version 3 of Windows can be used on any personal computer, with microprocessors ranging from 8086s to 80486s.

When Windows is run on an 80386-based computer, programs can be executed in *386 enhanced mode*. This capability provides programs with access to more memory than really exists—by temporarily swapping data from memory to disk. 386 enhanced mode also allows for multitasking of applications that are not Windows-based, for example, DOS programs that were not specifically written to take advantage of Windows.

To support Windows, you need the following system capabilities: DOS V3.1 or later, 640K of memory—with an additional 1024K of extended memory to take advantage of 386 enhanced mode, a hard disk with six to eight megabytes of space available, and a graphics display card (preferably EGA or better).

This section explores Window's Program Manager and File Manager and briefly reviews other Windows features. For more information on Windows, see *Using Microsoft Windows 3*, 2nd Edition, published by Que Corporation.

> *A note from the author...* Windows has been around for a number of years, and many of you have seen the product at one stage or another. Even if you looked at Windows in the past and decided not to use it, you should still take a look at Version 3. Windows has come a long way since its original release, and you may be surprised to learn just how much the product has improved.

Windows Fundamentals

When you execute the main WIN.EXE program from the DOS prompt, the Windows *desktop* is displayed (see fig. 12.21). The desktop is the entire screen display, and it may include individual windows and small icons.

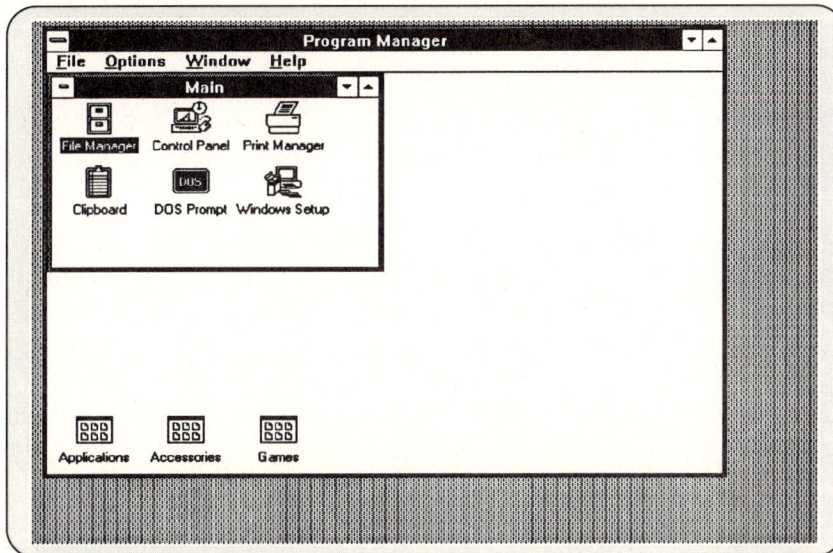

Fig. 12.21. *The Windows desktop.*

There are two types of windows. *Applications windows* contain programs that are running and active. The name of the application appears in the title bar at the top of the window. *Document windows* are generated and controlled by the application that is running.

Only programs written specifically to work with Windows have document windows. The File Manager is an example of a program that can create document windows. In this case, they are windows that display directory details (see fig. 12.22). Document windows cannot be moved outside the boundaries of the parent applications window.

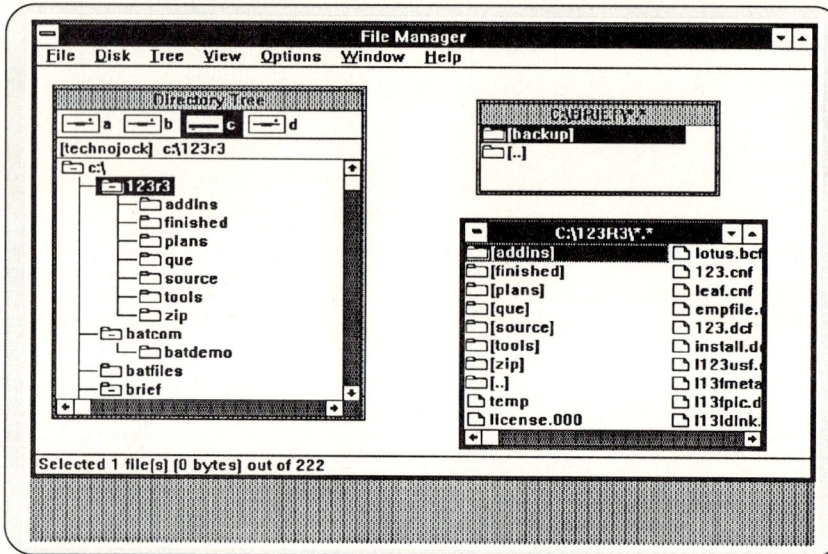

Fig. 12.22. *Applications and documents windows.*

Common Window Characteristics

All the applications windows share some common characteristics. Figure 12.23 illustrates the common parts of the window. By clicking the mouse on the various objects in the window perimeter, you can control the size, shape, and contents of the window. All these window adjustments can be achieved with the keyboard, but Windows is much easier to use with a mouse.

The attributes of applications windows highlighted in figure 12.23 are used as follows:

Control box. The control box (located in the top left of the window) is primarily for keyboard users. When activated, a pull-down menu displays a list of window operations, such as Minimize, Maximize, and Close. With a mouse, you can alternatively perform these actions by clicking on the various window objects. If you double-click on the Control box, the application is closed.

Control box   Title bar   Maximize box

                              Minimize box

    Scroll bar   Elevator

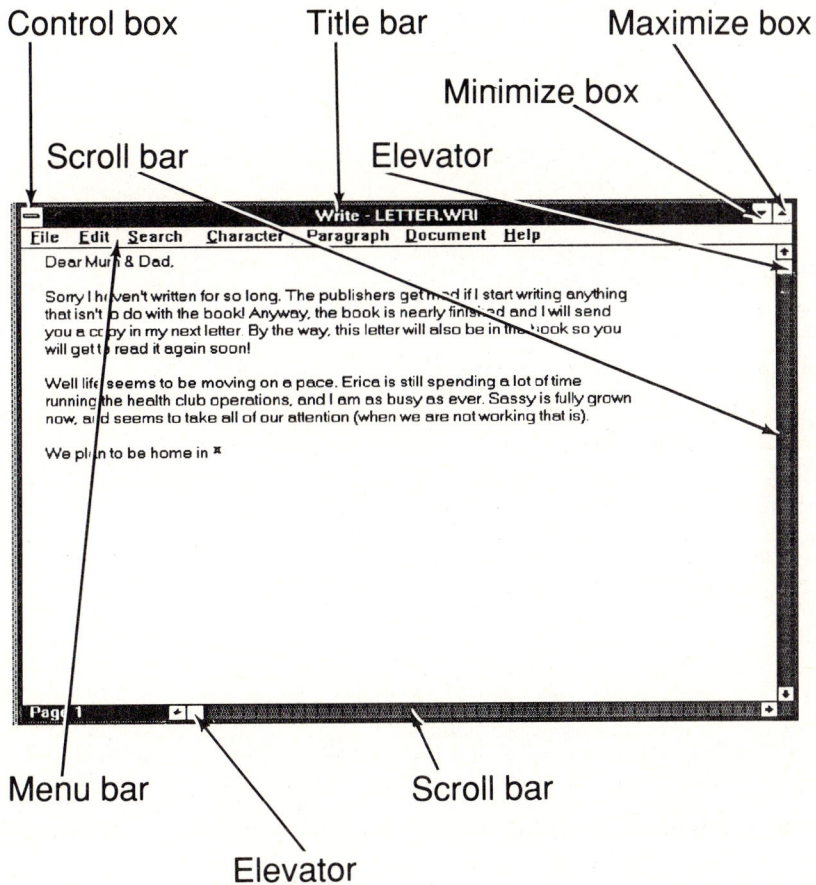

Menu bar   Scroll bar

            Elevator

Fig. 12.23. *The common elements of a window.*

Title bar. The title bar describes the application displayed in the window. By clicking the mouse on the title bar and dragging the mouse, you can move the window to another position on the desktop.

Minimize box. The downward-pointing arrow located at the upper right of the window is the Minimize box. By clicking on this box, you can shrink the entire window to an icon. (The icon can be restored to a window with8 a double-click of the mouse.)

Maximize box. The upward-pointing arrow located next to the Minimize box is the maximize box. If you double-click on this object, the window is expanded to fill the entire screen. When the window is maximized, the Maximize box is replaced with a Restore box, used to restore the window to its previous dimensions.

Menu bar. The menu bar is located immediately below the title bar, and indicates the major headings of the applications' pull-down menus. When you click on the menu headings, the pull-down menu is displayed.

Scroll bars. Along the right and bottom sides of the window, you may find scroll bars. When the window is too small to display all the relevant information, the scroll bars can be used to scroll vertically and horizontally through the information displayed in the body of the window. The scroll-bar elevators indicate the relative vertical and horizontal position of the data currently being displayed in the window. To scroll through the text, you can either click on the scroll bar directional arrows or drag the elevators.

Window border. By pressing and dragging the mouse on one side of the window border, the window can be shrunk and stretched. By dragging a window corner, two sides can be adjusted at once.

Window body. The body of the window, known as the *workspace*, is the main information displayed by the window. In figure 12.23, it is the text being edited with the Windows Write word processing program.

Not every window has every one of the above objects. For example, the Window's calculator does not have scroll bars and, because the calculator is of a fixed size and shape, the window cannot be maximized, shrunk, or stretched.

Window Icons

Icons are small graphical images about the size of a postage stamp, which represent program applications. Icons provide a convenient way of displaying multiple applications windows on the desktop without taking up too much room. By double-clicking on an icon, you can either start an application running or, if the application is already running, redisplay an application that was minimized. Windows supports three different types of icons: program item icons, applications icons, and document icons.

Program item icons are special icons, which are available only in the Program Manager (discussed in the next section). Each icon represents a program in a group. These icons can be moved from group to group, but they cannot be moved outside the boundaries of the Program Manager window.

Applications icons represent applications that have been activated and subsequently minimized. Applications icons are the only icons that appear on the desktop outside a window's borders. By default, icons are located at the bottom of the screen, but you can drag them anywhere on the desktop.

Document icons represent document windows that have been minimized. These icons can be moved anywhere inside the parent application's window.

Using the Program Manager

The Program Manager is the heart of the Windows desktop. It provides you with windows showing all the groups of programs can select and run. Remember that, unlike standard DOS, you can run multiple applications at the same time using Windows. For example, your word processing program might be printing a long document while you are entering details about new customers into your database. The Program Manager is designed to help you invoke multiple applications and switch between them once they are active.

The Program Manager can run applications written specifically to be run by Windows, as well as standard programs written to run under DOS. Unless you are using Windows in 386 enhanced mode, standard DOS programs run in Windows will take over the entire screen and look as though they were executed from the DOS prompt.

To go back to the Windows desktop from a full-screen application, press Ctrl-Esc. When you do so, the application is represented by an icon at the bottom of the desktop.

Not surprisingly, the Program Manager runs in a window (see fig. 12.24). Programs are organized into *groups*. When you install Windows, three or four groups will be created, depending on the options you selected during installation.

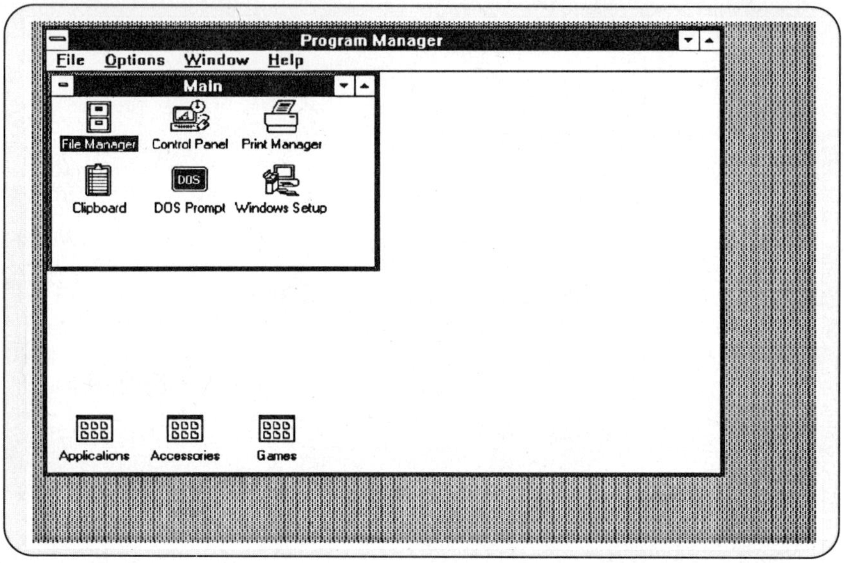

Fig. 12.24. *The Program Manager window.*

The group entitled Main Group contains all the Windows system programs included with the package: File System, Control Panel, Print Manager, and so on. The Accessories Group contains a collection of handy programs, including a calculator, calendar, cardfile, and clock. There is also a Games Group, which includes a great version of Solitaire and Reversi. You also may have two groups entitled Windows Applications and Non-Windows Applications. These groups are optionally created when you install Windows, and they contain all the applications found on your hard disk.

To start a program, you open a group window and double-click on the icon of the program you want to run. When you first start the Program Manager, the Main Group is displayed in a group window inside the main Program Manager window. The other groups are displayed as group icons at the bottom of the Program Manager window (see fig. 12.24).

You may have multiple group windows open at one time. To open a group, you can either double-click on the group icon or select the group from the Program Manager's Window pull-down menu. Group windows can be closed like any other window—by double-clicking on the Control Box at the top left of the window. If you have multiple group windows open, you can arrange them neatly by selecting Tile (see fig. 12.25) or Cascade from the Window pull-down menu.

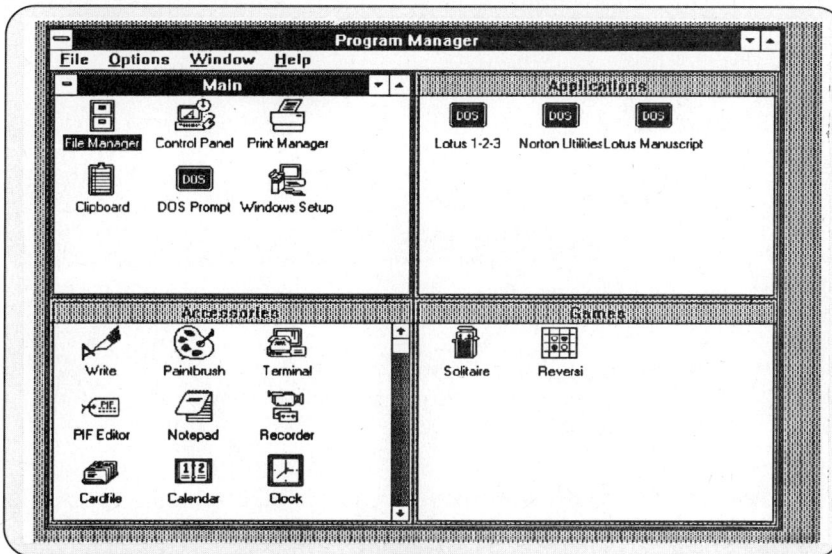

Fig. 12.25. *Multiple group windows can be opened.*

You can add, modify, and delete groups and programs within groups. To create a new group or program, select New from the File pull-down menu. If you are creating a group, the system prompts for a description and a file name, which will be used internally by the Program Manager. If you want to modify a group's settings, the group must not be in an active window, that is, it must be an icon. Highlight the group icon and select properties from the File pull down menu. You will then be able to change the description and the file name.

If you are creating a program within a group, the system prompts for a description and the command line to be executed when the program is selected, that is, the program name. If you cannot remember the file name or directory of the program, you can select the file from a browse window that displays all the files on your hard disk. Unlike the DOS Shell, the Program Manager does not allow you to add multiple commands on the command line or embed commands to pop up dialog boxes.

To move a program from one group to another is a snap. All you have to do is open the source and target group windows and drag the program from one window to the other.

Windows provides two other ways of executing a program besides selecting a program icon. You can select the Run option from the File pull-down menu and enter the program name, or you can double-click on the program file name in the File Manager window.

Using the File Manager

The File Manager replaces the DOS Executive from earlier versions of Windows and is executed from the Main group. The File Manager is designed to help you manage and organize the files on your hard disk. It is very similar to the file-management programs included with the DOS Shell and OS/2 Presentation Manager.

The File Manager allows you to manipulate files, either individually or in blocks. When the File Manager is started, a File Manager window is opened, and a Directory Tree window gives you a bird's eye view of the directory hierarchy of your hard disk (see fig. 12.26).

The Directory Tree window displays a set of icons identifying all the installed drives. The drive currently being viewed is highlighted. To select a different drive, click the mouse on a different drive icon. Immediately below the drive icons is the volume label and the drive and directory highlighted in the main directory tree. The body of the window displays the directory tree. By default, the File Manager displays a compressed tree showing only the level-one directories. To the left of each directory name is a small directory icon (shaped like a file folder). If a directory has further subdirectories that are not displayed, a plus sign appears inside the icon. This indicates that you can press the plus key to expand the tree one level. To expand the tree to all levels for the current directory, press *, or press the Ctrl-* key combination to display the entire directory tree. You can press the minus key to compress the tree if you want to display less detail.

To see and manipulate the files in a directory, you must open a directory window. Double-click the mouse on the directory name in the tree, and a directory window will be opened. This window will display a list of all the files in the directory. You can open multiple directory windows (see fig. 12.27).

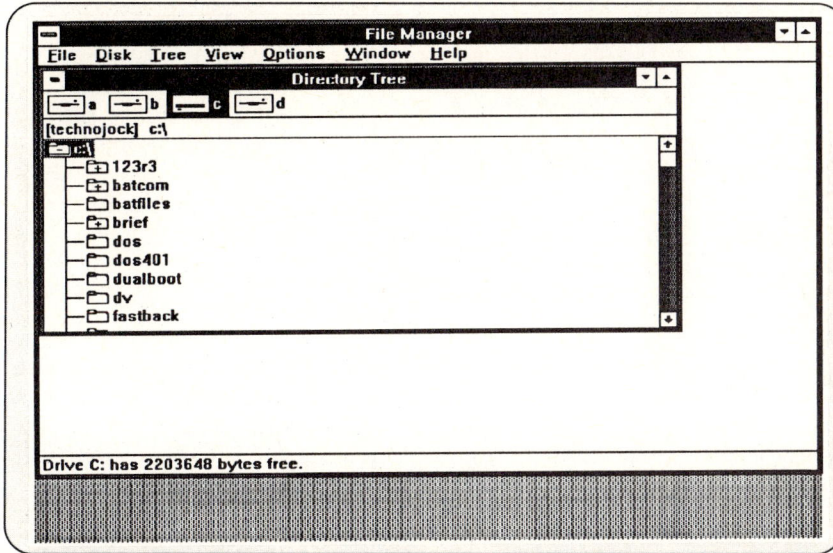

Fig. 12.26. *File Manager's Directory Tree window.*

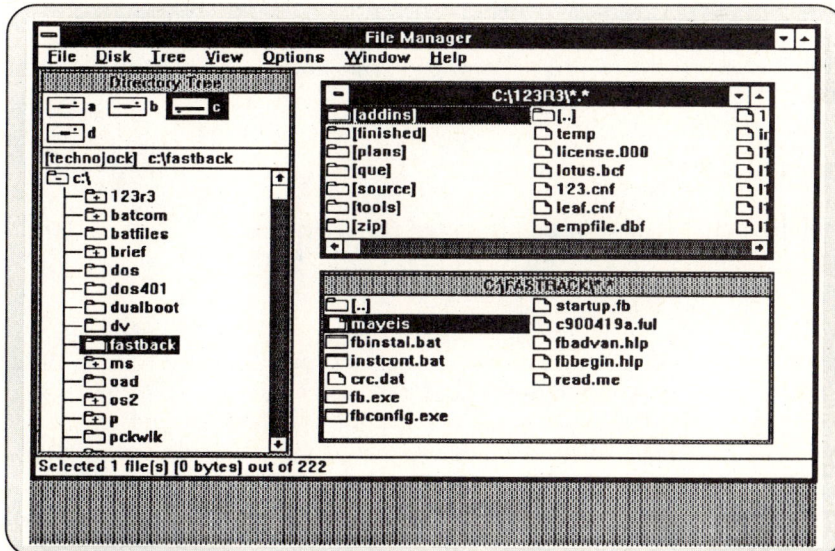

Fig. 12.27. *Multiple directory windows can be displayed.*

To the left of each file name is an icon describing the file type. As well as the directory icon, there are icons to represent program files, document files, and other files. Program files are any files with an EXE, COM, BAT, or PIF extension. A document file is a file that has been associated with a program. Using the Associate option from the File pull down menu, the File Manager can be instructed to recognize certain file extensions. For example, you can associate all files with a WK3 extension to the program Lotus 1-2-3 Release 3. The parent program can be executed by clicking on a document file associated to it. You can control which files are displayed in a directory window and the order in which they are displayed by accessing options on the View pull-down menu.

Double-clicking on a file in a Directory window indicates that you want to execute the file. If you double-click on a directory file, the directory will be selected and the Window will be refreshed to display all the files in the newly selected directory. If you double-click on a program file or a document file (associated with a program), the program will be executed. If you double-click any other file, an error message will be displayed indicating that the file cannot be executed.

You must *select* one or more files before it can be manipulated— copied, renamed, deleted, or printed. When a file is selected, it is displayed in different colors. To select a single file, click on the file name. To select more than one file name, hold down the control key and click on each file name in turn. To select a block of files, select the first file, hold down the Shift key, and select the last file. These two files and all the ones in between will be selected.

The File pull down menu can be used to perform the following operations on selected files: copy, move, delete, rename, change file attributes, associate, and print. Depending on the File Manager's options (set from the Options pull menu), you may be prompted for confirmation before each file is processed. The File pull-down menu also can be used to instruct the File manager to *search* the current directory, or the entire drive, for all files that match a file name (wild-card characters included).

The File Manager provides an alternative way to copy or move files. If the source and target directory windows are open, you can copy a file by dragging it from one window to the other. To move a file, hold down the Alt key while you drag the file from the source to the target directory. No dialog boxes. No menus. Just drag and drop.

The File Manager also includes options to format directories, change disk volume labels, and rename or delete entire directories, even when they contain files and other subdirectories.

Microsoft Windows 3.0 is a state-of-the-art operating environment that combines sophisticated memory-management capabilities with a rich set of utilities such as a Program Manager and a File System. It uses an elegant graphical user interface. Windows 3.0 appears to be setting the standards by which other operating environments are judged.

Using DESQview

DESQview, from Quarterdeck Office Systems, is a popular operating environment that supports multitasking. Multiple DOS applications can be run in individual windows, and data can be cut and pasted between applications. DESQview can utilize expanded memory or virtual memory (by swapping data in memory temporarily to disk) to provide each application with its own standard memory space. Each application program thinks it is being run in conventional memory, and this allows you to run more programs concurrently than would normally run in 640K of base memory.

As well as managing multiple programs in windows, DESQview provides a DOS Services tool, which can help you manage the files on your hard disk, and a keyboard macro facility for recording and playing back keystrokes.

Managing DESQview Applications

When you execute the main programs, DV.EXE, you are presented with the DESQview main menu (see fig. 12.28).

This menu is used to start programs and can switch between applications when multiple applications are active. The Open Windows option is used to start an application. During installation, DESQview scans the hard disk for popular programs, and it automatically adds these programs to the Open Windows menu. When you select the Open Windows option, a list of all known programs on the hard disk is displayed (see fig. 12.29).

To start an application, you click the mouse on the program name or scroll the cursor to the desired program and press Enter. The application is then started in a window. At any time, you can press the Alt key to pop up the DESQview main menu. You can select another application from the Open Window menu and run multiple applications. To swap from one application to another, press Alt to display the main menu and select Switch Windows. DESQview will display a list of all the active applications. Select one of the applications, and it will become the active application.

```
            DESQview

Open Window               O
Switch Windows
Close Window

Rearrange                 R
Zoom

Mark
Transfer
Scissors

Help for DESQview         ?
Quit DESQview             Q
```

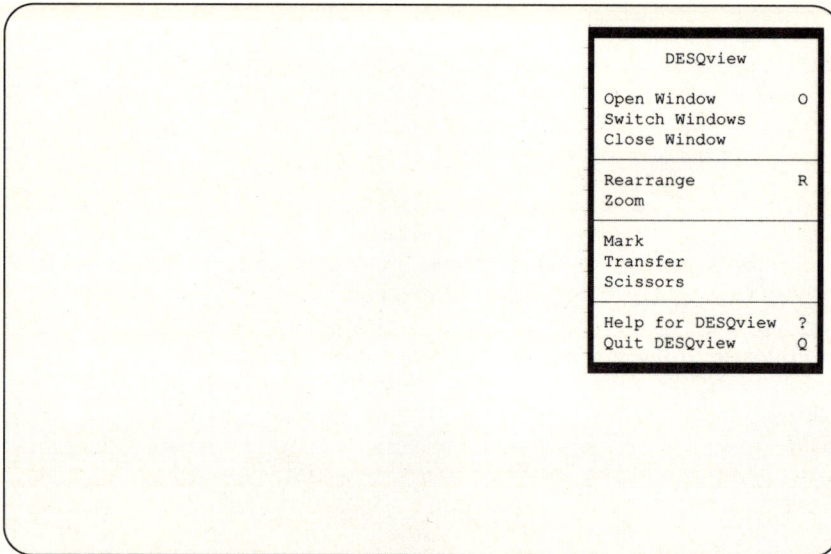

Fig. 12.28. *DESQview's main menu.*

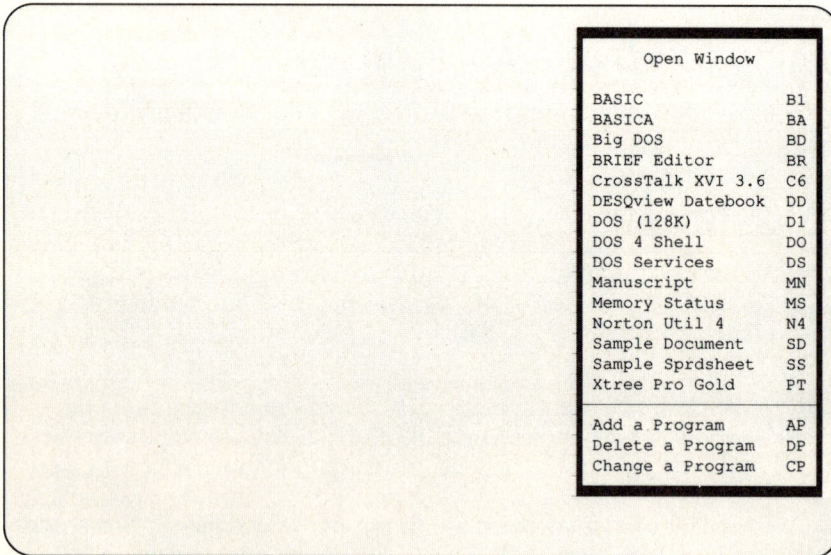

```
           Open Window

BASIC                    B1
BASICA                   BA
Big DOS                  BD
BRIEF Editor             BR
CrossTalk XVI 3.6        C6
DESQview Datebook        DD
DOS (128K)               D1
DOS 4 Shell              DO
DOS Services             DS
Manuscript               MN
Memory Status            MS
Norton Util 4            N4
Sample Document          SD
Sample Sprdsheet         SS
Xtree Pro Gold           PT

Add a Program            AP
Delete a Program         DP
Change a Program         CP
```

Fig. 12.29. *The Open Window menu list.*

The Rearrange option on the main menu is used to adjust the size and position of any of the applications windows. This feature allows you to view multiple applications at one time. DESQview allows up to 250 windows to be open at one time, but few of us are able to efficiently run more than three or four programs at once.

The Open Windows menu includes options to add new programs, as well as to modify or delete existing items. When you add a new program, you need to specify the program name and location and parameters that describe the memory requirements and display properties of the program. Two screens of information need to be specified. The initial Add-a-Program menu screen shows parameters you need to specify (see fig. 12.30A).

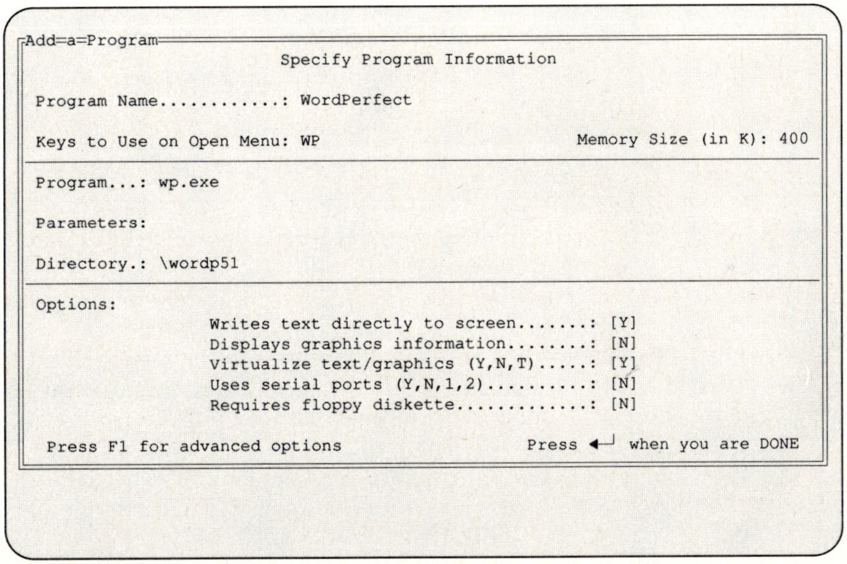

```
┌Add=a=Program══════════════════════════════════════════════════════
                         Specify Program Information

  Program Name...........: WordPerfect

  Keys to Use on Open Menu: WP                    Memory Size (in K): 400
 ───────────────────────────────────────────────────────────────────
  Program...: wp.exe

  Parameters:

  Directory.: \wordp51
 ───────────────────────────────────────────────────────────────────
  Options:
                  Writes text directly to screen.......: [Y]
                  Displays graphics information........: [N]
                  Virtualize text/graphics (Y,N,T).....: [Y]
                  Uses serial ports (Y,N,1,2)..........: [N]
                  Requires floppy diskette.............: [N]

  Press F1 for advanced options            Press ← when you are DONE
```

Fig. 12.30A. The initial Add-a-Program menu, showing parameters to specify.

Although the second screen assumes default values, you can optionally override the defaults. The screen in figure 12.30B shows the second Add-a-Program menu.

```
┌Add=a=Program──────────────────────────────────────────────────────┐
│                   Specify Program Information Advanced Options      │
│                                                                    │
│  System Memory (in K).......:   0   Maximum Program Memory Size (in K)..: │
│                                                                    │
│  Script Buffer Size.......: 1000    Maximum Expanded Memory Size (in K): │
│                                                                    │
│  Text Pages: 1  Graphics Pages: 0   Initial Mode:        Interrupts: 00 to FF │
│  ───────────────────────────────────────────────────────────────── │
│  Window Position:                                                   │
│      Maximum Height:  25     Starting Height:      Starting Row...: │
│      Maximum Width.:  80     Starting Width.:      Starting Column: │
│  ───────────────────────────────────────────────────────────────── │
│                            Shared Program                          │
│  Pathname..:                                                        │
│  Data......:                                                        │
│  ───────────────────────────────────────────────────────────────── │
│  Close on exit (Y,N,blank)......: [ ]  Uses its own colors.............: [N] │
│  Allow Close Window command.....: [Y]  Runs in background (Y,N,blank)...: [ ] │
│  Uses math coprocessor..........: [Y]  Keyboard conflict (0-4)..........: [0] │
│  Share CPU when foreground......: [Y]  Share EGA when foreground/zoomed.: [Y] │
│  Can be swapped out (Y,N,blank).: [ ]  Protection level (0-3)...........: [0] │
│                                                                    │
│   Press F1 for standard options              Press ◄┘ when you are DONE │
└────────────────────────────────────────────────────────────────────┘
```

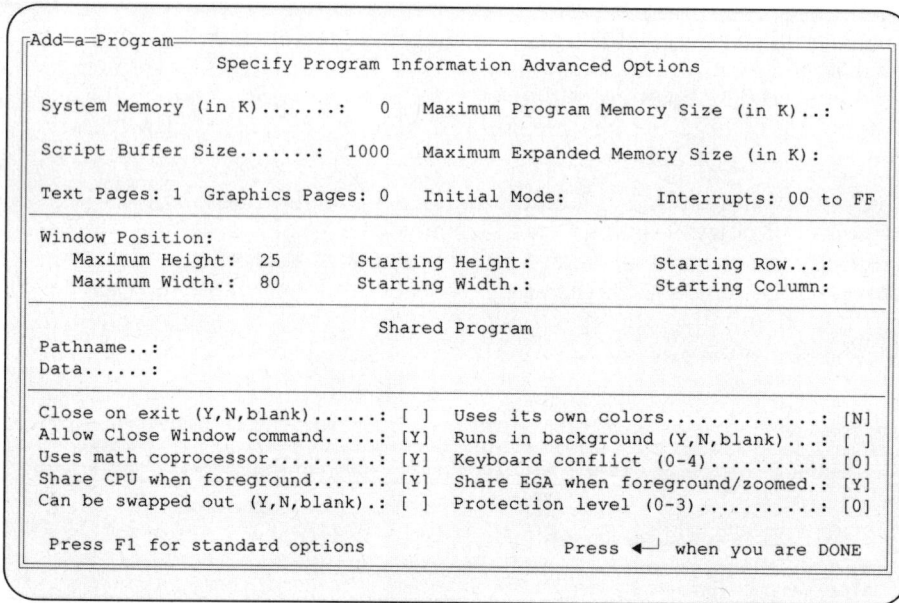

Fig. 12.30B. *The second Add-a-Program menu, showing optionally specified values.*

One of DESQview's most interesting features is Learn. Using Learn, you can record and edit a series of keystrokes. This series of keystrokes, or *script*, can then be assigned to a special key. When the special key is pressed, the recorded keystrokes are passed to the program as though you were typing them. You can permanently store as many scripts as you require. For example, you may have a script that records all the keystrokes you normally type into your database program to generate a report and another script that logs you into your electronic mail system and downloads your mail. You also can assign a script to any of the applications in the Open Window menu. When you start the application, the script is automatically played.

Using the DOS Services

The DOS Services application provides a modest but nonetheless useful set of routines to help you manage the data on your hard disk. The most commonly used DOS commands, such as COPY, RENAME, and DELETE can be selected via the DOS services. When you select the DOS Services application, the DOS Services Menu is displayed on the right side of the screen, and the DOS Services window is displayed on the left (see fig. 12.31). As you select commands from the menu, the results are displayed in the DOS Services window.

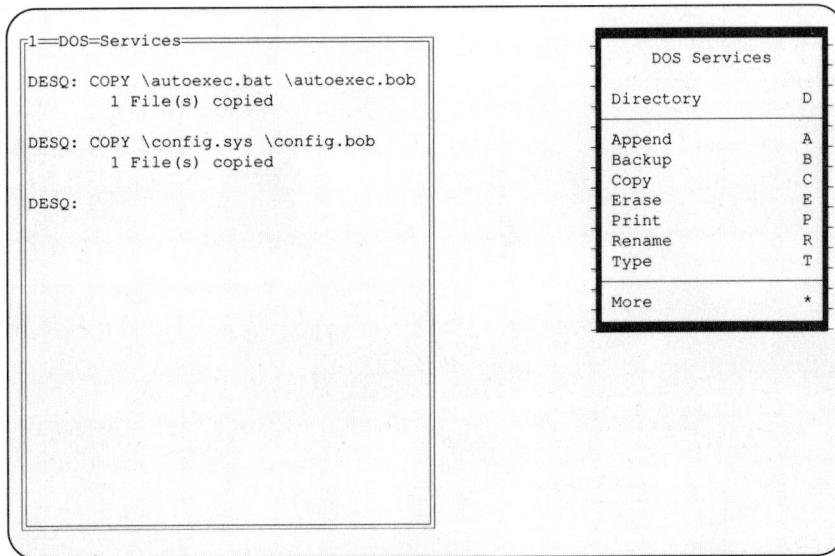

```
┌1══DOS═Services═══════════════════════┐        ┌────────────────────┐
│                                        │        │   DOS Services     │
│DESQ: COPY \autoexec.bat \autoexec.bob │        │                    │
│        1 File(s) copied                │        │ Directory        D │
│                                        │        ├────────────────────┤
│DESQ: COPY \config.sys \config.bob     │        │ Append           A │
│        1 File(s) copied                │        │ Backup           B │
│                                        │        │ Copy             C │
│DESQ:                                   │        │ Erase            E │
│                                        │        │ Print            P │
│                                        │        │ Rename           R │
│                                        │        │ Type             T │
│                                        │        ├────────────────────┤
│                                        │        │ More             * │
│                                        │        └────────────────────┘
│                                        │
│                                        │
│                                        │
│                                        │
│                                        │
│                                        │
└────────────────────────────────────────┘
```

Fig. 12.31. *The DOS Services window and menu.*

One advantage of the DOS Services is that the option application can be popped up while you are running another application. For example, if you wanted to save a file to a floppy disk from 1-2-3, but you didn't have a formatted diskette, you could use the DOS Services window to format the diskette while 1-2-3 is still active.

In addition to supporting basic file-management commands, the DOS Services application can display a list of files in a directory. You can control which files are to be displayed and in what order they will be displayed, for example, by name, size, date, and so on.

Selected files can be manipulated as a group. To select a file, you can click on the file name with the mouse, or highlight the file and press the space bar. A double chevron (>>) to the left of the file name identifies selected files. You can invoke any of the DOS services menu options, and each selected file will be processed in turn. Figure 12.32 illustrates a DOS Services directory window.

```
┌1══DOS═Services═══════════════
   PgUp  PgDn    ↑     ↓    ^Home   ^End
Directory of C:\  (TECHNOJOCK)
210056 bytes in 69 files, 8470528 free

  SPOOL              <DIR>   12-14-89    9:39p
  TEMP               <DIR>   12-15-89    8:37a
  U                  <DIR>   12-14-89    6:46p
  UTILS               3824    5-13-90    6:58p
  W                  <DIR>   12-14-89    6:46p
  WIN386             <DIR>   12-14-89    7:17p
  WINDOWS            <DIR>    5-08-90    7:16a
»AUTOEXEC  BAK        568     5-10-90   10:49a
»CONFIG    BAK        139     5-19-90    6:26p
»AUTO      BAT        231     2-22-90    6:40p
»AUTOEXEC  BAT        577     5-19-90    6:28p
  COLOR    BAT         75     2-22-90    7:02a
  COLORB   BAT         53     2-22-90    7:38a
  DV       BAT         51     3-22-89    2:25a
  MENU     BAT         40     4-26-90   12:57p
  RESET    BAT         43     2-22-90    7:03a
  WAIT     BAT        197     2-22-90    8:00a
  AUTOEXEC BOB        577     5-19-90    6:28p
  CONFIG   BOB        144     5-19-90    6:28p
```

```
┌─────────────────────────┐
│      DOS Services        │
│                          │
│  Directory           D   │
│──────────────────────────│
│  Append              A   │
│  Backup              B   │
│  Copy                C   │
│  Erase               E   │
│  Print               P   │
│  Rename              R   │
│  Type                T   │
│──────────────────────────│
│  Mark by Name        M   │
│  Only Show Marked    O   │
│  Unmark by Name      U   │
│──────────────────────────│
│  More                *   │
└─────────────────────────┘
```

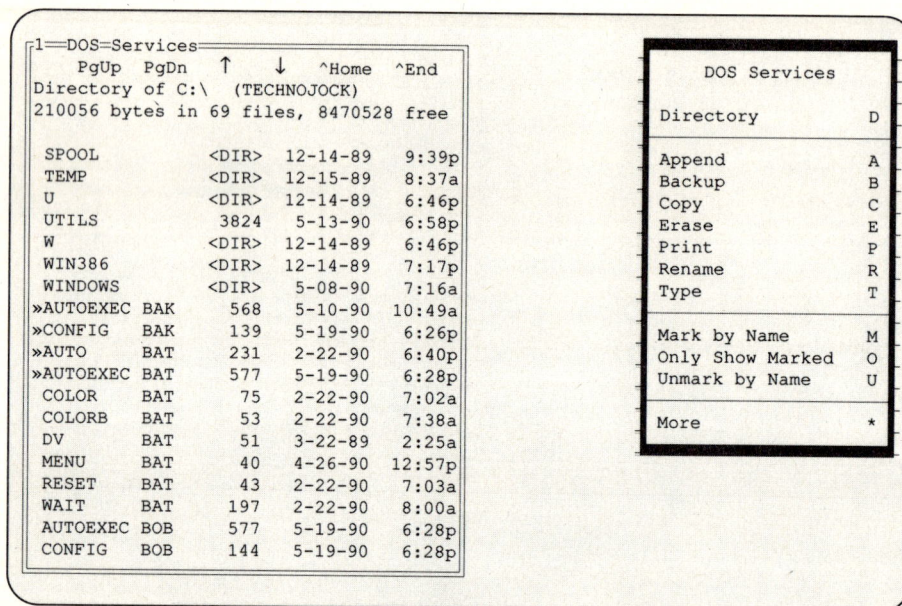

Fig. 12.32. The DOS Services directory display.

Summary

Whether supplied with the operating system or purchased separately, operating environments provide a layer between you and the base operating system. In this chapter you learned how operating environments use an intuitive interface to help you execute programs and manage the files on your hard disk. Many operating environments extend the normal capabilities of the operating system by allowing multiple programs to run simultaneously. They also can provide ways of transferring data between incompatible products. Many industry experts believe that operating environments will be a standard fixture on nearly all PCs in the next few years. Let's hope so.

This chapter concludes Part IV. In Part V you learn about hard disk integrity and security.

Part V

Maintaining Hard Disk Security

Keeping Data Backups

Avoiding Disk Disasters

Recovering from Disk Disasters

Securing Your Data

Safeguarding against Viruses

13

Keeping
Data Backups

Over time, you are sure to grow dependent upon your computer, and the data stored in your computer will be very valuable to you. This is especially true of a large hard disk, which you will come to rely on to hold vast quantities of information. We tend to think of computers as infallible machines that never go wrong, but, unfortunately, they sometimes do. Because of operator or computer error, important data files may be deleted or damaged. As the old computer saying goes, "There are two kinds of computer users—those who have lost precious files, and those who are going to." Until you have experienced losing a file you need, it is difficult to imagine the problems and heartache caused by lost files.

The primary way to minimize the impact of losing files is to keep a spare copy, a *backup*, of your files. Whether you are a new or an experienced computer user, you need to be diligent about data backups. In this chapter, you learn how to make data backups using operating system commands and using a commercial backup program.

This chapter discusses the following DOS commands:

- BACKUP
- RESTORE
- XCOPY

You also learn about the power and the advantages of using third-party backup programs, such as FASTBACK PLUS.

Understanding Data Backup Needs

Files do get accidentally corrupted or destroyed. But if you have a backup copy of the file on a diskette or tape, you can always retrieve the file and copy it onto the hard disk. To ensure that you always have a reliable and useful backup, you need to develop a backup habit. When you first start to make backups, you must decide which programs you will use to copy the files, how frequently you will back up, and where you will physically store the backup files. These topics are discussed in the following sections.

Backup Programs

A backup file is simply a copy of a file. All backup programs copy files from a disk to an external storage medium, such as a diskette, Bernoulli cartridge, or tape. Typically, the backup files are stored on diskettes.

Most backup programs use a special file format that squeezes files onto each diskette, thereby reducing the number of disks needed for a complete backup. These backup programs usually provide a special program that copies files from the backup set onto the hard disk and converts the file to its original file format.

Backup Frequency

One of the most important backup decisions to make is deciding how frequently to make backups. Most people do not make backups frequently enough.

Suppose, for example, that you back up your hard on the last day of every month, and your last backup was taken three weeks ago. During those three weeks, you completed the month-end financial reports, created a series of new batch files, and improved your menu system to make the computer much easier to use. In addition, you made a variety of small changes to the customer database. It's been a very hectic few weeks, so you take Friday as a vacation day. On Monday you turn on the computer and notice that the new menu system doesn't appear. In a few minutes you realize that all your directories have disappeared! The temporary employee, who used the computer on Friday, formatted the drive and destroyed all the files.

You decide to restore the files from the backups. The only problem is that the files are three weeks out of date. The work you completed in the past three weeks has been lost. Now you realize that a once-a-month backup is not frequent enough! You spend the next two weeks trying to duplicate the changes and updates you made. Imagine the problems you would have if you didn't have any backup at all.

✓ **NOTE**	In Chapters 14 and 15 you learn how you might be able to resurrect lost files using disaster-recovery programs. However, don't rely on these programs. The best insurance against losing data is a recent backup.

If you have a large hard disk, making a full backup can take anywhere from fifteen minutes to more than an hour. That seems like a long time, but it is a lot less than the time you would have to spend trying to recover from file loss if you have no backup.

To decide how often you should make a backup, you need to think about how much you use the computer and about how important the data is to you. If you use a computer every day, then you should take a backup at least once a week. Often you will need to take a backup more frequently.

Imagine, for example, that you are responsible for keeping a customer database that records the history of transactions with customers, as well as address details. In one week, you might make hundreds of changes to the database. Losing those changes might be catastrophic, especially if the changes were not recorded on data-input sheets. In this case a daily backup would be justified.

Incremental Backups

Many of the files on your hard disk do not change from week to week—applications program files, such as 123.EXE, and operating system external command programs, for example. If you are thinking that making backup copies of these files is not necessary, you are right.

In the discussion of files in Chapter 4, you learned that every file has attributes, which describe the properties of the file. One of these attributes is the *archive flag*; it is used by backup programs to determine whether a file needs to be backed up.

When a file is backed up, the attribute of the original file on the hard disk is marked to indicate that the file has been backed up. If any program subsequently modifies the file, the archive attribute is automatically switched off. The attribute now indicates that the file has been changed since it was last backed-up. Most backup programs can be instructed to perform an *incremental backup*, which means that they will select for backup only those files modified since the last backup. The backup program actually inspects every file's archive flag to see if the flag has changed since the last backup. If so, the program makes a backup copy of the file and sets the archive flag to indicate that the file has been backed up.

> **NOTE** Whenever a new file is created, the operating system automatically sets the archive attribute to indicate that the file has changed since the last backup. This action ensures that all new files are also included in an incremental backup.

Some backup programs allow you to copy all files modified since a particular date and time. For example, you might back up all the files modified since June 1. The backup programs simply check the time and date stamp of every file to determine whether the file should be included in the backup.

A good backup plan includes a frequent full backup—every file on the disk—as well as intermediate, incremental backups. The disadvantage of keeping many incremental backups is that the process of recovering a file from backup can be somewhat more complicated. The impact of incremental backups on the restore operation is addressed further in the discussion of the RESTORE command.

On heavily used computers, a full backup once a week and an incremental backup every day would be sensible. Alternatively, on less active computers, a full backup once a month and an incremental backup once a week might suffice. Ask yourself how much disruption would occur if you lost all the changes since your last backup. That should give you some indication of whether you are making backups frequently enough.

Multiple Backups

You should always keep more than one full backup copy of the files on your hard disk. Doing so will help you to recover from problems that go unnoticed between full backups.

For example, you might accidentally delete a file without realizing it, perhaps a worksheet you only use once a quarter. Two months later, you try to retrieve the worksheet and realize that it has disappeared. You go to your backup diskettes to recover the file and find that it's not there. The reason is that the last full backup was taken a week ago, and the file was missing long before then.

If you keep multiple backups, you have a much better chance of recovering from these subtle problems, which are not immediately obvious.

Keeping multiple backups does not cost you time. All it costs is the diskettes to store the files on. For example, if you take a full backup once a week, why not keep the most recent four weeks of backups on separate sets of disks? You might even consider keeping the backups taken at the end of each month or quarter for a year or more. To modify an old adage, "You can never be too rich, too thin, or take too many backups."

Storing Backups

The worst place to store a backup is on the hard disk itself. Some people have actually created a directory on their hard disks for storing the disk backup, because the backup program runs more quickly when the files are on the hard disk. This practice is useless. If the disk fails, you lose your files and your backup in one quick disaster!

It is good practice to store the backup files away from the computer. In the event the computer is damaged by fire or theft, there is less chance that the backup will be similarly afflicted. At a minimum, keep the backup disks in a different room, and preferably keep them off-site. You might consider storing a backup of your home computer at work, and vice versa. If you are responsible for storing backups of many different computers, you ought to consider buying a fire-proof disk storage cabinet.

Always be aware that anyone can use a backup to restore files to a different computer. If the files are confidential or classified, you need to treat the backup disks with the same care you use for confidential paper reports and dossiers. Keep them under lock and key. See Chapter 16 for more information about keeping files secure.

Restoring Backups

There is no point in keeping file backups if you are unable to restore them. Many people try to restore files for the first time when a problem has occurred, only to discover that the files were never saved in the first place. While you are developing a backup regimen, try to restore some files. You will learn the file restoration process and confirm that the files are actually backed up as well.

Using DOS Commands for Backups

Making data backups is a fundamental task for any computer user, and so DOS includes a number of external commands that can be used to make backups.

☑ UTILITY

Many programs developed by third-party vendors are designed to help you back up and restore files. Most of these programs are significantly easier to use, faster, and more flexible than the equivalent DOS command. Some of these programs are discussed in the section "Using Commercial Backup Programs."

DOS includes the commands BACKUP and RESTORE, which are designed specifically to make file backups. The command XCOPY has a wider usage than just file backup; nonetheless it provides an effective solution for some data backup needs.

Using BACKUP

The external operating system command BACKUP is used to back up data from the hard disk. BACKUP is like a file copy command that prompts you

to insert another floppy disk when the current one is full. BACKUP stores
the files on the floppy disk in a special format; the command RESTORE
(discussed in the following section) must be used to transfer one or more
files back from the floppy to the hard disk.

BACKUP can place part of a file on one disk, and if the disk becomes full,
it can put the rest of the file on the next disk. This is the only operating
system command that can split a large file and store it on multiple disks. If
a BACKUP operation uses more than one diskette, each diskette is
internally linked to the next diskette to form a backup set.

BACKUP is a selective command. You can use it to back up a single file, a
set of files matching a wild-card, one or more directories, or the whole hard
disk. You can also instruct BACKUP to select only files that have the
archive attribute set, that is, files that have been modified since the last
backup.

The syntax for the BACKUP command is

BACKUP *d1:path\filename.ext* **d2:** */switches*

where *d1:* is the optional name of the source drive you are backing up. If
you omit the drive source name, the default drive is assumed.

path is the name of the optional path to the files you are backing up. If you
omit the path name, the current directory of the specified (or default) drive
is assumed.

filename.ext is the optional name of the source file(s) you are backing up.
You may use wild-card characters, for example, *.WK3. If you omit the
file-name specifier, *.* is assumed. That is, all files in the directory are
backed up.

d2: is the name of the destination drive to which the backup files will be
written. If the destination drive name is omitted, the operating system issues
an error message.

/switches are optional switches that add additional control to the command.
Table 13.1 details the valid switch options, together with a description of
their purpose.

Table 13.1
The BACKUP Command's Optional Switches

Switch	Purpose
/A	*Adds* the backup files to the files already existing on the backup set.
/D	Includes the files created or modified on or after the specified date. The form of the switch is /D:mm-dd-yy or /D:mm/dd/yy.
/F:size	*Formats* the destination disk. The *size* parameter instructs the operating system which format to use—/F:360 for a 360K diskette, /F:720 for a 720K diskette, /F:1.2 for a 1.2M diskette, and /F:1.44 for a 1.44M diskette. The /F:size switch was added in DOS V4.
/L:filename	Writes a backup *log* entry (discussed later) in the file specified, or in the file \BACKUP.LOG if no filename is specified. This switch was added in DOS V3.3.
/M	Includes files whose archive attribute is set on, that is, *modified* files.
/S	Includes files from the specified directory and all *subdirectories* of the specified directory.
/T	Includes files created or modified on or after the *time* specified, using the format /T:hh:mm:ss. This switch was added in DOS V3.3.

The optional backup log (generated when the /L switch is specified) contains an inventory of all the files on the backup disks (see fig. 13.1). The first line of the backup log file lists the date and time of the backup. A line for each file backed up details the file name and the number of the backup disk on which the file resides. If the BACKUP.LOG file already exists, the new information for the current backup is added to the end of the file.

```
4-15-1990  19:31:27
001   \MS\MSEDIT.EXE
001   \MS\MSLOCAL.EXE
001   \MS\MSMACRO.EXE
001   \MS\MSMARKER.EXE
001   \MS\MSRDDOC2.EXE
001   \MS\MSWRDOC2.EXE
001   \MS\INSTALL.COM
001   \MS\INSTALL.MSG
001   \MS\INSTALL.VOL
001   \MS\MSFONT.EXE
001   \MS\MSINIT.EXE
001   \MS\CUSTOM.SPC
001   \MS\MSMPBIT.EXE
001   \MS\MSPREV.EXE
001   \MS\MSPRINT.ERR
001   \MS\MSPRINT.EXE
001   \MS\MSTABLES.EXE
001   \MS\HYAMAA05.EXC
001   \MS\HYAMAA05.HYP
001   \MS\MSEQNPDL.EXE
001   \MS\MSEQNPS.EXE
001   \MS\MSGMFPDL.EXE
```

Fig. 13.1. BACKUP can create a backup log when the /L switch is specified.

The Operation of the BACKUP Command

The following points summarize the operation of the BACKUP command.

- You select files to be backed up by leaving the default values unchanged or by indicating the drive, path, and file specifiers. The optional switches allow for additional selectivity.

- The contents of the root directory on the destination diskette will be overwritten in the backup operation unless the destination disk is a backup disk and you use the /A switch.

- DOS V4 automatically formats the destination diskette (if it is not already formatted) as though the /F switch had been used in DOS V3.3.

- If BACKUP is to format destination disks, the FORMAT command must be available in the current directory, or it must be located in one of the directories on the search path.

- BACKUP does not back up system or hidden files. The command processor COMMAND.COM also is not backed up.

- Do not use BACKUP if the drive you are backing up has been assigned, substituted, or joined with the ASSIGN, SUBST, or JOIN commands.

⚠ **WARNING**

Although fewer and fewer software companies copy-protect their programs, you need to be aware that BACKUP cannot back up special (and usually hidden) copy-protected files.

Making A Full Backup

If you are using a version of DOS prior to V3.3, you will have to format backup diskettes before you issue the BACKUP command. Label each disk "Full Backup" and mark the date of the backup. The number of diskettes you will need depends on the capacity of the diskette and the number of files on the hard disk (see table 13.1). A 20M hard disk may consume as many as 60 diskettes that have only a 360K capacity, so have plenty ready!

Table 13.2
Number of Floppy Disks Needed for a Backup.

Bytes To Back Up	Diskette Capacity			
	360K	720K	1.2M	1.44M
10M	29	15	9	8
20M	59	29	18	15
30M	83	44	27	22
40M	116	58	35	29
70M	200	100	60	50

To start the full backup, enter the following command:

BACKUP C:\ A: /S

This command tells BACKUP to start in the root directory of the hard disk and back up all subdirectories on the disk. When you issue the command, BACKUP displays the following warning message:

```
Insert backup diskette 1 in drive A:
Warning! Files in target drive
A:\ root directory will be erased.
Strike any key to continue.
```

This message warns you that any data stored in the root directory of the floppy disk, that will hold your backup files, will be overwritten.

Label the first diskette "Disk 1," as indicated in the screen message. Then insert the disk into the drive and press a key. As each file is backed up, the operating system displays the file name. When the first disk is filled, BACKUP repeats the insertion message, asking for the next disk. Again, mark the second disk's label with the sequential number that appears in the message and insert the second diskette into the drive.

Repeat these steps until the last file from the hard disk is backed up. When you have completed the backup, place the full set of disks in a safe storage place.

Note that if a directory other than the root is specified in the source path, only files in the specified directory will be backed up. The /S switch still can be used to instruct BACKUP to include all the subdirectories of the specified directory.

Making an Incremental Backup

Remember that an incremental backup is a backup of only those files that have changed since the last backup. The BACKUP command can determine which files to back up by checking each file's archive attribute.

To make an incremental backup of the entire disk, enter the following command:

BACKUP C:\ A: /S/M

The /S switch includes in the backup operation all directories on the hard disk; the /M switch selects files with their archive attribute switch set. The incremental backup proceeds in the same manner as the full backup. As with the full backup, mark each disk in the set with the diskette number and the date you did the incremental backup and label the disk "Incremental Backup." Store the completed set in a safe place and avoid mixing the disks with disks from another backup set.

You can make an *additive* incremental backup, in which you add the new files to files already on the backup diskette, rather than overwriting the existing backup files. To use the additive backup method, issue the BACKUP C:\ A: /S/M/A command. For the first incremental backup, insert disk 1 of the set first. For every other incremental backup besides the first one of the cycle, issue the BACKUP command as follows:

BACKUP C:\ A: /S/M/A

The /A switch instructs the BACKUP command to add the files to the end of the backup set. You then see the following prompt:

```
Insert last backup diskette in drive A:
Strike any key when ready . . .
```

You now insert the final disk from the last incremental backup. Don't start with the next reclaimed (unused in this cycle) disk. When the /A switch is used, BACKUP tries to fill any available space on the disk that was used last in the previous backup session. You must always insert the last disk that was used in the previous backup operation. When you have inserted the correct disk, press a key. The operation will proceed in the same manner as the full backup described previously.

Making a Partial Backup

You can use the BACKUP command to back up files that match a specific wild-card file name. For example, to back up all the files with an extension of .WK3 in the directory c:\123R3 and its subdirectories, enter the following command:

BACKUP C:\123R3*.WK3 A: /S

When you take partial backups, you might consider creating a log file that lists all the files included in the backup. The BACKUP command can be modified to write a backup log in the c:\123R3 directory as follows:

BACKUP C:\123R3*.WK3 A: /S/L:C:\123R3\WEEK3.LOG

Using RESTORE

The external command RESTORE is the sister command to BACKUP. It is used to transfer files from the backup diskettes back to the hard disk. RESTORE converts the files from the special backup format to the normal file format used on the hard disk.

By issuing a literal file-name parameter with RESTORE, you can restore a single file from a backup disk. With a directory parameter and a wild-card file-name parameter, you can restore selected files to the named directory. With the /S parameter, you can restore an entire hard disk, using only a source drive specifier. RESTORE puts the selection of files in your control. A number of examples that show how to use these switches are discussed later in this chapter.

Like BACKUP, the RESTORE command provides additional control through the use of numerous switches. With RESTORE's switches, you can use time, date, and presence or absence as selection criteria for files to be restored.

The syntax of the RESTORE command is

RESTORE d1: *d2:path\filename.ext /switches*

where **d1:** is the required source drive that holds the file(s) to be restored.

d2: is the drive that will receive the restored files.

path is the optional path to the directory that will receive the restored files. If the path specifier is omitted, the current directory of the destination disk is assumed.

filename.ext is the optional name of the file(s) to be restored. Wild-card characters are allowed in file names.

/switches are optional switches. See Table 13.2 for a list of the valid switches.

If RESTORE is to restore a file for which the original directory is no longer on the destination disk, RESTORE creates the directory before restoring the file.

Like the BACKUP command, RESTORE prompts you to insert the disks of the backup set. If you know the disk number containing the file(s) you want to restore, RESTORE will accept that disk as the first disk. Remember that you can use the /L switch with the BACKUP command to create a log file showing the names and disk numbers of all files in the backup set.

Table 13.2
The RESTORE Command's Optional Switches

Switch	Purpose
/A:date	Restores files created or modified on or *after* the date given, using the format /A:*mm-dd-yy* or /A:*mm/dd/yy*.
/B:date	Restores files created or modified on or *before* the date given, using the format /B:*mm-dd-yy* or /B:*mm/dd/yy*.
/E:time	Restores files created or modified *earlier* than or at the time given as /E:*hh:mm:ss*.
/L:time	Restores files created or modified *later* than or at the time given as /L:*hh:mm:ss*.
/M	Restores files *modified* or deleted since the last backup (by checking the archive attribute).
/N	Restores files that *no* longer exist in the same directory on the hard disk.
/P	*Prompts* you to confirm the restoration of a read-only file or a file modified since the last backup.
/S	Restores files to the specified (or default) directory and *subdirectories*.

Note that only the switches /P and /S are available in versions of DOS earlier than V3.3.

NOTE When the RESTORE command restores files that are no longer on the destination disk, it makes directory entries for the restored file in the file allocation table (FAT). If the destination disk is not newly formatted, the restored files may be spread all over the disk. For example, if you are restoring from an additive backup set files that have the same full path name, but different sizes, RESTORE allocates clusters for the first file of the duplicate name pair and subsequently allocates additional clusters for a larger file with the same name. The result can be a fragmented destination file. You recall that fragmentation doesn't affect the file's integrity, but it may slow disk performance.

The Operation of the RESTORE Command

- You must give a source drive name in the command line.

- All files restored from the backup set will be placed in their original directories on the destination disk. If a source directory does not exist, the directory will be created.

- Files selected for restoration are selected according to the destination drive, path, and file specifiers. Further selection of the files is based on the included switches.

- The destination disk must be formatted before you use RESTORE. Unlike the BACKUP command, RESTORE has no provision to format the destination disk.

- Files restored to a freshly formatted disk will not be fragmented.

- RESTORE automatically overwrites any files on the destination disk that have the same name, unless the /P switch is used.

- RESTORE in DOS V3.2 or earlier versions cannot restore files created by the BACKUP command in DOS V3.3 or V4.

- You cannot restore files to drives that have been assigned, joined, or substituted with an ASSIGN, JOIN, or SUBST command.

Performing a Complete Restore

On a few occasions, you might want to perform a complete restore—that is, restore every file on a backup set. For example, you may have taken a backup of an old disk before installing a new larger hard disk, or you may have accidentally formatted the hard disk and need to recover all the lost files.

If you have a single full-backup set, the following command will instruct RESTORE to restore all files from drive A to drive C:

RESTORE A: C: /S

The operating system will prompt you as follows:

```
Insert backup diskette 1 in drive A:
Strike any key when ready . . .
```

Put the first disk of the backup set into drive A and press a key. The operating system will respond as follows:

```
*** Files were backed up mm/dd/yy ***
```

The message shows the actual date you created the backup set. Then you will see the following prompt:

```
*** Restoring files from drive A: ***
```

The screen displays the full path names of the files as they are being restored. When all the files from the first disk are restored to the hard disk, the operating system prompts you for the next disk in the backup set. Repeat this process until you have restored all the files.

If you had also taken incremental backups after the full backup, you will now need to restore the incremental backup data. Because you want to restore all the files from the incremental backup set, you will use the same command as you used to restore the full backup set. The operation will proceed in the same fashion.

When an incremetal backup is taken, each file that has changed since the last backup is added to the incremental backup disks. BACKUP does not replace the previous version of the file in the backup; it adds another (more recent) copy of the file. This can result in one file being stored multiple times on the backup disk. When you are restoring files from an incremental backup, you must be careful to ensure that you have restored the most recently backed up version of the file. You will always restore the most recent version if you are careful to insert every disk used in the incremental backup set.

Performing a Selective Restore

The RESTORE command can be used to restore a single file, a set of files matching a wild-card file name, a single directory, or a directory and its subdirectories.

Listed below are some examples that illustrate the capability of the RESTORE command to selectively restore files. Note that RESTORE, by default, automatically (and without a warning prompt) overwrites any existing file of the same name as the file being restored. As a safety precaution, use the /P directive to instruct RESTORE to prompt you for confirmation if it finds that a file on the hard disk is more recent than the file of the same name in the backup.

To restore a specific file:

RESTORE A: C:\BATFILES\2.BAT /P

As with a complete restore operation, RESTORE will prompt for you to insert the first BACKUP disk into drive A. RESTORE will then search every disk in the backup set. When it finds the file C:\BATFILES\2.BAT it will restore the file to the hard disk.

To restore a set of files:

RESTORE A: C:\123R3\BUDGET*.WK3 /P

The command restores all files in the C:\123R3\BUDGET directory that have an extension of .WK3.

To restore all files in a subdirectory:

RESTORE A: C:\UTILS*.* /P

The command restores all the files in the C:\UTILS directory.

To restore a set of subdirectories:

RESTORE A: C:\DATA*.* /S /P

The command restores all the files in the C:\DATA directory and all subdirectories of \DATA.

To restore files based on the date:

RESTORE A: C:\ /A:09/01/90 /S /P

The command restores all files modified since Sept 1, 1990.

Remember that you must repeat the RESTORE command using the incremental backup set to ensure you get the most recent backup copy of the file. During the restore operation, the operating system searches every disk in the backup set, looking for files that match the files requested. If you are confident that the remaining disks in the backup set do not contain any more matching files, you can abort the operation by pressing Ctrl-Break or Ctrl-C. For safety's sake, however, you should insert all disks from an additive backup; more recent versions of a file may have been backed up towards the end of the set.

Using XCOPY

The external command XCOPY is used to copy files. XCOPY also has the capability of creating destination directories. Because XCOPY can create directories, the command is handy for copying a portion of your directory tree to another disk. The XCOPY command, introduced with DOS V3.2, addresses very well the needs of computer users who have hard disks.

XCOPY's syntax is similar to COPY's syntax, but the switches are more complex. XCOPY's syntax is as follows:

XCOPY *d1:path1\filename1.ext1*
    d2:path2\filename2.ext2 /V /P /W /S /E /A /M /D:date

The source files, designated by a 1, are the files to be copied. If you omit the disk drive name (*d1:*), the current disk drive is used. If you omit the path name (*path1*), the current directory on the drive is used. You can use wild-card characters in the file name (*filename1.ext1*). If you omit the file name, XCOPY assumes that you want to specify a wild card *.*, and all files in the given path will be copied. You must include at least one of the source parameters.

The destination files are designated by the 2 in the name. File names, disk drive names, and path names are taken from the operating system's current defaults if you do not specify them. If you omit a drive name (*d2:*), XCOPY uses the current disk drive. If you do not specify a path name (*pathd*), XCOPY uses the current directory. If you omit the file name (*filenamed.extd*), the copied files retain their names.

A subdirectory can contain a file with the same name as the subdirectory. In some XCOPY operations, this duplication can pose a problem. A destination name might be a path name or a file name; XCOPY asks you to indicate whether the destination is a file name or path name.

As an example, look at the following command:

XCOPY C:\WORDS*.* A:\WORDS

If you use this command to copy the files from C:\WORDS to the disk in drive A, and the disk in drive A does not have a directory called WORDS, XCOPY displays this message:

```
Does WORDS specify a filename
or directory name on the target
(F = file, D = directory)?
```

If the destination is a file name, answer F. If the destination is a directory, answer D. Unlike COPY, XCOPY creates directories on the destination disk as needed.

Understanding XCOPY's Switches

The switches available with the XCOPY command are summarized in Table 13.3.

Table 13.3
The XCOPY Command's Optional Switches

Switch	Purpose
/A	Copies files whose *archive* flag is on, but does not turn off the archive flag similar to the /M switch).
/D:date	Copies files that were changed or created on or after the date you specify. The date's form depends on the setting of the COUNTRY directive in the CONFIG.SYS file, but is typically /D:mm-dd-yy.###
/E	Creates parallel subdirectories on the destination disk, even if the created subdirectory is *empty*.

Switch	Purpose
/M	Copies files whose archive attribute is on (*modified* files) and turns off the archive attribute (similar to the /A switch).
/P	Causes XCOPY to prompt you for approval before copying a file.
/S	Copies files in all the *subdirectories* of the starting directory.
/V	Verifies that the copy has been recorded correctly.
/W	Causes XCOPY to prompt and wait for the correct source floppy disk to be inserted.

See *Using DOS*, published by Que Corporation, for a thorough explanation of the XCOPY command.

Using XCOPY for Backups

Because XCOPY can control which files should be copied by date or archive attribute, can copy complete subdirectory trees, and can confirm which files should be copied, the command is ideal for making selective backups of critical files.

XCOPY is practical to use if you want to make backup copies of less than a disk full of files from several directories. Rather than using BACKUP, you might prefer to use the XCOPY /A command to select files that have changed since the last backup.

This technique has one drawback, however. XCOPY cannot gracefully handle full disks. When the destination disk fills, XCOPY stops. To continue, you must change disks and restart the XCOPY process using the /A and /P switches to skip the files you have already copied. To avoid this problem, you should ensure that the files you want to back up will fit on one disk. Also, XCOPY cannot handle an individual file that is too big to fit on one destination disk. If you need to back up such a file, use the BACKUP command.

Suppose, for example, that you want to keep a copy of some important word processing files, and your word processing directory is \WPFILES. This directory has a few files in it. \WPFILES also has two subdirectories. The first, \WPFILES\MEMOS, contains your memos. The second,

\WPFILES\DOCS, contains your other document files. Because these three directories are the ones you modify most often, you want to keep a current set of duplicate of files in these directories. All the files fit on one floppy disk. To copy all the files in this directory branch to the floppy, you issue the following command:

XCOPY C:\WPFILES A:\WPFILES /S

The operating system responds as follows:

```
Does WPFILES specify a filename
or directory name on the target
(F = file, D = directory)?
```

When you press F, XCOPY immediately begins to process files, and you see the following display:

```
Reading source file(s)...
C:\WPFILES\LET9_1.WP
C:\WPFILES\LET9_2.WP
C:\WPFILES\LET9_3.WP
C:\WPFILES\LET9_4.WP
C:\WPFILES\LET9_5.WP
C:\WPFILES\DOCS\SCHEDULE.DOC
C:\WPFILES\MEMOS\SALES.MEM
        7 File(s) copied
```

Because you included the /S switch, XCOPY processes the files in C:\WPFILES, C:\WPFILES\MEMOS, and C:\WPFILES\DOCS. The A:\WPFILES path specifier causes XCOPY to ask whether the name specifies a directory or a file. \WPFILES could conceivably be a user file in the root directory. The full path name of each file is echoed to the screen as it is copied to drive A. When the command finishes, a copy of the \WPFILES directory branch exists on the disk in drive A.

The Operation of XCOPY

- XCOPY cannot copy hidden source files.

- XCOPY will not overwrite read-only destination files.

- If a file specifier is omitted in the XCOPY syntax, XCOPY assumes the *.* full wild-card pattern as the file specifier.

- If you include the /D switch, the date specifier must be entered in the format of the system's DATE command, or in the format indicated by the setting in the COUNTRY setting in the CONFIG.SYS file.

- To use the XCOPY command to copy empty source subdirectories, you must specify both the /S and the /E switches.

Using Commercial Backup Programs

Keeping up-to-date data backups is the ideal for any computer user, but in practice many users find the operating system's backup and restoration commands too slow and inflexible to use regularly. Soon after the first introduction of hard disks, independent software vendors wrote backup programs to simplify and speed-up the file backup and restoration process. Over the past few years, these programs have become extremely powerful and easy to use.

If your time is valuable, and you want to keep regular backups, consider using a third-party backup program in preference to the operating system commands. The faster and easier it is to do a backup, the more likely it is that you will do it. Backup programs cost from $50 to $200, and they offer one or more of the following advantages over the operating system commands:

- Special techniques are used to increase the speed at which data is transferred to the floppy disk, thereby reducing the overall time required to do a backup.

- Data compression techniques significantly reduce the number of floppy disks required to store a backup.

- All the files to be backed up may be archived into a single large file when you back up to another high capacity drive, for example a network drive or a Bernoulli drive.

- Multiple source *path\filename.ext* file specifications can be included in a single backup operation—for example, *.DOC and *.TXT for all directories.

- Files can be explicitly excluded from a backup.

- Hidden and system files can be backed-up.

- Selective restoration of files is simplified.

A note from the author... Nowadays, you can choose from dozens of very good backup programs. In this chapter, you read about a few that will help you manage your hard disk. These programs are clearly among the best and most popular in the marketplace, but many other equally good products exist. We simply do not have space enough to discuss them. Just because a program is not mentioned in the book does not mean that it is not a good program.

The primary goal of spotlighting one or two products is to give you specific insights into how independent software may help you get the most from your hard disk. For source information about the third-party programs and utilities mentioned in this book, see Appendix D.

Using FASTBACK PLUS

FASTBACK PLUS is a file backup program marketed by Fifth Generation Systems, Inc. When FASTBACK was first introduced, it revolutionized the whole backup process. The original program had breakneck backup speed as its primary goal, and it was truly outstanding. Since that time, the product has been revised and enhanced. The latest version (at press time) is 2.10, but because of the frequent changes that occur in operating systems, controllers, and disk drives, backup programs tend to be updated more frequently than most mainstream software.

In a comparison of backup operations, BACKUP took 15 minutes and 30 seconds to back up 12 megabytes of data on 11 high-density diskettes. FASTBACK took 4 minutes and 45 seconds to perform the same backup (with error-checking) and required only 7 high-density diskettes. Proof positive of FASTBACK's superiority.

Features of FASTBACK PLUS

The following list describes some of the main features of FASTBACK PLUS.

- A backup can be made either directly from the operating system prompt or interactively using FASTBACK PLUS' pull-down menu system. The menus can be configured for beginning, intermediate, or advanced users.

- Data is backed up at very high speeds; FASTBACK PLUS bypasses the normal disk read-write process and accessing the *direct memory access* (DMA) chip. This technique allows simultaneous reading of data from the hard disk and writing of data to the floppy and can result in backups that are more than twice as fast as normal.

- You can use multiple file specifications to both include and exclude files from the backup set.

- You have the option of saving files in compressed format to reduce the number of disks required to store the backed up files. Compression does, however, increase the time required to make the backup.

- Files can be selected for a backup or restore operation by moving a cursor bar through a list of all files to the appropriate file.

- FASTBACK PLUS performs extensive error checking to ensure high data integrity.

- You can make incremental backups based on the archive attribute or based on the date and time.

Installing FASTBACK PLUS

The FASTBACK PLUS distribution diskette includes a special program, FBINSTAL, which automatically installs the program files onto your hard disk. The installation process performs the following tasks:

- Transfers the FASTBACK files from the program disk to the hard disk.

- Modifies your CONFIG.SYS and AUTOEXEC.BAT files to ensure optimum backup performance.

- Asks you to identify the size and format of the disk drives installed on the computer.

- Tests the computer hardware (specifically, the DMA chip) to determine the maximum safe operating speed of the software. (Note that you will need to insert a diskette into a drive for this part of the installation. Any files on that disk will be erased.)

- Performs a quick backup of the newly created C:\FASTBACK directory, and then runs a comparison check to ensure the software has been correctly installed.

Installing FASTBACK PLUS is easy. The most difficult part of the process may be opening the package!

Making a Backup with FASTBACK

The main FASTBACK program is FB.EXE, and to start the program you change to the C:\FASTBACK directory and enter the FB command:

```
CD\FASTBACK
FB
```

The main FASTBACK menu displays. The menu has three main elements: BACKUP, RESTORE, and OPTIONS (see fig. 13.2).

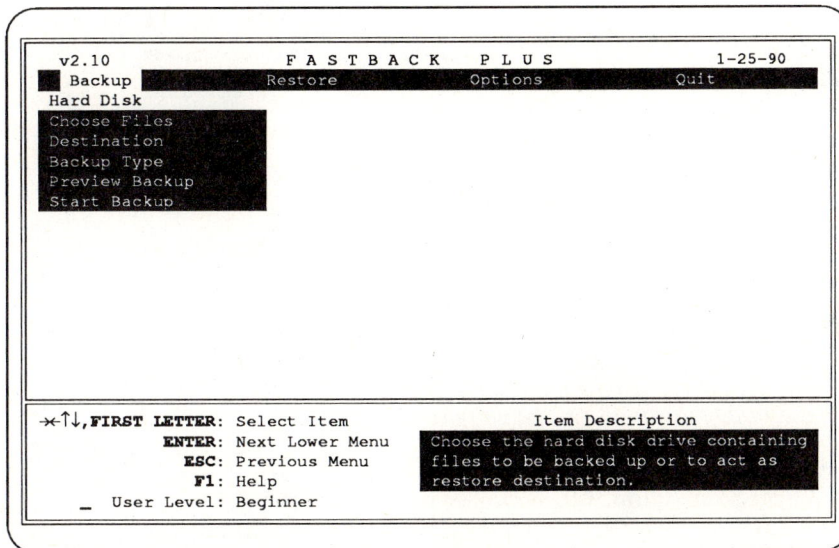

```
 v2.10              F A S T B A C K    P L U S        1-25-90
  Backup          Restore          Options          Quit
 Hard Disk
 Choose Files
 Destination
 Backup Type
 Preview Backup
 Start Backup




 ←↑↓,FIRST LETTER: Select Item              Item Description
          ENTER: Next Lower Menu    Choose the hard disk drive containing
            ESC: Previous Menu      files to be backed up or to act as
             F1: Help               restore destination.
 _  User Level: Beginner
```

Fig. 13.2. The FASTBACK PLUS start-up screen.

The first option in the Options menu is `User Level`. This option can be used to change the user level from beginner to intermediate or advanced. Using the more advanced settings provides access to more menu options. One of these options allows you to choose whether the backup should save time or save disks (see fig. 13.3). In other words, should the backup be as fast as possible, or should FASTBACK PLUS take more time, but compress the backup onto fewer disks?

```
v2.10              F A S T B A C K   P L U S          1-25-90
  Backup            Restore          Options              Quit
                              User Level
                              Installation
                              History Report
                              Old History Reports
                              Write Verify
                              Audible Prompts
                              Format Mode
                              Overwrite Warning
                              Compression of Data
                              Display Colors          ┌──────────────┐
                              Error Correction        │ Off          │
                              Password Protection     │ Save Time    │
                                                      │►Save Disks   │
                                                      └──────────────┘

  ──↑↓,FIRST LETTER: Select Item        Choose between reducing backup time
          ENTER: Next Lower Menu        and using the least disks.
            ESC: Previous Menu

  F1      F2      F3    F6      F7        F8        F9        F10
  Help  Settings  Dir   DOS  Save Keys  Play Keys  Load Setup  Save Setup
```

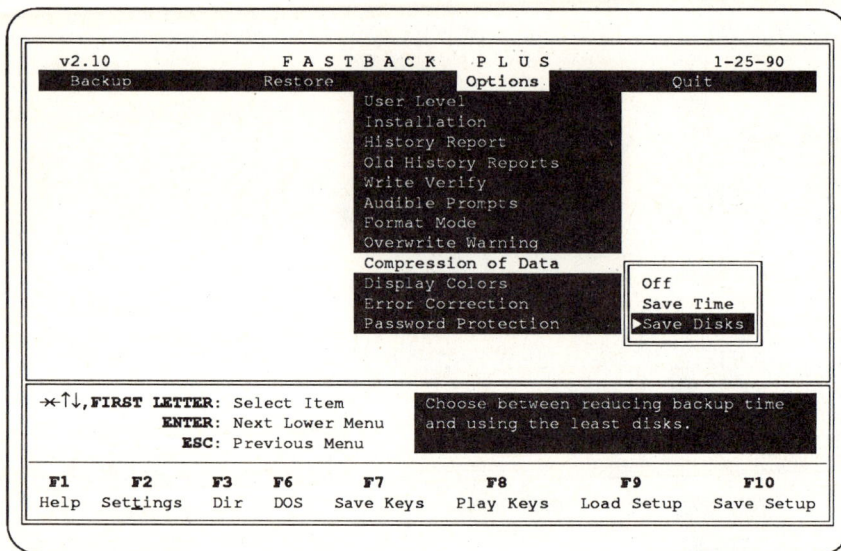

Fig. 13.3. The Options menu lets you choose the backup type.

The BACKUP menu is used to define precisely which files are to be backed-up. Options include the specifications of files to include in the backup; the files to exclude from the backup; whether files should be selected by modification date; and whether the backup is full or an incremental backup (see fig. 13.4).

When the file-selection options have been specified, you select the Start Backup option, and a special backup screen is displayed. From this screen, you may either select the backup estimate or instruct FASTBACK PLUS to start the backup operation. The estimate is very handy because it estimates how many disks are required and how long the operation will take.

During the backup operation, the program displays each filename as it is being backed up (see fig. 13.5). When one disk is full, the program prompts you to insert the next disk. If the disk is not formatted, FASTBACK PLUS automatically formats it. Note that to save valuable backup time, the disk drive motor continually spins, even when you are removing and inserting disks. This is one of the rare occasions when you should open the disk drive door while the drive light is on.

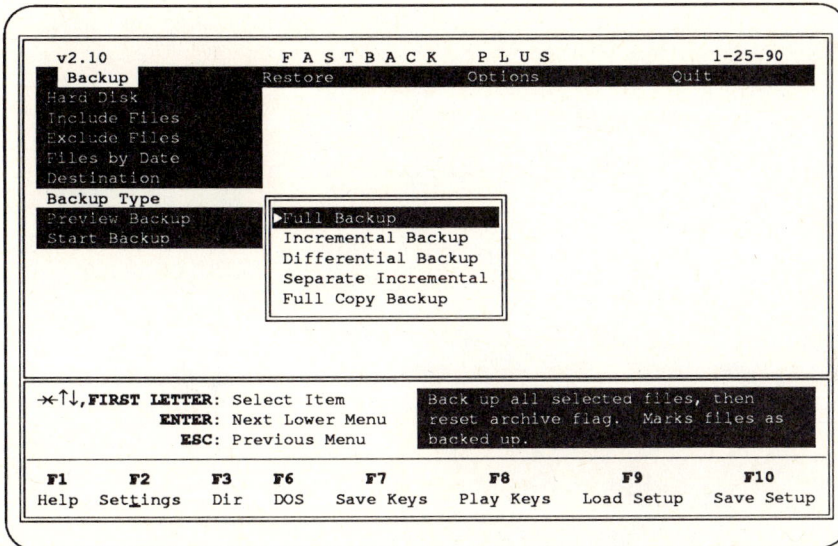

Fig. 13.4. FASTBACK PLUS supports various incremental backups.

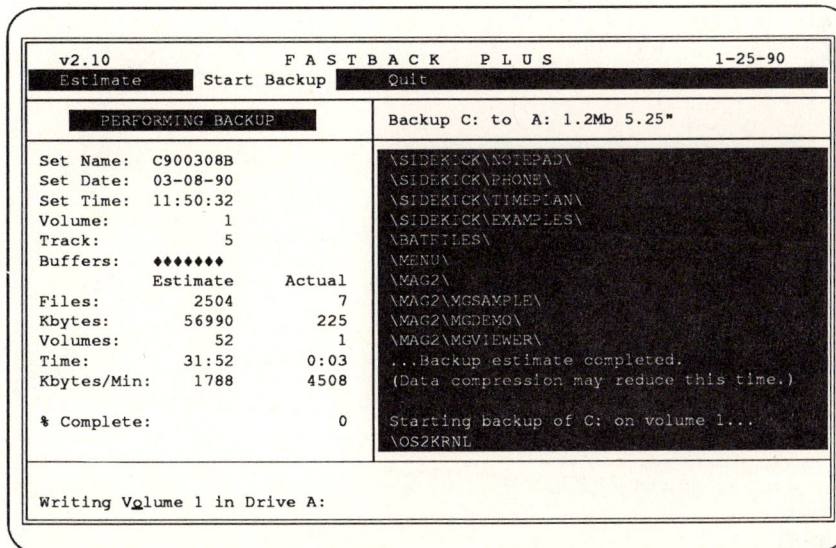

Fig. 13.5. Each file name is displayed as it is backed up.

As with the operating system command BACKUP, you should carefully mark each disk in the FASTBACK PLUS backup set and store the set in a safe place.

Restoring FASTBACK PLUS Files

The options on the RESTORE menu are similar to those on the BACKUP menu. You can select which file(s) you want to restore using wild-card file names to include and exclude multiple files, and you can set whether you want files to be automatically overwritten (see fig. 13.6).

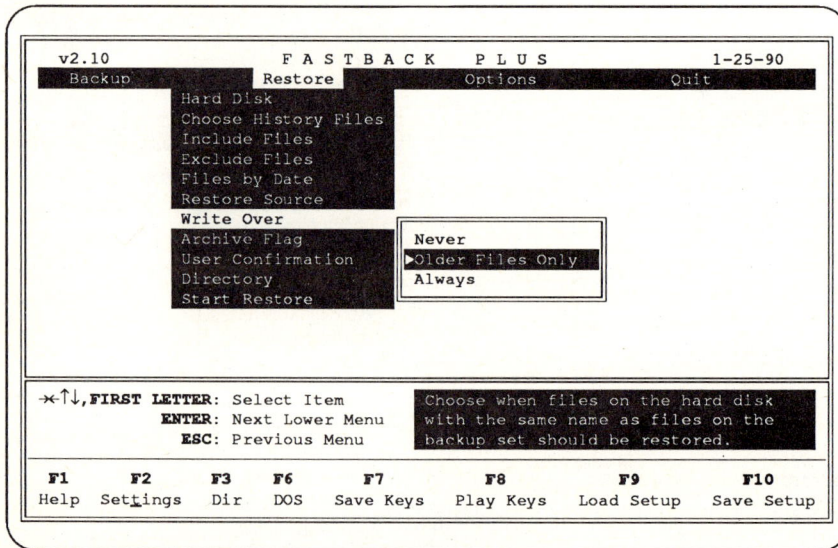

```
v2.10              F A S T B A C K   P L U S         1-25-90
   Backup         Restore            Options            Quit
                Hard Disk
                Choose History Files
                Include Files
                Exclude Files
                Files by Date
                Restore Source
                Write Over
                Archive Flag        Never
                User Confirmation  ▶Older Files Only
                Directory           Always
                Start Restore


  ⟶↑↓,FIRST LETTER: Select Item    Choose when files on the hard disk
          ENTER: Next Lower Menu    with the same name as files on the
            ESC: Previous Menu      backup set should be restored.

  F1      F2      F3    F6    F7        F8        F9          F10
  Help  Settings  Dir   DOS  Save Keys  Play Keys  Load Setup  Save Setup
```

Fig. 13.6. Setting the write-over warning option.

During the backup process, FASTBACK PLUS automatically creates a special log file that details all the files included in the backup. FASTBACK PLUS uses this file to simplify the selection of files to restore. If the special log file cannot be found, FASTBACK PLUS inspects each of the backup disks to determine the files contained on the disk.

Both the BACKUP and RESTORE custom options can be saved in separate configuration files. If at some future date you want to use the same options, you can just load the appropriate configuration file.

PC Tools' Backup Utility

PC Tools from Central Point Software is a versatile disk-management software package that includes a backup and restore program called PCBACKUP. While not quite as fast or flexible as the state-of-the-art dedicated backup programs, PCBACKUP is a very good backup and restore program that offers speed, flexibility, and ease of use.

The opening display of PCBACKUP shows the directory tree in graphic form in the left window and the files in the highlighted directory in the right window (see fig 13.7).

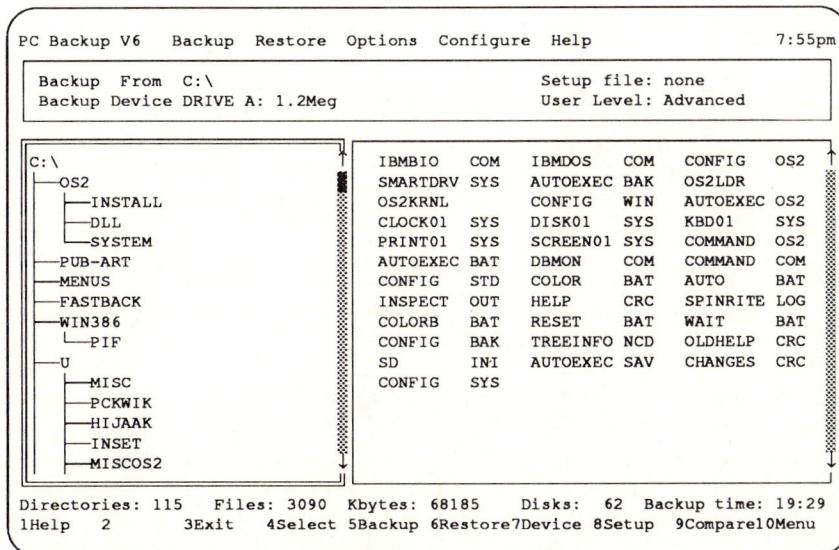

```
PC Backup V6    Backup  Restore  Options  Configure  Help            7:55pm

 Backup  From  C:\                        Setup file: none
 Backup Device DRIVE A: 1.2Meg            User Level: Advanced

 C:\                            IBMBIO   COM   IBMDOS   COM   CONFIG   OS2
  ┌─OS2                         SMARTDRV SYS   AUTOEXEC BAK   OS2LDR
  │  ├──INSTALL                 OS2KRNL        CONFIG   WIN   AUTOEXEC OS2
  │  ├─DLL                      CLOCK01  SYS   DISK01   SYS   KBD01    SYS
  │  └─SYSTEM                   PRINT01  SYS   SCREEN01 SYS   COMMAND  OS2
  ├─PUB-ART                     AUTOEXEC BAT   DBMON    COM   COMMAND  COM
  ├MENUS                        CONFIG   STD   COLOR    BAT   AUTO     BAT
  ├FASTBACK                     INSPECT  OUT   HELP     CRC   SPINRITE LOG
  ├WIN386                       COLORB   BAT   RESET    BAT   WAIT     BAT
  │  └─PIF                      CONFIG   BAK   TREEINFO NCD   OLDHELP  CRC
  ├U                            SD       INI   AUTOEXEC SAV   CHANGES  CRC
  │  ├──MISC                    CONFIG   SYS
  │  ├─PCKWIK
  │  ├─HIJAAK
  │  ├─INSET
  │  └─MISCOS2

 Directories: 115   Files: 3090   Kbytes: 68185    Disks:  62  Backup time: 19:29
 1Help    2       3Exit   4Select 5Backup 6Restore7Device 8Setup  9Compare10Menu
```

Fig. 13.7. *The opening display of the PC Tools PCBACKUP program.*

Like FASTBACK PLUS, PCBACKUP sports pull-down menus to specify the appropriate backup and restore options (see fig. 13.8). PCBACKUP has a variety of backup options: multiple file specifications can be included and excluded, files can be compressed as they are saved, files can be selected based on the archive attribute or the date/time the file was last modified, and so on.

```
PC Backup V6   Backup  Restore  Options  Configure  Help              7:55pm

Backup  From  C:\              Load setup...      ALT-L  none
Backup Device DRIVE A: 1.2Meg  Save setup...      ALT-S  Advanced

C:\                            Backup Method...       (Full)   CONFIG   OS2  ↑
 └─OS2                         Reporting...          (None)   OS2LDR        ▒
    ├─INSTALL                  Compress... (Minimize Time)  AUTOEXEC OS2   ▒
    ├─DLL                      Verify... (When Formatting)  KBD01    SYS   ▒
    └─SYSTEM                   Format Always                COMMAND  OS2   ▒
 ├─PUB-ART                   √ Error Correction             COMMAND  COM   ▒
 ├─MENUS                     √ Standard Format              AUTO     BAT   ▒
 ├─FASTBACK                  √ Subdirectory inclusion       SPINRITE LOG   ▒
 ├─WIN386                    √ Include/exclude files...     WAIT     BAT   ▒
 │ └─PIF                       Attribute exclusions...      OLDHELP  CRC   ▒
 └─U                           Date range selection...      CHANGES  CRC   ▒
    ├─MISC
    ├─PCKWIK                 √ Save History
    ├─HIJAAK                 √ Time display
    ├─INSET                  √ Overwrite warning                          ↓
    └─MISCOS2

Directories: 115  Files: 3090  Kbytes: 68185   Disks:  62  Backup time: 19:29
Load a pre-defined backup/restore setup file
```

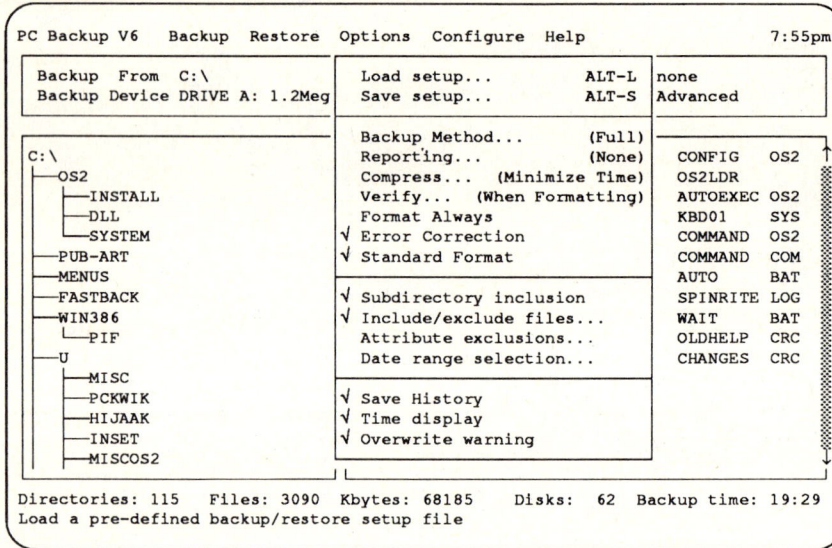

Fig. 13.8. PCBACKUP supports a variety of backup file-selection options.

Using Tape Backup Devices

Whether you use the operating system commands or a third-party backup program, constantly feeding diskettes into disk drives is a laborious process. With modern hard disks that store from 100 to 600 megabytes and more of data, a diskette-based backup system is, at best, clumsy.

A sensible alternative for owners of large hard disks is to save the backup data on a high-capacity storage device. One good alternative is a Bernoulli drive (see Chapter 3). Another solution is to use a tape backup device.

Tape backup devices come in a variety of shapes and sizes. The drives may be internal, fitting into a standard half-height floppy disk bay, or external, connected to a special card installed in the computer. The tape cartridge also comes in a variety of designs, ranging from a cassette, which is similar to an audio cassette, to a cartridge, which is similar to the eight-track cartridges you've got in the attic!

During the backup process, data is streamed onto the tape in a similar way sound is recorded on a music tape. The tape itself may be fed at rates of 90 to 120 inches per second, and data backup rates can be as high as 5 megabytes per minute. The data-storage capacity of tapes can range from 20 megabytes (20 million bytes) to more than a gigabyte (a billion bytes). The primary advantages of tapes are that each tape can store massive volumes of data, and the backup can run unattended.

Most tape systems ship with their own backup programs, and the overall speed of the backup operation is significantly influenced by the quality of the software. For optimum speed, a mirror image of a disk can be taken, but this technique retains all the file fragmentation that exists on the disk. Most programs back up the disk on a file-by-file basis to eradicate file fragmentation. A number of third-party backup programs are beginning to provide support for tape backup devices, including FASTBACK PLUS and PC Tools. If you have a high volume of important data, you should consider purchasing a special backup device like a Bernoulli drive or tape system.

Summary

Because data is the backbone of any computer system, backups should be a regular and frequent part of your computer activity. This chapter emphasized the following key points:

- Human error or system failure inevitably results in loss of data at one time or another, and data backups are the best insurance.

- The operating system includes the commands BACKUP and RESTORE, which specifically manage data backups.

- The versatile external command XCOPY provides a very powerful file-copying facility, which can be tailored to make backups of data files that fit on a single disk.

- Many third-party software programs provide excellent data-backup facilities.

- For very large data storage systems, consider installing a special backup device, such as a Bernoulli drive, or a tape system.

Chapter 14 discusses some of the common causes of data loss and how they might be avoided.

14

Avoiding
Hard Disk Disasters

In computing, as in health care, prevention is better (and usually easier) than cure. Many computer users, unfortunately, have had to learn this simple lesson the hard way. Cautious users, on the other hand, know that by taking steps to avoid computing disasters, and by being prepared in case a disaster actually happens, they also can avoid the cost and frustration of recovering lost data and programs. This chapter describes measures you can take to lessen the likelihood of disk and file catastrophes, such as inadvertent file deletion, and worse yet, the accidental formatting of a disk.

This chapter shows you how to use the ATTRIB command to protect specific files, how to avoid accidentally reformatting the hard disk, and how to use the CHKDSK command to check for cluster errors. The chapter's final sections introduce a few commercial programs that can analyze your hard disk's "health" and alert you to potential problems.

Preventing Hardware Failures

Computers contain thousands of transistorized circuits. Most of these circuits have a life expectancy of more than a century. A poor power source, excessive heat, or static discharges, however, can cause circuits to operate erratically or fail completely. A disk drive's mechanical parts, which are aligned and operate at extremely close tolerances, can fail for similar reasons. The potential always exists for hardware failures. By following a few common-sense precautions, however, you can reduce the chance of hardware failure.

Your computer's electrical environment should be stable and reliable. If the power flutters and lights flicker, you probably do not have a reliable source of constant power. Other electrical appliances also can pollute your power source; those of us who work at home learn not to compute when the washing machine is running! At the office, you might experience similar power drains when someone heats a sandwich in the company's microwave oven. Avoid using computers on an electrical circuit that also serves high-consumption electrical devices.

If you are stuck with a power source that suffers from these drops in electrical power, known as *brownouts*, you should buy a *line voltage regulator* from your computer dealer. Line voltage regulators smooth out the peaks and troughs in the power supply, and contain transformers and other circuitry that can bridge a momentary drop in voltage. If you work on highly sensitive data, or if any data loss could be catastrophic, you should consider buying an *uninterruptible power supply* (UPS). Typically, a UPS features a line voltage detector and a battery. If the normal power supply fails, the UPS sounds an alarm, and supplies the computer with power; some units can keep a computer operating for up to two hours. The UPS may be able to power the computer until the normal electrical supply resumes, but you should never count on such luck. If you have a UPS and normal electrical service is cut off, you should use this battery-powered "grace period" to save files, terminate applications, and shut down the computer gracefully, so that you can avoid data loss.

Whether or not the system suffers power fluctuations, you should at least protect your computer with a *surge protector*. Surge protectors do not help matters when the power is low, but they do stop harmful power surges, (called *spikes*) from damaging the circuitry. These power surges can be caused by nearby lightning strikes, faulty power equipment, or one of several other reasons. A spike can fry an unprotected computer's circuits instantly. Both line voltage regulators and uninterruptible power supplies provide surge protection.

You should check the computer periodically to see if it needs to be cleaned. If dust has built up in the unit, clean the air vents and fan so that the computer can breathe freely again. For routine cleaning, simply use a soft brush and a vacuum cleaner to remove dust and loose grime. You also can use canned compressed air to unseat dust and dirt, and blow it out of the computer. You can purchase cans of compressed air at most computer stores. Remember that built-up dust not only clogs the computer's air intakes, but also can act as insulation, causing components to retain heat. The computer can "act up" if it gets too hot. Overheated circuits are not reliable, and may cause data to become garbled. Make sure that your computer can breathe and keep its cool.

You should clean your floppy disk drive's read-write heads at least once a year. Floppy disk cleaning systems are available at most computer stores. These systems include a dummy disk, which you insert into the disk drive. Some head cleaning kits feature a wet disk that applies a cleaning fluid to the heads; others use a dry disk that cleans the heads by abrasion. The wet disk cleaners are generally recommended because they are gentler than dry cleaners, and are less likely to damage the drive heads.

Unlike a floppy disk drive, the hard disk drive is enclosed in a protective chassis that keeps dirt out. Do not tamper with the drive's seals; you should not try to get into the hard disk chassis to clean it. For more information on cleaning your personal computer's mechanical components and circuit boards, as well as tips on using liquid lubricants on your system, see *Upgrading and Repairing PCs*, published by Que Corporation.

If you cannot keep your computer in a clean environment, take extra precautions. Cover the computer with a protective jacket when it is not in use, and consider having your computer regularly cleaned by a professional.

Your body generates *static electricity* when humidity is low, when you wear synthetic fabrics, or when you walk on carpet. Just by touching your keyboard while carrying a static charge, you can send an electrical "shudder" through your computer. Such a charge may not even sting your finger, but inside the computer, it can jumble data or cause circuits to fail. Fortunately, you can avoid static problems by touching the keyboard. The best way to minimize static problems is to make sure that the computer is properly grounded. You also can place an anti-static mat underneath the computer and keyboard, before you touch the computer, touch the mat to discharge any static electricity you are carrying in your body. Be sure to discharge static electricity before touching electrical components or opening the computer for repairs or cleaning.

You would be surprised how many computers, especially keyboards, are ruined by spilled beverages. Computer manufacturers and repair centers need to start distributing bumper stickers that say "Don't drink and compute!" Although it sounds obvious, you should take care to keep all food and drink (as well as other kinds of liquids) at a safe distance from the computer. Accidents happen. If you use the computer in an industrial environment or in a high-traffic area, you should consider purchasing a see-through plastic "skin" that lays over the keyboard and protects it from contaminants.

Parking Drive Heads

Remember that the disk drive heads are positioned extremely close to the disk platter's surface. If the drive head actually touches the disk surface—this is called a *head crash*—data is destroyed. A head crash can result if the computer receives a physical jolt or is dropped, or if a contaminant (such as dust or hair) finds its way into the sealed drive. The drive head also suffers a little each time you turn on the computer. When you switch on the system, the drive head receives a brief pulse of power that, over time, can result in the loss of data.

To reduce the risk of data loss caused by head malfunctions, you should always move the drive heads away from the disk surface before turning off the computer. During this procedure, called *head parking*, the drive heads' arm is pulled aside from the platter's data area.

Because head parking is a simple and effective way of avoiding disk crashes, many newer disk drives automatically park the heads when the computer is turned off. Generally, drives that use a *stepper motor* do not automatically park the heads. Drives that use a *voice coil* usually do park the heads. If you are not sure whether your drive automatically parks the heads, check with the drive manufacturer.

Some manufacturers supply a parking utility with the computer. The program generally is located on the system's *diagnostics* or *setup* disk; you can activate the parking program by running the setup program.

The enclosed disk includes a generic head-parking program, called PARK, which works on virtually all types of hard drives. The program was provided by Gibson Research Corporation, the makers of SpinRite. To park the drive heads, simply type **PARK** at the operating system prompt.

The utility programs Mace Utilities and PC Tools (see fig. 14.1) also feature all-purpose head-parking utilities, which work with any type of hard drive.

```
 PC Shell V6  File  Disk  Options  Applications  Special  Help         3:08pm
 Drive A  B   C   D   E                                      Advanced Mode
 ──ID = TECHNOJOCK─────────────      ──────────C:\U\PCTOOLS\*.*──────────
   ├─INSET                   ↑        PCSHELL   CFG     PCSECURE  EXE    WPWORKS   VWR  ↑
   ├─MISCOS2                           PHONE     TEL     PCSECURE  HLP    DWRITE    VWR
   ├─DUPLICAT                          PCBACKUP  CF1     DISKFIX   EXE    SPREAD20  VWR
   ├─RCD                               OLDSHELL  CFG     MIRROR    COM    PARADOX   VWR
   ├─FB                                PCOLD     CFG     REBUILD   COM    WORKS     VWR
   ├─PCTOOLS                  ┌────────Hard Disk Head Parking────────┐    WORDPERF  VWR
   │  └─SAMPLES               │                                      │    DBASE     VWR
   ├─NORTON                   │  The hard drive heads are now parked. │    ARCHIVE   VWR
   ├─BAT                      │  You may now turn off your computer   │    PCXVIEW   VWR
   ├─XTGOLD                   │  and transport it. If you continue,   │    WORD      VWR
   ├─AUTOMENU                 │  the heads will no longer be parked.  │    LLQC      EXE
   ├─QFILER                   │                                      │    PCSHELL   HLP
   ├─QUE                      │  ┌──────────┐                        │    PCSHELL   OVL
   │  ├─PCUTIL                │  │  CANCEL  │                        │    PCRUN     COM
   │  ├─4DOS                  │  └──────────┘                        │    TEXT      VWR
   │  ├─PERFECT               └──────────────────────────────────────┘    BINARY    VWR
   │  ├─P                               PC-CACHE  COM     SPREAD1A  VWR    PARK      COM  ↓
                                        KILL      EXE     RBASE     VWR
   ┌──────────────────────────┐        ┌──────────────────────────────────────────────┐
   │  1,744,896 Bytes Free    │        │   105 Listed =    2,738,206 bytes             │
   └──────────────────────────┘        └──────────────────────────────────────────────┘
 C:\U\PCTOOLS>
  Select CANCEL to UN-Park heads and continue with PCSHELL.
```

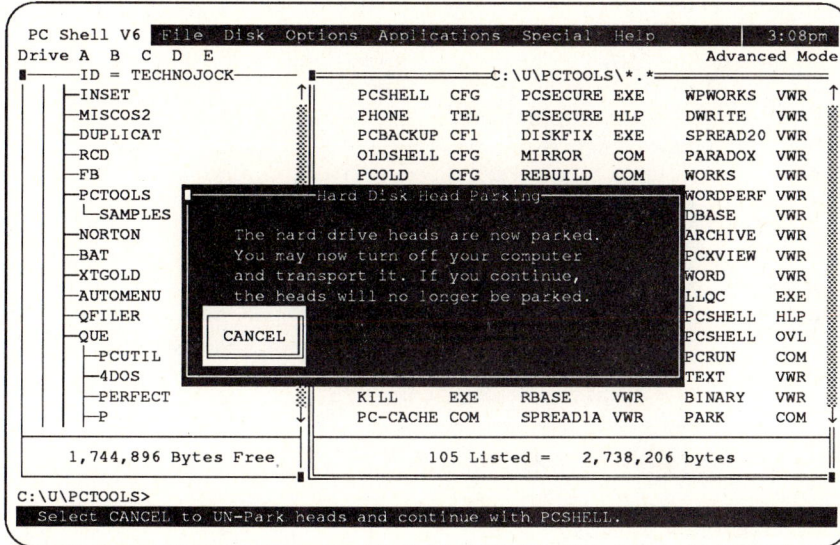

Fig. 14.1. *PC Tools includes a head-parking option in the program PCSHELL.*

Generally, you should run the head-parking program immediately before you turn off the computer. If you use a menu on your hard disk, create a menu option that executes the head-parking program. The more sophisticated programs enable you to use the computer after parking the heads, in case you change your mind about shutting down the computer. Other programs force you to turn the computer off, and then back on again, if you want to use the computer after the program has been run.

> ⊠ **WARNING**   Data loss may result if you install a head-parking utility that is not designed for use with your system's disk drives. Make sure that the utility is compatible with your drive before use.

Protecting Important Files with ATTRIB

Even if your concentration lapses for just a second, you can destroy valuable files while using operating system commands. You might delete the wrong files, for example, by using the wrong file mask in an ERASE or DEL operation. Similarly, you may inadvertently use the COPY command to copy one file on top of another file of the same name.

You can use the external operating system command ATTRIB to change a file's attributes, and to protect the file from accidental destruction. One file attribute is called the *read-only* attribute. If the operating system marks a file as read-only, the file cannot be deleted or overwritten; it can only be *read*. The ATTRIB command, therefore, is a simple means of protecting files that do not change much. You can activate the read-only attribute to protect important files, such as a budget spreadsheet or a word processing document that serves as a template for standard contracts. The command processor COMMAND.COM is another good candidate for this type of protection.

You also can use the ATTRIB command to set a file's *archive* attribute. You can issue the ATTRIB command in one of three ways. Use the following syntax to receive an on-screen report of any file's current attribute settings:

> **ATTRIB** *d:path***filename.ext** */S*

Use the following form of the command to set (turn on) one or both attributes for any file:

> **ATTRIB** *+R +A d:path***filename.ext** */S*

Use the following form to reset (turn off) one or both attributes for any file:

> **ATTRIB** *-R -A d:path***filename.ext** */S*

In these generic forms of the command, *d:path*\\ represents the optional drive and directory containing the selected files. If you do not specify a drive and path, the current drive and directory are assumed.

filename.ext is the name of the file whose attributes are being checked or set. You must specify a file name. You can use wild-card characters in the file name.

R and *A* represent the read-only and archive attributes, respectively. To turn on an attribute, prefix the letter with a plus sign (+). To turn off an attribute, prefix the letter with a minus sign (-).

If you do not supply either the *R* or the *A* attribute letters, ATTRIB displays a list of the current attributes for the files that match the specified file name.

The optional */S* switch (DOS V3.3 and later versions only) instructs ATTRIB to process all files that match the file specifier in all *subdirectories* beneath the specified (or default) directory.

As mentioned earlier, the COMMAND.COM file is a good example of a file that can be protected with a read-only attribute. Assuming that COMMAND.COM resides in the root directory of the default drive, enter the following command to make the file read-only:

ATTRIB +R \COMMAND.COM

This command instructs ATTRIB to turn on the read-only attribute for a file named COMMAND.COM, which resides in the root directory. COMMAND.COM is now a read-only file. To verify the setting, issue the following command:

ATTRIB \COMMAND.COM

The operating system responds with the following message:

```
R   C:\COMMAND.COM
```

Now, suppose that you try to delete the COMMAND.COM file by issuing the command **DEL \COMMAND.COM.** The operating system responds with the following message:

Access Denied

You should try the preceding experiment only if you have successfully completed the previous two commands. If the file is not marked as read-only, the DEL command will erase the file from the disk. If you erase COMMAND.COM, the disk becomes unbootable. Should this happen, you must boot the computer from a floppy disk, and copy COMMAND.COM from the master disk to the hard disk.

To return a file's read-only status to read/write, reverse the process. In the case of COMMAND.COM, issue the following command:

ATTRIB -R \COMMAND.COM

The following command turns on the read-only attribute for all the files in the \DOS directory:

ATTRIB +R \DOS*.*

Remember: you cannot modify any file that has been marked as read-only. If you activate the read-only attribute for a 1-2-3 worksheet file, for example, 1-2-3 cannot save any changes you make to the file. If you must modify such a file, you first must use ATTRIB to turn off the read-only attribute. Afterward, you can issue another ATTRIB command to reactivate the read-only attribute.

Note that the read-only attribute only protects files from being deleted or copied over. It does not protect the files in the event of hard disk failure or a FORMAT command.

> ☑ Many of the file-management programs discussed in Chapter 11,
> UTILITY as well as the popular disk utility programs (such as The Norton Utilities), include a facility for changing file attributes.

Avoiding a Hard Disk Format

One of the most common computing disasters is the accidental formatting of the hard disk. The external command FORMAT is used to prepare a disk for data storage. (For more information on disk formatting, see Chapter 7.)

The FORMAT command overwrites the file allocation table and root directory, destroying the disk's primary bookkeeping records, and effectively destroying the data. In fact, some versions of the FORMAT command also completely overwrite all data stored on the disk. Certain utility programs can help you try to recover data after a hard disk format. (The next chapter discusses these programs.) Even so, you should not assume that you can recover data after a format.

Before formatting a hard disk, more recent versions of DOS display a warning message similar to the following:

```
WARNING! ALL DATA ON NON_REMOVABLE DISK
DRIVE d: WILL BE LOST!
Proceed with Format (Y/N)?
```

Still, all you have to do is enter Y instead of N, and your data is destroyed. Some versions of the FORMAT command even prompt you to enter the disk's volume label before continuing. This procedure is a further reminder that you are about to perform a destructive operation. You can reduce the chances of an accidental hard disk format in several ways. You can build a batch file that is called in place of the FORMAT command, for instance, or use a commercial formatting program that replaces the operating system's FORMAT command.

Using a FORMAT Batch File

When you issue the FORMAT command, you must include a switch that tells the program which drive to format. To format a floppy disk in drive A, for example, you would enter the following command:

FORMAT A:

Suppose, however, that you mistakenly enter the following command:

FORMAT C:

If you issue this command, FORMAT ignores the disk in drive A, and formats drive C. By accidentally using a C rather than an A, you can cause a data catastrophe. You can prevent this sort of disaster, however, by taking the following two steps:

1. Rename the FORMAT.COM file with an unusual name, such as FORMAT$!.COM. (This file contains the commands that cause the FORMAT program to be carried out.)

2. Create a FORMAT.BAT file that first checks the parameters you issue with each FORMAT command, and then calls the program FORMAT$!.COM if the parameters do not affect the hard disk.

Assuming that the operating system commands are stored in the \DOS directory, you can rename the FORMAT command by issuing the following commands:

CD\DOS
RENAME FORMAT.COM FORMAT$!.COM

While you are still in the \DOS directory, create the FORMAT.BAT file with the following contents:

```
@ECHO OFF
IF "%1"=="c:" GOTO ERROR
IF "%1"=="C:" GOTO ERROR
FORMAT$! %1 %2 %3 %4 %5 %6 %7 %8 %9
GOTO END
:ERROR
ECHO You cannot FORMAT DRIVE C.
ECHO Enter FORMAT A: or FORMAT B:
:END
```

The batch file's second and third lines determine whether the user is trying to format drive C; the file even tests the user's entry for upper- and lowercase drive specifications. If the user specifies drive C in the FORMAT command, the batch file causes the operating system to ignore the command, and displays a two-line error message. If any other drive is specified, the batch file executes the renamed command FORMAT$!. All the parameters passed to the batch file are passed on to the command, and the floppy disk is formatted as requested. (For more information on batch files, see Chapters 6 and 9.)

If your system has more than one logical or physical hard disk, increase the number of IF statements to check for every hard disk specifier.

This simple but effective batch file ensures that you never accidentally use the FORMAT command to format the hard drive.

Using Commercial Formatting Programs

Most of the disk utility programs that include file undeletion tools provide their own variations of the operating system FORMAT command. These programs can help you guard against unintentional hard disk formats. Some utilities even provide a formatting program that only works on floppy disks; if you want to format the hard disk, these programs force you to use the FORMAT command from a diskette, and you are hardly going to do that by mistake! Further, the third-party formatting programs perform nondestructive formats. That is, the program only clears the FAT and root directory, and does not overwrite the data in each sector. If, in spite of your precautions, you accidentally format the hard drive, the nondestructive format makes recovery a possibility. File undeletion and format recovery are discussed in the next chapter.

Mace Utilities (Fifth Generation Systems) includes the following two special programs, which replace the operating system command FORMAT.

The FORMATF.EXE program is a fully functional replacement for FORMAT, with two major differences. First, you cannot use this program to format a hard disk. Second, FORMATF.EXE does not destroy any data on a floppy disk during formatting, because the program modifies only the FAT and the root directory. (If you accidentally use the operating system's FORMAT command to format a floppy disk, another Mace Utility program might be able to recover the data on the disk.)

The FORMATH.EXE program formats hard disks, using the same non-destructive format used by the FORMATF.EXE program.

The program documentation recommends that you delete all copies of FORMAT.COM from the hard disk, and then copy FORMATF.EXE onto the hard disk. If you do want to format a hard disk, you should execute the FORMATH.EXE program from a floppy disk.

You can specify switches with the FORMATF command, just as you can when issuing the FORMAT command. Otherwise, the program can be initiated through a full-screen menu system (see fig. 14.2).

```
                    Mace FORMATF version 1990
             Copyright (C) 1989 Fifth Generation Systems, Inc.
Begin Format Drive  Size  sYstem  Volume  Mode              Quit
Begin formatting the specified drive.


        Format Status                        Diskette Status
      ░░░░░░░░░░░░░░░░░░░           Diskette previously formatted!
                                                 Directory
                                      @7FF9.ADF
                                      @7FFA.ADF
                                      INSTALL.EXE
         Drive: A:
          Size: 1.2 MB
        System: No
        Volume: TECHNOJOCK
          Mode: Quick
```

Fig. 14.2. Mace Utilities includes a floppy-disk formatting program, FORMATF.EXE.

FORMATF allows you to specify the target drive, the type and size of the format, and the volume label. The program even offers a fast format option that quickly reformats a previously formatted floppy disk.

The Norton Utilities (Peter Norton Computing, Inc.) includes the program SF.EXE (for Safe Format), which provides features similar to the Mace Utilities programs. You can use the SF.EXE program, however, to format both floppy and hard disks.

PC Tools (Central Point Software) also includes a set of programs that performs nondestructive formatting on floppy and hard disks. These formatting facilities are included in the PCSHELL.EXE program.

Using CHKDSK

The operating system external command CHKDSK can analyze the hard disk, report disk fragmentation, and identify (and optionally fix) problems in the FAT and directories.

You should run CHKDSK periodically on your hard disk. Because the FAT and the hierarchical directory system work together to track file names and locations, a disaster may occur if a problem arises in the FAT or a directory. CHKDSK can fix most of the problems it finds in a disk's internal bookkeeping tables.

The CHKDSK program takes the following basic syntax:

CHKDSK *d:path\filename.ext* /F /V

In this generic syntax, *d:* is the name of the drive to be checked. If you leave the drive name out of the command, the current (default) drive is assumed.

path is the directory containing the files to be analyzed for fragmentation. If you do not specify a path, but do provide a file specifier in the command line, the default directory is assumed.

filename.ext is the optional file name and extension for the file you want to analyze for fragmentation. You can specify more than one file. If you do not supply a file name, CHKDSK does not check for fragmentation.

/F is the optional *fix* switch, which instructs CHKDSK to repair any problems encountered.

/V is the *verbose* switch, which instructs CHKDSK to display each file name as it is analyzed.

CHKDSK is the operating system's self-test command. CHKDSK checks for the following problems in the FAT:

- Unlinked cluster chains (lost clusters)

- Multiple linked clusters (cross-linked files)

- Invalid next cluster-in-chain values (invalid cluster numbers)

- Defective sectors where the FAT is stored

CHKDSK checks for the following problems in the directory system:

- Invalid cluster numbers (out of range)

- Invalid file attributes in entries (attribute values DOS does not recognize)

- Damage to subdirectory entries (CHKDSK cannot process these entries)

- Damage to a directory's integrity (its files cannot be accessed)

After checking for these problems, CHKDSK produces a screen report summarizing disk space and system RAM usage.

If you want to perform a general check of the hard disk, enter the CHKDSK command with no parameters, as shown in figure 14.3. Optionally, you can supply a drive path or file name, to instruct CHKDSK to check for disk fragmentation (see fig. 14.4).

```
C:\>CHKDSK
Volume TECHNOJOCK   created Mar 10, 1990 9:39a

 84123648 bytes total disk space
   380928 bytes in 7 hidden files
   401408 bytes in 96 directories
 65671168 bytes in 2584 user files
 17670144 bytes available on disk

   654336 bytes total memory
   447024 bytes free

C:\>
```

Fig 14.3. A typical report produced by CHKDSK, when the command is issued with no parameters.

```
C:\>CHKDSK \123R3\*.*
Volume TECHNOJOCK  created Mar 10, 1990 9:39a

 84123648 bytes total disk space
   380928 bytes in 7 hidden files
   401408 bytes in 96 directories
 65675264 bytes in 2585 user files
 17666048 bytes available on disk

   654336 bytes total memory
   447024 bytes free

C:\123R3\INSTALL.EXE
   Contains 6 non-contiguous blocks.
C:\123R3\INSDISK.RI
   Contains 3 non-contiguous blocks.
C:\123R3\123.EXE
   Contains 2 non-contiguous blocks.

C:\>
```

Fig 14.4. *A typical report produced when CHKDSK is issued with parameters to check for disk fragmentation.*

You should issue the CHKDSK command without the /F (fix) switch, in order to evaluate disk problems before attempting to repair them. That is, if you issue the command without the /F switch, CHKDSK makes a "dry run" and checks for problems without automatically fixing them. Even if you use CHKDSK without the /F switch, the program still prompts you when it finds a problem, just as though you had used the /F switch. You can take advantage of this "dry run" capability to assess reported problems. After assessing CHKDSK's findings and taking remedial steps (such as those described in the following sections), you can issue CHKDSK with the /F switch, so that the command can fix problems that it finds.

Starting at the root directory level, CHKDSK processes each directory individually, moving through the directory hierarchy. The program inspects each file's cluster chain, and compares the file's size to the number of clusters set aside for the file. During this process, CHKDSK determines how many clusters are allocated in the FAT for each file. The program expects to find enough chained clusters to accommodate the file, but not more than necessary. If CHKDSK finds that too many clusters are assigned to a file, it issues the following message:

Allocation error, size adjusted

If you included the /F switch when you issued the CHKDSK command, CHKDSK truncates the file. That is, the program de-allocates any excess clusters that were assigned to the file. Before using the /F switch, however, you should copy the reported file to another disk. This way, you will have a backup copy of the file, in case an incorrect number of bytes was indicated in the file's directory entry. If the directory entry incorrectly shows that too many clusters were assigned to the file, CHKDSK effectively chops off part of the file. If you have a backup copy of the file on another disk, you can recover in the unlikely event that the directory entry was wrong.

CHKDSK makes sure that each cluster is allocated only once. In rare circumstances, such as power problems or hardware failures, DOS can assign the same cluster to two different files. By checking each cluster chain for these *cross-linked* files, CHKDSK can report such mix-ups. When a cross-linked file is found, CHKDSK displays the following message:

```
filename is cross-linked on cluster X
```

When this message appears, copy the problem file to another disk. CHKDSK then repeats the message for another file; copy the second file to another disk, as well. The two files' contents probably will be mixed up, but you have a better chance of recovering the files if you save them to another disk before CHKDSK "fixes" the problem.

Although CHKDSK can remove the cross-linked entries from the FAT, the program may also corrupt each file. Further, the correction to the FAT will not correct each file's data problems. If you have a copy of the files on a diskette, you might be able to perform some manual surgery with help from a file recovery program (these programs are discussed in the next chapter).

Unfortunately, if CHKDSK encounters a file allocation chain that loops back on itself, CHKDSK runs in a circle reporting errors. Remember that a large file must be stored on more than one cluster, and the FAT identifies the chain of clusters in which the file is stored. Each of the FAT's cluster entries points to the next cluster in the chain. The last cluster in a chain usually is set to a special value, which marks it as the last cluster for the file. A loop occurs when one cluster entry points back to a cluster entry that already was included in the chain. For example, cluster A might point to cluster B, cluster B points to cluster C, and cluster C indicates that the next cluster is cluster A.

When this happens, CHKDSK keeps looping through these three clusters, without realizing that it is heading nowhere. If the /F switch is active, you can easily find your root directory flooded with CHKDSK-produced recovery files. Generally, when it is chasing a circular allocation chain,

CHKDSK stops only after all root directory entries have been filled (that is, when CHKDSK has created so many temporary files that the root directory becomes full). You can halt the process, however, by pressing Ctrl-C. If you suspect that a circular reference episode is taking place with CHKDSK, don't re-issue the command with the /F switch. Rather, you should try erasing the file and restoring it from a backup disk.

CHKDSK anticipates that every cluster in the FAT will be either available for allocation, part of a legitimate directory-based cluster chain, or marked as a bad cluster. If CHKDSK encounters any clusters or cluster chains that are not pointed to by a directory entry, CHKDSK issues the following message:

```
X lost clusters in Y chains
```

CHKDSK then prompts as follows:

```
Convert lost chains to files (Y/N)?
```

If the /F switch is active, CHKDSK turns each lost cluster chain into a file in the root directory, and assigns each newly created file the name **FILEnnnn.CHK**, in which **nnnn** is a consecutive number between 0000 and 9999. This number is incremented by 1 for each file created by the CHKDSK command's current execution. If the file is a text file, you can use the TYPE command to examine the file's contents, and you may be able to use a word processor to put the text back into its original file. You cannot use the TYPE command, however, to read the contents of a binary (program or data) file. If the problem is with a program file, you may need to use COMP or FC to compare your disk's binary files with their counterparts from your master disks.

If CHKDSK terminates because the root directory has no more entries available for converted chain files, clear the current **FILEnnnn.CHK** files by erasing them or copying them to another disk. When the files are cleared from the root directory, reissue CHKDSK.

Remember that the disk does not physically lose any sectors. A lost cluster report does not indicate that the clusters are bad, but means instead that DOS made a bookkeeping error in the FAT. The error causes one or more clusters to appear to be lost, as far as the operating system can tell. The clusters aren't tied to a directory entry, yet are marked as being in use.

Using Commercial Disk Analyzers

Many commercial utilities feature programs that can check the status of the hard disk. These programs, however, differ from CHKDSK. CHKDSK checks the logical relationship between the directory tables and the FAT, but most disk-checking programs perform one or more physical checks on the stored data.

Typically, a commercial disk utility reads and checks the data in each sector of the disk. If any sector is found to be bad, the utility moves the data to a different cluster. The program then places a marker in the FAT, identifying the faulty cluster as unusable.

If you purchase a commercial utility package that features a disk-checking program, you should execute the program regularly. If disk problems occur frequently in your system, then a more drastic problem may be looming. If your disk begins to act erratically, be sure to make frequent data backups, and consider having the disk and controller serviced by a professional.

Many different utility programs can be found on the market today. The following sections examine three of these packages: The Norton Utilities, Mace Utilities, and PC Tools. Each of these utilities includes a disk-checking program.

Using The Norton Utilities
To Analyze the Hard Disk

The Norton Utilities program DT.EXE (short for Disk Test) can be used to check a hard disk. By executing the program with one or more of the available switches (see fig. 14.5), you can specify which parts of the disk are checked.

Disk Test can run two tests on a disk: a *disk-read* and a *file-read*. The disk-read test reads every part of the disk; each area is read whether it is in use or not. The disk-read tests the boot record, FAT, root directory, and the entire data area of the disk, including active file space, erased file space, and unused file space. The file-read test reads either all the disk's active files, or those files matching a specified file name.

```
┌─────────────────────────────────────────────────────────────┐
│            ▗▛ The Norton Integrator ▜▖                        │
│  BE  Batch Enhancer    ┌───────────────────────────────────  │
│  DI  Disk Information   Disk Test      DT [d:] [filespec] [switches]
│  DS  Directory Sort        Test a disk or file for physical errors, move
│ ▐DT  Disk Test▌            questionable clusters, manually mark clusters.
│  FA  File Attributes                                          │
│  FD  File Date/Time    DT                                     │
│  FF  File Find             Run a Disk Test on the default drive.
│  FI  File Info         DT maybe.bad /M                        │
│  FR  Format Recover        Check maybe.bad, and relocate doubtful clus-
│  FS  File Size             ters. (Without /M, DT won't relocate clusters.)
│  LD  List Directories                                        │
│  LP  Line Print        Switches                               │
│  NCC Control Center        /B    Perform both a disk test and a file test
│  NCD Norton CD             /Cn   Mark Cluster n as bad        │
│  NDD Disk Doctor          /Cn-  Mark Cluster n as good; opposite of above
│  NU  Norton Utility        /D    Test entire Disk            │
│  QU  Quick UnErase        /F    Test files only              │
│  SD  Speed Disk           /LOG  Format output for printer or file LOGging
│  SF  Safe Format          /M    Move doubtful clusters to a safe location
│  SI  System Information   /S    Test subdirectories also     │
│                more...                                        │
│  ┌──────────────────────────────────────────────────────┐   │
│  │ )T                                                     │   │
│  └──────────────────────────────────────────────────────┘   │
│                                      ═ Press F1 for Help ═   │
└─────────────────────────────────────────────────────────────┘
```

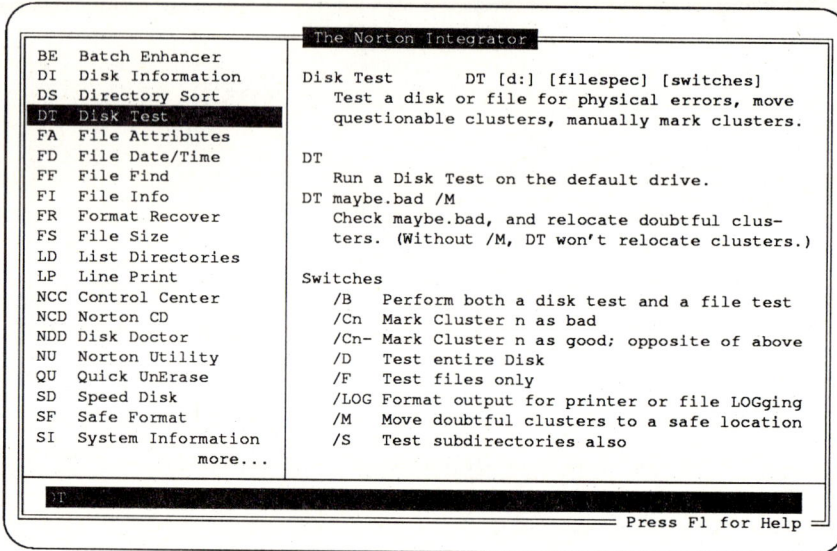

Fig 14.5. Accessing the Disk Test program from the Norton Integrator.

By default, DT simply displays a list of all the problem areas; the list can be written to a file or the printer. Or, if you like, DT can move all the data in the questionable clusters to a safe location, and then mark the bad clusters in the FAT. Even if the program relocates data from bad clusters, however, you are not guaranteed that the data can be successfully recovered, because DT may not be able to read all bad clusters. You can determine a relocated file's usability by trying to access the file in an application.

One interesting feature of the DT program is that it enables you to mark an individual cluster as bad or usable. You can control this and other features by using various switches as you issue DT commands.

Checking the Disk with Mace Utilities

Mace Utilities feature a disk-checking program called REMEDY.EXE. Unlike the Norton Utilities' DT program, REMEDY automatically tests the entire drive, including the system area and unused clusters.

You can instruct the program to run multiple tests, and to run tests without taking any corrective action. While REMEDY tests each cluster, the program's progress is displayed on a full-screen map of the disk (see fig. 14.6). If you want, REMEDY can store the test's results in an ASCII text file.

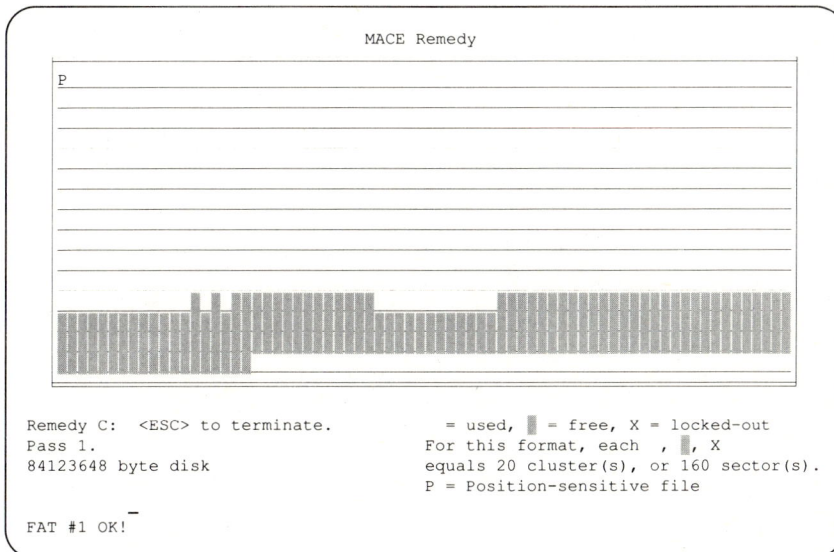

```
                              MACE Remedy

 P

         Remedy C:  <ESC> to terminate.        = used,  ▌ = free, X = locked-out
         Pass 1.                          For this format, each  ,  ▌, X
         84123648 byte disk               equals 20 cluster(s), or 160 sector(s).
                                          P = Position-sensitive file
                   ▔
         FAT #1 OK!
```

Fig. 14.6. REMEDY graphically shows the progress of the disk test.

If REMEDY has trouble reading a sector, the program reports that the sector's host cluster is bad, and then tries 10 times to read the data. If the read operation is successful, the program removes all data from the problem cluster, and places the data in a good cluster. REMEDY then updates the FAT, and locks out the cluster so that it cannot be used again.

If REMEDY is unable to read a sector that is part of a file, the missing data is replaced with asterisks in a new sector. If the file is a text file, you have to replace the asterisks with the original text (if you can remember the file's contents). If the file is a binary file (such as a worksheet), you may not be able to use it again.

Verifying Disk Integrity with PC Tools

The PC Tools program PCSHELL.EXE includes a disk-checking option,
called Verify Disk. This option checks every cluster on the disk. The Verify
Disk option, however, does not automatically correct the problems it finds
on the disk. This option is similar to the "test-only" options included in the
other products.

If you want to correct the problems encountered by the Verify Disk
program, you must execute another PC Tools program, named
COMPRESS. One COMPRESS option, Surface Analysis, can check
the status of all clusters (see fig. 14.7).

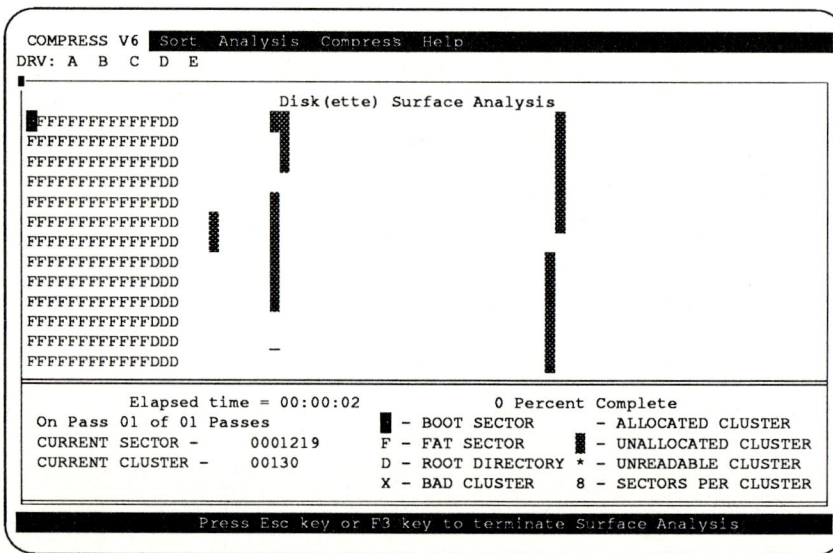

Fig 14.7. COMPRESS conducts a surface analysis.

The Surface Analysis option can check the disk one or more times, and
the program's output can be directed to a file. If COMPRESS finds a bad
sector, the sector's data is moved to a new location, and the faulty cluster is
marked as bad.

Using SpinRite II for a Low-Level Format

SpinRite II (Gibson Research Corporation) is a utility package that can help you ensure the integrity of your hard disk's data. SpinRite does not offer file undeletion, disk caching, or other file utilities. Rather, the package focuses on physical data storage on the disk.

SpinRite can perform rigorous disk surface integrity tests to ensure that each sector can store data correctly. The program also ensures fundamental drive/controller data compatibility, and optimizes the hard disk's sector interleave, permitting maximum data throughput.

SpinRite's most unique feature is the program's capability to perform low-level formatting on a hard drive, as well as data analysis and correction, *without* disturbing the data that is stored on the drive. If you own a copy of SpinRite, you should use the program about once every four months, to continually refresh and renew all the data on the hard disk.

SpinRite also can scan the disk's surface in only a few minutes, to verify SpinRite's compatibility with the hard disk and controller. You should run a quick surface scan as a precursor to low-level formatting.

When a hard disk undergoes low-level formatting for the first time, the disk surface is organized into tracks and sectors. At that time, the low-level formatting program writes sector identification data at the beginning of each sector. After this initial low-level formatting, the sectors normally are never written again; they are only read as the controller searches the disk. Over time, however, the disk drive heads may drift, so that the original sector IDs are no longer aligned with the data that is written into the sector. When alignment drift is severe, the drive head cannot read the sector identification data, and the operating system displays a `Sector not found` message. (For more information on sectors and alignment drift, see Chapter 7.) SpinRite can correct this problem by performing a new low-level format on the disk, and by realigning the sector IDs with the sector data.

During low-level formatting, SpinRite displays its progress graphically, as shown in figure 14.8. As part of the formatting process, SpinRite tests every sector on the disk. As it tests the sectors, the program bypasses the controller's built-in error-correction facility, which might hide a bad sector. When executed in "extremely thorough" mode, SpinRite writes 84 individual tests to every byte of storage space on the disk. The program checks sectors that are marked as bad, and enables you to mark them as usable, if each sector passes the test.

```
                                                    Track Map
 ┌─────────────────────────┐  ┌──────────────────────────────────────────────────┐
 │   Pattern Testing:      │  │    0 ●●●●●●●●●●●●●●●●●●●●●●●●●●●●●●●●●●●●●●●●●●●●    │
 │   C:  x:1  Depth:2      │  │  320                                               │
 │                         │  │  640                                               │
 └─────────────────────────┘  │  960                                               │
                              │ 1280                                               │
 ┌─────────────────────────┐  │ 1600                                               │
 │    Track Status:        │  │ 1920                                               │
 │                         │  │ 2240                                               │
 │      Reading/Wrting     │  │ 2560                                               │
 │      Formatting         │  │ 2880                                               │
 │  • O Patt Testing       │  │ 3200                                               │
 │  «   Relocating         │  │ 3520                                               │
 │  •   Format Okay        │  │ 3840                                               │
 │  cC  Correctable        │  │ 4160                                               │
 │  uU  Uncorrectable      │  │ 4480                                               │
 │  123 Defect Count       │  │ 4800                            4984               │
 │  B   Marked as Bad      │  │                                                    │
 ├─────────────────────────┤  ├──────────────────────┬─────────────────────────────┤
 │    See page 17-18       │  │ Complete:  286 ( 5%)  │ Remaining: 4699 (95%)       │
 └─────────────────────────┘  └──────────────────────┴─────────────────────────────┘

     Press [SPACE BAR] for Technical Log.  Press [B] to blank the display.
     Formatting may be suspended and resumed at a later time. Press ESC.
```

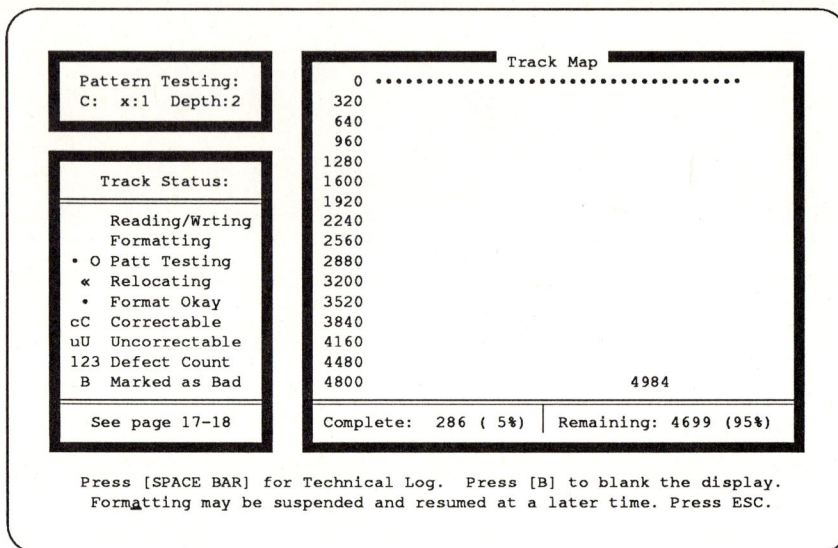

Fig 14.8. SpinRite reports its progress during low-level formatting.

If a bad sector is encountered during low-level formatting, that area of the disk is marked as bad in the low-level format region as well as in the FAT table. If the bad cluster contains data, the data is moved to another area of the disk.

Using SpeedStor's Disk Diagnostics

SpeedStor (Storage Dimensions, Inc.) is a hard disk utility program used primarily to perform hard disk preparation tasks such as low-level formatting and disk partitioning (these configuration steps are discussed in Chapter 7). Before the appearance of DOS V4, SpeedStor also was used extensively to break the 32M data access limit. SpeedStor also features advanced diagnostic tools, which can verify the integrity of the hard disk, and test the compatibility of the disk drive and the disk controller.

The program's Diagnostics menu is accessed from the SSTOR.EXE main menu (see fig. 14.9). You need to use these menu options with caution, because some of them can destroy data on the hard disk. Specifically, the Write Test and Media Analysis options write data to the hard disk; use these options only on new or fully backed-up disks.

```
            SpeedStor(TM)  Disk Integration Software, version 6.0.3
          Copyright(C) 1985-1989 Storage Dimensions, Inc.  All rights reserved
 ═══════════════════════════════════════════════════════════════════════════
                            D I A G N O S T I C S   M E N U
          NextDrive  Controller  SeekTest  ReadTest  WriteTest  MediaAnalysis  Quit

       Perform controller's internal test

       Drive   Manufacturer/Model      Cyls  Heads  Secs  Precomp  Lzone  TotalBytes
         1     <Standard Type 11>       925    7     17     128     924   56,357,888




                           To select a menu item:
          Use the arrow keys to highlight the desired selection and press <Enter>,
                   or type the first letter of the desired selection.

                        Press <Esc> to abort the current command.
                     From the Main Menu, <Esc> will exit the program.
```

Fig. 14.9. The SpeedStor diagnostics menu.

The Controller Test, the Seek Test, and the Read Test, however, are nondestructive tests.

The Controller Test checks the hard disk controller's internal buffers, and tests the controller's communication with the main computer. SpeedStor displays a **FAILED** or **PASSED** message after a few seconds of testing. If the **FAILED** signal appears, make sure that the controller card is properly seated in the motherboard. If these connections are sound, the controller is probably defective.

The Seek Test checks the communication between the hard disk controller and the hard disk, as well as the drive's mechanical operation. The program performs three different seek tests: drive calibration, extremes to middle, and random. These tests rigorously evaluate the drive actuator mechanism.

The Read Test makes sure that the disk drive can read the data on the hard disk. You can specify a range of tracks to be tested, or instruct the program to test the entire drive.

Viruses

This chapter discusses preventative measures that can be taken against disk disasters. In recent times a new hazard has surfaced: the computer virus. A virus is a program developed expressly to propagate itself within other program files, such as COMMAND.COM. At some stage during its "life," a virus probably will perform some unexpected act—like display a message, delete one or more files, or destroy large portions of the data on the disk.

You can use a number of techniques to identify and eradicate computer viruses. Chapter 17 discusses these techniques in detail.

Summary

Frequent backups are your best insurance against a disk disaster, but you also can take precautions to lessen the chances of hard disk problems. The following key points were raised in this chapter:

- Always use a surge protector, and avoid discharging static electricity into the keyboard or any circuitry.

- If your drive does not automatically park the drive heads, use a program to park the heads before turning off the computer.

- The external operating system command ATTRIB changes a file's archive and read-only attributes. If a file is flagged as read-only, it cannot be deleted or overwritten.

- You can avoid accidental hard disk formats by renaming the FORMAT command and creating a FORMAT.BAT file.

- The external operating system command CHKDSK verifies and can correct the cluster information stored in the FAT and the directories.

- Many commercial programs provide utilities designed specifically to validate the data integrity of the clusters on a hard disk.

The next chapter shows you how commercial disaster recovery programs can be used to repair disk and file problems.

15

Recovering from Disk Disasters

Even if you take sensible precautions to avoid disk disasters, the chances are good that something eventually will go wrong with your system's hard drive. To help users cope with disk problems, software manufacturers have introduced a variety of highly specialized data recovery programs, which can reduce a full-fledged disaster to a minor irritation. This chapter describes the capabilities of several popular data and disaster recovery tools.

The following sections show you how to use these commercial programs to undelete a file and to recover from an accidental disk format. This chapter focuses on the capabilities of three popular disk utility packages: The Norton Utilities (Peter Norton Computing, Inc.), Mace Utilities (Fifth Generation Systems, Inc.), and PC Tools (Central Point Software, Inc.).

While these three programs are widely acclaimed as excellent disaster recovery programs, remember that they are not the only such programs available. These programs have been selected to show you how disaster recovery programs work in general. Most disaster recovery programs provide a variety of features and capabilities beyond those discussed in the following sections, and you should select such a program according to your own unique needs.

Using Data Recovery Snapshots

Some data disasters, such as an accidental format, can be truly destructive and almost impossible to recover from. Recovery is easier, however, if you have installed extra bookkeeping software that maintains its own records of the data stored on the disk. The disk formatting process usually does not erase the data stored in each file, but simply obliterates the disk's bookkeeping records. A disaster recover program can scour the disk for the duplicate bookkeeping records, which are used in reconstructing the original file records.

The Norton Utilities, Mace Utilities, and PC Tools all include "snapshot" programs that maintain their own file records. These programs record vital information about the disk, and place the information in a special file, which is reserved for use by the data recovery programs. You should execute the snapshot program frequently, to keep the file information current and improve the chances of successful data recovery. Ideally, the program should be executed from the AUTOEXEC.BAT file, so that a snapshot is made every time you boot the computer. If you restructure the files or directories, you should immediately run the snapshot program to record the new information.

Making Snapshots with The Norton Utilities

The Norton Utilities include a dual-purpose program named FR.EXE (short for Format Recover), which you can use to save disk information in a special file, and to recover data after an accidental format. (The program's format recovery capabilities are discussed later.) You can execute the program from the operating system command prompt, or by placing the program in full-screen mode (see fig. 15.1).

You can execute the program from the operating system prompt by issuing the FR command. The command takes the following syntax:

FR *d: /SAVE /NOBAK*

In this generic syntax, *d:* is drive for which the data will be saved. If you do not specify a drive, the program saves the file information for the default drive.

/SAVE is an optional parameter, which instructs FR to save information about the disk's boot record, FAT, and root directory in a file. This option creates a file in the root directory, called FRECOVER.DAT. The program

also creates an optional backup file, named FRECOVER.BAK, which contains a copy of the program's previous output. Several Norton Utilities programs use the FRECOVER.DAT file to assist in data recovery. When used in recovery mode, the FR.EXE program needs the information stored in FRECOVER.DAT, as well.

/NOBAK is another optional parameter, which instructs FR not to keep a FRECOVER.BAK file.

If you do not specify any parameters with the FR command, the program switches into full-screen mode.

Full-screen mode provides all the same features and functions of command-line mode. Full-screen mode also is easier to use, because it frees you from using (and trying to remember) switches and other parameters that are required when you execute the program at the operating system prompt. The program's command-line version, however, is useful if you want to add the commands to the AUTOEXEC.BAT file (or any batch file), so that you can execute the program without being prompted for input.

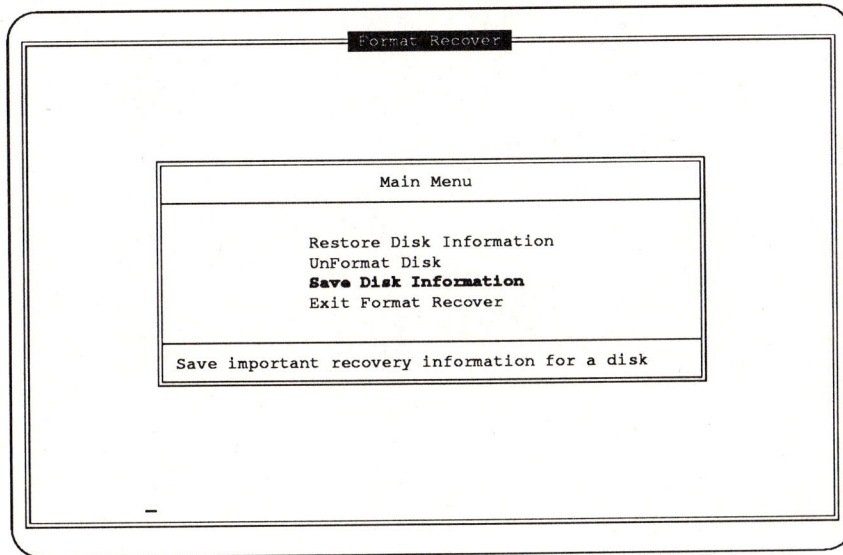

```
┌──────────────── Format Recover ────────────────┐
│                                                 │
│                                                 │
│                                                 │
│      ┌─────────────────────────────────┐       │
│      │           Main Menu             │       │
│      ├─────────────────────────────────┤       │
│      │                                 │       │
│      │    Restore Disk Information     │       │
│      │    UnFormat Disk                │       │
│      │    Save Disk Information         │       │
│      │    Exit Format Recover          │       │
│      │                                 │       │
│      ├─────────────────────────────────┤       │
│      │ Save important recovery         │       │
│      │ information for a disk          │       │
│      └─────────────────────────────────┘       │
│                                                 │
│   _                                             │
│                                                 │
└─────────────────────────────────────────────────┘
```

Fig. 15.1. *The Norton Utilities format recovery program FR.EXE.*

Storing Disk Information with Mace Utilities

The Mace Utilities package include a *recovery insurance program*, called RXBAK.EXE. You can execute the program from the operating system prompt by issuing the RXBAK command. The command takes the following syntax:

RXBAK *d: ...*

In this generic syntax, *d:* is the drive for which disk information will be saved. The ellipses (...) indicate that multiple drives can be specified. If no drive is specified, the current (default) drive is assumed.

The RXBAK program makes a copy of the disk's boot sector, the FAT, and the root directory, and stores the information in a file named BACKUP.M_U. This file is placed in the subject disk's root directory. If a file named BACKUP.M_U already exists, it is renamed OLDBACK.M_U.

Other Mace Utilities programs can use the BACKUP file's information to restore lost files. You can use the UNFORMAT command, for example, to restore the disk to the state it was in when RXBAK was last run. The UNDELETE program, also uses BACKUP.M_U to recover deleted files.

Like any such program, RXBAK should be run frequently, so that the BACKUP file is kept up to date. If you want, the Mace Utilities installation program can add a line to the system's AUTOEXEC.BAT file, so that RXBAK runs every time the computer is booted.

Tracking Disk Information with PC Tools

PC Tools also includes a snapshot program, called MIRROR.COM, which makes a backup of the boot sector, the FAT, and the root directory.

You can run MIRROR periodically as a stand-alone program, or you can install it as a memory-resident program. In memory-resident mode, MIRROR provides a *delete tracking* facility that maintains information about all deleted files. This information is kept in a special file, which is used by the PCSHELL program's file undeletion option (this option is discussed later). Note, however, that PCSHELL may be able to recover undeleted files, even if the delete tracking file is not available.

The MIRROR command takes the following syntax:

MIRROR *d: ... /1 /Td-nnn ...*

In this generic syntax, *d: ...* is one or more drives for which information will be recorded. If you do not name a drive, MIRROR records information for the default drive.

The optional */1* switch indicates that only *one* copy of the boot-FAT-root file should be maintained. If you omit this parameter, MIRROR maintains the current file, as well as a backup file containing the program's previous output.

/Td-nnn... indicates that the memory-resident Delete Tracking option should be installed. You can use one /T switch for each drive. The *d* is the letter of the drive to be tracked; the optional *-nnn* indicates the maximum number of files to be tracked. If you do not specify a value for *-nnn*, MIRROR uses a default value based on the type of drive being tracked.

You also can issue a third optional switch—/PARTN—which saves information about the disk's partition structure. PC Tools can use this information to recover from an `invalid drive specification` problem. You need to use the /PARTN switch only once, unless you redefine the hard disk's partitions.

Undeleting a File

One of the most common mini-disasters is accidental deletion of a file. The simplest (and least frustrating) way to recover from an accidental file deletion is to use a backup copy of the file. If you do not have a backup copy, you can try to undelete the file with the help of a data recovery program. Remember, however, that if you can recover the file only with the help of such a program, you should run the program as soon as possible after the file has been deleted. No operating system command can undelete a file that has been erased from the hard disk. If you do not have a data recovery program, and must use an operating system command, your only recourse is to use the RESTORE command to restore a copy of the file from a backup.

Do not install any of the utilities mentioned in this chapter if you are trying to recover a deleted file. The process of installing the software onto the hard disk may actually overwrite the very data you are trying to recover. Instead, run the file undeletion program from a floppy disk. You can install the software after you have recovered from this disaster, so that you will be ready for the next disaster.

Understanding How Files Are Undeleted

Before examining how a file can be undeleted, you should understand how the operating system deletes a file in the first place. Fortunately, when a file is deleted, the data is not actually erased. Rather, the operating system retains the file's directory entry, but replaces the file name's first character in the directory entry with the ASCII 229 character, called *sigma*. This special character marks the file as deleted, but all the other characters in the file's directory entry remain intact, such as the remaining characters in the name, the date and time, the file size, and the starting cluster's number. Once the sigma character is in place, the file does not appear in normal directory listings. After placing the sigma character in the file's directory entry, the operating system marks as free all the clusters that were allocated to that file. (For more information on the FAT and directory details, refer to Chapter 7.)

The directory entry is the key to recovering a deleted file. The first stage in the recovery process involves scanning the directory to find all the files that begin with the sigma character. Most undelete utilities display this character as a question mark (?). Typically, the program selects a specific file from the list of deleted files, and prompts you to supply the original first character of the file name. The program replaces the sigma with the specified character.

From the directory entry, the program determines the file's starting cluster, and then examines the FAT. If the starting cluster is still marked as free, then the cluster probably still contains part of the deleted file. If so, the first part of the file has been found.

The file's directory entry retains a record of the file's size. The number of bytes in a sector (usually 512 bytes) and the number of sectors in a cluster (often 4 or 8) can be determined by referencing the disk's boot sector. Using this data, the undelete program can easily compute the total number of bytes in a cluster. The program then divides this cluster size into the original file size, to determine the total number of clusters used by the file.

Now that the program has identified the starting cluster and calculated the total number of clusters occupied by the file, the next task is to determine remaining clusters' locations. Often, a file occupies the clusters adjacent to the starting cluster. If enough clusters are free, they are assumed to belong to the deleted file. The final stage of undeletion is to restore the file's directory entry (by replacing the sigma character with the alphabetic character supplied by the user), and to mark the cluster chain in the FAT. The deleted file is now undeleted.

Typically, an undeletion program requires you only to choose the file to be undeleted, and to supply the file name's first character. The program does the rest. This process is referred to as an *automatic recovery*, because the recovery program finds all the clusters together and unused.

Unfortunately, file recovery is not always so easy. The following two conditions that can significantly hinder file recovery:

1. If you save other files to the disk from which the file was deleted, one or more of the deleted file's clusters may be overwritten by a new file. When a cluster is reused, the operating system truly erases the data from that cluster, making complete recovery of the file impossible. For this reason, you must try to recover a deleted file as soon as you realize that it has been deleted. You also should avoid saving other files before recovering the deleted file.

2. If a disk is highly fragmented, the deleted file's clusters may be scattered all over the disk, rather than lined up in a neat contiguous block. The file recovery program can find the starting cluster easily enough (if the cluster hasn't been overwritten by a subsequent file save), but locating the remaining clusters is almost impossible, especially if the disk contains thousands of free clusters. If you ran one of the snapshot programs before the file was deleted, however, the undeletion program can read this backup copy of the FAT, and locate the file's cluster chain.

A sophisticated undeletion utility can determine when an automatic recovery is not possible, and then can switch to manual mode. In manual mode, most utilities show you each free cluster and ask you if you want to add it to the file. Even if you find the correct clusters (by recognizing some text in the data), you still have to put them in the right order.

If a file was deleted a long time ago, or if the disk is badly corrupted, you may be able to make only a partial recovery. In other words, an undeletion program may recover the file, but the recovered file may not contain all its data, and the data may be in the wrong order. In the case of ASCII files, some data is better than no data, and you can at least use the partial file as a starting point for re-entering the missing data. Partially restored binary files, such as .WK1 worksheets or .DBF database files, however, often are useless. In these kinds of files, data integrity relies on the logical and relative positioning of information within the file. If part of the data is missing, then the file is useless. (Specialized data recovery tools can restructure damaged files so that the files can at least be read by the parent program; these tools are discussed later in this chapter.)

Remember that subdirectories actually are special files that contain information about other files. If you accidentally delete a subdirectory (by using the RMDIR command), you may be able to restore the subdirectory by using the recovery programs described earlier. You then can use the newly restored subdirectory to restore the files that were contained in the subdirectory (all files in a directory must be deleted before the directory itself can be deleted). Complete data recovery is by no means a certainty, and the best safeguard for data loss—even better than the most expensive data recovery program—is a frequently updated backup.

Unerasing Files with The Norton Utilities

The Norton Utilities package includes a program named QU.EXE, for Quick Unerase, which can perform automatic file recovery. (The package's main program, called NU.EXE, can help you recover a file manually.) QU.EXE program is easy to use, and you can execute the program from the operating system's command prompt by issuing the command QU. The command takes the following syntax:

QU *filename* /A

where *filename* is the file or group of files (if wild cards are used), to be unerased.

The /A switch is optional, and tells the program to restore all erased files in a directory.

If you execute the QU command without any parameters, the program runs in interactive mode, and prompts you to select the erased files that must be restored. If QU cannot restore a file, the program displays a message advising you to use the NU command to unerase the file manually.

Figure 15.2 shows The Norton Utilities Quick Unerase screen as the program works in a directory that contains three deleted files. The first file is unerased, and the second file is skipped. The third file must be unerased with the NU program, because it cannot be recovered with QU.

NU.EXE enables you to edit any area of the disk, and offers a sophisticated file undelete program that enables you to control the manner in which a file is undeleted. NU.EXE is a full-screen, menu-driven program. After you select a file to unerase, the program prompts for the first character of the file name. The display includes an estimate of how successful an unerase will be (see fig. 15.3).

```
C:\BATFILES>\u\norton\qu
QU-Quick UnErase, Advanced Edition 4.50, (C) Copr 1987-88, Peter Norton

Directory of C:\BATFILES
   Erased file specification: *.*
   Number of erased files: 3
   Number that can be Quick-UnErased: 2

   Erased files lose the first character of their names.
   After selecting each file to Quick-UnErase, you will be
   asked to supply the missing character.

   ?ack_wk3.bak        411 bytes      2:33 pm  Tue Feb 20 90
'back_wk3.bak' Quick-UnErased

   ?etter.mom          423 bytes      1:19 pm  Fri Feb 23 90

   ?est.pix          1,750 bytes     11:50 am  Sat Feb 24 90
It is not possible to Quick-UnErase this file
Its data space is being used by another file
Press any key to continue...

C:\BATFILES>
```

Fig. 15.2. Restoring deleted files with The Norton Utilities QU.EXE program.

```
Menu 2.2 part 2        Complete selected erased file name

                     Name: ?est.pix
               Attributes: Archive
            Date and time: Friday, July 31, 1987, 12:00 am
  Starting cluster number: 2,997 (sector number 24,155)
                     Size: 3,170 bytes, occupying 1 cluster


          Successful UnErase: Unlikely
          The first cluster of this file is used by another file.


                        ?est.pix


             To restore the missing first character
                    press any letter or number key
                 Use the arrow keys to change files
```

Item type Erased file	Drive C:	Directory name \BATFILES	File name ?est.pix

Fig. 15.3. NU prompts for the input of the first character of the file name.

After you specify the file name's first character, the program lets you view clusters that might contain a portion of the file's data. You also can select clusters to add to the file (see fig. 15.4). You can instruct the program to select the next probable cluster, or to choose a specific cluster or sector. The program displays a count of the total number of required clusters, as well as the number of clusters already selected.

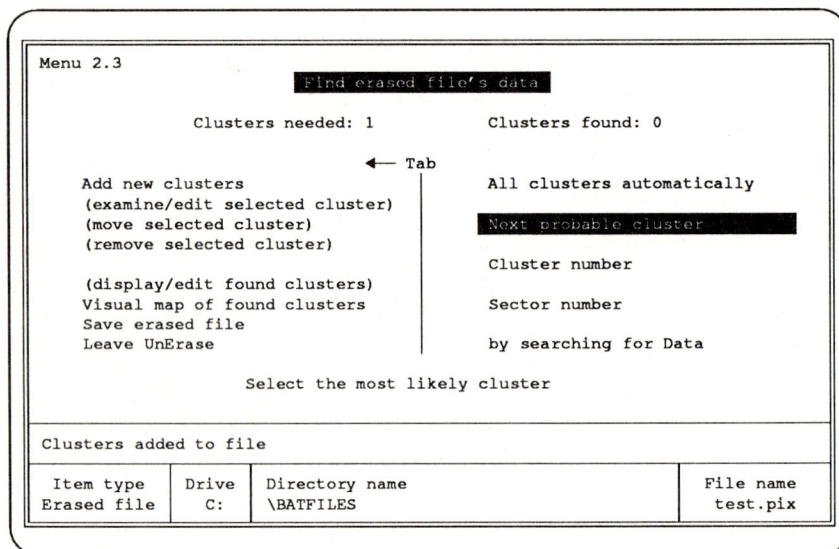

```
Menu 2.3
                        Find erased file's data

              Clusters needed: 1            Clusters found: 0

                               ←— Tab
      Add new clusters                   All clusters automatically
      (examine/edit selected cluster)
      (move selected cluster)            Next probable cluster
      (remove selected cluster)
                                         Cluster number
      (display/edit found clusters)
      Visual map of found clusters       Sector number
      Save erased file
      Leave UnErase                      by searching for Data

                  Select the most likely cluster


 Clusters added to file

 Item type    Drive   Directory name              File name
 Erased file  C:      \BATFILES                   test.pix
```

Fig. 15.4. NU.EXE lets you view clusters, and select clusters to add to the file.

When you have reconstructed as much of the file as possible, select the Save option; the program unerases the file and then adds the file to the directory and the FAT.

Undeleting Files with Mace Utilities

The Mace Utilities package includes an automatic file recovery program, called UNDELETE.EXE. You can execute the program from the operating system command prompt by issuing the command UNDELETE. The command takes the following syntax:

UNDELETE *d:path\filename*

In this generic syntax, *d:path* is the drive and directory containing the file to be unerased. If you do not specify a drive and directory, the program uses the default drive and directory.

You also can specify the name of the file you want to recover (*filename*). Wild cards are accepted in this file name. If you do not specify a file name, the program assumes *.* as the default file mask.

UNDELETE searches for all the deleted files that match the file name or file mask you specify. Each matching file is processed in turn; the program prompts you for the first character of each file's name, if you want to recover the file (see fig. 15.5).

```
BATFILES 1 of 4 eligible files recovered. [SPACE] skips. [ESC] quits.
 Alternate FAT information not available.

   Undeleted TM      BAT  Feb 23, 1990   3:51pm  24
   σETTER  MOM  Feb 23, 1990   1:19pm  423  probably erased.
   Correct first letter->σUESS   BAT  Feb 23, 1990  10:40am  39
   σACK_WK3BAK  Feb 20, 1990   2:33pm  411  probably erased.
   Check recovered files for accuracy.
   Press a key to return to DOS
```

Fig. 15.5. UNDELETE.EXE recovers files individually.

If UNDELETE determines that a file cannot be recovered automatically, you must try to recover the file manually by using a program called MUSE (short for Mace Utilities Sector Editor). Essentially, MUSE is an editor that enables you to modify any area of the disk. When you execute MUSE, the program presents a directory tree from which you choose a directory (see fig. 15.6).

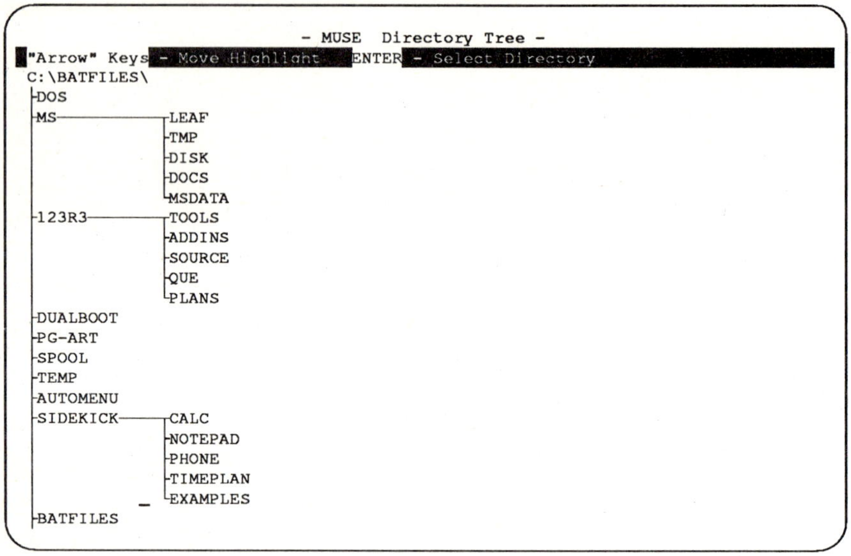

```
                    - MUSE  Directory Tree -
"Arrow" Keys - Move Highlight   ENTER - Select Directory
C:\BATFILES\
├DOS
├MS───────────┬LEAF
              ├TMP
              ├DISK
              ├DOCS
              └MSDATA
├123R3────────┬TOOLS
              ├ADDINS
              ├SOURCE
              ├QUE
              └PLANS
├DUALBOOT
├PG-ART
├SPOOL
├TEMP
├AUTOMENU
├SIDEKICK─────┬CALC
              ├NOTEPAD
              ├PHONE
              ├TIMEPLAN
           _  └EXAMPLES
├BATFILES
```

Fig. 15.6. *At start-up, MUSE presents a directory tree.*

When you select a directory, MUSE lists all the files in the directory, including deleted files (see fig. 15.7). You can undelete a file by moving the cursor to the first character (sigma) of a file name and replacing it with a valid character. The file is instantly undeleted, but data recovery may not be possible if the disk is fragmented or if some clusters have been overwritten. If this is the case, the file must be manually (and somewhat precariously) recovered through a chain facility that enables you to select individual clusters.

Undeleting Files with PC Tools

The PC Tools program PCSHELL includes an Undelete option on the main menu. With Undelete, you can undelete a file or a subdirectory, or create a new file from unused clusters (see fig. 15.8). If you select the file-recovery option, PCSHELL lists the deleted files in the current directory. To undelete a file from another directory, you must change directories before you activate the file-recovery program. A question mark (?) appears as the first character in the name of each deleted file (see fig. 15.9). If a file can be recovered automatically, an at-sign (@) character appears after that file's name. An asterisk (*) means that some—but not all—the file's clusters are available. In manual mode, the program enables you to view and select clusters to add to the file (see fig. 15.10).

```
         -  BATFILES\          Editing DIR entry 9         Data Cluster 08400 -
  ALT   ████i███F███████x███n███J█████M█████S████T████O████H████Q████

  File                        Attributes                      First
 ┌Name───────────Ext── Arc Dir Sys Hid R/O  Date   Time Cluster Length─┐
  B A C K _ W K 3  B A K                     02/20/90  14:33  8390  411

  A D D P A T H    B A T                      02/23/90  08:19  9882  17

  T M 4            B A T                      02/24/90  07:50  9465  56

  S H I F T I T    B A T                      02/23/90  09:37  13029 205

  F O U N D        B A T                      02/23/90  13:11  13810 36

  σ E M P          T X T                      02/22/90  13:21  15903 10905

  T M 2            B A T                      02/23/90  11:26  13764 164

  R N              B A T                      02/23/90  13:41  13829 447
```

Fig. 15.7. All directory entries are displayed, including deleted files.

```
 PC Shell V6  File  Disk  Options  Applications  Special  Help      8:44am
 Drive A  B  C  D  E                                          Advanced Mode
 ┌─ID = TECHNOJOCK──────┐  ┌──────────C:\BATFILES\*.*─────────┐
    └─FINISHED       ↑      BACK_WK3 BAT   TEST    EXE  COPYROOM BAT  ↑
  ─DUALBOOT                 SETSTART BAT   MENU    BAT  TEMPCD   BAT
  ─SPOOL                    ┌──────────Undelete──────────┐DBACK    BAT
  ─TEMP                                                    RNT     BAT
  ─AUTOMENU               Choose whether you are un-deleting a file,
  ─BATFILES               a sub-directory, or creating a file from
  ─MENU                   clusters of your choice.
  ─MAG2
    ─MGSAMPLE          ┌FILE┐  ┌SUB-DIR┐  ┌CREATE┐  ┌CANCEL┐
    ─MGDEMO
    ─MGVIEWER         └────────────────────────────────────┘
  ─OAD                      TM3      BAT   GETSTART BAT
  ─DOS401                   NEWPATH  BAT   CONFIG   2
  ─PCKWIK                   PROGS    BAT   AUTOEXEC 2
  ─BATCOM                   2        BAT   AUTOEXEC 1
    └─BATDEMO               OLDPATH  BAT   WHAT     EXE
  ─SAVE                     1        BAT   MENUWHAT BAT
 ┌────────────────────┐  ┌──────────────────────────────────┐
   1,478,656 Bytes Free        38 Listed =      15,983 bytes
 C:\BATFILES>
 Select the CANCEL button or press ESC to return.
```

Fig. 15.8. PC Tools prompts for the type of data to be recovered.

```
PC Shell V6  File  Disk  Options  Applications  Special  Help        8:39am
Drive A  B  C  D  E                                        Advanced Mode
■──────ID = TECHNOJOCK────── ■──────────────C:\BATFILES\*.*───────
         └─FINISHED            ^    ?R-77E1   MDS                        ^
      ─DUALBOOT                     ?EST      PIX
      ─SPOOL                        ?ETTER    MOM@
      ─TEMP
      ─AUTOMENU
      ─BATFILES
      ─MENU
      ─MAG2
         ─MGSAMPLE
         ─MGDEMO
         └─MGVIEWER
      ─OAD
      ─DOS401
      ─PCKWIK
      ─BATCOM
         └─BATDEMO
      ─SAVE                    v                                        v
 ───────────────────────────── ──────────────────────────────────────
     1,486,848 Bytes Free            3 Listed =      7,533 bytes

C:\BATFILES>
1Help  2Index  3Exit  4Unsel  5Go   6      7      8      9      10
```

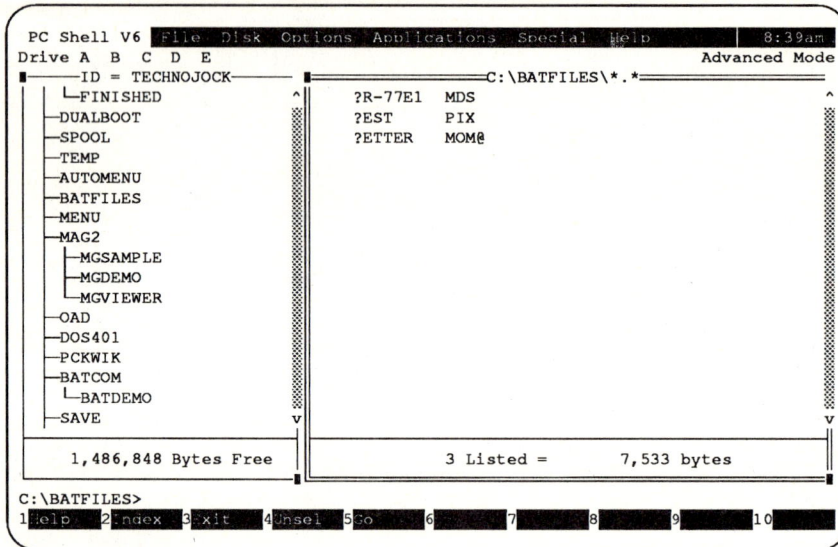

Fig. 15.9. All deleted files are displayed in a window.

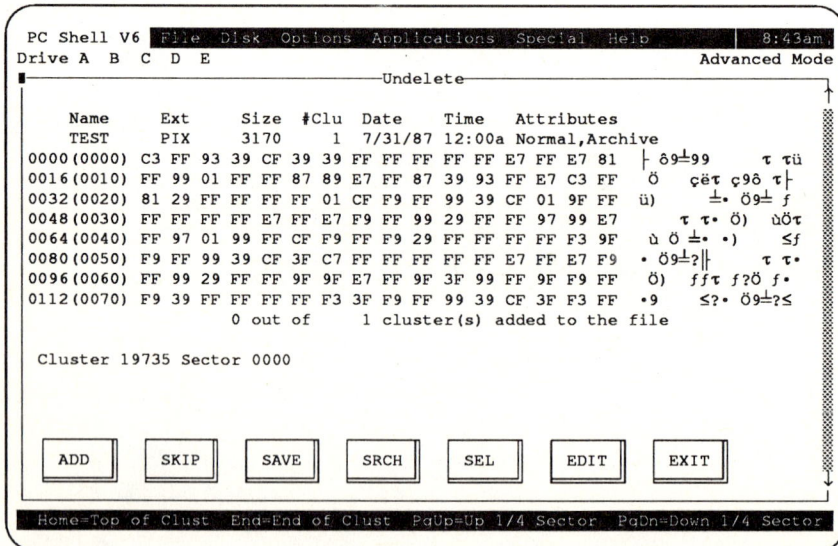

```
PC Shell V6  File  Disk  Options  Applications  Special  Help        8:43am
Drive A  B  C  D  E                                        Advanced Mode
■───────────────────────────Undelete───────────────────────────

   Name     Ext    Size  #Clu  Date     Time   Attributes
   TEST     PIX    3170    1   7/31/87  12:00a  Normal,Archive
0000(0000) C3 FF 93 39 CF 39 39 FF FF FF FF E7 FF E7 81   ├ δ9┴99    τ τü
0016(0010) FF 99 01 FF FF 87 89 E7 FF 87 39 93 FF E7 C3 FF  Ö  çëτ ç9δ τ├
0032(0020) 81 29 FF FF FF FF 01 CF F9 FF 99 39 CF 01 9F FF  ü)   ┴• δ9┴ f
0048(0030) FF FF FF FF E7 FF E7 F9 FF 99 29 FF FF 97 99 E7   τ τ• Ö) ùÖτ
0064(0040) FF 97 01 99 FF CF F9 FF F9 29 FF FF FF F3 9F  ù Ö ┴• •)   ≤f
0080(0050) F9 FF 99 39 CF 3F C7 FF FF FF FF FF E7 E7 F9  • δ9┴?|├    τ τ•
0096(0060) FF 99 29 FF FF 9F 9F E7 FF 9F 3F 99 FF 9F F9 FF  Ö)  ffτ f?Ö f•
0112(0070) F9 39 FF FF FF FF F3 3F F9 FF 99 39 CF 3F F3 FF  •9   ≤?• δ9┴?≤
                 0 out of    1 cluster(s) added to the file

   Cluster 19735 Sector 0000



   ┌─────┐  ┌─────┐  ┌─────┐  ┌─────┐  ┌─────┐  ┌─────┐  ┌─────┐
   │ ADD │  │SKIP │  │SAVE │  │SRCH │  │ SEL │  │EDIT │  │EXIT │
   └─────┘  └─────┘  └─────┘  └─────┘  └─────┘  └─────┘  └─────┘

 Home=Top of Clust  End=End of Clust  PgUp=Up 1/4 Sector  PgDn=Down 1/4 Sector
```

Fig. 15.10. Files can be created by manually selecting individual clusters.

Repairing Damaged Files

Binary files, such as spreadsheet and database files, have a highly structured
format. If part of a binary file is damaged or missing, then the program may
not be able to read the file. A binary file can be corrupted in a variety of
ways: the power might fail while a file is being saved to disk, a
memory-resident program might interfere during a file save, the file might
be partially recovered after being deleted, and so on. No matter how the
corruption occurs, however, the program cannot read a file even though 99
percent of the file's data is intact.

You can use many speciality programs to rebuild or repair damaged binary
files. Generally, these programs remove a small piece of data that does not
adhere to the normal file format, and rebuild the remaining data so that the
file can be read. In a spreadsheet, the program may remove data for some
cells; in a database file, the recovery program may remove a number of
damaged records. This slight or moderate damage, however, is certainly
preferable to the loss of an entire file.

To reconstruct the files, a repair program must have detailed information
about the binary file's specific format. In other words, the programs are
product-specific; a routine that recovers a spreadsheet file cannot recover a
word processing file. You can purchase file recovery programs for most of
the popular file formats, including files created by spreadsheet, database,
word processing, and graphics programs.

The following sections examine two popular data recovery programs. One
program, Rescue, specializes in recovering 1-2-3 spreadsheet files. The
other program, Mace Utilities, can recover dBase III database files. If you
use other programs, such as Excel or Paradox, you must use a different
recovery program. If you have a corrupted file, contact the program's
technical support staff; they may be able to recommend a file repair
program that works well with their files.

Repairing 1-2-3 Spreadsheets

If you need to recover damaged or lost 1-2-3 (WKS and WK1) or
Symphony (WRK and WR1) spreadsheet files, you can use the Rescue
utilities package (Intex Solutions, Inc.). The Rescue package's primary
program for repairing damaged spreadsheet files is called RESCUE.COM.

When you execute RESCUE, the program prompts you to enter the name of the file to be repaired. RESCUE then asks if the file is password protected; the program can recover spreadsheet files that have been encrypted with a password. You also can choose one of two modes of data recovery. Select the R (Regular) recovery option for normal data recovery. If the spreadsheet is severely corrupted, however, the S (Severe) option removes all non-data parts of the spreadsheet, such as global settings, in an attempt to recover only the spreadsheet data.

When RESCUE repairs a file, the program creates a new file, and prompts you to name the new file. With all the basic questions answered, the program begins the recovery process (see fig. 15.11).

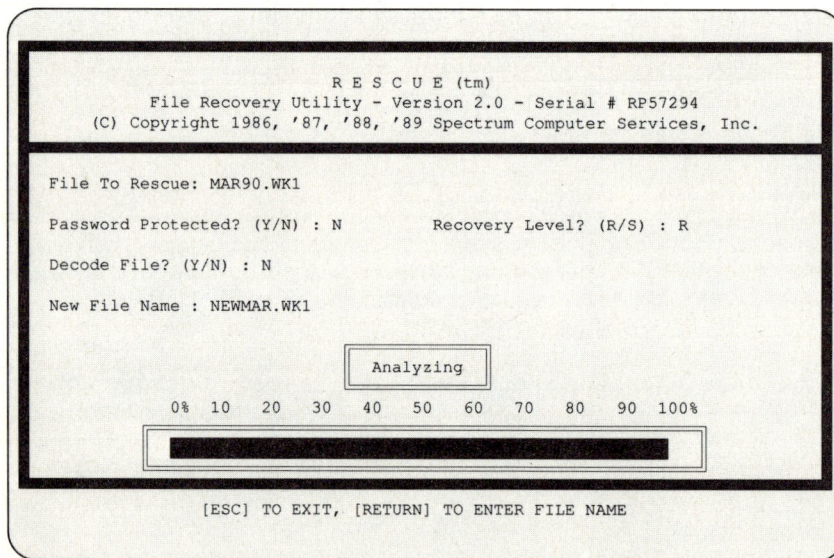

```
                       R E S C U E  (tm)
             File Recovery Utility - Version 2.0 - Serial # RP57294
          (C) Copyright 1986, '87, '88, '89 Spectrum Computer Services, Inc.


  File To Rescue: MAR90.WK1

  Password Protected? (Y/N) : N          Recovery Level? (R/S) : R

  Decode File? (Y/N) : N

  New File Name : NEWMAR.WK1


                        ┌─────────────┐
                        │  Analyzing  │
                        └─────────────┘

         0%  10   20   30   40   50   60   70   80   90  100%

              ████████████████████████████████████████


            [ESC] TO EXIT, [RETURN] TO ENTER FILE NAME
```

Fig. 15.11. RESCUE automatically recovers damaged spreadsheet files.

The Rescue package includes other helpful programs that you can use to undelete and create spreadsheets from unused clusters on the disk. These programs operate in much the same way as the general utilities described earlier in this chapter, with one significant exception.

The Rescue recovery programs search every cluster on the disk and can automatically identify clusters that contain spreadsheet data; you do not have to search clusters manually to find the data. The following spreadsheet recovery programs are included in the package:

ResQDisk This program searches all the unused clusters on the disk, and identifies all the clusters that contain spreadsheet data. ResQDisk then writes a detailed report to the printer. You can instruct the program to search for any clusters that contain spreadsheet data, or just for clusters with information stored at the start of a spreadsheet file. The program also can automatically undelete a recently deleted spreadsheet file.

ResQView This program presents a formatted display of the spreadsheet data stored in a specific cluster (see fig. 15.12). This capability enables you to review spreadsheet segments in an attempt to find all the missing pieces of a file.

ResQFile This is the program that actually reconstructs a spreadsheet from the cluster list generated by ResQDisk, and viewed by ResQView. The other programs are used to find the data, but ResQFile is used to build a working spreadsheet from the data.

ResQPass This utility retrieves spreadsheets that have been password protected, even if you have forgotten the password.

If you have ever corrupted an important spreadsheet, you can appreciate the value of a product like Rescue.

```
 Loc Rec Type    Lgth  Record Description/Contents      Drive C: Cluster  17004
 958 LABELFMT     1
 963 TITLES      16
 983 GRAPH      439
1426 LABEL       34     B1: ^March 1990 Income Statement
1464 FORMULA     27     C1: $7,325.30
                            @SUM(C8..C202)
1495 LABEL       28     B3: 'February Credit Cards
1527 BLANK        5     C3:
1536 LABEL       29     B4: 'Net March Direct Sales
1569 FORMULA     27     C4: $7,325.30
                            +C1-C3
1600 BLANK        5     C5:
1609 BLANK        5     C6:
1618 LABEL       11     A7: 'Date
1633 LABEL       11     B7: ^Name
1648 LABEL       14     C7: 'Amount
1666 LABEL       13     D7: 'Taxed?
1683 LABEL       14     A8: '3/16/90
1701 LABEL       15     B8: 'Rabobank
1720 NUMBER      13     C8: $64.95
1737 LABEL       14     A9: '3/16/90
1755 LABEL       18     B9: 'Hynes Shane
1777 NUMBER      13     C9: $54.95
 To View Use ↑↓ Home End   Commands: F1=Prev  F2=Next  F3=New Clust  Esc=Quit
```

Fig. 15.12. ResQView displays the spreadsheet information of any cluster.

Repairing dBase Files

The Mace Utilities package includes a program called DBFIX.EXE, which is designed specifically to repair damaged dBase files. The program also can find lost dBase data that is stored in unused clusters.

When you select the program's File Recovery option, DBFIX.EXE scans the specified drive and locates all the dBase files that have the DBF extension. You can scroll through this list of files and select a file to be validated and, if necessary, repaired. After you select a file, the program prompts you to select the type of operation you want to perform (see fig. 15.13).

One of the most critical elements of a dBase file is the file header located at the top of the file. The header provides dBase with the information it needs to read the rest of the file. One of the DBFIX options can check the file header; if the header is corrupted, the program steps you through a manual repair process.

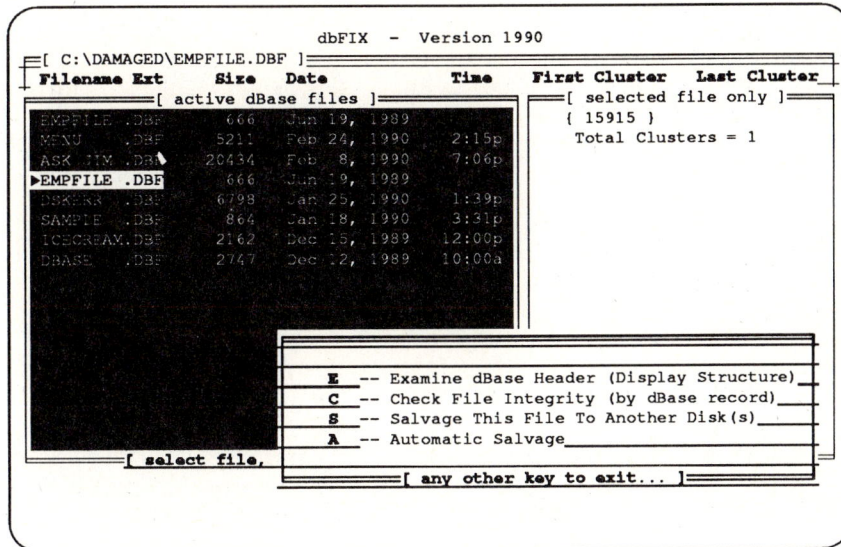

```
                        dbFIX  -   Version 1990
[ C:\DAMAGED\EMPFILE.DBF ]
 Filename Ext      Size   Date            Time    First Cluster   Last Cluster
            [ active dBase files ]                [ selected file only ]
  EMPFILE .DBF      666   Jun 19, 1989             { 15915 }
  MENU    .DBF     5211   Feb 24, 1990    2:15p       Total Clusters = 1
  ASK JIM .DBF    20434   Feb  8, 1990    7:06p
▶ EMPFILE .DBF      666   Jun 19, 1989
  DSKERR  .DBF     6798   Jan 25, 1990    1:39p
  SAMPLE  .DBF      864   Jan 18, 1990    3:31p
  ICECREAM.DBF     2162   Dec 15, 1989   12:00p
  DBASE   .DBF     2747   Dec 12, 1989   10:00a




                               E -- Examine dBase Header (Display Structure)
                               C -- Check File Integrity (by dBase record)
                               S -- Salvage This File To Another Disk(s)
                               A -- Automatic Salvage
  [ select file,
                              [ any other key to exit... ]
```

Fig. 15.13. DBFIX can validate and repair damaged dBase files.

The *salvage* option is the heart of the DBFIX program. This option attempts a record-by-record repair of the afflicted file, and writes the salvaged information to a new file on a separate (destination) disk. The salvage function first examines the file's header, and asks you to define a new header if the old one is corrupted. The program then reads the disk and recovers any records that match the header, and adds those records to the new file on the destination disk. If DBFIX finds a record that does not conform to the header, the program tries to adjust the record to make it acceptable. You can either accept, modify, or discard the adjusted record.

The DBFIX program also features an *automatic salvage* option, which functions just like the salvage option, but processes all records without prompting you for permission to continue, and automatically adjusts nonconforming (or damaged) records.

DBFIX does not repair database indexes. If a database file formerly had one or more indexes, you must go into dBase (or the program you use to manipulate dBase files) and re-index the file.

Undoing a Disk Format

Arguably, the FORMAT command is the single most destructive operating system command. As described earlier in this text, the FORMAT program prepares a new disk to receive data, and creates a boot record, a FAT, and a root directory. These bookkeeping files hold vital information about all the data files stored on the disk. If the disk already has been formatted and contains data files, a new format overwrites the existing FAT, boot record, and root directory. Therefore, if you format a hard disk that contains data files, you essentially destroy all the information about the files. The FORMAT command can wipe out an entire disk full of data in one swift operation.

You should take steps to avoid accidental hard disk formatting. See Chapter 14 for more information on the precautions you can take.

NOTE Most versions of the operating system command FORMAT only rebuild the FAT and the root directory, leaving the data area of the disk untouched. Special programs can help you recover from such *nondestructive* formats. Some versions of the FORMAT command, however, perform *destructive* formats that preclude data recovery, including all versions of COMPAQ DOS through V3.2, all versions of AT&T MS-DOS through V3.1, and some versions of Burroughs DOS. If you have one of these versions of the FORMAT command, you should consider replacing it with a third-party nondestructive equivalent. Chapter 14 explains how such third-party programs work.

Many data recovery programs include utilities that can attempt to rebuild the FAT and root directory after accidental formatting. As you can imagine, recovering every file on a hard disk is a mammoth task. The job is significantly simplified, however, if you frequently back up the FAT and root directory by using one of the snapshot programs discussed earlier in this chapter.

Without a backup copy of the FAT and root directory, the format recovery programs must reconstruct the disk from scratch. All the programs use the same basic technique to rebuild the disk's bookkeeping records. First, the programs scan each cluster of the hard disk for data that resembles a directory file. Once directory data is identified, a new directory file is created, and the salvaged data is assigned to the new file. The program continues searching until it has reconstructed all the directories. Because the program cannot ascertain the directories' original names, the replacement directories are given a temporary name that adheres to some simple naming convention, such as **DIR001**. The program then uses these newly created directory files to recover each file and subdirectory.

Format recovery programs generally attempt to recover individual files by using the same techniques employed for file undeletion, as described earlier in this chapter. If a disk was highly fragmented when it was formatted, the chances are slim that all the files will be successfully recovered.

A disk format destroys all the bookkeeping information about the root directory. But, by searching the disk's surface, a recovery program can recognize sectors that contain data that corresponds to a directory entry. The recovery programs use the directory data found on the disk to create level 1 directory entries. The original names of these directories cannot be ascertained, so the directories are assigned a name based on some simple naming convention; each recovery program uses its own method of naming the recovered level 1 directories. The recovery programs cannot recognize the other files that were originally stored in the root directory (such as AUTOEXEC.BAT), however, so these files cannot be recovered. After the recovery is complete, the new root directory contains only directory entries. Any files that originally were stored in the root directory must be recovered from backup, or reinstalled.

After you have unformatted the disk, you should run CHKDSK to make sure that the restored data has been logically reconstructed. You then can use a utility program to rename the new directories that were created during the recovery process.

Using The Norton Utilities' Format Recover Program

As mentioned previously, you can use The Norton Utilities' format recovery program, FR.EXE, to copy the FAT and root directory, and to recover from an accidental format. If the program locates the file FRECOVER.DAT, you can quickly reconstruct the disk. If the file is not found (because you didn't execute the **FR /SAVE** command to make a backup copy), FR.EXE searches the disk and recovers all the data it can.

You may be wondering why the FRECOVER.DAT file does not need to be saved to a floppy disk. The reason is that, even though this file's directory entry is erased when the disk is formatted, the file's data remains intact. When you execute FR to recover from a format, the program starts by searching the disk until it recognizes the FRECOVER.DAT file. The program then restores this file and uses its data to rebuild the other directory entries. Some special characters are saved at the head of the FRECOVER.DAT file to make it easy to identify.

When the recovery process is finished, the root directory contains a list of subdirectories named after the naming convention **DIRnnnn**. The first directory, therefore, is named DIR0000, the second is named DIR0001, and so on.

Using Mace Utilities' UNFORMAT Program

The Mace Utilities package includes the UNFORMAT.EXE format recovery program. UNFORMAT uses the sister program RXBAK.EXE (described earlier in this chapter) to maintain a copy of the FAT and root directory in the file named BACKUP.M_U.

When you execute UNFORMAT, the program searches for the file BACKUP.M_U. If the file is found, UNFORMAT can quickly recover the disk. If the file cannot be located, UNFORMAT rebuilds the FAT and root directory by scanning each cluster on the disk.

UNFORMAT recreates the main directories, and names them according to the naming convention **SUBnnn**. The first directory is named SUB000, the second is named SUB001, and so on.

Using PC Tools' REBUILD

The PC Tools program REBUILD.EXE can help you recover from an unintentional disk format. REBUILD searches the hard disk for files created by the sister program MIRROR (which was discussed earlier in this chapter), and uses this information to recover from the format.

If the MIRROR files are not found, or if you specify that these files are to be ignored (because they are out of date), REBUILD attempts to re-create the disk's root directory and FAT, based on the disk's contents. Like the other programs, REBUILD can at best recover directories; all other files in the root directory are lost.

REBUILD also can go through the motions of recovering from a format, without making any actual changes to the disk. By using the /TEST switch, you can run a "rehearsal" to verify that the recovery is possible and desirable. REBUILD sends a report of this dry run to the screen or a printer.

Recovering From a "Dead" Disk

If you ask a computer user to relate his worst experience, he might tell about the day one of the following messages appeared on-screen:

```
Bad or missing Command Interpreter

Disk boot failure

Error loading operating system

File allocation table bad

Non-System disk
```

Whatever the message, the problem is the same. The computer will not boot. Such a failure can be caused by a variety of situations, including the following:

- The hard disk has suffered a mechanical failure.

- The DOS partition table has been corrupted.

- The FAT, boot sector, or root directory has been corrupted.

- The wrong drive type has been specified in the Setup program.

- A bad device driver has been installed in the CONFIG.SYS file.

If any of these disasters strikes your system, boot the computer from a bootable floppy disk, and use one of the following utilities to solve the problem. All these utilities are easy to use. "Under the hood," however, they perform highly complex disk diagnoses and remedies.

Using Norton Disk Doctor

The Norton Disk Doctor is one of the most powerful programs in The Norton Utilities. The program automatically finds and corrects physical or logical errors on floppy or hard disks and checks the integrity of all copies of the FAT, the boot record, and the directory structure.

You can execute the Disk Doctor from the operating system command prompt, by issuing the command NDD. The NDD command takes the following syntax:

NDD *d: ... /QUICK /COMPLETE*

In this generic syntax, *d:* is the drive to be tested. The ellipses (...) mean that you can specify more than one.

The optional parameter */QUICK* instructs the program to omit the test for bad cylinders. The */COMPLETE* switch tells the program to search for bad cylinders.

You can run the Disk Doctor in either command-line mode or full-screen mode. If you execute the NDD command without any parameters, the program operates in full-screen mode. At the heart of the program is the Diagnose Disk option, which can identify and fix a variety of disk problems. This option can even make a disk bootable. When you select the Diagnose Disk option, the program automatically verifies the integrity of the disk (see fig. 15.14) and, if necessary, corrects any problems. You also can select the Common Solutions option from the Disk Doctor main menu. The Common Solutions sub-menu includes options that enable you to make a disk bootable, revive a defective diskette, and recover from the DOS RECOVER command.

> *A note from the author...* I recommend that you do <u>not</u> use the DOS RECOVER command. This operating system command can recover single files, entire directories, or the entire disk, when one or more sectors become defective. The program's main weakness, however, is that it moves all recovered files to the root directory, and renames them `filennnn.rec`, where `nnnn` is a sequential number starting with 0001. Should you use RECOVER to recover all the files in an entire directory or drive, you will have a real mess on your hands.
>
> Further, the files that were stored in bad sectors (that is, the files that actually needed recovering), will probably be unusable anyway. If you experience a problem caused by bad sectors, use one of the commercial data recovery programs rather than RECOVER. The Norton Utilities even provide a RECOVER "undo" facility, which restores files to their original names and directories, after the DOS RECOVER command has done its work!

```
┌──────────────────────────────────────────────────────────────────────┐
│                        ┤ Norton Disk Doctor ├                          │
│  ┌──────────────────────────────────────────────────────────────┐     │
│  │                                                                │     │
│  │              ┌───────────────────────────────────┐            │     │
│  │              │        Analyzing Drive C:         │            │     │
│  │              │                                   │            │     │
│  │              │ √ Analyzing DOS Boot Record       │            │     │
│  │              │ · Analyzing File Allocation Tables│            │     │
│  │              │   Analyzing Directory Structure   │            │     │
│  │              └───────────────────────────────────┘            │     │
│  │                                                                │     │
│  ├──────────────────────────────┬─────────────────────────────── ┤     │
│  │    Logical Characteristics   │   Physical Characteristics      │     │
│  │                              │                                 │     │
│  │     Drive Letter:  C:        │      Drive Number:  80h         │     │
│  │            Size:  82M        │            Heads:  6            │     │
│  │ Media Descriptor:  F8h       │        Cylinders:  831          │     │
│  │  Large Partition:  Yes       │ Sectors Per Track:  33          │     │
│  │        FAT Type:  16-bit     │     Starting Head:  1           │     │
│  │   Total Sectors:  164,505    │ Starting Cylinder:  0           │     │
│  │  Total Clusters:  20,538     │   Starting Sector:  1           │     │
│  │ Bytes Per Sector:  512       │       Ending Head:  5           │     │
│  │Sectors Per Cluster:  8       │   Ending Cylinder:  830         │     │
│  │   Number of FATs:  2         │     Ending Sector:  33          │     │
│  └──────────────────────────────┴─────────────────────────────── ┘     │
└──────────────────────────────────────────────────────────────────────┘
```

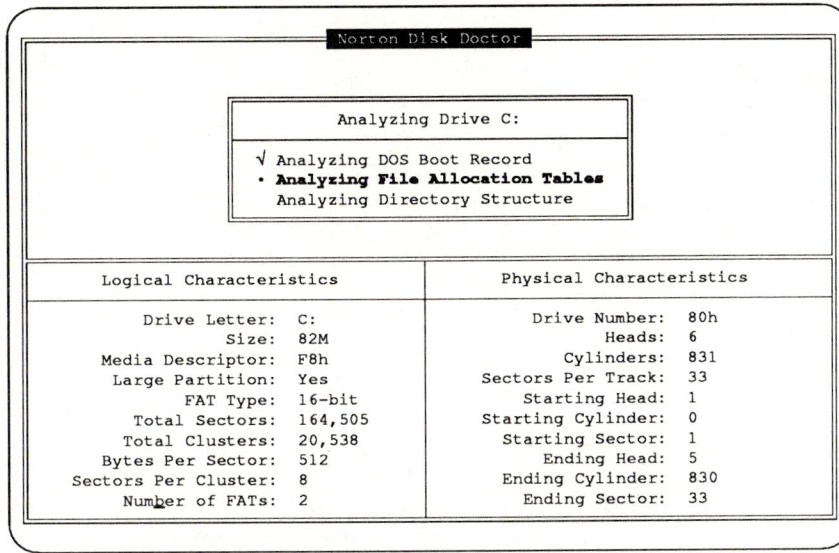

Fig. 15.14. The Diagnose Disk option verifies the integrity of the boot record, the FAT, and the directory structure.

Using Emergency Room

Emergency Room (ER.EXE) is the Mace Utilities program for rejuvenating a damaged disk. Like Disk Doctor, ER can diagnose and automatically fix problems with the boot record, FAT, and directory structure, and can make a disk bootable.

You can execute the Emergency Room program from the operating system command prompt, by issuing the command ER. The ER command takes the following syntax:

ER d: *mode_switch* /z /p

In this generic syntax, **d:** is the drive to be examined.

The *mode_switch* option is one of several switches that make the program more legible on non-standard displays.

The /z switch forces the program to replace the boot record, regardless of whether ER determines that the boot record is bad. Similarly, the /p switch forces the program to rebuild the partition table, even if ER determines that the partition table is bad.

Emergency Room has a special feature in that the program can undo any changes it made in the last session. Sometimes the cure may be worse than the illness; disk repair programs, in rare circumstances, can render a disk even less usable. You can use the Undo option to restore the disk to its previous state.

When you choose the Fix option, ER validates the partition table, boot record, FAT, and directory structure. The program corrects any problem it identifies. If ER encounters no problems, the program displays a summary of the disk diagnosis (see fig. 15.15).

```
- P A U L   M A C E ' S   E M E R G E N C Y   R O O M   v1990 -
   Copyright 1989, Fifth Generation Systems Inc.  All Rights Reserved
                  by Paul Mace and Bill Haynes

 System Recognizes 1 hard drive.        C: is formatted as follows:
                                            512 bytes per sector
 C: is volume #1 on hard drive #1,            8 sectors per cluster
    beginning  on cylinder #0,                1 sectors reserved for DOS
    and ending on cylinder #830.              2 copies of the FAT on disk
                                             81 sectors for each FAT
 There are                                  512 entries in ROOT directory
          2711 files                      20538 data clusters
           100 subdirectories                84 Mbytes capacity

                     No errors were found on drive C:.

                 ─[ Press any key to Continue ]─

 Analyzing: Directory Structure       Repairing:
 Current file:                        Current file:

 Current directory:
 C:\P\TURBO\TOT\TEMP\
```

Fig. 15.15. Emergency Room displays a summary of the disk diagnosis if no problems are encountered.

Using PC Tools' DISKFIX

DISKFIX is PC Tools' disk analysis and repair program. DISKFIX verifies a disk's integrity, and automatically tests the following seven areas of the hard disk (see fig. 15.16).

If DISKFIX encounters any problems during the disk analysis, the program prompts for permission to fix the problem. If any cluster errors are found during the media surface check, for example, DISKFIX reads as much of the cluster as possible, and transfers the data to a nondefective unused cluster. Any characters that cannot be recovered are replaced with dashes (-) in the newly written cluster.

Area	Description
DOS Boot Sector	DISKFIX checks for damage to the boot record, which is used during system start-up.
Media Descriptor	A special area of the FAT contains a media descriptor, which describes the type of installed drive. DISKFIX makes sure that the media descriptor and the actual disk type are the same.
FAT	Both FATs (the real FAT and the backup copy maintained by DOS) are analyzed to ensure they are readable and identical. FAT entries also are checked for logic; that is, DISKFIX ensures that no loops exist in any of the cluster chains.
Directories	All directories are checked for illegal filenames and file size errors.
Cross-linked Files	DISKFIX makes sure that no files are cross-linked; that is, that no two files share the same cluster.
Lost Clusters	The FAT is compared with the directory entries to ensure that no unused cluster is marked as "in use" in the FAT.
Media Surface	The program reads every cluster on the disk to guard against read errors.

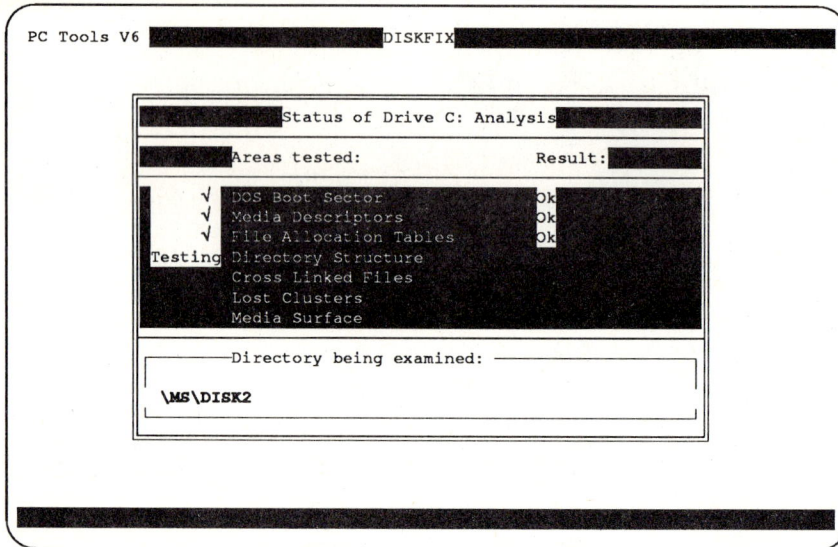

```
PC Tools V6                        DISKFIX

                    Status of Drive C: Analysis

               Areas tested:                    Result:

             √  DOS Boot Sector                   Ok
             √  Media Descriptors                 Ok
             √  File Allocation Tables            Ok
     Testing  Directory Structure
             Cross Linked Files
             Lost Clusters
             Media Surface

             ─Directory being examined: ─────────

     \MS\DISK2
```

Fig. 15.16. *DISKFIX analyzes seven areas of the hard disk.*

Editing a Disk Directly

A text editor provides a way of changing the contents of ASCII files. Some editors even enable you to edit binary files. Both The Norton Utilities and The Mace Utilities provide powerful editors that enable you to edit any byte on the hard disk, including files, directory entries, the FAT, the boot record, and the partition table.

Such tools permit microscopic alteration of data on the hard disk, and in the hands of experts, can be used to repair data on a disk that otherwise would be unusable. Remember, however, that the operating system maintains a detailed record of the data stored on a hard disk, and indiscriminate use of these editors can irreversibly corrupt the bookkeeping records. Sector-level editing should be performed only by an expert.

Summary

Even when adequate precautions are taken, hard disk disasters do occur. This chapter showed you how to use commercial disaster recovery programs to perform the following tasks:

- Maintain duplicate copies of the partition table, FAT, and root directory to assist in file and format recovery.

- Undelete files.

- Repair specific binary files, such as spreadsheets and databases.

- Recover from an accidental disk format.

- Revive a nonbootable or dead disk.

Of course, even the best error recovery programs are not foolproof. The simplest and best safeguard is to maintain frequent disk backups.

Chapter 16 shows you how to maintain the security of your disk-based data.

Securing Your Data

A great deal of valuable information is stored on personal computers. This information can range from harmless games to highly confidential and private information, such as details of credit cards, bank transactions, and personnel data. Whether you work in a large corporation or only use a computer at home for leisure, you need to be aware of data-security issues.

In this chapter you learn techniques for securing your disk-based data, including how to eradicate data so it cannot be "undeleted" and how to encrypt important files.

Understanding the Need for Security

As a rule, people tend to treat confidential information on a hard disk with less care than they treat the same information written down in black and white. For example, a confidential report is never left open on a desk at lunch time, and it is always stored in a locked file when it is not being used. But the same data in a word-processing file might be left for months (in its original form) on a hard disk.

Most people underestimate the value of the data stored on their computer. For example, an analyst's computer in a large corporation can include information about budgets, earnings forecasts, new ventures, return on investment, acquisition plans, and so on. Much of this information would be of great value to competitors. Similarly, a supervisor might store personnel information, such as an employee's performance-appraisal data, merit budget details, and other confidential information that should not be seen by subordinates. Even if you only use a PC at home, imagine what damage would be done if a thief could access your credit card information, bank account transactions, holiday plans, and the spare car key ID number.

It is all too easy to forget how much information a competent computer user can gather from a hard disk. In Chapter 15, you learned how deleted files can be undeleted and how data can be recovered from a formatted disk. Thus, even when data has been deleted, it is not truly secure.

The first stage in improving the security of your data is to be aware of the data that needs to be secured. Once you have an appreciation for the need for data security, you can take three main measures: physically secure the PC to prevent unauthorized access; store the data on removable media that can be locked away; or encrypt the data.

Bogus Security Techniques

Before you learn good security techniques, you should recognize that some crude security techniques are, at best, ineffective and will only give you a false sense of security. They are the electronic equivalent of hiding your life savings under the mattress. The main reason for discussing them is to make you aware of how ineffective they are and to encourage you to take more robust precautions.

Password-Protecting the AUTOEXEC.BAT File

Using some batch file tricks, it is possible to prompt the user for a password in an AUTOEXEC.BAT file. If the user does not enter the correct password, the batch file loops and prompts for the password again. This process repeats until the user enters the correct password. The problem with this technique is that the user can terminate the batch file by pressing Ctrl-C. Even if the display colors (using ANSI.SYS) are set to black-on-black, any competent user can set the colors to a visible combination, or call a file-management program that uses its own screen colors.

Excluding Programs from the Path and Menu

Programs are readily accessible when you add them to a menu system or add the program directory to the search path. Whereas these measures make the program easy to access, failing to do so does not protect the program from execution. For example, failing to add the item Bank Records to a menu does not prevent an intruder from searching all the directories and locating the \CHEKBOOK directory and from there executing the program. Remember that an experienced PC user can easily locate all the program and data files on a system.

Hiding Files

Every file has a set of attributes, which describe the properties of the file. You already know about the read-only and archive attributes. Another attribute indicates whether the file is hidden or not. A hidden file does not appear in a directory listing and is ignored by operating system commands, such as TYPE and COPY. A number of utilities are available that allow you to mark a file as hidden and subsequently to "unhide" the file so that it can be accessed by a program.

While these files are "invisible" to operating system commands, the majority of the file-management utilities discussed in Chapter 15 display hidden files and provide facilities to view and copy them. In fact, making a file hidden merely flags the file as being special and will probably draw the attention of an intruder.

Creating Hidden Directories

The ASCII character 255 is a valid, but non-displaying character. You may recall that this character is used with the ECHO batch subcommand to display a blank line from a batch file (see Chapter 9). This character also can be used to create a "hidden" directory. For example, if you type the command **MD**, hold down the Alt key and press the numbers 2 5 5 on the numeric keypad, and then press Enter, you create a directory with no name—it actually has the name ASCII 255, but it is not visible. To change to the directory, you have to use the CD command and specify Alt-255 as the directory name.

In the early days of PC hard disks, this little trick allowed you to create a directory that nobody could get to (nobody, that is, except somebody who knew how it was done). Now, all the file-management utilities are able to display such directories, and it is very easy to see the files contained in it. The days of Alt-255 providing adequate security are long gone.

Password-Protecting the System

Some systems, such as many COMPAQ models, have built-in security systems that include a power-on password facility as well as a keyboard password facility.

The power-on password requires you to enter a password each time the system is turned on. If the proper password is not entered, the system remains inoperative. You set the power-on password, using the SETUP facility, and it is operative until it is set to a new value or disabled.

The power-on password is automatically assigned to the keyboard password. The keyboard password allows you to lock or unlock the keyboard while the system is operating. For example, you may "lock" the keyboard temporarily while you go off to a meeting.

Many manufacturers of popular personal computers provide a power-on password facility, including IBM, AST, and COMPAQ. Most of these computers use similar password techniques. To illustrate their general approach, we will look at the COMPAQ's features.

With COMPAQ systems, the keyboard password program KP is located on the User Programs disk. The program should be copied to the hard disk to the C:\DOS directory. To lock the keyboard, enter the command **KP**. The program prompts for a password that will be used to unlock the keyboard (see fig. 16.1). If an intruder finds the keyboard "locked" and reboots the system, the power-on password will prevent further access.

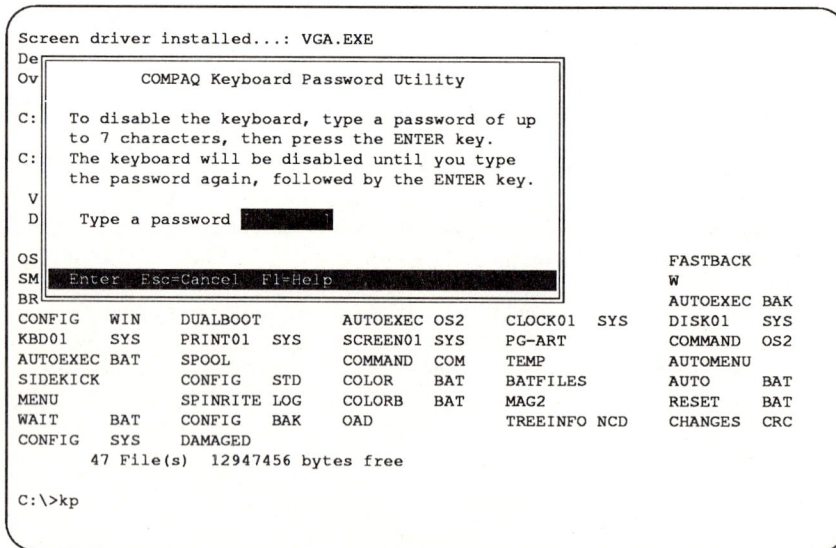

```
Screen driver installed...: VGA.EXE
De┌─────────────────────────────────────────────────┐
Ov│           COMPAQ Keyboard Password Utility        │
  │                                                   │
C:│   To disable the keyboard, type a password of up  │
  │   to 7 characters, then press the ENTER key.      │
C:│   The keyboard will be disabled until you type    │
  │   the password again, followed by the ENTER key.  │
V │                                                   │
D │      Type a password  ███████████                │
  │                                                   │
OS│                                                   │          FASTBACK
SM│   Enter  Esc=Cancel  F1=Help                      │          W
BR└─────────────────────────────────────────────────┘          AUTOEXEC BAK
CONFIG    WIN      DUALBOOT        AUTOEXEC OS2    CLOCK01  SYS   DISK01    SYS
KBD01     SYS      PRINT01  SYS    SCREEN01 SYS    PG-ART          COMMAND  OS2
AUTOEXEC BAT       SPOOL           COMMAND  COM    TEMP            AUTOMENU
SIDEKICK           CONFIG   STD    COLOR    BAT    BATFILES        AUTO      BAT
MENU               SPINRITE LOG    COLORB   BAT    MAG2            RESET     BAT
WAIT      BAT      CONFIG   BAK    OAD             TREEINFO NCD    CHANGES   CRC
CONFIG    SYS      DAMAGED
          47 File(s)   12947456 bytes free

C:\>kp
```

Fig. 16.1. COMPAQ systems include a keyboard-locking facility.

These built-in security facilities offer a modest form of data protection, but they are by no means fool-proof. Imagine that you forgot your password, and the computer manufacturer informs you that your $10,000 system has been rendered unusable!

To avoid such problems, a switch on the motherboard can be used to reset the password. This escape hatch provides a practical solution if you forget your password, but it also provides an intruder with a way of breaching the security. All the intruder has to do is remove the system unit's cover and trip the special switch. Your only solace is that at least you are aware that someone has modified the system password and has therefore been looking at your data. The fact that the intrusion is conspicuous may serve to discourage a casual intruder.

Built-in security features provide a reasonable level of security and should be habitually used, but if the data on the PC is highly confidential, other measures should also be taken. These include using computer locks, maintaining physical file security, obliterating data, and encrypting data.

Software/Hardware Computer Locks

Various third party software and hardware products are designed to password-protect the computer. They operate in a way similar to COMPAQ's built-in password protection scheme. However, most of these password-protection systems suffer from one of two problems:

- The software-only systems require the user to enter a password before the computer will boot. Often, however, the system can be breached by booting the PC from a floppy disk.

- Some sophisticated systems include a special card, which is installed in the motherboard of the computer. This card prevents booting from a floppy, but like the COMPAQ systems, there must be a way of circumventing the security if the password is forgotten. This might involve removing the special card or toggling a switch on the card. If you can override the security, so can an intruder.

Recently, some very secure hardware add-ons have been developed that provide a high degree of security. The data on the hard disk is stored in a special encoded form, which can be unscrambled only if the correct password is entered when the system is booted. A special disk controller performs the security coding/encoding. With such a security system, even if the hard disk is stolen, the data cannot be unscrambled without a password.

These special disk/controller combinations are not widely available at present and are mainly used by the government in situations where security is of paramount importance. With the increase in security awareness, we are likely to see these products more widely available in the next few years.

Physical File Security

One of the best forms of security is to lock the data away in a safe location. The computer itself may be located in a secure area, but relying on this security alone is still not advisable. How often would you leave confidential paper-based files open in such areas?

One of the best methods for ensuring data security is to store the information on removable media that can be locked away when it is not being used. The most readily available form of removable media is a floppy disk. If you have confidential memos, you can create and maintain them on a floppy disk. The floppy disk can be locked in a drawer, cabinet, or safe when it is not in use. As long as the floppy disk is secure, the information is secure.

The main drawback of keeping the data on a floppy disk is that system performance is slow if the computer is continually accessing a floppy disk, and there is a restrictive limit to the amount of data you can store on a single floppy disk. For example, you would not be able to store a large employee database on a single floppy disk.

If you keep confidential data on a floppy disk, there is the temptation to copy the data to the hard disk to improve performance. The normal practice would be to copy the updated file back to the floppy, and delete the file on the hard disk. But remember that a deleted file can be undeleted by an intruder. If you keep confidential data this way, be sure to "shred" the file on the hard disk after you transfer it to the floppy.

The ideal solution is to have a removable device for storing large volumes of data. A number of manufacturers sell removable disks, including Tandon and Plus Development. The Bernoulli Box from Iomega is excellent for storing confidential information. You can store 44M of data on a single 5 1/4-inch cartridge that is only 1/4 inch thick. (For more information on the Bernoulli box, see Chapter 3.)

If you keep regular data backups, the backups will most probably include confidential files. Be sure to treat the backups with as much caution as you do the main data. There is little point in keeping the master disks locked away if the backup disks are stored in your top drawer!

"Shredding" Hard Disk Data

In Chapter 15, you learned that files can be restored after they have been deleted, even after a disk has been formatted. While this capability is a valuable safety valve for recovering from accidental file deletion, it also provides an intruder with a loophole for accessing confidential data that you thought was deleted. A deleted file is not a secure file.

A number of utilities delete files and ensure that all the data is completely and irretrievably erased. When you deal with confidential files, you should always use one of these utilities. These programs delete a file in the normal manner, but they then overwrite every byte of the data in each sector the file formerly occupied. They are an electronic version of a paper shredder that actually destroys the file. Remember, however, that after you have shredded a file, there is no way a file-recovery program can bring it back.

As you can imagine, the U. S. government has a lot of confidential data in electronic form, and it issues guidelines and rules about how that data should be encrypted and erased. (Data encryption is discussed in the section "Encrypting Confidential Data Files.") All the good file-shredding programs can optionally use a government-endorsed procedure for erasing data. It is safe to assume that if you erase a file according to the government's guidelines, it is irrevocably erased. Both the Norton Utilities and the Mace Utilities optionally use file-shredding techniques that follow the Federal regulation DOD 5220.22-M for data erasure.

There are utilities to erase a file, overwrite all unused clusters of the disk, and even destructively format an entire disk so no files can be recovered. Both The Norton Utilities and the Mace Utilities provide such tools.

Using the Norton Utilities To Erase Data

The Norton Utilities includes two programs for erasing data: WIPEFILE and WIPEDISK.

WIPEFILE erases one or more files and uses the following syntax:

   WIPEFILE filename *switches*

where **filename** is the name of the file to be deleted. The filename may include a drive, path, and wild-card characters.

switches represents one or more of the following optional switches:

/Gn   Enforces government standards for data erasure. When the original data is overwritten, the replacement characters are combinations of zeros and ones. *n* specifies the number of times the 0/1 replacement pattern is repeated. If *n* is omitted, a default of 3 is used.

/LOG   Enables the logging of program output to the screen or printer.

/N   Deletes, but does not shred file (nonwiping mode).

/P   Pauses before each file is deleted to prompt for confirmation.

/Rn   Sets the number of times the data will be overwritten.

/S   Includes all files matching the file name in subdirectories below the specified (or default) path.

/Vn   Sets the value used to overwrite the data. *n* can be any number from 0 to 255. The default is 0 unless the /G switch also is invoked. If /G is in effect, the default for /V is 246.

WIPEFILE is a command-line program and can be run from the system prompt or from the Norton Integrator (see fig. 16.2).

Although WIPEFILE has seven optional switches, the program is very straightforward to use. In its default state (with no switches) the program functions just like the operating system command DEL. For example, to shred all the files in the current directory that have the extension PRV, enter the following command:

WIPEFILE *.PRV

If you use wild-card characters in the file name, using the /P switch to instruct the program to prompt before deleting any file is a good practice. Note that WIPEFILE automatically erases read-only, hidden, and system files that match the file name.

If you wanted to shred every file on the hard disk that has the extension CON, you would use the /S switch:

WIPEFILE *.CON /P /S

```
┌────────────────────────────────────────────────────────────────┐
│                              ▛▀▀The Norton Integrator▀▀▜           │
│                more...       ╚══════════════════════════╝          │
│  FR   Format Recover        WIPEFILE         WIPEFILE  filespec [switches] │
│  FS   File Size               Protect confidential data by wiping clear   │
│  LD   List Directories        (overwriting) selected files.               │
│  LP   Line Print                                                          │
│  NCC  Control Center        WIPEFILE *.ltr /P                             │
│  NCD  Norton CD               Wipe all *.ltr files in the current directory; │
│  NDD  Disk Doctor             pause for confirmation before wiping each one. │
│  NU   Norton Utility        WIPEFILE  B:\*.* /S/N                         │
│  QU   Quick UnErase           Erase (/N--No wipe) all files on the B: drive. │
│  SD   Speed Disk            WIPEFILE *.* /N                               │
│  SF   Safe Format             Erase all files, with prompting for each file. │
│  SI   System Information                                                  │
│  TM   Time Mark             Switches                                      │
│  TS   Text Search             /Gn  Follow certain government rules for wiping │
│  UD   UnRemove Directory      /LOG Format output for LOGing to printer or file│
│  VL   Volume Label            /N   Non-wiping mode; erase but do not wipe  │
│       WipeDisk                /P   Pause for wiping or deleting each file  │
│       WipeFile                /Rn  Repeat the wiping n times; default n=1  │
│       Quit NI                 /S   Wipe or delete files in subdirectories also│
│                               /Vn  Wipe Value; default n=0                │
│ ╔══════════════════════════════════════════════════════════════╗         │
│ ║:IPEFILE *.prv /P /R7                                          ║         │
│ ╚══════════════════════════════════════════════════════════════╝         │
│                                              ══ Press F1 for Help ══       │
└────────────────────────────────────────────────────────────────┘
```

Fig. 16.2. WIPEFILE can be run from the Norton Integrator.

The other data-erasing program in the Norton Utilities is WIPEDISK. This program can be used either to shred the entire disk or to shred the erased-file portion of the entire disk. The syntax of the WIPEDISK command is

WIPEDISK d: *switches*

where d: is the drive name of the disk to be shredded.

The optional switches include the same /Gn, /LOG, /Rn, /Vn switches used with WIPEFILE. Additionally, the /E switch specifies that only the unused portions of the data space (that is, the free clusters) is to be shredded.

When the WIPEDISK command is used with the /E option, all active data remains untouched; only free clusters are erased. This is the most common application of the program. It is important to realize that no deleted files can be subsequently recovered from a disk after it has been shredded, even if the /E option has been used. After all, erasing data permanently is the primary purpose for using WIPEDISK.

If the /E option is <u>not</u> specified, the entire disk is totally erased: the data files, the free clusters, all the system files, and the format data. To use the disk, you need to reformat it. WIPEDISK often is used in this way when a disk is being transferred to someone else.

Using the Mace Utilities' DESTROY

The Mace Utilities contains a single program, aptly named DESTROY, that can shred a file, a group of files, or the unused portions of a disk. The syntax of the DESTROY command is

> **DESTROY filename** *switches*

where **filename** is the name of the file to be deleted. The file name may include drive, path, and wild-card characters.

switches represents one or more of the following optional switches:

/A	Shreds files automatically, without prompting. By default, DESTROY prompts for confirmation before shredding a file.
/D	Includes all files matching the file name in subdirectories below the specified (or default) directory.
/E	Destroys all the data stored in the unused portion of a disk, leaving all other files intact.
/H	Destroys hidden files that match the file name.
/R	Destroys read-only files that match the file name.
/S	Destroys system files that match the file name.
/F	Uses the government-approved standards for data erasure.

DESTROY can be run from the command line or from the Mace Utilities command shell (see fig. 16.3).

```
  v1990                    Mace DESTROY                  12-15-89
 RUN   Drive   Path   Name   [Options]  Query
 DOD standard, Zap

    ┌─────────────────────────────┐
    │ Selecting:                  │
    │ [Options]   /F              │
    │                             │
    │                             │
    │                             │
    │                             │
    │                             │
    │ Required:                   │
    │ DESTROY Name                │
    └─────────────────────────────┘


 C:\U\MACE>DESTROY *.PRV /F

  Hilite:  ← →
  Accept:  ↵      F2:   Command line
  Escape:  ESC    HOME  Goto RUN
```

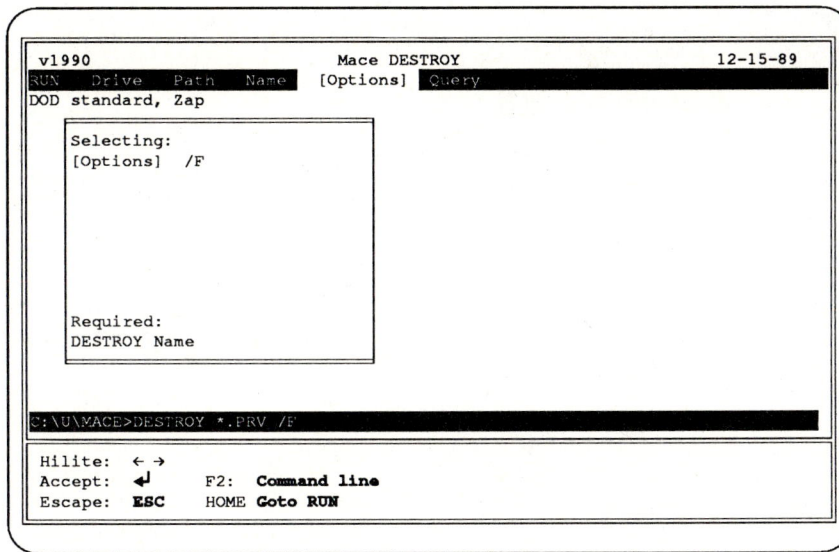

Fig. 16.3. DESTROY can be run from the MACE shell.

DESTROY does not automatically shred read-only, system, or hidden files; the necessary switch must be specified on the command line. If the /F option is used to use the government-approved algorithm, the data is overwritten seven times. As with Norton's WIPEDISK utility, a /E switch indicates that unused potions of the disk should be shredded. DESTROY does not include a switch to shred an entire disk.

Encrypting Confidential Data Files

One of the least disruptive and least expensive methods of securing important data files is to use a data-encryption program.

Cryptology is the study of how to code and scramble data so that it cannot be interpreted without the use of a code book or password key. When information is *encrypted*, it is scrambled; and when it is *decrypted*, it is translated back into its original state. The use of encryption for data-security purposes pre-dates computers by many centuries, and yet it is still one of the best forms of data security available.

The level of security afforded by encrypting data is wholly dependent upon the sophistication of the encryption algorithm—the formulae used to encrypt the information. With the introduction of high-powered computers, cryptanalysts have been able to break many data-encryption algorithms by experimenting with millions of tests to break the code.

In 1977, the National Bureau of Standards released a data-encryption standard referred to as *DES*. This standard provides a very detailed specification of how to encrypt data so that it is virtually impossible to decode. DES is the standard today. Many of the PC-based file-encryption programs optionally use a file-encryption technique that adheres to DES. All these programs require you to provide a special keycode or password, which is used to encrypt the file. The encryption program uses this keycode as part of the formula for encrypting the file. The only way the file can be decrypted is by providing the same keycode.

The degree of security provided by the file-encryption programs depends somewhat on the sensible selection of a keycode. If the keycode is obvious (such as your spouse's name), or if it is known by others, data security is significantly compromised. The same weakness is true of passwords used to access a mainframe system. The best technique is to choose a truly random selection of characters (not QWERTY!) that cannot be second-guessed.

Once you select it, don't forget the keycode—DES is designed to be foolproof, so your data can only be decrypted with the password.

When a file is encrypted, it is totally unintelligible and is therefore useless to an intruder. For example, the preceding paragraph appears like this after it has been encrypted:

```
%¬ëüÇr*LîLOM"**p|**%qv'^X^A\
≡H:YenπPqá^TG∞%1-oB|√ªτé*_n;^\
1%8Θ*Æ***5+19'îAY
ppe∩Σ!uFA^W^O*c#z**4εeτl*±Ev*
3!πaU*&≡ß%*,*3^GCΩê?5≡W2^A*
zClå*@í:"*)Iza6≡}^Q-*;^|σ*^[*^YΩ
;*qçO^T%*:F#xe*≥#*τNvé?G*/*ó>
*HNñ.*:*^G*tE*8g
[9¬ε$*dóº?"fF -me82J~*εt**c**[≥<
*^@Xv%q7,E^R ⌠FFδ*Op^_c*2$tfπ
*!ü}2*!ñ*Y-p$ú%8óP^@pz#å^XπU^
[σ*Zε*^T4'Q-y'*q*Ωy**yé**^Grv
%<5∩GM≡*G±*2-f**GñpA-∩é3$['：
$^G "^KA4*qëd[^Q*JÆw*;*?q***-
x$F:*>'*j*5vCX*5÷=σ*^G'üó3u4^
```

K"B$wT*5∞?Z*ê{*εH±ô**Pt
1/2x^T$
">EK$*F^*^E*qé'2*27n|M^],*v*qèv
*;Σ^L5
#*g*∩%ê$Ω(^W^^l^Tr*5<7.*h*^K7
Äm±
:?%whτ^Ls?p'ó2Θj*oê∞.1/2/U+j;#^
H**ü**αîμK*1 ⌠*1_≡&8-lq^H%ÆH
ä^K*∩*Fm<@7±p2=~N:]óMéZr~τ^
R{#q¿G*

✓
UTILITY

A number of shareware and public domain utilities can encrypt and decrypt files. Cipher, by Rex B. Ivie III, is a good example of a robust encryption utility.

Two popular commercial programs that provide good data-encryption facilities are SuperKey from Borland International and PC Tools from Central Point Software.

Using SuperKey

SuperKey is the ever-popular keyboard-enhancement program from Borland International. SuperKey is a multifeatured program that provides data-encryption facilities as well as cut-and-paste facilities, keyboard macros, a screen saver, and an editable DOS command stack.

SuperKey is a memory-resident program that must be installed into memory before the program's facilities can be accessed. There are two primary data-encryption programs: KEY and KEYDES. KEYDES is a special version of KEY that provides exactly the same facilities as KEY, except that the data-encryption algorithm adopts DES. KEY uses Borland's own encryption algorithm, which is not quite as secure as DES, but is considerably faster.

Whichever version of the program is installed, the operation is the same. The Alt-/ (forward slash) key combination displays SuperKey's main menu, which includes an encryption option. From the sub-menu, a file can be either encrypted or decrypted (see fig. 16.4).

```
┌──────────────────────────────────────────────────────────────────┐
│                                                                    │
│   Macros   Commands  Functions   Options   Defaults  Encryption Layout   Setup │
│                                                      ┌──────────────┐│
│                                              Encrypt file          ││
│                                              ┌───ENCRYPTION───┐     │
│                                            └─│ File:    CRYPT.TXT │  │
│                                              │ Keyword:    *****  │  │
│                                              │ Text mode? No      │  │
│                                              └────────────────────┘  │
│                                                                    │
│                                                                    │
│                                                                    │
│                                                                    │
│                                                                    │
│                                                                    │
│                                                                    │
│                                                                    │
│                                                                    │
└──────────────────────────────────────────────────────────────────┘
```

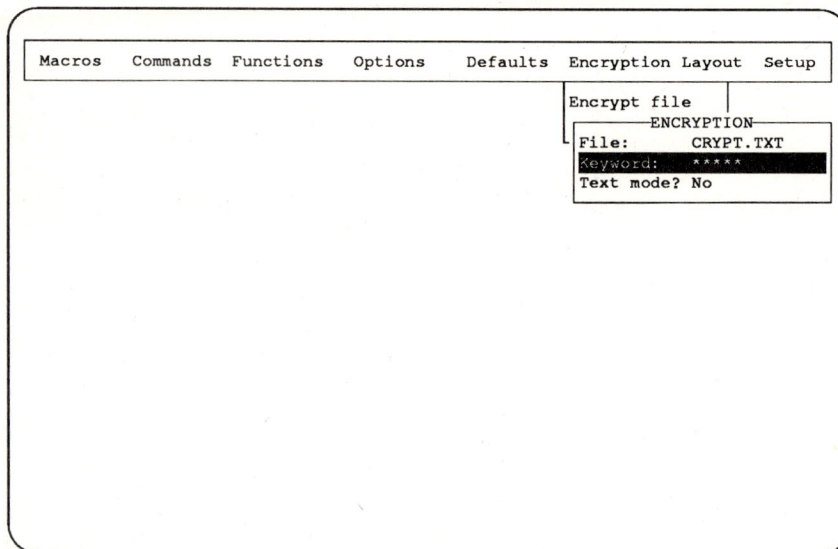

Fig. 16.4. The SuperKey menu includes an Encryption sub-menu.

SuperKey supports wild-card characters in the filename, allowing you to encrypt multiple files in one command, using the same keycode or password. Having selected the file(s), SuperKey prompts for a password and then prompts a second time for the password to ensure that you entered it correctly. The file is then encrypted or decrypted, as appropriate.

One additional option in SuperKey provides a way of forcing the encrypted file to be an ASCII text file. This feature is useful for modem communications when the communications program is capable of sending only text files. Note that files encrypted in text mode must also be decrypted in text mode.

Using PC SECURE

PC Tools from Central Point Software includes the excellent full-screen, menu-driven program PCSECURE.

PCSECURE is both a file-encryption and a file-compression program. The first time you execute PCSECURE, the program prompts for the input of a master password (see fig. 16.5). This password (or master key) can be used to decrypt files when you forget the individual file password. Note, however, that the master key *cannot* be used to decrypt a file encrypted with Expert Mode activated. Having entered the master password once, you are prompted by the program to enter it a second time to ensure that you didn't accidently press a key.

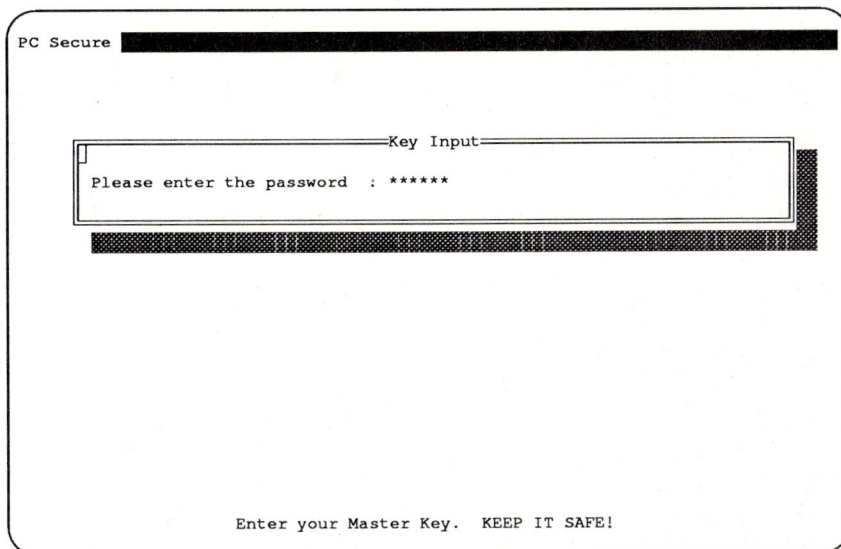

Fig. 16.5. PCSECURE first prompts for a master password.

You can use the Options menu to set the general operating parameters of PCSECURE (see fig. 16.6). PCSECURE provides two encryption methods: Quick Encryption and Full DES Encryption. Quick encryption (as you would imagine) is faster than DES encryption, but is not quite as secure from professional crytologists. An excellent feature of PCSECURE is its ability to compress, as well as encrypt a file. Not only is the file secured, it takes up much less disk space. In fact, an encrypted and compressed file may be only 40% of its original size.

The One Key option in the Options menu instructs PCSECURE to use the same key (or password) for every encryption and decryption operation during the session. PCSECURE can optionally hide the encrypted file and activate the read-only flag.

```
PC Secure  File   Options   Help (F1)                              4:22 p
                  √ Full DES Encryptio
                    Quick Encryption
                  √ Compression

                  √ One Key
                    Hidden
                    Read-Only
                  √ Delete Original File
                  √ Expert Mode

                    Save Preferences




                    Use Full DES for added security
```

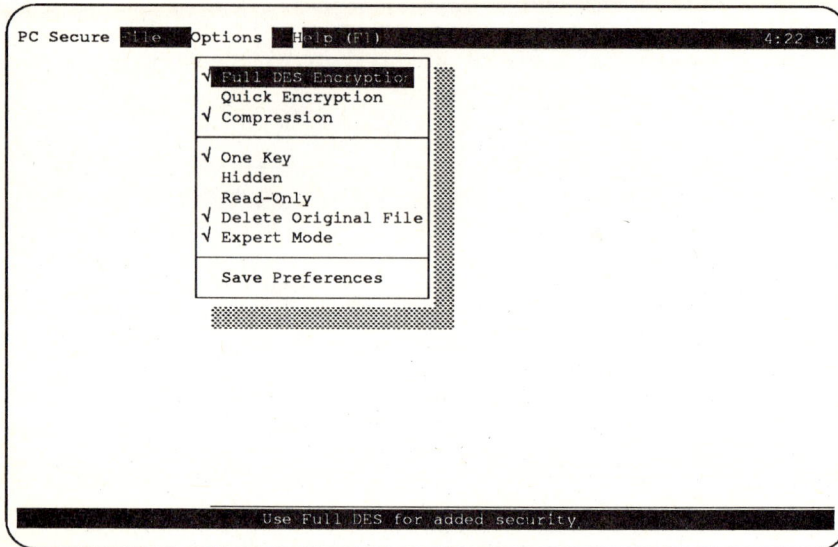

Fig. 16.6. The Options menu is used to select PCSECURE switches.

By default, PCSECURE erases the original file and replaces it with an encrypted file that has the same name. This facility is controlled with the Delete Original File option. If this option is turned off, PCSECURE creates another file using the same root name, but with an extension of SEC. The original file remains intact and is not encrypted.

If you are using PCSECURE to secure files, be sure that you have the Delete Original File option set on. You would normally select the Delete Original File option off only if the file were being encrypted to send a copy via modem or mail to another user.

The Expert Mode is used to suppress the option of decrypting the file using the master password. The Expert Mode should be enabled for very sensitive data: there is a chance that someone may know the master password and be able to decrypt the file. Be sure to remember the password, because there is no way to decrypt such a file without the password.

The File menu includes an option to encrypt files and another to decrypt files. When the Encrypt option is selected, PCSECURE displays a list of all the files in the default directory, as well as connected directories and other drives (see fig. 16.7). An individual file can be encrypted or, if a directory is highlighted, the option to encrypt all the files in the directory may be selected.

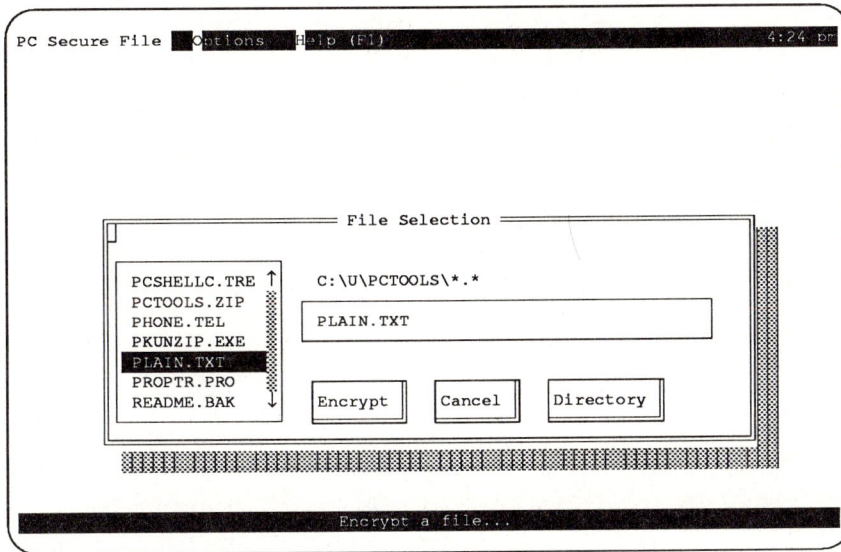

Fig. 16.7. PCSECURE displays a file list from which you can select the file to be encrypted.

Once you select a file or a directory, PCSECURE prompts you for the input of the encryption keycode or password. The key may consist of between 5 and 32 alphanumeric characters, or exactly 16 hexadecimal characters. The F9 key is used to switch into hexadecimal input. You enter the password a second time for verification; then PCSECURE begins the file encryption process, displaying a graphic depiction of the progress (see fig. 16.8). If an entire directory is selected instead of a file, PCSECURE prompts to see if you want to encrypt all the subdirectories as well.

The file and directory decryption process works in exactly the same way as the encryption option, except, of course, that the file is decrypted.

> **NOTE** The PCSECURE program that ships outside the United States does not include the encryption/decryption option. The USA and non-USA versions of PCSECURE are not compatible. You cannot decrypt with a non-USA version of secure a file encrypted with the USA version, and vice-versa.

```
PC Secure File  Options   Help (F1)                          4:24 p
```

```
╔══════════════════ Progress ══════════════════╗
║ Encrypting file : PLAIN.TXT                   ║
║                                               ║
║ ┌─────────────────────────────────────────┐  ║
║ │▓▓▓▓▓▓▓▓▓▓▓▓▓▓▓▓▓▓▓▓▓▓▓▓▓▓▓▓▓▓▓▓▓▓▓▓▓▓▓▓▓│  ║
║ └─────────────────────────────────────────┘  ║
║                                               ║
║ Reading 12 K out of 12 K total                ║
║                                               ║
║ Writing 6 K                                   ║
║                                               ║
║ *** Completed ***                             ║
║                                    ┌────────┐ ║
║                                    │  EXIT  │ ║
║                                    └────────┘ ║
╚═══════════════════════════════════════════════╝
```

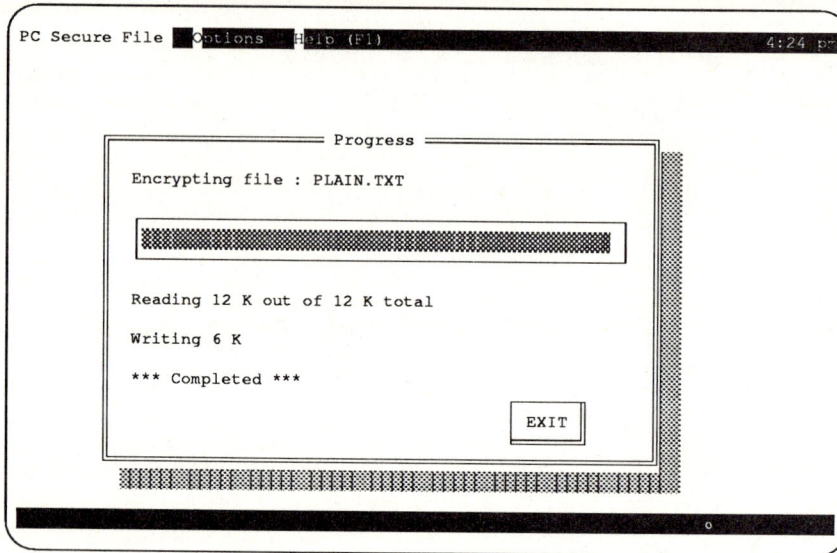

Fig. 16.8. The PCSECURE Options menu is used to select switches.

Password-Protecting Data Files

Over the past few years, more and more software developers have begun to provide customized data-encryption options in their programs. Popular spreadsheets, word processors, and database systems provide built-in file-encryption features.

The usual procedure is to encrypt a file by optionally specifying a password when the file is saved. This password is used as the data encryption key. In its encrypted form, the file is illegible, even if you use a binary file browser, such as the one provided with The Norton Utilities. When you try to retrieve the file, the program prompts you to enter the password. If you do not enter the correct password, the file will not load.

Database software programs often use a more sophisticated password-protection scheme, which can control user access to specific fields and records in the database. For example, one user may have full access; another may have access to the Name and Department fields, but not to the Salary field; and a third may be able to read the Name and Department fields, but not change them. Databases usually provide this additional degree of access control because they are often used in a multiuser environment where security is especially important.

Remember that these password schemes provide file encryption and decryption; they do not prevent anyone from using DOS commands to delete the file. Furthermore, while this form of data file encryption does afford some data security, it should not be relied upon for highly confidential or classified data. There are a number of utilities that you, or an intruder, can purchase that identify the password used to encrypt a file.

Three popular packages that provide built-in password protection are Lotus 1-2-3, WordPerfect, and Paradox from Borland International.

Password-Protecting 1-2-3 Worksheets

With the introduction of 1-2-3 Release 2, Lotus Development Corporation became one of the first major software companies to provide data-encryption facilities. You can protect a worksheet with a password, but not to DES standards.

The way to password-protect a worksheet is not obvious in 1-2-3. First, you select the /**F**ile **S**ave option. Then enter the name of the file to be saved, followed by a space and the letter "p." The program will prompt for a password. The password can be up to 15 characters long. As you enter the characters, 1-2-3 displays an asterisk for each character you type (to prevent anyone peeking over your shoulder from reading the password as you type it). The password is case-sensitive, so you must remember the exact combination of upper- and lowercase characters. 1-2-3 will prompt you to enter the password a second time—standard practice with password-protection schemes—to ensure that you know what you typed the first time. That is, that you didn't accidentally press a character.

Whenever you, or anyone else, tries to load the worksheet, 1-2-3 automatically prompts for the password. The only way to load the spreadsheet is to enter the correct password. You can, at a later stage, remove the password in the file-saving operation. When you save an already-protected file, 1-2-3 automatically displays the string `[PASSWORD PROTECTED]` after the filename. Before pressing Enter to save the file, press the Backspace key, and the password string will be deleted. Once the password has been deleted, you can use the file normally.

With the introduction of 1-2-3 Release 3, further password-protection facilities were added. In addition to the file passwords just described, the worksheet can be protected so that a user can access and read the spreadsheet, but certain data-changing commands are disabled. This process is referred to as *file sealing* and is activated from the /**F**ile **A**dmin **S**eal option. The worksheet is sealed with a password, and this prevents access to many of the major commands used to edit the file. File sealing restricts the user so that only data in unprotected cells can be modified. File sealing prevents users from modifying—accidentally or otherwise—formulas and macros and is ideal for worksheet templates where the integrity of the calculations must not be compromised. While password-protection of worksheets does afford some data security, it should not be relied upon for sensitive or classified data. There are a number of utilities that you, or an intruder, can purchase that will identify the password used to encrypt a file.

WordPerfect File Protection

WordPerfect provides file locking to password-protect documents. When a document is *locked*, no one can retrieve or print the file without knowing the password. When you lock a document, all files associated with it, such as backup files, move files, and virtual files, are all locked as well. Even the find facility, which searches multiple documents for a word or phrase, prompts you for the password before it searches a locked document file. A document is locked and unlocked from the Text In/Out menu (press Ctrl-F5), or from the File pull-down menu (see fig. 16.9).

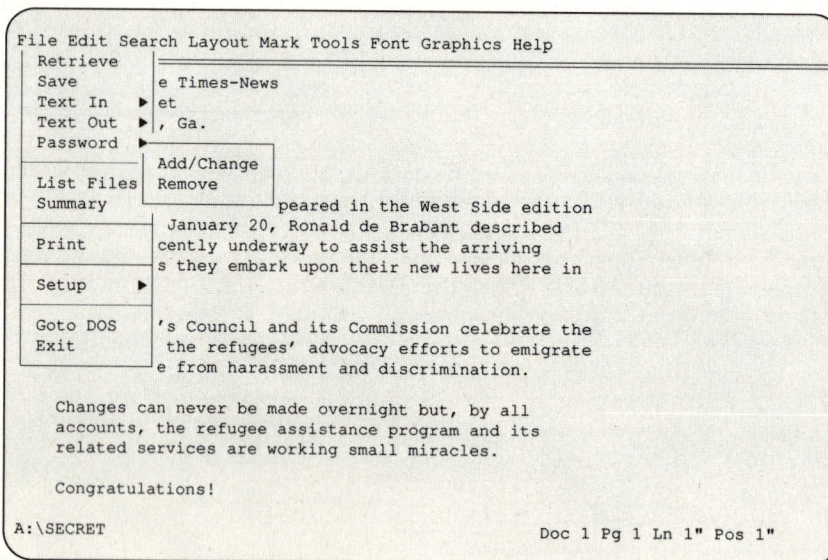

```
File Edit Search Layout Mark Tools Font Graphics Help
  Retrieve ┌──────────────────────────────────────────────────
  Save     │e Times-News
  Text In ▶│et
  Text Out▶│, Ga.
  Password▶│
           │  ┌────────────┐
  List Files│  │Add/Change  │
  Summary   │  │Remove      │peared in the West Side edition
           │  └────────────┘January 20, Ronald de Brabant described
  Print    │cently underway to assist the arriving
           │s they embark upon their new lives here in
  Setup   ▶│
           │
  Goto DOS │'s Council and its Commission celebrate the
  Exit     │ the refugees' advocacy efforts to emigrate
           │e from harassment and discrimination.

              Changes can never be made overnight but, by all
              accounts, the refugee assistance program and its
              related services are working small miracles.

              Congratulations!

A:\SECRET                              Doc 1 Pg 1 Ln 1" Pos 1"
```

Fig. 16.9. WordPerfect provides password protection for files.

The password can be up to 24 characters, and any of the standard or special compose characters are acceptable. You must enter the password twice for verification. The file can be unlocked by loading it and selecting Remove from the Text In/Out menu. The file must then be saved to disk to complete the unlocking.

Paradox Security Facilities

Paradox, Borland International's relational database, provides a sophisticated set of password-protection features. A table (database file) or a script (user program code) can be password-protected by selecting the [F10] Tools More Protect menu. This menu provides three options: *Password*, to encrypt a file; *ClearPasswords*, to reprotect passwords by erasing the passwords entered in the current session; and *Write-Protect*, to allow users to view, but not change, any data in the file.

```
Password  ClearPasswords  Write-protect                      Main
Set or remove passwords for a table or script.
SIGS══════════Sig name══════╦═CPE═╦════════Coordinator════════╦═HAL-PC id╦═Wo
     1 ║ ACT!               ║     ║ Don Boldman                ║          ║ 96
     2 ║ Accounting         ║  *  ║ Jim Harris                 ║    151   ║ 85
```

Fig. 16.10. Paradox's Protection menu from tables and scripts.

When you select Password, the system prompts you to select a file. You are then prompted to enter a password (twice) of up to 15 characters, including spaces. Once you enter the password, Paradox displays the Auxiliary Password form (see fig. 16.11). Assigning auxiliary passwords allows you to very specifically control access to the database, but it is entirely optional.

You can create as many auxiliary passwords as you need. Associated with each password is a set of access rules. When a password-protected table is opened with an auxiliary password, users will be able to access only those parts of the database you authorized in the Auxiliary Password form for that specific password. For example, with one password, a user may be able to view (but not modify) the database. And with a different password, a user may be able to add new records, but not delete or change existing records. You can even control whether a user will be able to modify or even see specific fields in the records.

To remove a password, select the password menu. When Paradox prompts for the password, enter the correct password, and Paradox will automatically prompt for the new password. To remove the password, just press Enter. Alternatively, you can enter a different password.

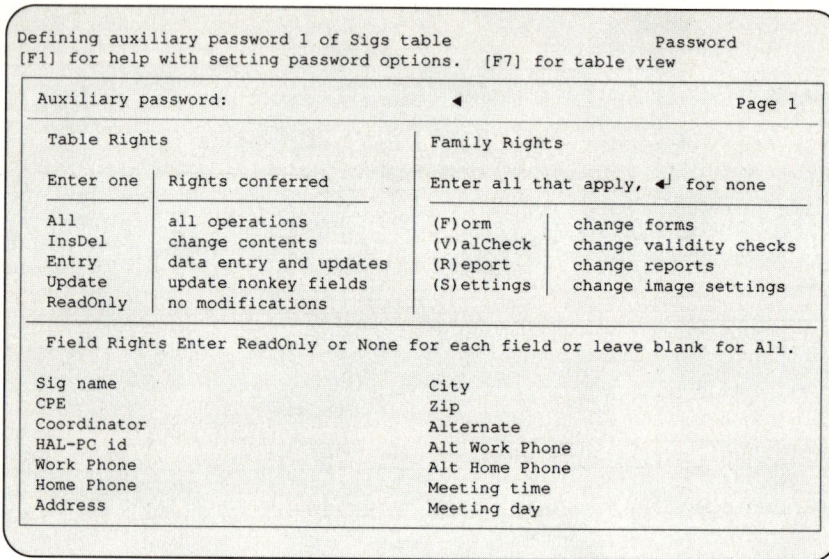

```
Defining auxiliary password 1 of Sigs table                    Password
[F1] for help with setting password options.   [F7] for table view

  Auxiliary password:                    ◄                    Page 1

    Table Rights                  │  Family Rights

    Enter one │ Rights conferred  │  Enter all that apply, ⏎ for none

    All       │ all operations    │  (F)orm      │ change forms
    InsDel    │ change contents   │  (V)alCheck  │ change validity checks
    Entry     │ data entry and updates │ (R)eport │ change reports
    Update    │ update nonkey fields │ (S)ettings │ change image settings
    ReadOnly  │ no modifications

    Field Rights Enter ReadOnly or None for each field or leave blank for All.

    Sig name                         City
    CPE                              Zip
    Coordinator                      Alternate
    HAL-PC id                        Alt Work Phone
    Work Phone                       Alt Home Phone
    Home Phone                       Meeting time
    Address                          Meeting day
```

Fig. 16.11. Auxiliary passwords provide specific control to the elements of the database.

Summary

Data security is an important issue, and most computers are storing files that should be secured. Try to avoid using simplistic security techniques that provide no real protection against an experienced intruder.

While PC hardware and software locks provide some degree of security, they can usually be breached by changing a dip switch or removing a special card from the PC.

The two best ways to secure data is to either store the files on removable media that can be locked away, or encrypt the files using a DES approved method. The secure encryption of data relies upon the selection of a random keycode or password that cannot be guessed and is not known by other people. Also, remember that the data backups must be treated with as much care as the original data.

A file can still be recovered even after it has been deleted. To ensure that deleted files are not recovered by an intruder, use an electronic file shredder that truly erases deleted files.

In Chapter 17, you learn about viruses: what they are, how to avoid them, and how to eradicate them if your system becomes infected.

Safeguarding against Viruses

It is possible to write computer programs that can perform destructive acts, such as erasing files, scrambling data, or destroying all the files on a disk. Obviously, none of us would want such a program!

These programs are designed to propagate undetected, spreading from one computer to another. After they have spread from one computer to connected computers, the programs often perform some destructive act. Such destructive programs have been present on mainframe computers since the 1960s, and with the increase in communication between PCs, the programs are now appearing in the personal computer world.

These programs, which use a number of different techniques to propagate, fall into three broad categories: worms, Trojan horses, and viruses.

Worms

A *worm* is a hostile program that spreads throughout a computer network. The predecessor to PC viruses, a worm exploits flaws in operating systems to propagate. Usually, worms are associated with mainframe and minicomputer systems, but they also may occur on personal computer networks.

A worm program tries to infiltrate a computer system and spread to other connected computers without being detected. One of the most widely publicized worm programs in computing history was unleashed on the Internet computer network in November 1988 by Robert Morris, Jr. (whose father is a computer-security expert). This worm, known as the Internet worm, exploited features (or flaws) in a UNIX electronic-mail system to propagate at frightening speed within many of the computers connected to the Internet network. In less than eight hours, the worm had infected more than 6,000 workstations across three networks, including the ARPAnet research network used by the Pentagon.

Fortunately, the intent of the worm was not directly malicious. That is, the worm contained no code to destroy files or data. It simply spread from computer to computer. However, the computer resources used by the worm to propagate brought the computer network to its knees—operations were taking 50 times longer than they should. In a much-publicized trial, Robert Morris, Jr., was found guilty of violating the Federal Computer Fraud and Abuse Act of 1986.

The responsibility for stopping worms and making operating systems foolproof lies with the staff of computer operations and with operating system developers. However, it is interesting to note that the Internet worm included 1,000 common passwords, and that twenty percent of the work stations were breached with one of those passwords! If you are connected to a PC network (or to a mini- or mainframe computer) you have a responsibility to use a random password. You may be interested to know that some of the most common passwords are PASSWORD, the logon ID, SECRET, and UNKNOWN.

Trojan Horses and Viruses

There has been extensive media coverage (and hype) regarding computer viruses. Viruses have been discussed on the front page of national newspapers and featured on national and local TV. Yet, despite the notoriety given to computer viruses, many people do not understand what they are and what problems they can cause. In this section, you learn what computer viruses are, what damage they can do, how they propagate, and how to eradicate them if your PC becomes *infected*.

When a program includes a sub-program designed to perform some hidden act, it is known as a *Trojan horse*. Often, but not always, the hidden purpose of the program is destructive. For example, a nondestructive Trojan Horse might display a political message or offensive text. A program which is destructive is referred to as *malignant*, and one that is non-destructive is *benign*.

One example of a malignant Trojan horse is a recreational game program, such as a chess game, that includes a hidden routine that deletes all the files in the root directory. (Don't assume, however, that all chess games are Trojan horses; they are not!) The destructive routine might be called as soon as the program is executed, or it might be triggered at a later date—for example, the third time the program is run, when you select a specific option in the program, or any time the program is run after 9 p.m., and so on.

A virus is a special form of Trojan horse. A computer virus is a program (with a hidden purpose) that can propagate and spread itself to other programs. These infected programs can then infect other programs; hence the term *virus*. The only way a computer virus can be activated, and therefore propagate, is through the execution of an infected program.

Some people would have you believe that computer viruses spread through air or are transmitted by radio waves. This is simply not true. A computer can only become infected if the virus program is transferred to the computer. The file can be transferred in a number of ways: it may be copied from a diskette, accessed when two computers are connected for file transfer, transferred from another computer on a local or wide-area network, or transferred via a modem. Many people assume, erroneously, that electronic bulletin boards are the only source of viruses. In fact, there have been instances of commercial shrink-wrapped (and popular) programs containing a virus.

Virus programs usually do not perform a destructive act immediately. Their objective is to infect other files and computers before being detected. The actual destructive aspect of the virus is usually triggered by some event. For example, the program may be activated when a program is executed on, or after, a specific date. The actual damage caused by a virus is dependent upon the particular strain of the virus. Damage can range from the corruption of a program to the complete erasure of a hard disk. Invariably, the damage is caused by the virus's writing information to the hard disk. This fact makes prevention possible, since programs can check for hard disk writes.

One of the first PC computer viruses that propagated worldwide was called the Pakistani Brain virus. Not surprisingly, this virus originated in Pakistan (in 1986) and is still evident on some computers. The virus does not destroy all the data on your disk, but it does corrupt the primary operating system file COMMAND.COM. It also marks as bad sectors on the drive, thereby destroying the data stored in the sector. The original virus was inserted into illegally copied versions of popular programs that were being sold on the black market. You will learn of some more recent and hostile PC virus programs in a later in this chapter.

Understanding why anyone would write malicious programs is difficult. One motivation appears to be the technical challenge of writing a program that can propagate undetected. Viruses are not simple to program (fortunately), and virus developers go to great technical lengths to write strains that are difficult to detect. Whatever the motivation, the act of writing a destructive virus is malicious and perpetrators may face heavy fines and even imprisonment.

The good news is that viruses are not spreading out of control; nor are they bringing the computer world to its knees. The fact is that more damage is caused by operator error, such as accidental deletion of files, than by computer viruses. However, destructive viruses are a reality, and you should consider preventative measures.

How Viruses Propagate

A computer virus program has two main elements: the part of the program that spreads the virus to other programs and the part that eventually is triggered and destroys data on the hard disk. When you execute a program, the operating system opens the program files (a file with an EXE or COM extension) and loads the program instructions into memory. Having loaded the program in memory, the operating system invokes the program, which you are then able to access. A virus works by modifying the (host) program, adding some extra code to the program file. When the infected program is executed, the virus code is also executed. Once executed, the virus can perform tasks and control the computer just like the host program. For example, it can create files, modify files, delete files and so on.

A virus spreads via executable program files. There is no point in a virus spreading itself to a data file, such as a spreadsheet or word-processor document, because the operating system provides no mechanism for the virus to propagate further or invoke file-destruction from a data file.

Viruses also may attach themselves to a special form of executable file referred to as an *overlay*. Overlay files include executable program code, but cannot be executed from the operating system prompt. They are executed by other (parent) programs. Overlays typically have a file extension beginning with the letter O, such as OVR and OVL. Files with the extensions BIN and SYS also include program instructions and can be infected by a virus.

When an infected program is executed, the program is loaded into memory as usual, along with the virus sub-program. Usually, the infected program operates normally, and you are unaware that the virus is active. When you terminate the program, the virus remains in memory. If you subsequently execute other programs, the virus attaches itself to the newly executed program file. The virus propagates only onto executable program files that are run after an infected program has been run.

Newly infected programs also function in an apparently normal way. If, during a later session, you execute a newly infected program, the virus remains in memory, ready to infect other programs that are subsequently executed. A virus may attach itself to a program multiple times—every time the program is executed.

Some of the early PC viruses attached themselves to the main operating system command processor, COMMAND.COM. Every time the computer is booted, COMMAND.COM is loaded into memory. Thus, a system with an infected COMMAND.COM command will always have the virus active in memory. Changes to COMMAND.COM are easy to identify, however, and most contemporary viruses avoid COMMAND.COM in order to remain inconspicuous.

The Damage Caused by Viruses

If a malignant virus goes undetected, some event will eventually trigger the virus program to perform a destructive act. By simply propagating, the virus may have already overwritten program code in the host program and thereby made the program unreliable, but this form of data loss is minor compared to the data destruction caused when the virus is triggered.

You may be wondering how a small piece of code can wreak havoc on a hard disk. The truth is that a small program can very easily destroy your partition table or scramble the file allocation table. Usually, viruses directly affect the hard disk's bookkeeping area in track 0. Virus software can even invoke the operating system commands to format the disk or erase all the files in a directory. One virus program, called AIDS, waits for ninety system reboots before formatting drive C.

The techniques used and the damage caused by these viruses varies from strain to strain, but all the malignant viruses cause significant data damage. There are over sixty known viruses, and each has been given a unique name: Pakistani Brain, Jerusalem-B, Dark Avenger, and so on.

How To Identify Viruses

Detecting a virus is possible because viruses propagate by attaching to program files. You would not normally identify this action, but once a virus attaches itself, the properties of the infected file change. Either the file will increase in size, or some of the code in the file will be overwritten by the program code of the virus. These subtle, but identifiable, changes are used to detect a virus.

> **NOTE** When a virus alters a program file, it normally does so without affecting the file's date and time entry in the directory. You cannot determine whether a file has been modified simply by looking at the date or time record.
>
> Making a file read-only or hidden does not protect it from a virus attack. A virus can alter the status of the file before attaching itself and then change the file attributes back again.

Logging Program Files

The most common evidence of an infected program is a modification of the size of a program file. Usually a virus only increases a file by a few thousand bytes. Over time, however, a file may be reinfected many times, and the size of the program can increase significantly.

Some virus-protection utilities scan a hard disk for all executable files (including overlays) and record information about the files in a special log file. The protection program can be executed later to see whether any of the executable files have been modified. If any files have changed, a virus may be active.

Not all file changes are caused by a virus, of course. Some programs are self-modifying; that is, they change themselves to reflect some change in program configuration. A program might modify itself to store new display colors selected by a user or to record a change in program defaults, such as the data-file directory. If you are in any doubt about the cause of a change in a program file, check with the manufacturer and/or run a virus-detection program to ascertain whether a virus is active. If multiple program files have changed, the chances are great that your hard disk has a virus infection.

Scanning Files for Patterns

Many virus programs have been identified and documented. Most of them add a specific sequence of data to a program file. These patterns are like fingerprints and are different for each virus. Some virus-protection utilities can scan all the program files to see whether any of the known data patterns are found in a file. If so, there is a high probability that the file is infected with a virus. The drawback to these programs is that they must be continually upgraded to search for new virus strains.

Unfortunately, some sophisticated virus programs now encrpyt themselves when they attach to a program and do not leave a detectable fingerprint.

Maintaining File Check Values

Some very inconspicuous viruses do not change the date and file stamp, do not increase the size of the file, and do not leave a detectable fingerprint. However, there is still a reliable technique that can identify a program infected with one of these elusive viruses.

Virus detection programs may use *check values* to monitor file changes. A check value is a single value derived by summing some source values mathematically. A simple check value on a file might be the sum of every byte value in a file. More sophisticated procedures use complex algorithms to derive a unique check value. By maintaining a list of program-file check values, a virus-protection utility program can determine whether the file has been modified in any way. If any data in the file changes, it is highly probable that the check-sum value also will change.

Anti-virus programs that use check-sum values to monitor changes to program files provide one of the most effective and fool-proof ways of determining whether a file has been infected.

Intercepting Suspicious Disk Writes

Some anti-virus programs run in memory and monitor disk activity. Any attempt to write data to the disk, without using the standard operating system facilities, is stopped, and a warning message is displayed. These programs identify both a virus trying to replicate and Trojan horse programs trying to perform destructive deletion on the hard disk.

You should be aware, though, that such programs also may intercept legitimate programs that are modifying disk data directly, including programs like CHKDSK /F and disk defragmenters.

Eradicating a Virus

If you identify or suspect that your system is infected by a virus, you should take immediate steps to fix the problem. These steps include rebooting the system, identifying the infected programs, and then either erasing the infected files or using special software to "cure" the infected files.

To prevent propagation of the virus, try to establish when and how your machine became infected. This determination can help warn others who may have become similarly infected. Document the files you think have become infected and also those programs you have executed recently.

Recall that viruses propagate by installing themselves in memory and attaching themselves to any program file executed. To ensure that you arrest any further propagation, turn off the computer and reboot from a _write-protected_ system disk. All floppy disks you subsequently use during the clean-up process should be write-protected. This stops the virus from infecting floppy disks.

The importance of this precaution is illustrated by the recent experience of a _Fortune 10_ company. The company identified a virus on a PC and used a program on an unprotected floppy disk to remove the virus. The same floppy disk was then used to check the other machines in the department. The virus had attached itself to the virus-checking program, and all the other machines checked with this disk became infected. This problem could have been avoided if the floppy disk had been write-protected.

Having booted from a protected floppy disk, do not execute any infected programs from the hard disk. If you are not sure which programs are infected, do not execute any program at all from the hard drive. If you have important data files on the hard disk, copy them to a floppy disk. (Remember that the floppy disk cannot be write-protected. If it is, you won't be able to copy the files to it.) Do not use a file-copy program located on the hard drive. If you boot from a floppy disk and avoid using all programs on the hard disk, the virus will remain dormant and will not further infect your computer—assuming that the programs you use on the floppy disk were not infected before you identified the virus problem.

The next stage consists of identifying the infected programs and eradicating the virus. One sure way to eradicate a virus is to format the entire disk, but this form of cure can be as bad as the illness, especially if you do not have a recent backup. You also can use a special virus cleanup program (see Appendix D for sources of anti-virus programs), or you can delete infected program files.

Virus cleanup programs try to remove the virus and restore the program file to its original state, but this is not always possible. If the file cannot be repaired, you should delete the file and reload a new copy from the original program disk. In the next section, we review software products that accomplish these tasks. A last-ditch remedy is to delete *all* the files (that is, reformat the hard disk) and start again.

If you eradicate a virus by reformatting the disk, you may be concerned about restoring data from a backup that also may be infected. Don't be. A virus cannot infect data files (non-program files), so you can use an infected backup to restore data files. But the program files should only be copied from the master program disks.

Viruses can be identified and eradicated successfully, but as a precaution, you should closely monitor the status of your computer for the next few weeks to ensure the virus was completely purged.

Using Virus-Protection and Eradication Utilities

The truth about viruses is that they do not make computers an endangered species. A far greater source of danger is operator error. Nonetheless, viruses are a constantly changing and evolving reality, and you may want to consider using one of the following programs to safeguard yourself.

Of the popular disk-utility programs reviewed in this book, only two include virus-detection tools: The Mace Utilities and Lotus Magellan. These programs use the check-sum value method of identifying when a program has become infected. They do not, however, provide any software to eradicate the virus once it has been spotted. McAfee Associates provide a number of virus eradication tools that both identify and remove viruses. All three products are discussed in the following section.

Using Mace Vaccine

Fifth Generation Systems markets the Mace Utilities as well as Mace Vaccine. Mace Vaccine is designed specifically to provide an early-warning system against viral attack. The Mace Vaccine programs are also bundled with the Mace Utilities, starting with version 1990. If you don't want to buy the Mace Utilities, you can purchase Mace Vaccine separately.

There are two anti-virus programs in the Mace Vaccine package: SURVEY and VACCINE.

The program SURVEY is used to maintain a detailed log of all the program files. To use SURVEY, you enter the command according to the following syntax:

SURVEY *d:*

where *d:* is an optional drive specifier.

SURVEY examines all files on the drive that have a BIN, COM, EXE, or OVL extension. Then it creates a special log file, HELP.CRC, in the root directory of the specified drive with information about all these program files.

The HELP.CRC file includes a list, by directory, of every program file name, together with the file size, date and time of last modification, and a special check-sum value that changes when any data in the file changes.

The following example is an extract from a HELP.CRC file:

```
C:\OS2\SYSTEM\
    DMPC.EXE          2798   Jul 25, 1989   12:00am   73e9
    HARDERR.EXE      15808   Jul 25, 1989   12:00am   f200
    SWAPPER.EXE       4660   Jul 25, 1989   12:00am   75f1
C:\MENUS\
    CONVERT.EXE      15472   Apr  4, 1989    8:33am   847f
    MAKEMENU.EXE     72752   Apr  7, 1989   10:29am   f833
    MEGAEDIT.EXE     28688   Apr  3, 1989    4:47pm   62f1
    EXEC.COM         18056   Jan 29, 1987    2:00pm   4684
    MEGAMENU.EXE     55200   Apr 11, 1989    7:53am   d0b3
```

```
    MEGAWIPE.COM     20356   Feb   4, 1988     1:20pm   44c2
C:\FASTBACK\
    FB.EXE          224160   Jan  25, 1990     9:32pm   3520
    FBCONFIG.EXE     65326   Jan  25, 1990     9:42pm    569
C:\WIN386\
    WIN200.BIN      230080   Feb   7, 1990     1:36pm   c1ce
    WIN200.OVL      257520   Feb   7, 1990     1:36pm   e2cf
    SPOOLER.EXE      14336   Mar  13, 1989    12:00am   d5ee
    WIN386.EXE       37404   Mar  13, 1989    12:00am   7f25
    CALC.EXE         28000   Mar  13, 1989    12:00am   96b7
    CALENDAR.EXE     38896   Mar  13, 1989    12:00am   2f0f
    CARDFILE.EXE     39264   Mar  13, 1989    12:00am   e76f
    CLIPBRD.EXE      10800   Mar  13, 1989    12:00am   18ff
```

If you use Mace Vaccine, you should re-execute the SURVEY program periodically. You should consider calling the SURVEY program from your AUTOEXEC.BAT file. Every program file is rechecked, and the values are compared with the original entries in the HELP.CRC file. SURVEY will warn you about any files that have changed (see fig. 17.1).

```
v1990                     MACE Survey                    12/15/89

  ┌─────────────────────────────────────────────────────────────┐
  │ OLDCURS.EXE      4816   Jan 28, 1990    2:44pm   dff8         │
  │C:\P\TURBO\MISCOOP\                                            │
  │ BEZIER.EXE      26368   Jan  3, 1990    4:30pm   18c1         │
  │ TESTFILE.EXE     7424   Jul 11, 1989    1:07am   61ea         │
  │C:\P\TURBO\CONOCO\                                             │
  │ PKUNZIP.EXE     22022   Oct  1, 1989    1:02am   392f         │
  │ BPT.EXE         49184   Dec 18, 1989   10:15am   aca3         │
  │ BPFULL.EXE     102048   Feb 24, 1990    2:22pm   71b6         │
  │ PSA.EXE         70512   May 16, 1989    5:04am   80f6         │
  │ BP.EXE         102048   Feb 24, 1990    2:22pm   71b6         │
  │C:\P\TURBO\TEDDY\                                              │
  │                                                               │
  │3-26-1990 9:29  PROGRAM FILE HAS BEEN CHANGED!                 │
  │FROM:                                                          │
  │ T2.EXE         42064 Mar 26, 1990  9:21am 4f3d                │
  │TO:                                                            │
  │ T2.EXE         42064  Mar 26, 1990    9:28am  dcc4            │
  │Press a key to continue.  [Esc to quit]                       │
  └─────────────────────────────────────────────────────────────┘

    -
```

Fig. 17.1. SURVEY identifies any changes in a program file.

All program-file changes are recorded in a separate file, CHANGES.CRC, in the root directory of the specified drive. All subsequent SURVEY updates are appended to this file, thereby providing a permanent record of all changes. If you want to start afresh using SURVEY, you have to copy the .CRC files to a floppy disk (for a permanent record), deleting them on the hard disk. The next time SURVEY is run, a new HELP.CRC file will be created.

Keep in mind that a change in a program file does not necessarily mean that a virus is active. Some self-modifying programs store user-changeable configuration information directly in the program file.

The sister program to SURVEY is VACCINE. VACCINE is a memory-resident program that monitors all disk activity and can identify any covert activity that may be a virus. The syntax of the VACCINE command is:

VACCINE *n*

or

VACCINE *ON/OFF*

where n is the number 1, 2 or 3, which instructs the program what level of protection to activate. If a level is not specified, level 1 is used.

Alternatively, the VACCINE program can be deactivated or re-activated using the *ON* or *OFF* switch. These switches do not remove VACCINE from memory.

VACCINE offers three levels of disk protection:

Level 1 interrupts any attempt to alter the master boot record and partition table of a disk and any direct (non-DOS) attempt to write to the system areas of a drive, including the FAT, root directory, COMMAND.COM, and the hidden system files. This level of protection is limited to the first hard disk in the computer.

Level 2 includes all the protection of Level 1 for every installed disk and additionally intercepts any attempt by a program to bypass DOS and write directly to any part of all the hard disks installed in the computer.

Level 3 retains all the Level 2 and Level 1 protection and, in addition, checks the program for alteration (by checking the HELP.CRC file) before executing the program (see fig. 17.2).

```
==============================[Mace VACCINE]===============================
 T2.EXE        is about to be executed. There is no survey file
 entry for this file, so there is no way to determine whether
 this program has been altered.
 Type Y to allow this operation, N to disallow it, or X to
 disable all protection.
=========================[Protection Level = 3]===========================
MENU          <DIR>        2-24-90    2:10p
INSPECT   OUT     11239    3-20-90    9:32a
OLDHELP   CRC     30207    3-26-90    9:27a
SPINRITE  LOG      3825    3-19-90    9:40a
COLORB    BAT        53    2-22-90    7:38a
MAG2          <DIR>        2-28-90   10:55a
RESET     BAT        43    2-22-90    7:03a
WAIT      BAT       197    2-22-90    8:00a
CONFIG    BAK       233    2-07-90    1:17p
OAD           <DIR>        3-10-90    8:48a
TREEINFO  NCD      1627    3-19-90    9:49a
HELP      CRC     19892    3-26-90    9:30a
CONFIG    SYS       111    2-07-90    1:30p
DAMAGED       <DIR>        3-15-90    4:34p
       49 File(s)  10276864 bytes free

C:\>\p\turbo\teddy\t2 autoexec.bat
```

Fig. 17.2. At Level 3, VACCINE checks all program files before they are executed.

SURVEY and VACCINE identify the presence of a virus and prevent any covert disk activity. These programs provide excellent protection against a virus, but they are of little value if your system has already become infected. In other words, if you discover you have a virus, rushing out and buying Mace Vaccine will not be of direct help. Mace Vaccine is designed as a preventative measure, not a cure.

Virus Detection with Lotus Magellan

Like Mace Vaccine, Lotus Magellan uses a check-sum value technique to identify when programs have become infected with a virus. The verify option (Ctrl-F7) is used to check for viral infection.

Magellan can check an individual file, a group of files, or all (program) files on your disk. When you select the verify option, Magellan computes a check-sum value (or signature) for the selected files (see fig. 17.3). If this is the first time the Verify option has been executed, Magellan will record the file details in a special log file, called MAGELLAN.CRC (see fig. 17.4). Whenever this file is subsequently verified, the newly computed check-sum value is compared to the value stored in the CRC file. Any differences may be the result of a virus, and Magellan will warn you.

As with Mace Vaccine, you should remember that not all file changes are the result of a virus. However, if an unexpected number of files are reported, you may have an infected system.

Using McAfee Associates Virus Products

John McAfee, of McAfee associates, has dedicated many man-months to the research of computer viruses and is recognized as a leading expert in the field. McAfee Associates distributes a number of well written programs that help identify and eradicate computer viruses. The software is available as shareware from many bulletin boards and shareware libraries and directly from the McAfee Associates' own bulletin board in California (see Appendix D for details).

The two main programs in the McAfee arsenal are SCAN and CLEAN. These programs are used to identify and eradicate viruses, respectively. The programs are frequently updated to combat the latest virus *strains*. At press time, these programs were up to version 62! The programs even include a self-check algorithm to ensure they have not been infected themselves.

SCAN is used to search a hard disk for viruses. Its syntax is

> **SCAN** *d: ... /M /D /A /E ext... /NOMEM /MANY*

where *d:...* is one or more drive specifiers.

/M instructs SCAN to scan memory for active viruses.

/D overwrites and destroys infected files.

/A scans all files, including data files.

/E ext ... specifies a list of up to three program-overlay file-name extensions that also should be searched, for example, /E .001 .002 .OVD.

/NOMEM causes SCAN to skip the memory scan.

/MANY scans multiple floppy disks if *d:* specifies a floppy drive.

```
_ Lotus Magellan      Use ↑↓ to select file, → to view           WAIT
  Explore: All files
  ANSI.SYS
  AUTOEXEC.BAT        ╤VPQRWU
  AUTOEXEC.OLD        IICC
  BUFFERS.COM         └╥
  COMMAND.COM         ╤PSQRVW
  CONFIG.OLD          *** (C) Copyright Compaq Computer Corporation 1987 ***
  CONFIG.STD
  CONFIG.SYS          ┌──────────────────────────────────┐
  CONFIG.WIN          │                                  │
  LOADHI.COM          │   Verifying SILVER.EXE.          │
  LOADHI.SYS          │   File 22 of 363.               │
  MOUSE.SYS           │                                  │
  MSMOUSE.COM         │   Press Ctrl-Break to stop.     │
  MSMOUSE.SYS         │                                  │
  NOEGA.COM           └──────────────────────────────────┘
  QEMM.COM
  QEMM.SYS
  RCD.SYS
  SMARTDRV.SYS
  TOEGA.COM
  File 1 of 2867      C:\ANSI.SYS              Text         1,709 Bytes
  F1      F2      F3      F4      F5      F6      F7      F8      F9      F10
  Help
```

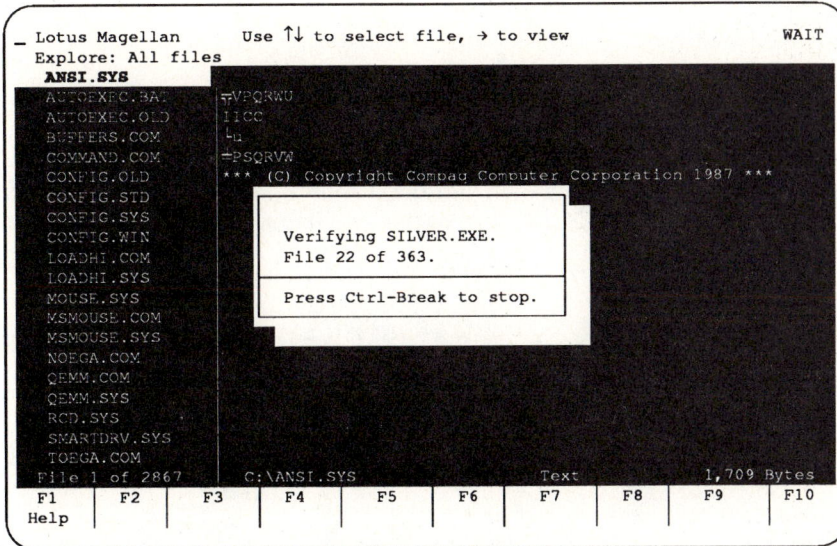

Fig. 17.3. Magellan computes check-sum values for each program file.

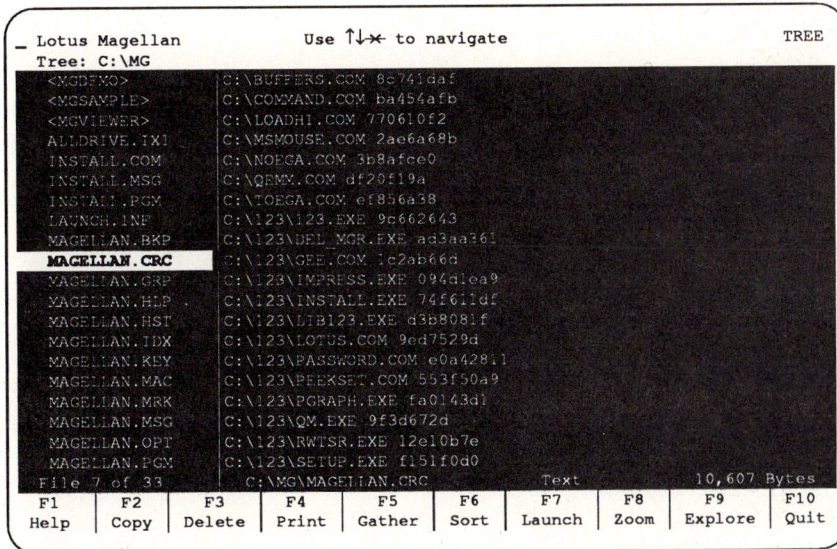

```
_ Lotus Magellan      Use ↑↓→ to navigate                        TREE
  Tree: C:\MG
  <MGDEMO>            C:\BUFFERS.COM 8c741daf
  <MGSAMPLE>          C:\COMMAND.COM ba454afb
  <MGVIEWER>          C:\LOADHI.COM 770610f2
  ALLDRIVE.IX1        C:\MSMOUSE.COM 2ae6a68b
  INSTALL.COM         C:\NOEGA.COM 3b8afce0
  INSTALL.MSG         C:\QEMM.COM df20f19a
  INSTALL.PGM         C:\TOEGA.COM ef856a38
  LAUNCH.INF          C:\123\123.EXE 9c662643
  MAGELLAN.BKP        C:\123\DEL_MGR.EXE ad3aa361
  MAGELLAN.CRC        C:\123\GEE.COM 1c2ab66d
  MAGELLAN.GRP        C:\123\IMPRESS.EXE 094d1ea9
  MAGELLAN.HLP        C:\123\INSTALL.EXE 74f611df
  MAGELLAN.HST        C:\123\LTB123.EXE d3b8081f
  MAGELLAN.IDX        C:\123\LOTUS.COM 9ed7529d
  MAGELLAN.KEY        C:\123\PASSWORD.COM e0a42811
  MAGELLAN.MAC        C:\123\PEEKSET.COM 553f50a9
  MAGELLAN.MRK        C:\123\PGRAPH.EXE fa0143d1
  MAGELLAN.MSG        C:\123\QM.EXE 9f3d672d
  MAGELLAN.OPT        C:\123\RWTSR.EXE 12e10b7e
  MAGELLAN.PGM        C:\123\SETUP.EXE f151f0d0
  File 7 of 33        C:\MG\MAGELLAN.CRC        Text      10,607 Bytes
  F1      F2      F3      F4      F5      F6      F7      F8      F9      F10
  Help    Copy    Delete  Print   Gather  Sort    Launch  Zoom    Explore Quit
```

Fig. 17.4. The program details are recorded in the file MAGELLAN.CRC.

To scan the entire hard disk for a virus, you would enter the following command:

SCAN C: /M /A

The program then searches all files on drive C and looks for the special fingerprints of the known viruses. The amount of time taken to scan the disk depends on the size of the disk and the type of computer. It may take from 5 to 30 minutes. SCAN displays each file's name as it is being checked and reports any viruses found (see fig. 17.5).

```
SCAN 3.1V59
Copyright 1989-90 by McAfee Associates.
(408) 988-3832
Scanning for known viruses.
Scanning C:\CKMATE\CM.COM
    Found Jerusalem Virus version B [Jeru]
Scanning C:\DOME90\DOME.EXE
    Found Jerusalem Virus version B [Jeru]
Scanning C:\LOTUS\IMPRESS.EXE
    Found Jerusalem Virus version B [Jeru]
Scanning C:\LOTUS\123.EXE
    Found Jerusalem Virus version B [Jeru]
Scanning C:\LOTUS\LIB123.EXE
    Found Jerusalem Virus version B [Jeru]
Scanning C:\LOTUS\GEE.COM
    Found Jerusalem Virus version B [Jeru]
Scanning C:\LOTUS\IMPRESS\IFL.EXE
    Found Jerusalem Virus version B [Jeru]
Scanning C:\NC\NCMAIN.EXE
    Found Jerusalem Virus version B [Jeru]
Scanning C:\NC\WPVIEW.EXE
    Found Jerusalem Virus version B [Jeru]

Disk C: contains 75 directories and 3400
files

Found 9 files containing viruses.
```

Fig. 17.5. SCAN checks every file and reports any confirmed viruses.

The infected files could be automatically destroyed by specifying the /D parameter when SCAN is executed. However, the program CLEAN might be able to eradicate the virus and restore the file to its original state. The syntax of the CLEAN command is as follows:

CLEAN *d:.. [virusname] /A /MANY*

where *d:...* is one or more drive specifiers.

[virusname] is the name of the virus identified by SCAN.

/A scans all files, including data files.

/MANY scans multiple floppies if *d:* specifies a floppy disk drive.

Part of the output from SCAN is the code name of the specific virus that has been identified, for example, [Jeru]. The same virus code name is specified as a parameter for CLEAN. For example, the command to eradicate a virus from the hard disk shown in fig. 17.5 is

CLEAN C: [JERU] /A

CLEAN will search each file for the specified virus. When an infected file is found, the virus is removed and CLEAN tries to rebuild the file to its original state. Fig. 17.6 illustrates the output from the preceding CLEAN command.

```
Scanning C:\NC\NCMAIN.EXE
  Found Jerusalem Virus version B [Jeru]
Scanning C:\NC\NCMAIN.EXE
  Found Jerusalem Virus version B [Jeru]
  Virus removed.
Scanning C:\NC\WPVIEW.EXE
  Found Jerusalem Virus version B [Jeru]
Scanning C:\NC\WPVIEW.EXE
  Found Jerusalem Virus version B [Jeru]
  Virus removed.

Disk C: contains 75 directories and 3430
files

Found 9 files containing viruses.
32 viruses were removed.
```

Fig. 17.6. CLEAN checks every file for a specific virus and tries to repair the file.

A file may be infected multiple times, and CLEAN will remove each layer of the virus. In the preceding example, only 9 files were infected, but there were 32 infections, because some files included multiple copies of the virus. In cases where CLEAN cannot restore a program to its original state, the program will be unusable, but the virus will be removed. If this occurs, you will need to erase the program and reinstall it from the master disks. Even if the file is not usable, you still have peace of mind knowing that the virus has been removed.

Summary

Operator error remains the most frequent cause of data loss. But viruses do occur and they can be very destructive. There are two main elements to a virus: propagation and destruction. Viruses propagate by installing themselves into memory when an infected program is run, and surreptitiously modifying any other program files that are subsequently executed.

Some event will trigger a virus to perform some (usually destructive) act, such as erasing files, or damaging the FAT. Viruses can be identified by monitoring program size and computing check-sum values for program files. If a virus is identified, it normally can be eradicated through the use of specialist software.

A note from the author. . . A hard disk is like a car engine in one respect: to get the most from your PC, you must keep the disk well-tuned and efficient. After all, it is where your programs and data are stored. The goal of this book has been to provide you with as much information as you need to make your disk a safe and easy-to-drive sports car!

Remember that the key to efficient hard disk usage is to have a simple and easy-to-use directory hierarchy. Don't forget that you can leverage your investment in the hard disk by buying disk-performance utilities, such as defragmenters and disk caches. They really do work.

And now that you have mastered disk management, you can concentrate on using your applications software. Isn't that what you bought the PC for anyway? And don't forget to make data backups!

Appendix A

Operating System Command Reference

APPEND
V4—External

The APPEND command instructs the operating system where to look for data files not found in the current directory. APPEND is especially useful on hard disks when data files are likely to be situated in many different subdirectories. APPEND is similar to the PATH command, which is used for program files.

SYNTAX

    *dc:pathc***APPEND** */X /E d1:path1;d1:path2;d2:path1;...*

DOS V4 additional switches:

    *dc:pathc***APPEND** */X:on /X:off /PATH:on /PATH:off*

dc:pathc are the disk drive and directory that hold the command.

d1:path1, d1:path2, d2:path1 are valid disk drive names and paths to the directories you want DOS to search for nonprogram or nonbatch files. The three periods (...) represent additional disk drive and path names.

SWITCHES

/X	Redirects programs that use the DOS function calls SEARCH FIRST, FIND FIRST, and EXEC.
/X:ON	Same as /X (DOS V4 only).
/X:OFF	Turns this feature off (DOS V4 only).
/E	Places the disk drive paths in the environment.
/PATH:ON	Turns on the search for files that have a drive or path specified (DOS V4 only).
/PATH:OFF	Turns off search for files that have drive or path specified (DOS V4 only).

NOTES

The first time you execute APPEND, the program loads from the disk and installs itself in DOS. APPEND then becomes an internal command and is not reloaded from the disk until you restart DOS. You can give the /X and /E switches only when you first invoke APPEND. You cannot give any path names with these two switches.

If an invalid path is encountered, such as a misspelled path or one that no longer exists, DOS skips the path and does not display a message.

Do not use APPEND with RESTORE. The RESTORE command searches for files in the directories on which you have used APPEND. If you use the /N or /M switch with RESTORE, the correct files may not be processed. Before you use RESTORE, be sure that you have deactivated APPEND.

EXAMPLES

APPEND is the complement of PATH. Whereas PATH searches for program and batch files, APPEND searches for all other files. Before using APPEND to set search paths, use the following form:

```
APPEND /E /X
```

After you run APPEND with the switches, you can tell APPEND the directories to search. For example, to search the directories C:\DOS and C:\DOS\UTILS, use the following form:

APPEND C:\DOS;C:\DOS\UTILS

To disable the APPEND command, use this form:

APPEND;

ASSIGN
V2, V3, V4—External

ASSIGN can be used to trick programs that normally look for files on a floppy drive to look on a hard disk instead. For example, if the program looks specifically on drive B for data files, you can assign the hard disk (drive C) to drive B. When the program thinks it is looking at drive B, it is really looking at the hard disk.

SYNTAX

To reroute drive activity, use the following form:

*dc:pathc***ASSIGN d1=d2 ...**

dc:pathc are the disk drive and directory that hold the command.

d1 is the letter of the disk drive the program or DOS normally uses.

d2 is the letter of the disk drive that you want the program or DOS to use instead of the usual drive.

The three periods (...) represent additional disk drive assignments.

NOTES

ASSIGN reroutes a program, causing it to use a disk drive that is different from the one the program intends. A program "thinks" that it is using a certain disk drive when, in fact, the program is using another. You should use ASSIGN primarily for programs that were written to work only with drives A: and B:, but you want to load and run from your hard disk.

Do not use a colon after the disk drive letter for d1 or d2. You can use a space on either side of the equal sign.

You can give more than one assignment on the same line. Use a space between each set of assignments, as in the following example:

    ASSIGN B=C A=C

EXAMPLES

To assign all activity for drive A: to drive C:, use the following form:

    ASSIGN A = C or ASSIGN A=C

To clear any previous drive reassignments, type only the command:

    ASSIGN

ATTRIB
V3, V4—External

This command is used to view and change a file's attributes. Setting the read-only attribute provides a useful security precaution for hard disk users.

SYNTAX

    *dc:pathc***ATTRIB** +R -R +A -A *d:path***filename.ext**

dc:pathc are the disk drive and directory that hold the command.

+R sets a file's read-only attribute on.

+A sets a file's archive attribute on.

-R sets a file's read-only attribute off.

-A sets a file's archive attribute off.

d:path are the disk drive and directory holding the files for which the attribute will be displayed or changed.

filename.ext is the name of the file(s) for which the read-only attribute will be displayed or changed. Wild-card characters are permitted.

SWITCH

/S   Sets or clears the attributes of the specified files in the specified directory and all subdirectories to that directory.

NOTES

With the DOS V3 addition of ATTRIB, users have more control over the DOS read-only and archive file attributes. ATTRIB sets or clears these attributes. When the file is marked as read-only, it cannot be altered or deleted. When the archive attribute is on, the file can be processed by using the commands BACKUP /M, XCOPY /M, or XCOPY /A.

EXAMPLES

Use the following to set the read-only and archive attributes for the file MEMO.TXT on:

    ATTRIB +R +A MEMO.TXT

To turn off the read-only attribute of MEMO.TXT, type:

    ATTRIB -R MEMO.TXT

To see the read-only and archive attributes for MEMO.TXT, type:

    ATTRIB MEMO.TXT

BACKUP
V2, V3, V4—External

If you have a hard disk, you should back up your files regularly. BACKUP backs up one or more files from a hard disk or floppy disk onto another disk.

SYNTAX

*dc:pathc***BACKUP** *d1:path\\filename.ext* **d2:** */S /M /A*
/D:date /T:time /F /L:dl:path1\\filename1.extl

dc:pathc are the disk drive and directory that hold the command.

d1:path are the hard disk or floppy disk drive and the directory to be backed up.

filename.ext specifies the file you want to back up. Wild-card characters are allowed.

d2: is the hard or floppy disk drive that receives the backup files.

SWITCHES

/S	Backs up all subdirectories, starting with the specified or current directory on the source disk and working downward.
/M	Backs up all files modified since their last backup.
/A	Adds the file(s) to be backed up to files already on the specified floppy disk drive.
/D:date	Backs up any file created or changed on or after the specified date.
/T:time	Backs up any file created or changed on or after the specified time on the specified date (given with the /D switch).
/F	Formats the destination floppy disk if the floppy disk is not formatted. DOS V4 formats the target floppy disks automatically without the use of this switch.

/F:size   with DOS V4, formats the destination floppy disk according
                 to the size specified. If you have a 1.2M disk drive, but only
                 360K floppy disks, you can specify /F:360 to format the
                 360K disk in the 1.2M drive.

/L:dl:path\\filenamel.ext Creates a log file.

NOTES

If you have a hard disk, you should become familiar with BACKUP and its
companion program RESTORE. BACKUP makes a copy of files from a
source disk to a destination disk. With BACKUP, you are prompted to
insert disks by number in sequential order until all specified files are backed
up. You should number each disk with the number that BACKUP assigns.

You must give both a source and a destination for BACKUP. Neither disk
can be a networked disk and neither can be used in an ASSIGN, SUBST, or
JOIN command.

If you back up onto diskettes with BACKUP from a version of DOS prior
to V3.3, you must have enough formatted diskettes before invoking the
BACKUP command. BACKUP does not work on unformatted or non-DOS
diskettes. If you have too few formatted diskettes, you will need to stop and
restart BACKUP. With V3.3 or V4 of DOS, you may use the /F switch to
format unformatted disks.

EXAMPLES

To back up the entire hard disk C: to floppy disks in drive A:, type:

    BACKUP C:\ A: /S

To back up all files as of a specified date, type:

    BACKUP C:\ A: /S /D:08/21/89

To back up all files modified since the last backup and add those files to the
last backup disks, use the following form:

    BACKUP C:\ A: /S /M /A

Batch Command
V1, V2, V3, V4—Internal

Executes one or more commands contained in a disk file.

SYNTAX

> *dc:pathc***filename** *parameters*

dc:pathc are the disk drive and directory that hold the command.

filename is the root name of the batch file.

parameters are the parameters to be used by the batch file.

NOTES

A batch file is an ASCII text file that contains DOS commands as well as the special batch subcommands. A batch file is useful for performing repetitive tasks, such as issuing commands to start programs.

Batch Subcommand—CALL
V3.3, V4

Runs a second batch file, then returns control to the first batch file. CALL is particularly useful in a hard disk menu system where you want to call a batch file, rather than an executable file.

SYNTAX

> **CALL** *dc:pathc***filename** *options*

dc:pathc are the disk drive and directory that hold the command.

filename is the root name of the called batch file.

options are the parameters to be used by the batch file.

NOTES

Use the CALL command to run a second batch file from another batch file.
When the second file is finished, DOS resumes processing the remaining
commands located in the first file.

Batch Subcommand—ECHO
V2, V3, V4

Controls the display of batch commands and other messages as DOS
executes batch subcommands. ECHO is used to good effect in hard disk
menu systems where you want to suppress the display of extraneous
information.

SYNTAX

To display a message, use the following form:

ECHO *message*

To turn off the display of commands and batch command messages, use the
form:

ECHO OFF

To turn on the display of commands and messages, use the form:

ECHO ON

To check the status of ECHO, use the form:

ECHO

message is the text of the message to be displayed on-screen.

NOTES

For unconditional on-screen display of a message, use the command ECHO
message. This means that the message you designate will be displayed
whether ECHO is on or off.

When ECHO is on, a batch file displays commands as DOS executes each line. The batch file also displays any messages from the batch subcommands.

When ECHO is off, a batch file does not display its commands as DOS executes them. The batch file also does not display messages produced by other batch subcommands. Exceptions to this rule are the `Strike a key when ready` message generated by the PAUSE subcommand and any ECHO message command.

Batch Subcommand—FOR..IN..DO
V2, V3, V4

Allows iterative processing of a DOS command. FOR..IN..DO can be used to good effect to list all files matching multiple file specifications.

SYNTAX

FOR %%variable IN (set) DO command

variable is a single letter.

set is one or more words or file specifications. The file specification is in the form d:path\filename.ext. Wild-card characters are allowed.

command is the DOS command to be performed for each word or file in the set.

NOTES

You can use more than one word or a full file specification in the set. You must separate words or file specifications by spaces or by commas.

%%variable becomes each literal word or full file specification in the set. If you use wild-card characters, FOR..IN..DO executes once for each file that matches the wild-card file specification.

Batch Subcommand—GOTO
V2, V3, V4

Transfers control to the line following a label in the batch file.

SYNTAX

GOTO label

label is the name used for a marker in a batch file. Although more than eight characters can be used, only the first eight characters of label are significant.

NOTES

When the command GOTO label is executed, DOS jumps to the line following the label and continues execution of the batch file. The label is used as a marker in a batch file and must be preceded by a colon. You do not use a colon in the GOTO statement, however.

Batch Subcommand—IF
V2, V3, V4

Allows conditional execution of a DOS command. IF can be used in batch files to test whether files exist in a directory on the hard disk. IF also can be used to test for program failures and string equality.

SYNTAX

IF *NOT* **condition command**

NOT tests for the opposite of condition and executes the command when the condition is false.

condition is the basis of the test and can be any of the following:

ERRORLEVEL number	DOS tests the exit code (0 to 255) of the program. If the exit code is greater than or equal to the number, the condition is true.
string 1 == string2	DOS compares these two alphanumeric strings to whether they are identical.
EXIST d:path\filename.ext	DOS tests whether *d:path***filename.ext** are in the specified drive or path (if given) or in the current disk drive and directory.

command is any valid DOS batch file command.

NOTES

For the IF subcommand, if condition is true, command is executed. If condition is false, command is skipped and the next line of the batch file is immediately executed. For the IF NOT subcommand, if condition is false, the command is executed. If condition is true, command is skipped, and the next line of the batch file is immediately executed.

For string1 == string2, DOS makes a literal, character-by-character comparison of the two strings. The comparison is based on the ASCII character set, and upper- and lowercase letters are distinguished.

When you are using string1 == string2 with the parameter markers (%0-%9), neither string may be null (empty, or nonexistent). If either string is null, DOS displays a syntax error message and aborts the batch file.

Batch Subcommand—PAUSE
V1, V2, V3, V4

Suspends batch file processing until a key is pressed and optionally displays a message.

SYNTAX

PAUSE *message*

message is a string of up to 121 characters.

NOTES

Regardless of the ECHO setting, DOS displays the message:

```
Strike a key when ready
```

DOS suspends processing of the batch file until you press any key. Afterward, DOS continues processing the batch file lines. To end processing of a batch file, press Ctrl-Break or Ctrl-C.

Batch Subcommand—REM
V1, V2, V3, V4

Displays a message within the batch file.

SYNTAX

REM *message*

message is a string of up to 123 characters.

NOTES

The optional message can contain up to 123 characters and must immediately follow the word REM. When DOS encounters a REM subcommand in a batch file, DOS displays the message if ECHO is on. If ECHO is off, DOS does not display the message.

Batch Subcommand—SHIFT
V2, V3, V4

Shifts command line parameters one position to the left when a batch file is invoked.

SYNTAX

SHIFT

NOTES

When you use SHIFT, DOS moves the command line parameters one position to the left. DOS discards the former first parameter (%0).

BREAK
V2, V3, V4—Internal

Determines when DOS looks for a Ctrl-Break sequence to stop a program. BREAK has the same effect as the BREAK command in the CONFIG.SYS file.

SYNTAX

To turn on BREAK, use the following form:

BREAK ON

To turn off BREAK, use the following form:

BREAK OFF

To determine whether BREAK is on or off, use the following form:

BREAK

NOTES

The setting of BREAK depends on the type of work you will be doing on the computer. When BREAK is on, DOS checks for a Ctrl-Break sequence whenever a program uses a DOS device. The Ctrl-Break key then causes the program to halt.

With BREAK set to off, the default setting, DOS checks for a Ctrl-Break key sequence only when the program writes to the screen or the printer, reads the keyboard, or reads/writes from the serial adapter. With BREAK set to off, a user is less likely to halt a program with Ctrl-Break.

CHDIR or CD
V2, V3, V4—Internal

Every hard disk should be organized into directories. The CHDIR or CD command is used to show the current directory, or to change the current directory.

SYNTAX

CHDIR *d:path*

or, using the short form:

CD *d:path*

d:path are valid disk drive and directory names.

NOTES

You have two methods for maneuvering through the hierarchical directories with CD: (1) starting at the root, or top, directory of the disk and moving down, or (2) starting with the current directory and moving in either direction.

To start at the root directory of a disk, you must begin the path with the path character (\), as in \ or B:\ When DOS sees \ as the first character in the path, the system starts with the root directory. Otherwise, DOS starts with the current directory.

EXAMPLES

To display the current directory, type the command:

CD

To move to the single directory \DOS, use:

CD \DOS

To move to the second-level directory \DATA\MEMOS, use this form:

CD \DATA\MEMOS

CHKDSK
V1, V2, V3, V4—External

Checks the directory and the file allocation table (FAT) of the disk and reports disk and memory status. CHKDSK can also repair errors in the directories or in the FAT.

SYNTAX

*dc:pathc***CHKDSK** *d:path\filename.ext* /F/V

dc:pathc are the disk drive and directory that hold the command.

d: is the disk drive to be analyzed.

path\filename.ext are the directory path and the file name(s) to be analyzed.

SWITCHES

/F   Fixes the file allocation table and other problems if errors are found.

/V   Shows CHKDSK's progress and displays more detailed information about the errors the program finds. (This switch is known as the verbose switch.)

NOTES

CHKDSK shows you the following items of information:

1. Volume name and creation date (only disks with volume labels)

2. Total disk space

3. Number of files and bytes used for hidden or system files

4. Number of files and bytes used for directories

5. Number of files and bytes used for user (normal) files

6. Bytes used by bad sectors (flawed disk space)

7. Bytes available (free space) on disk

8. Bytes of total memory (RAM)

9. Bytes of free memory

DOS V4, CHKDSK also reports the following:

1. Total bytes in each allocation unit

2. Total allocation units on the disk

3. The available allocation units on the disk

An allocation unit equates to a cluster.

CHKDSK checks a disk's directories and the FAT. The command also checks the amount of memory in the system and determines how much of that memory is free. If CHKDSK finds errors, it reports them on-screen before it makes a status report.

You must direct CHKDSK to make repairs to the disk by giving the /F switch. CHKDSK asks you to confirm that you want the repairs made before the program proceeds.

Do not combine different versions of CHKDSK and DOS. Do not, for example, use CHKDSK from any increment of DOS V2 with DOS V3 or later versions or you may lose files.

CHKDSK will not process a directory on which you used the JOIN, ASSIGN, or SUBST commands.

EXAMPLES

To analyze the current disk drive, type the command:

    CHKDSK

To analyze a disk in another drive and display all the files on the disk, use the form:

    CHKDSK B: /V

CLS
V2, V3, V4—Internal

Erases the display screen.

SYNTAX

    CLS

NOTES

This command clears all information on the screen and places the cursor at the home position in the upper left corner. This command affects only the active video display, not memory. CLS is frequently used in hard disk menu systems driven by batch files.

COMMAND
V2,V3,V4—External

Invokes a second copy of COMMAND.COM, the command processor. When used with the /C switch, it is similar to the CALL command introduced in DOS V3.3 and is used most frequently with batch files.

SYNTAX

*dc:pathc***COMMAND** */E:size /P /C string*

dc:pathc are the disk drive and the directory that hold the command.

string is the set of characters you pass to the new copy of the command interpreter.

SWITCHES

/E:size   Sets the size of the environment. Size is a decimal number from 160 to 32,768 bytes, rounded up to the nearest multiple of 16.

/P   Keeps this copy permanently in memory (until the next system reset).

/C   Passes the string of commands (the string) to the new copy of COMMAND.COM and returns to primary processor.

NOTES

COMMAND is an advanced DOS command not recommended for newcomers to DOS. Consult the DOS Technical Reference manual for more information about this command.

COMMAND is most often used with the SHELL directive. This combination allows you to relocate COMMAND.COM from the root directory of a disk to a subdirectory.

EXAMPLES

You can use COMMAND with DOS versions from V2.0 through V3.2 to emulate the CALL command found in V3.3 through V4.01. To use COMMAND in a batch file to call a batch file named MOVE.BAT, use the following form:

    COMMAND /C MOVE

COMP
V1, V2, V3, V4—External

Compares two sets of disk files. This command is not available with some DOS versions. If COMP is not available on your version of DOS, see the FC command.

SYNTAX

*dc:pathc***COMP** *d1:path1\\filename1.ext1 d2:path2\\filename2.ext2*

dc:pathc are the disk drive and the directory that hold the command.

d1:path1 are the drive and the directory containing the first set of files to be compared.

filename1.ext1 is the file name for the first set of files. Wild-card characters are allowed.

d2:path2 are the drive and the directory containing the second set of files to be compared.

filename2.ext2 is the file name for the second set of files. Wild-card characters are allowed.

Special terms:

d1:path1\filename1.ext1 is the primary file set.

d2:path2\filename2.ext2 is the secondary file set.

NOTES

COMP is the utility for comparing files. Use the command to verify that files on which you used the COPY command are correct. Also, use COMP to check a known good program copy against a questionable copy. If a program once functioned properly, but now acts strangely, check a good backup copy of the file against the copy you are using. If COMP finds differences, copy the good program to the disk you are using.

Files with matching names but different lengths are not checked. A message is printed indicating that these files are different.

After 10 mismatches (unequal comparisons) between the contents of two compared files, COMP automatically ends the comparison and aborts.

EXAMPLES

To compare the file IBM.LET that resides in the current directory of drive C: and in drive A:, use the form:

    COMP A:IBM.LET C:IBM.LET

To compare all the files in C:\WORDS\LETTERS with the files on drive A:, use the form:

    COMP C:\WORDS\LETTERS*.* A:*.*

or this form:

    COMP C:\WORDS\LETTERS A:

Configuration Subcommand—BREAK
V3, V4—Internal

Determines when DOS looks for a Ctrl-Break or Ctrl-C to stop a program.
See also the BREAK command.

SYNTAX

>   **BREAK = ON**

or

>   **BREAK = OFF**

NOTES

The setting for BREAK in the CONFIG.SYS file works in the same manner
as setting BREAK from the DOS prompt.

EXAMPLE

To set DOS to check for the Ctrl-Break key sequence, type the following in
your CONFIG.SYS file:

>   BREAK = ON

CONFIGURATION SUBCOMMAND—BUFFERS
V2, V3, V4—INTERNAL

Sets the number of disk buffers set aside by DOS in memory.

SYNTAX

>   **BUFFERS = nn**

If you are using DOS V4.0 or V4.01, use this form:

BUFFERS = nn,*mm* /X

nn is the number of buffers to set, in the range of 1 to 99. If you have DOS V4, you may set a maximum of 10,000 buffers, using the /X switch.

mm is the number of sectors, from 1 to 8, that can be read or written at a time. The default is one.

SWITCH

/X   Uses expanded memory for buffer storage.

NOTES

Buffers provide the memory for DOS to store data in transit between a disk drive and user RAM. The use of buffers is desirable as, when reading from a disk, DOS checks first to see if the information is in a buffer. The information, if found in the buffer, is transferred to user memory—the disk is not accessed and computer time is saved. For programs, such as database programs, that read/write the disk often, the more buffers you have, the more time you will save, because the data is more quickly accessible. A program that does not access the disk often, such as a spreadsheet program does not gain any speed from a greater buffers setting.

EXAMPLES

To set your CONFIG.SYS file so that DOS uses 20 disk buffers, enter the command in the following form:

BUFFERS = 20

Configuration Subcommand—DEVICE
V2, V3, V4—Internal

Instructs DOS to load, link, and use a special device driver. Many device drivers, such as disk cache and RAM disk drivers, have an impact on hard disk performance.

SYNTAX

DEVICE = *d:path***filename.ext** *options*

d:path are the disk drive and the directory that hold the device driver.

filename.ext is the root file name and optional extension of the device driver.

options are any parameters or switches that may be used with a device driver.

NOTES

The device command is used to attach devices to DOS. The device driver, as it is called, can be a program that controls a physical device attached to the computer, such as a mouse. Or the device driver can be a program that creates a logical, or non-real, device.

EXAMPLE

To install the ANSI.SYS in your CONFIG.SYS file, use this form:

DEVICE = C:\DOS\ANSI.SYS

This example assumes that ANSI.SYS is located in the drive C: \DOS subdirectory.

Configuration Subcommand—DRIVPARM V4—Internal

Defines or changes the parameters of a block device, such as a disk drive.

SYNTAX

> **DRIVPARM = /D:num** /C /F:type /H:hds /I /N /S:sec /T:trk

SWITCHES

/D:num
: specifies the drive number, num, ranging from 0 to 255, where drive A=0, drive B=1, drive C=2, etc.

/C
: specifies that the drive supports change-line, meaning that the drive has sensor support to determine when the drive door is open. When the drive door is open, the drive is sensed as empty.

/F:type
: is used to determine the type of drive. *type* is one of the following:

type	Drive specification
0	160K/320K/180K/360K
1	1.2M
2	720K
3	Single-density 8—dp disk
4	Double-density 8—dp disk
5	Hard disk
6	Tape drive
7	1.44M

Type 2 is the default if you do not specify /F.

/H:hds
: is used to specify the total number of drive heads, where hds is a number from 1 to 99. The default for hds is 2.

/I   is used if you have a 3 1/2-inch drive connected internally to
                your floppy drive controller, but your ROM BIOS does not
                support a 3 1/2-inch drive.

/N   specifies that your drive or other block device is not
                removable, or a hard disk, for example.

/S:sec   is used to specify the total number of sectors per side on the
                drive. sec can be a number from 1 to 999.

/T:trk   is used to specify the number of tracks per side of a disk or
                the total number of tracks per tape. trk can be a number from
                1 to 99.

NOTES

You have great flexibility in adding block devices to your computer. Make
sure that you specify the correct type of device, number of heads, and
number of sectors. Incorrect values will cause the device to work
incorrectly or not at all.

EXAMPLE

To specify an internal 3 1/2-inch, 1.44M drive that will be drive B: and will
support change-line, use the following form:

    DRIVPARM /D:1 /C /F:7 /I

Configuration Subcommand—FILES
V2, V3, V4—Internal

Specifies the number of file handles open at any given time. Many
programs designed to take full advantage of the hard disk expect the file
handles to be set to 20 or more.

SYNTAX

    FILES = nnn

nnn is the number, from 8 to 255, of file handles that may be open at any given time. The default value is 8.

NOTES

Starting with DOS V2.0, you use the FILES directive in the CONFIG.SYS file to specify the maximum number of files that DOS can have open at one time. For some programs such as spreadsheet programs, a setting of FILES = 15 may be adequate. With database programs, however, you should set FILES for 20 or greater. Database programs often open several files at a time.

DOS began using file handles rather than File Control Blocks, beginning with V2.0. The number of programs available that use FCBs is diminishing. All major commercial programs as of this printing use file handles. Still, you may find a DOS V1 program using FCBs that you find helpful, for which you will use the FCBS setting.

EXAMPLE

To allow as many as 20 files open at one time, type the following form in your CONFIG.SYS file:

    FILES = 20

Configuration Subcommand—INSTALL
V4—Internal

Starts program from CONFIG.SYS. Valid programs to start with INSTALL are FASTOPEN, KEYB, NLSFUNC, and SHARE.

SYNTAX

    INSTALL = *dc:pathc***filename.ext** *options*

dc:pathc are the disk drive and the directory that hold the command.

filename.ext is the name of the file, which may be FASTOPEN.EXE, KEYB.COM, NLSFUNC.EXE, or SHARE.EXE.

options are any parameters the filename.ext command requires to function.

NOTES

INSTALL gives DOS the ability to load some programs from CONFIG.SYS. When a program is loaded from CONFIG.SYS rather than at the DOS prompt, less memory is used.

EXAMPLE

To start SHARE.EXE in your CONFIG.SYS file using INSTALL, use the form:

    INSTALL = C:\DOS\SHARE.EXE

This directive assumes that SHARE.EXE is in the directory \DOS on drive C:.

Configuration Subcommand—LASTDRIVE V3, V4—Internal

Sets the last valid drive letter acceptable to DOS. This command is useful for reserving drive letters for RAM disks.

SYNTAX

    LASTDRIVE = x

x is the alphabetical character for the highest system drive. The highest default drive letter is E.

NOTES

If you use the SUBST command to assign drive letters to subdirectories, use the LASTDRIVE statement to increase the usable drive letters. Also, users of a local area network can use the LASTDRIVE statement to identify the highest letter that can be assigned as a drive letter to a subdirectory.

EXAMPLE

If you want to use a drive letter of J:, type in your CONFIG.SYS file the form:

    LASTDRIVE = J

Configuration Subcommand—SHELL
V3, V4—Internal

Changes the default DOS command processor. SHELL is most commonly used to increase the environment space.

SYNTAX

SHELL = *d:path***filename.ext** *parameters*

d:path are the drive and the directory where DOS can find the command processor to be used.

filename.ext is the root file name and optional extension of the command processor.

parameters are the optional parameters that the command processor uses.

NOTES

Most users will not replace COMMAND.COM with another command processor. However, many users wish to reposition COMMAND.COM to a subdirectory. The SHELL command can help accomplish this task.

EXAMPLE

To place COMMAND.COM in the \DOS directory on drive C:, use the following form:

    SHELL = C:\DOS\COMMAND.COM /P

COPY
V1, V2, V3, V4—Internal

Copies files between disk drives and/or devices, either keeping the file name or changing it.

SYNTAX

To copy a file, use the following form:

COPY */A/B d1:path1***filename1.ext1***/A/B*
d2:path2\filename2.ext2/A/B/V

To join several files into one, use the following form:

COPY */A/B d1:path1\filename1.ext1/A/B*
+d2:path2\filename2.ext2/A/B +...

d1:path1 and *d2:path2* are valid disk drive names and directories.

filename1.ext1 and *filename2.ext2* are valid file names. Wild-card characters are allowed.

The three periods (...) represent additional files in the form dx:pathx/filenamex.extx.

Special terms:

The file being copied from is the source file. The names containing 1 and 2 are the source files.

The file being copied to is the destination file. This file is represented by a 0.

SWITCHES

/V   Verifies that the copy has been recorded correctly.

The following switches have different effects on the source and the destination.

For the source file:

>   Treats the file as an ASCII (text) file. The command copies all the information in the file up to, but not including, the end-of-file marker (Ctrl-Z). Anything after the end-of-file marker is ignored.

>   Copies the entire file (based on its size, as listed in the directory) as if it were a program file (binary1). Any end-of-file markers (Ctrl-Z) are treated as normal characters, and the EOF characters are copied.

For the destination file:

/A   Adds an end-of-file marker (Ctrl-Z) to the end of the ASCII text file after it is copied.

/B   Does not add the end-of-file marker to this binary file.

NOTES

The meanings of the /A and /B switches depend on their positions in the line. The /A and /B switches affect the file immediately preceding and all following the switch until another /A or /B switch is encountered. When one of these switches is used before any file name, the switch affects all following files until contradicted by another /A or /B switch.

EXAMPLES

To copy the file MEMO.TXT from the current directory on the default drive A: to the directory C:\WORDS, use the form:

C:\WORDS

To copy the file MEMO.TXT from the current directory on drive C: to the current directory on drive A:, use the form:

COPY MEMO.TXT A:

To copy the file MEMO.TXT from \WORDS on the current drive to drive A: and change the name to MEMO.LTR, use the form:

COPY \WORDS\MEMO.TXT A:MEMO.LTR

DEL
V1, V2, V3, V4—Internal

Deletes files from the disk.

DEL is an alternative command for ERASE and performs the same functions. See ERASE for a complete description.

DIR
V1, V2, V3, V4—Internal

Lists any or all files and subdirectories in a disk directory.

SYNTAX

DIR *d:path\filename.ext /P/W*

d: is the drive holding the disk you want to examine.

path is the path to the directory you want to examine.

filename.ext is a valid file name. Wild-card characters are permitted.

SWITCHES

/P   Pauses when the screen is full and waits for you to press any key.

/W   Gives a wide (80-column) display of the file names. Information about file size, date, and time is not displayed.

NOTES

The DIR command displays the following information:

> Disk volume name, if any
> Name of the directory (its complete path)
> Name of each disk file or subdirectory
> Number of files
> Amount, in bytes, of free space on the disk

The DIR command, unless otherwise directed, also shows the following:

> Number of bytes occupied by each file
> Date/time of the file's creation/last update

The DIR command finds the disk files or subdirectories on the disk. This command shows only the files and subdirectories in the specified or the default directory.

EXAMPLES

To examine the directory of the current disk and current directory, type the command:

> DIR

To examine the \DOS directory on the current drive, and pause after each screen view of files, use the form:

> DIR \DOS /P

ERASE
V1, V2, V3, V4—Internal

Removes one or more files from the directory.

SYNTAX

You can use the command form:

   ERASE *d:path***filename.ext**

or the form:

   DEL *d:path***filename.ext**

With DOS V4, you can add the /P switch in the form:

   ERASE *d:path***filename.ext** /P

or with its alternative command:

   DEL *d:path***filename.ext** /P

d:path are the disk drive and the directory holding the file(s) to be erased.

filename.ext is the name of the file(s) to be erased. Wild-card characters are allowed.

SWITCH

/P   With DOS V4, this switch prompts you before erasing the file
            with the message `filename.ext, Delete (Y/N)?`

NOTES

ERASE, or its short form DEL (delete), removes files. The directory entry for each erased file is altered so that DOS knows the file is not in use. The space occupied by each file erased from the disk is freed.

If you specify *.* or no file name when you give a disk drive name and/or path name, DOS displays the following prompt:

    `Are you sure (Y/N)?`

If you answer Y, all files in the specified directory are erased; If you answer N, no files are erased.

You cannot ERASE either the current (.) or the parent (..) directory from a subdirectory. To remove a directory, you must use RMDIR.

EXAMPLES

To erase the file MEMO.TXT, use the following form:

    ERASE MEMO.TXT

or the alternative command form:

    DEL MEMO.TXT

To erase all the files in the directory C:\MEMOS, use the form:

    ERASE C:\MEMOS

or the form:

    DEL C:\MEMOS

To erase all the files in C:\MEMOS using DOS V4 and be prompted before each file is erased, use the form:

    ERASE C:\MEMOS /P

or this form:

    DEL C:\MEMOS /P

EXIT
V2, V3, V4—Internal

Leaves a secondary command processor and returns to the primary one. You usually use this command when you have "dropped to DOS" from within an application; that is, when you have temporarily suspended a program and left it in memory. For example, to return to Lotus 1-2-3 after selecting /System, you would issue the EXIT command.

SYNTAX

   EXIT

NOTES

This command has no effect if a secondary command processor is not loaded or was loaded with the /P switch.

FASTOPEN
V3.3, V4—External

FASTOPEN is a special form of disk cache that retains the hard disk's bookkeeping information in memory for fast access. It keeps directory information in memory so that DOS can quickly find frequently needed files.

SYNTAX

   *dc:pathc***FASTOPEN d:=***nnn* . . .

For DOS V4, additional syntax is as follows:

   *dc:pathc***FASTOPEN d:=***(nnn,mmm)* . . . */X*

dc:pathc are the disk drive and the directory that hold the command.

d: is the name of the disk drive containing directory information to be held in memory.

nnn is the number of directory entries to be held in memory (10 to 999).

mmm is the number of fragmented entries for the drive (1 to 999).

. . . designates additional disk drives in the forms d:=nnn or d:=(nnn,mmm).

SWITCHES

/X   tells DOS to use expanded memory to store the information buffered by FASTOPEN.

NOTES

FASTOPEN was added to DOS V3.3 and retained in DOS V4. This command caches directory information on files and can be used on any disk drive. The value of using the command on a RAM disk is questionable, however.

FASTOPEN works by keeping directory information in memory. Because disk buffers already hold the file allocation table information, FASTOPEN allows DOS to search memory for a file or a subdirectory entry, to locate quickly the corresponding FAT entry, and to open the file. If you have many files and use FASTOPEN effectively, you can increase DOS's performance significantly.

If you give nnn, the value must be between 10 and 999,inclusively. FASTOPEN's minimum value is 10 or the maximum level of your deepest directory plus 1, whichever value is greater.

The sum of nnn for all successful FASTOPEN commands cannot exceed 999.

EXAMPLE

To keep in memory the location of up to 90 files residing on drive C:, use the following form:

    FASTOPEN C:=90

With DOS V4, to track as many as 90 files in memory from drive C: that may be fragmented, you can use the following form:

FASTOPEN C:=(90,10)

FC
V2, V3, V4—External

This powerful command compares two files or two sets of files and displays any discrepancies found.

SYNTAX

*dc:pathc***FC** */A /B /C /L /LB x /N /T /W /x*
*d1:path1***filename1.ext1** *d2:path2***filename2.ext2**

dc:pathc are the disk drive and the directory that hold the command.

d1:path1 are the drive and the directory containing the first set of files to be compared.

filename1.ext1 is the file name for the first set of files. Wild cards are allowed.

d2:path2 are the drive and the directory containing the second set of files to be compared.

filename2.ext2 is the file name for the second set of files. Wild-card characters are allowed.

Special terms:

d1:path1\\filename1.ext1 is the primary file set.

d2:path2\\filename2.ext2 is the secondary file set.

SWITCHES

/A	Abbreviates ASCII comparison displays.
/B	Forces a binary file comparison.
/C	Causes DOS to disregard case of letters.
/L	Compares files in ASCII mode.
/LB x	Sets internal buffer to b lines.
/N	Displays line numbers for ASCII comparisons.
/T	Suppresses expansion of tabs to spaces.
/W	Compresses tabs and spaces.
/x	Sets the number of lines (1-9) to match (the default is 2).

NOTES

FC is a file comparison program similar to COMP, but more powerful (see COMP in this Command Reference). With FC, you can compare either source or binary files.

Source files are batch files, or files that contain text, such as program listings. Binary files are program files, usually bearing the extension .COM or .EXE.

EXAMPLES

To compare MEMO.LET to MEMO.BAK, use the form:

    FC MEMO.LET MEMO.BAK

To find the proper syntax for File Compare, type the command:

    FC

FIND
V2, V3, V4—External

FIND is a useful hard disk management tool that allows you to search text files for a specific word or phrase. The command then displays from the designated files all the lines that match or do not match (depending on the switches used) the specified string. This command also can display the line numbers.

SYNTAX

*dc:pathc***FIND** */V/C/N* **"string"** *d:path\filename.ext...*

dc:pathc are the disk drive and the directory that hold the command.

string is the set of characters you want to find. As shown in the syntax line, string must be enclosed in quotation marks.

d:path are the disk drive and the directory that hold the file.

filename.ext is the file you want to search.

SWITCHES

/V	Displays all lines not containing string
/C	Counts the number of times that string occurs and displays that number on the screen
/N	Displays the number of the line that contains string in front of the line that contains string

NOTES

FIND is one of several filters provided with DOS V3 and V4. The command can find either lines that contain string or those that do not. FIND also can number and count lines rather than display them.

This filter is useful when it is combined with DOS I/O redirection. You can redirect the output of FIND to a file by using the > redirection symbol. Because FIND accepts a sequence of files to search, you do not have to redirect the input to FIND.

If you use switches with FIND, you must place them between the word FIND and the string. Most DOS commands require you to place switches at the end of the command line.

You must enclose string in double-quotes. To use the double-quote character in the string, use two double-quote characters sequentially.

EXAMPLES

To display each occurrence of the string print in the file HELP.TXT, use the form:

> FIND "print" HELP.TXT

To find all files in a directory that were created or modified on July 9, 1989, use the following form:

> DIR | FIND "7-09-89"

FORMAT
V1, V2, V3, V4—External

Initializes a disk to accept operating system information and files; also checks the disk for defective tracks and optionally places DOS on the floppy or hard disk.

SYNTAX

> *dc:pathc***FORMAT d:** */S/1/8/V/B/4/N:ss/T:tt*

With DOS V4, you also may add the /V:label and /F:size switches:

> *dc:pathc***FORMAT d:** */S/1/8/V/B/4/N:ss/T:tt /V:label*
> */F:size*

dc:pathc are the disk drive and the directory that hold the command.

d: is a valid disk drive name.

SWITCHES

/S Places a copy of the operating system on the disk so that it can be booted.

/1 Formats only the first side of the floppy disk.

/8 Formats an eight-sector floppy disk (V1).

/V Writes a volume label on the disk.

/B Formats an eight-sector floppy disk, leaving the proper places in the directory for any operating system version, but does not place the operating system on the disk.

/4 Formats a floppy disk in a 1.2M disk drive for double-density (320K/360K) use.

/N:ss Formats the disk with ss number of sectors, with ss ranging from 1 to 99.

T:ttt Formats the disk with ttt number of tracks per side, with ttt ranging from 1 to 999.

/F:size	Formats the disk to less than maximum capacity, with size designating one of the following values:

Drive	*Allowable Values for size*
160K, 180K	160, 160K, 160KB, 180, 180K, 180KB
320K, 360K	All of above, plus 320, 320K, 320KB, 360, 360K, 360KB
1.2M	All of above, plus 1200, 1200K, 1200KB, 1.2, 1.2M, 1.2MB
720K	720, 720K, 720KB
1.44M	All of above, plus 1440, 1440K, 1440KB, 1.44, 1.44M, 1.44MB

/V:label	Transfers volume label to formatted disk. Replaces label with 11-character name for new disk.

NOTES

You must format each diskette or hard disk before using it. FORMAT actually performs several tasks. The program sets up each track and sector on the disk so that it accepts information. Special information is recorded, such as track headers (one for each track), sector headers (one for each sector), and CRC (cyclic redundancy check) bits to ensure that the recorded information is accurate.

FORMAT destroys information previously recorded on the diskette or hard disk, so do not FORMAT a diskette or hard disk that contains useful information.

EXAMPLES

To format the disk in drive A:, use the form:

    FORMAT A:

To format the disk in drive A: and transfer DOS to the disk, use the following form:

    FORMAT A: /S

To format a 720K diskette in a 1.44M drive A:, use the form:

    FORMAT A: /N:9 /T:80

With DOS V4, use the form:

    FORMAT A: /F:720

JOIN
V3.1, V3.2, V3.3, V4—External

Produces a single directory structure by connecting one disk drive to a subdirectory of another disk drive. JOIN is a disk *pretender* command designed to be used on systems with multiple hard disk drives.

SYNTAX

To connect disk drives, use the following form:

    *dc:pathc***JOIN d1:** *d2:***dirname**

To disconnect disk drives, use this form of the command:

    *dc:pathc***JOIN d1:** */D*

To show currently connected drives, use the following form:

    *dc:pathc***JOIN**

dc:pathc are the disk drive and the directory that hold the command.

d1: is the disk drive to be connected. DOS calls this drive the guest disk drive.

d2: is the disk drive to which d1: is to be connected. DOS calls *d2:* the host disk drive.

\dirname is a subdirectory in the root directory of d2:, the host drive. DOS calls \dirname the host subdirectory. \dirname holds the connection to d1:, the guest drive.

SWITCH

/D   Disconnects the specified guest disk drive from its host.

NOTES

The JOIN command, introduced with DOS V3.1, combines two disks into a single disk. The guest disk logically (apparently) becomes a subdirectory to the host disk.

JOIN does not affect the guest disk drive, only the way you access the files on that disk drive. You cannot exceed the maximum number of files in the guest disk's root directory. In the host subdirectory, size of a single file cannot exceed the guest disk's size. Similarly, a single file cannot span more than one disk.

Use the JOIN command with caution. When a JOIN is active, certain DOS commands work differently and some should not be used at all. While joined, the guest disk drive appears to be a host subdirectory. You cannot issue a DIR or CHKDSK command using the letter of the guest disk drive. You must first break the connection, then use DIR or CHKDSK on the former guest.

You must specify the host subdirectory name. This subdirectory must be a level-one subdirectory; that is, it must belong to the root directory of the host disk drive and not to another subdirectory. If the host subdirectory does not exist, JOIN creates one. If the subdirectory exists, it must be empty (it must have only the entries . and ..), or DOS displays an error message and aborts the connection. When you break the connection, the newly created subdirectory remains. You can use this subdirectory later for another JOIN command or delete the subdirectory by issuing the RMDIR command.

EXAMPLES

To join the diskette in drive A: to C:\MNT, use the form:

    JOIN A: C:\MNT

To display the current join status, type the command:

    JOIN

JOIN displays the current assignments. If the preceding example is in effect, DOS displays this message:

    A: => C:\MNT

To disconnect drive A: from the JOIN to C:\MNT, use the form:

    JOIN A: /D

LABEL
V3, V4—External

A disk's volume label appears at the top of directory listings. LABEL creates, changes, or deletes a volume label for a disk. The command also is used for verification during a hard disk format operation.

SYNTAX

   *dc:pathc***LABEL** *d:volume_label*

dc:pathc are the disk drive the directory that hold the command.

d: is the disk drive whose label will be changed.

volume_label is the disk's new volume label.

NOTES

You can easily identify your disks by giving each one a volume label, which is simply an electronic label for a disk. Volume labels appear when you use the DIR, TREE, or CHKDSK commands.

Do not use LABEL on a disk in any drive that is affected by the SUBST or ASSIGN commands, because DOS labels the "real" disk in the disk drive instead.

EXAMPLES

To change the current label, use the form:

    LABEL MY_DISK

To display the current label of the disk in drive B: and have the option to change the label, type the command:

    LABEL

MEM
V4—External

Displays the amount of used and unused memory, allocated and open memory areas, and all programs currently in the system.

SYNTAX

   *dc:pathc***MEM** */PROGRAM /DEBUG*

dc:pathc are the disk drive and the directory that hold the command.

SWITCHES

/PROGRAM   Displays programs that are in memory, including the address, name, size, and type of each file for every program. Also shows current free memory.

/DEBUG   Displays programs that are in memory, including the address, name, size, and type of each file for every program. Also displays system device drivers and installed device drivers, as well as all unused memory.

NOTES

You may use MEM to display information on how memory is being used. MEM displays statistics for conventional memory and also for extended and expanded memory if the latter two are available. You cannot specify /PROGRAM and /DEBUG at the same time.

EXAMPLES

To display the current memory usage, type the command:

    MEM

MKDIR or MD
V2, V3, V4 — Internal

One of the primary commands used to build a hard disk directory hierarchy, MKDIR creates a subdirectory.

SYNTAX

MKDIR *d:path***dirname**

or the short form:

MD *d:path***dirname**

d: is the disk drive for the subdirectory.

path\ indicates the path to the directory that will hold the subdirectory.

dirname is the subdirectory you are creating.

NOTES

MKDIR, or the short form MD, makes subdirectories. You can create as many subdirectories as you want, but remember that DOS accepts no more than 63 characters, including backslashes, for the path name. Do not create too many levels of subdirectories with long names, or the path to the directory may exceed 63 characters.

You cannot create a directory name that is identical to a file name in the current directory. For example, if you have a file named MYFILE in the current directory, you cannot create the subdirectory MYFILE in this directory. If the file is named MYFILE.TXT, however, the names will not conflict when you create the MYFILE subdirectory.

EXAMPLES

To create the subdirectory \WORDS on the current drive, use the form:

    MKDIR \WORDS

or the short form:

    MD \WORDS

MORE
V2, V3, V4—External

Displays one screen of information from the standard input device and pauses while displaying the message **--More--**. When you press any key, MORE displays the next screen of information.

SYNTAX

    dc:pathc**MORE**

dc:pathc\\ are the disk drive and the directory that hold the command.

NOTES

MORE is a DOS filter that enables you to display information without manually pausing the screen.

MORE is similar to the TYPE command, but automatically pauses after each screen of information.

One screen of information is based on 40 or 80 characters per line and 23 lines per screen. MORE, however, does not always display 23 lines from the file. Rather, the command acts intelligently with long lines, wrapping those that exceed the display width (40 or 80 characters). If one of the file's lines takes 3 lines to display, MORE displays a maximum of 21 lines from the file, pauses, and shows the next screen of lines.

EXAMPLES

To use redirection to display TEST.TXT one screen at a time, use the following form:

    MORE <TEST.TXT

To display a sorted directory one screen at a time, use the following form:

    DIR | SORT | MORE

PATH
V2, V3, V4—Internal

The directory search path instructs the operating system where to look on your hard disk for program files. PATH is used to set the search path. Every hard disk user should have a PATH command in the AUTOEXEC.BAT file.

SYNTAX

    PATH *dl :path1 ;d2 :path2 ;d3 :path3 ;...*

dl :, d2 :, and *d3 :* are valid disk drive names.

path1, *path2*, and *path3* are valid path names to the commands you want to run while in any directory.

The ellipsis (...) represents additional disk drives and path names.

NOTES

PATH is a useful command in hierarchical directories. Directories containing utility programs, system programs, or batch files can be established and used from anywhere on the disk. PATH enables the directories that you specify to be searched for your programs; you do not need to type the path each time.

Always specify an absolute path that starts with a disk's root directory (\) rather than a relative path starting with the current directory. By specifying an absolute path, you need not be concerned with the current directory.

If you specify more than one set of paths, the following rules apply:

   a. The path sets must be separated by semicolons.

   b. The search for the programs or batch files is made in the order in which you give the path sets. First, the current directory is searched. Then d1:path1 is searched, then d2:path2, d3:path3, and so on, until the command or batch file is found.

If you give invalid information when assigning a path, such as an invalid disk drive, a bad delimiter, or a deleted path, DOS does not display an error message. When the path is being searched for a program or batch file, DOS skips a bad or invalid path. If, however, you give an invalid disk drive name, DOS displays an `Invalid drive in search path` message when it searches the path for a program or batch file.

PATH affects the execution of only program (.COM or .EXE) files or batch (.BAT) files. This command does not work with data files, text files, or program overlays.

EXAMPLES

To set a search path for C:\DOS, C:\UTILS, and the root directory, use the form:

    PATH C:\DOS;C:\UTILS;C:\

To display the current path setting, type the command:

    PATH

PRINT
V2, V3, V4—External

Prints one or more text files in the background while you proceed with other tasks. The command includes options for placing files in the print queue, modifying the print queue, and cancelling already queued print jobs.

SYNTAX

> *dc:pathc*\PRINT /D:*device* /B:*bufsiz* /M:*maxtick* /Q:*maxfiles*
> /S:*timeslice* /U:*busytick d1:path1**filename1.ext1* /P/T/C
> *d2:path2**filename2.ext2*/P/T/C . . .

dc:pathc\ are the disk drive and the directory that hold the command.

d1: and *d2:* are valid disk drive names.

path1\ and *path2*\ are valid path names to the files for printing.

filename1.ext1 and *filename2.ext2* are the files you want to print. Wild-card characters are allowed.

The ellipsis (. . .) represents additional file names in the form dx:pathx\filenamex.extx.

SWITCHES

You can specify any one of the following switches, but only the first time you start PRINT:

/D:device   Specifies the device to be used for printing. *device* is any
                valid DOS device name. (You must list this switch first
                whenever you use it.)

/B:bufsiz Specifies the size of the memory buffer to be used while the files are printing. The size can be any number from 1 to 16,386.

/M:maxtick Specifies in clock ticks the maximum amount of time that PRINT has for sending characters to the printer each time PRINT gets a turn. (A tick is the smallest measure of time used on PCs. A tick happens every 1/18.2 [0.0549] seconds.) The value of maxtick can be any number from 1 to 255. The default is 2.

/Q:maxfiles Specifies the number of files that can be in the queue (line) for printing. The number can range from 4 to 32. The default is 10.

/S:timeslice Specifies the number of slices in each second. The timeslice can be a number from 1 to 255. The default is 10.

/U:busytick Specifies in clock ticks the maximum amount of time for the program to wait for a busy or unavailable printer. The value of busytick can be any number from 1 to 255.

You can specify any one of the following switches whenever you use PRINT:

/P   Queues up the files (places in the line) for printing.

/T   Terminates the background printing of any or all files, including any file currently being printed.

/C   Cancels the background printing of the file(s).

NOTES

PRINT controls the background printing feature of DOS V3 and V4. The command has been significantly improved since DOS V2.

During the background printing process, DOS orders a specified printer to print a disk-based file while the computer itself performs a separate task, such as running a program. Because the computer must devote most of its time and attention to the non-printing task, that task is in the foreground.

PRINT gets less attention from the computer, and therefore is called a background task. When the cursor sits at the system prompt (>), PRINT receives most of the computer's time.

You can specify any of the switches from the first set (/D, /B, /M, /Q, /S, and /U) only when PRINT is first used. If you give the /D switch, you must make it the first switch on the line. You can give the remaining five switches in any sequence before you specify a file name.

EXAMPLES

To enable background printing to the LPT1 device, use the form:

        PRINT /D:LPT1

Once PRINT is enabled, to start the files MEMO.TXT, LETTER.TXT, and REPORT.PRN printing, use the following form:

        PRINT MEMO.TXT /P LETTER.TXT REPORT.PRN

If the three files begin printing, to cancel LETTER.TXT, use the form:

        PRINT LETTER.TXT /C

To cancel all jobs that are queued for printing use this form:

        PRINT /T

PROMPT
V2, V3, V4—Internal

The most common use of the PROMPT command is to customize the DOS system prompt, which is displayed while the operating system is waiting for input. All hard disk users should set PROMPT in the AUTOEXEC.BAT file to display the current directory.

SYNTAX

PROMPT *promptstring*

promptstring is the text to be used for the new system prompt.

Special terms:

A meta-string produces a prompt that you designate. The meta-string is comprised of a $ character, followed by a single character ?. To use certain characters (for example, the < or > I/O redirection symbols), you must enter the appropriate meta-string to place the desired characters in your promptstring. Otherwise, DOS immediately attempts to interpret the character.

All meta-strings begin with the dollar sign ($) and have two characters, including the symbol $. The following list contains meta-string characters and their meanings:

Character	Meaning
$	$, the dollar sign
_ (underscore)	newline, (moves to the first position of the next line)
b	$vb, the vertical bar
e	The Escape character, CHR$(27)
d	The date, like the DATE command
h	The backspace character, CHR$(8), which erases the preceding character
g	>, the greater-than character
l	<, the less-than character
n	The current disk drive
p	The current disk drive and path, including the current directory

q	=, the equal sign
t	The time, like the TIME command
v	The DOS version number
Any other	Nothing or null; the character is ignored

NOTES

The PROMPT command gives users greater control over their systems, and in this case, the system prompt. With hierarchical directories, you will find it helpful to display the current path on your disk drive. For that reason, you may want to set the system prompt to the following:

    PROMPT $p

Any text entered for promptstring becomes the new system prompt. You can enter special characters by using the meta-strings. If you do not enter the promptstring, the standard system prompt reappears.

EXAMPLES

To set the current prompt to display the date, then the path in brackets on the next line, use the form:

    PROMPT D_[$P]

To return the prompt to the default (c> for example), type the command:

    PROMPT

RECOVER
V2, V3, V4—External

RECOVER is designed to recover files that contain data located in bad sectors. Use the command with caution, because the recovered files are relocated in the root directory and are renamed. Do not use wild-card characters to recover files. If you have many files with bad sectors, use a third-party disk utility.)

SYNTAX

To recover a file, use the following form:

> *dc:pathc***RECOVER** *d:path***filename.ext**

To recover a disk with a damaged directory, use this form:

> *dc:pathc***RECOVER d:**

dc:pathc\ are the disk drive and the directory that hold the command.

d:path\ are the disk drive and the directory holding the damaged file or floppy disk.

filename.ext is the file to be recovered.

NOTES

RECOVER attempts to recover either a file with a bad sector or a disk with a directory containing a bad sector. DOS tells you if a file has bad sectors by displaying a disk-error message when you try to use the file. To recover a file with one or more bad sectors, type RECOVER d:filename.ext.

If the damaged file is a program file, the program probably cannot be used. If the file is a data or text file, some information can be recovered. Because RECOVER reads the entire file, make sure that you use a text editor or word processor to eliminate any garbage at the end of the file.

EXAMPLE

To recover the file MEMO.TXT that contains a few bad sectors, use the form:

> RECOVER MEMO.TXT

RENAME or REN
V1, V2, V3, V4—Internal

Changes the name of one or more disk files.

SYNTAX

RENAME *d:path***filename1.ext1 filename2.ext2**

or the short form:

REN *d:path***filename1.ext1 filename2.ext2**

d:path\ are the disk drive and the directory holding the file(s) to be renamed.

filename1.ext1 is the file's current name. Wild-card characters are allowed.

filename2.ext2 is the file's new name. Wild-card characters are allowed.

NOTES

RENAME, or the short form REN, changes the name of a file on the disk. Because you are renaming an established disk file, the file's drive or path designation is given with the old name so that DOS will know which file to rename.

Wild-card characters are acceptable in either the old or the new name. Be careful, however, when you use these characters, because they can be troublesome. You may not be able to rename all files, as DOS may try to use duplicate names.

EXAMPLES

To rename the file MEMO.TXT to SMITH.MMO, use the form:

REN MEMO.TXT SMITH.MMO

To rename all the files in C:\LETTERS to change their extension from TXT to LTR, use the form:

REN C:\LETTERS*.LTR *.TXT

REPLACE
V3.2, V3.3, V4—External

Replaces files on one disk with files of the same name from another disk; adds files to a disk by copying them from another disk.

SYNTAX

*dc:pathc***REPLACE** *ds:paths***filenames**.*exts* **dd:***pathd* */A/P/R/S/W*

With DOS V4, you can add a /U switch:

*dc:pathc***REPLACE** *ds:paths***filenames**.*exts* **dd:***pathd* */A/P/R/S/W/*U

dc:pathc are the disk drive and the directory that hold the command.

ds:paths are the disk drive and directory holding the replacement file(s).

filenames.*exts* are the replacement files. Wild-card characters are allowed.

dd:pathd are the disk drive and the directory whose file(s) will be replaced.

In the fragment *ds:paths\filenames.exts, s* represents the source. The source is the file that will be added to a directory or that will replace an existing file in the directory.

In the fragment *dd:pathd, d* represents the destination. The destination can be either the file to be replaced or the disk and directory where a new file will be added. DOS refers to the destination as the target.

SWITCHES

/A   Adds files from the source disk that do not exist on the
             destination disk.

/P   Displays a prompt asking if the file should be replaced or
             added to the destination.

/R   Replaces files on the destination disk even though the files'
             read-only attribute is on.

/S   Replaces all files with matching names in the current
             directory and its subordinate subdirectories. The /S switch
             does not work with the /A switch.

/W   Causes REPLACE to prompt and wait for the source floppy
             disk to be inserted.

/U   Replaces only those files of a date and time earlier than the
             source files (DOS V4 and later).

NOTES

The REPLACE command, added with DOS V3.2, is a semi-intelligent
COPY program that can selectively update or add files to one or more
directories.

You can use this command to replace one or a few files that are duplicated
in several subdirectories. You also can use the command to update a major
application program or even DOS itself. REPLACE is especially useful
because it can search subdirectories for files to replace.

REPLACE replaces or adds files based on the matching of file names. The
command disregards drive names, directory names, and file contents,
searching only for the appropriate file names and extensions. By using this
exclusive search facility, you can quickly find older files and replace them
with their updated versions.

EXAMPLES

To search the current directory of drive A: for files with a .COM extension,
then copy over files with matching names in C:\DOS, use the following
form:

REPLACE A:*.COM C:\DOS

Any .COM file on A: is not copied if its name does not match a file in the directory C:\BIN.

To use the command above, to replace only matching files in C:\DOS and any directories below C:\DOS, use the form:

REPLACE A:*.COM C:\DOS /S

RESTORE
V2, V3, V4—External

RESTORE is a sister command to BACKUP, and together they form the backup utility supplied by the operating system. RESTORE is used to restore files from a backup diskette to the hard disk.

SYNTAX

*dc:pathc***RESTORE d1:** *d2:path\filename.ext /S /P /M /N*
/B:date /A:date /L:time /E:time

dc:pathc are the disk drive and the directory that hold the command.

d1: is the disk drive holding the backup files.

d2: is the disk drive that will receive the restored files.

path is the path to the directory that will receive the restored files.

filename.ext is the file that you want to restore. Wild-card characters are allowed.

SWITCHES

/S   Restores files in the current directory and all its subordinate subdirectories. When this switch is given, RESTORE re-creates any necessary subdirectories that have been removed, then restores the files in the re-created subdirectories.

/P   Causes RESTORE to prompt for your approval before restoring a file changed since the last backup or before restoring a file that is marked as read-only.

/M   Restores all files that have been modified or deleted since the backup set was made.

/N   Restores all files that no longer exist on the destination.

/B:date   Restores all files that were created or modified on or before the date you specify.

/A:date   Restores all files that were created or modified on or after the date you specify.

/L:time   Restores all files that were created or modified at or later than the time you specify.

/E:time   Restores all files that were created or modified at or earlier than the time you specify.

NOTES

BACKUP and RESTORE V3.3, V4.0, and V4.01 are radically different from earlier versions. BACKUP V3.3 and later versions place all backed-up files in one larger file and maintain a separate information file on the same disk. In V3.3 and later, RESTORE handles the new and old backup file formats, which means that these later versions will restore backups created by any version of BACKUP.

You can use the RESTORE command only on files that you have saved with the BACKUP command.

RESTORE prompts you to insert the backup diskettes in order. If you insert a diskette out of order, RESTORE prompts you to insert the correct diskette.

Be cautious when you restore files that were backed up while an ASSIGN, SUBST, or JOIN command was in effect. When you use RESTORE, clear any existing APPEND, ASSIGN, SUBST, or JOIN commands. Do not use RESTORE /M or RESTORE /N while APPEND /X is in effect. RESTORE attempts to search the directories for modified or missing files. APPEND tricks RESTORE into finding files in the paths specified to the APPEND command. RESTORE then might act on the wrong files and fail to restore files as you want. Give the APPEND; command to disable APPEND.

EXAMPLES

To restore an entire backup set of disks from drive A: to drive C:, use the form:

    RESTORE A: C:\ /S

To restore the file MEMO.TXT from the backup disks in drive A: to C:\LETTERS, use the form:

    RESTORE A: C:\LETTERS\MEMO.TXT

To restore all files from the disks in drive B: to C:\REPORTS, use this form:

    RESTORE B: C:\REPORTS\

RMDIR or RD
V2, V3, V4—Internal

This command removes (or deletes) empty directories that are no longer needed. If you restructure the files on your hard disk, you will make extensive use of RD and MD.

SYNTAX

    RMDIR *d:***path**

or the short form:

    RD *d:***path**

d: is the drive holding the subdirectory.

path is the path to the subdirectory. The last path name is the subdirectory you want to delete.

NOTES

RMDIR, or the short form RD, removes subdirectories from the disk. RMDIR is the opposite of MKDIR (make directory).

When you remove a subdirectory, it must be empty except for the current directory file (.) and any parent directory files (..). You cannot remove the current directory. To do this, you must first move to another directory, then use RMDIR to remove the previous current directory. If you attempt to remove a subdirectory that is not empty or is the current directory, DOS displays an error message and does not delete the directory.

EXAMPLES

To remove the directory C:\LETTERS when drive C: is the current drive, use the form:

    RD \LETTERS

or when drive A: is the current drive, use the form:

    RD C:\LETTERS

To remove the directory REPORTS (but *not* the directory DATA) from the path C:\DATA\REPORTS, use the form:

    RD C:\DATA\REPORTS

All directories must be empty before they can be removed.

SET
V2, V3, V4—Internal

SET is used to add text to the environment or to display the current environment contents.

SYNTAX

To display the environment, type the command:

SET

To add to or alter the environment, use this form:

SET name=*string*

name is the string you want to add to the environment.

string is the information you want to store in the environment.

The environment is the portion of RAM reserved for alphanumeric information that can be examined and used by DOS commands or user programs. For example, the environment usually contains COMSPEC, which is the location of COMMAND.COM; PATH, the additional paths for finding programs and batch files; and PROMPT, the string defining the DOS system prompt.

NOTES

SET puts information in memory for later use by invoked batch files or programs. The command is most commonly used to store the directory path to data files or program overlays. An invoked program examines the RAM where the SET information is stored, then issues the proper commands to find the needed data or program overlays.

EXAMPLES

To set an environment variable WPPATH to be equal to C:\WORDS\LETTERS, use the form:

SET WPPATH=C:\WORDS\LETTERS

To delete the environment variable WPPATH from the environment, use the form:

    SET WPPATH=

SHARE
V3, V4—External

Enables DOS support for file and record locking.

SYNTAX

   *dc:pathc***SHARE** */F:name_space /L:numlocks*

dc:pathc\ is the name of the disk drive and directory that holds the command.

SWITCHES

/F:name_spa   Sets the amount of memory space(name_space bytes large)
ce   used for file-sharing.

/L:numlocks Sets the maximum number (numlocks) of file/record locks to
                    use.

NOTES

SHARE is the DOS V3 and V4 program for file and record locking.

You use SHARE when two or more programs or processes share a single computer's files. After SHARE is loaded, DOS checks each file for locks whenever the file is opened, read, or written. If a file has been opened for exclusive use, an error message results from any subsequent attempt to open the file. If one program locks a portion of a file, an error message results if another program attempts to read or write the locked portion.

You must use SHARE if you use DOS V4.0 and V4.01 and have a hard disk formatted larger than 32M. For convenience, you can use INSTALL in the CONFIG.SYS file to activate SHARE.

EXAMPLES

To install SHARE with the default file space (/F) of 2048 bytes and number of locks (/L) of 20, type the command:

    SHARE

SORT
V2, V3, V4—External

Reads lines from the standard input device, performs an ASCII sort of the lines, then writes the lines to the standard output device. The sorting may be in ascending or descending order and may start at any column in the line.

SYNTAX

*dc:pathc***SORT** */R* */+c*

dc:pathc are the disk drive and the directory that hold the command.

SWITCHES

/R   Sorts in reverse order. Thus, the letter Z comes first, and the letter A comes last.

/+c   Starts sorting with column number c.

NOTES

SORT is a "semi-intelligent" general-purpose sorting program that has been changed significantly since DOS V2. With V3 and V4, SORT is a powerful filter, but it does have some limitations. One limitation, for example, is that it cannot sort a file larger than 63K.

SORT uses the ASCII sequence with some exceptions. SORT treats numbers as characters.

With DOS V3 and V4, SORT handles alphabetic characters intelligently, giving upper- and lowercase characters the same treatment. SORT V2 treats these characters differently. In the ASCII characters the uppercase A precedes the uppercase Z, but the lowercase a comes after the uppercase Z.

With V3 and V4, SORT also is intelligent in sorting certain ASCII characters in the range of 128 to 225, which includes foreign language characters and symbols. SORT V3 and V4 can handle most files containing non-English text.

EXAMPLES

To sort the lines in the file WORDS.TXT and display the result on the screen, use the form:

    SORT < WORDS.TXT

To sort the lines in the file WORDS.TXT and place the result of the sort on the file WORDS.SRT, use the form:

    SORT < WORDS.TXT > WORDS.SRT

To produce a sorted directory listing, use the form:

    DIR | SORT

To produce a directory listing sorted by extension, use this form:

    DIR | SORT /+10

SUBST
V3.1, V4—External

Creates an alias disk drive name for a subdirectory; used principally with programs that do not use path names.

SYNTAX

To establish an alias, use the following form:

    *dc:pathc***SUBST d1:** *d2:***pathname**

To delete an alias, use this form:

    *dc:pathc***SUBST d1: /D**

To see the current aliases, use this form:

    *dc:pathc***SUBST**

dc:pathc are the disk drive and the directory that hold the command.

d1: is a valid disk drive name that becomes the alias or nickname. d1: may be a nonexistent disk drive.

d2:pathname are the valid disk drive name and the directory path that will be nicknamed d1:.

SWITCH

/D   Deletes the alias.

NOTES

SUBST enables you to use a disk drive name rather than a disk drive name and directory path name. SUBST also enables you to use files in subdirectories with programs that do not allow path names, such as programs written for DOS V1.

If you need several SUBST commands, use the LASTDRIVE command in your CONFIG.SYS file. Without this command, the normal LASTDRIVE is E:.

While SUBST is in effect, certain DOS commands should be used with caution, others should be avoided, and some should not be used at all. When used on the alias disk, for example, MKDIR and RMDIR actually make or remove subdirectories from subdirectory dirname. Other commands that you should avoid or use with care are: CHKDSK, ASSIGN, JOIN, LABEL, BACKUP, DISKCOPY, DISKCOMP, FDISK, FORMAT, and RESTORE.

EXAMPLES

To assign the directory path C:\WORDS\LETTERS the drive designation E:, use the form:

SUBST E: C:\WORDS\LETTERS

To display all current substitutions, type the command:

SUBST

For the above substitution, you would see the message:

`E: => C:\WORDS\LETTERS`

To deactivate the above substitution, use the form:

SUBST E: /D

TREE
V2, V3, V4—External

Displays all the subdirectories on a disk and optionally displays all files in each directory.

SYNTAX

*dc:pathc***TREE** *d: /F*

With DOS V4, you may add the /A switch:

*dc:pathc***TREE** *d: /F /A*

dc:pathc\ are the disk drive and the directory that hold the command.

d: is the disk drive holding the disk you want to examine.

SWITCHES

/F   Displays all files in the directories.

/A   Graphically displays the connection of subdirectories.

NOTES

The TREE command displays all directories on a disk so that the user does not have to enter every directory, run a DIR command, and search for every <DIR> file (subdirectory). The /F option also displays the name of every file in every directory.

TREE shows one directory or file name on a line and can quickly scroll off the screen. If you want a copy of the entire tree, you can redirect the output to the printer.

EXAMPLES

To display a listing of all directories and subdirectories of the current disk drive, type the command:

    TREE

If you have DOS V4 and want a graphic display of your directory system, use the form:

    TREE /A

TYPE
V1, V2, V3, V4—Internal

This command displays the contents of a text file and is used frequently with the |MORE pipe to stop the text scrolling off the screen.

SYNTAX

    TYPE *d:path***filename.ext**

d:path are the disk drive and the directory holding the file that will be displayed.

filename.ext is the file that will be displayed on-screen. Wild cards are not permitted.

NOTES

The TYPE command displays a file's characters on the video screen. You can use TYPE to see a file's contents.

Strange characters appear on the screen when you use TYPE on some data files and most program files, because TYPE tries to display the machine-language instructions as ASCII characters.

The output of TYPE, like most other DOS commands, can be redirected to the printer by adding >PRN to the command line or by pressing Ctrl-PrtSc. (Don't forget to press Ctrl-PrtSc again to turn off the printing.)

You cannot predict what will happen if you print when you TYPE a program file or a data file that contains control characters. As a rule, if you have nonsense on-screen, your printout will also be nonsense.

EXAMPLES

To display the contents of the file MEMO.TXT that resides in the \WORDS directory, use the following form:

    TYPE \WORDS\MEMO.TXT

VERIFY
V2, V3, V4—Internal

Sets the computer to check the accuracy of data written to a disk to ensure that information is recorded properly, then shows whether the data has been checked.

SYNTAX

To show the verify status, type the command:

VERIFY

To set the verify status, use this form:

VERIFY ON

or the reverse form:

VERIFY OFF

NOTES

VERIFY controls new data, checking on the disk to ensure correct recording of the data. If VERIFY is off, DOS does not check the data; if VERIFY is on, DOS checks the data. VERIFY does not affect any other DOS operation.

Two factors affect the trade-off between VERIFY ON and VERIFY OFF. If VERIFY is on, data integrity is assured. If VERIFY is off, you can write to the disk faster. It usually is safe to leave VERIFY off. If you are working with very important data or are using BACKUP, you are wise to turn VERIFY on.

VOL
V2, V3, V4—Internal

Displays the disk's volume label, if a label exists.

SYNTAX

VOL *d:*

d: is the disk drive whose label you want to display.

NOTES

This command is similar to LABEL/ The main difference is that, whereas LABEL changes a disk label, VOL only displays the disk label.

EXAMPLE

If you want to display the label of the disk in drive A:, type

> VOL A:

XCOPY
V3.2 and later—External

Because of its power, XCOPY is like a big brother to the COPY command. It offers a great deal of flexibility for hard disk users.

SYNTAX

> *dc:pathc***XCOPY** *ds:paths****filenames.exts*** *dd:pathd\filenamed.extd*
> */A/D/E/M/P/S/V/W*

dc:pathc are the disk drive and the directory that hold the command.

ds:path are the source disk drive and the directory holding the file(s) that will be copied.

filenames.ext is the file that will be copied. Wild-card characters are allowed.

dd:pathd are the destination disk drive and the directory to receive the copied file(s). DOS refers to the destination drive as the target.

filenamed.extd is the new name of the file that is copied. Wild-card characters are allowed.

SWITCHES

/A	Copies files whose archive flag is on, but does not turn off the archive flag (similar to the /M switch).
/E	Creates parallel subdirectories on the destination disk even if the created subdirectory is empty.
/D:date	Copies files that were changed or created on or after the date you specify. The date's form depends on the setting of the COUNTRY directive in CONFIG.SYS.
/M	Copies files whose archive flag is on (modified files) and turns off the archive flag (similar to the /A switch).
/P	Causes XCOPY to prompt you for approval before copying a file.
/S	Copies files from this directory and all subsequent subdirectories.
/V	Verifies that the copy has been recorded correctly.
/W	Causes XCOPY to prompt and wait for the correct source floppy disk to be inserted.

NOTES

XCOPY is the extended COPY command. Although XCOPY runs more slowly than COPY, XCOPY offers more features and greater versatility. For example, XCOPY gives you greater control in selecting the files that will be copied. You can select the file's archive attribute and directory data and confirm the files individually before they are copied. The XCOPY command also enables you to copy through more than one directory. The command is most useful as an alternative to the DOS BACKUP command or when you want to maintain files between two computers that are "in sync" (two systems with hard disks or a "base" station and a laptop).

When the destination floppy disk is full, XCOPY pronounces the destination full and stops. Change floppy disks and reissue the command. The files that were copied have their archive attribute off, and XCOPY skips these files. XCOPY copies the files that have not yet been copied.

EXAMPLES

To copy all files from the root directory of drive C: to drive A:, use the form:

XCOPY C:\ A:

To copy all files from the directory C:\WORDS and all directories beneath C:\WORDS to the disk in drive A:, use the form:

XCOPY C:\WORDS A: /S

Any directories beneath C:\WORDS will be created on drive A:, and the associated files will be copied to their respective directories on drive A:.

To copy all files from the directory C:\WORDS with the extension TXT to the disk in drive A:, use the following form:

XCOPY C:\WORDS*.TXT A:

Appendix B

Selecting
a Hard Disk

Nowadays, many different suppliers sell hard disks, which come in varied shapes, sizes, and flavors. With so many varieties of hard disk available, determining which sort to purchase can be difficult.

Buying a hard disk is like buying a car. There are no hard and fast rules to tell you which specific model to buy. There are, however, a number of price/performance considerations that will narrow your choice to those models which meet your primary needs. Essentially, the final brand you choose is less important than the type of disk you buy.

If you are going to buy a hard disk for your PC, you need to consider the following questions:

- What size drive will fit in the computer?

- Will you need a power-supply upgrade?

- What storage capacity do you need?

- How fast should the disk be?

- Will you need to buy a controller card?

- Will you need a BIOS upgrade?

- Is the drive supported by your computer?

- Where should you buy the hard disk and which brand should you choose?

This appendix helps you find answers to these important questions.

Physical Drive Characteristics

One of the first things to determine is the physical size of disk you need. If you choose to buy an external drive, size is not critical, but most users will buy a hard disk to install inside the PC chassis. You must, therefore, make sure that the drive will fit.

The original IBM PC had two floppy disk drives and no hard disk. Each floppy disk drive was 5 1/4 inches wide and was full height. That is, it occupied the full height of the bay in which it was housed. When the IBM PC-XT was introduced, a 5 1/4-inch, full-height hard disk replaced one of the floppy disk drives. Since those early hard disk days, the size of hard disk drives has been reduced. Now they are available in 3 1/2-inch or 5 1/4-inch widths, and the drive may be full-height or half-height.

The 3 1/2-inch wide hard disks are designed to fit in the narrower bays used by many of the "smaller footprint" PCs. If you have such a computer, you will have to buy a 3 1/2 inch hard disk. There are, however, mounting kits that allow you to fit a 3 1/2-inch drive into a 5 1/4-inch bay.

Whether you purchase a full-height or half-height drive depends largely on the available space. Many PCs sold in the past two years have at least one half-height bay available for an extra device, such as a tape-drive unit or a hard drive. For earlier systems, you may need to make room for the hard disk. For example, if you are planning to add a hard disk drive to an original PC, you need to remove one of the floppy disk drives. Similarly, to add a second hard disk to an XT system, you may need to replace the full-height floppy disk drive with a half-height floppy disk drive and a half-height hard disk drive.

If there is a chance that you might add hard disks or devices to your PC in the future, you should consider buying a half-height drive, even if there is space for a full-height. This will leave room for future growth.

You should be aware that half-height drives usually cost more per magabyte than full-height ones. Thus, you may find that you get a better value if you elect to purchase a full-height drive.

If you are purchasing a hard disk to upgrade a PC or XT system, you will also need to consider buying a new power supply for your computer. A hard disk is a significant drain on power, and the power supply wattage in many of the early systems is inadequate. Many of the more modern PCs provide a high wattage power supply so that you can add additional devices without needing to upgrade. Make sure you check the power supply wattage in your system and compare it with the power rating of the drive you're buying.

Price/Performance Considerations

Two of the most important characteristics of a hard disk are its storage capacity (*size*) and the operating performance (*speed*). As a simple rule, the larger and faster, the better! But, as you might have guessed, greater storage and greater speed lead to greater cost.

The original hard disks for PCs had a storage capacity of 10M. Some top-of-the-line personal computers now ship with 650-megabyte drives. The likelihood is that your hard disk will need a storage capacity within these two extremes. You need enough room to store your programs and data. Clearly, the trend with most software developers is to write programs that are larger and larger. A few years ago, a major software program could be stored on one or two 360K floppy disks. Now, it is not uncommon for a program to be supplied on 10 or 15 high-density disks. For example, Microsoft Windows 3.0 consumes more than 5M of hard disk storage if you install all the options, and OS/2 can take more than 8M.

You may have very specific computing needs, and the amount of storage capacity you need will not expand appreciably in the future. For example, a writer may need only a word processing program and perhaps an accounting system to keep track of his great wealth (!). In this instance, a 20M drive might be adequate. Most of us, however, are less sure of potential computing needs and should buy a hard disk that gives us room to grow.

The average size of a hard disk purchased in 1989 was 40M. Unless your computing needs are very specific, you should consider buying a 40M hard disk or larger. There are no hard and fast rules about what size drive you should buy, however. You need to consider the number of applications you want to use on your computer. If you know that you will work with a large program (such as OS/2 or CADCAM), you need to consider buying a drive even larger than 40M. If possible, err on the side of a large drive. Most hard disk users say that no matter how big their disk is, they always seem to run out of space sooner or later.

The second big purchase consideration is drive speed. Usually, drive speed is measured in average access time, in milliseconds (ms). The hard disks in PC-XTs had an average access time of 80 to 110 milliseconds (ms). With the introduction of AT-class machines, the speed was improved to 65 ms. Today, any drive that operates at 65 ms or slower is considered a slow drive. Most popular hard disks offer either a 40 ms or 28 ms average access time, and many of the higher performance drives now sport drives with 22 ms or better access times. Basically, you should buy the fastest drive that you can afford; any drive with an access time of 28 ms or better is considered a good drive. But remember that it would be wasteful to buy a 15 ms drive and install it in a PC-XT that operates at 4.77 MHz. That would be like putting a jet engine into a Model T Ford. You would not be able to gain full advantage of the hard disk because the computer would not be fast enough to handle the throughput. For more information about the performance factors of disk drives, refer to Chapter 3.

Controller Considerations

Every hard disk needs a hard disk controller, and like hard disks, controllers come in a variety of types. Not all hard disks and controllers work together, however, and you need to make sure that yours are compatible.

If your system already has a hard disk, you already have a hard disk controller. Many 80286-based machines include a hard disk controller, even if you bought the system without a hard disk—you need a controller for the floppy drives, and most modern disk controllers include support for two floppies and two hard disks.

If you are planning to add a hard disk to a PC or XT, you probably need to buy a controller card. The original PCs had a floppy-only controller, and XT machines have controllers that support only 10M drives. You may also decide to replace your existing controller if you are installing a high-performance drive that requires a different controller type.

Controllers are available in three primary types: ST506, ESDI, and SCSI. The ST506 controller is the most common—the majority of PCs, XTs, and ATs with hard disks use ST506 controllers. The ST506 controller may use one of three data-encoding methods, which affect how data is actually stored on the disk surface and influence overall drive performance. These encoding methods are modified frequency modulation (MFM), run length limited (RLL), and advanced run length limited (ARLL).

The ESDI controller looks similar to an ST506, since it uses the same cables and connections. The controllers, however, are very different, and the two are not interchangeable. An ESDI drive requires an ESDI controller, and an ESDI controller cannot drive an ST506 drive. Many high-performance drives that have an access time of 22ms or better and a 1:1 interleave ratio use ESDI.

The SCSI interface is designed to support several peripheral devices, such as hard disks, tape systems, and CD-ROM drives. SCSI hard disks have the majority of the controller functions located on the drive itself. Nevertheless, there is a "host adaptor" card that needs to be plugged into the motherboard and connected to the drive. This card can support up to eight devices.

For more information on controller interfaces, encoding methods, and interleave ratios, refer to Chapter 3.

If your system already has a hard disk controller, you will save between $100 and $150 by buying a compatible drive. If you are looking for very high performance, you may decide to replace your ST506 controller with an ESDI or SCSI system. Whichever route you take, make sure that your drive and controller are compatible.

PC Compatibility

When you install a hard drive in a personal computer, you need to inform the computer about the main characteristics of the drive—how many cylinders are on the disk and how many read-write heads it has, for example. This information is usually defined by selecting one of the drive types from the PC's set-up program. The original Personal Computer ATs were configured to recognize 14 drive types.

If you try to install a drive not listed in your computer's set-up program, a problem arises. There are solutions, but they have drawbacks. One solution is to select a drive type that has the same number of read-write heads as the drive you want to install, but fewer cylinders. The primary drawback with this solution is that you will not be able to fully utilize your new drive's storage capacity—the extra cylinders are ignored and will remain unused. An even bigger problem occurs if no drive types listed by the set-up program come close to matching your new drive. In this instance, you may need to upgrade your PC's BIOS by installing new BIOS chips.

Chapter 8 describes third-party programs that help you to install incompatible drives with your system. These programs may even be included with your hard disk.

NOTE   High-performance COMPAQ computers (such as the 80386 series) use ESDI drives and ESDI controllers, but they use nonstandard modifications to ESDI, which means that standard ESDI drives cannot be added to the system. You cannot simply buy another ESDI drive and install it in your system. Even the third-party drive installation programs will not help.

You must either purchase a COMPAQ-approved drive or replace the existing drive and controller with a standard drive and controller.

Buying and Installing a Hard Disk

By now, you should have some idea what size, capacity, and speed hard disk to buy, and you should have determined whether you need to buy a new power supply and controller. The next question is: Where do you buy it, and what brand should you buy?

As you might expect, there are numerous places to buy a hard disk. The best way to determine the "going price" for a system is to purchase a personal computer magazine and look at the disks advertised by the mail-order companies. The hard disk market is very competitive, and you should find many suppliers offering significant discounts. Based on unit sales, by far the most popular brands of hard disk drives are Seagate and Miniscribe. There are many other reputable disk drive manufacturers as well, but you can use the Seagate and Miniscribe drives for a price/performance benchmark, against which you can compare other products.

The two common places to buy a hard disk are a computer store or by mail order. Both sources are popular and, as with any purchase, you should try to buy from a reputable company that has been in business for some years. If you buy locally, you should be able to secure a price similar to the ones offered by the major national mail-order companies.

Installing a hard disk is not a complex job. (I think it's easier than changing a faucet washer!) And most hard disks include installation instructions. For a very good blow-by-blow description of how to install a hard disk, see Scott Mueller's *Upgrading and Repairing PCs*, published by Que Corporation.

✓ **NOTE** This appendix focuses on traditional hard disk drives. Refer to Chapter 3 for a discussion of alternative storage devices that may better suit your needs. For example, if you want to add a hard disk to an original PC that has a low-wattage power supply, you might consider a hard card—a disk mounted on a card.

Appendix C

OS/2 and the Hard Disk

Many people know about the OS/2 operating system, but relatively few have used it. OS/2 is a powerful operating system that is still in its infancy. In 1985, many people expected that OS/2 would be the personal computer operating system of choice by 1990. But as history reveals, this did not happen and, with hindsight, it is easy to realize that the operating system needs considerably longer than five years to mature. If most industry experts are to be believed, OS/2 will become more popular than DOS by 1995.

The purpose of this appendix is to give you an awareness of what OS/2 is and the impact it has on hard disk management.

Overview of OS/2

To understand the origins of OS/2, you need to appreciate how the PC microprocessor has evolved.

The PC operating system (DOS) was developed to run on machines based on 8086/8088 chips. When the 80286 chip was released, there were already millions of PCs using 8086/8088 chips; so the 80286 was designed to run any software that would run on these earlier systems. When an 80286 chip is used like an 8086/8088 chip, it is said to be running in *real mode*. The 80286 chip also is capable of running applications in *protected mode*, which allows programs to access more memory than 640K and run multiple applications at the same time. DOS, however, uses the real mode of the 80286 chip. In other words, DOS only utilizes the 8086/8088 features of the chip; it does not benefit from the protected mode. The same is true of the newer 80386 and 80486 chips. DOS uses these very powerful microprocessors in real mode only—to DOS, the chips are just like very fast 8086s.

For many years, PC users have wanted to break the 640k memory limit and have wanted to run more than one application at one time. The protected mode of the 80286 (and later) microprocessors offers these capabilities. Microsoft and IBM have jointly developed an operating system, OS/2, designed to unleash the potential of protected mode on 80286 and (with OS/2 Release 2.0) 80386 computers.

The good news about this development is that OS/2 is specifically designed to access up to 16M of memory and provide you with multitasking capabilities. The bad news is that DOS programs have to be completely rewritten to take advantage of these OS/2 features. The slow growth in OS/2 applications software packages has largely been blamed for the slow growth of OS/2 sales. Why buy OS/2 if there are no applications that use it?

> **NOTE**
>
> You do not have to use a new operating system to take advantage of a fast microprocessor. In fact, a number of DOS based-applications programs are designed specifically to take advantage of protected mode. For example, Paradox 386 is designed to run in protected mode on 80386 computers. Windows 3.0 and DESQview also can run on top of DOS and provide multitasking capabilities on 80286 and 80386 computers.
>
> The introduction of these specialty products has contributed to the slow adoption of OS/2, but as OS/2 matures, the gap between OS/2 and the DOS-based protected mode software will widen. There is a limit to how much can be achieved without fundamental changes in the operating system, and over time OS/2-based programs will inevitably provide more power and features than DOS-based programs.

OS/2 is a sophisticated operating system that provides many features. The following list summarizes some of the main features of OS/2 from a user's perspective.

Multitasking. OS/2 is designed to allow multiple programs to run concurrently. For example, a database program can run a large query while a communications program is downloading your electronic mail and your spreadsheet is printing a long report. Remember, though, that the microprocessor has to run each of these tasks simultaneously, so the more tasks you are running, the slower they all run.

Memory. Applications can access up to 16M of memory, and the operating system will use virtual (disk-based) memory if random-access memory is insufficient.

DOS similarity. The designers of OS/2 knew that the majority of OS/2 users would already be familiar with DOS, so many of the OS/2 commands are very similar to their DOS counterparts. For example, the COPY, RENAME, and DELETE commands are all available in OS/2.

DOS compatibility. To allow users to run applications written for DOS, OS/2 has a DOS session or "compatibility box," which can be used to run a single DOS session. Most, but not all, programs written for DOS will run in the DOS compatibility box. With the introduction of OS/2 V2, an 80386 machine will be able to run multiple DOS sessions, as well as multiple OS/2 sessions.

Presentation Manager. The operating system includes a sophisticated graphical user interface designed to simplify file-management and program-execution commands. Presentation Manager is discussed in Chapter 12.

In addition to these basic features, IBM offers the *OS/2 Extended Edition*, which provides additional capabilities not normally associated with an operating system. This product includes a relational database manager, a communications manager, an OS/2 LAN (local-area network) server program, and other LAN communications features.

Installation Considerations

OS/2 is self-installing. When you first boot your computer with an OS/2 startup disk in the floppy disk drive, OS/2 will run the installation program. Like DOS, OS/2 installs some startup files in the root directory of your hard disk. It also creates subdirectories to store the majority of the operating system files. All told, the operating system will probably use more than 8M of hard disk space.

The root directory includes an OS/2 version of COMMAND.COM, as well as the startup files CONFIG.SYS, and STARTUP.CMD (the OS/2 equivalent of AUTOEXEC.BAT). DOS relied heavily on the personal computer's BIOS chips for much of its low-level interaction with the hardware, but OS/2 uses the BIOS very little. OS/2 accesses the BIOS-type data from special device-driver files, which have a SYS extension. The SYS files are stored in the root directory and include DISK01.SYS, KBD01.SYS, and SCREEN01.SYS. These device-driver files allow hardware manufacturers to write specific drivers to support their systems. The files are also the reason that some clones are unable to run IBM

OS/2—the SYS files are designed specifically to run on IBM computers. The root directory also contains some hidden files like OS2KNL and OS2LDR that are accessed during the booting process.

The OS/2 installation program creates an OS2 directory and at least three subdirectories: INSTALL, SYSTEM, and DLL. The main OS/2 directory contains all the operating system external commands, such as XCOPY, BACKUP, and RESTORE, as well as many of the Presentation manager program files. The INSTALL subdirectory is usually required only while OS/2 is being installed and can be removed after installation. The SYSTEM subdirectory holds a variety of the system files accessed directly by the operating system: SWAPPER.EXE, for example, which provides virtual memory support. The DLL subdirectory stores the dynamic link library (DLL) files.

DLLs allow developers to extend the capabilities of the operating system by writing re-entrant routines that can be accessed by multiple programs. DLLs are like special libraries of overlay files, which can be used by multiple programs. Most large OS/2 applications programs use DLLs. OS/2 is instructed where to find the DLL files by the LIBPATH statement in the CONFIG.SYS file.

The Presentation Manager includes a File System program, which can help you to manage your files and review the files in the directories. Refer to Chapter 12 for a detailed review of the OS/2 File System features.

The OS/2 High-Performance File System

Prior to V1.2 of OS/2, there are no major differences in the way DOS and OS/2 manage files. The same basic concepts of directories and the FAT are used in both systems, and the same file-naming conventions are used. But because users have complained for years about the restriction on the length of file names, OS/2 V1.2 introduced the *High Performance File System* (HPFS). The HPFS is the most significant enhancement made to the operating system since its first release.

The file system is the system of bookkeeping records that allows the operating system to store and retrieve files on such peripheral devices as hard disks. Traditionally, the file system has been an intimate part of the operating system, and the operating system therefore has by necessity dictated how files are accessed. With OS/2 V1.2 the rules changed. OS/2 V1.2 introduces the concept of *installable* file systems. In other words, the file system is not part of the operating system kernel, and third-party developers can create file systems independently from the operating system. OS/2 V1.2 will even support different file systems being used at one time! Each file system has to be installed on a separate disk or partition.

As well as providing the capabilities for third-party suppliers to develop their own file systems, OS/2 takes advantage of this new technology by introducing its own installable system, namely the HPFS. The following list summarizes some of the main features of the HPFS.

Long file names. No longer is a file name restricted to 8 characters with a three-character extension. The file name can be up to 254 upper- and lowercase characters, and it may include spaces and multiple period (.) delimiters. For example, the file name "A letter to T. L. Solomon" is a valid file name in the HPFS.

Time and date stamps. With the standard DOS file system, the date and time of last modification is recorded for each file. The HPFS records three dates and times: when the file was created, when the file was last modified, and when the file was last accessed.

Extended attributes. DOS files have a set of attributes, which describe some of the properties of the file. For example, the archive attribute shows whether the file has been modified since the last backup. These file attributes are still available in the HPFS (for compatibility), but a new mechanism of extended attributes has been introduced. These extended attributes are used to provide a wealth of information about the file. In fact, each file can have up to 64K of extended-attribute information. For example, the .TYPE is used to describe the type of file in much the same way that the file-name extension was used in DOS. For example, in DOS a Lotus 1-2-3 Release 3 file would have a WK3 extension. With the HPFS file system, the file name would not need an extension, and the spreadsheet program might look for any file with a .TYPE attribute of "Lotus 1-2-3 Release 3." Other attributes include .COMMENTS to allow you to make notes about the file, .HISTORY to keep a log of all changes made to the file, .KEYPHRASES for a list of keywords that could referenced by a file management program, and so on.

Applications software must be written to specifically take advantage of the HPFS. For example, the file-save option in your word processor must allow you to type in long file names and add information to the extended attributes. The HPFS represents a very significant change in the way personal computers manage files, but it will be some time before the major software packages are upgraded to take advantage of it.

The Future for OS/2

Arguably, one of the reasons for OS/2's poor acceptance is that it was written to run on 80286 based machines and did not take advantage of the capabilities of the 80386 microprocessor—even though the vast majority of computers using OS/2 are 80386-based.

OS/2 V2 (scheduled for release in 1990) is written specifically to take advantage of the 80386. Many observers believe that the introduction of OS/2 V2 will give a strong push to OS/2 sales. The biggest improvement in the new system is that it will be able to use a 32-bit memory-addressing scheme. To the user, this will translate into faster-running programs that can address phenomenal amounts of memory. The system also will support multiple DOS sessions, each of which can run in the background. For example, you will be able to run Lotus 1-2-3/G in an OS/2 session, Windows 3.0 in one DOS session (and a bevy of applications within Windows), and DESQview in another DOS session. The main advantage of running multiple DOS applications is that a DOS user can move to OS/2 without losing any of the capabilities he/she had in the DOS world.

Although OS/2 has been slow to catch on, it is likely that the improvements in the operating system, combined with a growth in OS/2 specific applications, will provide a healthy future for the operating system.

Appendix D

Sources of Programs

Listed below, in alphabetical order, are the names of commercial, shareware, and public domain programs featured in this book, with the names and addresses of the companies who market the products.

Automenu
Magee Enterprises, Inc.
P.O. Box 1587
Norcross, GA 30091
(404) 446-0271

Batcom
The Wenham Software
Company
5 Burley Street
Wenham, MA 01984
(508) 774-7036

Bernoulli Box
Iomega Corporation
1821 West 4000 South
Roy, UT 84067
(801) 778-1000

DESQview
Quarterdeck Office Systems
150 Pico Blvd.
Santa Monica, CA 90405
(213) 392-9701

Direct Access
Delta Technology
International
1621 Westgate Road
Eau Glaire, WI 54703
(715) 832-7575

Disk Manager
Ontrack Computer Systems,
Inc.
6321 Bury Drive #16-19
Eden Prairie, MN 55346
(612) 937-1107

FastBack Plus & Mace
Utilities & Mace Vaccine
Fifth Generation Systems, Inc.
10049 N. Reiger Rd
Baton Rouge, LA 70809
(504) 291-7221

FGREP
The Cove Software Group
P.O. Box 1072
Columbia, MD 21044
(301) 992-9371

LIST
Vernon D. Beurg
139 White Oak Circle
Petaluma, CA 94952
(707) 778-1811

Lotus 1-2-3 Release 2
Lotus 1-2-3 Release 3
Lotus 1-2-3 /G
Lotus Magellan
Lotus Development
Corporation
55 Cambridge Parkway
Cambridge, MA 02142
(615) 577-8500

Microsoft Windows 3.0
MS DOS
OS/2
Presentation Manager
Microsoft Corporation
One Microsoft Way
Redmond, WA 98052-6399
(206) 882-8080

MOVE
Bryan Higgins
1802 Channing Way
Berkeley, CA 94703-1725

Paradox
Borland International
800 Greenhills Road
P.O. Box 660001
Scotts Valley, CA
95066-0001
(800) 345-2888

PC Tools
Central Point Software
15220 NW Greenbriar Pkwy
#200
Beaverton, OR 97006
(503) 690-8090

PCOPY
Partriquin Utilities
P.O. Box 8623
San Bernadino, CA 92412

PKZIP
PKWARE, Inc.
7545 North Port
Washington Road
Glendale, WI 53217
(414) 352-3670

PowerMenu
Brown Bag Software, Inc.
2155 South Bascom Avenue
Suite 114
Campbell, CA 95008
(408) 559-4545

Q-Filer
Jamestown Software
2508 Valley Forge Drive
Madison, WI 53719
(608) 271-2090

66666666

66666666666

Rescue
Intex Solutions, Inc.
161 Highland Ave
Needham, MA 02194
(617) 449-6222

SpeedStor
Storage Dimensions
2145 Hamilton Avenue
San Jose, CA 95125
(408) 879-0300

SpinRite II
SPINTEST
SPINTIME
PARK
Gibson Research Corporation
22991 La Cadena
Laguna Hills, CA 92653
(714) 830-2200

Super PC KWIK & Power Disk
Multisoft Corporation
15100 S W Koll Pkwy
Beaverton, OR 97006
(503) 644-5644

Teddy
TechnoJock Software, Inc.
P.O. Box 820927
Houston, TX 77282
(713) 493-6354

The Norton Utilities
Norton Commander
Peter Norton Computing, Inc.
100 Willshire Blvd. 9th Floor
Santa Monica, CA 90401
(213) 319-2000

Viruscan & Clean
McAfee Associates
4423 Cheeney Street
Santa Clara, CA 95054
(408) 988-3832

VOPT
Golden Bow Systems
2665 Ariane Dr., Suite 207
San Diego, CA 92117

WordPerfect
WordPerfect Corporation
1555 N. Technology Way
Orem, UT 84057
(801) 225-5000

XtreePro Gold
Executive Systems, Inc.
4330 Sante Fe Road
San Luis Obispo, CA 93401
(416) 866-8592

Appendix E

Using the Programs Disk

The disk accompanying this book includes a variety of popular public-domain and user-supported shareware programs. This appendix explains how to install the programs on your hard disk and briefly describes the purpose of each program. Most of the programs are also discussed within the body of the book and can be easily identified by the special disk icon:

Note that some of the programs are included for evaluation only. If you continue to use the programs, you are expected to register your copy. Refer to the section "Understanding User-Supported and Shareware Programs" for further information.

Installing the Programs

The disk includes the programs in a compressed file, PROGRAMS.ZIP. The disk is a standard double-sided double-density (360K) disk. Run the program INSTALL.EXE to install the programs on your hard disk.

To install the programs, insert the disk into the floppy drive and enter the following commands:

        A:
        INSTALL A: C:

Note: The preceding commands assume that you are copying from drive A to drive C. If you use different drive names, substitute the appropriate drive letter. For example, to copy from drive B to drive E, you would type **B:** *and then* **INSTALL B: E:.**

The install program creates the directory \QUEDISK on the hard disk and transfers all the files from the floppy disk to this directory (see fig. E.1). The programs use approximately 700K of hard disk space. The installation will check that you have enough room for the files before proceeding.

```
┌─────────────────────────────────────────────────────┐
│   Using Your Hard Disk -- Program Installation     │
└─────────────────────────────────────────────────────┘

This program will copy files from A:\ to C:\QUEDISK.
Press Esc to abort, or any other key to continue...
Unzipping the files

PKUNZIP (tm)    FAST!    Extract Utility    Version 1.02    10-01-89
Copyright 1989 PKWARE Inc.  All Rights Reserved.  PKUNZIP/h for help

Searching ZIP: A:/PROGRAMS.ZIP
  Exploding: FGREP.DOC
  Exploding: FGREP.COM
  Exploding: FINDIT.COM
  Exploding: VTREE.COM
  Exploding: LICENSE.LST
  Exploding: LIST.DOC
  Exploding: LIST.HST
  Exploding: LIST.COM  _
```

Fig. F.1. *INSTALL places all the program files in the \QUEDISK directory on the hard disk.*

After the files have been installed, the default directory will be changed to the \QUEDISK directory on the target drive. You can then use the file-management program QFILER to review the program files. To do so, type **QFILER** and press Enter.

FGREP

FGREP is an excellent utility program that searches files for any character, word, or phrase. It was written by Chris Dunford, a developer at The Cove Software Group, which sells the excellent PCED utility package.

FGREP can search text or binary files for any sequence of characters. To try the program, enter the following command from the \QUEDISK directory:

FGREP "hard disk" *.DOC

FGREP will display all the files with a DOC extension that include the phrase *hard disk*. The file FGREP.DOC provides further information about FGREP. Also see Chapter 11 for a discussion of FGREP.

FINDIT

FINDIT is a public-domain utility that will search every subdirectory on a hard disk for any files that match a specified file name, including wild cards. This program is especially useful when you know a file is on the hard disk somewhere, but cannot remember the directory in which it is stored! For example, to instruct FINDIT to search for all files that begin with W, enter the following command from the QUEDISK directory;

FINDIT W*.*

See the discussion of FINDIT in Chapter 11 for more information. Note that if you enter the command FINDIT with no parameters, FINDIT displays a useful help screen describing its operation.

LIST

LIST is the excellent file-browsing program from Vernon Beurg. LIST can be used to browse any text or binary file. The file LIST.DOC describes the features and capabilities of the program. You can use LIST to display the contents of the file LIST.DOC by entering the following command in the \QUEDISK directory:

LIST LIST.DOC

Chapter 11 explains the syntax of the LIST command.

In the documentation for LIST, Vernon refers to three different versions of the program (LISTP, LISTR, and LISTS), and he recommends that you select whichever version you want and rename it LIST.COM. This has already been done. There was only space on the disk to include one version,

so LISTP.COM, the full-featured program, was selected and renamed
LIST.COM. If you continue to use the program, you should send a donation
to Vernon. See the file LICENSE.LST for further information.

MV

MV.EXE is Bryan Higgins' efficient file mover. It can be used to move
files between directories on the same disk drive or to different drives.
Optional switches allow you to control the operation and indicate whether
files should be automatically overwritten in the target directory, and so on.
Documentation for the MV command is included in the file MV.DOC. This
file also includes the address to send a donation if you find the program
useful.

PCOPY

PCOPY is a powerful shareware file-copying program from Norm
Partrequin. PCOPY is a full-screen program that makes safe file copying a
breeze. Using optional switches, you can strictly control which files are
copied and whether files in the target directory should be overwritten. For
example, you can copy all files modified since June 4th, or only copy files
that don't exist in the target directory, and so on.

The file PCOPY.DOC documents this command. If you execute the
PCOPY command with no parameters, a comprehensive help system is
invoked. See Chapter 11 for further information about PCOPY.

PKZIP

PKZIP is the name of the file-compression utilities from PKWARE, Inc.
The programs include PKZIP.EXE for creating and managing archived
files, PKUNZIP for extracting files from an archive, PKSFX for creating
self-extracting files, and PKZIP.DOC, which describes how to use the
programs. If you decide you want to continue using the program, you
should register your copy—details are included in the file PKZIP.DOC.

PKZIP is designed to combine a set of files into a single compressed file. It
is ideal for saving space and makes files easier to manage and distribute.
The PKZIP utilities were used to compress the files on this book's
companion disk—700K of files were compressed to fit on a 360K floppy
disk. See Chapter 11 for a further discussion of PKZIP.

QFILER

QFILER is the file-management program from Ken Flee at Jamestown Software. The main program is QFILER.EXE. There is also an installation program, QINST.EXE, which you can use to customize the program settings. QFILER includes mouse support, but you must enable it by executing QINST with a "/mouse" parameter on the command line.

You can use QFILER to peruse the files on your hard disk by typing the following command in the \QUEDISK directory:

QFILER

QFILER is a shareware program. The file QFILER.DOC describes all the features of the program, as well as how to register your copy. Further information about QFILER can be found in Chapter 11.

RAM

The file RAM.SYS is a device driver that creates a RAM disk. A good feature of RAM.SYS is that you can change the size of the RAM disk without rebooting the computer. The file RAM.DOC provides further information, and RAM.SYS also is discussed in Chapter 11.

T2

T2.EXE, for TEDDY II, is a public-domain text editor written by Bob Ainsbury. It is a simple, full screen editor that can be used to create and modify text files up to 64K in size. To execute the program, enter **T2**, followed by the name of the file you want to edit, for example, **T2 \AUTOEXEC.BAT.** If specified, the switch /BW forces the editor to use monochrome display attributes. While editing a file, you can press F1 to get help.

See Chapter 6 for a further discussion of TEDDY.

SPIN Programs

Gibson Research Corporation, makers of SpinRite, have provided two programs to test your hard disk: SPINTEST and SPINTIME. The file INTLEAVE.DOC provides instructions on how to use these programs.

The main program SPINTEST, determines how many disk revolutions your IBM compatible personal computer requires to read an entire track from its hard disk. SPINTEST therefore indicates your hard disk interleave ratio. For example, a disk that needs three revolutions to read an entire track has an interleave ratio of 3:1.

SPINTIME has two purposes: to determine the speed of your system's clock and to verify that your system's hard disk is spinning at close to the standard 3600 RPM standard.

The program PARK, also written by Gibson Research Corporation, is a general-purpose head-parking utility that can be used on any hard disk. See Chapter 14 for a discussion of the importance of disk head parking.

VTREE

VTREE is a public-domain utility that displays the directory tree structure of a drive. This feature was implemented in the TREE command starting with DOS V4. But if you use DOS V3.3 or earlier, you will appreciate the value of this simple program. To display the directory tree, enter VTREE. VTREE is described further in Chapter 11.

WHAT

WHAT is a public-domain batch file enhancer. It allows you to prompt the user to enter text, check the amount of free disk space, determine whether the printer is attached and on-line, and much more.

The file WHAT.DOC briefly describes the operation of the program. In addition, Chapter 9 discusses in detail how to use WHAT to improve your batch files.

Understanding User-Supported and Shareware Programs

Some of the programs on the accompanying disk are public domain. They are free and can be used and distributed to others at will.

Other programs, however, are user-supported or shareware. These are programs distributed so that you can use them to see if you like them. If you continue to use the programs, you should pay the program's author(s). This payment often is referred to as registering the product. It is a try-before-you-buy marketing concept, and the whole system relies upon the honesty of program users to register the products they use. If you decide you don't want to use a program, you are under no obligation to pay. The documentation files for these programs clearly describe the registration procedures.

There are many other excellent shareware programs—far too many to fit even a representative sampling on the disk. For further information about top-quality shareware, contact the Public (Software) Library at (713) 524-6394 or write to them at:

Public (Software) Library
P.O. Box 35705
Houston, TX 77235-5705

This excellent company specializes in shareware and public-domain programs. They have literally thousands of programs in their library.

Glossary of Hard Disk Terms

A

access time   The time that elapses between the time the operating system issues an order for data retrieval and the time the data is ready for transfer from the disk.

The access time of a disk drive is determined by the following: seek time (the time the heads take to settle down after reaching the correct track) and latency (the time required for the correct sector to swing around under the head).

For hard disks, access times usually are measured in milliseconds (ms).

algorithm   A specific set of well-defined mathematical and logical procedures that can be followed to solve a problem in a finite number of steps.

archive flag   A file attribute set to indicate that the file has been modified since it was last backed up. This flag is referenced by backup programs when an incremental backup is being made.

ASCII   (American Standard Code for Information Interchange) A standard computer character set (or computer alphabet) devised in 1968 to enable efficient data communication and achieve compatibility among different computer devices.

The standard ASCII code consists of 96 displayed upper- and lowercase letters, plus 32 nondisplayed control characters. An individual character code is composed of seven bits plus one parity bit for error checking. The code permits the expression of English-language textual data, but is inadequate for many foreign languages and technical applications. Because ASCII code includes no graphics characters, most modern computers use an extended character set.

attribute   In many word processing and graphics programs, a character emphasis, such as boldface and italic, and other characteristics of character formatting, such as typeface and type size. In Lotus Manuscript, for example, attributes include appearance attributes (boldface, underline, double underline, italic, shadow, small caps, and strikeout) and size attributes.

AUTOEXEC.BAT   In DOS, a batch file consulted by DOS when the system is started or restarted.

AUTOEXEC.BAT is not mandatory for IBM PC-compatible computers, but when you are running a hard disk loaded with several applications and a computer to which you have attached several peripherals, the file is all but essential for efficient operation. Common ingredients in AUTOEXEC.BAT are PATH command statements that tell DOS where to find application programs and the names of system-configuration programs that set up your computer for the use of peripherals, such as a serial printer and mouse. Such commands and programs do not remain in your computer's memory when you shut off the power. You must enter all this information manually at the start of every operating session. AUTOEXEC.BAT does the task for you.

B

back up   To copy a data or program file to a removable secondary storage device so that it can be kept in a safe off-site location.

basic input-output system (BIOS)   A set of programs encoded in read-only memory (ROM) in IBM PC-compatible computers. These programs facilitate the transfer of data and control instructions between the computer and peripherals, such as disk drives.

batch file   A file containing a series of DOS commands executed one after the other, as though you had typed them. Batch files are useful when you repeatedly need to type the same series of DOS commands. Almost all hard disk users have an AUTOEXEC.BAT file, a batch file that DOS loads at the start of every operating session. See **AUTOEXEC.BAT**.

binary file   A file containing data or program instructions in a format other than that of a text file, so that special software is required to display the file. See **text file**.

bit   The basic unit of information in a binary numbering system (BInary digiT).

boot   To initiate an automatic routine that clears the memory, loads the operating system, and prepares the computer for use.

The term "boot" is derived from the saying "pulling yourself up by your bootstraps." Personal computers must do just that because random-access memory (RAM) does not retain program instructions when the computer's power is shut off.

Buried within the computer's read-only memory (ROM) circuits is an auto-start program that comes into play when the power is switched on (a *cold boot*). Unlike RAM, ROM circuits retain data and program instructions without requiring power. The auto-start program instructs the computer's disk drives to search for the disk containing the computer's operating system.

After a system crash occurs, you usually must reboot the computer. With most systems, you can perform a *warm boot*, which restarts the system without the stress on electronic components caused by switching the power off and on again. See **cold boot** and **warm boot**.

buffer   A unit of memory given the task of holding information temporarily, especially when such temporary storage is needed to compensate for differences in speed between computer components.

byte   Eight contiguous bits, the fundamental data word of personal computers.

Computers work with binary numbers, and the internal circuit can represent one of the two numbers in a binary system: 1 or 0 . These basic either/or, yes/no units of information are called bits. Because building a reliable circuit that tells the difference between a 1 (represented by high current) and a 0 (represented by low current) is easy and inexpensive, computers are accurate in their internal processing capabilities.

C

cache   A storage space in memory that holds information about disk-based data. It is used to reduce the number of disk accesses and thereby speed up the overall system throughput. When a program requests data from the disk, the cache is checked to see whether the data is already loaded. If so, the data is extracted from the cache rather than from the disk.

cache memory   A special fast section of randomly accessed information stored in RAM.

CD-ROM   A read-only optical storage technology that uses compact disks.

CD-ROM disks can store up to 650M of data, all of which can be made available interactively on the computer's display. CD-ROM currently is used to make encyclopedias, dictionaries, and software libraries available to personal computer users. New compression techniques enable you to pack up to 250,000 text pages on one CD-ROM disk. See **compact disk** and **optical storage**.

central processing unit (CPU)   The computer's internal storage, processing, and control circuitry, including the arithmetic-logic unit (ALU), the control unit, and the primary storage.

Only the ALU and control unit are wholly contained on the microprocessor chip; the primary storage is elsewhere on the motherboard or an adapter on the expansion bus.

cluster   In a floppy disk or hard disk, a unit of storage that includes one or more sectors.

When DOS stores a file on disk, DOS breaks down the file's contents and distributes them among dozens or even hundreds of clusters. The file allocation table (FAT) tracks the connections between all the sectors on a disk.

command line   The complete text entered at the operating system prompt to invoke a program or operation.

COMMAND.COM   In DOS, an essential system disk file that contains the command processor. This file must be on the start-up disk for DOS to run.

command processor   The portion of a command-line operating system that handles user input and displays messages, such as prompts, confirmation messages, and error messages.

CON   In DOS and OS\2, the device name that refers to the console (that is, the keyboard and monitor).

concatenation   The combination of two or more units of information, such as text or files, so that they form one unit.

CONFIG.SYS   In DOS and OS\2, an ASCII text file that contains configuration commands.

The operating system consults this file at system start-up. If no CONFIG.SYS file is on the start-up disk, DOS uses the default configuration values. Most programs work well with the default configuration settings. Nonstandard peripherals and some application programs, however, may require that a CONFIG.SYS file be present in the root directory so that these configurations are modified.

copy protection   The inclusion in a program of hidden instructions intended to prevent you from making unauthorized copies of software. Because most copy-protection schemes impose penalties on legitimate owners of programs, such as forcing them to insert a specially encoded "key-disk" before using a program, most business software publishers have given up using these schemes. Copy protection is still common, however, in recreational and educational software.

crash   An abnormal termination of program execution, usually (but not always) resulting in a frozen keyboard or an unstable state. In most cases, you must reboot the computer to recover from a crash.

current directory   The directory that DOS or an application uses by default to store and retrieve files.

Within an application, the current directory is normally the one from which you start that application program. Some programs, however, enable you to change the current directory so that you can save data files in a directory other than the one in which the program's files are stored. Synonymous with **default directory.**

cyclic redundancy check (CRC)   A check made by the disk controller to ensure that data has been successfully read from the disk. At the end of each sector on the disk is a special value, which is like a subtotal of all the data written to the sector. When the data is subsequently read from the sector, the subtotal is computed from the data just read and compared to the value stored at the end of the sector.

cylinder   In disk drives, a unit of storage consisting of the set of tracks that occupy the same position.

On a double-sided disk, a cylinder includes track 1 of the top and the bottom sides. On hard disks, in which several disks are stacked on top of one another, a cylinder consists of the tracks in a specific location on all the platters.

D

data   Factual information stored on magnetic media. This information can be used to generate calculations or to make decisions.

default setting   A command option a program uses unless you specify another setting. In Lotus 1-2-3, for example, the default column width is nine characters.

defragmentation   A procedure in which all the files on a hard disk are rewritten so that each file's parts are stored in contiguous sectors. Defragmentation improves the disk's speed in retrieval operations.

delimiter   A symbol that marks the end of one section of a command and the beginning of another section.

device   Any hardware component or peripheral, such as a printer, modem, monitor, or mouse, that can receive and/or send data.

directory   An index to the files stored on a disk or a portion of a disk. The operating system maintains an updated record of the files stored on a disk, with ample information about the file's content, time of creation, and size. You can view a directory on-screen to determine the names and types of files it contains.

disk drive   A secondary storage medium such as a floppy disk drive or a hard disk. This term usually refers to floppy disk drives. A floppy disk drive is an economical secondary storage medium that uses a removable magnetic disk. Like all magnetic media, a floppy disk can be recorded, erased, and reused over and over. The recording and erasing operations are performed by read/write heads, which move laterally over the disk's surface, giving the drive its random-access capabilities.

Although floppy disk drives are inexpensive, they are too slow to serve as the main secondary storage medium for today's personal computers; for business applications, a minimum configuration is one hard disk and one floppy disk drive. (The floppy disk drive is needed to copy software and disk-based data onto the system and for backup operations.) See **floppy disk**, **random-access memory**, **read/write head**, and **secondary storage**.

diskette   A file-storage disk, also called a floppy disk. See **floppy disk.**

DOS   Acronym for disk operating system; refers to PC-DOS and MS DOS, the operating systems of IBM Personal Computers and compatibles.

drive name   The name assigned to each logical disk drive in the computer. The name is composed of a letter and a colon (:). Floppy drives usually are assigned the names A: and B:, and the first hard drive is named C:.

driver   A disk file that contains information needed by a program to operate a peripheral, such as a monitor or printer.

E

environment   The hardware and/or operating system for applications programs, such as the Macintosh environment.

ERRORLEVEL   A special code that is set when a program terminates. An ERRORLEVEL of zero indicates that the program terminated successfully. You can check the status of the last executed program with the help of a batch file that contains an "IF ERRORLEVEL *code*" statement.

external command   An operating system program that is not included in the COMMAND.COM file; a command that is not installed in memory when the computer boots. When an external command (such as XCOPY) is issued, the operating system searches for a program file with the same name and an extension of COM, EXE, or BAT.

F

file   A named collection of information stored as an apparent unit on a secondary storage medium, such as a floppy disk.

Although a file appears to be whole, the operating system may distribute the file among dozens or even hundreds of noncontiguous sectors on the disk. The operating system logs the connections (chains) among these sectors in a file allocation table. To the user, however, the file appears as a single unit in a disk directory and is retrieved and copied as a unit. See **file allocations table (FAT)** and **secondary storage**.

file allocation table (FAT)   On a disk, a hidden table that stores information about how files are stored in sectors.

file name   A name assigned to a file so that the operating system can find the file. You assign file names when the files are created. Every file on a disk must have a unique name.

In DOS and early versions of OS/2, file names have two parts: the file name and the extension.

file name extension   A three-letter suffix to a file name. A file extension often describes the file's contents.

filter   A program that reduces the amount of output from another program by filtering out information that doesn't meet some specific criterion. The FIND command is an example of a filter. See **pipe**.

floppy disk   A removable and widely used secondary storage medium that uses a magnetically sensitive flexible disk enclosed in a plastic envelope or case.

Floppy disks are the usual way in which programs and text files are communicated from one computer to another. At one time, they also were the only secondary storage medium for personal computers, but the availability of inexpensive hard disks has relegated floppy disks to the sidelines.

FORMAT   In DOS and OS/2, an external command that prepares a disk to accept files.

During the formatting operation, the computer's disk drive encodes a magnetic pattern consisting of tracks and sectors. The tracks are arranged concentrically around the disk's center, like the tracks of an LP album. The sectors are created by drawing electronic lines from the disk's center to its edge.

Caution: Version 3.1 and earlier versions of DOS may carry out an unintended format of a hard disk if not used with caution. Suppose that you have copied the FORMAT program to a directory on drive C, and without thinking, you type FORMAT and press Enter. Because you have not specified a drive name, DOS uses the current drive. If the current drive is C, these versions of DOS begin a formatting operation on the hard disk, erasing everything. If you are using an early version of DOS, always specify the drive designator after FORMAT, as in the following example:

FORMAT A:

fragmentation   The inefficient allocation of files in noncontiguous sectors on a floppy disk or hard disk. Fragmentation occurs because of multiple file deletions and write operations.

When DOS writes a file to disk, the operating system looks for available clusters. If you have created and erased many files on the disk, few files are stored in contiguous clusters; the disk drive's read/write head must travel longer distances to retrieve the scattered data. A process known as defragmentation can improve disk efficiency by as much as 50 percent, by rewriting files so that they are placed in contiguous clusters. See **defragmentation**.

G

graphical user interface (GUI)   A user interface that uses the mouse and a bit-mapped graphics display to make basic computer operations substantially easier for novices.

Standard features of the graphical user interface include alert boxes, a clipboard, desk accessories, the desktop metaphor, dialog boxes, scroll boxes, on-screen display of fonts, "what-you-see-is-what-you-get" (WYSIWYG) on-screen page representation, and multiple on-screen windows.

The graphical user interface has been criticized for slowing down the computer and insulating users from the nitty-gritty details of the operating system. Microprocessors such as the Intel 80386 and Motorola 68030, however, can run GUIs at speeds sufficient to satisfy most users, and the nitty-gritty details of the operating system ought to be transparent to the user.

H

hard disk   A secondary storage medium that uses several nonflexible disk platters coated with a magnetically sensitive material and housed, together with the recording heads, in a hermetically sealed mechanism.

A hard disk is a complex storage system that includes the disk, the read/write head assembly, and the electronic interface that governs the connection between the drive and the computer.

hardware platform   A computer hardware standard, such as IBM PC-compatible or Macintosh personal computers, in which a comprehensive approach to the computer solution of a problem can be based.

hidden file   A file whose file attributes are set so that the file name does not appear on the disk directory. You cannot display, erase, or copy hidden files.

I

internal command   In DOS and OS/2, a command such as DIR or COPY that remains in memory and is always available when the DOS or OS/2 prompt is visible on-screen.

K

kilobyte (K)   The basic unit of measurement for computer memory, equal to 1,042 bytes.

The prefix *kilo* suggests 1,000, but the computer world contains twos, not tens: $2^{10} = 1,024$. Because one byte is the same as one character in personal computing, a memory of 1K can contain 1,024 characters (letters, numbers, or punctuation marks).

Early personal computers (mid-1970s) offered as little as 16K or 32K of random-access memory (RAM), because memory chips were expensive. In IBM PC-compatible computing, 640K is considered a standard figure (the maximum under DOS); today, Macintosh computers are equipped with at least 1M of RAM.

L

log file   A file created by the operating system's BACKUP command. When BACKUP is used with the /L switch, the command creates a log file, which lists the name, date, and backup time of each file. Also, a file that records the activities performed on a computer. Log files often are created by a menu program to record programs accessed and to identify the user.

logical disk drive   A computer system's disk drives, which present themselves to the user as identical devices that retrieve and store data using the same file-management commands.

M

mainframe   A multiuser computer designed to meet the computing needs of a large organization.

Originally, the term mainframe referred to the metal cabinet that housed the central processing unit (CPU) of early computers. The term came to be used generally to refer to the large, central computers developed in the late 1950s and 1960s to meet the accounting and information-management needs of large organizations. The largest mainframes can handle thousands of terminals and use gigabytes of secondary storage.

megabyte (M)   A unit of memory measurement equal to approximately one million bytes (1,048,576 bytes).

megahertz (Mhz) A unit of measurement equal to one million electrical vibrations or cycles per second. Commonly used to compare the clock speeds of computers.

menu An on-screen display that lists the command choices available to the user.

microprocessor An integrated circuit that contains the arithmetic/logic unit (ALU) and control unit of a computer's central processing unit (CPU).

multitasking The execution of more than one program at a time on a computer system. Multitasking should not be confused with multiple program loading. In which two or more programs are present in RAM, but only one program executes at a time. The active or foreground task responds to the keyboard, while the background task continues to run (but without your active control).

In a multitasking operating system, terminate-and-stay resident (TSR) programs are unnecessary, because you simultaneously can run any programs you want to, as long as the computer has enough memory.

Among the operating systems or shells that provide multitasking are OS/2 and Microsoft Windows.

N

numeric coprocessor A microprocessor support chip that performs mathematical computations—specifically those using binary-coded decimal (BCD) and floating-point calculations—at speeds up to 100 times faster than a microprocessor alone.

The Intel numeric coprocessors (8087, 80287, and 80387) are designed to work with their microprocessor counterparts (the 8087 is designed to work the 8088 and 8086, and the 80287 and 80387 are designed to work with the 80286 and 80386, respectively).

Otherwise, all three Intel numeric coprocessors are similar; they are designed to work with 80 bits at a time so that a programmer can express a number of sufficient length to ensure accurate calculations. An innovative feature of the Intel 80486 chip is the placement of the numeric coprocessor's circuitry directly on the microprocessor chip.

O

operating system   A master control program that manages the computer's internal functions and provides you with a means to control the computer's operations.

The most popular operating systems for personal computers include DOS, OS/2, and the Macintosh System.

optical disk   A secondary storage medium for computers in which you store information of extremely high density on a disk in the form of tiny pits, the presence or absence of which corresponds to a bit of information read by a tightly focused laser beam.

Optical storage technologies are expected to play a significant role in the secondary storage systems of the 1990s. CD-ROM disks and CD-ROM disk drives offer an increasingly economical distribution medium for read-only data and programs. Write-once read-many (WORM) drives enable organizations to create their own huge in-house databases.

Erasable optical disk drives, such as the 256M drive included with the NeXT computer, offer more secondary storage than hard disks, and the CDs are removable.

Optical storage disk drives, however, are more expensive and much slower than hard disks.

overlay files   A file containing program code, but which cannot be directly executed from the operating system prompt. Overlay files are called (behind the scenes) by other programs. They often have an extension of OVR or OVL. Overlay file-programming techniques reduce the total amount of memory required by a program.

overwrite   To write data on a magnetic disk in the same area where other data is stored (destroying the original data).

P

parameter   A value or option that you add or alter when you give a command, so that the command accomplishes its task in the way you want. If you do not state a parameter, the program uses a default value or option.

For example, most programs enable you to type the name of the file you want to work with when you start the program. If you type **WORD REPORT1.DOC**, for example, Microsoft Word and the document file called REPORT1.DOC load at the same time. In this case, the file name is the parameter. If you do not type the file name, Word starts and opens a new, blank document file.

partition   A section of a hard disk physically divided from other sections during the formatting operation and treated by the operating system as if it were a separate disk.

password   A security tool used to identify authorized users of a computer program or computer network and to define their privileges, such as read-only, reading and writing, or file copying.

path   1) the full directory name, which specifies precisely in which directory a file is stored, for example \123R3\BUDGET; 2) the list of directories searched for programs when the program is not found in the current directory.

peripheral   A device, such as a printer or disk drive, connected to and controlled by a computer but external to the computer's central processing unit (CPU).

pipe   In DOS and OS/2, an operator (a vertical line symbol) that redirects the output of one command so that it becomes the input of another command.

platter   An aluminium disk used to store data in a hard disk drive. Most hard disks include two or more platters stacked in a vertical column.

primary storage   The computer's main memory directly accessible to the central processing unit (CPU), unlike secondary storage, such as disk drives.

In personal computers, primary storage consists of the random-access memory (RAM) and the read-only memory (ROM).

print screen (PrtSc)   The key pressed to send a copy of the screen to the printer.

prompt   A symbol or phrase that appears on-screen, informing you that the computer is ready to accept input.

public-domain software   Software not copyrighted, which can be freely distributed without obtaining permission from the programmer or paying the programmer a fee.

R

random-access memory (RAM)   The computer's primary working memory, in which program instructions and data are stored so that they are accessible directly to the central processing unit (CPU). To perform computations at high speeds, the computer's processing circuitry must be able to obtain information from the memory directly and quickly. Computer memories, therefore, are designed to give the processor random access to the contents.

RAM often is called read/write memory to distinguish it from read-only memory (ROM), the other component of a personal computer's primary storage. In RAM, the CPU can write and read data. Most application programs set aside a portion of RAM as a temporary work space for your data, enabling you to modify (rewrite) as needed until the data is ready for printing or storage on disk.

RAM disk   An area of electronic memory configured by a software program to emulate a disk drive. Data stored in a RAM disk can be accessed more quickly than data stored on a disk drive, but this data is erased whenever you turn off or reboot the computer.

read-only memory (ROM)   The portion of a computer's primary storage that does not lose its contents when the current is switched off. ROM contains essential system programs, which neither you nor the computer can erase.

read/write head   In a hard disk or floppy disk drive, the magnetic recording and playback device that travels back and forth across the surface of the disk, storing and retrieving data.

redirection In DOS and OS/2, the routing of input and output operations to a file, the printer, or another device rather than the console (keyboard and monitor).

response time The time the computer needs to respond and carry out a request.

Response time is a better measure of system performance than access time, because it more fairly states the system's throughput. See **access time**.

revolutions per minute (RPM) The number of times a device rotates in sixty seconds. Hard disks revolve at 3,600 RPM.

root directory The top-level directory on a disk, the one DOS creates when you format the disk.

S

secondary storage A nonvolatile storage medium, such as a disk drive, which stores program instructions and data even when the power is switched off.

sector In a floppy disk or hard disk, a segment of one of the concentric tracks encoded on the disk during a low-level format.

In IBM PC-compatible computing, a sector usually contains 512 bytes of information. See **cluster**.

sequential access An information storage and retrieval technique in which the computer must move through a sequence of stored data items to reach the desired one.

Sequential access media, such as cassette tape recorders, are much slower than random-access media. See **random access**.

serial number A unique number used to identify a piece of equipment or hardware. The DOS V4 FORMAT command assigns an identifying volume serial number when a disk is formatted.

shareware Copyrighted computer programs made available on a trial basis; if you like and decide to use the program, you are expected to pay a fee to the program's author.

software   System, utility, or application programs expressed in a computer-readable language.

storage   The retention of program instructions, initial data, and intermediate data within the computer so that this information is available for processing purposes.

string   A series of alphanumeric characters.

subdirectory   In DOS, OS/2, and UNIX, a directory listed within a directory that, when opened, reveals another directory that may contain files and additional subdirectories.

switch   A code typed after a command name to indicate the specific way a command is to be used. See **parameter.**

syntax   All the rules that specify precisely how a command, statement, or instruction must be given to the computer so that the machine can recognize and process the instruction correctly.

system file   A program or data file that contains information needed by the operating system—distinguished from program or data files used by applications programs.

T

terminate-and-stay-resident program (TSR)   An accessory or utility program designed to remain in the computer's random-access memory (RAM) at all times so that the user can activate it with a keystroke, even if another program also is in memory.

With its protected mode processing, OS/2 enables the simultaneous execution of two or more programs without the peril of system crashes.

text file   A file consisting of nothing but the standard ASCII characters (with no control characters or higher-order characters).

toggle   A key that switches back and forth between two modes.

track   In a floppy disk or hard disk, one of several concentric rings, encoded on the disk during low-level formatting, which defines a distinct area of data storage on the disk.

transfer rate   The number of bits of data transferred per second between a disk and the computer after the drive head reaches the place where the data is located. See **access time**.

tree structure   A way of organizing information into a hierarchical structure with a root and branches.

U

utility   A program designed to enhance a specific aspect of computer operation. FGREP, a program to search text files for a specific word or phrase, is a good example of a utility.

V

variable   In computer programming, a named area in memory that stores a value or string assigned to that variable.

virtual memory   A method of extending the apparent size of a computer's random-access memory (RAM) by using part of the hard disk as an extension of RAM.

Many application programs, such as Lotus Manuscript, routinely use the hard disk instead of memory to store data or program instructions. A true virtual memory system, however, is implemented at the operating system level, so that the memory is available to any and all programs. Under virtual memory, even a program such as WordPerfect, which insists that the entire document be placed in RAM, can work with documents of unlimited length (or length limited by the capacity of a hard disk, rather than the capacity of RAM).

Tip: Virtual memory techniques currently are being implemented for most personal computers, but RAM is significantly faster than a hard disk. Virtual memory may result in delays of up to half a minute or more while the microprocessor waits to retrieve needed information from disk. With RAM chip prices at a reasonable level, equip a computer with additional RAM rather than relying on virtual-memory techniques.

volume label   In DOS and OS/2, the unique, identifying name assigned to a disk and displayed on the first line of a directory. The name must be no more than 11 characters. You assign the volume label when you format the disk.

W

wait state   A null processing cycle, during which nothing occurs. A wait state is programmed into a computer system to enable other components, such as random-access memory (RAM), to catch up with the central processing unit (CPU).

A microprocessor with a fast clock speed, such as 25MHz, can outrace the main memory, particularly if the memory is composed of dynamic random-access memory (DRAM) chips. Wait states, therefore, are programmed into the machine to rule out the serious errors that can occur if DRAM does not respond to the microprocessor fast enough.

Wait states can be eliminated (resulting in a "zero wait state" machine) by using fast (but expensive) cache memory, interleaved memory, page-mode RAM, or static RAM chips. See **random-access memory (RAM)** and **central processing unit (CPU)**.

warm boot   A system restart performed after the system has been powered and operating: a restart is the electronic equivalent of turning on the system because it clears the memory and reloads the operating system.

A warm boot is preferable to a cold start after a system crash because it places less strain on the system's electrical and electronic components. With IBM PC-compatible computers, you restart the system by pressing Ctrl-Alt-Del, although sometimes this command does not unlock the system.

wild-card characters   Characters, such as asterisks and question marks, that stand for any other character that may appear in the same place.

DOS recognizes two wild-card characters: the asterisk (*), which stands for any character (and any number of characters), and the question mark (?), which stands for any one character.

windowing environment   An applications program interface (API) that provides the features commonly associated with a menu, on-screen fonts, and scroll bars or scroll boxes, and makes these features available to programmers of application packages.

write-protect   To modify a floppy disk so that the computer cannot write on the disk or erase the information on it.

Z

^Z   The end-of-file marker

zip   To combine one or more files into a single compressed file.

Index

% sign, 160-165
80286 microprocessor, 11
80386 microprocessor, 11
80386SX microprocessor, 11
80486 microprocessor, 11
8088 microprocessor, 11
> redirector symbol, 88, 96, 156
@ symbol in batch files, 150
. directory entry, 113
.. directory entry, 113

A

---

access time, 615
AIDS virus, 502
algorithm, 615
ANSI.SYS device driver, 221, 538
    screen colors, 235-239
APPEND DOS command, 38, 296, 515-517
    /E switch, 516
    /PATH:OFF switch, 516
    /PATH:ON switch, 516
    /X switch, 516
    /X:OFF switch, 516
    /X:ON switch, 516
applications,
    managing from DESQview, 379, 381-382
    relationship to operating system, 29

archive flags, 615
    backing up data, 390
ARLL (advanced run length limited) data
    encoding method, 68
Arrange menu, DOS Shell, 355
ASCII (American Standard Code for
    Information Interchange), 615-616
    files, 93-94, 310
        text editors, 470
        undeleting, 449
    graphics characters, 231-235
ASK.COM Norton Utilities program,
    250-252
ASSIGN DOS command, 38, 132-133, 396,
    401, 517-518
ATTRIB DOS command, 38, 423-426,
    518-519
    /S switch, 424, 519
AUTOEXEC.BAT file, 36, 226-228, 410,
    444-446, 474, 507, 564, 568, 616
    multiple boot configurations, 241-243
    password-protecting, 474
AUTOMAKE.EXE file, 310
Automenu, 309-311, 603
    menu definition files, 310
AUX (communications port) device name,
    83

B

background printing, 97
backing up data, 387-417, 616
   additive incremental backup, 398
   archive flag, 390
   complete restore, 401-402
   DOS commands, 392-408
   FASTBACK PLUS, 411-414
   frequency, 388-389
   full backup, 396-397
   incremental backup, 389-391, 397
   partial backup, 398
   restoring data, 398-404
   selective restore, 403
   storing backups, 391-392
   tape backup devices, 416-417
BACKUP DOS command, 23-24, 38,
   392-398, 520-521
   /A switch, 394-395, 398, 520
   /D:date switch, 394, 520
   /F:size switch, 394, 395, 520-521
   /L:filename switch, 394, 521
   /M switch, 394, 397-398, 520
   /S switch, 394, 397-398, 520
   /T:time switch,394, 520
backup files, restoring, 575-577
backup programs, 23-24, 388, 408-415
   FASTBACK PLUS, 409-414
   PCBACKUP, 415
BACKUP.LOG file, 394
BACKUP.M_U file, 446, 464
Basic Input/Output System see BIOS
BAT file extension, 144-145, 239-241, 351,
   378, 565, 621
batch files, 22, 139, 145-148, 303, 522-528,
   616-617
   @ symbol, 150
   ASK.COM Norton Utilities program,
     250-252
   AUTOEXEC.BAT, 226-228
   Batcom batch file compiler, 253-255
   BE.EXE Norton Utilities program,
     249-252

BEEP.COM Norton Utilities program,
   252-253
beeping, 153
branching, 165-167
calling
   other batch files, 156-159
   programs, 234-235
comments, 151-153
comparing strings, 167-168
displaying
   messages, 527
   program files, 239-241
DOSSHELL.BAT, 356-359
ECHO DOS command, 149-153
editing, 140-144
error levels, 169-170
executing, 146
extending search path, 244-245
FORMAT.BAT, 427-428
menu system, 230-239
   calling programs, 234-235
   menu screen, 231-235
   screen colors, 235-239
multiple boot configurations, 241-243
passing parameters, 160-165
pausing, 154-155
redirecting messages, 156
running another batch file from a,
   522-523
shifting parameters, 527-528
subcommands, 144-160
suspend processing, 526-527
temporary, 303, 310
testing for missing parameters, 168-169
transferring control, 525
WHAT.EXE public domain program,
   246-249
Batcom batch file compiler, 253-255, 603
BE.EXE Norton Utilities program, 249-252
BEEP.COM Norton Utilities program,
   252-253
beeps in batch files, 153
Bernoulli box, 16-17, 70-71, 603
BIN file extension, 501, 506
binary files, 617
   repairing damaged, 457

BIOS (basic input-output system), 33-34, 616
bits, 80
block devices, changing parameters, 539, 540
boot record, 56
booting, 34, 617
    AUTOEXEC.BAT, 36
    cold boot, 35-36
    CONFIG.SYS file, 36
    multiple boot configurations, 241-243
    warm boot, 35-36
BREAK DOS configurations subcommand, 215-217, 528-529, 536
buffers, 217-220, 617
    default number, 218
    expanded memory, 219-220
    look-ahead, 219-220
BUFFERS DOS configurations subcommand, 217-220, 536-537
    /X switch, 537
byte, 19, 617

C

cache, 618
    controllers, 69
    memory, 618
cache programs
    CACHE.EXE, 269-271
    Mcache, 276
    PC-CACHE, 277-278
    SMARTDRV.SYS, 272
    SuperPC-Kwik, 273-276
CACHE.EXE program, 269-271
CALL DOS batch subcommand, 140, 157-159, 522-523
cathode ray tube (CRT), 12
CD DOS command, 38, 113-115, 475
CD-ROM, 71-72, 618
central processing unit (CPU), 10, 618
    see also microprocessors
CGA (color graphics adapter), 13
CGM file extension, 319
CHANGES.CRC file, 508

characters
    meta-string, 569-570
    wild-card, 633-634
CHCP DOS command, 38
CHDIR DOS command, 38, 113-115, 529-530
CHKDSK DOS command, 38, 430-435, 463, 530-532
    /F switch, 430, 432-434, 530
    /V switch, 430, 530
CLEAN virus eradication utility, 510, 512-514, 605
    /A switch, 513
    /MANY switch, 513
clock, 12
CLS DOS command, 38, 154-155, 532
clusters, 28, 56-58, 618
    errors, 64
cold boot, 35-36
    power-on reset (POR), 35-36
    power-on self test (POST), 35-36
colors, ANSI.SYS device driver, 235-239
COM file extension, 239-241, 351, 378, 500, 506, 565, 574, 621
COM (serial communications port) device name, 83
COMMAND DOS command, 533-534
    /C switch, 533
    /E:size switch, 533
    /P switch, 533
command line, 618
command processors, 619
    changing default, 543-544
    returning to primary from secondary, 550
command syntax, 37
COMMAND.COM command interpreter, 34, 38, 395, 424-425, 508, 543-544, 599, 618
    /C switch, 140, 158-159
    invoking second copy, 533-534
    viruses, 500-501
Commander Link, 321
commands
    defining with Direct Access, 313
    Direct Access prompting, 313

external, 621
internal, 624
interrupting, 216-217
invoking in XtreePro Gold, 322
comments in batch files, 151-153
COMP DOS command, 38, 140, 534-535
COMPRESS disk analyzer program, 438
compressing files, 332-333
CON (console) device name, 83, 619
concatenating files, 125-126, 619
CONFIG program, 366-367
CONFIG.SYS file, 36, 213-226, 316, 405,
    407, 410, 528, 536-538, 541-542, 580,
    599, 619
    ANSI.SYS device driver, 221
    BREAK directive, 215-217
    BUFFERS directive, 217-220
    DEVICE directive, 220-222
    device drivers, 214, 220-222
    directives, 214-225
    DISPLAY.SYS device driver, 221
    DRIVER.SYS device driver, 221
    editing from Presentation Manager, 366
    FILES directive, 222-223
    LASTDRIVE directive, 223
    multiple boot configurations, 241-243
    PRINTER.SYS device driver, 221
    RAMDRIVE.SYS device driver, 221
    SHELL directive, 224-225
    SMARTDRV.SYS device driver, 221
    starting programs, 541-542
controllers, 17-18
    cache controllers, 69
    ESDI standard, 67
    SCSI standard, 67
    ST506/ST412 standard, 66-67
COPY DOS command, 38, 120-128
    /A switch, 125-126, 545
    /B switch, 125-126, 545
    /V switch, 121, 123, 545
copy protection, 619
copying files, 120-121, 331, 544-546,
    588-590
    from directory to directory, 122-123
    from disk to disk, 122, 281-282
    to devices, 126-128

COUNTRY directive, 405, 407
CPU see central processing unit and
    microprocessors
crash, 619
cross-linked files, 64, 433
CRT (cathode ray tube), 12
Ctrl-Break keys, stopping program, 528-529
CTTY DOS command, 38
current directory, 110-111, 619
cyclic redundancy check (CRC), 619-620
    errors, 63-64
cylinders, 49, 620

D

data, 620
    backups, 387-417
    checking accuracy, 586-587
    DES encryption, 484
    restoring backed up files, 398-404
    security, 24, 473-494
data encoding
    ARLL method, 68
    MFM method, 68
    RLL method, 68
data encryption programs
    KEY, 485
    KEYDES, 485
    PCSECURE, 486-489
data erasing programs
    DESTROY, 482-483
    WIPEDISK, 479, 481
    WIPEFILE, 479-480
data recovery snapshot programs, 444-445
    FR, 444-445
    MIRROR, 446-447
DATE DOS command, 38, 80, 407
date/time stamp, 80
dBASE III, repairing files, 460-461
DBF file extension, 319
DBFIX, 460-461
default
    number of buffers, 218
    setting, 620
defect mapping in low-level format,
    179-180

defragmenting hard disks, 21-22, 285-295, 620
    Mace Utilities UNFRAG, 293-294
    Norton Utilities Speed Disk, 294-295
    PC Tools COMPRESS, 292-293
    Power Disk, 289-290
    VOPT, 290-291
DEL DOS command, 38, 303, 382, 423, 425, 480, 546
deleting
    directories, 118-120
    files, 60, 546
    subdirectories, 118-120
delimiters, 620
    file names, 81-82
DES data encryption, 484
DESQview, 338-382, 603
    managing applications, 379, 381-382
DESTROY data erasing program, 482-483
    /A switch, 482
    /D switch, 482
    /E switch, 482-483
    /F switch, 482-483
    /H switch, 482
    /R switch, 482
    /S switch, 482
DEVICE DOS configurations subcommand, 220-222, 538
device drivers, 538
    ANSI.SYS, 221, 235-239, 538
    CONFIG.SYS, 214, 220-222
    DISPLAY.SYS, 221
    DRIVER.SYS, 221
    IBMCACHE.SYS, 268-269
    PRINTER.SYS, 221
    RAM.SYS, 284, 285
    RAMDRIVE.SYS, 221, 282-283
    SMARTDRV.SYS, 221
devices, 620
    AUX (communications port), 83
    COM (serial communications port), 83
    CON (console), 83
    copying files to, 126-128
    device names, 82-83
    LPT (parallel communications port), 83
    NUL (null device), 83

PRN (printer), 83
diagnostics disk, 422
dialog boxes, customizing in DOS Shell, 341, 346-348
DIR DOS command, 38, 78, 85-93, 116, 307, 546-547
    /P switch, 86-87, 547
    /W switch, 86-87, 547
    wild cards, 89-93
Direct Access, 311-313, 603
    activity-logging feature, 313
    menu creation, 311-312
direct memory access (DMA) chip, 410
Direct Net program, 313
directives, 214-225
    see also DOS batch subcommands
    BREAK, 215-217
    BUFFERS, 217-220, 296
    DEVICE, 220-222
    COUNTRY, 405, 407
    FILES, 222, 223
    LASTDRIVE, 223
    SHELL, 224-225, 533
directories, 20, 58-60, 78, 84-85, 109-115, 206-209, 212-213, 620
    . directory entry, 113
    .. directory entry, 113
    checking, 530-532
    copying files from one to another, 122-123
    current directory, 110-111, 113-115, 619
    directory tree, 207-209
    displaying structure, 117-118, 529-530
    DOS Shell, 353
    File System, 349
    fixing problems, 430-432
    hidden, 475
    hierarchical structure, 108
    improving performance, 295-296
    installing software, 211-212
    KEEP directory, 212
    listing, 546-547
        files with DIR command, 85-93
    Microsoft Windows 3.0 tree, 376
    moving files among, 329-330

parent directory, 110-111
paths, 109-110, 128-130
printing DIR listing, 88-89
removing, 118-120, 577-578
    files, 548-549
restoring files, 403
root, 56, 106-108, 209, 630
searching for files, 515
subdirectories, 84-85
TEMP directory, 212-213
tree builder, 334
\QUEDISK, 608
XCOPY DOS command, 404
directory tree, 313
Directory Tree window in Microsoft
    Windows 3.0, 376
disk analyzer programs, 435-438
    COMPRESS, 438
    DT, 435-436
    REMEDY, 436-437
disk caches, 21, 263-278
    CACHE.EXE cache program, 269-271
    IBMCACHE.SYS device driver, 268-269
    Mcache cache program, 276
    memory use, 266-267
    mirroring, 264
    PC-CACHE cache program, 277-278
    redundancy checking, 266
    SMARTDRV.SYS cache program, 272
    SuperPC-Kwik cache program, 273-276
    track buffering, 265
    troubleshooting, 267-269
    write buffering, 265-266
disk drives, 620-621
    heads, 44-47
    logical, 625
Disk Manager, 307-308, 603
disk interleave, 47, 52-54
disk-read test, 435
DISK01.SYS file, 599
diskette, 621
DISKFIX program, 469
Disk Manager utility, 193-194
DISKCOMP DOS command, 38
DISKCOPY DOS command, 38

disks
    diagnostics, 422
    displaying volume label, 587-588
    floppy see floppy disks
    hard see hard disks
    joining to subdirectory, 558-560
    optical, 627
    Programs, 607-612
    RAM, 629
    setup, 422
    volume label, 560-561
display adapters, 13
display hardware
    CRT (cathode ray tube), 12
    display adapters, 13
    gas plasma displays, 12
    liquid crystal displays (LCD), 12
    resolution, 13
DISPLAY.SYS device driver, 221
DOS (disk operating system), 20, 621
    compatibility to OS/2 operating system,
        599
    environment setting, 130-132
    installing, 199-201
    similarity to OS/2 operating system, 599
    versions, 30-32, 181, 183-192
DOS batch subcommands, 144, 522-524
    see also directives
    CALL, 140, 157-159, 522-523
    ECHO, 38, 148-153, 475, 523-524
    FOR..IN..DO, 170-172, 524
    GOTO, 39, 140, 159-160, 165-166, 525
    IF, 39, 140, 159-160, 166-170, 525-526
    PAUSE, 39, 140, 154-155, 526-527
    REM, 39, 140, 151, 527
    SHIFT, 40, 164-165, 527-528
DOS command reference, 515-590
DOS commands
    APPEND, 38, 296, 515-517
        /E switch, 516
        /PATH:OFF switch, 516
        /PATH:ON switch, 516
        /X switch, 516
        /X:OFF switch, 516
        /X:ON switch, 516
    ASSIGN, 38, 132-133, 396, 401, 517-518

ATTRIB, 38, 423-426, 518-519
    /S switch, 424, 519
backing up data, 392-408
BACKUP, 23-24, 38, 392-398, 520-521
    /A switch, 394-395, 398, 520
    /D switch, 394
    /D:date switch, 520
    /F switch, 520-521
    /F:size switch, 394-395, 521
    /L switch, 521
    /L:filename switch, 394
    /M switch, 394, 397-398, 520
    /S switch, 394, 397-398, 520
    /T switch, 394
    /T:time switch, 520
CHDIR or CD, 38, 113-115, 475,
    529-530
CHCP, 38
CHKDSK, 38, 430-435, 463, 530-532
    /F switch, 430-434, 530
    /V switch, 430, 530
CLS, 38M 154-155, 532
COMMAND.COM command interpreter,
    34, 38
    /C switch, 140, 158-159
COMMAND, 533-534
    /C switch, 533
    /E:size switch, 533
    /P switch, 533
COMP, 38, 140, 534-535
conditional execution, 525-526
COPY, 38, 120-128, 331, 353, 382, 423,
    475, 544-546
    /A switch, 125-126, 545
    /B switch, 125-126, 545
    /V switch, 121, 123, 545
CTTY, 38
DATE, 38, 80, 407
DEL, 38, 303, 382, 423, 425, 480, 546
DIR, 38, 78, 85-93, 116, 307, 546-547
    /P switch, 86-87, 547
    /W switch, 86-87, 547
    wild cards, 89-93
DISKCOMP, 38
DISKCOPY, 38
EDLIN, 140-142

ERASE, 38, 423, 548-549
    /P switch, 548
EXE2BIN, 38
EXIT, 38, 550
FASTOPEN, 38, 297-298, 550-552
    /X switch, 551
FC, 39, 552-553
    /A switch, 553
    /B switch, 553
    /C switch, 553
    /L switch, 553
    /LB x switch, 553
    /N switch, 553
    /T switch, 553
    /W switch, 553
    /x switch, 553
FDISK, 39, 61, 181, 183-192
FIND, 39, 78, 98-102, 554-555
    /C switch, 98-100, 554
    /N switch, 98-100, 554
    /V switch, 98-100, 554
FOR, 39, 140, 159-160
FORMAT, 39, 56, 197-199, 303, 395,
    426-428, 462, 555-558, 622-623
    /1 switch, 556
    /4 switch, 556
    /8 switch, 556
    /B switch, 556
    /F:size switch, 557
    /N:ss switch, 556
    /S switch, 556
    /T:tt switch, 556
    /V switch, 556
    /V:label switch, 557
GRAFTABL, 39
GRAPHICS, 39
iterative processing, 524
JOIN, 39, 133-135, 396, 401, 558-560
    /D switch, 559
KEYB, 39
LABEL, 39, 560-561
MEM, 39, 561-562
    /DEBUG, 562
    /PROGRAM, 561
MKDIR or MD, 39, 56, 111-113, 475,
    562-563

MODE, 39
MORE, 39, 78, 94-95, 563-564
NLSFUNC, 39
PATH, 39, 128-130, 296, 564-566
PRINT, 39, 78, 96-97, 351, 566-568
 /B:bufsize switch, 567
 /C switch, 567
 /D:device switch, 566
 /M:maxtick switch, 567
 /P switch, 567
 /Q:maxfiles switch, 567
 /S:timeslice switch, 567
 /T switch, 97, 567
 /U:busytick switch, 567
 background printing, 97
PROMPT, 39, 115-116, 140, 236-239,
 568-570
RECOVER, 39, 466, 570-571
RENAME or REN, 40, 382, 572-573
REPLACE, 40, 573-575
 /A switch, 574
 /P switch, 574
 /R switch, 574
 /S switch, 574
 /U switch, 574
 /W switch, 574
RESTORE, 23-24, 40, 398-404, 447, 516,
 575-577
 /A:date switch, 400, 576
 /B:date switch, 400, 576
 /E:time switch, 400, 576
 /L:time switch, 400, 576
 /M switch, 400, 576
 /N switch, 400, 576
 /P switch, 400-401, 403, 576
 /S switch, 399-400, 575-576
RMDIR or RD, 40, 118-120, 450,
 577-578
SELECT, 40
SET, 40, 244-245, 579-580
 /F:name_space switch, 580
 /L:numlocks, 580
SHARE, 40, 580-581
SORT, 40, 581-582
 /+c switch, 581
 /R switch, 581

SUBST, 40, 135-136, 396, 401, 582-584
 /D switch, 583
SYS, 40
TIME, 40, 80
TREE, 40, 117-118, 334, 584-585
 /A switch, 117-118, 585
 /F switch, 117, 585
TYPE, 40, 78, 93-96, 328, 434, 475,
 585-586
VERIFY, 37, 40, 297-298, 586-587
VOL, 40, 587-588
XCOPY, 40, 331, 404-408, 588-590
 /A switch, 405-406, 589
 /D:date switch, 405, 407, 589
 /E switch, 405, 408, 589
 /M switch, 406, 589
 /P switch, 406, 589
 /S switch, 406-408, 589
 /V switch, 406, 589
 /W switch, 406, 589
DOS configuration subcommands
 BREAK, 528-529, 536
 BUFFERS, 536-537
  /X switch, 537
 DEVICE, 538
 DRIVPARM, 539-540
  /C switch, 539
  /D:num switch, 539
  /F:type switch, 539
  /H:hds switch, 539
  /I switch, 540
  /N switch, 540
  /S:sec switch, 540
  /T:trk switch, 540
 FILES, 540-541
 INSTALL, 541-542
 LASTDRIVE, 542-543
 SHELL, 543-544
DOS prompt and Norton Commander, 320
DOS Services application, 382-384
DOS Shell, 338-359
 adding programs to groups, 345-348
 associating files with file extensions, 351
 changing file attributes, 353
 copying, deleting, or renaming files,
  352-353

creating
    directories, 353
    groups, 343-345
    menus, 342-343
customizing
    dialog boxes, 346-348
    DOSSHELL.BAT batch file, 358-359
dialog boxes, 341
display modes, 340
file
    display options, 353
    information, 354-355
    management, 342, 348-355
    options, 354
File System, 348-355
Main Group menu, 341
moving files, 352
opening files, 350-351
printing files, 351
pull-down menus, 340-341
selecting and deselecting files, 353
viewing files, 353
DOSSHELL.BAT batch file, 356-359
    customizing DOS Shell, 358-359
DRIVER.SYS device driver, 221
drivers, 621
drives
    changing in File System, 349
    head alignment, 62-63
    name, 621
    selecting in Microsoft Windows 3.0, 376
    setting last valid number, 542-543
DRIVPARM DOS configurations
    subcommand, 539-540
    /C switch, 539
    /D:num switch, 539
    /F:type switch, 539
    /H:hds switch, 539
    /I switch, 540
    /N switch, 540
    /S:sec switch, 540
    /T:trk switch, 540
DT disk analyzer program, 435-436
DV.EXE program, 379
dynamic link library (DLL) files, 600

E

ECHO DOS batch subcommand, 38,
    148-153, 475, 523-524
editing
    batch files, 140-144
    sector-level, 470
EDLIN text-editing program, 303
    commands, 140-142
EGA (enhanced graphics adapter), 13
Emergency Room, 467-468
    /p switch, 468
    /z switch, 468
encrypting files, 483-489
encryption programs, 24
end-of-file marker (^Z), 634
enhanced small device interface see ESDI
environments, 621
    extending search path, 244-245
    setting, 130-132
ERASE DOS command, 38, 423, 548-549
    /P switch, 548
ERRORLEVEL, 621
ESDI interface standard, 67
EXE file extension, 239-241, 351, 378, 500,
    506, 565, 621
EXE2BIN DOS command, 38
EXIT DOS command, 38, 550
expanded memory
    buffers, 219-220
    disk caches, 266-267
extended DOS partition, 188-190
extended memory, disk caches, 266-267
external commands, 621

F

FASTBACK PLUS, 409-414, 604
    backing up data, 411-414
    direct memory access (DMA) chip, 410
    installing, 410
    restoring files, 414
FASTOPEN DOS command, 38, 297-298,
    550-552
    /X switch, 551

FAT *see* file allocation table
FB.EXE file, 411
FBINSTAL program, 410
FC DOS command, 39, 552-553
    /A switch, 553
    /B switch, 553
    /C switch, 553
    /L switch, 553
    /LB x switch, 553
    /N switch, 553
    /T switch, 553
    /W switch, 553
    /x switch, 553
FDISK DOS command, 39, 61, 181-192
FGREP, 326-327, 604, 608-609
file allocation table (FAT), 56-60, 622
    checking, 530-532
    fixing problems, 430, 432-435
    restoring files, 400
file extensions
    .BAT, 239-241, 351, 378, 565, 621
    .BIN, 501, 506
    .CGM, 319
    .COM, 239-241, 351, 378, 500, 506,
        565, 574, 621
    .DBF, 319
    .EXE, 239-241, 351, 378, 500, 506, 565,
        621
    .GIF, 319
    .MDF, 310
    .MEU, 343
    .OVL, 501, 506
    .OVR, 501
    .PCX, 319
    .PIF, 378
    .SEC, 488
    .SYS, 501
    .ZIP, 332-333
file fragmentation, 285-295
File Manager, Microsoft Windows 3.0,
    376-378
file manager programs, 22, 301, 314-325
    communications, 316
    copying, erasing, and moving groups,
        315
    DOS Shell, 348-355

    editing files, 316
    finding files, 315
    graphical disk map, 315
    laptop connectivity, 316
    menu building, 316
    program launching, 316
    tagging files, 315
    text searching, 315
    viewing files, 315-316
File System in DOS Shell, 348-355, 363-366
    changing drive or directory, 349
    listing files, 348-349
file utilities, 325-334
file-read test, 435
files, 14, 145-148, 622
    ASCII, 93-94, 310
    associating with file extensions, 351
    attributes, 518-519
        DOS Shell, 353
    AUTOEXEC.BAT, 36, 226-228, 241-243,
        410, 444-446, 474, 507, 564, 568,
        616
    AUTOMAKE.EXE, 310
    AUTOMENU.COM, 309
    backing up, 520-521
    BACKUP.LOG, 394
    BACKUP.M_U, 446, 464
    batch, 22, 139, 303, 522-528, 616-617
        @ symbol, 150
        beeping, 153
        branching, 165-167
        calling other batch files, 156-159
        comments, 151-153
        comparing strings, 167-168
        ECHO DOS command, 149-153
        editing, 140-144
        error levels, 169-170
        executing, 146
        passing parameters, 160-165
        pausing, 154-155
        redirecting messages, 156
        subcommands, 144, 159-160
        testing for missing parameters,
            168-169
    binary, 617
    CHANGES.CRC, 508

check values in virus searching, 503
combining, 332
COMMAND.COM, 395, 424-425, 500-501, 508, 533-534, 543-544, 599, 618
comparing, 534-535, 552-553
compressing, 319, 332-333
concatenating, 125-126
CONFIG.SYS, 36, 213-226, 241-243, 316, 366, 405, 407, 410, 528, 536-538, 541-542, 580, 599, 619
copying, 120-121, 331, 544-546, 588-590
    deleting, or renaming in DOS Shell, 352-353
    directory to directory, 122-123
    disk to disk, 122, 573-575
    erasing, and moving groups, 315
    to devices, 126-128
cross-linked files, 64, 433
date/time stamp, 80
deleting, 60, 546
directories, 20, 58-60, 78, 84-97, 106-108
    . directory entry, 113
    .. directory entry, 113
    changing current, 113-115
    displaying directory structure, 117-118
    hierarchical structure, 108
    paths, 109-130
    subdirectories, 84-85, 106-115
DISK01.SYS, 599
displaying, 93-96, 353, 584-856
dynamic link library (DLL), 600
editing, 316
    Lotus Magellan, 319
encrypting, 483-489
FB.EXE, 411
FGREP.DOC, 326
finding, 315, 327
    FIND command, 98-100
fragmentation, 21-22
FORMAT.COM, 429
FRECOVER.BAT, 445
FRECOVER.DAT, 444-445, 463-464

handles, 540-541
HELP.CRC, 506-508
hidden, 475, 624
indexing, 318
INSTALL.EXE, 607
KBD01.SYS, 599
LIST.DOC, 329
listing
    DIR command, 85-93
    File System, 348-349
LISTP.COM, 328
LISTR.COM, 328
LISTS.COM, 328
locking, 580-581
log, 625
MAGELLAN.CRC, 510
management, 22, 28-29
    DOS Shell, 342
    Microsoft Windows 3.0, 376-378
    Presentation Manager, 364-366
menu definition, 310
Microsoft Windows 3.0 document, 378
moving among directories, 329-330
moving in DOS Shell, 352
MV.EXE, 329
names, 79-80, 622
    .BAT file extension, 144-145
    delimiters, 81-82
    legal characters, 81-82
    reserved names, 82-83
OLDBACK.M_U, 446
opening in DOS Shell, 350-351
options in DOS Shell, 354
overlay, 501, 627
password-protecting data files, 490-494
PCOPY.DOC, 331
physical security, 478
printing
    DIR listing, 88-89
    DOS Shell, 351
    PRINT command, 96-97
    redirection symbol, 96-97
program overlay, 280-281
PROGRAMS.ZIP, 607
protecting, 423-426
read-only attribute, 424-426

reading, 58-59
recovering in bad sectors, 570-571
removing from directory, 548-549
renaming, 572-573
repairing damaged, 457-461
restoring, 403, 575-577
    FASTBACK PLUS, 414
root directory, 56
saving, 59-60
scanning for patterns, 503
SCREEN01.SYS, 599
search path, 564-566
searching, 319
    directories, 515
    for word or phrase, 554-555
    text, 326-327
selecting, 315
    DOS Shell, 353
    Microsoft Windows 3.0, 378
size, 79-80
STARTUP.CMD, 599
system, 631
tagging, 315, 321-322
temporary, 280
text, 631
undeleting, 447-456
unerasing, 450-452
viewing, 315-316, 322, 328-329
    DOS Shell, 353
FILES DOS configurations subcommand,
    222-223, 540-541
filters, 622
FIND DOS command, 39, 78, 98-102,
    554-555
    /C switch, 98-100, 554
    /N switch, 98-100, 554
    /V switch, 98-100, 554
FINDIT, 327, 609
firmware, 11
fixed disks see hard disks
floppy disks, 14, 622
    copying files between, 281-282
    formatting, 428-429, 555-558
FOR DOS command, 39, 140, 159-160
FOR..IN..DO DOS batch subcommand,
    170-172, 524

FORMAT DOS command, 39, 56, 197-199,
    303, 395, 426-428, 462, 555-558,
    622-623
    /1 switch, 556
    /4 switch, 556
    /8 switch, 556
    /B switch, 556
    /F:size switch, 557
    /N:ss switch, 556
    /S switch, 197, 556
    /T:tt switch, 556
    /V switch, 197, 556
    /V:label switch, 557
format recovery programs
    FR, 463-464
    REBUILD, 464
    UNFORMAT, 464
FORMAT.BAT batch file, 427-428
FORMAT.COM file, 429
FORMATF.EXE formatting program,
    428-429
FORMATH.EXE formatting program,
    428-429
formatting
    floppy disks, 428-429, 555-558
    hard disks, 28, 428-429, 555-558
        low level, 439-440
        preventing, 426-428
    high-level, 51, 56, 197-199
    logical, 51, 56, 197-199
    low-level, 51, 55-56, 178-180
formatting programs
    FORMATF.EXE, 428-429
    FORMATH.EXE, 428-429
    PCSHELL.EXE, 429
    SF.EXE, 429
FR data recovery snapshot program,
    444-445, 463-464
    /NOBAK switch, 445
    /SAVE switch, 444-445
fragmentation, 21-22, 623
FRECOVER.BAT file, 445
FRECOVER.DAT file, 444-445, 463-464
function keys, 13-14
    Norton Commander, 320-321

G

gas plasma displays, 12
GIF file extension, 319
glossary, 615-634
GOTO DOS batch subcommand, 525
GRAFTABL DOS command, 39
graphical
    disk map, 315
    hard disk shown as tree, 307
    user interface (GUI), 623-624
graphics, creating with ASCII characters,
    231-235
GRAPHICS DOS command, 39
groups
    DOS Shell, 343-345
    Microsoft Windows 3.0, 374-376
    Presentation Manager, 361-362
GOTO DOS command, 39, 140, 159-160,
    165-166

H

hard cards, 70
hard disks
    analyzing, 430-432
    and the OS/2 operating system, 597-602
    backup programs, 23-24
    boot record, 56
    buffers, 217-220
    buying and installing, 596
    clusters, 28, 56-58, 64
    configuring, 177-201
    controllers, 17-18, 594-595
        cache controllers, 69
        ESDI standard, 67
        SCSI standard, 67
        ST506/ST412 standard, 66-67
    CRC errors, 63-64
    cylinders, 49
    data encoding
        ARLL method, 68
        MFM method, 68
        RLL method, 68
    data recovery snapshots, 444-445

diagnostics, 440-441
directories, 56-60
disk analyzer programs, 435-438
disk cache, 21
disk drive heads, 44-47, 62-63
disk interleave, 47, 52-54
disk-read, 435
ESDI controller, 594-595
failure, 465-469
file allocation table (FAT), 56-60
file-read, 435
formatting, 28, 428-429, 555-558
fragmentation, 21-22
full-height, 16
graphical tree, 307
half-height, 16
head crash, 47, 65, 422
heads, 17-18
high-level formatting, 51, 56, 197-199
improving performance, 261-298
installing
    operating systems, 199
    second, 201
logical
    drives, 181-182
    formatting, 51, 56, 197-199
low-level formatting, 51, 55-56,
    178-180, 439-440
management programs, 301-334
parking drive heads, 422-423
partitions, 60-61, 180-196
platters, 44
PC compatibility, 595
physical characteristics, 592
preventing formatting, 426-428
price/performance considerations,
    593-594
    problems, 419
recovering from disasters, 443-470
removable, 16-17
repairing damaged files, 457-461
SCSI controller, 594-595
searching for programs, 306
sectors, 17, 49-51
selecting, 591-596
shredding data, 479-483

speed, 19-20, 54-55, 593-594
stepper motor, 422
ST506 controller, 594-595
storage capacity, 16, 19, 593
testing sectors, 439
tracks, 17, 48-51
undeleting files, 447-456
undoing formatting, 462-464
viruses, 442
voice coil, 422
hardware
    display hardware, 12-13
    floppy disk drives *see* floppy disks
    hard disk drives *see* hard disks
    keyboards, 13-14
    microprocessors, 10
    peripheral, 10
    preventing failures, 419-421
    platform, 624
    requirements, Microsoft Windows 3.0,
      368
    system, 10
head crash, 47, 65
HELP.CRC file, 506-508
hidden
    directories, 475
    files, 475, 624
hierarchical directory structure, 108
High Performance File System (HPFS),
  600-601

I

IBMCACHE.SYS device driver, 268-269
icons
    Microsoft Windows 3.0, 373, 378
    Presentation Manager, 365-366
IF DOS configuration subcommand, 39,
    140, 159-160, 166-170, 525- 526,
    541-542
INSTALL.EXE file, 607
installing
    device drivers in CONFIG.SYS file,
      220-222
    DOS, 199-201

FASTBACK PLUS, 410
    operating systems, 199-201
    second hard disk, 201
    software, 210-212
    UNIX, 200-201
interleave, 47, 52-54
internal commands, 624
interpreter, 33-34

J–K

JOIN DOS command, 39, 133-135, 396,
    401, 558-560
    /D switch, 559
KBD01.SYS file, 599
KEY data encryption program, 485
KEYDES data encryption program, 485
kilobyte (K), 624-625
KEEP directory, 212
kernel, 33-34
KEYB DOS command, 39

L

LABEL DOS command, 39, 560-561
laptop computers, 282
    connectivity, 316
LASTDRIVE DOS configurations
    subcommand, 223, 542-543
latency, 55
line voltage regulator, 420
liquid crystal displays (LCD), 12
LIST, 328-329, 604, 609-610
listing files with DIR command, 85-93
LISTP.COM file, 328
LISTR.COM file, 328
LISTS.COM file, 328
log file, 625
logical
    drives, 181-182, 625
    formatting, 51, 56
look-ahead buffers, 219-220
Lotus 1-2-3
    password-protecting worksheets,
      491-492

repairing spreadsheets, 457-459
Lotus 1-2-3 /G, 604
Lotus 1-2-3 Release 2, 604
Lotus 1-2-3 Release 3, 604
Lotus Magellan, 318-319, 604
low-level formatting, 51, 55-56, 178-180
LPT (parallel communications port) device
    name, 83

M

Mace Utilities, 428, 436-437, 446, 452-454,
    460-461, 464, 467- 468, 479, 482-483,
    604
    UNFRAG defragmentation program,
        293-294
Mace Vaccine, 506-509, 604
MAGELLAN.CRC file, 510
mainframe, 625
Mcache cache program, 276
MDA (monochrome display adapter), 13
MDF file extension, 310
megabyte (M), 19, 625
megahertz (Mhz), 626
MEM DOS command, 39, 561-562
    /DEBUG switch, 562
    /PROGRAM switch, 561
memory
    and menu programs, 302-303
    disk buffers, 536-537
    disk caches, 266-267
        directory information, 550-552
    displaying used and unused, 561-562
    expanded, 219-220
    Microsoft Windows 3.0 requirements,
        368
    OS/2 operating system, 598
    random-access (RAM), 629
    read-only (ROM), 629
    virtual, 632-633
menu definition files, 310
menu programs, 23, 302-303
    and memory, 302-303
    automatically adding applications, 303
    built-in file manager, 305

logging activities, 304
mouse support, 304
network support, 305
password protection, 303-304
PowerMenu, 306
screen blanking, 304
virus detection, 304
menus, 302, 626
    automatic creation, 303
    batch file menu system, 230-239
    building, 316
    DOS Shell pull-down, 340-343
    excluding programs, 474-475
meta-string characters, 569-570
MEU file extension, 343
MFM (modified frequency modulation)
    data encoding method, 68
microprocessors, 10, 626
    80286, 11
    80386, 11
    80386SX, 11
    80486, 11
    8086, 11
    8088, 11
Microsoft Windows 3.0, 338, 368-382, 604
    386 enhanced mode, 368
    applications windows, 369
    desktop, 369
    Directory Tree window, 376
    document files, 378
    document windows, 369
    File Manager, 376-378
    groups, 374-376
    hardware requirements, 368
    icons, 373, 378
    managing files, 376-378
    memory requirements, 368
    operating system requirements, 368
    Program Manager, 373-376
    starting programs, 374
    window characteristics, 370-372
MIRROR data recovery snapshot program,
    446-447
    /1 switch, 447
    /Td-nnn switch, 447
mirroring, 264

MKDIR or MD DOS command, 39, 56,
111-113, 475, 562-563
MODE DOS command, 39
modified frequency modulation *see* MFM
MORE DOS command, 39, 78, 94-95,
563-564
mouse, accessing menus, 304
MOVE, 329-330, 604
MS DOS, 20, 604
multitasking, 20, 626
MUSE undeletion program, 453-454
MV, 329, 610

N

networks
support from menu programs, 305
worms, 497-498
NLSFUNC DOS command, 39
Norton Commander, 316, 319-321, 605
and DOS prompt, 320
function keys, 320-321
windows, 320
Norton Disk Doctor, 465-466
/COMPLETE switch, 466
/QUICK switch, 466
Norton Utilities, 429, 435-436, 444-445,
450-452, 463-466, 479- 481, 605
Speed Disk defragmentation program,
294-295
NU undeletion program, 450-451
NUL (null device) device name, 83
numeric coprocessor, 626

O

OLDBACK.M_U file, 446
operating environments, 337-384
DESQview, 338, 379-382
DOS Services application, 382-384
DOS Shell, 338-359
Microsoft Windows 3.0, 338, 368-382
Presentation Manager, 338, 359-367
operating systems, 27-29, 627
command reference, 515-590

command syntax, 37
DOS, 20, 30-32
MS DOS, 604
file management commands, 28-29
installing, 199-201
interpreter, 33-34
kernel, 33-34
multitasking, 20
operating environments, 339
OS/2, 20, 30-32, 604
relationship to applications programs,
29
requirements, Microsoft Windows 3.0,
368
UNIX, 32-33
utilities, 33-34
optical disk, 627
OS/2 operating system, 20, 30-32, 597-600,
604
and hard disk, 597-602
compatibility to DOS, 599
High Performance File System (HPFS),
600-601
installation considerations, 599-600
memory, 598
multitasking, 598
Presentation Manager, 599
real mode, 597
similarity to DOS, 599
overlay files, 501, 627
OVL file extension, 501, 506
OVR file extension, 501

P

Paradox, 604
password-protecting database, 493-494
parameters, 37, 628
parent directory, 110-111
PARK, 422, 605
partitioning hard disks, 60-61, 180-196,
628
active partition, 183, 189-190
changing partition settings, 190-192
Disk Manager utility, 193-194
extended DOS partition, 188-190

logical drives, 181-182
partition tables, 182-183
primary DOS partition, 187-189
SpeedStor utility, 195-196
password protection, 303-304
AUTOEXEC.BAT file, 474
files, 490-494
PowerMenu, 307
system, 475-477
passwords, 498, 628
PATH DOS command, 39, 128-130, 296, 564-566
paths, 109-110, 128-130, 628
excluding programs, 474-475
extending search path, 244-245
PAUSE DOS batch subcommand, 39, 140, 154-155, 526-527
PC DOS, 20
PC Tools, 316, 323, 415, 429, 438, 446-447, 454-456, 464, 469, 486-489, 604
COMPRESS defragmentation program, 292-293
file-display windows, 323
PCBACKUP backup program, 415
PC-CACHE cache program, 277-278
PCOPY, 331, 604, 610
as backup program, 331
PCOPY.DOC file, 331
PC-Kwik RAM disk program, 283-284
PCSECURE data encryption program, 486-489
PCSHELL, 323, 429, 446, 454-456
PCX file extension, 319
peripherals, 10, 628
physical file security, 478
PIF file extension, 378
piping (|), 94-95, 628
pixels, 12
PKUNZIP program, 333
PKZIP, 332-334, 604, 610
platters, 44, 628
Power Disk defragmentation program, 289-290, 605
PowerMenu, 306-309, 604
power-on reset (POR), 35-36

power-on self test (POST), 35-36
Presentation Manager, 338, 359-367, 604
editing CONFIG.SYS file, 366
File System, 363-366
groups, 361-362
icons, 365-366
managing files, 364-366
OS/2 operating system, 599
swapping tasks, 362, 363
task icons, 360
Task Manager, 360, 362-363
utilities, 366-367
windows, 360-361
PRINT DOS command, 39, 78, 96-97, 351, 566-568
/B:bufsize switch, 567
/C switch, 567
/D:device switch, 566
/M:maxtick switch, 567
/P switch, 567
/Q:maxfiles switch, 567
/S:timeslice switch, 567
/T switch, 97, 567
/U:busytick switch, 567
background printing, 97
print screen, 629
PRINTER.SYS device driver, 221
printing
DIR listing, 88-89
DOS Shell files, 351
files, 96-97
text files in background, 566-568
PRN (printer) device name, 83
program files
displaying with batch files, 239-241
logging, 502-503
program overlay files, 280-281
Program Manager Microsoft Windows 3.0, 373-376
programs
adding to DOS Shell groups, 345-348
AUTOMAKE text editor, 310
Automenu, 309-311, 603
backup, 388, 408-415
Batcom, 603
Clean, 605

Commander Link, 321
CONFIG, 366-367
DBFIX, 460-461
DESQview, 603
Direct Access, 311-313, 603
Direct Net, 313
Disk Manager, 307-308, 603
DISKFIX, 469
DV.EXE, 379
EDLIN text-editing, 303
Emergency Room, 467-468
excluding from menus and paths, 474-475
FastBack Plus, 604
FBINSTAL, 410
FGREP, 604, 608-609
file managers, 314-325
FINDIT, 609
hard disk management, 301-334
launching, 316
LIST, 604, 609-610
Lotus 1-2-3 /G, 604
Lotus 1-2-3 Release 2, 604
Lotus 1-2-3 Release 3, 604
Lotus Magellan, 318-319, 604
Mace Utilities, 428, 436-437, 446, 452-454, 460-461, 464, 467- 468, 479, 482-483, 604
Mace Vaccine, 506-509, 604
menu, 302
Microsoft Windows 3.0, 604
MOVE, 604
MV, 610
Norton Commander, 316, 319-321, 605
Norton Disk Doctor, 465-466
Norton Utilities, 429, 435-436, 444-445, 450-452, 463-466, 479-481, 605
Paradox, 604
PARK, 422, 605
PC Tools, 316, 323, 415, 429, 438, 446-447, 454-456, 464, 469, 486-489, 604
PCOPY, 604, 610
PCSHELL, 323, 446
PKUNZIP, 333
PKZIP, 604, 610

Power Disk, 605
PowerMenu, 306-309, 604
Presentation Manager, 604
QFILER, 324-325, 604, 608, 611
RAM, 611
rerouting to look for files on hard disk, 517-518
Rescue, 457-459, 604
ResQDisk, 459
ResQFile, 459
ResQPass, 459
ResQView, 459
searching hard disk for, 306
shareware, 612-613
SHELLB.COM, 357
SpeedStor, 440-441, 604
SpinRite II, 439-440, 605
SPINTEST, 605, 611-612
SPINTIME, 605, 611-612
stopping with Ctrl-Break or Ctrl-C, 528-529, 536
stub, 306
Super PC KWIK, 605
SuperKey, 485-486
T2, 611
Teddy, 303, 605
terminate-and-stay-resident (TSR), 631
Trojan Horse, 498-499
UNDELETE, 446
undeletion, 448-456
Viruscan, 605
VOPT, 605
VTREE, 612
WHAT, 612
WIN.EXE, 369
WordPerfect, 605
XtreePro Gold, 321-322, 605
Programs disk, 607-612
installing programs, 607-608
PROGRAMS.ZIP file, 607
PROMPT DOS command, 39, 115, 116, 140, 236-239, 568-570
prompts, 629
protected mode, 597
protecting files, 423-426
public-domain software, 246-249, 629

Q

QFILER, 324-325, 604, 608, 611
  displaying file listings or directory trees,
    324
QU undeletion program, 450-452
  /A switch, 450
QUEDISK directory, 608

R

RAM disks, 278-285, 629
  copying files between floppy disks,
    281-282
  laptop computers, 282
  PC-Kwik program, 283-284
  program overlay files, 280-281
  RAM.SYS device driver, 284-285
  RAMDRIVE.SYS device driver, 282-283
  spell checkers, 281
  temporary files, 280
RAM.SYS device driver, 284-285
RAMDRIVE.SYS device driver, 221, 282-283
random-access memory (RAM), 11-12, 15,
  611, 629
read-only file attribute, 424, 425-426
read-only memory (ROM), 629
read/write head, 629
real mode, 597
REBUILD format recovery program, 464
  /TEST switch, 464
records, locking, 580-581
RECOVER DOS command, 39, 466,
  570-571
recovery insurance programs
  RXBAK, 446
redirection, 630
redundancy checking, 266
REM DOS batch subcommand, 39, 140,
  151, 527
REMEDY disk analyzer program, 436-437
RENAME or REN DOS command, 40, 382,
  572-573

REPLACE DOS command, 40, 573-575
  /A switch, 574
  /P switch, 574
  /R switch, 574
  /S switch, 574
  /U switch, 574
  /W switch, 574
Rescue, 457-459, 604
resolution, 13
response time, 630
ResQDisk, 459
ResQFile, 459
ResQPass, 459
ResQView, 459
RESTORE DOS command, 23-24, 40,
  398-404, 447, 516, 575-577
  /A:date switch, 400, 576
  /B:date switch, 400, 576
  /E:time switch, 400, 576
  /L:time switch, 400, 576
  /M switch, 400, 576
  /N switch, 400, 576
  /P switch, 400, 401, 403, 576
  /S switch, 399, 400, 575-576
revolutions per minute (RPM), 630
RLL (run length limited) data encoding
  method, 68
RMDIR or RD DOS command, 40, 118-120,
  450, 577-578
ROM BIOS (Basic Input/Output System),
  33-34
root directory, 106-108, 209, 630
RXBAK recover insurance program, 446
run length limited see RLL

S

saving files, 59-60
SCAN virus eradication utility, 510, 512
  /A switch, 510
  /D switch, 510, 512
  /E switch, 510
  /M switch, 510
  /MANY switch, 510
  /NOMEM switch, 510

screen colors, ANSI.SYS device driver,
    235-239
SCREEN01.SYS file, 599
SCSI interface standard, 67
SEC file extension, 488
secondary storage, 630
sector-level editing, 470
sectors, 17, 49-52, 630
SELECT DOS command, 40
sequential access, 630
serial number, 630
SET DOS command, 40, 244-245, 579-580
    /F:name_space switch, 580
    /L:numlocks, 580
setup disk, 422
SF.EXE formatting program, 429
SHARE DOS command, 40, 580-581
shareware programs, 612-613, 630
SHELL DOS configurations subcommand,
    224-225, 533, 543-544
    /E switch, 225
    /P switch, 224-225
SHELLB.COM program, 357
SHIFT DOS batch subcommand, 40,
    164-165, 527-528
small computer system interface see SCSI
SMARTDRV.SYS device driver, 221, 272
software, 11, 631
    backup programs, 23-24
    batch files, 22
    encryption programs, 24
    file managers, 22
    installing, 210-212
    menu programs, 23
    operating systems, 20, 27-29
    public-domain, 629
    utilities, 21
software/hardware computer locks,
    477-478
SORT DOS command, 40, 581-582
    /+c switch, 581
    /R switch, 581
SpeedStor, 195-196, 440-441, 604
spell checkers, 281
SpinRite II, 439-440, 605

SPINTEST, 605, 611-612
SPINTIME, 605, 611-612
ST506/ST412 interface standard, 66-67
STARTUP.CMD file, 599
static electricity, 421
storage, 631
strings, 631
    comparing in batch files, 167-168
stub, 306
subdirectories, 84-85, 109-115, 206-209,
    212-213, 562-563, 631
    . directory entry, 113
    .. directory entry, 113
    alias disk drive name, 582-584
    current directory, 110-115
    directory tree, 207-209
    displaying structure, 117-118, 584-585
    installing software, 211-212
    KEEP directory, 212
    listing files with DIR command, 85-93
    parent directory, 110-111
    paths, 109-110, 128-130
    printing DIR listing, 88-89
    recovering, 450
    removing, 118-120
    restoring files, 403
    root directory, 106-108, 209
    TEMP directory, 212-213
SUBST DOS command, 40, 135-136, 396,
    401, 582-584
    /D switch, 583
Super PC KWIK, 273-276, 605
SuperKey, 485-486
surge protectors, 420
SURVEY virus detection program, 506-509
switches, 37, 631
syntax, 631
SYS DOS command, 40
SYS file extension, 501
system
    file, 631
    hardware, 10
    password protecting, 475-477
    prompt, customizing, 568-570

T

T2 program, 611
tape backup devices, 416-417
Task Manager, 360, 362-363
TEDDY text-editing program, 303, 605
TEMP directory, 212-213
terminate-and-stay-resident (TSR) programs, 631
text
    adding to environment, 579-580
    ASCII sorting, 581-582
    locating with FIND command, 98-100
    searching, 315, 326-327
text editors
    AUTOMAKE, 310
    editing batch files, 143-144
text files, 93-94, 631
    background printing, 566-568
TIME DOS command, 40, 80
toggle, 631
tracks, 17, 48-51, 632
transfer rate, 55, 632
TREE DOS command, 40, 117-118, 334, 584-585
    /A switch, 117-118, 585
    /F switch, 117, 585
tree structure, 632
Trojan Horse program, 498-499
TYPE DOS command, 40, 78, 93-96, 328, 434, 475, 585-586

U

UNDELETE program, 446, 452-453
undeleting files, 447-456
undeletion programs, 448-456
    automatic recovery, 449
    MUSE, 453-454
    NU, 450-451
    PCSHELL, 454-456
    QU, 450-452
    UNDELETE, 452-453
unerasing files, 450-452
UNFORMAT format recovery program, 464

uninterruptable power supply (UPS), 420
UNIX, 32-33
    installing, 200-201
utilities, 21, 325-334, 632
    Disk Manager, 193-194
    drive head parking, 422
    FGREP, 326-327
    FINDIT, 327
    LIST, 328-329
    MOVE, 329-330
    PCOPY, 331
    PKZIP, 332-334
    PowerMenu, 307
    Presentation Manager, 366-367
    operating systems, 33-34
    SpeedStor, 195-196
    VTREE, 334

V

VACCINE virus detection program, 506-509
variables, 632
VERIFY DOS command, 37, 40, 297-298, 586-587
VGA (video graphics array), 13
virtual memory, 632-633
virus detection programs
    Lotus Magellan, 509-510
    SURVEY, 506-509
    VACCINE, 506-509
virus eradication utilities
    CLEAN, 510, 512-514
    SCAN, 510, 512
Viruscan, 605
viruses, 304, 442, 497-514
    AIDS, 502
    damages, 501-502
    eradicating, 504-514
    identifying, 502-504
    intercepting disk writes, 504
    propagation, 500-501
    protection from, 505
VOL DOS command, 40, 587-588
volume label, 560-561, 633

VOPT, 290-291, 605
VTREE, 334, 612

W

wait states, 12, 633
warm boot, 35-36, 633
WHAT public domain software, 246-249, 612
wild-card characters, 89-93, 633-634
WIN.EXE program, 369
windowing environment, 634
windows
　characteristics in Microsoft Windows 3.0, 370-372
　displaying file listings or directory trees, 324
　file-display, 323
　Microsoft Windows 3.0 application and document, 369
　Norton Commander, 320
　Presentation Manager, 360-361
WIPEDISK data erasing program, 479, 481
　/E switch, 481
　/Gn switch, 481
　/LOG switch, 481
　/Rn switch, 481
　/Vn switch, 481
WIPEFILE data erasing program, 479-480
　/Gn switch, 480
　/LOG switch, 480
　/N switch, 480
　/P switch, 480
　/Rn switch, 480
　/S switch, 480
　/Vn switch, 480
WordPerfect, 605
　password-protecting documents, 492-493
word processors, editing batch files, 142-143
worms, 497-498
write-protecting, 634
write buffering, 265-266

X

XCOPY DOS command, 40, 331, 404-408, 588-590
　/A switch, 405-406, 589
　/D:date switch, 405, 407, 589
　/E switch, 405, 408, 589
　/M switch, 406, 589
　/P switch, 406, 589
　/S switch, 406-408, 589
　/V switch, 406, 589
　/W switch, 406, 589
　creating directories, 404
XtreePro Gold, 321-322, 605

Z

^Z (end-of-file) marker, 634
zip, 634
ZIP file extension, 332-333

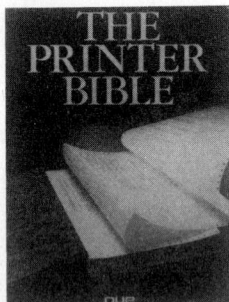

The Printer Bible
by Scott Foerster

From basic printer concepts and purchasing analysis to networking, maintenance, and troubleshooting, *The Printer Bible* is the ultimate printer information resource! Covers all kinds of printers —including laser-jet and dot matrix—and provides troubleshooting tips and a glossary of printer terms. A definite best-seller!

Order #1056
$24.95 USA
0-88022-512-2, 550 pp.

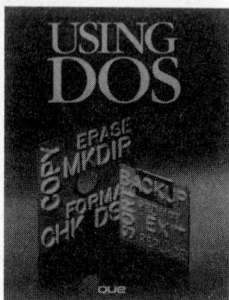

Using DOS
Developed by Que Corporation

The most helpful DOS book available! Que's *Using DOS* teaches the essential commands and functions of DOS Versions 3 and 4 —in an easy-to-understand format that helps users manage and organize their files effectively. Includes a handy **Command Reference**.

Order #1035
$22.95 USA
0-88022-497-5, 550 pp.

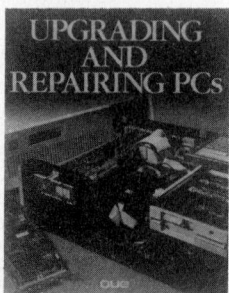

Upgrading and Repairing PCs
by Scott Mueller

The ultimate resource for personal computer upgrade, repair, maintenance, and troubleshooting! This comprehensive text covers all types of IBM computers and compatibles—from the original PC to the new PS/2 models. Defines your system components and provides solutions to common PC problems.

$27.95 USA
Order #882
0-88022-395-2, 750 pp.

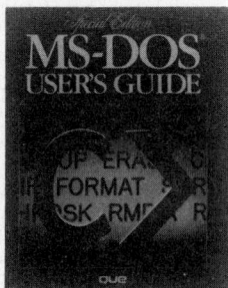

MS-DOS User's Guide, Special Edition
Developed by Que Corporation

A special edition of Que's best-selling book on MS-DOS, updated to provide the most comprehensive DOS coverage available. Includes expanded EDLIN coverage, plus **Quick Start** tutorials and a complete **Command Reference** for DOS Versions 3 and 4. A **must** for MS-DOS users at all levels!

Order #1048
$29.95 USA
0-88022-505-X, 900 pp.

More Computer Knowledge from Que

Lotus Software Titles

1-2-3 Database Techniques	24.95
1-2-3 Release 2.2 Business Applications	39.95
1-2-3 Release 2.2 Quick Reference	7.95
1-2-3 Release 2.2 QuickStart	19.95
1-2-3 Release 2.2 Workbook and Disk	29.95
1-2-3 Release 3 Business Applications	39.95
1-2-3 Release 3 Quick Reference	7.95
1-2-3 Release 3 QuickStart	19.95
1-2-3 Release 3 Workbook and Disk	29.95
1-2-3 Tips, Tricks, and Traps, 3rd Edition	22.95
Upgrading to 1-2-3 Release 3	14.95
Using 1-2-3, Special Edition	24.95
Using 1-2-3 Release 2.2, Special Edition	24.95
Using 1-2-3 Release 3	24.95
Using Lotus Magellan	21.95
Using Symphony, 2nd Edition	26.95

Database Titles

dBASE III Plus Applications Library	24.95
dBASE III Plus Handbook, 2nd Edition	24.95
dBASE III Plus Tips, Tricks, and Traps	21.95
dBASE III Plus Workbook and Disk	29.95
dBASE IV Applications Library, 2nd Edition	39.95
dBASE IV Handbook, 3rd Edition	23.95
dBASE IV Programming Techniques	24.95
dBASE IV QueCards	21.95
dBASE IV Quick Reference	7.95
dBASE IV QuickStart	19.95
dBASE IV Tips, Tricks, and Traps, 2nd Edition	21.95
dBASE IV Workbook and Disk	29.95
dBXL and Quicksilver Programming: Beyond dBASE	24.95
R:BASE User's Guide, 3rd Edition	22.95
Using Clipper	24.95
Using DataEase	22.95
Using Reflex	19.95
Using Paradox 3	24.95

Applications Software Titles

AutoCAD Advanced Techniques	34.95
AutoCAD Quick Reference	7.95
AutoCAD Sourcebook	24.95
Excel Business Applications: IBM Version	39.95
Introduction to Business Software	14.95
PC Tools Quick Reference	7.95
Smart Tips, Tricks, and Traps	24.95
Using AutoCAD, 2nd Edition	29.95
Using Computers in Business	24.95
Using DacEasy	21.95

Using Dollars and Sense: IBM Version, 2nd Edition	19.95
Using Enable/OA	23.95
Using Excel: IBM Version	24.95
Using Generic CADD	24.95
Using Harvard Project Manager	24.95
Using Managing Your Money, 2nd Edition	19.95
Using Microsoft Works: IBM Version	21.95
Using PROCOMM PLUS	19.95
Using Q&A, 2nd Edition	21.95
Using Quattro	21.95
Using Quicken	19.95
Using Smart	22.95
Using SmartWare II	24.95
Using SuperCalc5, 2nd Edition	22.95

Word Processing and Desktop Publishing Titles

DisplayWrite QuickStart	19.95
Harvard Graphics Quick Reference	7.95
Microsoft Word 5 Quick Reference	7.95
Microsoft Word 5 Tips, Tricks, and Traps: IBM Version	19.95
Using DisplayWrite 4, 2nd Edition	19.95
Using Freelance Plus	24.95
Using Harvard Graphics	24.95
Using Microsoft Word 5: IBM Version	21.95
Using MultiMate Advantage, 2nd Edition	19.95
Using PageMaker: IBM Version, 2nd Edition	24.95
Using PFS: First Choice	22.95
Using PFS: First Publisher	22.95
Using Professional Write	19.95
Using Sprint	21.95
Using Ventura Publisher, 2nd Edition	24.95
Using WordPerfect, 3rd Edition	21.95
Using WordPerfect 5	24.95
Using WordStar, 2nd Edition	21.95
Ventura Publisher Techniques and Applications	22.95
Ventura Publisher Tips, Tricks, and Traps	24.95
WordPerfect Macro Library	21.95
WordPerfect Power Techniques	21.95
WordPerfect QueCards	21.95
WordPerfect Quick Reference	7.95
WordPerfect QuickStart	21.95
WordPerfect Tips, Tricks, and Traps, 2nd Edition	21.95
WordPerfect 5 Workbook and Disk	29.95

Macintosh/Apple II Titles

The Big Mac Book	27.95
Excel QuickStart	19.95
Excel Tips, Tricks, and Traps	22.95
Using AppleWorks, 3rd Edition	21.95
Using AppleWorks GS	21.95
Using dBASE Mac	19.95
Using Dollars and Sense: Macintosh Version	19.95
Using Excel: Macintosh Verson	22.95
Using FullWrite Professional	21.95

Using HyperCard:	24.95
Using Microsoft Word 4: Macintosh Version	21.95
Using Microsoft Works: Macintosh Version, 2nd Edition	21.95
Using PageMaker: Macintosh Version	24.95
Using WordPerfect: Macintosh Version	19.95

Hardware and Systems Titles

DOS Tips, Tricks, and Traps	22.95
DOS Workbook and Disk	29.95
Hard Disk Quick Reference	7.95
IBM PS/2 Handbook	21.95
Managing Your Hard Disk, 2nd Edition	22.95
MS-DOS Quick Reference	7.95
MS-DOS QuickStart	21.95
MS-DOS User's Guide, Special Edition	29.95
Networking Personal Computers, 3rd Edition	22.95
Norton Utilities Quick Reference	7.95
The Printer Bible	24.95
Understanding UNIX: A Conceptual Guide, 2nd Edition	21.95
Upgrading and Repairing PCs	27.95
Using DOS	22.95
Using Microsoft Windows	19.95
Using Novell NetWare	24.95
Using OS/2	23.95
Using PC DOS, 3rd Edition	22.95

Programming and Technical Titles

Assembly Language Quick Reference	7.95
C Programmer's Toolkit	39.95
C Programming Guide, 3rd Edition	24.95
C Quick Reference	7.95
DOS and BIOS Functions Quick Reference	7.95
DOS Programmer's Reference, 2nd Edition	27.95
Power Graphics Programming	24.95
QuickBASIC Advanced Techniques	21.95
QuickBASIC Programmer's Toolkit	39.95
QuickBASIC Quick Reference	7.95
SQL Programmer's Guide	29.95
Turbo C Programming	22.95
Turbo Pascal Advanced Techniques	22.95
Turbo Pascal Programmer's Toolkit	39.95
Turbo Pascal Quick Reference	7.95
Using Assembly Language	24.95
Using QuickBASIC 4	19.95
Using Turbo Pascal	21.95

For more information, call

1-800-428-5331

All prices subject to change without notice. Prices and charges are for domestic orders only. Non-U.S. prices might be higher.

If your computer uses 3 1/2-inch disks . . .

While most personal computers use 5 1/4-inch disks to store information, some newer computers are switching to 3 1/2-inch disks for information storage. If your computer uses 3 1/2-inch disks, you can return this form to Que to obtain a 3 1/2-inch disk to use with this workbook. Simply fill out the remainder of this form, and mail to:

Using Your Hard Disk
Disk Exchange
Que Corporation
11711 N. College Ave.
Carmel, IN 46032

We will then send you, free of charge, the 3 1/2-inch version of the workbook software.

Name _____ Phone _____

Company _____ Title _____

Address _____

City _____ St _____ ZIP _____